Encyclopedia of
PSYCHOLOGY
& LAW

Encyclopedia of
PSYCHOLOGY
& LAW

Volume 1

Brian L. Cutler ▪ Editor
University of North Carolina at Charlotte

A SAGE Reference Publication

SAGE Publications
Los Angeles • London • New Delhi • Singapore

For information:

 SAGE Publications, Inc.
2455 Teller Road
Thousand Oaks, California 91320
E-mail: order@sagepub.com

SAGE Publications Ltd.
1 Oliver's Yard
55 City Road
London EC1Y 1SP
United Kingdom

SAGE Publications India Pvt. Ltd.
B 1/I 1 Mohan Cooperative Industrial Area
Mathura Road, New Delhi 110 044
India

SAGE Publications Asia-Pacific Pte. Ltd.
33 Pekin Street #02-01
Far East Square
Singapore 048763

Printed in the United States of America.

Library of Congress Cataloging-in-Publication Data

Encyclopedia of psychology and law/editor, Brian L. Cutler.
    p. cm.
Includes bibliographical references and index.
ISBN 978-1-4129-5189-0 (cloth)

   1. Law—Psychological aspects—Encyclopedias. 2. Law—United States—Psychological aspects—Encyclopedias. 3. Forensic psychology—Encyclopedias. 4. Forensic psychology—United States—Encyclopedias. I. Cutler, Brian L.

K346.E53 2008
340′.19—dc22   2007029845

This book is printed on acid-free paper.

07   08   09   10   11   10 9 8 7 6 5 4 3 2 1

Publisher:	Rolf A. Janke
Acquisitions Editor:	Jim Brace-Thompson
Developmental Editor:	Diana E. Axelsen
Reference Systems Manager:	Leticia Gutierrez
Production Editor:	Kate Schroeder
Copy Editor:	QuADS Prepress (P) Ltd.
Typesetter:	C&M Digitals (P) Ltd.
Proofreaders:	Penny Sippel, Dennis Webb
Indexer:	Janet Perlman
Cover Designer:	Janet Foulger
Marketing Manager:	Amberlyn Erzinger

Contents

List of Entries

Reader's Guide

This list is provided to assist readers in locating entries on related topics. Some entry titles appear in more than one category.

Criminal Competencies

Adjudicative Competence of Youth
Capacity to Waive Rights
Capacity to Waive *Miranda* Rights
Checklist for Competency for
  Execution Evaluations
Competence Assessment for Standing Trial for
  Defendants With Mental Retardation (CAST*MR)
Competency, Foundational and Decisional
Competency, Restoration of
Competency Assessment Instrument (CAI)
Competency for Execution
Competency Screening Test (CST)
Competency to Be Sentenced
Competency to Confess
Competency to Stand Trial
Competency to Waive Appeals
Competency to Waive Counsel (Proceed Pro Se)
Delusions
Evaluation of Competence to Stand Trial–Revised
  (ECST–R)
Fitness Interview Test–Revised (FIT–R)
Georgia Court Competence Test (GCCT)
Grisso's Instruments for Assessing Understanding
  and Appreciation of *Miranda* Rights
Gudjonsson Suggestibility Scales
Hallucinations
Interdisciplinary Fitness Interview (IFI)
MacArthur Competence Assessment Tool for
  Criminal Adjudication (MacCAT–CA)
Psychotic Disorders

Criminal Responsibility

Aggravating and Mitigating Circumstances,
  Evaluation of in Capital Cases
American Bar Association Resolution on Mental
  Disability and the Death Penalty
Automatism
Battered Woman Syndrome
Battered Woman Syndrome, Testimony on
Criminal Responsibility, Assessment of
Criminal Responsibility, Defenses and Standards
Delusions
Diminished Capacity
Dissociative Identity Disorder
Extreme Emotional Disturbance
Guilty but Mentally Ill Verdict
Hallucinations
Insanity Defense Reform Act (IDRA)
Mens Rea and Actus Reus
Mental Illness and the Death Penalty
Mental Retardation and the Death Penalty
M'Naghten Standard
Psychotic Disorders
Rogers Criminal Responsibility Assessment
  Scales (R–CRAS)

Death Penalty

Aggravating and Mitigating Circumstances,
  Evaluation of in Capital Cases
Aggravating and Mitigating Circumstances in
  Capital Trials, Effects on Jurors

Source Monitoring and Eyewitness Memory
Stress and Eyewitness Memory
Training of Eyewitnesses
Unconscious Transference
Verbal Overshadowing and Eyewitness Identification
Voice Recognition
Weapon Focus
WITNESS Model

Forensic Assessment in Civil and Criminal Cases

Ackerman-Schoendorf Parent Evaluation
  of Custody Test (ASPECT)
Adjudicative Competence of Youth
Adult Attachment Interview (AAI)
Aggravating and Mitigating Circumstances,
  Evaluation of in Capital Cases
American Bar Association Resolution on Mental
  Disability and the Death Penalty
Americans with Disabilities Act (ADA)
Antisocial Personality Disorder
Automatism
Battered Woman Syndrome
Capacity to Consent to Treatment Instrument (CCTI)
Capacity to Waive Miranda Rights
Capacity to Waive Rights
Checklist for Competency for Execution Evaluations
Child Abuse Potential (CAP) Inventory
Child Custody Evaluations
Child Maltreatment
Child Sexual Abuse
Civil Commitment
Classification of Violence Risk (COVR)
Competence Assessment for Standing Trial for
  Defendants With Mental Retardation (CAST*MR)
Competency, Foundational and Decisional
Competency, Restoration of
Competency Assessment Instrument (CAI)
Competency for Execution
Competency Screening Test (CST)
Competency to Be Sentenced
Competency to Confess
Competency to Stand Trial
Competency to Waive Appeals
Competency to Waive Counsel (Proceed Pro Se)
Conduct Disorder
Conflict Tactics Scale (CTS)

Consent to Clinical Research
Criminal Responsibility, Assessment of
Criminal Responsibility, Defenses and Standards
Danger Assessment Instrument (DA)
Delusions
Diminished Capacity
Disability and Workers' Compensation Claims,
  Assessment of
Disparate Treatment and Disparate Impact
  Evaluations
Dissociative Identity Disorder
Divorce and Child Custody
Domestic Violence Screening Instrument (DVSI)
Ethical Guidelines and Principles
Ethnic Differences in Psychopathy
Evaluation of Competence to Stand Trial–Revised
  (ECST–R)
Extreme Emotional Disturbance
Financial Capacity
Financial Capacity Instrument (FCI)
Fitness-for-Duty Evaluations
Fitness Interview Test–Revised (FIT–R)
Forensic Assessment
Georgia Court Competence Test (GCCT)
Grisso's Instruments for Assessing Understanding
  and Appreciation of Miranda Rights
Gudjonsson Suggestibility Scales
Guilty but Mentally Ill Verdict
Hallucinations
Hare Psychopathy Checklist–Revised
  (2nd edition) (PCL–R)
Hare Psychopathy Checklist: Screening Version
  (PCL:SV)
Hare Psychopathy Checklist: Youth Version
  (PCL:YV)
HCR–20 for Violence Risk Assessment
Hopkins Competency Assessment Test (HCAT)
Insanity Defense Reform Act (IDRA)
Interdisciplinary Fitness Interview (IFI)
Jail Screening Assessment Tool (JSAT)
Litigation Stress
MacArthur Competence Assessment Tool for
  Criminal Adjudication (MacCAT–CA)
MacArthur Competence Assessment Tool for
  Treatment (MacCAT–T)
MacArthur Violence Risk Assessment Study
Malingering
Malingering Probability Scale

Juvenile Offenders

Mental Health Law

Forcible Medication

Guardianship

Institutionalization and Deinstitutionalization

Mandated Community Treatment

Mental Health Courts

Mental Health Law

Mental Health Needs of Juvenile Offenders

Outpatient Commitment, Involuntary

Patient's Rights

Proxy Decision Making

Psychiatric Advance Directives

Substance Abuse Treatment

Therapeutic Jurisprudence

Psychological and Forensic Assessment Instruments

Ackerman-Schoendorf Parent Evaluation of Custody Test (ASPECT)

Adult Attachment Interview (AAI)

Capacity to Consent to Treatment Instrument (CCTI)

Checklist for Competency for Execution Evaluations

Child Abuse Potential (CAP) Inventory

Classification of Violence Risk (COVR)

Competency Assessment Instrument (CAI)

Competency Screening Test (CST)

Conflict Tactics Scale (CTS)

Danger Assessment Instrument (DA)

Domestic Violence Screening Instrument (DVSI)

Evaluation of Competence to Stand Trial–Revised (ECST–R)

Financial Capacity Instrument (FCI)

Fitness Interview Test–Revised (FIT–R)

Georgia Court Competence Test (GCCT)

Grisso's Instruments for Assessing Understanding and Appreciation of *Miranda* Rights

Gudjonsson Suggestibility Scales

Hare Psychopathy Checklist–Revised (2nd edition) (PCL–R)

Hare Psychopathy Checklist: Screening Version (PCL:SV)

Hare Psychopathy Checklist: Youth Version (PCL:YV)

HCR–20 for Violence Risk Assessment

Hopkins Competency Assessment Test (HCAT)

Interdisciplinary Fitness Interview (IFI)

Jail Screening Assessment Tool (JSAT)

MacArthur Competence Assessment Tool for Clinical Research (MacCAT–CR)

MacArthur Competence Assessment Tool for Criminal Adjudication (MacCAT–CA)

MacArthur Competence Assessment Tool for Treatment (MacCat–T)

Malingering Probability Scale

Massachusetts Youth Screening Instrument–Version 2 (MAYSI–2)

Miller Forensic Assessment of Symptoms Test (M–FAST)

Millon Clinical Multiaxial Inventory–III (MCMI–III)

Minnesota Multiphasic Personality Inventory–2 (MMPI–2)

Minnesota Multiphasic Personality Inventory–2 (MMPI–2) Validity Scales

Minnesota Sex Offender Screening Tool–Revised (MnSOST–R)

Novaco Anger Scale

Parent-Child Relationship Inventory (PCRI)

Parenting Satisfaction Scale (PSS)

Parenting Stress Index (PSI)

Psychological Inventory of Criminal Thinking Styles

Psychopathic Personality Inventory (PPI)

Rapid Risk Assessment for Sexual Offense Recidivism (RRASOR)

Risk-Sophistication-Treatment Inventory (RSTI)

Rogers Criminal Responsibility Assessment Scales (R–CRAS)

Sex Offender Needs Assessment Rating (SONAR)

Sex Offender Risk Appraisal Guide (SORAG)

Sexual Violence Risk–20 (SVR–20)

Short-Term Assessment of Risk and Treatability (START)

Spousal Assault Risk Assessment (SARA)

STABLE–2007 and ACUTE–2007 Instruments

STATIC–99 and STATIC–2002 Instruments

Structured Assessment of Violence Risk in Youth (SAVRY)

Structured Interview of Reported Symptoms (SIRS)

Suicide Assessment Manual for Inmates (SAMI)

Test of Memory Malingering (TOMM)

Uniform Child Custody Evaluation System (UCCES)

Validity Indicator Profile (VIP)

Violence Risk Appraisal Guide (VRAG)

Parole Decisions
Presentence Evaluations
Prison Overcrowding
Probation Decisions
Public Opinion About Sentencing
    and Incarceration
Sentencing Decisions
Sentencing Diversion Programs
Stanford Prison Experiment
Substance Abuse Treatment
Suicide Assessment and Prevention in Prisons
Suicide Assessment Manual for Inmates (SAMI)
Supermax Prisons
Therapeutic Communities for Treatment of
    Substance Abuse
Treatment and Release of Insanity Acquittees

Symptoms and Disorders Relevant to Forensic Assessment

Antisocial Personality Disorder
Automatism
Battered Woman Syndrome
Child Maltreatment
Child Sexual Abuse
Conduct Disorder
Delusions
Dissociative Identity Disorder
Hallucinations
Malingering
Mild Traumatic Brain Injury, Assessment of
Mood Disorders
Pedophilia
Personality Disorders
Posttraumatic Stress Disorder (PTSD)
Psychopathy
Psychotic Disorders
Substance Use Disorders

Trial Processes

Aggravating and Mitigating Circumstances in
    Capital Trials, Effects on Jurors
Alibi Witnesses
Alternative Dispute Resolution
Amicus Curiae Briefs
Bail-Setting Decisions

Battered Woman Syndrome, Testimony on
Chicago Jury Project
Children's Testimony
Children's Testimony, Evaluation by Juries
Complex Evidence in Litigation
Confession Evidence
CSI Effect
Damage Awards
Death Qualification of Juries
Domestic Violence Courts
Drug Courts
"Dynamite Charge"
Elderly Defendants
Expert Psychological Testimony
Expert Psychological Testimony, Admissibility
    Standards
Expert Psychological Testimony, Forms of
Expert Psychological Testimony on Eyewitness
    Identification
Expert Testimony, Qualifications of Experts
Fingerprint Evidence, Evaluation of
Hearsay Testimony
Inadmissible Evidence, Impact on Juries
Insanity Defense, Juries and
Judges' Nonverbal Behavior
Juries and Eyewitnesses
Juries and Joined Trials
Juries and Judges' Instructions
Jury Administration Reforms
Jury Competence
Jury Decisions Versus Judges' Decisions
Jury Deliberation
Jury Nullification
Jury Questionnaires
Jury Reforms
Jury Selection
Jury Size and Decision Rule
Jury Understanding of Judges' Instructions
    in Capital Cases
Legal Authoritarianism
Legal Negotiation
Legal Socialization
Leniency Bias
Litigation Stress
Mental Health Courts
Parole Decisions
Plea Bargaining

Victim Reactions to Crime

Violence Risk Assessment

About the Editors

General Editor

Brian L. Cutler, Ph.D., is Professor and Chair of the Department of Psychology at the University of North Carolina at Charlotte. He conducts research on eyewitness identification and the effectiveness of safeguards designed to protect defendants from erroneous conviction resulting from mistaken identification. He is the author of *Mistaken Identification: Eyewitnesses, Psychology, and the Law* (with Steven Penrod, 1995) and over 60 book chapters and articles on eyewitness memory and legal safeguards. He serves as Editor-in-Chief of *Law and Human Behavior*, the official journal of the American Psychology-Law Society. He also serves as an expert witness and testifies on the psychology of eyewitness memory. He received his doctoral degree in social psychology from the University of Wisconsin–Madison in 1987.

Associate Editor

Patricia A. Zapf, Ph.D., is currently Associate Professor in the Department of Psychology at John Jay College of Criminal Justice, the City University of New York. She is Associate Editor of *Law and Human Behavior* and was appointed Fellow of the American Psychological Association in 2006 for outstanding contributions to the field of law and psychology. She has published over 60 articles and chapters, mainly on the assessment of criminal competencies. In addition to her research, she serves as a consultant to various criminal justice and policy organizations and maintains a private practice in forensic assessment. She received her doctoral degree in clinical forensic psychology from Simon Fraser University in Canada in 1999.

Managing Editor

Sarah Greathouse, M.S., is currently working on her Ph.D. in psychology at the City University of New York. To date, her research has focused on issues relevant to jury decision making and eyewitness identification. She recently served as the editorial assistant for *Law and Human Behavior*, the official journal of the American Psychology-Law Society. She received her master's degree in legal psychology from Florida International University.

Contributors

Jeffrey Abracen
Correctional Service of Canada

Meera Adya
Syracuse University

Ani A. Aharonian
University of Nebraska–Lincoln

John J. B. Allen
University of Arizona

Scott W. Allen
Miami-Dade Police Department

Lia Amakawa
Fordham University

Paul S. Appelbaum
Columbia University

Elizabeth Arias
*John Jay College of Criminal Justice,
City University of New York*

Julie E. Artis
DePaul University

Else-Marie Augusti
University of California, Davis

Stella Bain
Glasgow Caledonian University

Nancy Lynn Baker
Fielding Graduate University

Albert Bandura
Stanford University

Trevor H. Barese
Roger Williams University

D. David Barnard
Graduate Center, City University of New York

Patrick Bartel
Youth Forensic Psychiatric Services of British Columbia

Jennifer L. Beaudry
Queen's University

Michelle I. Bertrand
Queen's University

Peter Blanck
Syracuse University

Arthur W. Blume
University of North Carolina at Charlotte

Marcus T. Boccaccini
Sam Houston State University

Douglas P. Boer
University of Waikato

James Bopp
Rockland Psychiatric Center

Brian H. Bornstein
University of Nebraska–Lincoln

Randy Borum
University of South Florida

Robert K. Bothwell
University of Louisiana at Lafayette

Bette L. Bottoms
University of Illinois at Chicago

Neil Brewer
Flinders University

Jocelyn M. Brineman
University of North Carolina at Charlotte

Johann Brink
*BC Mental Health & Addiction Services,
University of British Columbia*

Jessica Broderick
University of British Columbia

Ray Bull
University of Leicester

Barry R. Burkhart
Auburn University

Tom Busey
Indiana University, Bloomington

Julia C. Busso
*John Jay College of Criminal Justice,
City University of New York*

Brooke Butler
University of South Florida Sarasota-Manatee

Lisa Callahan
Sage Colleges

Philip J. Candilis
University of Massachusetts Medical School

Nathalie Castano
Florida International University

Elizabeth Cauffman
University of California, Irvine

Yoojin Chae
University of California, Davis

Jared Chamberlain
University of Nevada, Reno

Steve D. Charman
Florida International University

H. Lyssette Chavez
University of Nevada, Reno

Nicola Cheyne
Griffith University

Makenzie Chilton
University of British Columbia

Jason M. Chin
University of British Columbia

M. Cherie Clark
Queens University of Charlotte

Steve E. Clark
University of California, Riverside

Jacqueline K. Coffman
California State University, Fullerton

Ellen S. Cohn
University of New Hampshire

Lois Oberlander Condie
Harvard Medical School

Mary Connell
Private Practice

Virginia G. Cooper
*University of South Carolina,
South Carolina Dept. of Mental Health*

Ryan W. Copple
*John Jay College of Criminal Justice,
City University of New York*

Mark Costanzo
Claremont McKenna College

Kellina M. Craig-Henderson
National Science Foundation

Caroline B. Crocker
*John Jay College of Criminal Justice,
City University of New York*

Mark Douglas Cunningham
Private Practice

Brian L. Cutler
University of North Carolina at Charlotte

Anne K. Cybenko
University of California, Riverside

Tarika Daftary
Graduate Center, City University of New York

Michael R. Davis
Monash University

Kenneth Allan Deffenbacher
University of Nebraska at Omaha

Melissa Y. De Jesus
University of Pennsylvania

George J. Demakis
University of North Carolina at Charlotte

Susan Dennison
Griffith University

Sarah L. Desmarais
Simon Fraser University

Jennifer L. Devenport
Western Washington University

Dennis J. Devine
Indiana University, Purdue University

Mandeep K. Dhami
University of Cambridge

Shari Seidman Diamond
Northwestern University

Bridget M. Doane
University of Alabama

Catherine M. Dodson
Southern Methodist University

Dennis M. Doren
Sand Ridge Secure Treatment Center

Kevin S. Douglas
Simon Fraser University

Amy Bradfield Douglass
Bates College

Eric York Drogin
Harvard Medical School, Franklin Pierce Law Center

Rachel Duros
Nova Southeastern University

G. Donald Dutton
University of British Columbia

Jennifer L. Dvoskin
Argosy University

Joel A. Dvoskin
University of Arizona

Jennifer E. Dysart
*John Jay College of Criminal Justice,
City University of New York*

John F. Edens
Texas A&M University

Eric B. Elbogen
Duke University

Douglas L. Epperson
Iowa State University

Edna Erez
Kent State University

Caroline Everington
Winthrop University

David L. Faigman
University of California, Hastings College of the Law

Keith A. Findley
University of Wisconsin

Ronald Fisher
Florida International University

Heather D. Flowe
University of California, San Diego

Paul W. Foos
University of North Carolina at Charlotte

William E. Foote
University of New Mexico

Haley L. Ford
University of Alabama

Adelle E. Forth
Carleton University

Nicci Bowman Fowler
University of California, Irvine

Patricia A. Frazier
University of Minnesota

Richard I. Frederick
U.S. Medical Center for Federal Prisoners

Mary Ellen Fromuth
Middle Tennessee State University

I. Bruce Frumkin
Forensic and Clinical Psychology Associates, P.A.

Solomon M. Fulero
Sinclair College

Fiona Gabbert
University of Abertay, Dundee

Jennifer L. Gagné
Nova Southeastern University

Frank J. Gallo
Western New England College

Maryanne Garry
Victoria University

L. Beth Gaydon
University of Nevada, Reno

Simona Ghetti
University of California, Davis

Renée Gobeil
Carleton University

Stephen Golding
University of Utah

Naomi E. Sevin Goldstein
Drexel University

Gail S. Goodman
University of California, Davis

Pär Anders Granhag
Gothenburg University

Sarah Greathouse
*John Jay College of Criminal Justice,
City University of New York*

Edith Greene
University of Colorado at Colorado Springs

Michael P. Griffin
University of Alabama

Timothy Griffin
University of Nevada, Reno

Ross D. Grimes
University of Alabama

Jennifer Groscup
*John Jay College of Criminal Justice,
City University of New York*

John Louis Guidubaldi
Kent State University

Laura S. Guy
Simon Fraser University

Thomas L. Hafemeister
University of Virginia Law School

Craig Haney
University of California, Santa Cruz

Paula L. Hannaford-Agor
National Center for State Courts

David J. Hansen
University of Nebraska–Lincoln

Robert D. Hare
Darkstone Research Group, Ltd.

Andrew J. R. Harris
Forensic Assessment Group

Grant T. Harris
Mental Health Centre Penetanguishene

La Tonya Harris
University of California, Davis

Stephen D. Hart
Simon Fraser University

Lisa E. Hasel
Iowa State University

Katina R. Hebert
University of Alabama at Birmingham

Krystal Hedge
University of Denver

Marsha Anne Hedrick
Private Practice

Kirk Heilbrun
Drexel University

Larry Heuer
Barnard College, Columbia University

Virginia Aldigé Hiday
North Carolina State University

Charles Robert Honts
Boise State University

Irwin A. Horowitz
Oregon State University

Harmon M. Hosch
University of Texas at El Paso

Matthew T. Huss
Creighton University

Elizabeth L. Jeglic
*John Jay College of Criminal Justice,
City University of New York*

Alayna Jehle
University of Nevada, Reno

Nicole M. Johnson
University of Alabama

Kevin M. Jolly
University of Texas at El Paso

Rachel Kalbeitzer
Drexel University

Saul M. Kassin
Williams College

Patrick J. Kennealy
University of California, Irvine

Norbert L. Kerr
Michigan State University

Ryan P. Kilmer
University of North Carolina at Charlotte

Eva Kimonis
University of California, Irvine

Stuart M. Kirchner
*John Jay College of Criminal Justice,
City University of New York*

Lauren L. Kong
University of Arizona

David Kosson
Rosalind Franklin University of Medicine and Science

Margaret Bull Kovera
*John Jay College of Criminal Justice,
City Universty of New York*

L. Thomas Kucharski
*John Jay College of Criminal Justice,
City Universty of New York*

James Michael Lampinen
University of Arkansas

Edward E. Landis
Federal Medical Center

Jennifer Langhinrichsen-Rohling
University of South Alabama

Martin Langhinrichsen-Rohling
University of South Alabama

Daniel D. Langleben
University of Pennsylvania

Kimberly A. Larson
Drexel University, Villanova School of Law

G. Daniel Lassiter
Ohio University

Cindy Laub
University of Nebraska

Jennifer A. A. Lavoie
Simon Fraser University

Deah S. Lawson
University of Alabama, Huntsville

Sharon Leal
University of Portsmouth

Christie A. Ledbetter
University of Alabama

Zina Lee
University of Alabama

Jill S. Levenson
Lynn University

Lora M. Levett
University of Florida

Joel D. Lieberman
University of Nevada, Las Vegas

Scott O. Lilienfeld
Emory University

D. Stephen Lindsay
University of Victoria

R. C. L. Lindsay
Queen's University

Daniel Linz
University of California, Santa Barbara

Paul D. Lipsitt
Boston University

Thomas R. Litwack
*John Jay College of Criminal Justice,
City Universty of New York*

Elizabeth F. Loftus
University of California, Irvine

Vivian B. Lord
University of North Carolina at Charlotte

Jennifer Eno Louden
University of California, Irvine

Ruth Luckasson
University of New Mexico

Arthur J. Lurigio
Loyola University Chicago

Robert J. MacCoun
University of California, Berkeley

Doris Layton MacKenzie
University of Maryland

Otto MacLin
University of Northern Iowa

Roy S. Malpass
University of Texas at El Paso

Sarah Manchak
University of California, Irvine

Samantha Mann
University of Portsmouth

Jamal K. Mansour
Queen's University

Jessica L. Marcon
University of Texas at El Paso

Diane Marsh
University of Pittsburgh at Greensburg

Dorothy F. Marsil
Kennesaw State University

Daniel C. Marson
University of Alabama at Birmingham

Mary-Lou Martin
McMaster University

Hunter A. McAllister
Southeastern Louisiana University

Richard D. McAnulty
University of North Carolina at Charlotte

Kathy McCloskey
University of Hartford

Kaitlyn McLachlan
Simon Fraser University

Christian A. Meissner
University of Texas at El Paso

Amina Memon
University of Aberdeen

Cynthia Calkins Mercado
*John Jay College of Criminal Justice,
City Universty of New York*

Anna Mestitz
Research Institute on Judicial Systems

Richard Metzger
University of Tennessee at Chattanooga

Richard L. Michalski
Hollins University

Peter Miene
Winona State University

Holly A. Miller
Sam Houston State University

Monica K. Miller
University of Nevada, Reno

Joel S. Milner
Northern Illinois University

Kathryn L. Modecki
Arizona State University

John Monahan
University of Virginia

Gary Moran
Florida International University

Sarah Mordell
Simon Fraser University

Jessica Morgan
University of Alabama

Stephen J. Morse
University of Pennsylvania

Pam Mueller
Harvard University

Bryan Myers
University of North Carolina, Wilmington

Lavita Nadkarni
University of Denver

Cynthia J. Najdowski
University of Illinois at Chicago

Kamela K. Nelan
University of Virginia School of Law

Kally J. Nelson
University of California, Irvine

Jeffrey S. Neuschatz
University of Alabama at Huntsville

Eryn Newman
Victoria University of Wellington

Tonia L. Nicholls
*British Columbia Mental Health & Addiction
Services*

Raymond W. Novaco
University of California, Irvine

Kevin M. O'Neil
Florida International University

Maureen O'Sullivan
University of San Francisco

James R. P. Ogloff
Monash University and Forensicare

J. Gregory Olley
University of North Carolina at Chapel Hill

Elizabeth A. Olson
University of Wisconsin–Whitewater

Randy K. Otto
University of South Florida

Barbara A. Oudekerk
University of Virginia

Ira K. Packer
University of Massachusetts Medical School

Douglas Paton
University of Tasmania

Pedro M. Paz-Alonso
University of California, Davis

Michael L. Perlin
New York Law School

John Petrila
University of South Florida

Kathy Pezdek
Claremont Graduate University

Amy Phenix
Private Practice

Janice Picheca
Correctional Service of Canada

Kerri L. Pickel
Ball State University

Lisa D. Piechowski
Private Practice

Gianni Pirelli
*John Jay College of Criminal Justice,
City University of New York*

Judith Platania
Roger Williams University

Natalie H. Polvi
Regional Psychiatric Centre (Prairies)

Mina Popliger
McGill University

Norman G. Poythress
University of South Florida

Joanna D. Pozzulo
Carleton University

Jennifer Pryor
Hollins University

Ethel Quayle
University College Cork

Vernon L. Quinsey
Queen's University

Jennifer J. Ratcliff
Ohio University

J. Don Read
Simon Fraser University

Margaret C. Reardon
Florida International University

Allison D. Redlich
Policy Research Associates

Kim Reeves
Simon Fraser University

Alan Reifman
Texas Tech University

David Reitman
Nova Southeastern University

Michelle R. Resor
Uniersity of North Carolina at Charlotte

Marnie E. Rice
Mental Health Centre Penetanguishene

Jennifer K. Robbennolt
University of Illinois

Julian Roberts
Oxford University

Amanda L. Robinson
Cardiff University

Ronald Roesch
Simon Fraser University

Richard Rogers
University of North Texas

Barry Rosenfeld
Fordham University

J. Peter Rosenfeld
Northwestern University

David F. Ross
University of Tennessee at Chattanooga

David B. Rottman
National Center for State Courts

R. Barry Ruback
Pennsylvania State University

Melissa B. Russano
Roger Williams University

Michael J. Saks
Arizona State University

Karen L. Salekin
University of Alabama

Randall T. Salekin
University of Alabama

C. Gabrielle Salfati
John Jay College of Criminal Justice,
City University of New York

Larissa A. Schmersal
University of Texas at El Paso

Bethany Schneider
Indiana University–Bloomington

Jonathan W. Schooler
University of British Columbia

Regina A. Schuller
York University

Carolyn Semmler
Flinders University

Ralph C. Serin
Carleton University

Michael C. Seto
Centre for Addiction and Mental Health

John S. Shaw III
Lafayette College

Daniel W. Shuman
Southern Methodist University

Sarah L. Shurbert
Winona State University

Leigh Silverton
University of California, Los Angeles

Diane Sivasubramaniam
John Jay College of Criminal Justice,
City University of New York

Jennifer L. Skeem
University of California, Irvine

Candice A. Skrapec
California State University, Fresno

Amy E. Smith
San Francisco State University

Brian C. Smith
Graceland University

Brooke A. Smith
Univerity of Texas at El Paso

Samuel R. Sommers
Tufts University

F. Caitlin Sothmann
John Jay College of Criminal Justice,
City University of New York

Loretta J. Stalans
Loyola University

Barbara Stanley
John Jay College of Criminal Justice,
City University of New York; New York State
Psychiatric Institute/Columbia University

Nancy K. Steblay
Augsburg College

Dennis J. Stevens
Sacred Heart University

Veronica Stinson
Saint Mary's University

Tania Stirpe
Correctional Service of Canada

Leif A. Strömwall
Göteborg University

Christina A. Studebaker
ThemeVision LLC

Alicia Summers
University of Nevada, Reno

Kyle J. Susa
University of Texas at El Paso

Jeffrey W. Swanson
Duke University

Marvin S. Swartz
Duke University

Victoria Talwar
McGill University

Tom N. Tombaugh
Carleton University

Allison Tome
Nova Southeastern University

Glenn Took
University of New South Wales

Joseph Toomey
John Jay College of Criminal Justice,
City University of New York

Jennifer M. Torkildson
John Jay College of Criminal Justice,
City University of New York

Colin G. Tredoux
University of Cape Town

John Turtle
Ryerson University

Lori Van Wallendael
University of North Carolina at Charlotte

John Vanderkolk
Indiana State Police Laboratory

Jose H. Vargas
University of Nevada, Reno

Sarah Vidal
University of California, Irvine

Jodi L. Viljoen
Simon Fraser University

Gina M. Vincent
University of Massachusetts

Aldert Vrij
University of Portsmouth

Lenore E. Walker
Nova Southeastern University

Glenn D. Walters
Federal Correctional Institution-Schuylkill

Lezlee J. Ware
Ohio University

Kelly A. Watt
University of Illinois at Urbana-Champaign

Christopher Webster
Simon Fraser University, University of Toronto

Rebecca A. Weiss
Fordham University

Gary L. Wells
Iowa State University

David B. Wexler
University of Arizona, University of Puerto Rico

Jennifer Wheeler
Private Practice

Karen E. Whittemore
Forensic Psychiatric Services

Michelle R. Widows
Psychological Assessment Resources, Inc.

Richard L. Wiener
University of Nebraska–Lincoln

Tisha R. A. Wiley
University of Illinois at Chicago

Kipling D. Williams
Purdue University

Kirk R. Williams
University of California, Riverside

Catherine M. Wilson
Simon Fraser University

Kathryn R. Wilson
University of Nebraska

Bruce J. Winick
University of Miami

Roselle L. Wissler
Arizona State University

Dan Yarmey
University of Guelph

Matt C. Zaitchik
Roger Williams University

Patricia A. Zapf
*John Jay College of Criminal Justice,
City University of New York*

Heather Zelle
Drexel University

Philip G. Zimbardo
Stanford University

Laura A. Zimmerman
Klein Associates

Introduction

Why an Encyclopedia of Psychology and Law?

Psychology and law is a relatively young field of scholarship. Conceptualized broadly, the field encompasses diverse approaches to psychology. Each of the major psychological subdivisions has contributed to research on legal issues: cognitive (e.g., eyewitness testimony), developmental (e.g., children's testimony), social (e.g., jury behavior), clinical (e.g., assessment of competence), biological (e.g., the polygraph), and industrial-organizational psychology (e.g., sexual harassment in the workplace). Scholars from university settings, research institutions, and various government agencies in several continents have contributed substantially to the growth of empirical knowledge of psychology-law issues. Though young, the field shows clear signs of maturation. These signs include scientific journals devoted exclusively to psychology-law research; the publication of psychology-law research in highly prestigious psychology journals; professional associations devoted to psychology and law in the United States, Canada, Europe, and Australia; annual professional conferences; and hundreds of books on psychology and law topics.

Psychology and law is also a practice. Clinical psychologists who practice in forensic arenas provide assessment and treatment services in a wide variety of criminal and civil matters and in law enforcement. Social psychologists employ their knowledge of psychology and law as trial consultants, assisting attorneys with jury selection and trial preparation. Clinical and experimental psychologists serve as expert witnesses in criminal and civil trials. These are but a few examples of practice in psychology and law. Practitioners draw on the tools and knowledge supplied by the traditional domains of psychological inquiry and the specialized domains of psychology and law.

Psychology and law play a significant role in postgraduate education and professional development. Psychology-law courses are increasingly common in undergraduate psychology programs, and many such offerings are filled to capacity with undergraduate students weaned on justice- and crime-themed media and literature. Attracted by the compelling application of psychology to real-world criminal investigations and trials, undergraduate students frequently volunteer as research assistants in psychology and law laboratories. Master's and doctoral programs focusing on various aspects of psychology and law have been developed and provide the research and service industries with additional intellectual capital. Postdoctoral training and professional certification options in forensic psychology support the development of a profession that is uniquely qualified to address mental health issues in a wide variety of legal contexts.

The development of psychology and law as a field of scholarship, practice, and education has numerous societal benefits and is consistent with the trend toward interdisciplinary inquiry. Although welcome in these respects, the marriage between these two broad disciplines poses several boundary challenges. Psychology and law is interdisciplinary in that it encompasses the fields of psychology and law. It is also inter-subdisciplinary in that it encompasses all the traditional subdisciplines of psychology. Given the lack of "ownership" of this field by any one discipline or subdiscipline, the lack of comprehensive references sources (e.g., textbooks, handbooks, encyclopedias) is particularly acute. A comprehensive encyclopedia of psychology and law represents an attempt to help fill this substantial gap in the holdings of academic, professional, and personal libraries. It is our hope that this resource will be of immense help for scholars, practitioners, and students of psychology and law.

Organization of the *Encyclopedia of Psychology and Law*

The *Encyclopedia of Psychology and Law* addresses the interface of the two named disciplines and draws from the related discipline of criminal justice. As is typical of encyclopedias, the entries in the *Encyclopedia of Psychology and Law* are listed in letter-by-letter order, in this case from the Ackerman-Schoendorf Parent Evaluation of Custody Test (ASPECT) to Wrongful Conviction (our efforts to identify key concepts in "X," "Y," or "Z," were unsuccessful). The enthusiastic reader who tackles this two-volume set from beginning to end will learn a great deal about the trees but little about the forest, for alphabetical order corresponds with no other meaningful organizing principle among these headwords.

Readers are strongly advised, therefore, to study or at least consult the Reader's Guide. The Reader's Guide organizes the headwords into meaningful themes as follows:

- Criminal Competencies
- Criminal Responsibility
- Death Penalty
- Divorce and Child Custody
- Education and Professional Development
- Eyewitness Memory
- Forensic Assessment in Civil and Criminal Cases
- Juvenile Offenders
- Mental Health Law
- Psychological and Forensic Assessment Instruments
- Psychology of Criminal Behavior
- Psychology of Policing and Investigations
- Sentencing and Incarceration
- Symptoms and Disorders Relevant to Forensic Assessment
- Trial Processes
- Victim Reactions to Crime
- Violence Risk Assessment

Each entry falls into at least one of the Reader's Guide categories, and many entries appear in multiple categories. The Reader's Guide itself provides one approach to partitioning the field of psychology and law. Although we make no claims that our list of headwords is exhaustive, the relative size of the Reader's Guide categories probably provides an estimate of the relative attention paid to these topics in the scholarly literature. For example, Eyewitness Memory is a very popular field of study and a very well-populated Reader's Guide category.

Brewing the *Encyclopedia*

Developing the list of headwords was a most unusual task. We used somewhat of an "hourglass" approach in developing the headword list. First, we developed the Reader's Guide—that is, the set of categories under which the entries would be classified. Guided by a variety of resources at our disposal (e.g., psychology and law textbooks, journals, library databases), we developed a set of categories that seemed to us to span the breadth of psychology and law. Using these categories, we developed several drafts of a headword list to the point at which we were ready to receive additional expert input.

To obtain such input, we assembled an advisory board consisting of 17 distinguished scholars and practitioners from the United States, Canada, Europe, and Australia. The scholarship and practice interests of this group are diverse and span the broad field of psychology and law. This distinguished group included previous and current editors of psychology and law journals, past presidents of professional organizations of psychology and law, authors of numerous books and articles on psychology and law topics, and experienced practitioners in the forensic arenas. Members of the advisory board were sent the draft list of headwords and asked to recommend additions, deletions, and modifications to the list and to nominate authors for the headword entries. Their responses were enormously helpful in refining the list of headwords and identifying experts as potential contributors. The advisory board played a very significant role in shaping the content of the *Encyclopedia of Psychology and Law*. Its members also demonstrated strong enthusiasm for the project as a whole, confirming my belief that this resource will be important and useful.

The suggestions provided by the advisory board were integrated, and a near-final draft of the headword list was developed. We also developed our list of potential contributors. We sent contributors formal invitations to write entries, together with instructions and information on the *Encyclopedia of Psychology and Law*. Many contributors graciously accepted our invitations; others, for a variety of reasons, were unable to do so. Fortunately, the rich information provided by the members of the advisory board contained numerous backup options, and over time we obtained commitments from contributors for all the entries. During this phase, the contributors, who had access to the full list of headwords, made additional excellent suggestions for new headwords, and we made some additional revisions to the headword list.

The resulting list of contributors is impressive. The list includes distinguished scholars—individuals responsible for the first or most impressive scholarship on the topics about which they wrote. It also includes distinguished practitioners—psychologists and lawyers with extensive experience in these topics in actual cases. The list includes many junior and midcareer scholars and practitioners well on their way toward establishing distinguished careers in psychology and law. Finally, the list includes the very important voices of graduate students in psychology and law. The American Psychology-Law Society, a primary affiliation of many psychology and law scholars, has historically been warmly receptive and encouraging to graduate student members and continues to be so. Training the next generation of psychology and law scholars has been a very high priority for members of the Society. Many contributors to these volumes asked if their graduate students could be included as co-authors—sometimes as first authors—of their entries, and such requests were granted. We are delighted that the voices of graduate students are represented in this project.

Well before all the invitations were accepted and the headword list completed, we started to receive draft entries. The Editor read each entry as it was received, occasionally requesting peer review from the Associate Editor or other scholars with relevant expertise. Modifications were requested as necessary. Once the entries were accepted, they were forwarded to our Developmental Editor, Diana Axelsen, for her expert review and were eventually submitted for copyediting and publication. The quality of the entries is excellent. Contributors provided hundreds of well-organized, well-written, balanced descriptions of the numerous psychology and law topics covered in the *Encyclopedia*. Once the entries were complete we revisited the Reader's Guide and made some modifications based on full knowledge of the content received.

The end result is an outstanding collection of entries describing a very broad array of contemporary and historical psychology and law topics. It is our hope that these volumes will serve their intended purpose—that is, to inform scholars, practitioners, and students who share the interests of my editorial team, the advisory board, and the hundreds of contributors to this exciting field of scholarship and practice.

Acknowledgments

Several individuals are due recognition for their efforts on behalf of this project. Michael Carmichael and Rolf Janke of Sage were instrumental in launching this project. Diana Axelsen, Developmental Editor, provided immense expertise, collegiality, and social support from the project's inception to its completion. Sanford Robinson and Kate Schroeder lent their expertise as editors. Letitia Gutierrez, Reference Systems Manager at Sage, expertly managed the publication software that kept this project organized and on track.

The University of North Carolina at Charlotte and John Jay College of Criminal Justice, City University of New York, must be recognized for supporting the editorial team throughout this project. The Cutler, Zapf, and Greathouse families also supported the editorial team as they no doubt substituted family time for work time to pursue this project, and they deserve our gratitude. A special thanks is also due to Dr. Steven Rogelberg, a colleague and close friend, who as editor of the previously published *Encyclopedia of Industrial and Organizational Psychology* generously provided expertise and social support, which enhanced the quality and efficiency of our work.

Brian L. Cutler
Patricia A. Zapf
Sarah Greathouse

ACKERMAN-SCHOENDORF PARENT EVALUATION OF CUSTODY TEST (ASPECT)

The Ackerman-Schoendorf Parent Evaluation of Custody Test (ASPECT) was among the first forensic assessment instruments developed specifically for use in the area of parenting disputes. Its design requires the user to develop multiple data sources. The ASPECT laid the foundation for further search for objective, data-intensive assessment in this highly complex area of forensic work.

Description of the Instrument

The ASPECT is designed specifically to assist the evaluator in gathering information to be used in court-related assessments. It was one of the first instruments to be developed for the complex purpose of assessing a family when parenting time and responsibility are in dispute. This instrument relies on multiple data sources, including some psychological measures with good psychometric properties. It provides a structured approach to data collection and assimilation, ensures that the same evaluative criteria are applied to both parents, and attempts to quantify the results in a way that allows for comparison of their parental competency. In its conception and design, some effort was made to ensure that it was a reliable and valid measure that would convert the highly subjective child custody evaluation process to a more objective, deliberate, and defensible forensic technique.

The ASPECT comprises 56 items to be answered by the evaluator after a series of interviews, observations, and tests have been completed. The tests include the Minnesota Multiphasic Personality Inventory–2 (MMPI–2), the Rorschach, the Thematic Apperception Test/Children's Apperception Test (TAT/CAT), projective questions, projective drawings, and intellectual and achievement testing. Parents also complete a 57-item Parent Questionnaire. Selected data from the tests comprise the answers to 15 of the 56 evaluator questions; the other 44 questions address material to be deduced from the Parent Questionnaires, interviews, and observations. There are 12 critical items that are said to be significant indicators of parenting deficits. The 56 items are, according to the authors, equally weighted based on a rational approach and are combined to form a Parental Custody Index (PCI) for each parent. The three subscales, the Observational Scale, the Social Scale, and the Cognitive-Emotional Scale, have not proven to be useful, according to the authors, and should not be used for interpretation.

The mean PCI is 78, and the standard deviation is 10. The authors suggest that if parents' PCI scores are within 10 points of one another, joint custody with substantially equal placement is recommended; if they are more than 20 points apart, the higher-scoring parent is substantially more fit to parent, and primary placement with the possibility of sole custody should be explored. When scores are between 10 and 20 points apart, the authors recommend more closely scrutinizing collateral information to determine the appropriate custody arrangement. The standardization demographic ($n = 200$) of the ASPECT was predominately white and relatively homogeneous.

The test manual for the ASPECT reports high levels of interrater reliability. As evidence of validity, the authors claim that in judicial dispositions of 118 of the 200 cases in the normative sample for which outcome data were available, there was a 91% hit rate of dispositions matching recommendations.

Limitations of the ASPECT

There are significant weaknesses in the basic conceptualization and the psychometric properties of the ASPECT, as its authors concede. Critics have noted that there was inadequate research to establish the constructs to be measured and their relevance to competent parenting. Instrument selection for its component parts was done without sufficient analysis to determine whether the data collected added incremental validity to the assessment of parenting strengths. Although a number of the factors to be considered by the user may seem to be logically associated with parenting, some clearly lack such inferential connectedness, and no empirical link is provided.

Further research is needed to support the cut score recommended by the authors, as well as to support the ideas that high PCI scorers are more effective parents, that sole custody is the best arrangement for children of parents who have disparate PCI scores, and that 20 points is sufficiently disparate for a recommendation of sole custody. Finally, further data are needed to support the implicit notion that the ASPECT takes into account all relevant data to be considered by the evaluator in formulating recommendations, if any, to be offered to the court for apportionment of parenting time and responsibility. The ASPECT's relevance and reliability have not been adequately demonstrated to justify its use for the court-referred assessments for which it was designed.

Mary Connell

See also Divorce and Child Custody

Further Readings

Ackerman, M. J. (2005). The Ackerman-Schoendorf Scales for Parent Evaluation of Custody (ASPECT): A review of research and update. *Journal of Child Custody, 2*(1/2), 179–193.

Connell, M. A. (2005). Review of "The Ackerman-Schoendorf Scales for Parent Evaluation of Custody" (ASPECT). *Journal of Child Custody, 2,* 195–209.

Heinze, M. C., & Grisso, T. (1996). Review of instruments assessing parenting competencies used in child custody evaluations. *Behavioral Sciences and the Law, 14,* 293–313.

Otto, R. K., & Edens, J. F. (2003). Parenting capacity. In T. Grisso (Ed.), *Evaluating competencies: Forensic assessments and instruments* (2nd ed., pp. 229–307). New York: Kluwer Academic/Plenum.

ADJUDICATIVE COMPETENCE OF YOUTH

Although the early juvenile justice system did not require that adolescent defendants be able to understand and participate in their legal proceedings, courts have increasingly required that adolescent defendants, like adult criminal defendants, be competent to proceed to adjudication (competent to stand trial). This has raised a unique set of challenges for the courts and mental health clinicians. Research has indicated that young adolescents have high rates of deficits in competence-related legal capacities in comparison with adults. As described below, however, little is known about assessing and treating adjudicative incompetence in youth, and legal standards regarding youths' adjudicative competence remain unclear.

Legal Standards for Juvenile Competence

Since the 1700s, the legal system has required that adult defendants tried in criminal courts be competent to proceed to adjudication. More specifically, the law requires that criminal defendants be able to understand the nature of the legal proceedings, appreciate the significance and possible consequences of these proceedings, communicate with their attorney, and reason about relevant legal decisions, such as how to plead. If defendants lack these capacities, they can be found incompetent, in which case their adjudication is typically suspended, and they are treated in an effort to restore their competence.

The early juvenile justice system, which was developed in Illinois in 1904, did not require that *adolescent* defendants be competent to proceed to adjudication. Because early juvenile justice was designed to be rehabilitative rather than punitive, it was not considered necessary that youth be able to understand and participate in their legal proceedings. However, during the 1990s, public concerns about youth violence rose to significant levels and drove a series of key legislative changes that allowed the transfer of adolescents to adult court to become easier and more common and for juveniles tried in juvenile court to be given harsher penalties.

Given the adultlike penalties that can now be given to youth, courts have increasingly required that adolescent defendants be competent to proceed to adjudication. At present, the specific nature of competence standards in juvenile courts remains unsettled. Although courts have generally required that adolescents have the same types of legal capacities as adults, some jurisdictions have held that lower levels of these capacities may suffice for adolescents in juvenile court.

Another issue that remains undetermined pertains to possible bases for findings of incompetence among adolescents. Although mental disorders and mental retardation are the most commonly recognized sources of incompetence, some adolescents may be incompetent owing to developmental immaturity rather than mental disorders or mental retardation. However, it is currently unclear whether jurisdictions will recognize developmental immaturity as a legitimate basis for a finding of incompetence.

Possible Sources of Adjudicative Incompetence in Youth

Legal deficits in youth may stem from very different sources. One possible cause of incompetence may be mental disorders. For instance, a young girl with a thought disorder may have a paranoid delusion that her attorney is conspiring against her and thus refuse to tell her attorney critical information regarding her case, a youth with symptoms of attention-deficit/hyperactivity disorder may have difficulty attending to court proceedings and managing his courtroom behavior, and a young girl with a depressive disorder may be unmotivated to adequately defend herself due to feelings of worthlessness.

A second possible cause of incompetence is mental retardation or severe cognitive deficits. Research has found that youth who have cognitive deficits are much more likely than other youth to demonstrate deficits in legal capacities relevant to adjudication. In addition to mental disorders and cognitive deficits, however, adolescents may also have impaired legal capacities simply due to normal developmental immaturity. Evidence for maturity-related legal deficits is provided by the MacArthur Juvenile Adjudicative Competence study. In this important study, Thomas Grisso and his colleagues examined the legal capacities of 927 adolescents and 466 adults from detained and community sites. Results indicated that young adolescents were more likely to demonstrate legal impairments than adults. Specifically, one third of youth aged 11 to 13 and one fifth of youth aged 14 to 15 demonstrated significant impairments in the understanding of legal proceedings and/or legal reasoning. In addition, young adolescents performed in a manner that suggested that they are less likely to recognize the risks and long-term consequences of legal judgments than older individuals.

While it is often assumed that experience with the legal system will mitigate any limitations in youths' legal capacities, this is not necessarily the case. Considerable research has indicated that simply having court experience does not equate to having adequate legal capacities.

The high rates of legal deficits in young adolescents may, in part, stem from the fact that youths' cognitive capacities may not yet have reached their adult potential. In addition, experts, including Elizabeth Scott, Lawrence Steinberg, and colleagues, have emphasized that psychosocial immaturity may also contribute to age-related impairments in competence-related legal capacities. Specifically, developmental psychology provides evidence that adolescents are more likely than adults to have difficulties in recognizing the consequences of their decisions, are more likely to be influenced by peers, and tend to act in an impulsive manner.

The research findings on youths' legal capacities raise a number of important issues for the legal system. While the legal system automatically assumes that adolescents, including young adolescents, are competent to stand trial unless proven otherwise, the high rate of legal impairments among young adolescents questions the appropriateness of this presumption. In addition, given that a high rate of young adolescents could show limited legal capacities, there is a considerable need for methods to assess adolescents who may be incompetent to proceed to adjudication and for strategies to remediate youths who are found incompetent.

Assessment of Youths' Adjudicative Competence

When an attorney or judge has concerns about a particular youth's adjudicative competence, the court will order that the youth be evaluated by a mental health professional to assess the youth's competence. These assessments differ considerably from general mental health evaluations in that they focus on youths' competence-related capacities as opposed to general mental health issues. In addition, juvenile competence assessments require procedures that differ somewhat from adult competence assessments. Specifically, juvenile evaluations should carefully assess youths' developmental maturity and consider contextual issues that are unique to adolescents, including possible caretaker involvement in legal proceedings.

As described by the leading expert in this field, Thomas Grisso, a key goal of juvenile competence evaluations is to describe the youths' functional legal capacities. In particular, competence reports should describe youths' understanding of important aspects of legal proceedings (e.g., understanding of the role of judges and attorneys), appreciation of the significance of legal proceedings (e.g., appreciation of the possible penalties that could be applied to them if found guilty), ability to communicate with counsel (e.g., the ability to disclose important information about their cases to their attorneys), and legal reasoning (e.g., the ability to weigh various plea options).

In evaluating youths' functional legal abilities, evaluators should consider how a specific youth's legal capacities match with the nature of his or her particular case. A finding of incompetence occurs when there is a significant mismatch between a particular defendant's legal capacities and the demands created by his or her particular case. For instance, if a youth who is charged with aggravated assault is going to be tried in adult court, where he or she will likely have to testify for lengthy periods of time, it will be important that the youth have the capacity to testify relevantly, an understanding of the transfer process, and an appreciation of the types of penalties that may be given to him or her in adult court. In contrast, if this youth's case was being handled in juvenile court and he or she had decided to accept a plea bargain instead of standing trial, it would not be as critical that he or she have a high level of testifying capacities, but it would be essential that he or she have a good understanding of plea bargains.

If a youth is found to have significant legal deficits in one or more the relevant areas (e.g., understanding, appreciation, communication with counsel, reasoning), the evaluator should attempt to provide information on possible causes of these legal deficits, such as whether the legal deficits appear to stem from a particular mental disorder and/or developmental immaturity. In addition, if a youth is found to have legal deficits, evaluators should offer opinions and recommendations regarding possible interventions to address these legal deficits.

Until recently, there have been no tools specifically for assessing youths' legal capacities. However, in 2005, Grisso developed a guide, called the Juvenile Adjudicative Competency Interview, to help structure assessments of youths' competence. The Juvenile Adjudicative Competency Interview is not currently a standardized instrument but instead functions as a guide to help ensure that clinicians consider key developmental and legal issues in assessing juveniles' adjudicative competence.

While some instruments that have been developed for adult defendants may have relevance to juvenile competence evaluations, caution is needed in applying adult instruments to youth; instruments that have been found to be reliable and valid with adults cannot be assumed to be reliable and valid with adolescents. Research has provided some preliminary support for the psychometric properties of the Fitness Interview Test–Revised when used with adolescents. Also, a number of evaluators report using the Competence Assessment for Standing Trial for Defendants with Mental Retardation with adolescent defendants, because its format is thought to be easier for adolescents to understand. However, research has yet to examine the psychometric properties of this tool with adolescent defendants.

Interventions for Remediating Incompetent Youth

After a competence evaluation has been conducted, the court must decide whether to find a youth incompetent. If a youth is found incompetent and is believed to be remediable, the trial will be suspended until he or she is considered to be competent. If the youth is considered to be unremediable, then his or her charges may be dropped and/or he or she may be referred to alternative services, such as inpatient mental health treatment.

At the present time, very little is known about how to remediate youth who are found incompetent to stand trial. However, there is reason to believe that this process may be challenging, especially when youth are found incompetent on the basis of mental retardation and/or developmental immaturity. Some research, using data from the MacArthur Juvenile Adjudicative Competence study, has found that young adolescents may be less likely than older individuals to benefit from brief teaching interventions targeted at improving their understanding of basic legal concepts, such as the role of judges and attorneys. It may be even more difficult to teach youth how to apply legal concepts to their own cases and how to reason about legal decisions. Given the high rates of legal deficits among young adolescents and the increasing numbers of adolescents who are being found incompetent, research in this area is greatly needed.

Jodi L. Viljoen

See also Capacity to Waive Rights; Juvenile Offenders; Mental Health Needs of Juvenile Offenders

Further Readings

Grisso, T. (2005). *Evaluating juveniles' adjudicative competence: A guide for clinical practice.* Sarasota, FL: Professional Resource Press.

Grisso, T., Steinberg, L., Woolard, J., Cauffman, E., Scott, E., Graham, S., et al. (2003). Juveniles' competence to stand trial: A comparison of adolescents' and adults' capacities as trial defendants. *Law and Human Behavior, 27,* 333–363.

Scott, E. S., Reppucci, N. D., & Woolard, J. L. (1995). Evaluating adolescent decision making in legal contexts. *Law and Human Behavior, 19,* 221–244.

Viljoen, J. L., & Grisso, T. (in press). Prospects for remediating juveniles' adjudicative incompetence. *Psychology, Public Policy, and the Law.*

ADULT ATTACHMENT INTERVIEW (AAI)

The Adult Attachment Interview (AAI), developed by Mary Main and associates, has been identified as an effective, psychometrically sound instrument with which to measure an individual's internal working model or state of mind regarding childhood attachment. The potentially detrimental influences of poor recall, social desirability, and naive lying associated with self-report measures of childhood attachment are substantially bypassed with the AAI. The AAI does not make classifications based primarily on reported events in childhood but rather on the thoughtfulness and coherency with which the adult is able to describe and evaluate these childhood experiences and their effects.

The AAI is a structured, semiclinical 20-question interview designed to elicit the individual's account of his or her childhood attachment experiences, together with his or her evaluations of those experiences on present functioning. It explores the quality of these childhood relationships and the memories that might justify them. The AAI is transcribed verbatim, with all hesitations carefully recorded and with only the transcript used in the analysis of the interview.

The AAI results in five classifications of state of mind regarding childhood attachment, which parallel those derived from M. D. S. Ainsworth's system, which is based on the "Strange Situation." Briefly, this procedure entails having the child enter an unfamiliar laboratory setting with a stranger present, filled with toys, with his or her caregiver. The caregiver then leaves twice and returns twice over a 20-minute period. Based on their responses, individuals are classified into one of the five attachment categories described below. Individuals with a Secure state of mind regarding attachment value relationships and grow to desire intimacy with others. Individuals classified as Dismissing tend to be devaluing of relationships. Such individuals may idealize relationships from their past but are cut off from related feelings or dismiss their significance. They may also be derogating of attachment in that they demonstrate a contemptuous dismissal of attachment relationships. Individuals with a Preoccupied state of mind are described as confused and unobjective. They may seem passive, vague or angry, conflicted, and unconvincingly analytical. The Unresolved category deals specifically with loss and abuse, and the Cannot Classify category is used when an individual does not fit clearly into any of the other classifications. Individuals categorized into one of the two disorganized patterns (i.e., Unresolved or Cannot Classify) of attachment can always be assigned to a best-fitting organized (Secure, Dismissing, Preoccupied) classification as well. That is, all individuals are believed to have one overriding organized state of mind regarding childhood attachment.

Several studies have examined the psychometric properties of the AAI (see Marinus H. van Ijzendoorn and Marian J. Bakermans-Kranenburg, 1996, for a summary). The AAI state-of-mind classifications are stable across 5-year periods, within 77% to 90%. One study found that individuals' response to the Strange Situation at 1 year of age was highly correlated (80%) to their AAI classification 20 years later. The AAI has been found to be unrelated to measures of intelligence, to both long- and short-term memory, to discourse patterns when individuals are interviewed on other topics, to interviewer effects, and to social desirability. Meta-analytic work has also supported the use of the AAI across several populations, including high-risk groups.

Tania Stirpe and colleagues employed the AAI with various groups of sexual offenders, examining five groups of subjects: extrafamilial child molesters (child molesters), intrafamilial child molesters (incest offenders), and sexual offenders against adult females (rapists) and two nonsexual offender comparison groups (violent and nonviolent). In addition, groups were compared with reference to normative data on the AAI. Results indicated that the majority of sexual offenders were insecure in their state of mind regarding attachment, representing a marked difference from normative samples. Although insecurity of attachment was common to all groups of offenders rather than specific to sexual offenders, there were important differences between groups with regard to the type of insecurity. Most notable were the child molesters, who were much more likely to be Preoccupied in their state of mind regarding attachment. Rapists, violent offenders, and, to a lesser degree, incest offenders, were more likely to have a Dismissing state of mind regarding attachment. Although still most likely to be judged Dismissing, nonviolent offenders were comparatively more likely than the other groups to be Secure. There were no differences between groups when Unresolved and Cannot Classify AAI classifications were considered. These findings provide evidence for the specificity of insecure attachment with regard to sexual offending, over and above its possibly more general influence on criminality.

Implications and Areas for Future Study

Research using the AAI has implications for the assessment and treatment of sexual offenders. Identifying the state of mind regarding attachment, together with its associated beliefs and interpersonal strategies, may provide valuable insight into the motivational strategies underlying offenses. As S. W. Smallbone and associates have argued, the intimacy problems faced by an individual whose offending is characterized by a devaluing of attachment are very different from those faced by one who fears rejection and offends in an attempt to cultivate a "relationship" with the victim.

Research suggests that early insecure attachment experiences may place some men at risk for later

offending. More specifically, some have suggested that these early experiences may contribute to sexual offending within a particular interpersonal context. Further research is required; however, the current empirical literature represents an important step in incorporating attachment theory into the etiology of sexual offending and in acknowledging that sexual offending may be constructively understood in terms of the relationship context in which it takes place. The AAI is the "gold standard" in attachment research but has rarely been used with forensic populations.

Tania Stirpe, Jeffrey Abracen, and Janice Picheca

See also Parent-Child Relationship Inventory (PCRI); Sex Offender Assessment; Sex Offender Treatment

Further Readings

Main, M., & Goldwyn, R. (1998). *Adult attachment rating and classification systems: Adult attachment coding manual.* Unpublished scoring manual, Department of Psychology, University of California, Berkeley.

Smallbone, S., & Dadds, M. (1998). Childhood attachment and adult attachment in incarcerated adult male sex offenders. *Journal of Interpersonal Violence, 13*(5), 555–573.

Stirpe, T., Abracen, J., Stermac, L., & Wilson, R. (2006). Sexual offenders' state-of-mind regarding childhood attachment: A controlled investigation. *Sexual Abuse: A Journal of Research and Treatment, 18,* 289–302.

van Ijzendoorn, M. H., & Bakermans-Kranenburg, M. J. (1996). Attachment representations in mothers, fathers, adolescents, and clinical groups: A meta-analytic search for normative data. *Journal of Consulting and Clinical Psychology, 64*(1), 8–21.

Ward, T., Hudson, S., Marshall, W., & Siegert, R. (1995). Attachment style and intimacy deficits in sexual offenders: A theoretical framework. *Sexual Abuse: A Journal of Research and Treatment, 7*(4), 317–335.

AGGRAVATING AND MITIGATING CIRCUMSTANCES, EVALUATION OF IN CAPITAL CASES

If a defendant is found guilty of a capital crime, the triers of fact are called on to weigh the significance of the aggravating and mitigating factors of the case and to use such judgments to decide whether the defendant will receive the death penalty or a life sentence. During the sentencing phase, the prosecution presents the relevant aggravating factors of the case, while the defense is charged with the duty of providing mitigation factors. Although no standard model exists to offer procedures for the investigation of mitigating factors, scholars, clinicians, and researchers have offered recommendations concerning the common types of information needed and the appropriate ways to present it to the jury. In all cases, a mitigation evaluation is conducted with the goal of humanizing the defendant to the jury, in the hope that they will not recommend the death penalty.

During the penalty phase of a capital offense trial, the triers of fact (i.e., the judge or jury depending on the state) are presented with two types of information: (1) *aggravating factors* (i.e., facts from the case that make it especially serious or heinous) and (2) *mitigating factors* (i.e., facts from the case that may reduce the defendant's moral culpability). As set forth in *Ring v. Arizona* (2002), to come forward with a recommendation for death, the jury must first be convinced beyond a reasonable doubt that the state has met its burden of proof with respect to the presence of one or more aggravating factors. Once this has been done, the defense is required to present mitigating factors with the goal of convincing the trier of fact that this individual does not deserve the penalty of death. The driving force behind this practice is the U.S. Supreme Court's assertion in *Furman v. Georgia* (1972) that sentences in capital cases should be individualized and should not be disproportionate or inappropriate given the mitigating factors in the case.

Aggravating factors in a capital case are often readily apparent from the circumstances of the crime. Like other states, the state of Texas has statutory aggravating factors that are precisely defined. Three examples of the criteria set forth by the Texas Penal Code are (a) if the person murders more than one person during the same criminal transaction; (b) if the person murders an individual under 6 years of age; and (c) if the person intentionally commits a murder in the course of committing (or attempting to commit) kidnapping, burglary, robbery, aggravated sexual assault, arson, or obstruction or retaliation.

In contrast to aggravating factors, which are established by statute, mitigating factors can be anything the defense chooses to present that it believes may sway the trier of fact to determine that life without parole is

the proper and just sentence in the particular case. The following list provides just a few examples of the most common mitigating factors that are brought forward in a capital trial: history of neglect and/or abuse during the formative years, the presence of a mental illness, youthfulness, and a limited history of involvement with the legal system. It was in *Lockett v. Ohio* (1978) that the U.S. Supreme Court decided that limiting the type and amount of mitigating factors that can be presented to the trier of fact is unconstitutional.

When deciding the sentence for a defendant who has been found guilty, jurors are asked to weigh the aggravating circumstances against the mitigating circumstances of the case. Each state has its own laws regarding how jurors are instructed to weigh aggravating and mitigating circumstances, but in all states, each individual juror must weigh the circumstances and decide whether the defendant is sentenced to death or life in prison. In many states, the death penalty can be imposed only if the jury returns a unanimous decision.

With respect to the process of conducting a mitigation evaluation, the onus is on the defense team to conduct a thorough investigation of all possible mitigating factors. To complete such an investigation, it is recommended that the defense team hire one or more professionals to carry out the various tasks required for the investigation and presentation of mitigating circumstances. In *Wiggins v. Smith* (2003), the U.S. Supreme Court ruled that failure on the part of the defense team to properly investigate and introduce mitigating evidence can result in a finding of ineffective assistance of counsel, leaving open the possibility that the verdict will be overturned on appeal.

Perhaps the most traditional form of investigation is that carried out by a professional known as a *mitigation specialist*. Although social workers often serve in this role, other professionals, such as paralegals, legal researchers, and attorneys, also work in this capacity. Regardless of the profession, the role of the mitigation specialist requires a commitment to uncover all possible mitigating factors, and to do this, it is imperative that he or she has a wide repertoire of knowledge and skills. For example, it is expected that the specialist be well versed in the field of human development and be skilled in the areas of data collection, interviewing, and putting together a person's life history. At a minimum, the mitigation specialist should request and receive records that are reflective of the defendant's life history (e.g., medical records, mental health records, and school records), conduct interviews with a variety of individuals who are familiar with the defendant (e.g., parents, siblings, friends, employers, teachers, therapists), and conduct multiple interviews with the defendant. In many cases, it is also critical that the mitigation specialist investigate the life histories of the defendant's parents and other members of their immediate and extended family. Such information is important with respect to being able to evaluate both genetic and environmental influences on the defendant's development. Given the breadth of the investigation required, it is recommended that it be initiated long before the trial is set to begin.

The goal of the mitigation specialist is to compile information concerning the defendant's life history that will offer insight into how the defendant's life experiences have shaped his or her development. Presentation of such information is aimed at humanizing the individual to the degree that the trier of fact recommends a life sentence. It should be clear, however, that the goal of mitigation is not to excuse the defendant's behavior but instead to explain how an individual can become the type of person who could be in a position to commit a capital offense.

Depending on their credentials and the role that they have been asked to play, mitigation specialists may or may not testify as to the information gathered. In cases where they do not testify, the information they gather is provided to one or more appropriate professionals. These individuals not only will present the information to the court but also will be expected to present it in such a way that it is accessible to the jury. For example, a psychologist or a social worker may testify about the defendant's childhood development, the impact of childhood abuse, the impact of being raised without a father figure in the home, and any mental illness he or she may have experienced. A neuropsychologist may provide expert opinions regarding the influence of traumatic brain injury on the defendant's functioning, and an anthropologist or sociologist may testify to the effects of sociological or economic factors related to the defendant's neighborhood that may have influenced the defendant's developmental trajectory.

Regardless of who presents the mitigation information to the court, recent literature has recommended that the presentation of such information be structured on the concepts of risk factors, protective factors, and resiliency. In brief, risk factors can be described as events in an individual's life that have been scientifically linked to negative outcomes in functioning. Examples of common risk factors in capital defendants

include childhood or adult trauma, childhood abuse or neglect, poverty, substance abuse, negative peer groups, cognitive impairment, and a diagnosis of conduct disorder in childhood or adolescence. Research has shown that individuals who have experienced multiple risk factors during their development are at a greater likelihood of exhibiting dysfunction in multiple domains. The individuals who are retained to testify about such risk factors have an obligation not only to deliver their findings to the court but also to illustrate how those risk factors influenced the development of this defendant.

To further the defense team's endeavor of obtaining a non–death sentence, the mitigation expert(s) should also discuss the relevant protective factors that the defendant has experienced. Protective factors can be described as those events or experiences in the defendant's life that may have lessened the likelihood that the defendant would have engaged in violent or dangerous behavior in the past. Examples of common protective factors include social support from family and friends, prior involvement in mental health treatments, and financial stability. It is quite typical for an expert to discuss how the absence of protective factors negatively affected the defendant's developmental trajectory and if protective factors were present, why they did not buffer the defendant against the negative influence of the risk factors.

The final dimension of mitigation presentation should include a discussion of the defendant's lack of resilience in the context of his or her experience with risk and protective factors. Resilience refers to the ability of individuals who have experienced great adversity to overcome such experiences and live a functional life in adulthood. Since only a small minority of individuals who face great adversity during their development actually go on to exhibit severe dysfunction in adulthood, it is important to convey to the jury how the defendant's unique combination of risk and protective factors, along with his or her response to them, led to the violent behavior for which the defendant has been convicted.

To date, research has not found any one strategy that is successful in all cases, nor has research identified any one mitigating factor that influences juror decision making in all cases. On the contrary, it is likely that the success of mitigation relates to the quality of the investigation and the presentation of information that is unique to the case. As such, it would be inappropriate for defense attorneys and other members of the defense team to think that there is a template that can be applied to these investigations. Finally, it should be noted that even the most eloquent presentation of mitigation evidence can be insufficient to counteract the effects of intrinsic juror biases, impairments in understanding the concept of aggravating and mitigating factors, and misinterpretation of instructions to the jury regarding how to weigh the evidence presented to them.

Bridget M. Doane and Karen L. Salekin

See also Aggravating and Mitigating Circumstances in Capital Trials, Effects on Jurors; Death Penalty; Expert Psychological Testimony, Forms of; Mental Illness and the Death Penalty; Mental Retardation and the Death Penalty

Further Readings

Connell, M. A. (2003). A psychobiographical approach to the evaluation for sentence mitigation. *Journal of Psychiatry and Law, 31,* 319–354.

Fabian, J. M. (2003). Death penalty mitigation and the role of the forensic psychologist. *Law and Psychology Review, 27,* 73–120.

Furman v. Georgia, 408 U.S. 238 (1972).

Lockett v. Ohio, 438 U.S. 586 (1978).

Miller, J. (2003). The defense team in capital cases. *Hofstra Law Review, 31,* 1117–1141.

Ring v. Arizona, 536 U.S. 584 (2002).

Salekin, K. L. (2006). The importance of risk factors, protective factors, and the construct of resilience. In M. Costanzo, D. Krauss, & K. Pezdek (Eds.), *Expert psychological testimony for the courts.* Thousand Oaks, CA: Sage.

Schroeder, J., Guin, C. C., Pogue, R., & Bordelon, D. (2006). Mitigating circumstances in death penalty decisions: Using evidence-based research to inform social work practice in capital trials. *Social Work, 51,* 355–364.

Wiggins v. Smith, 539 U.S. 510 (2003).

Aggravating and Mitigating Circumstances in Capital Trials, Effects on Jurors

Aggravating factors are elements of the crime or the defendant's prior criminal record that not only make the defendant eligible for the death penalty but also serve to make the defendant more likely to receive the death penalty. *Mitigating factors* are elements of the crime or the defendant's character and background that could make the defendant less likely to receive the death penalty. Statutes across the United States list many aggravating and mitigating factors that could be presented at trial. The existing research in psychology and law shows that jurors are sensitive to some factors but not to others. Experimental research has compared hypothetical cases in which various aggravating and mitigating factors are either present or absent. Other research, especially the Capital Jury Project, has surveyed or interviewed jurors who served in a death penalty case about what factors they considered important when making their decision.

Aggravating Factors

Jurors are more likely to sentence to death defendants who have committed a heinous, brutal, or cruel murder. Such crimes include those involving a single victim who suffers a lot of pain before death and also crimes with multiple victims. The brutality of a murder triggers jurors' desire for retribution, or punishing someone for the harm that he or she has caused. Several lines of research show that jurors treat more severe crimes more harshly when assigning punishment in general, not just in death penalty cases. Jurors may not understand what the words heinous or atrocious mean, or they may believe that all murders are heinous. Thus, courts must instruct jurors that this aggravating factor is limited in some way, so that they are supposed to apply it only in cases involving torture, very serious physical abuse, or extreme depravity. However, even without such extreme case facts, jurors will sentence a defendant to death more often if the crime is more severe and causes more harm. Usually, in death penalty trials, a separate listed factor is included for murders with multiple victims, because heinousness is a specific legal term measuring how much suffering occurred before the victim's death.

Jurors also consider the future dangerousness of a defendant—whether he or she is likely to commit another serious crime. In some states, jurors are specifically asked to decide whether the defendant is likely to re-offend, but even when not asked, jurors often bring this issue up during deliberations. The more the jurors fear that the defendant could re-offend, or even be released on parole, the more likely they are to sentence the defendant to death. Similarly, if the defendant has a prior criminal record that includes violent crimes, he or she will be seen as more dangerous, and jurors are more likely to sentence that defendant to death than defendants with no prior record.

Jurors are also affected by victim characteristics and *victim impact statements*. If the victim is a public figure or a policeman, jurors are more likely to sentence the defendant to death. The murder of such a person causes more harm to the community and deserves a more severe punishment. Furthermore, jurors are allowed to consider whether the victim was particularly vulnerable—for instance, because of young or old age or disability. Some research supports an increase in death verdicts in cases of child victims, but little research exists on other aspects of victim vulnerability. Jurors can also consider the effect that the murder has on the victim's surviving family, friends, and the community. Several studies have found that jurors are more likely to give the death penalty when there is a large amount of suffering by the victim's family and the community. Courts and researchers debate whether these effects are the result of jurors' sensitivity to an increase in the amount of harm caused or instead an emotional reaction to the testimony.

Victim characteristics can be important even without victim impact statements. Some legal scholars and social scientists worry that jurors may be improperly considering the "worth" of the victim, or distinguishing between a good victim and a bad victim, which the law says they are not supposed to do. However, interviews with jurors suggest that jurors' verdicts are different not necessarily because of a distinction between a good victim and a bad one but rather because of the similarity between the victim and themselves. Jurors can identify or empathize more with a normal victim chosen at random than a victim who is part of the crime or involved in a risky situation. In fact, that the victim is the defendant's accomplice or otherwise part of the crime is often a mitigating factor. Overall, victim characteristics are weighed heavily a lot by jurors.

Many other aggravating factors exist in death penalty cases, such as committing the murder for financial gain, in the course of another felony, or after substantial planning. However, research has not yet addressed the effect of these aggravating factors on jurors' decisions.

Mitigating Factors

Although jurors have trouble understanding the legal definition of mitigating factors, there are some factors that affect their decisions. The factors that have the largest effect are, generally speaking, those that are out of the defendant's control, are more severe, and reduce the defendant's responsibility for the murder.

Mental illness is the most powerful mitigating factor, even if it is not enough to make the defendant legally insane. Recognizing this large effect, the American Bar Association has recently called for the exclusion of severely mentally ill defendants from eligibility for the death penalty. Jurors likewise believe that a mental disorder can make a defendant less responsible for his or her crime. However, all mental disorders are not the same. Severe and typical disorders, such as schizophrenia and delusional disorders, will reduce the likelihood of a death sentence. Most studies also show that low IQ and "borderline" mental retardation also reduce death sentences, and defendants who are legally mentally retarded are not eligible for the death penalty at all. Disorders such as depression, antisocial personality disorder, or bipolar disorder have less effect on jurors, if any. Not much research has addressed these types of mental illness.

Researchers and courts recognize the fact that some mental disorders can be aggravating factors. The fact that a defendant has an antisocial personality disorder or a low IQ may cause jurors to think that that the defendant is dangerous, so jurors may be *more* likely to impose the death sentence. Specific symptoms that may influence jurors are the defendant's inability to control violent impulses or to learn from mistakes. Not enough research currently exists to clarify when these disorders will be treated as aggravating and when they will be treated as mitigating.

Drug or alcohol addiction and intoxication are forms of mental disorder because drug use impairs the decision-making capacity of the defendant and can induce other disorders. In many states, voluntary intoxication cannot be used as a legal defense to a crime but can still be a mitigating factor. Two studies have shown that intoxication at the time of the crime can reduce the likelihood of the death penalty.

Having been abused as a child or having had a difficult childhood and background is also commonly presented as a mitigating factor, but again, this factor could produce mixed reactions in jurors. Very severe physical and verbal abuse reduces the likelihood of a death sentence, but less severe abuse or a troubled childhood may not affect verdicts. Some courts, legal scholars, and social scientists assert that a troubled childhood could also be seen as an aggravating factor if the defendant's background includes violent acts or previous arrests. This again suggests that jurors are more concerned about a defendant's dangerousness than about a defendant's mitigating evidence.

Because jurors are concerned about the defendant's dangerousness and likelihood to be violent, evidence that the defendant has been or will be a well-behaved and model prisoner can also reduce the likelihood of the death verdict. Only one (as yet unpublished) study has found this result, but this could be a very important mitigating factor. Likewise, the lack of a prior criminal record reduces jurors' perceptions of dangerousness and, therefore, also decreases jurors' likelihood of sentencing the defendant to death.

Interviews with jurors who have given a verdict of death penalty show that jurors will give the death penalty less often if the defendant expresses remorse for his or her crime. However, no experimental study has found an effect of remorse in death penalty trials. A defendant's silence, or even a statement that he or she is not remorseful, could have an aggravating effect, producing more death penalty verdicts. A defendant's remorse is often presented along with a religious plea, or testimony that the defendant has become more religious while in prison and is asking for forgiveness. At least one study suggests that a defendant's conversion to religion can affect jurors and sensitize them to other mitigating factors as well.

Little research has addressed the effect of a defendant's "good character," such as serving the community, going to church, or previous good acts. Jurors may have difficulty considering this evidence if there are serious aggravating factors. Research shows that, during their deliberations, jurors focus much more on the crime than on the defendant's character. Jurors also tend to focus on the circumstances that formed a defendant's character rather than examples of previous good acts.

In the case of *Roper v. Simmons* in 2005, the Supreme Court banned the execution of defendants who committed their crime before the age of 18. Research conducted before that decision found that jurors did give the death penalty less often to juvenile offenders. Research also suggests that an 18- or 19-year-old defendant will be sentenced to death less often, but the mitigating effect of being a youthful defendant declines quickly beyond the age of 20.

Interviews with death penalty jurors have also found that jurors give the death penalty less often if there is any lingering or residual doubt about the defendant's guilt, though in most cases, there is no such doubt. This type of evidence can be restricted in death penalty sentencing hearings, but jurors may carry over such doubt from the guilt phase of the trial.

Kevin M. O'Neil

See also Aggravating and Mitigating Circumstances, Evaluation of in Capital Cases; Death Penalty; Juries and Judges' Instructions; Jury Understanding of Judges' Instructions in Capital Cases; Juveniles and the Death Penalty; Mental Illness and the Death Penalty; Mental Retardation and the Death Penalty

Further Readings

Durham, A. M., Elrod, H. P., & Kinkade, P. T. (1996). Public support for the death penalty: Beyond Gallup. *Justice Quarterly, 13,* 705–736.
Garvey, S. P. (1998). Aggravation and mitigation in capital cases: What do jurors think? *Columbia Law Review, 98,* 1538–1575.
Roper v. Simmons, 543 U.S. 551 (2005).
Sundby, S. E. (2003). The capital jury and empathy: The problem of worthy and unworthy victims. *Cornell Law Review, 88,* 343–381.

ALCOHOL INTOXICATION

See Substance Abuse and Intimate Partner Violence; Substance Use Disorders

ALCOHOL INTOXICATION, IMPACT ON EYEWITNESS MEMORY

Alcohol consumption has a significant effect on eyewitness identification abilities, including the accuracy of perpetrator descriptions and identification accuracy in showups (an identification procedure where only one individual is shown to the witness) and lineups (an identification procedure where several individuals, usually six in the United States, are shown to the eyewitness). Understanding the effects of alcohol consumption on memory is critical for the police, investigators, prosecutors, defense counsel, judges, and jurors to be able to judge the veracity of statements and evidence that are put forward in cases where alcohol consumption was present.

The research to date that has examined the effects of moderate levels of alcohol intoxication on eyewitness memory and identification accuracy has found that intoxicated witnesses are less likely to be accurate in their descriptions of events and people but are just as likely as sober witnesses to make a correct identification decision. In addition, intoxicated witnesses may be more susceptible to suggestion and suggestive procedures than are sober witnesses. However, as research has suggested, this finding should not necessarily be taken to imply that intoxicated witnesses are always less reliable than their sober counterparts.

Ethyl alcohol, or ethanol, is a depressant that is produced by the fermentation of yeast, sugars, and starches and is most commonly found in beer, wine, and liquor. After it is ingested, alcohol is metabolized by enzymes in the liver. However, because the liver can only metabolize small amounts of alcohol at a time, the remaining alcohol is left to circulate through the body until it can be processed. Alcohol impairs judgment and coordination as well as attention level, and the more alcohol consumed, the greater the impairment. For example, in all states in the United States, the maximum level of blood-alcohol concentration (BAC) that is permitted to be under the "legal limit" for driving a motor vehicle is 0.08% (80 mg/dl). However, the effects of alcohol intoxication as described above are likely to be present at BACs much lower than is set by the legal limit.

Although scientists and researchers know that alcohol consumption causes reduced coordination and impaired judgment, the effects of alcohol intoxication on memory has received little attention from psychology and law researchers. One of the potential reasons for this is that previous research has focused on the effects of alcohol from a public safety perspective (i.e., setting legal limits for driving) and not from a victim or witness perspective. However, given that there are more than 450,000 violent crimes in bars and nightclubs every year in the United States (and therefore more than 450,000 victims/witnesses who are likely to have consumed at least some alcohol), research on this topic is extremely valuable. The general findings from the few research studies that have investigated the memory and identification abilities of intoxicated witnesses are described below after a brief review of alcohol decision-making theory and a description of the research methodologies that are used in this field of research.

Theoretical Review

Not long ago, researchers believed that alcohol acted as a general disinhibitor that resulted in risky decision making, best characterized by the phase "throwing caution to the wind." However, the *disinhibition hypothesis* was unable to account for the finding that in some situations an intoxicated individual would become aggressive, whereas at other times the same individual would become depressed or happy. In an attempt to account for these disparate reactions to alcohol consumption, *alcohol myopia theory* was proffered. According to this theory, intoxicated persons, due to their limited cognitive capacity as a result of their alcohol consumption, are able to attend only to the most salient aspect in their environment. For example, a sober person is capable of having a conversation with another person while attending to other events in the surroundings, such as a new person entering the room. An intoxicated person having the same conversation, however, is much less likely to notice peripheral details in the environment. Similarly, intoxicated persons are more likely than sober persons to take into account only the immediate cues in their environment and to have a limited capacity to consider or bring to awareness other information, such as the consequences of their behavior.

Alcohol Research Methodologies

Although the research literature on this topic is limited, a discussion of the types of research methodologies that are most common when investigating the effects of alcohol on eyewitness memory is warranted. Two of the most common techniques are laboratory research and field studies.

Laboratory Research

Laboratory research on this topic involves (a) prescreening participants for any factor that would make them ineligible for alcohol consumption research (e.g., underaged participant or pregnant female), (b) obtaining the consent to participate, and (c) administering alcohol. The amount of alcohol given is calculated on a participant-by-participant basis and takes into consideration the following factors: the desired BAC, the concentration of the alcohol being administered, and the participant's sex and weight. The alcohol is generally administered over a period of 30 to 45 minutes, and after a short period of time (for adsorption), the stimulus (e.g., video clip of a taped mock crime or an interaction with a confederate) is then presented to the participant. Next, depending on the particular research question, the participants may be asked to complete the dependent measures while still intoxicated, or they may be asked to return for a follow-up session, where they will be sober when they complete the dependent measures. Regardless of the research question, for safety purposes, all participants in this type of research must be relatively sober before they are permitted to leave the research lab. To ensure that participants' BAC is low enough for them to be excused (usually 0.03% or lower, as set by individual institutional review boards), a breathalyzer is used. It should be noted that although a blood-test analysis could also be conducted in lieu of a breathalyzer, this practice is not normally used by psychology and law researchers. Also, laboratory research is limited with regard to the amount of alcohol that can be safely administered to participants. Although there may be exceptions depending on the location (country) of data collection, the research question, and individual IRBs, generating BACs in the lab greater than 0.08% is rarely permitted.

Field Studies

Field studies, on the other hand, do not normally screen participants for characteristics that would make them ineligible for lab studies because participants in field studies are obtained in bars or drinking establishments and have consumed alcohol, presumably on their own volition, prior to taking part in the research study. Also, because participants have consumed alcohol on their own, obtaining participants with BACs higher than 0.08% is common. Overall, there are few differences between field and lab research with regard to the presentation of stimuli or measuring of dependent variables. One important difference, however, should be noted. Due to the fact that participants in field studies are intoxicated at the time when consent to participate is given, they must be provided with an opportunity to withdraw their participation at a later time (i.e., when they are sober).

Intoxicated Eyewitnesses: Experimental Findings

Researchers have been examining the effects of alcohol on eyewitness memory since the early 1990s. Early experiments examined the effects of alcohol on memory by comparing groups that were either sober or intoxicated at the time of encoding and then testing all participants on a different day when all participants were sober. The results from these studies suggested that intoxicated participants were less accurate when asked to recall the features of a target person and less accurate about describing the events that took place

during the critical encoding period than were sober witnesses. However, participants who were intoxicated during encoding were just as accurate at identifying a target person in an identification task as witnesses who had not consumed alcohol. Although these studies were not specifically testing alcohol myopia theory, the results are consistent with alcohol myopia theory predictions.

Later research examined the effects of alcohol intoxication at the time of encoding and at the identification task. Although it is possible to conduct this research by having participants return to the lab a second time to become intoxicated again (i.e., context reinstatement), this body of research administered the dependent variables (e.g., a showup) relatively soon after the viewing of the target person and while the participants were still intoxicated. This research was unique from earlier studies in that it allowed researchers to study alcohol myopia theory by manipulating (a) the behavior of the investigator and (b) the identification procedure. This research was relevant to real police practice because the police often encounter intoxicated individuals in the course of their investigations and there had been no research on the potential vulnerabilities of intoxicated witnesses to police practices. The findings of these studies suggest that intoxicated participants are more susceptible to minor changes in police procedure, such as the instructions that are given to a witness prior to viewing a showup (e.g., "Please be careful when making your decision.") and biased identification procedures (e.g., when the suspect is shown wearing similar clothes to those worn by the perpetrator). Ultimately, however, intoxicated witnesses could, under the circumstances of these research studies, be more accurate than sober witnesses. In addition, correct identification decision rates were in the neighborhood of 90%—a notably high rate even for sober witnesses in eyewitness identification research.

Jennifer E. Dysart

See also Eyewitness Descriptions, Accuracy of; Eyewitness Memory; Identification Tests, Best Practices in

Further Readings

Dysart, J. E., Lindsay, R. C. L., MacDonald, T. K., & Wicke, C. (2002). The intoxicated witness: Effects of alcohol on identification accuracy. *Journal of Applied Psychology, 87,* 170–175.

Read, J. D., Yuille, J. C., & Tollestrup, P. (1992). Recollections of a robbery: Effects of arousal and alcohol upon recall and person identification. *Law and Human Behavior, 16,* 425–446.

Steele, C. M., & Josephs, R. A. (1990). Alcohol myopia: Its prized and dangerous effects. *American Psychologist, 45,* 921–933.

Yuille, J. C., & Tollestrup, P. (1990). Some effects of alcohol on eyewitness memory. *Journal of Applied Psychology, 75,* 268–273.

ALIBI WITNESSES

An *alibi,* in its most basic form, is a plea that one was not present when a crime was being committed. In practice, alibis can be considerably more complex than a simple narrative story. In the criminal justice system, alibis function as exculpatory evidence—a good alibi should rule out the alibi provider as a potential suspect in a case or provide reasonable doubt as to a defendant's guilt in a criminal trial. Psychological research into the study of alibis is a relatively new area in psychology and law. This entry summarizes some of the major findings and introduces the terminology of the existing psychological literature.

It is unclear how alibis are used in the early stages of criminal investigations, and the rules about how and when alibi evidence can be used in the court system vary greatly across jurisdictions. To function as exculpatory evidence, alibis must contain both a believable story and credible proof of the alibi provider's whereabouts. Psychology is in a unique position to study alibis from both sides of the criminal process: *Alibi generation* relies largely on the memory of alibi providers and corroborating witnesses, and *alibi evaluation* occurs as the police, attorneys, and jurors decide the exculpatory worth of the alibi. The study of alibi generation can be informed by autobiographical memory research, and alibi evaluation can benefit from deception detection and suspect interrogation research. However, psychological research on alibis specifically is still relatively new and has focused thus far on the evaluation of alibis.

Alibis are evaluated according to their believability by detectives, prosecutors, defense attorneys, and jury members at different stages of the criminal process. For an alibi to be judged believable, credible proof of the alibi provider's whereabouts is essential, and it can take one of two forms: physical evidence and person evidence. Credible physical evidence ties the alibi provider to a specific place and time; for example, an airline boarding pass includes time and location information and requires identification, making it highly unlikely that someone other than the ticket holder would be able to obtain the pass. The research to date has indicated that physical evidence corroborating an alibi carries considerable weight with alibi evaluators; mock jurors have rated alibis with supporting physical evidence as more believable than alibis without such evidence. However, evaluators do not seem to differentiate between physical evidence that might be easily fabricated, such as a cash receipt, and evidence that is more difficult to fabricate, such as a security video. Person evidence consists of testimony by an alibi corroborator, or alibi witness, as to the whereabouts of the alibi provider. Preliminary research has shown that mock jurors are quick to distinguish among alibi corroborators according to the corroborator's relationship to the alibi provider. Specifically, corroborators who could conceivably have a motivation to lie for the alibi provider (such as a close relative or a good friend) are viewed as less credible than corroborators who have no relationship to the alibi provider. Some research has suggested that having someone close to a defendant as an alibi corroborator could be no better than having no alibi at all—mock jurors voted guilty just as often when the corroborating witness was a motivated other as when the defendant had no alibi defense at all.

Skepticism on the part of alibi evaluators may work well when evaluators are dealing with fabricated alibis offered by guilty defendants. However, difficulties may arise when evaluators are faced with alibis offered by innocent alibi providers. Innocent alibi providers could potentially fall a victim to normal memory errors, such as misremembering a date or time for a particular activity or failing to correctly recall their companions for a particular day. Unlike in a normal recollection situation, however, a normal memory mistake could look suspicious in the context of a criminal investigation. Preliminary investigations into the strength of alibis produced by innocent alibi providers suggest that people frequently misremember their actions for a previous date and have considerable difficulty producing any kind of proof for their whereabouts. Anecdotal evidence from past criminal cases suggests that evaluators may use a weak alibi as incriminating evidence, which could be especially worrisome for innocent alibi providers.

Continued research into the psychology of alibis will shed additional light on how police detectives, attorneys, and jury members deal with alibis in the context of more complex criminal cases. For example, it is unclear how evaluators would deal with multiple pieces of alibi evidence or how they would look upon innocent alibi providers who need to change their alibis in some way. Although the psychological research is limited at present, the literature is growing and will continue to uncover how alibis interact with other pieces of evidence in criminal trials.

Elizabeth A. Olson

See also Detection of Deception: Use of Evidence in; Detection of Deception in Adults; Interrogation of Suspects; Police Decision Making; Postevent Information and Eyewitness Memory; Reconstructive Memory

Further Readings

Burke, T., Turtle, J., & Olson, E. A. (2007). Alibis in criminal investigations and trials. In M. Toglia, J. D. Read, M. Ross, & R. C. L. Lindsay (Eds.), *The handbook of eyewitness psychology: Vol. 1. Memory for events* (pp. 157–174). Hillsdale, NJ: Lawrence Erlbaum.

Culhane, S. E., & Hosch, H. M. (2004). An alibi witness' influence on mock jurors' verdicts. *Journal of Applied Social Psychology, 34,* 1604–1616.

Olson, E. A., & Wells, G. L. (2004). What makes a good alibi? A proposed taxonomy. *Law and Human Behavior, 28,* 157–176.

ALTERNATIVE DISPUTE RESOLUTION

Alternative dispute resolution (ADR) has come to refer broadly to a range of processes (e.g., bilateral negotiation, fact finding, mediation, summary jury trial, arbitration) that are used in transactional (e.g., design contracts, develop regulations), dispute prevention, and dispute resolution contexts. ADR processes operate in public and private settings, such as courts, government agencies, community mediation centers, schools, workplaces, and private providers, to address an array of substantive issues (e.g., custody, torts, contracts, misdemeanors, environmental issues).

This entry focuses on a subset of ADR processes: those that involve a neutral third party and serve as an alternative to court adjudication of civil, divorce, and minor criminal disputes. The processes that are most commonly used are described in the following section.

The goals and asserted benefits of ADR include enhancing disputants' satisfaction with the resolution process and its outcome; producing better outcomes and increased compliance; improving the disputants' relationship and reducing future disputes; providing faster, less expensive, and confidential case resolution; increasing disputants' access to a hearing on the merits; and reducing caseloads and the use of court resources. These goals do not all apply to, and are not of equal importance in, every ADR process and setting. Criticisms of ADR, particularly when its use is mandatory, include that it lacks procedural safeguards, decreases public participation and scrutiny, reduces the available legal precedents and reference points, creates pressures to settle, provides second-class justice, and impedes access to trial by adding another step in the litigation process. Empirical field research on the efficacy of ADR, and on the impact of process, third-party, and dispute characteristics, is discussed in a subsequent section.

Third-Party ADR Processes

Third-party ADR processes fall into two main categories. The first involves processes such as arbitration, in which the third party decides the case for the disputants. The second category involves processes such as mediation, in which the third party assists the disputants in reaching their own resolution. If the disputants reach an agreement, it is legally enforceable; if they do not, the case continues in litigation. Although most disputes settle before trial, a neutral third party can help disputants overcome the logistical, strategic, and cognitive barriers to bilateral negotiation that often impede early or optimal settlements.

Disputants can enter ADR as the result of a predispute contractual agreement to use ADR or, after a dispute has arisen, as a result of mutual agreement, judicial referral of a specific case, or court-mandated use for an entire category of cases. In both court-connected and private ADR, the proceedings are private, and the content of any agreement reached is confidential and not reported to the court. Below is a general description of several commonly used processes. How each is implemented varies with the type of setting and disputes, as well as with the specific ADR provider.

Arbitration involves a hearing during which the disputants' lawyers present evidence and arguments to a single arbitrator, or sometimes a panel of three arbitrators, who renders a decision. In voluntary private arbitration, the arbitrator's decision typically is binding, but the disputants determine that as well as other features of the process by agreement. Mandatory court-connected arbitration is nonbinding: The disputants may reject the arbitrator's decision and proceed to trial de novo. If they accept the arbitrator's decision, it becomes a court judgment.

The arbitration hearing typically is held after discovery has been substantially completed. Compared with a trial, an arbitration hearing tends to be less formal and to permit the broader admissibility of evidence. Court-connected arbitration usually involves a single session lasting several hours; private arbitration can involve multiple daylong sessions spread over weeks. Arbitrators are either lawyers or nonlawyers with expertise in the subject matter of the dispute. Although disputants often attend arbitration hearings, their participation is limited to providing evidence.

Mediation is a process in which a mediator, or sometimes a pair of mediators, facilitates the disputants' discussion of issues and options to help them reach a mutually acceptable resolution of their dispute. Accordingly, disputant participation in the mediation process and in determining the outcome is viewed as critical. The mediator's approach can vary with the setting, as well as with the individual mediator's preferences and the nature of the particular dispute. Some mediators view their primary objective as enabling the disputants to better understand their own interests and the other side's perspective. Most mediators, however, do not consider enhancing the disputants' understanding as an end in itself but as a means to helping them reach an agreement that meets their needs.

Mediators differ in how actively they intervene during the session: whether they focus the disputants' discussion narrowly on the instant dispute and legally relevant issues or expand it to include broader issues and considerations and whether they help the disputants assess various options or offer their own evaluation of the merits of the disputants' positions and proposals. The timing of mediation (e.g., before a claim is filed, shortly after filing, after discovery is completed), the number and length of sessions, who the mediators are (e.g., lay people, mental health professionals, lawyers), and whether the attendance of the disputants' lawyers is required or prohibited vary with the setting and types of disputes.

Neutral case evaluation is used less frequently than mediation. Following each lawyer's brief presentation of the case, the third party assesses the strengths and weaknesses of each disputant's position and facilitates settlement discussions. The evaluator, who usually is a lawyer, also might offer an assessment of liability and a valuation of damages, suggest a reasonable settlement value, or predict the likely trial outcome to facilitate settlement. If no settlement is reached, the evaluator might explore ways to streamline pretrial discovery and motions. Neutral case evaluation typically involves a single several-hour session that is held relatively early during litigation and is attended by the disputants and their lawyers.

Judicial settlement conferences may be conducted by the judge assigned to the case or by another judge and usually take the form of neutral case evaluation or narrow, settlement-focused, evaluative mediation. A settlement conference typically involves a single session that lasts several hours and is held when the case is essentially ready for trial. Although some judges require disputants to attend, usually only the lawyers are present and participate in the discussions. Courts generally consider judicial settlement conferences to be ADR, but some commentators regard them as a component of traditional litigation.

Empirical Field Research on ADR

Few general statements about the research findings can be made that apply consistently across ADR processes, settings, and dispute types. Even within the same process and setting, the findings are mixed as to whether ADR performs better than, or simply as well as, litigation.

Most of the research has examined mediation and arbitration in court-connected programs; few published studies have examined other ADR processes or private ADR. The primary data sources include court or ADR program records and questionnaires completed at the end of the session by disputants, lawyers, and neutrals. Few studies have included observations of sessions or long-term follow-up with disputants. Many studies do not include a comparison group of non-ADR cases; those that do seldom assign cases randomly to ADR and non-ADR groups. Drawing conclusions across studies is further complicated because different studies use different non-ADR comparison groups: Some use only cases settled via negotiation, others use only tried cases, and still others include all disposition types.

The Efficacy of ADR

In divorce, small claims, and community mediation, from 50% to 85% of cases settle. In general jurisdiction civil cases, from one fourth to two thirds of cases that use mediation, neutral evaluation, or arbitration settle. A majority of studies find that the settlement rate in mediation cases is higher than in comparable cases that do not use mediation, but other studies find no differences between mediated and litigated cases in settlement rates. Studies of court-connected arbitration tend to find a lower settlement rate in arbitrated cases than in comparable nonarbitrated cases. Because arbitration hearings divert cases from settlement but not from trial, arbitration increases disputants' access to a hearing on the merits. Studies generally find that judicial settlement conferences do not increase the rate of settlement but that lawyers think they do.

Some studies find that compared with traditional litigation, ADR resolves cases faster; reduces discovery, motions, pretrial conferences, and trials; and reduces disputants' legal fees and litigation costs. Other studies, however, find no differences between ADR and litigation in these measures. No study has found that judicial settlement conferences resolve cases faster. In mediation and neutral evaluation, time and cost savings are more likely in cases that settle than in cases that do not settle. In court-connected arbitration, however, cases that settle before the arbitration hearing often are not resolved more quickly than cases resolved by the arbitrator's decision; cases that appeal the decision take substantially longer to conclude, regardless of whether they eventually settle or are tried.

Most disputants and lawyers who participate in ADR have highly favorable assessments of the process (e.g., they feel that it was fair and gave them sufficient opportunity to present their case), the third party (e.g., they think that she or he was neutral, understood their views and the issues, did not pressure them to settle, and treated them with respect), and the outcome (e.g., they feel that it was fair, and they were satisfied with it). Thus, ADR tends to get high ratings on procedural justice and its correlates. Whether ADR participants' assessments are as favorable as or more favorable than those of non-ADR participants, however, varies across studies and settings. In most settings, disputants in mediation who settle have more favorable assessments than disputants who do not settle. Disputants in arbitration who have a hearing have more favorable views of the process, but not necessarily of the outcome, than disputants who settle before the arbitration hearing.

Studies involving divorce and small claims cases tend to find that disputants in mediated cases report a higher rate of compliance with the outcome, less anger, improved relationships, and less relitigation than disputants in litigation. These benefits associated with divorce mediation tend to disappear after several years, although disputants remain more satisfied. In general civil cases, most studies find no differences between mediated and nonmediated cases in terms of postresolution compliance or relationships. Several studies suggest that postresolution outcomes are less strongly influenced by whether disputants use mediation or litigation than by antecedent characteristics of the disputants, such as their ability to pay or their level of anger or adjustment.

The few studies that have examined the relative efficacy of different ADR processes tend to find no differences among them. However, because these studies do not involve the random assignment of cases to processes, these findings might simply reflect the "correct" matching of disputes to processes for which they are best suited.

Despite ADR performing at least as well as litigation, there is relatively little voluntary use of ADR after disputes have arisen. This appears to say less about disputants' or lawyers' preferences regarding dispute resolution procedures and more about the logistical, strategic, cognitive, and economic barriers to using ADR once litigation has begun. Rules designed to overcome these barriers by requiring lawyers to inform their clients about ADR or to discuss ADR with opposing counsel have had mixed success in increasing early settlements or voluntary ADR use.

The Effect of Process, Third-Party, and Dispute Characteristics

The mixed research findings regarding ADR's efficacy might reflect, in part, differences across studies in how the ADR process was implemented or in the mix of disputes handled. A small number of studies have examined the relationships between ADR outcomes and characteristics of the process, third party, and disputes, though few have systematically varied these characteristics.

Process Characteristics

Studies find that several benefits are associated with holding the ADR session sooner after the legal complaint is filed: Cases are resolved faster; fewer motions are filed; and, as found in some studies, more cases settle. Delaying ADR until after discovery is substantially completed is not associated with an increased rate of settlement. Most studies find no differences in settlement rates or participants' assessments associated with whether mediation use is voluntary or mandatory, but some studies find that voluntary use of mediation is associated with more favorable outcomes.

Third-Party Characteristics

A majority of studies find that when the mediator or neutral evaluator plays a more active role during the session in helping disputants identify issues and options, settlement is more likely and disputants have more favorable assessments of the process. Mediator actions associated with these positive outcomes include actively structuring the process, getting disputants to express their views and to assess different options, and providing their own views about the disputants' positions and proposals. If the mediator recommends a specific settlement, however, disputants are more likely to settle but less likely to view the mediation process as fair. Only a few studies have examined whether the third party's general approach or specific actions appear to be differentially effective in different types of disputes. These studies show, for instance, that some mediator approaches that are effective in resolving less intense conflicts are not effective in resolving more intense conflicts and some approaches that are effective in divorce cases are not effective in general civil cases.

Greater third-party familiarity with the substantive issues in the case is related to lawyers' viewing the arbitration process and decision as more fair. In mediation, the third party's substantive expertise is not related to settlement or to disputants' or lawyers' assessments. How well the mediator understood the disputants' views, however, is related to their assessments. Disputants' and lawyers' perceptions that the third party was not biased and was prepared for the session are associated with favorable assessments of the process and outcome of all ADR processes.

Dispute and Disputant Characteristics

Research examining which dispute and disputant characteristics are associated with better outcomes has been conducted primarily on the mediation process. The contentiousness of the disputants' relationship impedes settlement in divorce and community mediation but not in general civil and small claims mediation, which involves few intimate or ongoing relationships. In addition, divorcing couples with a more contentious relationship are more likely to be dissatisfied with the settlement, remain bitter, and bring subsequent lawsuits.

Across mediation settings, other indicators of more intense conflicts, such as poor communication, greater disparity in the disputants' positions, and the denial of liability, also are associated with a lower likelihood of settlement.

Not surprisingly, the greater the disputants' motivation to settle and the less disparity between the disputants in that motivation, the more likely they are to settle. Disputants who misunderstand the goals of mediation or whose goals are inconsistent with those of mediation are less satisfied and less likely to settle. Similarly, lawyers whose expectations about how the neutral case evaluation session will be conducted are closer to the approach actually used are more satisfied with the process. Disputants who are better prepared for mediation by their lawyers tend to be more likely to settle and to feel that the process is fair, perhaps because preparation modifies their expectations or their actions during the session.

Few studies have examined how antecedent dispute characteristics affect what goes on during the mediation session and how that, in turn, affects outcomes. These studies find that disputants who have a less contentious relationship or who are more motivated to settle are more likely to be cooperative and to engage in productive joint problem solving during mediation. These behaviors, in turn, are associated with disputants being more likely to settle, view the mediation process and outcome as fair, and report improved relationships. More active disputant participation during mediation also is associated with more favorable outcomes. The few studies that have examined lawyers' impact on mediation suggest that how cooperative the lawyers are during the session is related to settlement and to disputants' assessments of the process.

The research findings are mixed with regard to whether or not there is a relationship between settlement and dispute complexity, which has been defined in different studies as the number of disputants, the number of disputed issues, or the complexity of the issues in dispute. A majority of mediation studies find that legal case type categories (e.g., tort, contract) and the size of the monetary claim are not related to settlement or to disputants' assessments of mediation. A majority of arbitration studies, however, find that disputants are more likely to appeal the arbitrator's decision in cases involving larger dollar claims and in tort rather than contract cases.

Roselle L. Wissler

See also Legal Negotiation; Procedural Justice

Further Readings

ADR and the vanishing trial [Special issue]. (2004, Summer). *Dispute Resolution Magazine, 10.*

Brazil, W. A. (1985). *Settling civil suits: Litigators' views about appropriate roles and effective techniques for federal judges.* Chicago: American Bar Association.

Conflict resolution in the field: Assessing the past, charting the future [Special issue]. (2004, Fall–Winter). *Conflict Resolution Quarterly, 22.*

Folberg, J., Milne, A. L., & Salem, P. (Eds.). (2004). *Divorce and family mediation: Models, techniques, and applications.* New York: Guilford.

Menkel-Meadow, C. J., Love, L. P., Schneider, A. K., & Sternlight, J. R. (Eds.). (2005). *Dispute resolution: Beyond the adversarial model.* New York: Aspen.

Wissler, R. L., & Dauber, B. (2005). Leading horses to water: The impact of an ADR "confer and report" rule. *Justice System Journal, 26,* 253–272.

Wissler, R. L., & Dauber, B. (2007). Court-connected arbitration in the Superior Court of Arizona: A study of its performance and proposed rule changes. *Journal of Dispute Resolution 1,* 65–100.

AMBER ALERT SYSTEM

The AMBER Alert system was designed to help rescue missing children. Law enforcement entities release information about the child and the perpetrator through public announcements on television, roadside signs, and the Internet. Citizens are expected to remember the information and report sightings to the police. Although the system has not been well evaluated, a number of social science methods used in other areas (e.g., eyewitness memory research, bystander effect) may be applicable. Concerns have been raised that the program has been overused by the authorities, who issue alerts in nonserious cases, and that alerts are most "effective" when relatively little threat is posed, such as when a child is abducted by a parent.

AMBER Alert and Social Science

The AMBER Alert system makes many assumptions about human behavior that remain untested. The system assumes that individuals have the ability to remember the information presented in the alert and to identify the perpetrator or the child at a later time. Research on cognitive load and exposure duration suggests that brief messages presented while the recipient is busy (e.g.,

driving a car) may not be acquired, although these notions have not been tested with AMBER Alert messages. Retention failure and memory reconstruction may also make it difficult to properly remember the alert message. Retrieval problems, such as source attribution errors, may also make it difficult for citizens to fulfill their role in the AMBER Alert system. Eyewitness memory research has indicated that individuals are not always able to recognize a face seen before; this can be especially true for faces of another race. These research techniques could be used to test citizens' ability to become informants.

Social influences and individual differences could affect one's willingness to report. Informants may feel that they are too busy to get involved with an investigation, or they could decide that because other citizens will report the sighting, there is no need for them to report (i.e., the bystander effect). The people around informants could doubt their memory, influencing them not to report. On the other hand, the high severity of a crime may make informants more likely to report. Gender, race, and past experiences with the police have also been shown to affect one's willingness to help. Although these studies were not conducted using AMBER Alert as a framework, they may suggest avenues for future study.

There is also concern that AMBER alerts will lead to "AMBER fatigue," a phenomenon in which individuals stop paying attention to the alerts because they have seen so many of them. There is also concern that the great number of alerts could lead to a heightened level of public fear and to perceptions that abductions are more common than they actually are, as suggested by research on the availability heuristic and social construction of fear by the media. Alternately, the presence of the AMBER Alert system could convince people that the system is deterring abductions; this could lead to a reduction in the perceived need for prevention programs. Stories of abductions by strangers (which AMBER Alert was designed to address) may lead to a neglect of the more frequent problem of abductions by family members. Counterfactual thinking and hindsight bias can affect perceptions of the system: A rescue after an alert was issued or a child's death after a failure to issue an alert may seem like inevitable outcomes, thus bolstering the system's perceived effectiveness.

Finally, AMBER alerts can affect perpetrators. It is possible that alerts can deter criminals or encourage them to return the child safely. It is, however, also possible that they will encourage copycat abductions by publicity-seeking criminals. Seeing an alert could also lead a criminal to kill and dispose of the child more quickly than he or she had planned.

AMBER Alert Research

A few researchers have attempted to test the effectiveness of the system. An examination of 233 AMBER alerts issued in 2004 revealed that, despite the intention of focusing AMBER alerts on only serious abduction cases (which generally involve strangers), 50% of the alerts studied involved familial abductions, another 20% involved hoaxes or confusions, and only 30% actually involved abduction by strangers. The researchers recommended stricter adherence to the restrictive issuance criteria recommended by the U.S. Department of Justice to avoid overuse of the system.

There has also been one attempt to determine how effective AMBER Alert is in accomplishing its key goal, which is saving abducted children's lives in the worst cases (often called "stereotypical" abductions). The researchers found that, despite claims by some practitioners that AMBER alerts have helped rescue hundreds of children, successful recovery is most likely when the victim is abducted by a parent and least likely when the child is abducted by a stranger. Since prior research has shown that most children abducted by parents are not harmed (regardless of whether an alert was issued or not), researchers questioned the effectiveness of alerts and their ability to "save" lives.

In addition to these issues, there might be obstacles to AMBER alerts routinely functioning as intended. For practical reasons, it is very difficult to learn of an abduction and issue an alert within the small, critical window of opportunity that exists in the worst cases. Despite the reasonableness of insisting that AMBER alerts only be issued in serious scenarios, there is an inherent dilemma in determining the level of threat actually posed when a child is missing and might or might not have been abducted.

Monica K. Miller and Timothy Griffin

See also Eyewitness Memory; Reporting Crimes and Victimization; Sex Offender Community Notification (Megan's Laws); Victimization

Further Readings

Griffin, T., Miller, M. K., Hammack, R., Hoppe, J., & Rebideaux, A. (2007). A preliminary examination of AMBER Alert's effects. *Criminal Justice Policy Review.*

Hargrove, T. (2005). *False alarms endangering future of Amber Alert system.* New York: Scripps Howard News Service.

Miller, M. K., & Clinkinbeard, S. S. (2006). Improving the AMBER Alert system: Psychology research and policy recommendations. *Law and Psychology Review, 30,* 1–21.

Miller, M. K., Griffin, T., Clinkinbeard, S. S., & Thomas, R. M. (2006, April). *The psychology of AMBER Alert: Unresolved issues and policy implications.* Paper presented at the Western Social Science Association Conference, Phoenix, AZ.

AMERICAN BAR ASSOCIATION RESOLUTION ON MENTAL DISABILITY AND THE DEATH PENALTY

The question of how individuals with severe mental disabilities should be sentenced when they are convicted of capital (death penalty) crimes is a vexing one in U.S. society. On one hand, the death penalty is an established part of the criminal justice system in the United States, which exists in part as a reflection of our society's outrage in response to certain kinds of violent crime. On the other hand, in the words of former U.S. Supreme Court Chief Justice Earl Warren, a society's "evolving standards of decency that mark the progress of a maturing society" require that we recognize that there must be exceptions to this most extreme form of punishment. This entry describes the Resolution of the American Bar Association on Mental Disability and the Death Penalty, which was endorsed by the American Psychological Association and other professional organizations, and the Resolution's approach to the difficult problem of mental disability and capital punishment.

The American Bar Association (ABA) formed an interdisciplinary task force to consider this problem. The Task Force on Mental Disability and the Death Penalty (hereinafter "Task Force") was established by the ABA's Section of Individual Rights and Responsibilities and chaired by Ronald Tabak (Task Force, 2006). Many of the 24 members of the Task Force were attorneys, including representation from the National Alliance on Mental Illness, but there were also representatives from the American Psychological Association (the three authors of this entry) and the American Psychiatric Association. The Task Force worked for 2 years

(April 2003 to March 2005) on considering, debating, and crafting the Resolution that is quoted in this entry. It was approved by the ABA in August 2006, after having previously been endorsed by the American Psychological Association, the American Psychiatric Association, and the National Alliance on Mental Illness.

One of the important initial questions facing the Task Force was whether mental disability should constitute a per se bar to capital punishment—that is, whether individuals with certain kinds of mental disability should not need to demonstrate anything further in order to be excluded from consideration for the death penalty. There were differing views among Task Force members on this question. The vast majority of questions in mental health law require consideration not only of mental disability but also of specific functional legal capacities that vary according to the legal question, and the relationship between the mental disability and the functional capacities. For example, an individual with a severe mental disability would not be adjudicated incompetent to stand trial only on the basis of that disability; the court would also consider the functional legal criteria involving a rational and factual understanding of the individual's legal situation and the capacity to assist counsel in his or her own defense. The defendant who experiences deficits in these functional legal capacities that are caused by symptoms of a severe mental disability is much more likely to be adjudicated incompetent to stand trial by a court.

So it did not appear sufficient to craft a resolution on the theme that those with mental disability should be excluded from the death penalty on that basis alone. Throughout most of the Resolution, the Task Force used the consideration of mental disability, functional legal criteria, and causal connection in formulating its language.

To complicate matters further, however, there is some important case law, in the form of decisions by the U.S. Supreme Court, indicating that in some instances the defendant's mental condition or age is sufficient *by itself* to exclude that individual from capital punishment. In *Atkins v. Virginia* (2002), the U.S. Supreme Court decided that the Eighth Amendment of the Constitution bars capital punishment for individuals with mental retardation on the basis that it is a cruel and unusual punishment. This decision was followed by another case, *Roper v. Simmons* (2005), in which the Supreme Court held that execution of those under the age of 18 at the time of the offense was also constitutionally prohibited under the Eighth Amendment.

Faced with the choice of whether to apply "mental disability" to capital punishment as the Supreme Court did in *Atkins* and *Roper*, with the disability itself constituting sufficient grounds for an exclusion, or to use the more established approach used in virtually all other questions in mental health law, the Task Force adopted a two-dimensional approach. Consistent with *Atkins*, the first prong of this Resolution proposes that those with significant limitations in their intellectual functioning and adaptive behavior (criteria associated with mental retardation) be excluded from consideration for capital punishment on that basis alone. However, individuals with "severe mental disorder or disability" would need to demonstrate both the existence of such a disorder/disability and the resulting impairment in functional legal capacities at the time of the offense (the Resolution's second prong) or following sentencing (the third prong). This two-dimensional approach has the advantage of not only recognizing the Court's holding that a specific kind of disability (mental retardation) is sufficient in itself to exclude defendants with this disability from capital sentencing but also acknowledging the longstanding demand for considering both nature of disability and relevant functional legal capacities in other areas of mental health law.

Finally, the Task Force sought to fill an important gap in the law regarding competence for execution, which applies when a defendant who receives a death sentence begins to demonstrate symptoms of a severe mental disability after sentencing but before execution. In *Ford v. Wainwright* (1986), the U.S. Supreme Court held that execution of an incompetent prisoner constitutes cruel and unusual punishment, which is proscribed by the Eighth Amendment. However, the Court did not specify what criteria should be used to determine whether the prisoner is incompetent for execution. The Resolution provides suggested criteria that expand on the language used by Justice Lewis Powell, in his concurring opinion in *Ford*, to the effect that the prisoner's understanding of the nature of capital punishment and why it is imposed in this particular case ought to be the relevant test. (Since Justice Powell's opinion concurred with the majority on many points but was not part of the majority opinion, his language regarding the criteria for competence for execution did not become officially recognized as part of the *Ford* decision and hence applicable to other cases involving competence for execution. Some states have adopted this language as part of their law in this area, but they are not required to do so as they would have been if the language had been included in the majority's decision.)

The Resolution (Quoted From the Task Force)

RESOLVED, That the American Bar Association, without taking a position supporting or opposing the death penalty, urges each jurisdiction that imposes capital punishment to implement the following policies and procedures:

1. Defendants should not be executed or sentenced to death if, at the time of the offense, they had significant limitations in both their intellectual functioning and adaptive behavior, as expressed in conceptual, social, and practical adaptive skills, resulting from mental retardation, dementia, or a traumatic brain injury.

2. Defendants should not be executed or sentenced to death if, at the time of the offense, they had a severe mental disorder or disability that significantly impaired their capacity

    a. to appreciate the nature, consequences or wrongfulness of their conduct,

    b. to exercise rational judgment in relation to conduct, or

    c. to conform their conduct to the requirements of the law.

A disorder manifested primarily by repeated criminal conduct or attributable solely to the acute effects of voluntary use of alcohol or other drugs does not, standing alone, constitute a mental disorder or disability for purposes of this provision.

3. Mental Disorder or Disability after Sentencing

    a. *Grounds for Precluding Execution.* A sentence of death should not be carried out if the prisoner has a mental disorder or disability that significantly impairs his or her capacity

       i. to make a rational decision to forgo or terminate post-conviction proceedings available to challenge the validity of the conviction or sentence;

       ii. to understand or communicate pertinent information, or otherwise assist counsel, in relation to specific claims bearing on the validity of the conviction or sentence that cannot be fairly resolved without the prisoner's participation; or

       iii. to understand the nature and purpose of the punishment, or to appreciate the reason for its imposition in the prisoner's own case.

Procedures to be followed in each of these categories of cases are specified in (b) through (d) below.

    b. *Procedure in Cases Involving Prisoners Seeking to Forgo or Terminate Post-Conviction Proceedings.* If a court finds that a prisoner under sentence of death who wishes to forgo or terminate post-conviction proceedings has a mental disorder or disability that significantly impairs his or her capacity to make a rational decision, the court should permit a next friend acting on the prisoner's behalf to initiate or pursue available remedies to set aside the conviction or death sentence.

    c. *Procedure in Cases Involving Prisoners Unable to Assist Counsel in Post-Conviction Proceedings.* If a court finds at any time that a prisoner under sentence of death has a mental disorder or disability that significantly impairs his or her capacity to understand or communicate pertinent information, or otherwise to assist counsel, in connection with post-conviction proceedings, and that the prisoner's participation is necessary for a fair resolution of specific claims bearing on the validity of the conviction or death sentence, the court should suspend the proceedings. If the court finds that there is no significant likelihood of restoring the prisoner's capacity to participate in post-conviction proceedings in the foreseeable future, it should reduce the prisoner's sentence to the sentence imposed in capital cases when execution is not an option.

    d. *Procedure in Cases Involving Prisoners Unable to Understand the Punishment or Its Purpose.* If, after challenges to the validity of the conviction and death sentence have been exhausted and execution has been scheduled, a court finds that a prisoner has a mental disorder or disability that significantly impairs his or her capacity to understand the nature and purpose of the punishment, or to appreciate the reason for its imposition in the prisoner's own case, the sentence of death should be reduced to the sentence imposed in capital cases when execution is not an option.

Discussion

This Resolution does not take a position on the death penalty generally. Neither the ABA, which organized the Task Force and ultimately approved the Resolution, nor organizations such as the American Psychological Association, the American Psychiatric Association, or the National Alliance on Mental Illness intended their endorsement to reflect a broader position on capital punishment applicable beyond the scope of the Resolution.

In some respects, this Resolution is largely consistent with established law. In Prong 1, for example, the Resolution language is quite consistent with the Supreme Court's decision in *Atkins*, although it does expand the possible reasons for significantly limited intellectual functioning and adaptive behavior so that it now includes mental retardation as well as other possible sources of deficit (e.g., dementia, brain injury).

In other respects, however, the Resolution goes well beyond what is presently established under the law. It proposes to exempt from capital punishment those who, at the time of the offense or prior to execution, display both severe mental disability and impaired functional legal capacities. It does so in a traditional fashion, without the per se bar of a specific kind of mental disability or the defendant's age. However, there is no question that what is proposed in the Resolution's second and third prongs would change the law in some significant ways if the Resolution's language were adopted by state legislatures and used by appellate courts.

This Resolution should not be interpreted as an attempt to absolve offenders of responsibility for their actions or exempt them from punishment. But it does recognize that there are degrees of culpability for very serious offenses and that severe mental disability may reduce that culpability somewhat. Even for those who might meet the criteria described in this Resolution, however, the reduction in sanction is from a death sentence to life incarceration—an attempt to balance our society's interest in punishing the guilty with the importance of punishing them as culpability and fairness dictate.

Kirk Heilbrun, Joel Dvoskin,
and Diane Marsh

See also Competency for Execution; Death Penalty; Mental Illness and the Death Penalty

Further Readings

Atkins v. Virginia, 536 U.S. 304 (2002).
Bonnie, R. (2005). Mentally ill prisoners on death row: Unsolved puzzles for courts and legislatures. *Catholic University Law Review, 54,* 1169–1193.
Ford v. Wainwright, 477 U.S. 399 (1986).
Heilbrun, K., Radelet, M., & Dvoskin, J. (1992). The debate on treating individuals incompetent for execution. *American Journal of Psychiatry, 149,* 596–605.
Roper v. Simmons, 543 U.S. 551 (2005).
Task Force on Mental Disability and the Death Penalty. (2006). Recommendation and report on the death penalty and persons with mental disabilities. *Mental and Physical Disability Law Reporter, 30,* 668–677.
Trop v. Dulles, 356 U.S. 86 (1958).

AMERICANS WITH DISABILITIES ACT (ADA)

Psychologists may become involved with the Americans with Disabilities Act (ADA) through consultations with employers and workers or as an expert witness in litigation involving the act. In all these roles, the psychologist must gain an understanding of the many definitions in the act and the Equal Employment Opportunity Commission (EEOC) regulations mandated by it. The ADA not only is a valuable tool for use by disabled people against discrimination but also an arena of practice for forensic psychologists. Although the ADA is a complex mixture of definitions and rules, the forensic practitioner may enter this arena using many of the skills developed in tort cases or in civil rights cases involving sex or race. This entry describes the ADA, discusses the roles that psychologists may play in workplace consultations, and examines the use of psychological evaluations in litigation related to disability.

Background of the ADA

The ADA was signed into law in 1990 and came into effect 2 years later. The law was designed to eliminate discrimination against people with disabilities. The statute (42 U.S.C. 12101, Section 2 b (1), 1992) enabled the development of regulations by the EEOC and has been shaped by a number of U.S. Supreme Court decisions. The most obvious impact of the ADA is seen in its transformation of buildings, roads, side-walks, buses, and restrooms into places where people with disabilities may function with fewer barriers.

However, the advocates of disabled people who framed the ADA were more ambitious. The law intends to prevent individuals with disabilities from being discriminated against in hiring, training, compensation, and benefits. Under the ADA, it is illegal to classify an employee on the basis of disability or to participate in contracts that have the effect of discriminating against people with disabilities. The use of tests or other qualification standards that are not job related but result in screening out individuals with disabilities is also banned. Like the Civil Rights Act of 1964, the ADA protects workers who file complaints with the EEOC or other agencies from retaliation by their employers. Under the ADA, employers are required to provide "reasonable accommodation" for workers with disabilities who could qualify for jobs with appropriate assistance.

Mental Disabilities in the ADA

Forensic psychologists working in cases involving the ADA must have an understanding of the specific definitions that shape how the act is used. An important definition in the act is the definition of disability: (1) a physical or mental impairment that substantially limits one or more of the major life activities of an individual, (2) a record of such an impairment, or (3) being regarded as having such an impairment.

A *qualified individual with a disability* is a person with a disability who has the basic qualifications for the job, including the skills, experience, education, and other job-related requirements required for the position the person either currently holds or wishes to obtain. In the context of the ADA, a qualified individual with a disability, with or without reasonable accommodation, can perform the essential functions of that job.

An *impairment* becomes a disability when it adversely affects one or more major life activities. One first considers the impact of the disability on non-work-related activities, which include self-care, sleeping, reading, and concentrating. If none of those basic human activities are affected, the inquiry shifts to work-related activities. The impairment must be considered *severe* enough to "substantially limit a major life activity." How much restriction on essential life activity is caused by the disability is one metric, but the act also allows for consideration of the duration of the disability. Temporary disability is not considered, and chronic and recurring conditions must be considered substantially limiting while they are active.

Mental impairment refers to "any mental or psychological disorder, such as . . . emotional or mental illness." The ADA provides examples of mental or emotional illnesses, such as major depression, bipolar disorder, anxiety disorders, and schizophrenia. Although not listed in the ADA itself, EEOC regulations also include personality disorders as potentially disabling conditions and point to the *Diagnostic and Statistical Manual of Mental Disorders* (currently the *DSM-IV-TR*) as the appropriate reference for determining the symptoms associated with mental disorders. The ADA specifically excludes conditions related to sexuality, such as homosexuality, bestiality, transvestism, transexualism, pedophilia, exhibitionism, voyeurism, or gender identity disorders not related to physical impairments. In addition, the act excludes other behaviors of which Congress did not approve, including compulsive gambling, kleptomania, pyromania, and psychoactive substance abuse disorder resulting from the illegal use of drugs.

In general, the disabled worker must conduct himself or herself in the workplace just like other workers, unless the disability is causing conduct problems on the job. In those situations, the employer must provide *reasonable accommodations* that would allow the worker to meet conduct requirements. If a worker's behavior constitutes "a significant risk of substantial harm to the health and safety of the individual or others that cannot be eliminated or reduced by reasonable accommodation," it may be considered a *direct threat*. The ADA allows workers who pose a direct threat to be fired or removed from the affected position.

The ADA treats the abuse of illegal substances differently than the abuse of legal ones. Current illegal drug use, including abuse of prescription drugs, is not protected by the ADA. Rehabilitated illegal drug users are protected, and the existence of a history of illegal drug use may not be a basis for discharge or discipline, although a relapse may legitimately trigger discharge. Workers who have addictions to legal drugs, such as alcohol, must experience a substantial limitation in a major life activity to be covered by the ADA. Alcohol-dependent workers with excessive absenteeism who report to work drunk or who endanger other workers because of their dependence are subject to the same discipline as other workers.

Psychological Consultations With Employers and Workers

Accommodation Plans

The ADA mandates that an employer work with each disabled employee to develop a plan that takes into account the worker's disability, the worker's strengths, and the nature of the job. Psychologists may assist the employer to help craft an accommodation plan to allow the worker to function in the workplace. This may be done through changes in work hours or supervision levels or by simply providing time off for psychotherapy sessions.

Return-to-Work Evaluations

Workers with mental disabilities may experience fluctuations in their illnesses that result in extended absences from the workplace. In these situations, the employer may require that the worker undergo a psychological evaluation to determine if the worker may effectively return to the workplace without irremediable deficits in work functioning or dangers to the worker or others. In these situations, the psychologist obtains information concerning the demands of the job. The next task is to determine if the worker can perform essential job functions with or without reasonable accommodation.

The psychologist may provide information about what accommodations may be made, which might include altering the interpersonal demands of the workplace, changing the environmental conditions, changing the worker's shift, and eliminating distractions. In addition to reviewing the worker's documented medical and mental records, the examining psychologist may administer a battery of tests. Cognitive assessment may be required in situations in which the mental disability may affect attention, concentration, or the ability to work quickly. Personality assessment may add additional information about existing patterns of psychopathology in relation to the worker's history or the symptom picture that predicated the worker's departure from the workplace. A full clinical history and interview is part of this assessment and should include a detailed vocational history to determine whether the presented impairments have caused the worker problems in the past. A history of relationships, both on and off the job, will illuminate the existence of interpersonal impairments that could limit vocational functioning.

The assessment should result in the psychologist's opinion about whether the worker is disabled under the definitions of the ADA. Then, the psychologist determines if the worker's disability is amenable to reasonable accommodation within the range of alternatives that are feasible for that employer. This decision, as all others in relation to the ADA, is related to the nature of the employer's business, the number of employees, the cost of the accommodations, and other factors. For a small employer, changes in the worker's schedule may not be reasonable, while for a large employer, more extensive changes in the workplace may be practical.

The psychologist's active participation in discussions with the employer and the worker can result in a return-to-work plan that meets the worker's needs and allows for the employer to return a trained and functioning employee to duty. The psychologist should listen to all the parties to craft a viable course of action for the employee's return to work.

Litigation-Related Evaluations and Consultations

Failure to Provide Reasonable Accommodation

The ADA allows workers to sue employers for a number of acts and omissions in relation to the ADA. The worker may claim that the employer has failed to provide reasonable accommodation for a disability or has refused to hire a disabled employee. Assessment of plaintiffs in these cases involves evaluations similar to those used in return-to-work contexts because the psychologist is called on to compare the worker's skills with the job requirements to determine if changes in the workplace would allow the worker to perform essential job functions. Employers may claim that no amount of accommodation would bring the worker up to a functional level, that the proposed accommodations are not feasible or would impose an undue hardship on the employer, that reasonable accommodation has been offered to the worker but was rejected, or that no effective accommodation exists for that worker in that job setting.

These evaluations should meet the standards for any litigation-related evaluation and include gathering a thorough history, reviewing the appropriate job, mental health, and medical records, appropriate psychological testing, and collateral interviews. The psychologist should prepare a report consistent with professional standards and be prepared to be questioned in deposition or in open court.

Disparate Treatment and Disparate Impact Evaluations

If a worker is disabled according to the ADA and has not been hired, has been denied promotion, or has been fired, and nondisabled workers who are similarly situated have been treated more favorably, the disabled worker may have a claim for *disparate treatment.* If the disabled worker has experienced an adverse job action that is not a result of the employer's overt discrimination but is a result of a policy that was designed to be neutral toward people with disabilities, the worker may have a claim for *disparate impact.*

Psychological evaluation in these cases focuses on the impact of the nonhire, firing, or nonpromotion. Emotional damages may flow from these adverse job actions, and the impact of changes in income and lost future job opportunities may be considered. Psychological evaluations in these cases may more closely resemble evaluations in personal injury or workers' compensation cases, as reasonable accommodation is not an issue. Interviews with family members and friends may assist in determining if the worker has suffered emotional harm because of the employer's actions.

Reprisal for Protected Conduct

If a worker files a complaint with the EEOC or other similar agency and is subsequently the recipient of adverse treatment or discharge from his or her employer, that employee may file a claim for reprisal. Psychological evaluation of these cases may follow the parameters of evaluations in disparate treatment and impact cases.

Disability Harassment and Hostile Work Environment

In some situations, disabled individuals experience harassment or hostile work environments because of their disability status. In these situations, the plaintiff must show that he or she is disabled and that because of the disability, he or she was subjected to physical or verbal conduct so offensive that a reasonable person would consider the work situation to be a hostile work environment. Also, the plaintiff must show that the

employer failed to take prompt remedial action to stop the harassment. Evaluations for hostile work environment would follow the same pattern as outlined above.

William E. Foote

See also Disparate Treatment and Disparate Impact Evaluations; Forensic Assessment; Return-to-Work Evaluations

Further Readings

Foote, W. E. (2000). A model for psychological consultation in cases involving the Americans with Disabilities Act. *Professional Psychology: Research and Practice, 31*(2), 190–196.

Foote, W. E. (2003). Forensic evaluation in Americans with Disabilities Act cases. In A. D. Goldstein & I. B. Weiner (Eds.), *Comprehensive handbook of forensic psychology: Vol. 11. Forensic psychology.* New York: Wiley.

U.S. Equal Employment Opportunity Commission. (2000). Questions and answers on amending the interpretive guidance on Title I of the Americans with Disabilities Act. Retrieved June 4, 2007, from http://www.eeoc.gov/policy/regs/1630-mitigating-qanda.html

AMICUS CURIAE BRIEFS

Amicus curiae literally means "friend of the court," and the author of an amicus curiae brief is an entity who wishes to provide legal, scientific, or technical information to a court to aid its decision. An amicus is not a party to the case entitled to be heard as a matter of right but an individual or an organization granted discretionary leave to file a written brief to provide insight into an issue that the parties to the case may not be able to have because of lack of time, space, or expertise. Amicus curiae briefs have influenced the outcomes of many landmark legal cases. The American Psychological Association (APA) regularly seeks leave to file amicus briefs, as do a host of other individuals and organizations.

Overview

The U.S. adversarial legal system looks to the parties to present the information necessary for the judge or jury to decide the questions presented by a case. The amicus curiae brief is a vehicle for people or organizations, not joined as parties or otherwise entitled to be heard in the case, to provide the judiciary with insights or analysis that would otherwise be lacking in decisions of significant import.

Amici lack important rights that parties enjoy. For example, amici have no right to settle or refuse to settle claims, to raise a claim or a defense that the parties did not, or even to join a person that the parties did not. There is no constitutional right to file an amicus brief. The opportunity to be heard as an amicus rests with the discretion of the court before whom the case is pending or, in federal court, the consent of the parties or permission of the court. Typically, amicus briefs are thought to address transcendent questions of law decided at the appellate stage of a case. But it is within the discretion of the court to accept an amicus brief at trial as well as on appeal, whether labeled a pure or a mixed question of law or fact.

A Brief History

Authors such as Simpson and Vasaly have traced the roots of the amicus curiae brief to ancient Rome, where briefs were submitted to provide legal expertise directly to the judiciary at their discretion. Seventeenth-century England provides the first known occurrence of what is now understood as an amicus brief to aid judges in avoiding legal errors and maintaining judicial honor. The first known instance in the United States was when an amicus curiae brief was requested of House Speaker Henry Clay in 1812 by the Supreme Court to aid the Court in the application of law to a land dispute between two states. It was not long after this use of an amicus curiae brief that the practice of filing amicus briefs in appellate courts began in earnest. Although the core purpose of the amicus curiae brief has always been a nonpartisan effort to educate the court and not to advance the interests of a specific party, there has always been a tension between these motivations.

The amicus curiae brief may seek to serve numerous functions categorized by Simpson, include the following: (a) to address issues of policy; (b) to provide a more appealing advocate; (c) to support the granting of a Supreme Court review; (d) to supplement the brief of a party; (e) to give a historical perspective; (f) to provide technical or scientific aid; (g) to endorse a particular party in the case; and (h) to try and correct, limit, publish, or "depublish" an issued judicial opinion. These functions are not mutually exclusive; thus an amicus curiae brief may serve multiple purposes.

Prevalence and Influence of the Amicus Curiae Brief

The prevalence of amicus curiae briefs submitted to the courts, and the Supreme Court in particular, has increased over time. During the first few decades of the 20th century, Kearney and Merrill found that amicus curiae briefs were only filed in approximately 10% of the Supreme Court's cases. This practice has increased dramatically. For example, in the most recent decades, at least one amicus curiae brief has been filed in at least 85% of the Court's cases that incorporated oral arguments. Thus, today, cases with no amicus curiae filings have become the anomaly.

As the number of amicus curiae briefs filed has increased over time, so has the ability of the amicus curiae brief to influence the outcome of court cases, especially where there are many amicus curiae briefs that aid the parties in strong calls for change in the areas of social policy. Amicus curiae briefs that focus on social policy instead of pure legal argument have come to be known as "Brandeis briefs," named for the first filing by Louis Brandeis, later appointed a Supreme Court justice. Brandeis's use of a nonlegally oriented brief to highlight social science data has become a model for presenting such information.

Perceptions of the Amicus Curiae Brief

Perceptions of the use and utility of amicus curiae briefs vary widely within the legal profession. From one point of view, the amicus curiae brief is a beneficial vehicle, providing arguments, technical information, or authorities not included by the parties. Those agreeing with this view point to the numerous references to amicus curiae briefs in many court opinions to suggest that courts find amicus curiae briefs helpful.

Some members of the legal community hold an opposite view. Many judges report that amicus curiae briefs replay the arguments put forth by the parties and provide the court little or no assistance. Those who subscribe to this view contend that amicus curiae briefs are a nuisance, burdening judges and their staffs yet providing few, if any, benefits. For those who view the amicus curiae brief in this way, either prohibiting or limiting the submission of amicus curiae briefs would improve the judicial system.

Finally, a middle ground regarding the amicus curiae brief acknowledges its prevalence and its potential utility but cautions that amicus curiae briefs are most often filed by large, resourceful organizations. While amicus curiae briefs may prove helpful, researchers including Kearney and Merrill caution that inequality in organizational power, interest, and influence should be considered when contemplating an amicus curiae brief.

The APA as a Friend of the Court

The APA has been a prolific author of amicus curiae briefs. It has submitted amicus curiae briefs in cases presenting issues that can potentially affect the internal practices of the APA or its membership as well as external issues of social import that may affect the welfare of populations served by the APA. The topics of APA amicus briefs cover a wide gamut, ranging from scientific research and testing, psychological practice, and treatment of the mentally ill to abortion, sexual orientation, affirmative action, and the death penalty. While the wide range of amicus curiae brief topics are as diverse as the United States itself, in each specific case, the APA perceived either an important social value or an internal necessity in speaking as a "friend of the court."

The APA offers full-text copies of numerous amicus curiae briefs on its Web site, including briefs submitted in "landmark" cases. As an example, in *Planned Parenthood of Southeastern Pennsylvania v. Casey* (1992), the APA presented amicus briefs containing extensive psychological research to assist the Supreme Court's scrutiny of a Pennsylvania law requiring married women to obtain consent from their husbands before obtaining an abortion. The APA's amicus brief presented research that such a restriction supplants a woman's rational choice and places an unfair and potentially harmful burden on women who have compelling reasons not to inform their husbands of their choice. The Supreme Court found that the Pennsylvania law placed an unacceptable burden on women and declared the law unconstitutional.

In the Court's 2005 decision in *Roper v. Simmons*, which presented the constitutionality of imposing the death penalty on someone who was under 18 when the murder was committed, the APA presented research on juvenile behavior, maturity, decision-making ability, and criminology. In a 5:4 decision, in which the research presented by APA was central, the Supreme Court held that the Eighth Amendment of the Constitution prohibits the imposition of the death penalty on juveniles under the age of 18 when the crime was committed.

Daniel W. Shuman

See also Expert Psychological Testimony; U.S. Supreme Court

Further Readings

Barrett, G. V., & Morris, S. B. (1993). The American Psychological Association's amicus curiae brief in *Price Waterhouse v. Hopkins*: The values of science versus the values of the law. *Law and Human Behavior, 17,* 201–215.

Ennis, B. J. (1984). Symposium on Supreme Court advocacy: Effective amicus briefs. *Catholic University Law Review, 33,* 603.

Fiske, S. T., Bersoff, D. N., Borgida, E., Deaux, K., & Heilman, M. E. (1991). Social science research on trial: Use of sex stereotyping research in *Price Waterhouse v. Hopkins. American Psychologist, 46,* 1049–1060.

Kearney, J. D., & Merrill, T. W. (2000). The influence of amicus curiae briefs on the Supreme Court. *University of Pennsylvania Law Review, 148,* 743.

Krislov, S. (1963). The amicus curiae brief: From friendship to advocacy. *Yale Law Journal, 72,* 694.

Planned Parenthood of Southeastern Pennsylvania. v. Casey, 505 U.S. 833 (1992).

PsycLAW: APA's amicus briefs. (n.d.). Retrieved January 28, 2007, from http://www.apa.org/psyclaw/amicus.html

Roper v. Simmons, 543 U.S. 551 (2005).

Simpson, R. W., & Vasaly, M. R. (2004). *The amicus brief: How to be a good friend of the court* (2nd ed.). Chicago: American Bar Association.

Walbot, S. H., & Lang, J. H. (2003). Amicus briefs: Friend or foe of Florida courts? *Stetson Law Review, 32,* 269.

ANTISOCIAL PERSONALITY DISORDER

Antisocial personality disorder (ASPD) is characterized by a lifelong pattern of behavior that violates the law and other people's rights. Its primary relevance to the field of psychology and law stems from its association with criminal and violent behavior, as well as its implications for attempting to reduce the risk thereof through treatment. This entry reviews the diagnostic criteria for ASPD, its phenomenology (common attitudinal, cognitive, emotional, and behavioral features), assessment approaches, treatment issues, etiological factors, and current controversies.

Description

There are a number of definitional elements to personality disorder (PD) generally that apply to ASPD. A PD is a pattern of inflexible interpersonal relations, behavior, and internal experiences (emotional, cognitive, or attitudinal tendencies) that is stable across the life span and starts in adolescence (or early adulthood). It is inconsistent with cultural norms or expectations and involves distress or impairment to the individual. The core of ASPD involves consistently disregarding social norms or rules and violating other people's rights.

The official diagnostic criteria for ASPD, as with all PDs, are provided by the *Diagnostic and Statistical Manual of Mental Disorders*, currently in its fourth edition, which includes a textual revision (*DSM-IV-TR*), published by the American Psychiatric Association. To receive a diagnosis of ASPD, an individual must be at least 18 years old; there must be evidence of conduct disorder (CD) with an onset before the age of 15; antisocial behavior must not be limited in its occurrence solely within the course of schizophrenia or a manic episode; and there must be a pattern of violating or disregarding others' rights since the individual was 15 years old.

More specifically, an individual must meet three of seven diagnostic criteria—as specified in the *DSM-IV-TR*—since the age of 15. Paraphrasing, these include (1) repeated criminal behavior; (2) frequent lying or manipulation; (3) impulsive behavior; (4) aggression, including physical violence; (5) jeopardizing other people's safety (e.g., driving while intoxicated); (6) being irresponsible (i.e., refusing to pay one's bills or debts); and (7) not experiencing remorse for one's harmful behaviors.

In addition to meeting at least three of these seven criteria since age 15, an individual must also have shown evidence of CD prior to the age of 15. Although the *DSM-IV-TR* does not specify the number of CD symptoms required to satisfy this diagnostic criterion, some experts, and common assessment instruments (see below), have suggested that as few as 2 (of 15) CD symptoms would suffice. The 15 symptoms of CD include, among others, aggressive behaviors (e.g., stealing, fighting, using weapons, robbery, sexual assault), destroying property, lying, and other rule-breaking behavior (e.g., skipping school, running away from home).

Phenomenology, Associated Features, and Correlates

Attitudinally, individuals with ASPD may hold disparaging views of others and consider them to be avenues to fulfill their own needs (e.g., for money, sex, pleasure). They tend to have a hostile and distrustful view of the world, believing that others may be out to harm or deceive them and hence their own harmful or deceptive behavior is justified. ASPD is associated with negative views of societal institutions such as law enforcement, the judiciary, or the government. Procriminal attitudes that support, condone, or justify criminal behavior are common.

Cognitively, ASPD is associated with impulsive decision making involving little forethought, even if negative consequences are serious and probable. People with ASPD also may show poor concentration abilities and an impaired ability to devote sustained attention to routine activities. On the other hand, they may indeed be able to devote attention to activities that they consider pleasurable or exciting (e.g., gambling).

Emotionally, some, though not all or even the majority of, people with ASPD show serious deficits in the depth and breadth of emotional experience. That is, they tend not to experience extremes (positive or negative) of emotion, such as despair or love, to the same degree as people without ASPD. This type of emotional poverty would be most likely to occur in individuals with ASPD who also meet definitions of the more classic form of antisocial personality pathology—namely, psychopathy, a hallmark of which is emotional detachment.

People with ASPD commonly are prone to negative emotionality, or the tendency to have feelings of anger, irritability, hostility, dissatisfaction, unhappiness, displeasure, and anxiety. Such an emotional disposition may account, in part, for the tendency of people with ASPD to have problems initiating or sustaining positive interpersonal relationships. Furthermore, such emotional tendencies could explain the increased risk of suicide-related behavior in ASPD.

Behaviorally, there are numerous correlates of ASPD that span all domains of life functioning. Perhaps most notably, ASPD is commonly associated with criminal and violent behavior. This observation is complicated by the fact that crime and violence form part of its diagnostic criteria, and hence, not surprisingly, individuals with ASPD have more crime and violence in their histories than those without ASPD. However, ASPD also is predictive of future criminal behavior once persons are released from prisons or forensic institutions. In addition to criminal behavior, risk-taking behavior is common. This can take a variety of forms, such as problematic substance use that is associated with adverse outcomes, such as crime, injury, personal neglect, or financial difficulties. It also may include irresponsible behaviors, such as reckless driving, failing to care for children adequately, sexual behavior that puts others' safety at risk, or gambling problems.

In terms of more general life functioning, the effects of ASPD are notable as well. For instance, ASPD is associated with low socioeconomic attainment, poor employment records and performance, low educational attainment and success, and unstable interpersonal relationships. The latter may include broken ties with one's family, abuse and other mistreatment within romantic relationships, and having only friends of convenience. Furthermore, ASPD predicts increased morbidity and mortality associated with accidental death and injury, as well as suicide.

Association With Other Disorders

Most PDs are associated with other PDs, and ASPD is no exception. It is common for people with ASPD to show symptoms of other PDs involving dysregulation of affect and impulsive behavior, such as borderline, narcissistic, or histrionic PDs. In addition, perhaps stemming from the high degree of negative emotionality commonly present in ASPD, some depressive and anxiety disorders are overrepresented in ASPD. Substance-related disorders also are disproportionately present in persons with ASPD relative to those without.

Assessment

Both self-report and interview-based measures are available to assess ASPD. Although conducting an interview is regarded as meeting a higher standard of clinical care when assessing personality (or other) pathology, self-report tools may be desirable additions to an assessment because they tend to be relatively brief, may be appropriate for group administration, and do not require an examiner with advanced credentials. On the other hand, self-reports require cooperation from the examinee and a minimum level of literacy.

Several (semi)structured interviews exist for assessing ASPD, including the Diagnostic Interview for *DSM-IV* Personality Disorders, the Structured Interview for

DSM-IV Personality Disorders, the Personality Disorder Examination, the Diagnostic Interview Schedule, and the Composite International Diagnostic Interview. Perhaps the most widely used and researched semistructured interview schedule for use by trained clinicians in assessing ASPD (and other PDs) is the Structured Clinical Interview for *DSM-IV* Axis II Personality Disorders (SCID–II). Each symptom criterion is assessed by an item that the interviewer rates using a 3-point scale (1 = *absent or false*; 2 = *subthreshold*; and 3 = *threshold or true*). Research indicates acceptable levels of internal consistency, test-retest reliability, and interrater reliability for the SCID–II ASPD module.

Several self-report measures that include modules for assessing ASPD also have been developed, such as the Personality Diagnostic Questionnaire–4 (PDQ–4), the Assessment of *DSM-IV* Personality Disorders Questionnaire, and the Wisconsin Personality Disorders Inventory. Self-reports whose items closely track the diagnostic criteria, such as the PDQ–4, have greater clinical relevance to the assessment of ASPD than those that do not. Although many self-report personality measures and diagnostic inventories include scales for assessing features of ASPD (e.g., the California Psychological Inventory, the Minnesota Multiphasic Personality Inventory–2, the Millon Clinical Multiaxial Inventory–III, and the Personality Assessment Inventory), they often emphasize conceptualizations of delinquent personality other than ASPD (e.g., psychopathy). These scales typically demonstrate low concordance with SCID–II diagnoses of ASPD, which likely is related to their lack of representation of the *DSM* criteria for ASPD. Compared with interview-based measures, self-reports tend to yield elevated prevalence rates of ASPD. Furthermore, an actual diagnosis of ASPD must be made by a qualified mental health professional, who interprets whatever tests and measures are used, rather than simply relying on scores on a test or measure.

Research studies comparing the utility of self-report and interview measures for ASPD generally conclude that whereas agreement for dichotomous diagnostic classification tends to be poor, concordance is much higher when a dimensional perspective is considered. Although knowing the rates of categorical classification is attractive from a clinical perspective, there nevertheless is substantial empirical support for the use of dimensional representations of PDs. In terms of relevance to applied practice, information regarding the severity of symptoms (i.e., a dimensional perspective) can be useful for treatment planning and case management.

Despite the ease of use and availability of self-report measures and (semi)structured interviews, clinicians should be aware of the circumstances under which a diagnosis of ASPD is not warranted. First, a diagnosis of ASPD should not be given to individuals who display antisocial behavior only during acute phases of psychotic or mood disorders (e.g., a manic episode). In cases where the examinee has a substance use disorder and adult antisocial behaviors are observed, ASPD should be diagnosed only if features of the disorder were present during childhood. Also, given the high degree of comorbidity between PDs, differentiating between features of ASPD that are similar to those of other PDs is critical. Of course, ASPD also needs to be differentiated from certain Axis I disorders with similar symptoms (e.g., grandiosity and impulsivity, observed in bipolar disorder). Finally, collateral information is useful to consider in assessments in light of the characteristic deceitfulness of individuals with the disorder.

Treatment

ASPD is extremely difficult to treat, and at present, the prognosis for antisocial individuals typically is considered poor. The empirical treatment literature bearing on ASPD is in its infancy, with few controlled studies having been conducted. In addition, research in this area tends to examine the outcomes of interventions for behaviors associated with ASPD, such as substance abuse and violence, rather than treatments aimed at altering the underlying personality features of the disorder. In addition, relatively little research has examined intervention outcomes with women— and when women are included in samples, results typically are not disaggregated by gender. Nevertheless, the body of literature on this topic has grown over the past decade, and some broad trends are apparent.

Several studies have investigated the outcomes of substance abuse treatment among individuals with ASPD. Most results indicate that persons with co-occurring substance abuse problems and ASPD make treatment gains on par with those of individuals in substance abuse treatment without ASPD. However, other studies on this topic suggest less improvement in individuals with ASPD than in others. Furthermore, research suggests that broad classifications such as "substance abuser" may be too generic and that differences based on an individual's drug of choice and the severity of the impact on daily functioning may be important to treatment outcome.

Given the nature of the diagnosis, it is not surprising that most treatment outcome studies on ASPD have been conducted with offender samples. Although at this time, research data do not endorse a specific type of treatment for ASPD, there is strong empirical support for the effectiveness of certain guiding principles. The principles of *risk, need,* and *responsivity* indicate that treatment outcome will be maximized as a function of a treatment program's match with an individual's level of risk, criminogenic needs (changeable risk factors), and learning style. Meta-analytic reviews indicate that the strongest predictor of success across different correctional programs and offender groups—including both men and women—is treatment that adheres to these three principles.

Another aspect of treatment with empirical support is the *multimodal hypothesis,* which suggests that correctional treatment is most effective when multiple need areas of an offender are targeted. Research demonstrates that multimodal programs that incorporate cognitive-behavioral and social learning strategies are associated with substantially larger treatment gains than are nonbehavioral interventions. In addition, there is a positive association between the number of criminogenic needs targeted for intervention and subsequent reductions in recidivism. In contrast, approaches that are contraindicated for treating ASPD because they are viewed as unresponsive to offenders' criminogenic needs and/or learning style include traditional "talk" psychotherapy of the psychodynamic, client-centered, and insight-oriented ilk.

Programs that include a relapse prevention element are associated with enhanced reductions in recidivism. Relapse prevention is a cognitive-behavioral approach to self-management that entails teaching individuals alternate (more effective) responses to high-risk situations. Components of relapse prevention that seem to be especially effective in reducing recidivism include identifying one's offense-chain and high-risk situations and, subsequently, role-playing alternate (more effective) ways of handling such situations.

Etiology

Specifying etiological mechanisms for ASPD is difficult because of the nonspecificity of the disorder. That is, there are innumerable symptom combinations that can give rise to a diagnosis. Furthermore, a diagnosis can arise almost solely from a person having engaged in chronic criminal and violent behavior. That is, there are no pathognomonic, necessary, or sufficient signs of ASPD. Therefore, almost anything that predicts chronic crime and violence ostensibly could be considered a candidate etiological factor for ASPD.

Nevertheless, there is evidence for certain genetic, biological, and environmental etiological mechanisms in ASPD. Large-scale twin and adoption research shows a high degree of heritability for PDs generally, as well as for ASPD specifically. An interesting line of research by Robert Krueger and colleagues has shown that ASPD might be construed as part of a heritable externalizing spectrum of psychopathology that includes antisocial personality features and behavior, substance use problems, conduct problems, sensation seeking, and low constraint.

Potential biological mechanisms include neurochemical imbalances, such as low serotonin levels, that are related to impulsive and aggressive behavior. Some biological etiological mechanisms have been advanced more specifically for psychopathy, which includes additional interpersonal and emotional deficits. For instance, some experts propose that psychopathy, and as such some cases of ASPD, is associated with functional brain deficits, such as a diminished ability to process emotion or impaired information processing. Other mechanisms could include temperamental deficiencies, such as decreased startle potentiation. Structural, as opposed to functional, neuroanatomic models have been proposed as well, including deficits in prefrontal and temporal lobe gray matter. It is important to note that all such research on the biological mechanisms of psychopathy and ASPD is in its infancy and cannot yet support definitive statements about clear etiological factors.

Environmental factors also may elevate the risk of development of ASPD. For instance, abusive, inconsistent, or permissive parental disciplinary styles predict delinquency and adult criminality. Similarly, other family-of-origin and formative experiences predict delinquent and criminal behavior, such as parental criminality, violence, and substance use problems. Social learning theory would posit that such parental behaviors model criminal behavior for children, who then learn to use crime and violence in their own lives.

Of course, many such parental factors could be acting as mere proxies for genetic etiological mechanisms, and future research will need to disentangle genetic from environmental risk factors. Some interesting emerging research has started to do so. For instance, parental physical maltreatment of children has been found to predict antisocial behavior above and beyond the heritable aspects of parental antisociality. Furthermore, research is starting to address

gene-environment interactions vis-à-vis antisocial behavior and personality, which posit that genetic and environmental factors might be multiplicative in their influence on such outcomes rather than merely additive.

Controversies

The ASPD diagnosis has generated controversy on several fronts. The debate that has received the most commentary pertains to whether the diagnostic criteria should emphasize objective behaviors or personality features. The introduction of ASPD into the DSM was intended to reflect the clinical disorder known as psychopathy, which includes features such as callousness, remorselessness, guiltlessness, superficiality, and shallow affect. The ASPD criteria were written with a behavioral focus in the service of the decreasing subjectivity involved in rating personality features, thereby increasing reliability. In the current diagnostic nomenclature, ASPD is presented as being largely the same as psychopathy—even though many of the descriptors traditionally associated with psychopathy are absent from the diagnostic criteria. That the two disorders are not in fact synonymous is highlighted by the results of contemporary prevalence studies demonstrating that about three quarters of prisoners meet the criteria for ASPD whereas only about one quarter, or less, meets the criteria for psychopathy.

Additionally, the criteria have been criticized for lacking specificity; for instance, meeting diagnostic criteria may arise from a boggling number of permutations of the 7 adult disorder and 15 CD symptoms. An important impact of the imprecision with which the outcome of ASPD is delineated is that it renders investigation into the disorder's causal factors much more challenging, as noted above. Moreover, the validity of ASPD has been challenged in light of the paucity of available longitudinal data. Critics of the ASPD criteria also argue that they are underinclusive (in that individuals will not be identified who have the core antisocial personality features but have not been criminally sanctioned or who demonstrate antisociality during adulthood but for whom there is no evidence of CD). In contrast, others advance concerns that the criteria are overinclusive (in that there likely are several etiological bases for antisociality, only one of which may be psychopathy). As noted earlier, the criteria largely reflect the behavioral difficulties associated with crime and substance use. This is noted to be problematic because behaviors can be influenced by external circumstances, whereas personality traits are viewed as being more reflective of underlying pathology.

Another controversy surrounding the diagnostic criteria is the apparent diagnostic biases they invoke. Although the prevalence of ASPD genuinely may be higher among men (estimated at 3% of the population) than among women (estimated at 1%), research has documented elevated rates among men even when men and women do not differ in symptomatology. Some researchers have argued in favor of amending the diagnostic criteria to include behaviors associated specifically with antisociality in women in an effort to make the criteria more gender neutral. Finally, concerns also have been raised that ASPD may be disproportionately overdiagnosed among prisoners and persons with substance use problems in light of the behavioral focus of the criteria.

Kevin S. Douglas and Laura S. Guy

See also Aggravating and Mitigating Circumstances, Evaluation of in Capital Cases; Alcohol Intoxication; Community Corrections; Conduct Disorder; Criminal Behavior, Theories of; Ethnic Differences in Psychopathy; Forensic Assessment; Hare Psychopathy Checklist–Revised (2nd edition) (PCL–R); Juvenile Offenders, Risk Factors; Juvenile Psychopathy; Personality Disorders; Psychopathic Personality Inventory (PPI); Psychopathy; Psychopathy, Treatment of; Psychopathy Checklist: Youth Version; Violence Risk Assessment

Further Readings

American Psychiatric Association. (2000). *Diagnostic and statistical manual of mental disorders* (4th ed., text revision). Washington, DC: Author.

Fowler, K. A., & Lilienfeld, S. O. (2006). Antisocial personality disorder. In J. E. Fisher & W. T. O'Donohue (Eds.), *Practitioner's guide to evidence-based psychotherapy* (pp. 57–67). New York: Springer.

Krueger, R. F., Markon, K. E., Patrick, C. J., & Iacono, W. G. (2005). Externalizing psychopathology in adulthood: A dimensional-spectrum conceptualization and its implications for *DSM-V. Journal of Abnormal Psychology, 114,* 537–550.

Moffitt, T. E. (2005). The new look of behavioral genetics in developmental psychopathology: Gene-environment interplay in antisocial behaviors. *Psychological Bulletin, 131,* 533–554.

Patrick, C. J. (2006). *Handbook of psychopathy.* New York: Guilford.

Widiger, T. A., Cadoret, R., Hare, R., Robins, L., Rutherford, M., Zanarini, M., et al. (1996). *DSM-IV* antisocial personality disorder field trial. *Journal of Abnormal Psychology, 105,* 3–16.

APPEARANCE-CHANGE INSTRUCTION IN LINEUPS

Prior to viewing a lineup, eyewitnesses to crimes are often given various instructions by lineup administrators. Among these is the appearance-change instruction, which is used to inform the eyewitness that the criminal's appearance in the lineup may be different from his or her appearance at the time of the crime. Generally, this alteration in appearance would be the result of features that might have changed over time (such as head or facial hair). This instruction is especially likely to be given, and is presumed to be most beneficial, if a significant period of time has passed between the crime and the lineup or if the suspect's appearance is somehow at odds with the witness's description of the criminal. Although frequently administered in an attempt to increase identifications of the criminal, preliminary research suggests that the appearance-change instruction does not increase correct identifications but instead increases false identifications of innocent lineup members.

Eyewitness Evidence: A Guide for Law Enforcement (a set of guidelines distributed to all law enforcement agencies across the United States) recommends that lineup administrators instruct a witness that "individuals present in the lineup may not appear exactly as they did on the date of the incident because features such as head and facial hair are subject to change" (p. 32). Although recommended, this instruction is not mandatory; consequently, various police departments and individual lineup administrators may word the instruction differently or may omit it altogether. The purpose of this instruction is to ensure that the witness does not fail to identify the criminal simply because the witness does not appreciate that the criminal's appearance might have changed since the crime. Therefore, it is implicitly assumed that administering the appearance-change instruction will lower witnesses' expectations that the criminal's appearance in the lineup will exactly match his or her appearance at the time of the crime. This should, in turn, increase the probability of correctly identifying the actual criminal when the criminal is in fact in the lineup.

Empirical research on the effects of the appearance-change instruction is scarce. Preliminary studies suggest, however, that the instruction may not be as beneficial as previously assumed. Although it has been shown experimentally that witnesses who receive an appearance-change instruction do make more lineup identifications, this did not result in an increased number of *correct* identifications. Instead, the appearance-change instruction was shown to increase the number of incorrect identifications of fillers (i.e., lineup members who are known to be innocent) without increasing the number of correct identifications of the criminal. Although it is uncertain whether these findings will be replicated by future studies, they do nonetheless challenge the basic assumption underlying the use of the appearance-change instruction. Such an increase in false identifications without a concomitant increase in correct identifications means that lineup identifications made following an appearance-change instruction were, as a whole, less accurate than identifications made without an appearance-change instruction. Additionally, the appearance-change instruction has been shown to increase the length of time it takes witnesses to make an identification and to decrease the confidence with which witnesses report making an identification.

Although it is as yet not known why the appearance-change instruction increased false identifications without a concomitant increase in correct identifications, two hypotheses have been advanced. Both are predicated on the assumption that a lineup identification occurs when the similarity of a lineup member to the witness's memory of the criminal surpasses a minimum level.

The first hypothesis is that the instruction may simply lower a witness's decision criterion (the minimum level of similarity needed to result in an identification). Witnesses who are given an appearance-change instruction might conclude that due to possible appearance change they should not expect a high degree of similarity between the criminal in the lineup and their memory of the criminal. However, because even innocent lineup members may bear some moderate resemblance to the criminal, if a witness's decision criterion is low enough, even these innocent people may be falsely identified.

The second hypothesis that explains the effects of the appearance-change instruction is that the instruction may lead witnesses to mentally alter various facial features of the lineup members. For example, witnesses may imagine what the lineup members would look like with different facial hair, different hairstyles, or a chubbier face. If witnesses mentally alter the various lineup members' appearance in an effort to match the lineup members to their memory of

the criminal, then even innocent lineup members may come to resemble the actual criminal. Thus, the appearance-change instruction would make it even more likely that the similarity between an innocent lineup member and the criminal surpasses the witness's decision criterion, thereby leading to a false identification.

Whether the effects described here are replicable and whether they generalize across variations in the wording of the appearance-change instruction, across different witnessed events, and across various other lineup manipulations remain open empirical questions. A greater understanding of the effects of the appearance-change instruction, and the explanation of those effects, awaits further research.

Steve D. Charman

See also Estimator and System Variables in Eyewitness Identification; Eyewitness Identification: Effect of Disguises and Appearance Changes; Eyewitness Memory; Instructions to the Witness; WITNESS Model

Further Readings

Charman, S. D., & Wells, G. L. (2007). Eyewitness lineups: Is the appearance-change instruction a good idea? *Law and Human Behavior, 31,* 3–22.

Douglass, A. B., & Gerety, M. (2005). Eyewitness accuracy as a function of lineup instruction and expectation. Unpublished manuscript.

Technical Working Group for Eyewitness Evidence. (1999). *Eyewitness evidence: A guide for law enforcement.* Washington, DC: U.S. Department of Justice, Office of Justice Programs.

AUTOMATISM

Automatism is an excuse defense against criminal liability for defendants who committed a presumptively criminal act in a state of unconsciousness, semiconsciousness, or unawareness. Medically, the term automatism refers to motor behavior that is automatic, undirected, and not consciously controlled. The use of automatism as a legal defense is relatively rare and is typically claimed in cases where the defendant's conscious awareness is compromised by epilepsy, brain injury, somnambulism (sleepwalking), or trauma. The automatism defense is recognized as a viable defense in U.S. and British courts, but the definitions and applications of the defense vary widely and are often inconsistent. The basis for the defense is that a defendant should not be held responsible for presumptively criminal actions because of the involuntary nature of the behaviors, leading to lack of criminal intent and voluntary criminal action.

Excuses and Justifications

In criminal law, there is a general rule that individuals are to be held legally responsible for their actions. Our fundamental and longstanding societal values and moral traditions allow for several exceptions in situations in which it would not be fair or just to hold persons criminally liable. These exceptions are discussed under the general heading of defenses, which, in turn, have been distinguished as justifications and excuses. Justifications seek to establish that even though the prosecution may have fulfilled its required burden to prove the basic facts of the offense, the act committed by the defendant was not criminal because, for example, it was done in defense of self, others, or property. Excuses essentially concede the wrongfulness of the act but seek to establish that the defendant is not criminally responsible because the act took place, for example, under conditions of duress or compulsion, immaturity, or insanity.

Automatism is an excuse defense that has been characterized as similar to the excuse of ignorance. That is, an automatism can be defined as an action taken without any knowledge of acting or without consciousness of what is being done. Automatism, however, is not simply a matter of acting out of ignorance. In the case of ignorance, a defendant may be acting based on an erroneous belief (e.g., the defendant believes that he or she is administering first aid but is, rather, exacerbating a medical condition of the victim), but in the case of automatism, the defendant is unaware that he or she is acting at all.

Actus Reus and Mens Rea

Except in cases of strict liability, any crime contains two elements: the *actus reus* ("guilty act") and *mens rea* ("guilty mind"). The automatism defense seeks to prove that the defendant made physical actions (automatisms) that led to a bad outcome but did not perform a guilty act. As such, the automatism defense is the only excuse defense that is based on the actus reus element rather being purely a mens rea excuse defense (e.g., insanity). In an insanity defense, the defense acknowledges the guilty act but claims that the

defendant should not be held blameworthy due to the lack of a guilty mind or intent.

Another way of understanding these two elements would be to consider if the presumptively criminal act was *intentional* or *voluntary*. Actions directed toward a goal are typically considered to be intentional. An automatism defense, however, claims that the actions taken are automatic and, therefore, not intentional. In the case of some automatic movements (e.g., loss of muscular control during a grand mal seizure), the absence of intentionality is obvious. In some cases, however, this judgment can be exceedingly difficult. For example, intentionality is far less obvious in a defendant who engaged in goal-directed aggression during a period of postictal confusion following a nocturnal partial complex seizure when the defendant appeared to be sleepwalking. The issue of volitional control (voluntariness) goes directly to the heart of the automatism defense. The Model Penal Code of the American Law Institute states that a defendant is not criminally liable if he or she does not commit a "voluntary act," which is defined to exclude "reflex or convulsion" or actions taken during "unconsciousness." There can be no actus reus when the defendant does not commit a voluntary act. Typically, courts have required that volitional dyscontrol be total; that is, the actor (defendant) has no control over his or her actions.

The Automatism Defense: Case Law

Although its use is relatively rare, the automatism defense has been established as a criminal defense in courts in the United States and Britain. Courts vary widely, however, in definitions and applications of the defense. In the United States, for example, some courts have applied the rationale of an insanity defense, interpreting the involuntary behaviors associated with automatisms as a defect in reason that prevented the defendant from knowing the nature and quality of his or her act, therefore making an automatism defense a mens rea defense. Other courts have stressed the involuntary nature of the defendant's actions, focusing on the lack of actus reus. British courts have made a distinction between sane and insane automatism. A defense of insane automatism requires that the defendant meet all three conditions of the British insanity defense (the M'Naghten standard), where the automatism would be the "disorder of reason" caused by a "disease of the mind," leading to the defendant not knowing the "nature and quality of his act or that it was wrongful." Defendants who raise an automatism defense and who meet M'Naghten standards would be adjudicated under the "not guilty by reason of insanity" (NGRI) standard. The defendant who raises the defense and who does not meet the standard would be claiming sane automatism, seeking to challenge that his or her behavior was simply not a voluntary act. If such a defense were successful, the defendant would be acquitted and not subjected to the possible consequences (e.g., commitment to a psychiatric facility) faced by an NGRI acquittee. British courts have indicated that sane automatism is an acceptable defense when the defendant has suffered from a defect of reason but not a disease of the mind, usually due to some external physical factor. The sequelae of a head injury or confusion as a result of the administration of drugs would be examples of such external causes of automatisms.

Matt C. Zaitchik

See also Criminal Responsibility, Assessment of; Criminal Responsibility, Defenses and Standards; Insanity Defense, Juries and

Further Readings

Borum, R., & Appelbaum, K. L. (1996). Epilepsy, aggression, and criminal responsibility. *Psychiatric Services, 47*(7), 762–763.

Reznek, L. (1997). *Evil or ill? Justifying the insanity defense.* London: Routledge.

Schopp, R. F. (1991). *Automatism, insanity, and the psychology of criminal responsibility: A philosophical inquiry.* Cambridge, UK: Cambridge University Press.

B

BAIL-SETTING DECISIONS

The bail-setting decision is one of the early court decisions made in a case, and it has attracted attention from researchers studying legal decision making. When a case is adjourned (postponed), the court must decide what to do with the defendant until the next hearing of the case—basically, should the defendant be released on bail or not? The main goal of the bail decision is to ensure that the defendant appears at court for the next hearing. The bail decision also can affect later decisions in a case. Although laws govern the bail decision-making process, they are typically vague and ill defined, thus allowing courts considerable discretion. Past research on bail decision making has mostly been conducted in the United States and the United Kingdom; researchers have aimed to describe how courts make bail decisions as well as to evaluate efforts to improve bail decision making.

Because it arises each time a case is adjourned for trial, sentence, or appeal, the bail decision is one of the most frequent legal decisions made by the criminal courts. The primary goal is to ensure that the defendant surrenders to the court at the next hearing of the case and so does not abscond. A secondary goal is that the defendant does not threaten community safety (e.g., offend) while released on bail. In the United States, the court sets a monetary amount of bail. A defendant may either be required to provide a security (deposit the amount with the court) before release, which is forfeited if he or she fails to appear in court, or be released on recognizance, which is a promise to appear, so the amount is paid only if he or she fails to appear. (For a fee, bail bondsmen can act as a surety, a third party

who agrees to pay the forfeited amount to the court.) Nonfinancial conditions, such as curfew and surrendering firearms, may also be applied to bail. In the United Kingdom, defendants can be bailed (released) unconditionally; bailed with nonfinancial conditions or financial conditions, such as surety or security; or denied bail and remanded into custody. Whereas in the United States the bail decision is commonly measured on a continuous scale reflecting the monetary amount at which bail is set, in the United Kingdom the decision is typically measured as categorical because financial bail is uncommon. In most jurisdictions, bail jumping (skipping bail or absconding) is an offense.

The bail decision-making process is often governed by legislation, which is periodically revised. For instance, in the United States, currently there is the Federal Bail Reform Act of 1984 (state laws vary); in the United Kingdom, there is the Bail Act of 1976. It has often been recommended that the practice of bail decision making should adhere to the principles of due process rather than crime control. Thus, there is typically a general right to bail or pretrial liberty. However, there are exceptions if the court decides that the defendant may pose a risk of absconding or offending. The laws typically recommend that the court considers several factors (e.g., the defendant's offense, community ties, previous convictions, prior bail record, and strength of the prosecution's case) when judging these risks and consequently making bail decisions. Beyond this, the court is afforded considerable latitude in making bail decisions in terms of how it weights and integrates these and other factors.

The bail decision can have significant negative ramifications for defendants and their families if a defendant is denied bail or cannot raise the bail amount. For instance, defendants may lose their homes, employment, contact with their families, and their reputations, as well as experience the adverse effects of custody. In addition, evidence suggests that the bail decision may influence later decisions on a case, such as the decision to plea, convict, and sentence. Here, defendants who do not get bail are more likely to plead guilty or be convicted and are also more likely to receive a custodial sentence than their bailed counterparts.

Much of the past research, as noted previously, has investigated bail decision making in the United States and the United Kingdom. Studies have been conducted by psychologists, sociologists, criminologists, and legal scholars using methodologies such as experiments involving decision makers being presented with simulated cases, interview and questionnaire surveys of decision makers, courtroom observations of bail hearings, analyses of bail records and statistics, and analyses of bail laws. While most of this body of research has aimed to describe and explain how bail decisions are made, several studies have explored efforts to improve bail decision making. Overall, the research has yielded consistent findings.

Describing and Explaining Bail Decisions

Researchers have aimed to describe and explain bail decisions in terms of the variations in decision making and the factors that influence bail decisions. Studies have documented the variation in bail decisions made across cases and across jurisdictions (courts or decision makers), as well as within jurisdictions (courts or decision makers). There are apparent disparities in how cases that vary in their extralegal characteristics, such as the defendant's gender and race, are dealt with. In addition, different jurisdictions (courts or decision makers) may disagree on how to deal with cases that are similar. Beyond this, there is variability where the same jurisdiction (court or decision maker) is inconsistent in dealing with similar cases on different occasions.

Research has shown that bail decisions may be influenced by both legal and extralegal factors. Legal factors include the nature and seriousness of the offense the defendant is charged with, the defendant's previous convictions, and the strength of his or her community ties. Specifically, bail is more likely to be denied or set at a high amount if the defendant is charged with a serious offense, has previous convictions, or has weak community ties. The extralegal factors that have been found to affect bail decisions include the defendant's gender and race and the police and prosecution's recommendations. Here, denial of bail or its high amount is more likely to be associated with the defendant being male or non-White and a recommendation to deny bail.

In addition to identifying the factors that may influence bail decision making, some psychological studies have examined how the information is processed to form a decision. Here, there is evidence to suggest that the bail decision is the result of a simple strategy where only a few factors are considered rather than a more complex strategy involving weighting and integration of several factors.

Improving Bail Decisions

Researchers and policymakers have attempted to improve bail decision making by reducing discretion and increasing the availability of relevant information. As mentioned, the law affords the court considerable discretion in how it makes bail decisions. There have been attempts to reduce variability in bail decisions and the influence of extralegal factors as well as increase the accountability, transparency, and equity of bail decisions by limiting this discretion through the introduction of more precise guidelines. For example, in the United States, bail guidelines that specify the factors that the court should use and how they should make their risk assessments have been developed and implemented in several jurisdictions since the early 1980s. John Goldkamp and colleagues have evaluated the utility of such guidelines using randomized controlled trials and pre-post analyses. They found that decisions made under guidelines differed from those made without guidelines in several respects, including that under guidelines the bail amount was lower, there was an increase in the use of nonfinancial conditions, and there was a reduction in the time in pretrial custody. However, the impact of guidelines appears to differ across jurisdictions as they are applied and used differently.

There have also been efforts to increase the effectiveness of bail decisions by improving the court's ability to judge the defendant's risk of absconding on bail. The idea is that low-risk defendants, such as those who have strong ties to the community and thus may be unlikely to abscond, can be appropriately released. For example, in the United States, the Manhattan Bail Project (later renamed the New York Release on Recognizances Project) involved the collection, verification, and scoring of information on a defendant's community ties (e.g., residence, employment, and family situation) and then providing a recommendation directly to the court concerning the defendant's suitability for bail. In a randomized controlled trial involving real cases, the Vera Institute of Justice in 1963 found that defendants in the experimental group for whom a recommendation was provided were more likely to be bailed than those in the control group for whom the recommendation was withheld. In the United Kingdom, Bail Information Schemes provide largely positive information about a defendant's community ties to the prosecution and defense, who then can relay it to the court. In 2002, in an experiment involving simulated cases, the author found, however, that such schemes did not have a statistically significant effect on the bail decisions made.

Mandeep K. Dhami

See also Parole Decisions; Probation Decisions; Sentencing Decisions

Further Readings

Dhami, M. K. (2002). Do bail information schemes really affect bail decisions? *Howard Journal of Criminal Justice, 41,* 245–262.

Dhami, M. K. (2005). From discretion to disagreement: Explaining disparities in judges' pretrial decisions. *Behavioral Sciences and the Law, 23,* 367–386.

Dhami, M. K., & Ayton, P. (2001). Bailing and jailing the fast and frugal way. *Journal of Behavioral Decision Making, 14,* 141–168.

Goldkamp, J. S., & Gottfredson, M. R. (1985). *Policy guidelines for bail: An experiment in court reform.* Philadelphia: Temple University Press.

Goldkamp, J. S., Gottfredson, M. R., Jones, P. R., & Weiland, D. (1995). *Personal liberty and community safety. Pretrial release in the criminal court.* New York: Plenum Press.

BATTERED WOMAN SYNDROME

Battered woman syndrome (BWS), first proposed in the 1970s after research demonstrated the psychological impact from domestic violence on the victim, has undergone further clarification since its inception. This entry reviews the historical issues concerning domestic violence and its victims in the criminal justice system (including the criminal and family courts), describes psychological theories about domestic violence victims and the BWS, and discusses the application of the BWS in legal context.

History of Domestic Violence and the Law

Domestic violence is defined as the physical, sexual, and/or psychological abuse by one person (mostly men) of another person (mostly women) with whom there is an intimate relationship, in order to get that person to do what the abuser wants without regard for that person's rights. Domestic violence is also called *intimate partner violence* by some, while the term *family violence* encompasses child and elder abuse as well as intimate partner abuse.

Some have suggested that the family and monogamous relationships originated to protect women and children from physically and sexually aggressive nomadic men. Unfortunately, the family has not been a safe haven for some women and children. Laws condoning the practice of wife beating were common in the United States and other countries until very recently. Since men were given the legal responsibility of protecting their wives and children, they also had the right to discipline them. When women demanded their own legal and social rights during the renewed women's movement that began in the early 1970s in the United States, they also began to demand that the laws better protect them from men's physical and sexual violence.

Battered Women in the Criminal Justice System

The first area that received attention was the need for law enforcement to better protect women who were being abused by intimate partners. Typical reports were that the man would batter the woman and leave the scene if the police were called. Even if he was still present, the police would hesitate to intervene and make an arrest in what was said to be a family matter and instead would typically take the man for a walk around the block in an attempt to calm him down. Women told of how this rarely worked and that they would be beaten even worse after the law enforcement officers left. Police officers complained that prosecutors didn't take these cases seriously; but prosecutors claimed that women dropped the charges and refused to cooperate and judges didn't know how to handle these domestic matters. Two areas for reform became clear. First, domestic assaults should be prosecuted just like any other assault, without placing the burden on the woman to file or drop charges. Second, women needed protection from further abuse from all legal, social, and medical institutions and agencies. The barriers that women faced in all society's institutions became more visible as cases began to be heard in courts around the world. It became clear that it would require cooperation from all levels of society to better protect women and children.

The criminal justice system began to introduce several different reforms, including vertical prosecution of domestic violence cases and the development of pro-prosecution strategies, including special problem-solving domestic violence courts where perpetrators could be diverted into treatment. Other reforms included making restraining orders easier to obtain and strengthening their enforcement with penalties, as well as removing the ability of those arrested to bond out without first being in front of a judge. Research suggested that spending the night in jail and getting a stern message from the judge was a sufficient deterrent for most known batterers, and pro-arrest policies began to be adopted in many cities across the United States. Later research showed that some batterers, particularly those who had few community ties, such as a job or a social network, might actually become more violent after an arrest, and as batterers began to enter treatment programs, it became clear that they were as demographically diverse a population as were the women they abused.

Dependency and Family Courts

It also became clear that both men and women involved in domestic violence often had psychological and substance abuse problems. Although battered woman advocates in shelters and support groups disagreed about the origin of these problems, most agreed that availability of appropriately trained mental health providers was important. In the beginning, few psychiatrists, psychologists, social workers, or psychiatric nurses were trained in working with domestic violence victims or perpetrators. Protocols were developed for those in the medical and psychology fields, and large-scale government funding went into training victim advocates, shelter workers, and legal and mental health professionals. The battered woman shelter became the organizing point for policies and services in the United States and other countries. In the United States, the legal system and, in particular, the criminal justice system remained the gatekeeper for services for both perpetrators and victims, while in other countries, where the public health system had more impact, services were provided through that system.

Although the emphasis had been on protection of women from abusers, it was also necessary to focus on protection of children from abuse. Studies found that an overlap of anywhere from 40% to 60% of cases of child abuse occurred in families with known domestic violence. Child protection workers who had been trained to blame the mother for the actual abuse or failure to protect the child had to relearn how to work with moms who were also being battered and who tried to protect their children with little help from agencies in the community. The issue of protection of children is still unsolved, with cases going between criminal, dependency and neglect, and family courts, and children are often inadequately served by any of them.

Many advocates for battered women believe that batterers often use the family courts to continue their contact and control over the woman long after the marriage is dissolved by insisting on shared parental responsibility. They further believe that the court declines to use its power to empower the battered woman and assist her in the protection of the child. When the court does not intervene, the batterer is not stopped from his continued psychological abuse of both the woman and the child. An example of how batterers may use the court to their advantage is by filing numerous court motions, which become a major psychological and financial drain on women who earn less money than do men. To further complicate matters, mental health professionals hired by lawyers on both sides of highly contested divorce and custody cases may introduce constructs, such as Parental Alienation Syndrome and Psychological Munchausen by Proxy, that have questionable validity. These questionable constructs have been ruled inadmissible in criminal courts but are admissible in family courts.

Women Who Kill in Self-Defense

Approximately 1,000 women in the United States are known to have killed their abusive partners in what they claim was self-defense. In contrast, more than 4,000 women are reportedly killed by their partners each year. The self-defense laws had to be re-formed to enable these women to plead not guilty using a justification defense in criminal court. From the late 1970s to the early 1990s, states began the admissibility process through case law and legislation, so that women's perception of danger and, in particular, the battered woman's perception of danger would be accepted at trial. Until these cases began to be heard, self-defense was thought to be similar to two men having a fight in a bar. To help the triers of fact—the judges and juries who heard these cases—better understand the battered woman's perception of danger, especially when the woman killed the man when he was asleep or was just starting his dangerously escalating abuse, the dynamics of domestic violence and psychological theories, such as learned helplessness and BWS, were introduced into court testimony.

Psychological Theories About Domestic Violence and Battered Women

Dynamics of Domestic Violence

In the past 30 years, the assessment of behavior that is or is not considered to be domestic violence has been a major challenge for advocates and professionals. This difficulty may in large part be due to battered women having to maintain secrecy in order to protect themselves from their abuser, which leads them to minimize or cover up their pain, both emotional and physical. However, as the women began to receive legal protection and services, they have been able to describe the dynamics that occur in their homes, and as batterers began to talk in the offender-specific intervention programs into which they were sent by the courts, they confirmed much of the women's descriptions. Lenore Walker first found that battering did not occur all the time in homes where domestic violence existed but that it was not random either. Rather, the women described a cycle of violence that followed a courtship period that was mostly made up of loving behavior.

This cycle included three phases: (1) the tension-building period, (2) the acute battering incident, and (3) a period of loving contrition or absence of battering. Each time a new battering event occurred, the memory of fragments of the previous battering incidents added heightened fear, which guided the woman's response, usually to try to calm down the batterer and prevent further escalation of the violence. However, at times, when the woman saw signs that the batterer's violence was escalating no matter what she did, she engaged in actions to protect herself. Occasionally, this resulted in her intentionally or unintentionally killing the abuser.

Learned Helplessness

When evaluating battered women who killed their abusers, it became necessary to understand why a woman would use a gun or a knife against a man who was sleeping or at the beginning of a violent event. Why wouldn't she simply leave? The answer to this question is most important, both for specific cases and generally. The theory of learned helplessness helps explain how someone can learn to believe that her actions will not have a predictable effect and, therefore, that leaving will not stop the violence toward her. Research shows that many women are seriously injured or killed at the point of separation. The batterer who tells his partner that he will follow and harm her wherever she goes and who uses his power and control to enforce isolation, intrusiveness, and overpossessiveness reinforces her belief in his omnipotence. When battering continues unabated and the batterer suffers no consequences for his actions, he confirms her belief in his dominance over her. The loss of contingency between the victim's behavior and the battering leads to learned helplessness.

Battered women who experience learned helplessness experience the loss of their belief that they can escape to protect themselves. This learned helplessness is sometimes misunderstood as actual helplessness or the actual inability to escape the battering. The theory of learned helplessness, together with the cycle theory of violence and the BWS, has helped juries understand why women do not simply walk out of their homes and leave the batterer. In some of the legal opinions, the BWS is actually described as including the dynamics of abuse together with learned helplessness rather than the collection of psychological signs and symptoms that typically make up a syndrome according to the *Diagnostic and Statistical Manual of Mental Disorders* (fourth edition, text revision; *DSM-IV-TR*; American Psychological Association, 2000). However, this is part of the tension between the advocates who wish to eliminate any discussion of mental disorders as part of BWS and psychologists who understand that exposure to repeated trauma may well cause emotional difficulties, including posttraumatic stress disorder (PTSD), of which BWS is considered a subcategory.

Trauma Theory and Battered Woman Syndrome

The complexity of symptomatology and the clinical presentation of battered women has made it challenging for both legal and clinical disciplines. Over the years, these complexities have been widely studied, and a trend across cultures has been identified in the way women experience various forms of violence against them, including sexual assault and rape, domestic violence and sexual exploitation, and harassment. These abuses are perceived by most women as traumatic events, and therefore, a combination of feminist theory, to attempt to account for the power and control issues, and trauma theory, to deal with the abuse underlying BWS, is required.

BWS can best be conceptualized as a combination of posttraumatic stress symptomatology, including reexperiencing a traumatic event (i.e., battering episode); numbing of responsiveness; and hyperarousal, in addition to a variable combination of several other factors. These additional factors include, but are not limited to, disrupted interpersonal relationships, difficulties with body image, somatic concerns, as well as sexual and intimacy problems. Over the past few years, an attempt has been made to clearly define the hypothesized constituents of BWS for research purposes. As such, some variables were isolated and include PTSD symptoms, power and control issues, body image distortion, and sexual dysfunction, using data collected with the use of the Battered Woman Syndrome Questionnaire developed by Lenore Walker.

In the literature from the past 30 years, one of the most contemplated components of BWS is PTSD. When the original research was designed, PTSD had not yet been tested and entered into the *DSM* diagnostic system. In general, criticisms suggest that the trauma model does not include sufficient context of the woman's life so that it makes it appear that she has a mental illness rather than her symptoms being a logical response to being abused. While that is true for some women, studies indicate that there are numerous women who come to a therapist because the symptoms do not go away despite the fact that they are no longer being battered. PTSD, which is characterized by reexperiencing of the trauma from stimuli that are both physically and not physically present, can account for this phenomenon.

The Battered Women Syndrome Questionnaire

To gain insight into BWS and its effect on women across cultures, Lenore Walker and colleagues are continuing the validation process for the Revised Battered Woman Syndrome Questionnaire 2003 (BWSQ–3). Given the violence against women as a universal phenomenon, it is essential to interview women from various cultures. Consequently, data from interviews have been gathered from Russia, Spain, Greece, Colombia, and South Florida. Furthermore, the research has recently begun to take into account incarcerated women who report a history of battering relationships.

The original version of the Battered Women Syndrome Questionnaire was developed more than 25 years ago by Lenore Walker. The most recent version, the Battered Women Syndrome Questionnaire–3, and its predecessors serve as comprehensive tools to gather valuable information regarding the field of domestic violence research and treatment. Establishing the reliability and validity of BWSQ–3 will enable future clinicians to use a semistructured clinical interview to assess women who report a battering relationship. The assessment also has the potential to help guide clinicians treating battered women, as the interview allows for an individualized overview of the woman's history and battering relationship. In addition, researchers have begun to investigate the dynamics of battering relationships as experienced by women who become involved in the criminal justice system, for the purpose of identifying the unique needs of this population. Current research by the authors and their colleagues using the BWSQ–3 has shown similar patterns of experience, including a high endorsement of PTSD symptomatology, across cultures.

Application of Battered Woman Syndrome in Legal Contexts

As was described above, in a legal context, the term *battered woman syndrome* is most frequently used as an explanation of a woman's perception of threat leading her to commit a criminal offense in self-defense. Criminal offenses may also include spousal assault (i.e., in cases in which battered women fight back without killing their partners) or any other crime they may co-commit under the influence of their battering partners. In fact, the use of BWS extends beyond the criminal justice system, to include family court (e.g., child custody cases) or even civil court (e.g., in rare cases when the woman is suing the batterer for physical and emotional damages).

BWS is generally applied in the form of evidence being presented during a criminal trial where the battered woman killed her abusive partner in self-defense. The goal of introducing BWS is to obtain either an acquittal or a downgrading of a first-degree murder charge to second-degree murder or manslaughter. The burden carried by the defense includes presenting evidence that the woman was—or perceived herself to be—in imminent danger. The defense usually attempts to establish this with the help of an expert witness who testifies concerning the dynamics of an abusive relationship and how a woman's perception can be influenced by a history of abuse and PTSD symptomatology. In addition, because the expert conducts a comprehensive assessment of the defendant, he or she is likely able to discuss possible comorbid mental health disorders.

Because of BWS's broad range of applications within the legal system, and the need for psychological evaluation and/or expert testimony across legal settings, the term *battered woman syndrome* has traditionally been used in both a legal and a clinical context, with an understanding that the wide-ranging effects of battering are physiological, behavioral, cognitive, and emotional.

Lenore E. Walker, Rachel I. Duros,
and Allison Tome

See also Domestic Violence Courts; Intimate Partner Violence; Posttraumatic Stress Disorder (PTSD); Victimization

Further Readings

American Psychiatric Association. (2000). *Diagnostic and statistical manual of mental disorders* (4th ed., text revision). Washington, DC: Author.

Browne, A. (1987). *When battered women kill*. New York: Free Press.

Brownmiller, S. (1975). *Against our will: Men, women and rape*. New York: Simon & Schuster.

Koss, M. P., Goodman, L. A., Browne, A., Fitzgerald, L. F., Keita, G. P., & Russo, N. F. (1994). *No safe haven: Male violence against women at home, work, and in the community*. Washington, DC: American Psychological Association.

Walker, L. E. (1979). *The battered woman*. New York: Harper & Row.

Walker, L. E. A. (1984/2000). *The battered woman syndrome*. New York: Springer.

Walker, L. E. A., Arden, H., Tome, A., Bruno, J., & Brosch, R. (2006). *Battered Woman Syndrome Questionnaire: Training manual for interviewers*.

BATTERED WOMAN SYNDROME, TESTIMONY ON

The most common form of syndrome testimony that has been introduced in the courtroom is battered woman syndrome testimony. For the most part, this testimony has been offered in homicide trials of battered women who have killed their abusers. Most often, the expert witness, typically a clinical psychologist, offers the testimony on behalf of the defense, with the testimony being of relevance to jurors' evaluation of the woman's claim of self-defense. The courts have been quite receptive to this form of expert testimony, and it has now been admitted with some frequency in not only courtrooms across the United States but also in courtrooms in Canada, Britain, Australia, and New Zealand. Battered woman syndrome evidence has been used in other contexts as well (e.g., duress defenses, sentencing, civil actions), but the research examining its impact on jurors is confined primarily to cases involving battered women who have killed their abusers. This research suggests that the introduction of battered woman syndrome evidence is associated with positive effects for a battered woman on trial, but findings also point to some shortcomings of its use.

The term *battered woman syndrome* was first coined in the late 1970s by Dr. Lenore Walker, who pioneered much of the research on the topic. The syndrome describes the pattern of violence found in abusive relationships and the psychological impact that this violence can have on a woman. Drawing on her clinical work, as well as on interviews she conducted with hundreds of battered women, Walker identified a repetitive three-phase cycle that characterizes the battering relationship. The first phase, referred to as the *tension-building* phase, is characterized by "minor" abusive incidents (e.g., outbursts, verbal threats). These more minor incidents of abuse, however, eventually build up to the second, *acute battering* phase, which is then followed by the third, *loving contrition* phase. It is in this final phase that the abuser professes his love, promising never to harm the woman again. Believing his promises, the woman is provided some hope that the violence will cease. Eventually, however, the cycle repeats itself.

Alongside the cycle of violence theory, Walker proposed a *psychological rationale* to explain how battered women can become psychologically trapped in an abusive relationship. Given the repetitive, yet unpredictable nature of the violence and the impending imminence of harm that it presents to the woman, she is eventually reduced to a state of *psychological helplessness*, perceiving that there is little she can do to alter the situation. In her more recent writings, Walker characterizes the battered woman syndrome as a subcategory of posttraumatic stress disorder (PTSD), a clinical diagnostic disorder included in the *Diagnostic Statistical Manual of Mental Disorders-IV*.

Since its inception in the psychological literature in the late 1970s, psychologists have been asked to provide expert testimony pertaining to battered woman syndrome in homicide trials of battered women who have killed their abusers. As the content of the testimony suggests, battered woman syndrome testimony speaks of the woman's mental state and provides a context for understanding why she perceived herself to be in imminent danger at the time of the killing. The courts have also found the expert testimony on battering and its effects to be relevant to the jurors' understanding of the seemingly puzzling behavior and actions of the woman, most notable among these being why she remained in the relationship.

In contrast to its reception in the courts, within the psychological and legal communities, the admissibility of this form of expert testimony has sparked much debate and controversy. Since its introduction into the courtroom, some scholars and battered women's advocates have challenged the validity and applicability of the syndrome evidence to battered women's claims of self-defense. Methodological shortcomings in the research as well as the theories underlying the syndrome evidence have been critiqued by various researchers and legal scholars. Although numerous studies have documented the profound impact of battering and its effects on a woman's physical and mental health, there does not appear to be overwhelming support for a singular profile. As researchers have noted, the singular portrayal of the battered woman as a passive and helpless victim conveyed via battered woman syndrome testimony fails to take into account the variability in battered women's reactions and responses and is at variance with the help-seeking behavior of battered women. As such, scholars have warned against the dangers of adopting such a restrictive conceptualization of the responses of battered women.

As early as the mid-1980s, critics of the testimony voiced the concern that the "syndrome" terminology was likely to be interpreted by the jurors as an illness or a clinical disorder. Thus, as opposed to providing a framework that normalizes the battered woman and her actions, she is characterized as an "irrational and emotionally damaged" woman. As suggested below, a review of the empirical research examining the impact of battered woman syndrome evidence on jurors' judgments and verdict decisions indicates that there may be some validity in these concerns.

Empirical research on the impact of battered woman syndrome evidence began in the late 1980s, with much of this work employing juror simulation techniques. Using this methodology, mock jurors are presented with a simulated or mock trial and asked to render a verdict and provide various judgments about the defendant and the case. Within the trial presentation, the presence or absence of the expert testimony is varied, and comparisons of the mock jurors' responses (e.g., judgments, verdicts) across these different versions of the trial are made to assess the impact of the testimony. The findings of this research are somewhat mixed. While some simulation studies have found little evidence for the impact of battered woman syndrome evidence, studies conducted by Regina Schuller and her colleagues suggest that exposure to the testimony does result in more lenient verdicts and more favorable evaluations of the defendant. In a series of studies, these researchers found that compared with mock jurors who were not exposed to battered woman syndrome evidence, mock jurors provided with expert testimony pertaining to battered woman syndrome were more likely to believe the defendant's claim of self-defense (e.g., perceptions of fear, few options) and more likely to render a not guilty verdict. Although verdict decisions were more favorable to the defendant when battered woman syndrome evidence was presented, there was also evidence consistent with the notion that battered woman syndrome evidence is likely to be associated with interpretations of psychological dysfunction. Lending some support to the concern that battered woman syndrome evidence may lead to interpretations of dysfunction, mock jurors provided with the battered woman syndrome evidence, as opposed to no expert testimony, viewed the woman as more psychologically unstable and were more likely to support a plea of insanity.

In response to the criticism that battered woman syndrome evidence characterizes battered women as psychologically damaged and fails to capture the variation in battered women's experience, Mary Ann Dutton recommends that the term *battered woman syndrome* itself be dropped from the testimony and reference instead be made to expert testimony on "battering and its effects." Moreover, Dutton, one of the authors of a review of battered woman syndrome evidence undertaken at the direction of Congress, notes that the testimony should incorporate the diverse range of traumatic reactions described in the psychological literature and should not be limited to an examination of learned helplessness, PTSD, or any other single reaction or "profile."

Using juror simulation techniques, researchers have explored the impact of such a reformulation of the expert testimony. Specifically, the impact of an alternative form of testimony that eliminated reference to the syndrome terminology, as well as references to learned helplessness and PTSD, on mock jurors' decisions was examined in a series of studies conducted by Schuller and her colleagues. This alternative form of the testimony placed greater emphasis on the battered woman's agency (i.e., effortful and active rather than passive and helpless) and social realities (e.g., lack of social support). The results of this research indicate that, like the battered woman syndrome evidence, the inclusion of this expert evidence resulted in more lenient verdicts than when this evidence was omitted. Moreover, the presence of the expert testimony, compared with the no-expert condition, led to more favorable evaluations of the defendant's claim. Finally, and in contrast to the impact of battered woman syndrome evidence on mock jurors' evaluations of the defendant's psychological stability, the alternative form was not associated with interpretations of psychological dysfunction. In short, the research suggests that an alternative form of testimony that emphasizes the social aspects of the battering relationship and omits references to the term *battered woman syndrome*, learned helplessness, and PTSD may be as successful as battered woman syndrome evidence in terms of verdict decisions. Also, it appears to avoid some of the potential pitfalls associated with the syndrome evidence.

Regina A. Schuller

See also Battered Woman Syndrome; Expert Psychological Testimony; Expert Psychological Testimony, Admissibility Standards; Expert Psychological Testimony, Forms of; Expert Testimony, Qualifications of Experts

Further Readings

Dutton, M. (1993). Understanding women's responses to domestic violence: A redefinition of battered women syndrome. *Hofstra Law Review, 21,* 1191–1242.

Parrish, J. (1996). Trend analysis: Expert evidence on battering and its effects in criminal cases. In *The validity and use of evidence concerning battering and its effects in criminal trials* (Section 2). Washington, DC: DOJ, NIJ, USDHHS, and NIMH. Retrieved January 3, 2007, from http://www.ncjrs.org/pdffiles/batter.pdf

Schuller, R. A., & Jenkins, G. (2007). Expert evidence pertaining to battered women: Limitations and reconceptualizations. In M. Costanzo, D. Krauss, &

K. Pezdek (Eds.), *Expert psychological testimony for the court* (pp. 203–225). Mahwah, NJ: Lawrence Erlbaum.

Schuller, R. A., & Rzepa, S. (2002). The battered women syndrome and other psychological effects of domestic violence against women. In D. L. Faigman, D. H. Kaye, M. J. Saks, & J. Sanders (Eds.), *Modern scientific evidence: The law and science of expert testimony* (Vol. 2, 2nd ed., chap. 11, pp. 37–72). St. Paul, MN: West.

Walker, L. E. (1992). Battered women syndrome and self-defense. *Notre Dame Journal of Law, Ethics & Public Policy, 6,* 321–334.

Walker, L. E. (2000). *The battered woman syndrome* (2nd ed.). New York: Springer.

BEHAVIOR ANALYSIS INTERVIEW

The behavior analysis interview (BAI) is a set of 15 predetermined standardized questions designed to elicit differential responses from innocent and guilty suspects at the outset of a police interview. Police investigators who are reasonably certain of a suspect's guilt may submit the suspect to persuasive interrogation techniques meant to break down the suspect's resistance; because such interrogation techniques may lead to false confessions, it is important not to submit innocent suspects to these techniques. For this reason, BAI forms an important first step in police interviewing. Some evidence, however, refutes the basic assumptions of the BAI that guilty suspects will feel less comfortable and be less helpful than innocent suspects. This raises doubts about the ability of the BAI protocol to determine successfully which suspect is guilty and which suspect is innocent.

The BAI starts with the question "What is your understanding of the purpose of this interview?" followed by questions such as "Did you commit the crime?" or "Do you know who committed the crime?" or "Who would have had the best opportunity to commit the crime if they had wanted to?" and "Once we complete our entire investigation, what do you think the results will be with respect to your involvement in the crime?" Despite its name, *behavior analysis interview,* the BAI predicts that guilty and innocent suspects will differ in their nonverbal behavior and also in their verbal responses.

Regarding the *nonverbal responses,* it is assumed that liars feel more uncomfortable than truth tellers in police interviews. Guilty suspects should therefore show more nervous behaviors, such as crossing their legs, shifting about in their chairs, performing grooming behaviors, or looking away from the investigator while answering questions such as "Did you commit the crime?" Regarding the *verbal responses,* it is assumed that compared with guilty suspects, innocent suspects expect to be exonerated and therefore should be more inclined to offer helpful information. Thus, truth tellers should be less evasive in describing the purpose of the interview, more helpful in naming possible suspects when asked who they think may have committed the crime, and more likely to divulge who had an opportunity to commit the crime, and they should express more confidence in being exonerated when asked what they believe the outcome of the investigation will be.

Investigators who use the BAI protocol acknowledge that not every response to a BAI question will consistently match the descriptions presented for guilty and innocent suspects. Consequently, investigators should evaluate the responses to the entire BAI rather than to the 15 questions individually. There is only one study with real-life suspects that used the BAI protocol successfully. When only conclusive decisions were scored, 91% of the deceptive suspects and 80% of the innocent suspects were classified correctly. Although these results appear impressive, the authors themselves noted an important limitation of the study: They could not establish with certainty that the guilty suspects were truly guilty and the innocent suspects were truly innocent.

The BAI assumption that guilty suspects will feel less comfortable than truth tellers in a police interview is not universally accepted by the scientific community. For instance, in situations where the consequences of being disbelieved are severe, both liars and truth tellers will be concerned about not being believed. The prediction that guilty suspects will show more nervous behaviors than innocent suspects is not supported by deception research. In a mock theft laboratory study, where guilty and innocent suspects were interviewed via the BAI protocol, guilty suspects (those who had taken the money) did not differ from innocent suspects (those who had not taken the money) in eye contact. With other behaviors, just the opposite of the BAI prediction occurred: Guilty suspects displayed *fewer* movements than innocent suspects. A meta-analysis reviewing more than 100 deception studies showed exactly the same pattern: Eye contact is not related to deception, and liars tend to *decrease* rather than *increase* their movements. This pattern was also obtained in a real-world study

examining the nonverbal responses of suspects in police interviews. The decrease in movements often found in deception research could be the result of liars (guilty suspects) having to think harder than truth tellers (innocent suspects). Numerous aspects of lying add to mental load. For example, liars must avoid making slips of the tongue, should not contradict themselves, and should refrain from providing possible leads. If people are engaged in cognitively demanding tasks, their overall animation is likely to decrease. An alternative explanation of liars' decreased movements is that liars typically experience a greater sense of awareness and deliberateness in their performance, because they take their credibility less for granted than do truth tellers. Although truth tellers are also keen to be seen as truthful, they typically do not think that this will require any special effort or attention. As a result, liars are more inclined than truth tellers to refrain from exhibiting excessive movements that could be construed as nervous or suspicious.

This latter *impression management* explanation (liars put more effort into making a convincing impression than truth tellers) conflicts with the BAI's prediction that guilty suspects will be less helpful than innocent suspects. The impression management hypothesis states that guilty suspects will be keener than innocent suspects to create a favorable impression on the investigator, because liars will be less likely to take their credibility for granted. Indeed, the results from the mock theft laboratory study in which the BAI protocol was used showed just that pattern: Guilty suspects were *more* helpful than innocent suspects.

Aldert Vrij, Samantha Mann,
and Ronald Fisher

See also Detection of Deception: Nonverbal Cues; Detection of Deception in High-Stakes Liars; False Confessions; Interrogation of Suspects; Reid Technique for Interrogations

Further Readings

Horvath, F., Jayne, B., & Buckley, J. (1994). Differentiation of truthful and deceptive criminal suspects in behavior analysis interviews. *Journal of Forensic Sciences, 39,* 793–807.

Inbau, F. E., Reid, J. E., Buckley, J. P., & Jayne, B. C. (2001). *Criminal interrogation and confessions* (4th ed.). Gaithersburg, MD: Aspen.

Vrij, A., Mann, S., & Fisher, R. (2006). An empirical test of the behaviour analysis interview. *Law and Human Behavior, 30,* 329–345.

BIAS CRIME

Bias crime represents the nadir of intergroup relationships and contact. Prejudice and bigotry give rise to bias crime, and bigotry accompanies bias offenses. Protected categories of victims according to the bias crime statutes include ethnic, racial, religious, and sexual minorities as well as those with mental or physical disability status. Although debate about the criminalization of bias motives abounds, most of those who study bias crime agree that combating these types of offenses is important. This is because bias crime is different from similarly egregious crimes; the effects of bias crime extend well beyond the initial victim. There are physical, psychological, financial, and societal costs associated with this from of criminal activity.

Most people have a sense of what is meant by *prejudice*, and social scientists use the term to refer to a negative attitude that occurs when people prejudge disliked others. Those who are the targets of prejudice are disliked and perceived to be members of a particular social group. The term *bigotry* refers to extreme, and often blatant, forms of prejudice. Although both terms refer to a bias in the perception of others, prejudice can in rare cases refer to positive attitudes and reactions, whereas bigotry is exclusively reserved for negative attitudes. It is the latter set of reactions to a disliked individual or group of individuals (i.e., bigotry) that is most likely to spawn bias crimes.

Bias crimes involve a unique form of illegal, antisocial (and sometimes aggressive) behavior perpetrated primarily because of what the intended target represents. Definitions of bias crime vary, but definitions such as that of the Anti-Defamation League of B'nai B'rith (ADL) tend to focus on the motivation of the offender as well as the group status of the targeted victim. According to the Federal Bureau of Investigation (FBI) of the U.S. Department of Justice, a bias crime is "a criminal act that targets a person, property, or society and is motivated, in whole or in part, by the offender's bias against a race, religion, disability, sexual orientation, or ethnicity/national origin." Bias crimes "are traditional offenses motivated by the offender's bias."

The negative sentiment that drives bias crime offenders is so central and distinguishing a feature that the term *hate crime* is often used to describe these actions. Hate crime puts the extreme negative emotion (i.e., the affective state) front and center. Although

most people can readily identify with an offense characterized as a hate crime because of an almost visceral familiarity with that very negative emotion, some scholars debate the accuracy of this label. They argue that it is not always the case that the sentiment that motivates bias crime offenders is hate. Indeed, as the specialists James Jacobs and colleagues contend, hate crime is less about "hate" per se and more about bias or prejudice.

To be sure, the problem of bias crime is real, and because of the inherently social aspect of these offenses, they must be viewed within a particular context. According to Gregory Herek and colleagues, bias offenses generally occur "against a backdrop of intolerance." They represent the manifestation of deep-seated resentment and bigotry coupled with opportunity and disinhibition. *Disinhibition* has long been regarded as a necessary psychological feature in a person's decision to actually commit an antisocial or aggressive action. For the bias crime offender, disinhibition can occur in several ways. Potential bias crime offenders become disinhibited (i.e., releasing the proverbial brake) when they are prompted by like-minded others, when they can rationalize and justify their aggression, or when they believe that conventional authority figures condone their actions.

Bias Crime in the United States

According to recent statistics released by the FBI, 7,163 criminal incidents involving 8,380 offenses were reported in 2005 as a result of an extreme prejudice or bias. The greatest proportion of these incidents resulted from racial and ethnic animus (there were 3,919), with African Americans representing the most frequently targeted racial group. This is not surprising given that racial (i.e., anti-Black) prejudice has played so prominent a role in determining the nature of intergroup relations within the United States and because skin color represents a primary and salient marker for racial status.

Bias crimes in the United States have assumed many forms and have ranged from nonviolent to egregious and harmful. They include physical and verbal transgressions stemming from a perpetrator's bigotry or extreme prejudice. These transgressions can include defamation, threat and intimidation, verbal abuse, and physical assault or homicide, as well as offenses to property including arson, defacement, and vandalism. Many bias crimes against property assume the form of obscene or hurtful verbiage spray painted on private or public property.

Victims of bias crime are targeted because of their perceived race, ethnicity/national origin, religion, sexual orientation, gender, and physical disability. Whether victims actually are members of the targeted group matters little to their offenders; it is the perception that they do that drives offenders. Most targeted groups also tend to be singled out for negative stereotypes. Given the established relationship between stereotypes and prejudice, it is not surprising that members of the most negatively stereotyped social groups are also members of groups most frequently targeted by bias crime offenders. Thus, victims of bias crime disproportionately involve racial, ethnic, sexual, and religious minorities.

In the FBI's 2005 Hate Crime Statistics report, of the 8,380 reported bias offenses, 4,691 were racially motivated, 1,171 were instigated because of offenders' perceptions about their victims' sexual orientation, 1,314 resulted from religious prejudice, 1,144 were due to ethnicity/national origin prejudice, and 53 targeted victims because of a disability they were believed to possess. These numbers remain relatively consistent, although they reveal a slight drop from the 9,035 offenses reported in the 2004 statistics report.

It is worth noting that reluctance and fear on the part of certain immigrants and ethnic minorities may serve to stifle reports of certain bias offenses. Indeed, like many forms of criminal activity, many bias crimes that occur are not reported. Additionally, underreporting may be particularly likely in the case of victims of antigay bias crimes who, like rape victims, may not be willing to risk disclosure or be subjected to investigation by insensitive or unhelpful law enforcement personnel. Moreover, whether an actual bias crime is recorded as such is very much at the discretion of the individual law enforcement officer. Findings from one federally funded study, reported in Lu-in Wang's published work, found significant variation among police officers in their decisions to categorize incidents as bias crimes as well as within the state agencies charged with reporting to federal agencies.

Criminalizing Bias Crime

In recent years, criminologists and legal scholars have debated the usefulness of criminalizing bias, and debates about the constitutionality of legislation that penalizes

it abound. Of course, crimes that are motivated by bias are not new. The history of bias as an instigator and motive in criminal activities occurring within the United States predates the establishment and enactment of any legislation in the country. The legal scholar Brian Levin notes that "status-based deprivations" such as slavery were in place at the very same time that deliberations about the Constitution and Declaration of Independence were under way. What is new about today's form of bias crime, however, is the existing legislation as well as the corresponding efforts aimed at enacting additional legislation penalizing these activities. The term *bias crime,* first used by journalists and politicians, is well entrenched in today's academic and juridical circles.

Most jurisdictions see bias crime as emanating from a perpetrator's bias targeting some feature of the victim (e.g., racial status or sexual orientation). Although the Hate Crime Statistics Act (initially promulgated in 1990) mandates that all jurisdictions report the number of bias offenses that have occurred, there is substantial variance in the extent of participation across states. Like other offenses included in the FBI's Uniform Crime Reports, bias crimes are voluntarily reported by local jurisdictions.

In 2005, several members of the House of Representatives introduced a bill that would represent an amendment to the law that mandates the FBI's collection of bias crime information to include gender as a protected category (called the Hate Crime Statistics Improvement Act of 2005). Historically, gender has not been included in the FBI's definition of bias crime. The bill never became a law, and the current Federal Hate Crimes Statistics Act does not require the FBI to collect data on crimes that may manifest evidence of a gender bias. However, of the 41 states that have crime statutes, 19 of them include gender-based hate crimes in their hate crimes laws.

Importantly, where bias crimes were formerly limited to the actual physical presence of an offender (e.g., an assault) or the offender's sentiment (e.g., graffiti or vandalism), widespread usage of the Internet has enabled offenders to transcend the boundaries of space and time. According to a representative of the ADL, "the majority of Internet hate crime cases result from e-mails containing threats." Indeed, because of the proliferation of biased sentiment throughout the Internet, "cyber hate" is now investigated and tracked by advocacy groups, such as the ADL, as well as the FBI.

Bias Crime Versus "Normal" Offenses

Bias offenses differ from other similarly egregious offenses in several ways. First, because bias crimes indicate an offender's bias, they serve symbolic and instrumental functions. The targeted victim is symbolic of a despised out-group. An out-group is a social group composed of people whom an offender perceives to be outsiders. Symbolically, the bias crime effectively communicates a message to an entire community, neighborhood, or group. The message is extremely negative and reminds anyone who identifies as a member of the victim's social group of their own vulnerability.

Bias crime serves an instrumental function in that it curtails the behaviors and movement of members of large numbers of people, including members of the victim's and offender's groups. Bias offenses restrict the behaviors and choices of people because members of the victim's and offender's groups will tend to avoid certain locations and interactions with outgroups. For example, people who are personally unacquainted with the victim but who perceive themselves to be members of the victim's social group are likely to restrict their activities. They will think twice about being in geographic proximity of the location where the bias offense is known to have occurred. Members of the offender's group who sympathize with victims are also likely to be anxious about the prospect of intergroup interaction. Without realizing it, offenders can affect far greater numbers of people than the actual victim(s) of the offense.

The bias crime is also distinguished from the "normal" offense (i.e., the nonbias crime) in that the bias crime is a reflection of a perpetrator's bigotry or hatred, or both. Such clarity about an offender's thinking is a feature of the bias crime and not readily apparent in many other types of offenses. However, it should be noted that legal scholars debate the constitutionality of bias crime statutes because they argue that characterization of an offense as a bias offense is based on penalizing thoughts and motives. Although there may be some ambiguity for certain offenses, law enforcement, legislators, and prosecutors generally consider the presence of one or more specific indicators during the commission of an offense to be evidence of a bias motive. These indicators serve to disambiguate the circumstances surrounding the incident because they suggest that the offender's actions were motivated, in whole or in part, by bias.

A clear difference in group status between the victim(s) and offender(s) that has historically involved relations fraught with strife is often taken as an indicator of a bias motive. When the incident occurs in the context of an event that makes the group status of the victim particularly salient, prosecutors will likely suspect a bias motive. Moreover, when there are obvious items present, used in, or produced as a result of the offense (e.g., graffiti, bias-related gestures or expressions, and written materials) or when the offenders are members of organized hate groups (e.g., the Ku Klux Klan), the incident is likely to be characterized as a bias offense.

Costs Incurred

There are a number of costs associated with bias crimes. Those who are targeted by offenders (i.e., victims) may incur physical, psychological, and financial costs. Victims of hate crime who are physically assaulted suffer injuries that may lead to permanent bodily damage, and in several high-profile cases (e.g., the murders of James Byrd and Mathew Sheppard), these injuries have resulted in death. Psychologically, the victim of a bias crime may experience posttraumatic stress disorder (PTSD). In fact, research by Gregory Herek and colleagues provides evidence of long-term PTSD symptoms. That research examined the experiences of victims of antigay bias crimes and found that in some cases the victims needed as many as 5 years to overcome the effect of their victimization.

Even when victims are able to function "normally" following a bias crime, they may harbor intense fear. They may fear their attackers, and they may also fear anyone who resembles their attackers. Although this can be debilitating, it can be most problematic for the fearful victims who feel compelled to move from their residence, change jobs, or restrict their activities. Thus, an additional outcome of bias crime victimization can involve very real financial costs. To the extent to which victims decide to suddenly change their place of employment or residence, there is likely to be a significant change in financial well-being. In addition, bias crime involving property offenses creates financial costs for property owners who resolve to return their property to its original state.

Although the most obvious costs are incurred by the actual victims of the offense, there are also societal costs associated with bias crime activities. Bias crimes create a climate of suspicion and fear. They effectively contribute to deterioration in intergroup relations. Those who may perceive themselves to be members of the victim's social group will fear others who happen to be members of the offender's social group, and members of the latter may feel anger and guilt leading them to avoid interaction with those perceived to be members of the victim's group. In addition, particularly visible incidents can potentially trigger subsequent hate crime offenses, setting off a wave of retaliatory offenses.

Profile of Offenders

According to the U.S. Department of Justice's *Policymaker's Guide to Hate Crime*, hate crime offenders can be categorized according to their motives. In some cases, offenders perceive themselves to be exacting vigilante justice. These types of offenders blame the targets of their offenses for what they perceive to be wrong with the world or their immediate circumstances. In other cases, offenders perceive their actions to be a part of a greater mission—one in service of ridding the world of the social evil that their victim represents. An additional motive believed to account for some hate crime offenses involves the excitement and "rush" of committing the offenses. For these frenetic offenders, who are referred to as "thrill seekers," any targeted outgroup will do. In these incidents, willing offenders have the right set of circumstances, potential victims, and disinhibiting factors present at just the right time.

Although it would be useful to have a more detailed description of offenders, there is some variability among those who commit bias crimes. For example, the Hate Crime Statistics report of 2005 reveals that racial minorities are represented among racist bias crime offenders. Nevertheless, representatives from some local jurisdictions have noted that bias crime offenders are overwhelmingly young, White, and male.

Preventing Bias Crimes

Bias crimes, though extremely problematic, are not inevitable. When one considers that of the infinite number of interactions possible among the 34 million people living in California, for example, fewer than 2,500 resulted in reports of hate-motivated offenses, it is clear that bias crime occurrence is actually rare relative to its nonoccurrence. That said, recent events reflecting bias and bigotry underscore the importance of continued attention to this problem. Researchers, advocates, legislators, and law enforcement personnel have roles to play in attenuating the problem of bias crime. The greatest responsibility, however, rests with the lay public, which is composed of both victims and offenders. Eliminating bigotry and the problem of bias crime requires vigilant, continuous, and cross-cutting efforts, and it involves education, intergroup interaction, and legislation.

Kellina M. Craig-Henderson

See also Racial Bias and the Death Penalty; Reporting Crimes and Victimization; Victimization

Further Readings

Anti-Defamation League of B'nai B'rith. (1994). *Hate crime laws. A comprehensive guide.* New York: Author.

Craig-Henderson, K. M. (2004). A review of the debate over hate crime legislation: Do hate crime statutes work for the common good? In R. R. Miller & S. L. Browning (Eds.), *For the common good: A critical examination of law and social control* (pp. 230–236). Durham, NC: Carolina Academic Press.

Federal Bureau of Investigation. (2006). *Hate crime statistics 2005.* Washington, DC: U.S. Department of Justice.

Herek, G. M., & Berrill, K. T. (Eds.). (1992). *Hate crimes. Confronting violence against lesbians and gay men.* Newbury Park, CA: Sage.

Jacobs, J. B., & Potter, K. (1998). *Hate crimes: Criminal law and identity politics.* New York: Oxford University Press.

Levin, J., & McDevitt, J. (2002). *Hate crimes revisited. America's war on those who are different.* Boulder, CO: Westview Press.

Wang, L.-I. (2003). *Hate crimes law.* St. Paul, MN: Thomson/West.

CAPACITY TO CONSENT TO TREATMENT

The capacity to consent to treatment, also known as *treatment consent capacity* (TCC) and *medical decision-making capacity*, is a civil legal capacity with important ethical, legal, and functional aspects. TCC is a fundamental aspect of personal autonomy and self-determination and refers to a person's cognitive and emotional capacity to consent to medical treatment. TCC involves the capacity not only to accept a treatment but also to refuse a treatment, or to select between treatment alternatives. Legally, TCC forms the cornerstone of the medical-legal doctrine of informed consent, which requires that a valid consent to treatment be not only *informed* and *voluntary* but also *competent*. Functionally, TCC may be viewed as an "advanced activity of daily life" that is an important aspect of health and independent living skills in both younger and older adults. As such, it is a critical functional and life skill considered by probate courts conducting guardianship determinations.

From a legal standpoint, TCC is a distinctive civil capacity. Issues of TCC generally arise in a medical setting and usually involve a physician, a psychologist, or some other clinician, not a legal professional, as decision maker. These clinical judgments of TCC are rarely subject to judicial review. Accordingly, while clinicians do not determine TCC in a formal legal sense, their decisions often have the same effect insofar as a patient can effectively lose decisional authority.

Over the past 30 years, consent capacity has emerged as a distinct field of legal, ethical, clinical, and behavioral research. Clinical and cognitive models

of TCC, and associated assessment instruments, have been developed for evaluating TCC. TCC is often tested using four standards drawn from case law and the psychiatric literature: the capacities to

1. "evidence" or express a treatment choice (*expressing choice*),

2. "appreciate" the personal consequences of a treatment choice (*appreciation*),

3. "reason" about treatment (*reasoning*), and

4. "understand" the treatment situation and choices (*understanding*).

There is also a fifth consent ability of making a "reasonable" treatment choice (*reasonable choice*), which is used experimentally but not clinically. These consent abilities represent different legal thresholds for evaluating TCC and have served as the conceptual basis for instrument development and clinical and cognitive studies.

Legal Aspects of TCC

TCC is a fundamental aspect of personal autonomy in our society. Clinicians are ethically and legally obligated to respect patients' right of self-determination with respect to medical care. The doctrine of informed consent protects this right of self-determination by requiring that a legally valid consent to treatment be informed, voluntary, and competent. As such, a diagnostic or therapeutic intervention that is performed on a person lacking the capacity to consent—regardless of its intended benefit—may often represent a technical battery and be actionable under the law.

Medical-Legal Model of Consent Capacity

As discussed above, a medical-legal model of TCC incorporating specific consent abilities, or standards, has been developed from case law and the psychiatric literature. These standards are set forth below in order of proposed difficulty for patients with dementia:

S1. The capacity simply to "evidence" or express a treatment choice

S2. The capacity to make a "reasonable" treatment choice (this is not a clinically accepted consent standard because of concerns about the arbitrariness of the operative term *reasonable*; it is thus for experimental use only and is accordingly referenced with brackets)

S3. The capacity to "appreciate" the personal consequences of a treatment choice

S4. The capacity to reason about treatment and provide "rational reasons" for a treatment choice

S5. The capacity to "understand" the treatment situation and treatment choices

The above standards represent different thresholds for evaluating TCC. For example, S1 (*expressing choice*) requires nothing more than the subject's communication of a treatment choice. [S2] (*reasonable choice*) calls for the individual to demonstrate a reasonable treatment choice, particularly when the alternative is unreasonable. S3 (*appreciation*) requires the individual to appreciate how a treatment choice will affect him or her personally. S4 (*reasoning*) evaluates the individual's capacity to supply rational reasons for the treatment choice. S5 (*understanding*) is a comprehension standard and requires the individual to demonstrate conceptual and factual knowledge concerning the medical condition, its symptoms, and the treatment choices and their respective risks/benefits. Standards 3 to 5 are the standards generally applied in clinical settings. It should be noted that this medical-legal model can be readily applied to other consent capacities, such as the capacity to consent to research, and to decisional capacity generally.

In using this model and selecting applicable standards, clinicians should consider the potential risks and benefits of a proposed treatment and the consequences of refusing treatment. For instance, a patient who consents to a relatively low-risk medical procedure expected to yield significant benefits may be judged using a lower or more liberal standard of TCC. A more stringent threshold (e.g., S4, reasoning, and/or S5, understanding) should be considered as the risks associated with a medical procedure or with refusing treatment increase. Due to its short-term memory and other cognitive demands, S5 may be the most stringent legal standard, particularly for older adults and persons with amnesic disorders.

Cognitive Model for Consent Capacity

TCC may also be conceptualized cognitively as consisting of three core tasks: comprehension and encoding of treatment information, information processing and internally arriving at a treatment decision, and communication of the treatment decision to a clinical professional. These core cognitive tasks occur in a specific context: a patient's dialogue with a physician, a psychologist, or some other health care professional about a medical condition and potential treatments. The comprehension/encoding task involves oral and written comprehension, and encoding, of novel and often complex medical information presented verbally to the patient by the treating clinician. The information-processing/decision-making task involves the patient processing the consent and other information presented, integrating this information with established personal knowledge, including values and risk preferences, reasoning about and weighing this information, and arriving internally at a treatment decision. The decision communication task involves the patient communicating his or her treatment decision to the clinician in some understandable form (e.g., oral, written, and/or gestural expression of consent/nonconsent).

Clinical Assessment of TCC

Problems in Assessment

Despite the relevance of issues of TCC in medical settings, there is little academic or clinical education in this area. Medical and graduate schools, as well as residency, internship, and fellowship programs, have not traditionally offered formal training in capacity assessment. There has also been a general lack of practical clinical guidelines on which to base capacity assessments. Until recently, clinicians have had to rely almost exclusively on subjective clinical impressions and brief mental status testing in reaching a judgment regarding TCC.

Physician judgment has traditionally represented the accepted criterion or gold standard for determining TCC in medical and legal practice. However, studies involving older adults and persons with AD have raised the concern that physician judgments of TCC may be both subjective and unreliable. Specifically, experienced physicians have been found to be highly inconsistent in their judgments of TCC in older adults with mild AD. This inconsistency may reflect issues of lack of clinical training, differing conceptual approaches, and the conflation of mental status results with capacity status in older adults. One response to these issues of clinical accuracy and consistency in capacity judgments has been the development of standardized assessment measures.

Instruments for Assessing TCC

In recent years, investigators have used the above models of TCC to develop standardized, norm-referenced psychometric instruments for assessment of TCC in different patient populations. These instruments include the MacArthur Competence Assessment Tool for Treatment (MacCAT–T), the Hopemont Capacity Assessment Instrument, and the Capacity to Consent to Treatment Instrument (CCTI). These standardized measures assist clinicians by offering specific definitions of the TCC construct and by operationalizing standards or thresholds for testing capacity. In addition to measuring capacity performance, some instruments also identify capacity status (capable, marginally capable, or incapable) using cut scores derived from control performance. Thus, these measures provide objective, norm-referenced information concerning an individual's TCC that can inform and guide clinical decision making.

The limitations of these assessment instruments should also be considered. First, instrument-based deficits in TCC should not be construed as necessarily reflecting clinical or legal impairments or incompetency. Second, and related, clinical determination of TCC is ultimately a judgment made by a clinician and not an instrument performance score. Assessment instruments can provide objective information about

consent abilities but are not substitutes for clinical judgment. No capacity instrument can satisfactorily take into account the myriad medical, legal, ethical, and social considerations that inform a clinical or legal capacity judgment. For this reason, standardized measures of TCC are intended to support, but certainly not replace, the decision making of the clinician.

Research on TCC in Clinical Populations

Impairment and loss of TCC have been studied in multiple clinical populations, including persons with schizophrenia and other psychiatric illnesses, Alzheimer's disease (AD), mild cognitive impairment (MCI), Parkinson's disease (PD), and traumatic brain injury (TBI). Initial pioneering clinical studies of TCC were carried out in psychiatric populations by Appelbaum, Roth, Grisso, and colleagues and have documented clearly the effects of mental illness on informed consent capacities in these patients. Over the past 15 years, there have been an increasing number of studies of TCC in older adult populations with dementia. Due to its relentless progressive nature and the well-characterized stages of neurocognitive and functional change, AD has proven to be a useful prism for understanding impairment and loss of TCC. Studies have shown that the minimal standards of consent capacity, such as expressing choice (S1) and making a reasonable choice [S2], are relatively preserved in patients with mild to moderate AD, whereas the clinically relevant standards of appreciation (S3), reasoning (S4), and understanding (S5) already show significant impairment. TCC also shows significant longitudinal decline over a 2-year period in patients with mild AD. A very recent study has suggested that older patients with MCI, the prodrome or transitional stage to AD, also experience significant deficits in TCC. Other studies have identified deficits in TCC in patients with PD and cognitive impairment and dementia. In contrast to these dementia studies, an investigation of TCC in moderate to severely injured patients with TBI found significant initial impairment but also subsequent partial recovery of consent abilities 6 months following TBI. Thus, trajectories of consent capacity impairment and change over time can differ enormously across disease states.

Cognitive Studies of TCC

TCC assessment instruments have also provided a useful psychometric criterion for investigating the neurocognitive changes associated with impairment of TCC in neurocognitive disorders such as dementia. Findings suggest that multiple cognitive functions are associated with the loss of consent capacity in patients with AD. For example, deficits in conceptualization, semantic memory, and probably verbal recall appear to be associated with the significantly impaired capacity of both mild and moderate AD patients to understand a treatment situation and choices (S5). A factor analysis of TCC in an AD population revealed a two-factor solution comprising *verbal reasoning* and *verbal memory*, which was subsequently validated using a form of neuropsychological confirmatory analysis. In contrast, in studies of patients with PD and dementia, executive function measures have emerged as the primary predictors of impairments of TCC.

Daniel C. Marson and Katina R. Hebert

See also Capacity to Consent to Treatment Instrument (CCTI); Competency, Foundational and Decisional; Consent to Clinical Research; End-of-Life Issues; MacArthur Competence Assessment Tool for Clinical Research (MacCAT–CR); MacArthur Competence Assessment Tool for Treatment (MacCAT–T)

Further Readings

Dymek, M. P., Atchison, P., Harrell, L. E., & Marson, D. C. (2001). Competency to consent to medical treatment in cognitively impaired patients with Parkinson's disease. *Neurology, 56,* 17–24.

Grisso, T. (2003). Competence to consent to treatment. In *Evaluating civil competencies: Forensic assessment and instruments* (2nd ed., pp. 391–458). New York: Kluwer Press.

Grisso, T., & Appelbaum, P. S. (1995). The MacArthur Treatment Competence Study. III: Abilities of patients to consent to psychiatric and medical treatments. *Law and Human Behavior, 19,* 149–169.

Grisso, T., & Appelbaum, P. S. (1998). *Assessing competence to consent to treatment.* New York: Oxford University Press.

Kim, S. Y., Karlawish, J. H., & Caine, E. D. (2002). Current state of research on decision-making competence of cognitively impaired elderly persons. *American Journal of Geriatric Psychiatry, 10,* 151–165.

Marson, D. C., Chatterjee, A., Ingram, K., & Harrell, L. (1996). Toward a neurologic model of competency: Cognitive predictors of capacity to consent in Alzheimer's disease using three different legal standards. *Neurology, 46,* 666–672.

Marson, D. C., Dreer, L. E., Krzywanski, S., Huthwaite, J. S., DeVivo, M. J., & Novack, T. A. (2005). Impairment and partial recovery of medical decision-making capacity in traumatic brain injury: A 6-month longitudinal study. *Archives of Physical Medicine and Rehabilitation, 86,* 889–895.

Marson, D. C., Ingram, K., Cody, H., & Harrell, L. (1995). Assessing the competency of Alzheimer's disease patients under different legal standards: A prototype instrument. *Archives of Neurology, 52*(10), 949–954.

Moye, J., Karel, M. J., Azar, A. R., & Gurrera, R. J. (2004). Capacity to consent to treatment: Empirical comparison of three instruments in patients with and without dementia. *The Gerontologist, 44*(2), 166–175.

CAPACITY TO CONSENT TO TREATMENT INSTRUMENT (CCTI)

The Capacity to Consent to Treatment Instrument (CCTI) is a standardized psychometric instrument designed to assess the treatment consent capacity (TCC) of adults. The CCTI evaluates five different consent abilities or standards and has been shown to be a reliable and valid measure of TCC. The measure discriminates well between cognitively intact adults and persons with Alzheimer's disease (AD), Parkinson's disease dementia syndrome, and traumatic brain injury. The CCTI has application to all adult patient populations in which issues of neurocognitive impairment and consent capacity arise. Research using the CCTI has provided insight into the relationships between cognitive change and different thresholds of decisional capacity.

Structure and Administration of the CCTI

The CCTI was first developed in 1992 to empirically investigate patterns of consent capacity impairment in patients with mild and moderate AD. The measure consists of two clinical vignettes that present hypothetical medical problems and their symptoms (brain tumor, atherosclerotic heart disease) as well as treatment alternatives with the associated risks and benefits. The CCTI is administered in a way that simulates an informed consent dialogue between the physician and the patient. The vignettes are presented simultaneously in oral and written format using an uninterrupted disclosure method. They are written at a fifth- to sixth-grade reading level, with low syntactic complexity and a moderate information load.

After each vignette is presented, the written stimulus is removed, and patients are asked to answer a series of questions that test distinct consent abilities. These consent abilities are derived from psychiatric literature and case law and reflect four well-established standards (S) for decisional capacity: *evidencing a choice* for or against treatment (S1), *appreciating* the personal consequences of a treatment choice (S3), *reasoning about treatment*, or making a treatment choice based on rational reasons (S4), and *understanding* the treatment situation and choices (S5). The CCTI also assesses the capacity to make a *reasonable choice* (S2). This is an experimental standard that has not received legal or clinical acceptance due to arbitrariness in determining what constitutes a "reasonable" treatment choice.

Administration time for the CCTI is about 20 to 25 minutes for both vignettes.

CCTI Scoring System

The CCTI has a detailed and well-operationalized scoring system that yields information regarding both capacity performance and capacity status. Capacity performance is the quantitative score that a patient receives for each standard. Scores across vignettes are summed to create a composite score for each standard. There is no CCTI total score.

Capacity status refers to the categorical outcome (capable, marginally capable, or incapable of consenting to treatment) obtained on a particular standard. Depending on the standard, capacity status on the CCTI is operationalized using either predetermined cut scores or psychometric cutoff scores derived from the performance of cognitively intact older adults. CCTI capacity outcomes must be used cautiously insofar as they are derived from cut scores and do not represent legal or clinical competency findings.

Reliability and Validity of the CCTI

The CCTI has reliability and validity as a measure of consent capacity. Three separate raters trained in administration and scoring of the CCTI achieved high interrater reliability for interval scales (>.83, p < .0001; S3–S5) and categorical scales (96% agreement; S1 and S2). The CCTI demonstrates face and content validity. The medical content of each vignette was reviewed and approved by a neurologist specializing in aging and dementia. The CCTI has been found to discriminate well between cognitively intact older adults and persons with both mild and moderate AD. The CCTI also discriminates well between older controls and patients with Parkinson's disease and dementia. With respect to construct validity, factor analysis of the CCTI in an AD sample revealed a two-factor model of verbal reasoning and verbal memory, which was subsequently confirmed using neuropsychological factor analysis. In addition, the CCTI has demonstrated utility as a psychometric criterion for investigating the neurocognitive changes associated with loss of TCC.

Clinical and Research Utility

The CCTI provides a standardized and norm-referenced basis for evaluating TCC in individual patients and across different patient populations. For this reason, it has very good research application. In addition, by objectively evaluating different consent abilities, it provides clinicians with flexibility in a particular case to consider different standards of capacity in relation to the risks and benefits of a particular treatment situation.

Limitations

The CCTI has three key limitations. First, because it uses standardized, hypothetical clinical vignettes (brain tumor, heart disease), the CCTI does not directly assess specific issues of TCC presenting clinically (e.g., in the treatment of bone cancer). Instead, it provides objective, norm-referenced information about a patient's treatment consent abilities that the clinician can consider as part of his or her overall assessment of TCC. Thus, the CCTI gives up clinical specificity for standardization. A second limitation of the CCTI is its use of hypothetical medical vignettes. Patients dealing with real, personal medical problems arguably may display treatment consent abilities that differ somewhat from those demonstrated when responding to hypothetical medical situations. Finally, the CCTI and its performance and outcome scores are intended to support but not replace clinical judgment. Determination of consent capacity is ultimately a judgment made by a clinician.

Daniel C. Marson and Katina R. Hebert

See also Capacity to Consent to Treatment; Competency, Foundational and Decisional; Competency Assessment Instrument (CAI); Consent to Clinical Research; End-of-Life Issues; Hopkins Competency Assessment Test (HCAT); MacArthur Competence Assessment Tool for

Clinical Research (MacCAT–CR); MacArthur Competence Assessment Tool for Treatment (MacCAT–T)

Further Readings

Dymek, M., Marson, D., & Harrell, L. (1999). Factor structure of capacity to consent in Alzheimer's disease. *Journal of Forensic Neuropsychology, 1,* 27–48.

Griffith, R., Dymek, M., Atchison, P., Harrell, L., & Marson, D. (2005). Medical decision-making capacity in two neurodegenerative disorders: Mild AD and PD with cognitive impairment. *Neurology, 65,* 483–485.

Marson, D. C., Dreer, L., Krzywanski, S., Huthwaite, J., DeVivo, M., & Novack, T. (2005). Impairment and partial recovery of medical decision-making capacity in traumatic brain injury: A six month longitudinal study. *Archives of Physical Medicine and Rehabilitation, 86,* 889–895.

Marson, D. C., Ingram, K. K., Cody, H. A., & Harrell, L. E. (1995). Assessing the competency of patients with Alzheimer's disease under different legal standards: A prototype instrument. *Archives of Neurology, 52,* 949–954.

CAPACITY TO WAIVE *MIRANDA* RIGHTS

Prior to interrogating a suspect, police officers must inform individuals of their legal rights. Mental health professionals are frequently called on to evaluate the extent to which criminal suspects have understood their legal arrest rights and made valid decisions with respect to waiving those rights. For individuals to knowingly, intelligently, and voluntarily waive their rights, they must both understand and appreciate those rights. Research has consistently indicated that rights comprehension is significantly more impaired for younger adolescents than for older adolescents and adults. Furthermore, comprehension is most impaired among younger adolescents with lower intellectual abilities.

Miranda Warnings

Miranda v. Arizona (1966) required states to inform suspects prior to interrogation or questioning of several rights, which includes informing them of their right to remain silent, that anything they say can be used against them in a court of law, their right to the presence of an attorney, and the right to free counsel

if they cannot afford the cost of an attorney. These warnings were viewed as strengthening an individual's protection against self-incrimination during police interrogation. The rights provided to adults in *Miranda* were extended to juveniles in the cases of *Kent v. United States* (1966) and *In re Gault* (1967). For those individuals who opt to waive these rights and undergo interrogation, any statements they make can be admitted as evidence against them in future court proceedings provided that the waiver is valid.

While the specific rights guaranteed to suspects prior to arrest and interrogation are outlined in *Miranda,* the specific wording and language employed in rights warnings vary between jurisdictions and police forces. Each warning typically contains the four prongs outlined in *Miranda*. A fifth warning prong has been added in many jurisdictions, which informs suspects that they can choose to stop questioning and consult with an attorney at any time. Additionally, some jurisdictions have included cautionary statements to juveniles regarding the possibility of having their case remanded to adult court or serving an adult sentence. Research has demonstrated significant variability in the language and readability of *Miranda* warnings across states, with Flesch-Kincaid Grade reading levels ranging from 4.0 to 9.9 in one study. The typical *Miranda* warning is at about the seventh-grade reading level, which is above the reading level of many intellectually impaired individuals. Also, the reading level of many adolescents in the juvenile justice system is below that of their peers. Many states employ separate *Miranda* warning cards for juveniles in an effort to simplify the warnings and increase comprehension.

Statements made by individuals who have waived their rights can be ruled inadmissible if a judge determines that certain conditions have not been met. Several U.S. Supreme Court decisions have established a *totality of circumstances* test for evaluating the validity of a rights waiver decision. This requires the court to consider both the suspect's capacities and the procedures and circumstances surrounding the waiver. This includes whether the individual knowingly, intelligently, and voluntarily waived his or her rights. The knowing component requires understanding verbally or in writing the wording used in the warning. The intelligent component goes beyond simple understanding and requires that a suspect appreciate the significance of a particular right in his or her particular situation. For example, suspects may clearly understand a statement informing them that they can consult with a lawyer prior to interrogation, but without an appreciation of the role and function of a lawyer this understanding is rendered meaningless. Finally, the waiver must be made voluntarily, which requires that a suspect waive his or her rights independently, free from coercion from the police.

Research

Researchers have investigated the influence of numerous factors on adult and juvenile *Miranda* rights comprehension, including age, IQ, ethnicity, prior police contact and criminal justice experience, socioeconomic status, psychopathology and symptoms, special education classes, psychosocial maturity, and interrogative suggestibility. Results from these studies consistently indicate that rights comprehension is significantly more impaired for younger adolescents than for older adolescents and adults. Furthermore, comprehension is most impaired among younger adolescents with lower IQ. Adults with mental retardation have also been shown to demonstrate poor *Miranda* rights comprehension, resulting in the most frequent waiver challenges in court. Results from studies evaluating the influence of the other factors have been less clear. It is important to bear in mind that although research has been helpful in identifying areas in which capacity may be impaired, these studies have important limitations. They have typically been conducted in laboratory settings and have used hypothetical scenarios and noncriminal samples, thereby limiting the extent to which the true stressful nature of police interrogations is captured. Under stressful circumstances, suspects' understanding, appreciation, and reasoning about interrogation rights may be poorer than these findings suggest. Indeed, prior studies have shown that many adolescents in stressful or fearful situations, such as a police interrogation, will not be able to use their highest level of cognitive reasoning.

The choice whether to waive or exercise arrest rights represents the first step in a series of difficult decision points that individuals face when undergoing a police investigation. In addition to investigating the factors influencing arrest rights comprehension and waiver, researchers have examined the relationship between arrest rights comprehension and other possible outcomes arising from police interrogations. For example, researchers have begun to examine poor arrest rights comprehension as both a possible predictor of the decision to waive arrest rights and submit to police interrogation without assistance or advice as well as a predictor of the likelihood of offering a false confession. One recent study found that *Miranda* comprehension correlated negatively with false confessions in a juvenile sample, where juveniles were less likely to offer a false confession in response to a series of hypothetical vignettes as their *Miranda* comprehension improved.

Developmental Considerations

Results from research have generally demonstrated that younger adolescents with poor intellectual ability fail to comprehend adequately their *Miranda* rights. However, much of the variability in understanding can still be attributed to individual differences between people. A bright 12- or 13-year-old may demonstrate excellent understanding of *Miranda* rights, while a less intellectually capable adult may struggle to comprehend the content of typical *Miranda* warnings. However, adolescents are different from adults in one important way. They are at a stage of development in which they are still undergoing important maturational changes. Adolescence is marked by significant physical maturation, budding sexuality, an increased awareness of and sensitivity toward peers, and an increased desire for independence and identity development, to name only a few. One compelling explanation for the differences in understanding between adolescents and adults is that the cognitive capacities of adolescents are simply underdeveloped. Empirical evidence demonstrates that cognitive development continues throughout adolescence, and that it is only by age 17 that adolescents' raw cognitive abilities become more comparable with those of adults.

In addition to developmental differences in cognitive factors, research shows that adolescents differ in other important ways relevant to legal competencies. Particularly, adolescents differ in their level of psychosocial maturity and in the way they reason and make decisions. Younger adolescents with intellectual abilities comparable with those of adults have less life experience to draw on, which may influence their reasoning and decision-making processes. Younger children and adolescents are generally less likely to think strategically about their decisions; they are less future oriented, are less likely to weigh the consequences of their decisions, and often act impulsively. Thus, even if a young person adequately understands the meaning of a *Miranda* warning, his or her appreciation of the consequences of the decision to waive or exercise those rights may suffer given his or her relative level of maturity and development. It is perhaps not surprising, then, that research demonstrates that the majority of young persons opt to waive their rights when being questioned by the police. Interestingly, results from Canadian and U.S. studies have shown that with increased rights understanding, young persons are more likely to refuse to waive their rights in the context of a criminal investigation.

Assessing Capacity to Waive *Miranda* Rights

It is important to clarify that the term capacity to waive *Miranda* rights does not refer to a specific legal disposition but rather to the capacity of the defendant to understand and waive his or her legal rights. Grisso has described three areas of functioning pertinent to the evaluation of capacity to waive rights, including a suspect's understanding of the rights warnings, the suspect's perceptions of the intended functions of the *Miranda* rights, and the suspect's capacities to reason about the probable consequences of waiver or nonwaiver decisions. Researchers and evaluators have typically assessed the suspect's understanding of the rights warnings by examining an individual's understanding of the phrases included in a standard rights warning. Grisso conceptualizes appreciation of the significance of rights to comprise three main parts. First, suspects must recognize the interrogative nature of police questioning. Second, suspects must perceive the defense attorney as an advocate who will defend and advise them, and be willing to disclose confidential information to him or her (appreciation of the right to counsel). Finally, suspects must perceive the right to silence as a right that cannot be revoked and that statements made by them can be used in court (appreciation of the right to silence).

Grisso's *Instruments for Assessing Understanding and Appreciation of* Miranda *Rights* were developed to assist mental health professionals to examine the capacities of individual youths or adults to waive their *Miranda* rights knowingly and intelligently at the time of their police interrogation. Three instruments assess the individual's understanding of a typical arrest by asking examinees to paraphrase the meaning of each right, compare the four elements of a typical rights warning with a pool of statements including accurate and inaccurate rewordings of each of the sentences, and provide definitions of six words contained in the interrogation warnings. Appreciation of the warnings is evaluated in a fourth instrument, which assesses appreciation of the importance of rights in an interrogation and in legal situations generally by asking examinees to respond to pictures and vignettes describing youths interacting with various criminal justice figures. The instruments provide normative data against which evaluators can compare an examinee's responses on the instruments; however the normative data are based on a sample of juveniles in Saint Louis, Missouri, in 1980. An updated version of these instruments, *The* Miranda *Rights Comprehension Instruments,* is currently being developed.

Consequences

Current findings from the literature underscore the need for the provision of appropriate assistance or improvement in the rights communication and the waiver processes. Results from research conducted on juveniles' *Miranda* rights comprehension findings strongly suggest that although a majority of youths involved in police questioning and interrogation waive their rights, many of them, particularly younger adolescents, may not have the capacity to provide a valid waiver. The consequences of poor understanding and appreciation of arrest rights, in combination with a highly suggestible young person and coercive interrogation conditions, may be far ranging and logically include a greatly increased likelihood of offering a false confession. Youths, especially younger adolescents and preteens, may be especially vulnerable to making false confessions due to immaturity and poor judgment.

Ronald Roesch and Kaitlyn McLachlan

See also Capacity to Waive Rights; False Confessions; Forensic Assessment; Grisso's Instruments for Assessing Understanding and Appreciation of *Miranda* Rights; Interrogation of Suspects; Videotaping Confessions

Further Readings

Feld, B. C. (2000). Juveniles' waiver of legal rights: Confessions, *Miranda*, and the right to counsel. In T. Grisso & R. G. Schwartz (Eds.), *Youth on trial: A developmental perspective on juvenile justice* (pp. 105–138). Chicago: University of Chicago Press.

Goldstein, N. E., Condie, L. O., Kalbeitzer, R., Osman, D., & Geier, J. L. (2003). Juvenile offenders' *Miranda* rights comprehension and self-report likelihood of offering false confessions. *Assessment, 10,* 359–369.

Grisso, T. (1998). *Instruments for assessing understanding and appreciation of* Miranda *rights.* Sarasota, FL: Professional Resources.

Grisso, T. (2003). Evaluating competencies: Forensic assessment and instruments. New York: Plenum Press.

Helms, J. (2003). Analysis of *Miranda* reading levels across jurisdictions: Implications for evaluating waiver competency. *Journal of Forensic Psychology Practice, 3,* 25–37.

In re Gault, 387 U.S. 1 (1967).

Kent v. United States, 383 U.S. 541 (1966).

Miranda v. Arizona, 384 U.S. 436 (1966).

Viljoen, J. L., & Roesch, R. (2005). Competency to waive interrogation rights and adjudicative competence in adolescent defendants: Cognitive development, attorney contact, and psychological symptoms. *Law and Human Behavior, 29,* 723–742.

Capacity to Waive Rights

With the Fifth Amendment right against self-incrimination and the Fourteenth Amendment right to due process as its grounding, the U.S. Supreme Court, in *Miranda v. Arizona* (1966), established important procedural protections for criminal suspects in custodial interrogations. Aware of the inherently coercive nature of interrogations and of suspects' risk of self-incrimination, the *Miranda* Court mandated that the police notify suspects of their right to silence and legal representation. The Court further ruled that a suspect may waive these rights, but the waiver would be considered valid only if it were provided *knowingly, intelligently*, and *voluntarily*.

To determine the validity of a *Miranda* waiver, courts typically examine the *totality of circumstances* under which the waiver was given, including both situational characteristics (e.g., length of the interrogation, strategies used to obtain the confession) and characteristics of the defendant (e.g., age, intelligence, prior criminal history). However, the question of how to weigh each of these factors in determining the validity of a waiver is left to the discretion of the judge. Thus, a judge or an attorney may request a forensic evaluator to aid the court in determining a defendant's capacity to meet the requirements of a valid waiver of rights.

Identification of Relevant Capacities

The first two elements of the standard, *knowing* and *intelligent*, are related to individuals' cognitive abilities: the ability to understand the meaning of the rights and to appreciate the consequences of waiver and non-waiver decisions. Thus, forensic evaluators are able to conduct clinical and psychological assessments and inform the courts about individuals' specific abilities or deficits in these areas (e.g., whether they have the cognitive developmental and/or intellectual capacities to grasp the concept of a right as an entitlement rather than as a privilege that can be revoked). The *voluntariness* element, however, is more speculative because it considers the interaction between the situational characteristics of the interrogation (e.g., coercive police interrogation strategies used to extract a confession) and individual characteristics that may influence a defendant's waiver decision (e.g., susceptibility to suggestion by authority figures, psychosocial immaturity). Because forensic evaluators have little additional information to offer the courts about the situational characteristics, they typically address the issue of voluntariness less directly; they examine the capacities related to the knowing and intelligent elements and provide information about defendants' specific vulnerabilities that may influence their waiver decisions.

To meet the knowing and intelligent requirements of a valid waiver, one must demonstrate three primary capacities. First, one must demonstrate the ability to *comprehend* the meaning of the *Miranda* warnings. Simply, does the suspect understand the basic meaning of each of the warnings?

Second, one must be able to *appreciate the significance* of the rights. Slightly more complex than the first capacity, this ability is related to whether suspects are able to appreciate the importance of the warnings within the context of the legal process. For example, suspects may understand that they have the right to remain silent. However, if they lack an understanding of the adversarial nature of the criminal proceeding and mistakenly believe that exercising the right to silence will make them appear guilty, then their misunderstanding might impair their ability to benefit from the right.

Last, one must display the *ability to reason about choices* to make a waiver decision. This more complex ability, compared with the previous capacities, requires individuals to consider various options throughout the interrogation process (e.g., whether to talk with the police about the crime) and to weigh the short- and long-term consequences of each option (e.g., talking with the police now may lead to immediate release, but it also may result in one's statements being used against one in court at a later date).

Assessment of Relevant Capacities

In the 1970s, Thomas Grisso developed a series of instruments, the *Instruments for Assessing Understanding and Appreciation of* Miranda *Rights,* designed to assess the capacities previously described. Briefly, these instruments are composed of four discrete measures to assess different capacities.

First, Comprehension of *Miranda* Rights (CMR) is designed to assess examinees' basic understanding of each of the warnings. Examinees are read out each warning and asked to paraphrase the meaning of the warning. Second, Comprehension of *Miranda* Rights–Recognition (CMR–R) is also designed to assess examinees' understanding of their rights, but this measure does so without reliance on verbal expressive abilities; examinees must only identify whether a series of statements means the same thing as, or something different from, the warnings. Thus, it provides the opportunity for examinees with difficulties articulating their understanding to demonstrate their comprehension. Third, Comprehension of *Miranda* Vocabulary (CMV) evaluates examinees' understanding of six words found in the *Miranda* warnings by asking them to define the following terms: consult, attorney, interrogation, appoint, entitled, and right. Last, the Function of Rights in Interrogation (FRI) is the only measure that assesses examinees' appreciation of the significance of the warnings. Evaluators present four short vignettes with illustrations of police, legal, and court proceedings to examinees. After reading each vignette, examiners ask open-ended questions about the vignette (e.g., If the judge finds out that the defendant would not talk to the police, then what would happen?).

The first three measures of the *Instruments for Assessing Understanding and Appreciation of* Miranda *Rights,* the CMR, CMR–R, and CMV, assess capacities related to the knowing element of the standard for a valid waiver of rights. The final measure in the instruments, the FRI, primarily assesses capacities related to the intelligent element of the standard.

Importantly, questions about the validity of a defendant's waiver of rights may be raised at any point during the legal process, even weeks, months, or years after the waiver was provided. Consequently, the instruments provide direct information about examinees' understanding and appreciation of their rights at the time of the evaluation, not at the time of testing; data from testing must be extrapolated to estimate understanding and appreciation at the time the actual *Miranda* waiver was provided.

To increase the accuracy of a defendant's estimated capacities at the time of the *Miranda* waiver, forensic evaluators generally consider idiographic information in conjunction with the information obtained from Grisso's instruments. Additional measures typically include a clinical interview and measures of intellectual functioning, academic achievement, and symptoms of mental illness. In addition, collateral interviews are conducted and relevant records reviewed. For juvenile defendants, specific measures related to cognitive functioning and developmental maturity are also often administered.

Naomi E. Sevin Goldstein
and Rachel Kalbeitzer

See also Capacity to Waive *Miranda* Rights; Forensic Assessment; Grisso's Instruments for Assessing Understanding and Appreciation of *Miranda* Rights

Further Readings

Grisso, T. (1998). *Forensic evaluation of juveniles.* Sarasota, FL: Professional Resource Press.

Grisso, T. (1998). *Instruments for assessing understanding and appreciation of* Miranda *rights.* Sarasota, FL: Professional Resource Press.

Capital Mitigation

Capital mitigation consists of evidence that is presented in a death penalty trial to obtain a sentence other than death. In the bifurcated trial process that characterizes modern capital cases (in which a second penalty or sentencing phase occurs only if the defendant has been convicted of a crime for which the death penalty may be imposed), mitigation typically is introduced in the second stage of the trial. Its purpose is to lessen the jury's perceived need, desire, or rationale to return a death verdict. Under the death penalty statutes that govern most states, jurors are instructed to "weigh" mitigating factors (which lessen the tendency to punish with death) against aggravating factors (which increase that tendency).

Nature and Scope of Capital Mitigation

The scope of potential mitigation in a capital case is quite broad. In fact, unlike aggravating factors, which typically are limited in capital-sentencing statutes to certain prescribed categories of evidence (such as prior felony convictions), mitigating factors or evidence has been repeatedly defined by the courts as consisting of "anything proffered by the defendant in support of a sentence less than death."

Conceptually, mitigation falls into several broad categories. Capital defense attorneys often seek to introduce evidence and testimony that tend generally to humanize the defendant—that is, to emphasize the defendant's personhood and establish points of commonality between the defendant and the jurors who sit in judgment and decide his or her fate. Because many jurors enter the courtroom with stereotypic views of violent criminality, defense attorneys seek to overcome preexisting tendencies to demonize or pathologize the defendant in ways that will facilitate condemning him or her to death. Mitigating evidence that humanizes the defendant challenges the notion that extreme violence is perpetrated only by dehumanized, anonymous figures or human monsters rather than real people with very problematic and troubled lives.

Capital mitigation can provide jurors with a broader and more nuanced view of the causes of violence and deepen their understanding of the person whose life they are being asked to judge. In addition to the introduction of mitigating evidence that generally humanizes the defendant, defense attorneys also typically introduce background or social history testimony that places the defendant's life in a larger social and developmental context. Background and social history testimony can be used to explain the various ways in which the nature and direction of a defendant's life have been shaped and influenced by events and experiences that occurred earlier, often in childhood. This may include childhood trauma, parental mistreatment, and exposure to other developmental "risk factors" that are known to increase the

likelihood that someone will engage in criminal behavior later in life.

The presentation of a mitigating social history in a capital penalty trial also may include testimony about broader community-based risk factors and larger sociological forces to which the defendant was exposed and that helped shape his or her life course. Poverty, racism, "neighborhood disadvantage" (the surrounding environments characterized by unemployment, instability, and crime), and other social contextual factors may help explain the patterns of criminal behavior in which the defendant engaged. In that sense, they represent a form of mitigation. Similarly, testimony about mental health problems or disorders from which the defendant suffered, his or her cognitive limitations or deficits, or evidence of neurological abnormalities—especially if they help account for criminal behavior—are mitigating in nature. Capital mitigation also may focus on the circumstances that led up to, or helped precipitate, the capital crime itself. That is, showing that the crime was the product of a unique set of situational forces or circumstances that are unlikely to recur—at least in a prison setting (where a capital defendant who is not sentenced to death will be sent)—is a form of mitigation.

Another common but very different category of mitigation includes testimony about a capital defendant's positive qualities, good deeds, or accomplishments or the defendant's potential to make useful contributions in the future. Often this includes evidence of the defendant's positive (or, at least, unproblematic) adjustment to prison in the past, testimony about his or her potential to adjust well in the future, and even evidence that the defendant is likely to make useful contributions to prison life during his or her long-term incarceration. In these instances, the nature of the mitigating significance of the evidence derives from demonstrating the complexity of human nature (i.e., that even people who have done very bad things have other positive qualities that are unrelated to their criminality) and reminding jurors that even persons convicted of a very serious violent crime can make contributions to others that would be lost if they were sentenced to death.

In sum, the structure of capital mitigation generally involves the message that the defendant is a person, there are reasons why his or her life took the course that it did (ones that involve powerful psychological and sociological forces over which the defendant had little or no control), and the positive qualities and future contributions of the defendant would be sacrificed if he or she were to be sentenced to death.

Legal Doctrines Governing Capital Mitigation

The explicit use of mitigation as a key element in the death-sentencing process was first acknowledged by the U.S. Supreme Court in *Gregg v. Georgia* (1976) and its companion cases. Here, the Court approved a number of new state death-sentencing statutes that had been enacted in response to the Court's earlier declaration in *Furman v. Georgia* (1972) that the death penalty was unconstitutional as it was then being applied in the United States. The *Gregg* opinion endorsed a framework for capital sentencing that appeared in several of the revised state death penalty statutes that the Court reviewed and that was derived from the American Law Institute's *Model Penal Code* (1962). The *Model Penal Code* provided a list of mitigating and aggravating circumstances that it suggested jurors should "take into account" in deciding whether to impose a death sentence. The Court endorsed this approach as an acceptable way to attempt to guide the discretion of the jury.

Two years after *Gregg*, in *Lockett v. Ohio* (1978), the Supreme Court provided an expansive interpretation of the scope of admissible capital mitigation, indicating that the sentencer in a death penalty case (at that time, either a judge or a jury) must "not be precluded from considering," as mitigating factors, "*any* aspects of a defendant's character . . . that the defense proffers as a basis for a sentence less than death." In a long line of cases that followed, the Court continued to endorse the principle that capital defendants should be permitted to introduce a very broad (indeed, seemingly limitless) range of mitigating evidence. These opinions repeatedly established the right to introduce a wide range of mitigating evidence by declaring unconstitutional any statutes, procedures, or rulings that precluded or limited defendants from doing so. However, the Court nonetheless failed to impose any requirement, standard, or guideline governing whether and when capital attorneys *should* introduce mitigating testimony (or what remedy, if any, defendants were entitled to if their attorneys failed to do so). As a result, although defendants were entitled to present virtually unlimited mitigating evidence, many attorneys—because they lacked the training, experience, or resources—managed to present little or none on their client's behalf.

Nearly 25 years after *Gregg* was decided, however, the Court took steps to remedy this problem. Thus, in *Williams v. Taylor* (2000), it reversed a death sentence because a capital defense attorney had failed to investigate, assemble, and present important and available mitigating evidence in a death penalty case. Specifically, the Court found that the defense attorney had rendered "ineffective assistance of counsel" because he had failed to "conduct a thorough investigation of the defendant's background." As a result, he did not uncover and introduce potentially important mitigating evidence at trial, including the fact that the defendant had endured a "nightmarish childhood," had been raised by criminally negligent and physically abusive alcoholic parents, had been committed to an abusive foster home, and was borderline mentally retarded. The trial attorney also failed to introduce available evidence about the defendant's positive prison adjustment, including his prior good behavior in prison and extremely low violence potential in structured institutional settings.

In several subsequent decisions, the Court reaffirmed the constitutional mandate that capital attorneys must diligently pursue and present available mitigation on behalf of their clients. In perhaps the most important of these cases, *Wiggins v. Smith* (2003), the Court indicated that defense attorneys must investigate, analyze, and, where appropriate, present mitigating social history evidence. *Wiggins* emphasized that evidence of a seriously troubled background is highly relevant to what has been called "the assessment of a defendant's moral culpability" and acknowledged that when juries are confronted with such evidence, they are likely to return a sentence less than death. The Court concluded that the American Bar Association *Guidelines* (2003) for competent representation in capital cases help establish "prevailing professional norms," thereby making it incumbent on defense attorneys to investigate, analyze, and consider presenting "all reasonably available mitigating evidence," including the defendant's "medical and educational history, employment and training history, family and social history, prior adult and juvenile correctional experience, and religious and cultural influences."

Psychological Underpinning of Capital Mitigation

The doctrine of mitigation is decidedly not a doctrine of legal excuse. It allows jurors to acknowledge defendants' legal responsibility for their actions and to punish them for those actions. However, in a capital context, it provides a justification for imposing a punishment other than death. The underlying psychological rationale for this has several separate components. First, many mitigating factors that are introduced into a capital-sentencing trial serve to reduce defendants' level of moral culpability for the crime(s) they have been found responsible for committing. That is, exposure to traumatic, deprived, or otherwise criminogenic background factors may help account for a defendant's criminality, making him or her less personally blameworthy than otherwise. Similarly, a defendant whose behavior is significantly affected by mental health problems, cognitive or neurological impairments, or other maladies may be seen as less culpable than others not similarly afflicted. In a capital trial, depending on the nature and amount of those criminogenic forces or impairments, the defendant's moral culpability may be reduced, so that the jury decides that a death sentence is not warranted.

Humanizing testimony and evidence that illustrates the defendant's positive qualities and prior good acts are mitigating in a different way. This kind of capital mitigation speaks to the complexity of human nature, the fact that a life can be judged on the basis of more than the worst thing(s) someone has done, and encourages jurors to reflect comprehensively on the value of the life they are being called on to take. Mitigation about future adjustment, potential contributions to prison life, and the defendant's connections and importance to family and loved ones speaks to the psychological and social cost of a death verdict and encourages jurors to weigh these factors in the sentencing equation they employ.

Craig Haney

See also Aggravating and Mitigating Circumstances, Evaluation of in Capital Cases; Aggravating and Mitigating Circumstances in Capital Trials, Effects on Jurors; Death Penalty

Further Readings

American Bar Association. (2003). Guidelines for the appointment and performance of defense counsel in death penalty cases. *Hofstra Law Review, 31,* 913–1090.

American Law Institute. (1962). *Model penal code.* Philadelphia, PA: Author.

Fabian, J. (2003). Death penalty mitigation and the role of the forensic psychologist. *Law & Psychology Review, 27,* 73–120.

Furman v. Georgia, 408 U.S. 238 (1972).

Goodpaster, G. (1983). The trial for life: Effective assistance of counsel in death penalty cases. *New York University Law Review, 58,* 299–362.

Gregg v. Georgia, 428 U.S. 153 (1976).

Haney, C. (1995). The social context of capital murder: Social histories and the logic of capital mitigation. *Santa Clara Law Review, 35,* 547–609.

Haney, C. (2005). *Death by design: Capital punishment as a social psychological system.* New York: Oxford University Press.

Lockett v. Ohio, 438 U.S. 586 (1978).

Miranda v. Arizona, 384 U.S. 436 (1966).

Note, Eighth Amendment—Death penalty: Weighing of aggravating and mitigating factors. (2006). *Harvard Law Review, 120,* 144–154.

Wiggins v. Smith, 539 U.S. 510 (2003).

Williams v. Taylor, 529 U.S. 362 (2000).

CAPITAL PUNISHMENT

See DEATH PENALTY

CHECKLIST FOR COMPETENCY FOR EXECUTION EVALUATIONS

To date, very few instruments have been developed for the purpose of assisting evaluators in the assessment of competency for execution. One of the first—the Checklist for Competency for Execution Evaluations—is described in this entry. The checklist consists of four sections that describe important and relevant psycholegal criteria to be considered in this type of forensic assessment. The purpose of the checklist is to guide evaluators through the interview portion of a competency for execution evaluation. At present, there is no available research that examines the reliability or validity of this checklist.

Evaluations of competency for execution are probably the least common type of criminal forensic evaluation conducted, simply because of the relatively small number of individuals who have been sentenced to death (as compared with the population of criminal defendants); however, the repercussions of this type of evaluation are literally a matter of life and death for the inmate whose competence has been questioned. Utmost care needs to be taken in conducting this type of evaluation.

In 2003, Patricia Zapf, Marcus Boccaccini, and Stanley Brodsky published a checklist to be used in the evaluation of competency for execution. This checklist was developed after a review of the available literature on criminal competencies, including a review of the available case law on competency for execution, and after conducting interviews with professionals involved in conducting evaluations of competency for execution.

The checklist is divided into four sections: (1) understanding the reasons for punishment, (2) understanding the punishment, (3) appreciation and reasoning (in addition to simple factual understanding), and (4) ability to assist the attorney. These four sections are representative of the legal criteria for competency for execution that have been set out in various jurisdictions.

Most jurisdictions model their statutes pertaining to competency for execution after the criteria set out in the decision by the U.S. Supreme Court in the case of *Ford v. Wainwright* (1986) and, therefore, only consider the prisoner's ability to understand the punishment that is being imposed and the reasons why it is being imposed. The first two sections of the checklist parallel these two *Ford* criteria. The first section targets the offender's understanding of the reasons for punishment—that is, his or her understanding of the crime and other conviction-related information. Specific topic areas include the offender's understanding of the reasons why he or she is in prison; his or her place of residence within the prison; the crime for which he or she was convicted, including an explanation of the criminal act and victim-identifying information; the perceived justice of the conviction; and the reasons why other people are punished for the same offense and also any self-identified, unique, understandings of the offense and the trial that the offender might have.

The second section targets the offender's understanding of the punishment: that is, that the punishment he or she is facing is death. Specific topic areas include the offender's understanding of the sentence, the meaning of a sentence of death, what it means for a person to be dead, and the reasons for execution and also specific understandings about death from execution. Questions about death are asked from a number of different angles (e.g., the meaning of death, specific understandings about death from execution) so as to facilitate a thorough evaluation of any irrational beliefs or ideas that the offender may hold regarding death.

The literature on other types of competencies (e.g., competence to consent to medical treatment) indicates that there is often a relationship between the severity of the consequences (to the individual being assessed) and the stringency of the standard used to evaluate competence. Thus, given the gravity of the consequences in the particular instance of competency for execution, it seems appropriate and important to assess the offender's appreciation and reasoning abilities (in addition to simple factual understanding). Therefore, the third section of the checklist lists topic areas specific to the assessment of an offender's appreciation and reasoning abilities with respect to death and execution—areas that may go above and beyond the specific *Ford* criteria but that are arguably important to a comprehensive evaluation of competency for execution. Specific content areas in this section include the offender's appreciation of the personal importance of the punishment and the personal meaning of death; the offender's rationality or reasoning about the physical, mental, and personal changes that occur during and after execution; his or her beliefs regarding invulnerability; inappropriate affect; the offender's acceptance of or eagerness for execution; and his or her beliefs against execution. Although the *Ford* criteria are often interpreted as dealing with the offender's *factual* understanding, it appears justified that mental health professionals involved in competency for execution evaluations should also assess the offender's appreciation and reasoning and leave it to the court to determine how to interpret the *Ford* (or other relevant) criteria in each specific case.

The last section of the checklist identifies issues related to the offender's ability to assist his or her attorney. This section is especially relevant in jurisdictions that rely on criteria that are broader in nature than those outlined in *Ford,* such as the capacity to comprehend the reasons that might make the capital sentence unjust and to communicate these reasons effectively. Specific topic areas in this section include the identity of the offender's attorney and the amount of time that the attorney has been working for the offender, the offender's trust in the attorney, his or her awareness of the execution date, the status of the appeals, what the attorney is attempting to accomplish through the appeals, how the appeals will be processed and assessed, the actual substance of the appeals, important content that the offender may have withheld from the attorney, and any pathological reasons for not planning or discussing appeals.

Patricia A. Zapf

See also Competency for Execution

Further Readings

Brodsky, S. L., Zapf, P. A., & Boccaccini, M. T. (2001). The last competency: An examination of legal, ethical, and professional ambiguities regarding evaluations of competence for execution. *Journal of Forensic Psychology Practice, 1,* 1–25.

Brodsky, S. L., Zapf, P. A., & Boccaccini, M. T. (2005). Competency for execution assessments: Ethical continuities and professional tasks. *Journal of Forensic Psychology Practice, 5,* 65–74.

Ford v. Wainwright, 477 U.S. 399 (1986).

Heilbrun, K. S. (1987). The assessment of competency for execution: An overview. *Behavioral Sciences and the Law, 5,* 383–396.

Zapf, P. A., Boccaccini, M. T., & Brodsky, S. L. (2003). Assessment of competency for execution: Professional guidelines and an evaluation checklist. *Behavioral Sciences and the Law, 21,* 103–120.

CHICAGO JURY PROJECT

The Chicago Jury Project was a large-scale social science research initiative in the 1950s. This entry provides a descriptive portrait of the project, followed by a brief summary of the primary studies associated with it, and then a discussion of the project's legacy and its impact on the field of psychology and law. In essence, the Chicago Jury Project was a groundbreaking scientific endeavor that employed a variety of social science methods and anticipated a host of current research streams. It remains an impressive accomplishment and can fairly be said to represent the inaugural event in the scientific study of jury decision making.

Overview

The Chicago Jury Project, also known as the American Juries Project, was conceived as an innovative effort to study the American legal system using behavioral science methods. Initiated in 1953 with funding from a $400,000 grant from the Ford Foundation, the project was housed at the University of Chicago. A variety of research studies were undertaken with the aid of project funding, not all of which were concerned with juries (e.g., arbitration). The project was led primarily by three individuals: Harry Kalven (a law professor), Hans Zeisel (a sociologist, statistician, and law professor), and Fred Strodtbeck (a social psychologist), although more than 20 other individuals were affiliated

with the project, including Dale Broeder and Rita James Simon. The initial funding was spent by 1956, which triggered a review of project activities and findings by the Ford Foundation. A second round of funding from Ford enabled some arms of the project (most notably the work on juries) to continue until 1959, at which point active data collection ceased. A bibliography published in 1966 listed more than 60 journal articles published by researchers associated with the project. In-depth summaries of selected project initiatives were subsequently published in three book-length volumes titled *Delay in the Court* (1959), *The American Jury* (1966), and *The American Jury: The Defense of Insanity* (1967). The physical records of the project are currently held in 10 boxes at the Special Collections Research Center at the University of Chicago's Law School.

Few social science research projects receive public attention, and even fewer achieve any that is sustained, but the Chicago Jury Project actually caused something of a national scandal at one point in its existence. One early initiative involved audiotaping the deliberations of five civil jury trials in the federal district court in Wichita, Kansas. Although this was done with the assent of the trial judge and counsel for both sides, the jurors were unaware that their discussion was being recorded. When this became public knowledge in the summer of 1955, uproar ensued. The methodology was publicly censured by the Attorney General of the United States, a special hearing was initiated by the Senate Judiciary Committee, and more than 30 jurisdictions subsequently enacted statutes prohibiting the direct observation or recording of jury deliberations.

Project Studies and Results

As noted above, the Chicago Jury Project consisted of a number of different research initiatives involving several major methodological strategies: (a) analysis of archival data on court system functioning, (b) surveys, (c) intensive interviews with attorneys and jurors, and (d) experimental research with mock juries. This section briefly summarizes the project activities and findings within each methodological domain.

Archival Research

Much of the early work associated with the project involved taking stock of the descriptive research already done by others. One line of inquiry was comparative in nature and attempted to identify what had been learned about legal systems in general and the jury in particular in Western Europe. An effort was also made to collect and examine jury trial statistics from several major metropolitan areas in the United States in order to estimate the frequencies associated with defendants' waiving their right to jury trial, the occurrence of hung juries, and the number of annual jury trials in the United States. Existing data were also gathered on the extent to which judges agreed with the verdicts of their juries as well as the nature of cases heard by judges and juries. In the end, this archival research set the stage for a number of later project activities and produced the following conclusions: (a) there did not exist much data on juries outside the United States; (b) defendant waiver rates varied considerably across jurisdictions within the United States; (c) criminal "hung jury" rates varied across jurisdictions but on average occurred about 5% of the time; (d) judges and juries agreed on the appropriate verdict in about 75% to 85% of cases; (e) when trial complexity was taken into account, juries were about on par with judges in terms of the time needed to resolve cases; and (f) about 55,670 jury trials occurred in the United States in 1955 (which is considerably higher than current estimates).

Interview Research

Researchers associated with the Chicago Jury Project made extensive use of interview methodology in the course of their work. One notable study involved having one of the project researchers (Dale Broeder, a law professor) accompany a federal district court judge on his circuit for the better part of a year. During this time, he conducted intensive interviews with 225 jurors and many of the attorneys involved in 20 jury trials. Attorneys were asked about their strategies during voir dire and their reasons for challenging particular jurors; jurors were questioned about their attitudes toward the jury system in general, their service, and their preferences for particular kinds of trials. One finding from this line of work was that many jurors were not looking to serve, but those that did tended to be positively influenced by their experience and more supportive of the jury system afterward. This labor-intensive endeavor resulted eventually in a number of essays highlighting commonalities in deliberation across cases, most of which were published in law journals.

One of the most well-known findings associated with the Chicago Jury Project arose from a massive field study featuring interviews with more than 1,500 jurors from 225 criminal jury trials in Chicago and Brooklyn. Among the goals of this study was reconstruction of the distribution of juror votes on the first ballot taken during deliberation. The result—surprising at the time but often replicated since—was that the verdict preferred by the majority of the jury on the first ballot ended up being the jury's final verdict approximately 90% of the time regardless of the demographic composition of the majority and minority factions. Furthermore, the minority factions that did manage to prevail were typically fairly large (i.e., three or more jurors), not lone "hold-out" individuals. Project researchers concluded from this that most criminal cases were decided during the trial as opposed to deliberation, and they likened deliberation to the role of the dark room in photography—the image (verdict) was set at the moment of exposure (i.e., the conclusion of the trial), but deliberation served as the developmental process that brought the image to light. This line of work also produced some interesting generalizations about juror voting preferences as a function of ethnic/national background, as well as some of the first empirical evidence that jurors do not always fully understand their instructions.

Survey Research

Perhaps the most famous research associated with the Chicago Jury Project, however, concerned the extent to which it makes a tangible difference to the outcome whether bench trials or jury trials are used. To examine this question, project researchers assembled a comprehensive listing of judges who presided over jury trials and then invited all the 3,500 or so individuals on the list. In the end, 555 trial judges from every state (except Rhode Island) as well as the federal courts participated. Essentially, the participating judges were asked to fill out a brief questionnaire for each jury trial they presided over during the study and return it by mail. Sample I was collected during 1954 to 1955 using the first version of the questionnaire ($k = 2,385$ trials); Sample II was collected during 1958 using a revised and elaborated form ($k = 1,191$ trials). Although additional information was collected (especially on the second form), the focus was on three things: (1) the jury's actual verdict, (2) the judge's indication of what he or she thought was the appropriate verdict, and (3) the judge's perceived reasons for any discrepancy between the first two.

The spotlight finding of this massive study was that judges and juries agreed on the appropriate verdict in 75.4% of the 3,576 criminal trials when hung juries were treated as disagreements (and 78% of the trials when they were distributed evenly between "agree" and "disagree"). This figure for criminal jury trials was remarkably close to the corresponding figure for the approximately 4,000 civil jury trials for which data were obtained in the same fashion. Criminal juries were found to be more lenient than judges (i.e., they acquitted when the judge would have convicted) in 19% of the cases and more severe than judges in 3% of the cases. Intensive analysis yielded five broad categories of reasons for the discrepancies supplied by the judges: (1) evidence factors, (2) facts known to the judge but not to the jury, (3) disparity of counsel, (4) jury sentiments about the defendant, and (5) jury sentiments about the law. This research also produced a wealth of descriptive data on juries that would serve as a benchmark for later research, including estimates of the overall conviction rate for juries (64%), the overall "win" rate for plaintiffs (59%), and the frequency of "hung juries" (5.5%), as well as profiles of the different types of evidence presented by the prosecution and the defense.

Another survey study associated with the project but less well-known involved examining variation in damage awards as a function of region. Six model cases were created and submitted to 600 claims adjusters of three large insurance companies operating throughout the United States. Using the reports of claims adjustors as a proxy for jury awards, this study anticipated the now well-established finding that damage awards vary considerably by jurisdiction and region.

Experimental Research With Mock Juries

After the commotion caused by the taping of actual jury deliberations, project researchers were forced to seek an alternative method for studying jury deliberation and subsequently invented a staple methodology in the jury-decision-making literature: the mock jury. Four different cases (or scenarios) were created for use with mock juries to study the impact of manipulations associated with, for instance, the weight of the evidence, knowledge of the defendant's insurance status in civil cases, the legal definition of negligence in civil cases (comparative vs. contributory) and insanity in criminal cases, as well as the use of special verdict forms with interrogatories. In the end, 160 mock civil juries were run using two kinds of cases (auto negligence and product liability), whereas 98 mock criminal juries heard either a burglary or an incest case. The research on criminal juries was perhaps the first to show that an element of the jury's instructions (e.g, the definition of insanity) could influence jury verdicts; in contrast, little influence was associated with the provision of expert testimony or the fate of the defendant. Despite the focus on the effects of the manipulated independent variables, this line of research is perhaps most notable for the descriptive portrait it provided of jury deliberation. In particular, this research suggested that forepersons were usually selected quickly, with little discussion or campaigning, and the choices could be explained well using only three variables: prior jury experience, social status, and seat position around the table. Another conclusion was that speaking during deliberation was not egalitarian, but rather, a small set of jurors tended to do most of the talking (often males and those with more social prestige), while some jurors typically said little or nothing.

Project Legacy and Impact

It is common for scholarly papers on jury decision making to reference the Chicago Jury Project, and it is fair to ask if this exalted status is warranted. In other words, what lasting impact has the project had on the field of psychology and law? Arguably, the project's most fundamental contribution was in establishing the precedent that social science methods could be used to understand and ultimately improve the legal system. As natural and obvious as this may seem today, there was nothing inevitable about it. There are many institutions that have not received the same attention from psychologists; for example, there are no thriving subdisciplines for psychology and government, psychology and medicine, or psychology and the arts as there is for psychology and law. A second contribution was in showing that the full spectrum of social science methods could be brought to bear on the study of the legal system. Indeed, most of the major methodologies used to study juries today (with the exception of the Internet) were first used by the Chicago Jury Project, and it also put the use of mock juries on the map. Project researchers also stumbled on the limits of the legal system's tolerance for social science methods via their seemingly innocuous audiotaping of five civil jury deliberations in 1955; the door to the jury room was literally closed to researchers for basically the next 50 years (and it is only now starting to reopen).

Other lasting contributions associated with the Chicago Jury Project include the initiation of research on a remarkably diverse set of legal topics, devoting attention to civil as well as criminal juries, using a multidisciplinary approach with individuals from various fields, and publishing project findings in legal as well as psychology journals. By any standard, the number of publications resulting from the project's work is impressive, and there is no doubt that their widespread dissemination in different outlets is a major reason why the Chicago Jury Project is still so well-known today. These publications provided a number of descriptive findings based on large samples that provided empirical benchmarks for later work, including estimates of the frequency of jury trials, hung juries, and judge-jury agreement and a first portrait of deliberation that included foreperson selection and the power of early majority.

Alas, one unfortunate aspect of the project may have stemmed from the fairly cynical view of deliberation offered in *The American Jury* (1966). The colorful yet deterministic "dark room" metaphor may have inadvertently dissuaded a generation of jury scholars from taking an active interest in the dynamics of deliberation, and in some respects, it may continue to dampen interest in what happens behind the closed door of the jury room. Nonetheless, even 50 years later, the scope and accomplishments of the Chicago Jury Project remain remarkable, and it truly deserves its lustrous reputation as a seminal event in the field of psychology and law.

Dennis J. Devine

See also Insanity Defense, Juries and; Jury Decisions Versus Judges' Decisions; Jury Deliberation; Jury Selection

Further Readings

Broeder, D. (1958). The University of Chicago Jury Project. *Nebraska Law Review, 38,* 744–760.

Kalven, H., Jr., & Zeisel, H. (1966). *The American jury.* Boston: Little, Brown.

Simon, R. J. (1967). *The jury and the defense of insanity.* Boston: Little, Brown.

Strodtbeck, F. L., & Lipinski, R. M. (1985). Becoming first among equals: Moral considerations in jury foreman selection. *Journal of Personality and Social Psychology, 49,* 927–936.

Zeisel, H., Kalven, H., Jr., & Buchholz, B. (1959). *Delay in the court.* Boston: Little, Brown.

CHILD ABUSE POTENTIAL (CAP) INVENTORY

Psychologists are often asked to evaluate and to provide testimony about parental capacity. The Child Abuse Potential (CAP) Inventory, a measure originally designed to screen parents for child physical abuse risk, is frequently used as a measure of general parental capacity. The CAP Inventory is a 160-item, forced-choice (agree/disagree) self-report questionnaire. It contains a 77-item physical abuse scale, six descriptive factor scales (distress, rigidity, unhappiness, problems with child and self, problems with family, and problems from others), and three validity scales (lie, random response, and inconsistency). The three validity scales are used in different combinations to form three response distortion indexes (faking good, faking bad, and random response). The CAP Inventory also contains two special scales: the ego-strength and loneliness scales. The Inventory has been translated into more than 25 languages, including multiple Spanish translations. Although the available data on the translated versions of the CAP Inventory are generally positive, the amount of published data on the reliability and validity of the CAP Inventory translations is highly variable.

Background

An original pool of CAP Inventory items was developed following an exhaustive review of the theoretical and empirical literature that described parental psychological and interpersonal risk factors thought to be associated with child physical abuse. In constructing the CAP Inventory, an effort was made to avoid using items that represented static risk factors. Items were included in the current 77-item abuse scale based on their ability to distinguish between known child physical abusers and matched comparison parents in validation studies. Furthermore, in selecting the final list of abuse scale items, an effort was made to exclude items that were correlated with demographics characteristics.

Reliability

Internal consistency estimates for the CAP Inventory physical abuse scale range from .92 to .96 for general population parents and from .95 to .98 for child physical abusers. Internal consistency estimates are similar across gender, ethnic, and educational groups. Temporal stability (test-retest reliability) estimates for the CAP physical abuse scale are .91, .90, .83, and .75 for 1-day, 1-week, 1-month, and 3-month intervals, respectively.

Validity

Extensive construct validity data indicating the expected relationships between CAP Inventory abuse scores and risk factors have been reported. For example, the expected relationships have been found between a respondent's CAP abuse scores and his or her childhood history of observation and receipt of abuse, and the respondent's childhood history of observing marital violence. CAP abuse scores also are associated (in the expected manner) with psychophysiological reactivity, neuropsychological problems, social isolation/lack of social support, negative family interactions, adult attachment problems, low self-esteem/ego-strength, stress/distress, inadequate knowledge of child development, belief in corporal punishment, negative perceptions of child behaviors, negative evaluations of child behaviors, low expectations of children, negative attributions (e.g., hostile intent), authoritarianism, depression, anxiety, anger/hostility, aggression, mental health problems/psychopathology, alcohol/drug use, problems in coping, lack of empathy, problems in parent-child interactions, use of harsh discipline strategies, and lack of positive parenting behaviors.

Concurrent validity studies report abuse scale correct classification rates in the 80% to low 90% range. Predictive validity data indicate that elevated abuse scores in high-risk parents (where participants were tested before interventions) are significantly related to later cases of child physical abuse. In addition, numerous studies have reported that elevated parental CAP abuse scores are predictive of child problems. For example, in a prospective study, before and after controlling for obstetric risk factors, scores on an abbreviated version of the CAP abuse scale were predictive of neonatal morbidity. In another prospective study, before and after controlling for problematic parenting orientations, CAP abuse scores were predictive of children's later intelligence and adaptive behaviors.

In summary, although elevated CAP Inventory abuse scores have been shown to be predictive of later confirmed cases of child physical abuse, the large body of available construct validity data supports the view that the CAP abuse scale may have even more utility in detecting parents who are at high risk for a broad array of parenting problems (as outlined above) and is useful in detecting parents who are likely to have children who have problems in their physical and psychosocial development. Independent evaluations of the CAP Inventory psychometric data have produced similar conclusions. For example, with respect to testimonial admissibility, the CAP Inventory has been judged to meet the Daubert standard as a measure of parental capacity.

Joel S. Milner

See also Child Custody Evaluations; Child Maltreatment; Divorce and Child Custody; Parenting Stress Index (PSI)

Further Readings

Milner, J. S. (1986). *The Child Abuse Potential Inventory: Manual* (2nd ed.). DeKalb, IL: Psytec.

Milner, J. S. (2006). *An interpretive manual for the Child Abuse Potential Inventory* (2nd ed.). DeKalb, IL: Psytec.

Yanez, Y., & Fremouw, W. (2003). The application of the Daubert standard to parental capacity measures. *American Journal of Forensic Psychology, 22*(3), 5–28.

CHILD CUSTODY EVALUATIONS

Child custody evaluation (also known as evaluation of parental responsibility) refers to the use of the legal system to resolve questions of the distribution of decision-making responsibility and time with children, often but not always in the context of marital dissolution. This process exists to resolve disputes between two or more adults who have an interest in providing parenting to a child and who cannot agree about how the child's care should be divided between or among them. They may be divorcing or may have never lived together in the same household (such as when grandparents vie for the right to parent a grandchild whose biological parent is unavailable or when a child is born to two biological parents who were never involved in a live-in or marriage relationship). When adults with a potentially legitimate legal stake in parenting a child cannot agree on how time and responsibility for a child will be divided, the court, acting as parens patriae, must resolve the dispute. Society's interests are served by ensuring that a child's care is provided by caregivers who are able and willing to put the child's best interests ahead of their own.

Best Interests of the Child

All 50 states focus on the best interests of the child in making determinations regarding parenting time and responsibility. The "best interests of the child" standard is, however, an indeterminate one. States may define the child's best interests by statute or may leave the determination to the judge to make on a case-by-case basis. Child custody matters are decided by judges in 49 states; in Texas, either party can elect to put the matter before a jury.

In 1973, the National Conference of Commissioners on Uniform State Laws published the Uniform Marriage and Divorce Act, in anticipation of its adoption in a large number of jurisdictions, and in the years that followed, a number of states adopted parts of the act to assist courts in custody determinations. Section 402 of that act specifies that the court consider, as relevant to determining the child's best interests, the wishes of the child; the wishes of the parents; the interaction of the child with parents and siblings; the child's adjustment to home, school, and community; and the mental and physical health of all persons involved. Many courts continue to rely on these or variants of these factors in deciding parenting time and responsibility disputes.

A Historical Review of Custody of Children

In English common law, children were considered to be chattels, or possessions of their parents. They were a commodity or resource when they were able to work or otherwise generate income for their parents and a liability when they were not productive. Since the property of a married couple was considered to belong to the man of the house, children were their father's possession.

This notion of children as chattels carried forth to the United States, and the government was loathe to intervene in matters regarding the care and control of children, perceiving those matters to be of concern to their owners, their parents, or more particularly their father. However, with an awakened appreciation of the importance of the mother in meeting the needs of infant children, the tender years doctrine, holding that children of tender years generally required the care of

their mother because she was endowed with those natural qualities that were important in the nurture of young children, gradually displaced the children-as-chattels doctrine. With increasing frequency, mothers were awarded custody in contested cases. Coincident with the rising divorce rates in the United States, mothers began almost universally to win custody of the child unless fitness could be successfully challenged. Fathers ordinarily bore an inordinate proportion of financial responsibility, taxed to them in the form of alimony or child support. Their access to the child was often restricted to "visitation," which marginalized their involvement in parenting to the point that visiting fathers were referred to by Michael Lamb as "Disneyland Dad."

The pendulum began to swing away from the tender years doctrine, however, with several societal changes. As more women entered the workforce, parents increasingly shared responsibility for the home and child care. When marriages ended in divorce, involved fathers sought meaningful postdivorce contact with children reflective of their preseparation child care roles. Second, the roles of children had changed substantially—from field hands in the agrarian life of colonial America or workers in the Depression era middle class to emotionally cherished members of the family. With the postwar societal interest in improving the quality of life, Dr. Spock's advice on parenting, and a proliferation of self-help books to enhance emotional fulfillment, there was increased attention paid to children's emotional needs and to the role that each parent played in meeting those needs. Divorcing parents argued for a stake in childrearing based on their claimed fitness to meet various facets of the growing child's emotional needs.

Thus, the two-parent workforce, the shift in fathers' roles, and the recognition of the child's emotional attachment to both parents all converged to usher in a new era. State legislators increasingly recognized that it no longer made sense for the child to be in the sole custody of one parent, with contact with the other parent occurring through weekend visitation. Joint custody, in some form, became an option in every state. Disputing parents might be awarded either equivalent or joint legal decision-making power, equal or near-equal time with the child, or both, unless one parent was demonstrably incapable of providing such responsibility or care. There was increasing recognition of the importance of both parents in the child's healthy development, and the courts searched for ways to maximize the positive contributions of each parent in postdivorce or coparenting arrangements.

High-Conflict Families

The migration from sole to joint or shared custody outcomes has been a rough journey. It is understood that among divorcing parents, the vast majority resolve questions of parenting without the court's assistance, and only a small number seek the court's resolution of the dispute. Among those who need assistance, some return again and again, filing further motions for modifications of earlier rulings or alleging contempt of court, alleging failure to follow the court's orders. These high-conflict parents may also appeal against rulings of the court, and their disputes take up about 95% of the family court's time and resources.

Of primary concern with high-conflict families, however, is not the monopoly of the court's time but the great damage done to the children who are subjects of the ongoing child custody litigation and conflict. Exposure to preseparation and postseparation conflict between their parents is the most reliable predictor that children will develop emotional and behavioral problems stemming from divorce. The courts, recognizing this toll on the children, have sought ways to assist the high-conflict families to find more constructive and successful paths to resolving their difficulties.

Currently, there is a trend under way, manifested by the removal of the language of "custody" and "visitation" in the statutes of several states, to try to move these matters away from the climate of adversary proceedings, where the winner takes all and the loser—the marginalized parent who is allowed to visit with his or her child—goes away almost empty-handed (often nevertheless paying the greater portion of child care costs). Statutes in these states refer to parenting time and responsibility determinations and strive to find a solution that best reflects the sharing of parenting, with each parent making a meaningful contribution to the child's well-being. The courts may require or at least solicit parenting plans to be submitted by each parent, to increase the parents' involvement in decision making and to help the parents focus on the needs of the child and the long-term commitment to shared parenting. The courts may order mediation or some other form of dispute resolution to attempt to provide the family with a nonadversarial method for resolving the question of how this coparenting will occur, presently and as the children grow older.

The Role of the Psychologist

Psychologists' participation in these matters began with therapists offering opinions to the courts about a child's needs or wishes, or an adult client's presumed fitness to parent. The other parent in such matters soon discovered the value of obtaining expert testimony to rebut that of the therapist and would take the child to another therapist in search of helpful testimony. The emergence of dueling experts soon burdened the court with trying to determine which expert opinion seemed to have more credibility or to deserve greater weight. Before long, both psychologists and judges recognized the value of a court-appointed expert serving in a neutral role to assess the parents and children in the matter, in order to investigate the claims of each parent about the parenting capacity of the other parent or the child's needs or wishes. Between the mid-1970s and late 1980s, it became increasingly common to see court-appointed custody evaluators taking the place of testifying therapists in these matters. It is now well accepted that the therapist may have limited data on which to base actual recommendations regarding parenting time or responsibility.

Comprehensive Evaluation of Parental Responsibility

When disputes about parenting time and responsibility are not resolved by early interventions, such as having each parent propose a parenting plan, mediating the areas in dispute, and working to resolve issues through other forms of intervention, the next step is the court-ordered child custody or parenting responsibility evaluation. Since the more benign matters are resolved through these lower levels of contention, what remains for the custody evaluator are the most intransigent matters. These often involve allegations of sexual abuse of a child; alienation by one parent of the child's affections toward the other parent; allegations of domestic violence; or requests by one parent to relocate, with the child, to another city or state or even, in some matters, a different country. These difficult cases may be referred by the court for a comprehensive custody evaluation or evaluation of parental responsibility.

The comprehensive evaluation may take place over several weeks or even months. The process is preceded by a full disclosure to the parties of the purpose and nature of the evaluation, the limits of confidentiality, the potential range of outcomes, and the fee arrangements. The evaluator schedules appointments with each adult caregiver who is party to the suit and each child for an interview and testing, observation of interactions, and follow-up inquiry regarding matters in dispute. Collateral or third-party sources of information are sought, including records of previous court hearings, school records, mental health treatment records, and medical records for issues relevant to the dispute. Additionally, the parties may present other records, such as records of their communications with one another, recordings of exchanges, and other such materials. The psychologist may also consult teachers, child care workers, coaches, pediatricians, therapists, neighbors, and relatives who may have relevant information.

Psychological Testing

While psychological testing is not explicitly required in these evaluations, it is often included in the assessment techniques. Although no specialized tests of the best interests of the child or child custody fitness have been developed that meet established psychometric standards, some efforts have been advanced. When psychological measures are employed, instrument selection is driven by an appreciation of the importance of the relevance and reliability of the instrument for the purpose. Commonly used instruments include the Minnesota Multiphasic Personality Inventory–2 (MMPI–2), the Personality Assessment Inventory (PAI), and the Millon Clinical Multiaxial Inventory–III (MCMI–III) for assessing personality characteristics of the parents; the Parent-Child Relationship Inventory, the Parenting Stress Index, or some other measure of parental attitudes; and the Child Behavior Checklist or Behavior Assessment System for Children for children. Other instruments may be helpful to address special issues such as domestic violence allegations, substance abuse, or childhood depression and anxiety. Comprehensive social history and parenting history questionnaires may also be used to collect parent input in a somewhat standard way. When the inferential leap is too great from what the test measures to the matter at bar, it is advised that the test not be used.

Report of Findings

Finally, the data that have been collected are analyzed to develop information useful to the court in its determination of sharing of parenting responsibility and time. The psychologist may stop short of making specific recommendations about how parenting responsibility and time should be apportioned, recognizing the final determination to be a matter for the court to decide. When there are sufficient data to substantiate a specific recommendation, however, there is no legal bar to offering it.

Variations on the Nature and Forms of Families

Disputes regarding parenting time and responsibility are not limited to divorcing biological parents. Adoptive parents, noncohabiting parents, grandparent caregivers, estranged grandparents of a child with a deceased or incapacitated parent, gay and lesbian parents, and many other configurations of families may seek the court's assistance in settling matters in controversy when children's best interests are at stake. Families may enjoy unique cultural milieus, or there may be specialized concerns, such as a child with special needs or a parent with specific disabilities; all these issues may tax the court's resources in making particularized and customized determinations that best address the needs of the family whose child's best interests are in question. The psychologist may also be taxed by these special issues but may also have greater time and resources to invest in investigating their significance. Psychologists are helpful to the trier of fact by accomplishing this comprehensive, case-specific evaluation of parenting time and responsibility.

Mary Connell

See also Alternative Dispute Resolution; Child Sexual Abuse; Divorce and Child Custody; Parens Patriae Doctrine; Substance Abuse and Intimate Partner Violence; Tender Years Doctrine

Further Readings

American Psychological Association. (1994). Guidelines for child custody evaluations in divorce proceedings. *The American Psychologist, 49,* 677–680.

Association of Family and Conciliation Courts. (2007). Model standards of practice for child custody evaluation. *Family Court Review, 45,* 70–91. Available at http://www.afccnet.org

Connell, M. A. (2006). Notification of purpose in child custody evaluation: Informing the parties and their counsel. *Professional Psychology: Research and Practice, 37,* 446–451.

Greenberg, S. A., & Shuman, D. W. (1997). Irreconcilable conflict between therapeutic and forensic roles. *Professional Psychology: Research and Practice, 28,* 50–57.

Otto, R., Buffington-Vollum, J., & Edens, J. F. (2003). Child custody evaluation. In A. M. Goldstein (Ed.), *Handbook of psychology: Vol. 11. Forensic psychology* (pp. 179–208). New York: Wiley.

Sparta, S. N., & Koocher, G. P. (Eds.). (2006). *Forensic mental health assessment of children and adolescents.* New York: Oxford.

CHILD MALTREATMENT

Child maltreatment extends across class, culture, ethnicity, and nationality. In the United States alone, upward of 3 million cases of child abuse are reported annually, and more than 1,000 children die each year as a result of abuse. However, these numbers are likely underestimates of the scope of the problem because, as most experts agree, child maltreatment is underreported. The term *child maltreatment* itself is broad, encompassing neglect, emotional abuse, physical abuse, and sexual abuse. Scientific and clinical evidence indicates that child maltreatment detrimentally affects children's cognitive, social, and emotional development. Psychological models specifying the mechanisms by which child maltreatment imparts its adverse effects include attachment theory (e.g., child maltreatment distorts children's internal working models of self and others) and psychophysiological theories (e.g., chronic elevation of an abused child's biological stress response may influence the child's developing brain and, thus, the child's behavior and functioning). Research also points to the importance and influence of contextual factors that may promote resilience in maltreated children.

Over the years, the United States has enacted a complex patchwork of laws for protecting children against abuse. Child protection agencies exist to intervene when child abuse is suspected or substantiated and to prevent child maltreatment through means such as education for families at risk and awareness campaigns for the public at large. The criminal justice system also acts to protect maltreated children, most notably by prosecuting offenders. Fortunately, these prevention and intervention efforts may well have been effective, given the recent declines in the rates of child abuse reporting. This entry elaborates on the definitions of child maltreatment, provides more information about its incidence, discusses what is known about the causes and consequences of child maltreatment, and suggests ways to prevent this serious social problem.

Defining Child Maltreatment

Neglect is the most common form of confirmed child maltreatment (comprising more than 60% of all cases), followed by physical abuse (18%), sexual abuse (10%), and psychological or emotional abuse (7%). Defining child maltreatment is sometimes controversial, but generally, neglect is an act of omission—a caretaker's failure to provide basic necessities such as food, shelter, emotional support, medical attention, education, or a safe haven from harmful situations. Although neglect is the most common child maltreatment case that comes to the attention of authorities and enters the juvenile or family court system, its perpetrators are rarely prosecuted in criminal court. A condition known as nonorganic failure to thrive is often considered a type of child neglect. It refers to a condition in which an otherwise healthy baby, while under his or her parent's care, loses weight and stops growing. Psychological, social, and/or economic problems within the family typically prompt failure to thrive.

Sexual and physical abuse reflect acts of commission. Child sexual abuse occurs when children are involved in sexual activities with an adult. Adults often use coercion or deception to lure children into such activities, but it is worth noting that coercion and deception are unnecessary elements of this crime because children are not considered legally or developmentally capable of consenting to sexual activities with adults. Child sexual abuse sometimes involves physical contact such as penetration or fondling, but physical contact is not always necessary. For example, exhibitionism, forcing children to watch or make pornographic material, or encouraging sexual promiscuity is also considered sexually abusive to minors. Child sexual abuse cases are particularly likely to bring child victims into contact with court systems, both juvenile and criminal. In fact, most children who testify in criminal court do so in the context of child sexual abuse cases.

Physical abuse, which is most often perpetrated by parents and guardians, can be more difficult to define than sexual abuse. That is, while all forms of sexual contact between an adult and a child are considered socially inappropriate across most cultures, mild to moderate physical punishment applied as a disciplinary tactic is often socially sanctioned. Nevertheless, research shows that corporal punishment can have negative outcomes and that serious physical child abuse sometimes results from escalated corporal punishment. There is agreement that deliberate acts resulting in physical harm to a child, such as when an angry or frustrated parent hits, shakes, burns, or throws a child, constitute physical abuse. In many cases, the fact that physical abuse has taken place is relatively clear because of visible injuries to the child. Medical examination can confirm, to a certain extent, whether certain bruises, broken bones, bites, and burns are caused by accident (e.g., a child falling downstairs) or are a deliberate infliction of harm. In other cases, however, intentional physical abuse is hard to detect.

Psychological or emotional maltreatment involves acts of commission or omission that hinder children's psychological development. It can include acts of terrorizing, isolating, corrupting, and denigrating, as well as ignoring children or other acts that signal to children that they are unwanted, worthless, or unloved. Psychological abuse often accompanies other forms of child maltreatment, but it can also take place independently. It is typically quite hard to discover, and children experiencing such maltreatment rarely get appropriate therapeutic help. Less legal attention is also paid to this kind of abuse. This is unfortunate, because research indicates that psychological abuse can have detrimental effects on children's development and well-being.

Incidence of Child Abuse

Children from birth to 3 years of age are most at risk of being victims of reported child abuse and neglect. Of all cases reported and investigated, approximately one third are supported by enough evidence for authorities to determine that abuse actually occurred. The remainder lack evidence sufficient to support legal action, which does not necessarily mean that abuse did not take place. In fact, trends in re-referral rates (i.e., children reported as maltreated on multiple occasions) suggest that many unsubstantiated cases probably represent real abuse. Furthermore, even the total number of reported cases is likely to be a serious underestimate of the actual occurrence of child abuse, because child victims are often reluctant to disclose their experiences. For example, research reveals that about a quarter of young adults who experience child

sexual abuse and a third of those who experience physical abuse never tell anyone about their maltreatment. Among those who do tell, fewer than 10% report the abuse to authorities.

Throughout the 1980s, mandatory reporting laws increased the number of child maltreatment cases that were reported and that entered the child protection and criminal justice systems. Reporting levelled off during the 1990s and has even been declining in recent years. Research suggests that this decline, at least in part, reflects an actual decrease in the incidence of child maltreatment, suggesting that societal prevention efforts have been successful.

Potential Effects of Child Maltreatment

Many maltreated children are remarkably resilient and lead normal, healthy lives. Even so, child maltreatment often does have very serious short- and long-term physical and psychological consequences, leaving physical and psychological scars that can last well after the abuse or neglect has ended. Children who experience maltreatment can suffer immediate physical consequences, including broken bones, burns, bruises, abrasions, sexually transmitted diseases, pregnancy, malnutrition, declining health, or even death. Long-term psychological and behavioral outcomes can include internalizing behaviors (withdrawal, depression, anxiety) and externalizing behaviors (aggression, bullying, promiscuity). Child maltreatment can also increase the likelihood of development of serious psychopathology such as posttraumatic stress disorder (PTSD). Children who are maltreated may have difficulties establishing trusting relationships with their peers and adults. Moreover, experiencing maltreatment is associated with deficits, on average, in children's cognitive development, which, in addition to socioemotional deficits, also directly affects academic performance and school achievement. Children who have been maltreated are at an elevated risk of becoming delinquents, substance abusers, and victims of additional crimes.

Researchers struggle to identify the relations between particular forms of child abuse and specific outcomes, especially since different forms of maltreatment often co-occur. With careful analysis, however, some patterns have begun to emerge. For example, it is clear that sexual abuse is a risk factor for later substance abuse, depression, and attentional problems. Additionally, women who are victims of child sexual abuse are more likely than women who have not been sexually abused to engage in prostitution. Physical abuse is associated with substance abuse and aggressive behaviors. Neglect victims tend to perform poorly on cognitive tests and may be socially withdrawn. Neglect is often associated with extreme poverty, which itself has detrimental consequences for children's cognitive, social, and emotional development, as well as for their academic achievement.

Many factors moderate the impact of maltreatment on children's short- and long-term outcomes, including the child's gender, the child's age at abuse onset and offset, the frequency and severity of abuse, the child's coping ability, the abuser-victim relationship, and many broader family and community factors. For instance, there is some evidence that maltreated boys have poorer outcomes than maltreated girls. Social scientists have proposed a variety of explanations for this, such as male genetic vulnerability or the fact that behavioral difficulties are more easily measured in boys, who tend to exhibit externalizing rather than internalizing problem behaviors. A younger age at abuse onset is also thought to be related to especially adverse outcomes, although a firm pattern has not been established. Children who are younger when abuse occurs may not recall as much detail about their abuse, but it may be implicitly retained and expressed in their personality development. Moreover, child outcomes may be influenced by the cumulative effects of maltreatment. A child who suffers less severe or chronic abuse may be less likely to have poor psychological or behavioral outcomes than a child who experiences more extensive, frequent, and varied types of abuse.

How does maltreatment cause these varied effects? Scientists currently propose several different mechanisms. For example, because children's brains develop more rapidly during the first year of life than at any other point, some researchers theorize that the developing brain is particularly susceptible to traumatization, which may explain the negative impact of very early abuse.

Another explanation involves the influence of abuse on children's personality development. Young children are forming key attachments with others, and if this process is challenged, children's perceptions or expectations of others can be permanently affected. That is, according to attachment theory, infants form secure or insecure attachments with their caregivers based on the caregivers' sensitivity and responsiveness. Children's early experiences with caregivers shape children's developing mental models of how they can expect to be treated by others in the future. Thus, these first key relationships influence children's later relationships with peers and romantic partners, and even their approach to work, religion, and other major facets of life. Children who grow up in an abusive or neglectful environment, which is typically characterized by an absence of or inconsistency in sensitivity and responsiveness, are quite likely to develop insecure attachment styles, such as avoidant or disorganized attachment. Research shows that children who are insecurely attached are more likely to develop poor emotion regulation abilities and deficient interpersonal skills than do children who are securely attached to their caregivers. Children with disorganized attachments are at particular risk of mental health problems.

Another common explanation for the psychological difficulties that result from maltreatment focuses on the adverse influence of PTSD on children's psychological, social, and cognitive development. Many children who experience abuse suffer from PTSD, an acute syndrome characterized by intrusive thoughts, flashbacks, and hypervigilance. PTSD occurs in some individuals who experience an extremely traumatic event or situation, typically one that threatens the individual's health and safety. Psychological research has demonstrated that PTSD is associated with deficits in certain areas of memory performance, language ability, and attentional capacity (although such deficits are not necessarily global). Of note, people who suffer from PTSD have selective attention or memory bias for information that is trauma related, which can result in particularly accurate memories of trauma experiences. PTSD does not appear to affect IQ, although IQ and other cognitive factors are thought to be related to PTSD. Some researchers currently contend that suffering from PTSD may cause neuroanatomical changes in regions of the brain associated with memory and learning (e.g., the hippocampus), in areas associated with cognitive control (e.g., the prefrontal cortex), or in the entire cerebral cortex. Yet the effects of maltreatment and PTSD on the human brain are not easy to determine, and it is unclear whether PTSD causes changes in the brain structure or whether preexisting structural anomalies or preexisting behavioral or cognitive capabilities cause PTSD.

Finally, and of particular importance, research has identified a number of factors that promote resilience (or better than expected psychological or behavioral outcomes) in maltreated children, including having histories characterized by secure attachments and quality relationships with supportive adults or peers, an active or approach-oriented coping style, good social problem-solving skills, and greater sociability. Children who have at least one adult who cares for them in a positive way and children who receive effective therapeutic treatment are particularly likely to have the best outcomes. Understanding such factors can lead to better therapeutic interventions aimed at alleviating the effects of child maltreatment.

Causes of Child Maltreatment

The causes of child maltreatment are varied; there is likely no single cause. For instance, social learning theory suggests that child maltreatment is a learned behavior. Thus, parents who were maltreated as children may have learned, through their own childhood experiences, coercive forms of discipline or neglectful patterns rather than learning appropriate, nonabusive parenting practices. In this way, child maltreatment can be transmitted intergenerationally. In fact, a higher percentage of children who experienced maltreatment themselves, as compared with children who did not experience maltreatment, go on to abuse their own children later in life. Note that this does not mean, contrary to popular belief, that most children who have been abused go on to abuse their own children. The majority of adults who were abused as children are not abusive. Thus, there are many other potential contributors to child abuse and neglect, including an abundance of life stressors (e.g., poverty, lack of community resources, social isolation), individual personality or psychopathological traits, child-specific factors (e.g., a child's temperament or disability), cultural or community acceptance of maltreatment, and even religious beliefs about eschewing modern medical care and applying strict corporal discipline.

Prevention and Intervention

How should society act to prevent and deter child maltreatment? Characteristics of the child, the abuser, and the family, as well as the broader social context in which the abuse takes place, all play a role in causing child maltreatment. Thus, prevention efforts must take each of these factors into consideration. A host of interventions and changes are needed at the individual and societal levels to prevent child maltreatment. One obvious and effective societal-level strategy is to establish laws that make child abuse illegal. In some countries, even spanking a child is prohibited. With the current U.S. laws, if child maltreatment is discovered and reported, it may lead to the child or family's involvement with the criminal justice system and/or the child protective services system. Criminal court actions, which sometimes require the testimony of child victims, can stop existing abuse and prevent new maltreatment by sending perpetrators to jail and by deterring other potential perpetrators with the threat of similar prosecution. Child protective services actions against familial perpetrators can prevent further maltreatment through a range of actions, from requiring that parents attend parenting classes to temporary or even permanent removal of the child from its home, with parents sometimes losing parental rights and the child being put into the foster care system. If a child is young and not disabled, the likelihood is increased that he or she might be adopted into a new home. Unfortunately, however, many foster care children become immersed in juvenile court (e.g., dependency) actions and find themselves being bounced from foster home to foster home, which are sometimes themselves settings for additional abuse. Children's involvement in the legal and child welfare systems (e.g., multiple foster care placements, repeated testimony in criminal court) can have negative effects on their emotional well-being.

Other laws aimed at prevention of child sexual abuse include sex offender registration and community notification laws, which require perpetrators of sexual abuse, after they have finished serving their prison sentence, to register publicly as a sex offender everywhere they subsequently live. These laws are controversial because of civil rights issues, and there is no solid evidence that they really reduce child maltreatment. Other societal-level reform strategies involve efforts to educate the public and change attitudes, behaviors, and even public policy, often through media campaigns. For example, educational media campaigns such as those aimed at teaching parents not to shake babies have also achieved some success in the effort to decrease child physical abuse.

Whatever the means, the importance of preventing child maltreatment is underscored by the wide-ranging costs of child maltreatment, which ripple across a broad spectrum of social structures, including the medical and health systems, the legal and correctional systems, public health services, child welfare services, and educational institutions.

Given all these potential negative outcomes, some suggest that child maltreatment is one of the greatest social evils of our time, one that must be fought with a great deal of financial and human resources. Even so, as mentioned earlier, there is hope: Child maltreatment rates have begun to decline, at least in the United States. And many victims, although not unaffected by their experiences, nevertheless grow up to lead productive lives as good parents and citizens.

Bette L. Bottoms, LaTonya Harris,
Else-Marie Augusti, Gail S. Goodman,
Barbara A. Oudekerk, and Tisha R. A. Wiley

See also Child Abuse Potential (CAP) Inventory; Children's Testimony; Children's Testimony, Evaluation by Juries; Child Sexual Abuse; Conduct Disorder; Conflict Tactics Scale (CTS); Criminal Behavior, Theories of; Eyewitness Memory; False Memories; Intimate Partner Violence; Juvenile Offenders, Risk Factors; Mental Health Needs of Juvenile Offenders; Mood Disorders; Parens Patriae Doctrine; Parent-Child Relationship Inventory (PCRI); Parenting Stress Index (PSI); Pedophilia; Reporting Crimes and Victimization; Victimization

Further Readings

Appleyard, K., Egeland, B., Van Dulmen, M., & Sroufe, A. (2005). When more is not better: The cumulative role of risk in child behavior outcomes. *Journal of Child Psychology and Psychiatry, 3,* 235–245.

Bottoms, B. L., & Quas, J. A. (Eds.). (2006). Emerging directions in child maltreatment research. *Journal of Social Issues, 62,* 653–863.

Cicchetti, D., & Toth, S. L. (2006). A developmental psychopathology perspective on preventive interventions with high risk children and families. In A. Renninger & I. Sigel (Eds.), *Handbook of child psychology* (6th ed.). New York: Wiley.

Goodman, G. S., Emery, R., & Haugaard, J. (1997). Developmental psychology and law: Divorce, child maltreatment, foster care, and adoption. In I. Sigel & A. Renninger (Eds.), *Handbook of child psychology: Vol. 4. Child psychology in practice* (5th ed., pp. 775–876). New York: Wiley.

Myers, J. E., Berliner, L., Briere, J., Hendrix, C. T., Jenny, C., & Reid, T. (Eds.). (2002). *The APSAC handbook on child maltreatment.* Thousand Oaks, CA: Sage.

Schwartz-Kenny, B. M., McCauley, M., & Epstein, M. A. (Eds.). (2001). *Child abuse: A global view.* Westport, CT: Greenwood Press.

Sroufe, L. A., Carlson, E. A., Levy, A. K., & Egeland, B. (2003). Implications of attachment theory for developmental psychopathology. In M. Hertzig & E. A. Farber (Eds.), *Annual progress in child psychiatry and child development: 2000–2001* (pp. 43–61). New York: Brunner-Routledge.

CHILDREN'S TESTIMONY

Children may experience or witness crime and may need to provide reports to authorities. Children's eyewitness accounts can contain critical information about serious acts such as murder, domestic violence, kidnapping, and assault. Child sexual abuse is particularly likely to bring children into contact with the criminal justice system because the case may boil down to the child's word against that of the accused. Although even young children can provide accurate accounts of their experiences, including highly traumatic incidents, such children on average are both less complete in their memory reports and more suggestible than older children and adults.

Like adults' accounts, children's accounts are influenced by numerous factors, including cognitive, social, and individual ones. Developmentally appropriate interview protocols may contribute to obtaining complete and accurate accounts while reducing inaccuracies in a child's testimony. As part of a forensic interview, children may have to identify culprits from photo lineups. Children 5 years and older can perform quite well if the culprit is pictured in the lineup; however, in "target-absent" lineups, even older children have a strong tendency to guess. Children's emotional and attitudinal reactions to providing eyewitness testimony in criminal cases can be long lasting. For example, testifying multiple times, especially in severe intrafamilial child sexual abuse cases, is associated with adverse emotional and attitudinal reactions into adulthood. Children in such cases may need additional legal protections.

Memory and Suggestibility in the Child Witness

During the past several decades, there has been an exponential increase in the number of children who provide statements in legal cases, thus magnifying the need to determine the credibility of their testimony.

In general, older children are more accurate in eyewitness reports than are younger children, although even preschool-age children can provide accurate accounts of salient or personally meaningful events, including their own victimization. When asked free recall and open-ended questions, preschoolers can recall relevant and accurate information, but on average they are less responsive and provide fewer spontaneous statements than older children and adults. Because young children's free reports are generally relatively brief and incomplete, they are often exposed to specific and leading questions in forensic situations, which are indeed more likely to elicit the child's memory of an event. On the negative side, however, children are less accurate than adults in response to specific questions and more vulnerable to interviewers' implied suggestions. Particularly, closed questions, such as yes/no and forced-choice questions, can be problematic for young children, because they may guess instead of providing "I don't know" responses. Children also often have considerable difficulty in using standardized units of measurement, such as minutes and months, and in indicating the number of times highly repeated acts have occurred, even though such information can be vital in a legal case.

Usually, children's testimony is required for crimes or experiences that are negative, if not traumatic. Although this is a subject of debate, considerable research with adults suggests that for stressful compared with nonstressful events, central features (e.g., the main stressors) are retained particularly well, whereas peripheral details are less well remembered. Several studies confirm such findings for children; however, the results of developmental studies are mixed.

Child sexual abuse often involves trauma to child victims, leading to feelings of self-blame and helplessness. These characteristics have contributed to make child sexual abuse situations of special interest in debates about trauma and memory. Research suggests that memory of traumatic events, in many ways, follows the same cognitive principles as memory of distinctive nontraumatic events. However, there is debate as to whether "special memory mechanisms" (e.g., repression) are also involved.

Some of the main theoretical accounts of trauma and memory suggest that traumatized individuals remember trauma-related information particularly well. Empirical evidence confirms that traumatized individuals, especially those who have developed posttraumatic stress disorder, overfocus on trauma cues, have difficulty ignoring trauma stimuli, and remember their trauma experiences. In contrast, other theories indicate that trauma victims, such as incest survivors, may experience amnesia for the trauma and that children who have suffered a larger number of traumatic events tend to forget or remember more poorly those experiences compared with children who have been exposed to a single traumatic event.

Children's memory and testimony about negative emotional experiences also depend on individuals' coping strategies. Avoidant coping strategies lead children to evade thoughts, conversations, or reminders about the traumatic experiences. Parents' attempts to minimize or ignore their own or their children's distress facilitate avoidant coping. These postevent avoidance processes may prevent the creation of a complete, detailed, and verbally accessible account of the traumatic experience and the integration of these memories with the individual's other autobiographical memories. In contrast, positive parent-child interactions provide an opportunity for rehearsal and reactivation of event details, which may help maintain and strengthen memory traces, thus reducing the effects of decay while enhancing long-term retention. For example, children who received maternal support after disclosure of child sexual abuse and who discussed the event with their mothers provided more accurate reports, with fewer omission errors, of their maltreatment experiences years after the abuse reportedly ended compared with those who did not.

Children's suggestibility in the forensic context has been a flash point in the debate over children's testimonial competence. Suggestibility concerns the degree to which the encoding, storage, retrieval, and reporting of events can be influenced by a range of internal (e.g., developmental, cognitive, and personality) and external (e.g., social and contextual) factors. False information given before, during, and after an event can lead to difficulty in retrieving the original (true) information, alteration of true memory representations, and/or conscious acquiescence to social demands. Young children, specifically preschoolers, are disproportionately susceptible to the effects of leading questions and suggestions. However, of importance in the legal context, children are often less suggestible about negative than positive or neutral events.

Both cognitive and social factors can underlie developmental differences in eyewitness memory and suggestibility. Due to a less complete knowledge base and more limited capabilities of using memory strategies, young children have greater difficulty recalling events on their own. Also, compared with adults' memories, children's memories of the original event may be weaker and thus more vulnerable to being altered or overwritten by the suggestions of others. "False memory" may occur when the erroneous suggestion is particularly strong, such as in multiple suggestive contexts where not only misleading questions but also an accusatory context is involved. In addition, preschoolers are less able to distinguish between different sources of memories and thus misattribute an interviewer's suggestions to actual experiences. Moreover, without understanding the ramifications of their statements, children may adopt suggestions to gain the adult investigator's approval and avoid negative reactions, perceiving pressure to conform to the suggestions of the authority figure.

Although there is consensus that misleading questions and highly suggestive contexts are to be avoided when interviewing children, such questioning does not necessarily lead to false reports. For example, if the child's memory is strong, blatantly misleading questioning in a highly misleading context can actually bolster resistance to misinformation, at least compared with the effects of such questioning after a long delay, when the child's memory traces have weakened. However, with such questioning, the risks of memory contamination are potentially great, and the child's credibility may be destroyed in the process.

Individual Difference Factors

Although chronological age is almost always the strongest predictor of suggestibility, with preschool children being the most suggestible, even adults are suggestible. Moreover, there is much variability within age groups depending on the characteristics of the individual. However, findings concerning individual differences tend to be somewhat inconsistent, and the predictive power of individual difference factors tends not to be strong. That said, global, comprehensive measures of language ability are sometimes associated with preschool-age children's suggestibility. Children with mental retardation are more suggestible than typically developing children with normal intelligence, although intelligence is not significantly related to suggestibility within the normal population. Young children with poor self-concepts or poor supportive relationships with their parents are at risk of being more suggestible. Children raised by secure and

supportive parents may develop positive self-concepts, which in turn may make them resistant to suggestions that are inconsistent with their own experiences. Cultural factors may also play a role; in cultures where children are trained to be especially polite or obedient to adult authority, they may have more difficulty disagreeing with adult interviewers who falsely suggest information.

Interview Techniques and Protocols

How likely children are to disclose crimes such as child sexual abuse when simply asked free-recall and open-ended questions is the subject of debate. Researchers have developed child interview techniques and standardized child interview protocols intended to increase the likelihood of disclosure as well as the amount and accuracy of the information obtained, while reducing inaccuracies. These protocols (e.g., cognitive interview, narrative elaboration) derive from the application of mnemonic, communication, and social facilitative techniques to forensic practice and can in principle be used to interview child witnesses about a wide variety of events; however, some protocols are specifically designed for interviewing alleged child victims of child sexual abuse (e.g., the National Institute of Child Health and Human Development [NICHD] structured interview protocol). Overall, interview protocols and interview guidelines (e.g., the guidelines developed by the American Professional Society on the Abuse of Children) recommend that forensic interviewers rely as much as possible on free-recall/open-ended prompts. However, the use of some specific questioning is typically also allowed. We review a subset of the protocols/techniques next.

The cognitive interview (CI) relies on well-established principles of encoding specificity (i.e., how the items to be retrieved were encoded and stored determines the effectiveness of a particular retrieval cue) and varied retrieval. According to these principles, the original CI (developed for adults) included four mnemonic techniques: (1) "mental reinstatement" of the external and internal contexts of the experienced event; (2) the "report everything" instruction; (3) the "reverse-order-recall" instruction, which refers to recalling the event in an alternative temporal order; and (4) the "change perspective" instruction, which refers to recalling the event from an alternative perspective. Also, to avoid the common problems observed during the administration of the CI by professionals, the revised CI includes several social techniques intended to facilitate communication (e.g., rapport building, no interruptions). Compared with control interviews, the developmentally adapted CI for children ranging in age from 4 to 12 years, tends to elicit more correct information, although the reverse-order-recall and change perspective instructions may increase the reporting of incorrect details by young children. Moreover, the mental reinstatement and report everything mnemonics appear to be useful in reducing the negative effects of misinformation even in preschool-age children (i.e., 4–5 years).

Rather than supplying specific cues derived from the event itself, narrative elaboration (NE) provides child witnesses with pre-interview training, instructions, and techniques that could be applied to any event of interest. NE's main objective is to help overcome potential developmental limitations in communication and memory, such as lack of knowledge about the expectations of the listener and ineffective use of memory search strategies, by training children about the level of detail required and by providing picture cards as external cues to report forensically important categories of information. Overall, NE is helpful in enhancing children's eyewitness recall without increasing the amount of inaccuracies provided by 3- to 11-year-old children.

Similarly, after an initial rapport-building phase, the NICHD interview protocol incorporates training of children to respond to open-ended prompts during the presubstantive phase of the investigative interview. Next, the interviewer attempts to shift the child's focus to the substantive issue in a nonsuggestive manner (e.g., "Tell me why you came to talk to me today"), so that the recollection process can begin. During this substantive phase, interviewers maximize the use of open-ended questions and probes, introducing focused questions only after exhausting the open-ended-question modes. At the end of the session, interviewers may use option-posing questions to obtain essential information. This protocol is flexibly structured and aimed to translate research-based recommendations into operational guidelines to enhance children's retrieval using recall-memory prompts. It has been extensively investigated with real alleged child victims of sexual offenses, and it appears to be useful with children 4 years and older.

Basic and applied research underlies the development of interview techniques and protocols. However, further research on the accuracy of children's eyewitness memory—for example, concerning highly emotional and embarrassing information—is necessary to elucidate how extensive these benefits are. And, of special relevance, improved strategies and tools that can be effectively used with young children (e.g., 3-year-olds) to obtain evidence about specific details of an event without compromising the accuracy of their reports are still needed.

Props and Cues

Children typically have more information in memory than they report in response to free-recall or open-ended questions. Props such as real objects, scale models, dolls, toys, photographs, and drawings can provide concrete external retrieval cues for young children. They also can potentially extend memory retrieval by engaging children in the forensic interview for a longer period than do mere verbal prompts. According to the principle of encoding specificity, the effectiveness of a particular retrieval prop or cue depends on its match with the items to be retrieved with regard to how they were encoded and stored. Especially for younger children, an optimal match should include the original sensory/perceptual features as well as a clear symbolic correspondence.

Overall, props can facilitate children's reports but also increase the number of errors children make (e.g., if they are too young to understand dual representations). The extent to which props facilitate or compromise children's testimony depends on factors such as the nature of the event and of the prop, the mode of presentation, and the time that has elapsed between the event and the interview. And the age of the child may be critical in determining the influence of these factors.

Real props have maximal overlap with event information and can effectively aid retrieval for 3- to 10-year-olds. Real props and scale models increase the correct information that children report, but they also introduce additional errors, especially for younger children. In contrast to real props, toys and dolls, including anatomically detailed dolls, can increase commission errors and decrease accuracy, especially when preschool-age children are interviewed with misleading questions or when "distractor" or play-evoking props are involved. Under certain circumstances (i.e., in combination with specific but nonleading prompts), drawings can facilitate the completeness and accuracy of 5-years-olds' and older children's accounts, although there are mixed findings in relation to the effectiveness of drawings with preschool children. Finally, human figure drawings can produce a considerable amount of new details during the interview, especially for children aged from 4 to 7 years, but at the same time, these drawings may also increase inaccuracies in children's testimony.

In summary, research has shown that props and drawings can, under certain circumstances, facilitate memory accuracy in children older than 5 years, whereas they may add error to the reports of younger children. Although there is currently no "gold standard" method of interviewing children, different combinations of free-recall, specific, and prop-assisted questions are being researched to determine which of them facilitates the most accurate and complete memory reports from children.

Photo Lineups

When interviewed in forensic situations, children may be presented with photographic lineups to identify culprits. A lineup may include a criminal (target-present lineup) or only innocent individuals (target-absent lineup). When they are shown a target-present lineup, preschool-age children are less likely than adults to make correct identifications, although children around age 5 and above are typically comparable with adults in making correct identifications. Shown a target-absent lineup, however, even early adolescents are inferior to adults, making fewer correct rejections and more false identifications. As with leading questions, the photo lineup may entice children to guess.

Witnesses are usually shown a simultaneous lineup, in which all lineup members are presented at once and only one decision is made. This method has been criticized for encouraging a relative judgment, whereby witnesses compare all lineup members and choose the member who looks most like the criminal relative to other members. Although this strategy is successful in target-present lineups, it may lead to errors in target-absent lineups. Fortunately, fairly simple training techniques can reduce guessing on target-absent lineups in older children.

An alternative procedure is the sequential lineup, in which witnesses are shown photographs one at a time and make a decision for each photograph. Compared with simultaneous lineups, sequential lineups reduce adults' false identifications by increasing correct rejections of target-absent lineups while having a minimal effect on correct identifications from target-present lineups. When they are shown a sequential lineup, witnesses might make an absolute judgment for each photograph by comparing the photograph with their recollection of the criminal. However, target-absent errors by children are not reduced in sequential compared with simultaneous procedures.

Children in the Courtroom

As a result of involvement with legal authorities, children may experience social and emotional distress. Although repeated interviewing of children can keep accurate memories alive, child victims report that being interviewed multiple times by legal authorities is stressful for them. Speaking about traumatic experiences (particularly in open court), lack of parental support, harsh cross-examination, facing the defendant, and not being believed add to children's distress and may reduce significantly the amount of information provided by child witnesses. Moreover, in child sexual abuse cases, a child's initial disclosure of the abuse to a parent, teacher, or other trusted adult may include a more detailed account than the testimony that the child gives in court months or even years later. Although testifying may be helpful for some children, it causes others to recover from the criminal and legal experience more slowly than their nontestifying counterparts. Child sexual abuse victims who had to testify multiple times in severe intrafamilial cases tend to have the most negative long-term emotional effects and are thus most in need of protection during criminal prosecutions. To remedy these negative consequences, procedural modifications (e.g., testifying via closed-circuit television) and multidisciplinary investigations, conducted at child advocacy centers and involving teams of legal professionals (e.g., the police, prosecuting attorneys, and child protective services workers), who coordinate their efforts into a single interview of the child victim/witness, are being developed and tested in the United States and abroad.

Having an adult (e.g., a mother, social worker, or police officer) recount children's out-of-court statements (e.g., hearsay) at trial has recently attracted research and legal interest. In criminal trials regarding child sexual abuse, hearsay is often introduced in addition to the child's live testimony. Although hearsay is normally discouraged in the American legal system, there are special hearsay exceptions, some of which apply specifically to children's statements. However, a recent U.S. Supreme Court ruling suggests that if the out-of-court statement was made to an authority (e.g., a forensic interviewer) and is thus "testimonial," the authority cannot testify in place of the child.

Mock jurors find children's statements more credible when the child testifies live in court than if the child is replaced by a hearsay witness. Mock jurors also find children less credible if they testify via closed-circuit television instead of face-to-face at trial. Both hearsay and closed-circuit television are potential ways to protect children from the stress of testifying live in court and are used in many European countries.

*Pedro M. Paz-Alonso, Yoojin Chae,
and Gail S. Goodman*

See also Child Maltreatment; Children's Testimony, Evaluation by Juries; Child Sexual Abuse; Cognitive Interview; Expert Psychological Testimony; Eyewitness Memory; False Memories; Hearsay Testimony; Lineup Size and Bias; Postevent Information and Eyewitness Memory; Reporting Crimes and Victimization; Repressed and Recovered Memories; Simultaneous and Sequential Lineup Presentation; Witness Preparation

Further Readings

Bruck, M., & Melnyk, L. (2004). Individual differences in children's suggestibility: A review and synthesis. *Applied Cognitive Psychology*, *18*, 947–996.

Castelli, P., Goodman, G. S., Edelstein, R. S., Mitchell, E. B., Paz-Alonso, P. M., Lyons, K. E., et al. (2006). Evaluating eyewitness testimony in adults and children. In I. B. Weiner & A. K. Hess (Eds.), *The handbook of forensic psychology* (3rd ed., pp. 243–302). Hoboken, NJ: Wiley.

Ceci, S. J., & Bruck, M. (1995). *Jeopardy in the courtroom: A scientific analysis of children's testimony*. Washington, DC: American Psychological Association.

Eisen, M. L., Quas, J. A., & Goodman, G. S. (2002). *Memory and suggestibility in the forensic interview*. Mahwah, NJ: Lawrence Erlbaum.

Pipe, M.-E., Lamb, M., Orbach, Y., & Cederborg, A.-C. (2006). *Child sexual abuse: Disclosure, delay, and denial*. Mahwah, NJ: Lawrence Erlbaum.

Poole, D. A., & Lamb, M. E. (1998). *Investigative interviews of children: A guide for helping professionals*. Washington, DC: American Psychological Association.

Pozzulo, J. D., & Lindsay, R. C. L. (1998). Identification accuracy of children versus adults: A meta-analysis. *Law and Human Behavior*, *22*, 549–570.

CHILDREN'S TESTIMONY, EVALUATION BY JURIES

When children are involved in trials as witnesses, victims, or defendants, jurors must decide whether they are credible and how to weigh their testimony in reaching a verdict. Thus, although much psychological research focuses on the *actual* accuracy of children's eyewitness testimony, it is also important to consider their *perceived* accuracy. Research reveals that jurors consider many factors when making decisions about children's testimony. In this entry, we review what is known about jurors' perceptions of testimony given by children and adolescents who are bystander witnesses, alleged child abuse victims/ witnesses, and juvenile defendants.

Can jurors determine whether child witnesses are accurate or inaccurate, telling the truth or lying? Some research reveals that adults are not very adept at discerning children's actual accuracies from inaccuracies or at detecting lies from the truth, although adults can detect children's (especially older children's) lies with slightly greater than chance accuracy. Consistent with findings from the adult eyewitness literature, part of the problem is that jurors appear to overuse the dubious marker of child confidence in judging child accuracy, which is misleading because the relation between child confidence and child accuracy is not always strong. More research is needed to ensure that these results hold true in situations where children give incorrect or false testimony about events of great personal significance, which has not been the case with most research on this topic. Even so, existing research is converging on the conclusion that adults cannot detect children's actual level of accuracy well. A growing body of research has thus focused on identifying the factors other than actual accuracy that affect jurors' perceptions of children's eyewitness testimony.

Perceptions of Bystander Witnesses

Gail Goodman and her colleagues conducted the first studies of jurors' perceptions of child witnesses. They evaluated jurors' reactions to bystander testimony given in the context of vehicular homicide and murder cases. Although all jurors read the same testimony, some were told that the key prosecution witness was an adult, while others were told that the witness was a child. Individual jurors perceived child witnesses to be less credible than adult witnesses, an effect that was not tempered by jury deliberation. This research provided the first evidence that jurors—and juries— are skeptical of children's ability to provide accurate testimony, presumably because jurors doubt young children's cognitive abilities to encode and retrieve details of events accurately. Even so, witness age did not directly affect jurors' ratings of the defendant's guilt. Instead, jurors based their verdicts primarily on witness testimony only when the witness was an adult. When the witness was a child, jurors gave greater consideration to other case evidence. Thus, although jurors often report that they consider corroborating evidence when making decisions, this is especially true when the primary source of evidence is child testimony. In fact, later research showed that jurors perceive individual child witnesses more positively when their testimony is corroborated by other credible child witnesses.

Perceptions of Alleged Victims of Child Maltreatment

After the first studies of jurors' perceptions of child bystander witnesses, research quickly turned to jurors' perceptions of child victim witnesses—specifically alleged child sexual abuse victims. This shift reflected the increased societal attention in the 1980s to child sexual abuse, as well as the fact that child sexual abuse is usually perpetrated in secret, with little corroborating evidence, making child victim testimony key to its prosecution. This research has revealed that jurors' decisions are influenced by many factors. For example, jurors generally find child sexual abuse victims who are younger than about 13 years more believable than older children. Why? Jurors' belief that younger children are less cognitively competent than older children (which hurts the perceived credibility of child bystander witnesses) actually works to the advantage of child sexual abuse victims. That is, compared with older children, younger children are perceived as sexually naive and therefore less cognitively capable of fabricating allegations of sexual abuse that did not actually occur. Younger children are also seen as more honest and therefore less likely to lie about such matters. In fact, for the same reasons, jurors perceive intellectually disabled (i.e., mentally retarded) teenaged sexual abuse victims to be more credible than children of average intelligence. In fact, intellectually disabled children are sexually victimized more often than nondisabled children, but prosecutors might hesitate to prosecute such cases, fearing that jurors will not believe disabled witnesses.

A number of other factors also influence jurors' perceptions of child sexual abuse victims, including victim and defendant factors such as gender and race, case factors such as whether the child's disclosure of abuse was portrayed as delayed or repressed, and juror individual difference factors such as gender and attitudes. For example, one of the most robust findings in this field is that compared with men jurors, women are on average more likely to convict defendants and to perceive children as credible witnesses. This may be driven by the fact that compared with men, women empathize more with child victims and have somewhat more prochild and anti-child-abuse attitudes.

Recently, attention has begun to turn to adults' reactions to children who are alleged victims of other forms of child maltreatment. For example, studies in which adults consider brief vignettes of maltreatment situations indicate that neglect is perceived to be more severe when a victim is younger rather than older, perhaps reflecting people's awareness that compared with older children, younger children are less able to care for themselves and may experience more adverse consequences from neglect. In contrast, people perceive psychological abuse to be more severe when the victim is older rather than younger, perhaps reflecting the belief that older children are more likely to experience damage to their self-concept. Perceptions of physical abuse severity are not influenced by age, suggesting that people disapprove of physically abusing children of any age. Although the possibility has not yet been tested within a mock trial paradigm, jurors may be similarly influenced by these variables in trials involving these forms of child maltreatment.

Psychologists are sometimes allowed to testify as expert witnesses in trials about issues of psychological relevance that jurors do not intuitively understand. Scholars disagree about the conditions under which expert psychological testimony about children's actual eyewitness abilities should be allowed. Surveys reveal that some portion of the jury pool is knowledgeable about children's actual memory, suggestibility, and tendency to disclose sexual abuse, but other jurors are not. Most jurors have a poor understanding of the clinical symptoms exhibited by abused and nonabused children, forensic interview techniques that increase the risk of false allegations versus those that promote true disclosures of abuse, and whether children are prone to confabulate and internalize false memories of abuse. (Women and more highly educated jurors are more knowledgeable about such issues than other jurors.) Some argue that expert testimony would be a valuable tool for countering jurors' ignorance, while others fear that expert testimony will increase unfounded skepticism about children's abilities.

Research by Margaret Kovera and her colleagues has shown that expert testimony is useful in educating jurors about at least one particular issue: the hazards of basing credibility judgments on child witnesses' non-verbal cues and countenance. That is, jurors expect abused children to be emotionally upset when testifying about their sexual victimization, and when this expectation is not met, jurors doubt the veracity of abuse allegations. Expert testimony can inform jurors that most child victims have repeated their stories so many times before appearing in court that some no longer appear emotionally distraught. Such testimony can reduce jurors' otherwise negative bias against child sexual abuse victim witnesses, which results from incorrect assumptions about the relation between emotion and accuracy.

Regardless of how they appear, testifying in court can be a traumatic experience for some child witnesses. To protect children from this potential trauma, the U.S. Supreme Court declared it constitutionally permissible under some conditions for children to testify using innovative techniques that shield them from the defendant. For example, rather than testifying in an open courtroom in front of the defendant, child victim witnesses may testify elsewhere in the courthouse while their testimony is transmitted to the courtroom via closed-circuit television (CCTV). Or child witnesses can give their testimony in court with their view of the defendant blocked by a screen. How do such accommodations affect jurors' perceptions of child testimony? Although defense attorneys fear that jurors will infer a defendant's guilt from the use of accommodations and give undue weight to testimony presented under such circumstances, ironically, mock trial research suggests that jurors perceive child witnesses to be less credible when testimony is presented via CCTV than when children testify live in court. This may result from accommodated children appearing less stressed than children who testify in full view of the court, which may signal the need for psychological expert testimony for the reasons discussed previously.

Perceptions of Child Defendants

Recent research has begun to consider jurors' perceptions of children who are accused of committing crimes. This has become increasingly important because more and more teenagers are being tried in adult criminal court instead of juvenile or family court, and their cases are being decided by jurors rather than by juvenile court judges. Unfortunately, research suggests that trying a juvenile in adult criminal court is inherently prejudicial. For example, jurors infer that juveniles tried in adult criminal court have been convicted of past crimes, and this inference increases the likelihood of conviction. In reality, most felony juvenile offenders (i.e., juveniles whose cases are most likely to go to trial in adult criminal court) have never been arrested before. Jurors' judgments are also influenced by the severity of the crime (jurors perceive juveniles as more competent and render more severe sentences when the crime and its outcome are more severe) and by inferences regarding a juvenile's intent to commit a crime, understanding of wrongfulness, and recidivism potential. Many psychologists are concerned that jurors might not understand juveniles' actual capabilities in these regards and that jurors are insensitive to the fact that juveniles are less cognitively competent and mature than adults. Research on this issue is mixed. Although some jurors appear to set lower standards of proof for juveniles tried in adult criminal court than for adults, jurors are less likely to convict younger juveniles than older juveniles, perhaps because they believe that younger juveniles are less competent to stand trial. Under some conditions, however, jurors perceive younger and older juveniles to be equally competent. Meanwhile, other research has identified juror and case characteristics that influence jurors' perceptions of child and adolescent offenders. For example, as in child sexual abuse cases, women jurors appear to have more positive perceptions of juvenile offenders than men do. Also, situational trial factors can influence trial outcomes: Attorneys' pleas for jurors to empathize with a juvenile offender lead jurors to be more sensitive to mitigating factors, perceive the juvenile to be less responsible for the crime, and render more lenient judgments relative to jurors who are not asked to empathize.

Future Research

Future research will provide an even better understanding of the factors that influence jurors' perceptions of children in the courtroom and, importantly, the processes by which those perceptions influence jurors' verdicts. Psychologists hope that this knowledge can be used to inform a legal policy that ensures justice for all parties involved in trials.

Cynthia J. Najdowski and Bette L. Bottoms

See also Child Maltreatment; Children's Testimony; Child
    Sexual Abuse; Hearsay Testimony; Juries and
    Eyewitnesses; Juvenile Offenders

Further Readings

Bottoms, B. L., Golding, J. M., Stevenson, M. C., Wiley, T. R. A., & Yozwiak, J. A. (2007). A review of factors affecting jurors' decisions in child sexual abuse cases. In M. P. Toglia, S. J. Read, D. F. Ross, & R. C. L. Lindsay (Eds.), *The handbook of eyewitness psychology: Vol. 1. Memory for events* (pp. 509–543). Mahwah, NJ: Lawrence Erlbaum.

Ghetti, S., & Redlich, A. D. (2001). Reactions to youth crime: Perceptions of accountability and competency. *Behavioral Sciences and the Law, 19,* 33–52.

Goodman, G. S., Golding, J. M., Helgeson, V. S., Haith, M. M., & Michelli, J. (1987). When a child takes the stand: Jurors' perceptions of children's eyewitness testimony. *Law and Human Behavior, 11,* 27–40.

Kovera, M. B., Gresham, A. W., Borgida, E., Gray, E., & Regan, P. C. (1997). Does expert testimony inform or influence juror decision-making? A social cognitive analysis. *Journal of Applied Psychology, 82,* 178–191.

CHILD SEXUAL ABUSE

Although definitions can vary across legal, clinical, and research contexts, sexual abuse is commonly defined as sexual acts between a youth and an older person (e.g., by 5 years or more) in which the dominance of the older person is used to exploit or coerce the youth. Behaviors may include noncontact (e.g., exposure) and contact (e.g., intercourse) offenses.

The prevalence of sexual abuse is difficult to determine, but estimates suggest that as many as 20% of women and 5% to 10% of men report having been sexually abused as a child. The number of substantiated cases has dropped significantly in recent years, possibly due to a combination of factors, including changes in definitions and reporting and an actual decline in incidence. Sexual abuse occurs across all income levels and racial, cultural, and ethnic groups. Victims are identified via child self-disclosure, medical or physical evidence (e.g., trauma, sexually transmitted disease), behavioral and emotional changes that prompt inquiry, and investigations stemming from assault of other youths. Careful forensic interviews are often important for documenting abuse, protecting children, and successfully prosecuting perpetrators.

All states have mandatory reporting laws that require professionals to report suspected child maltreatment, including sexual abuse. Failure to report can lead to legal charges and ethical complaints. The statutes provide civil and criminal immunity from liabilities for reports made in good faith.

The impact of sexual abuse varies considerably, and there is no common symptom that is found in all victims. The possible consequences include internalizing (e.g., anxiety, depression, poor self-esteem) and externalizing (e.g., delinquency, substance abuse, sexual behavior) problems. Posttraumatic stress disorder (PTSD) is the most common clinical syndrome. A substantial number of young people do not show measurable clinical symptoms, although for some of them problems may appear later. Nonoffending parents and siblings may experience significant distress and may require treatment as well.

A variety of treatment approaches are used for reducing the consequences of abuse. Interventions may focus on the abused child, nonoffending parents, and nonabused siblings, in individual and group formats.

Only a small percentage of cases result in a sexually abused child testifying in court. Court preparation programs help make the experience less stressful and improve the child's participation.

Definitional Issues

Child sexual abuse is surprisingly difficult to define as no universally accepted criteria have been identified. Definitions generally consider the sexual behaviors involved and the ages of the victim and the perpetrator.

While force or coercion may occur, it is not always present. Younger children are not considered capable of consenting to sexual activities with older persons; thus, sexual acts between individuals with age differences of 5 years or more are generally seen as abusive. Legal definitions often emphasize that the perpetrator should be an adult in a position of dominance or authority over the youth for the behavior to be considered an act of abuse. Noncontact offenses include genital exposure, voyeurism, showing a child pornographic material, or having a child undress or masturbate. Contact offenses include genital touching; oral sex; and digital, object, or penile penetration (vaginal or anal).

If the perpetrator is a family member, including distant relations, in-laws, and step-relations, then the abuse is considered "intrafamilial" sexual abuse. If the perpetrator is not a family member by marriage or blood, then it is usually considered "extrafamilial."

Child sexual abuse has been challenging to define as each word in the term has been operationalized differently across legal, clinical, and research contexts.

While some behaviors are clearly sexual (e.g., intercourse), other behaviors (e.g., touching) can lie across a continuum, and the context can influence decisions regarding whether it is abusive. In clinical and research contexts, the term *sexual abuse* is sometimes used to describe the victimization of young people by similar-age peers, though in legal contexts this may be more likely to be viewed as "assault." Similarly, from a clinical and research standpoint, perpetration by an adult stranger or nonfamily member may be considered sexual abuse, but within the legal system it may be treated as sexual assault.

Incidence and Prevalence

Definitional challenges contribute to the difficulty in accurately identifying the incidence and prevalence of sexual abuse. Records from child protective services agencies in the United States in recent years indicate that approximately 1.2 children per 1,000 experience sexual abuse each year. This is an underestimate because it reflects only cases known to relevant agencies, and many instances of abuse are not identified or reported.

Overall, the number of cases of sexual abuse substantiated by child protective service agencies dropped by approximately 40% during the 1990s. This is likely due to a combination of factors, including increasing conservatism on what is substantiated as abuse, exclusion of cases that do not involve caretakers, changes in data collection methods, less reporting due to concerns about backlash, and possibly a real decline in incidence.

Although sexual abuse occurs across all income levels and racial, cultural, and ethnic groups, it is more commonly reported among families of lower socioeconomic status. Children of all ages are victimized, with risk of sexual abuse increasing around age 10. Girls are significantly more likely to experience sexual abuse than boys. In addition, children with physical or cognitive disabilities appear to be at increased risk.

Identification of Victims

Because of the covert and coercive nature of sexual abuse and the frequent absence of physical evidence, a child's self-disclosure is the primary means of identifying an abusive situation. When children do disclose sexual abuse, they are most likely to tell a parent, usually their mother.

Research has identified numerous factors that inhibit disclosure. Perpetrators often use manipulative and coercive methods to maintain their victim's compliance and silence. Children may be embarrassed, concerned about retaliation from the perpetrator or others, or worried about being blamed or punished. Unfortunately, such worries are often justified in that disclosures are sometimes met with disbelief and family upheaval. Boys are less likely to disclose due to concerns about being stigmatized if the abuse was perpetrated by a male, and they may not perceive sexual acts with older girls or women as abusive. Children are more likely to disclose if the abuse was perpetrated by a stranger. Older children are more likely to purposefully disclose (i.e., seek out someone to disclose to), while younger children may be more likely to disclose after questioning.

Medical or physical evidence sometimes leads to identification of sexual abuse. This may include trauma to the genitals or mouth, genital or rectal bleeding, sexually transmitted diseases, pregnancy, and complaints of discomfort in the genital or rectal area. In most cases, there are no physical indications of the abuse. However, positive medical findings are valuable for substantiation of an abusive act.

Sometimes there are significant behavioral or emotional changes that might provide an indication that something has happened. For example, a child might suddenly withdraw or act out, show signs of sexualized behavior, or avoid individuals or settings, and this might prompt questioning or investigation. At other times, abuse may be discovered as a result of an ongoing investigation of other victims, as perpetrators commonly have multiple victims.

Once abuse is suspected, it is common to conduct a forensic interview with the potential victim. These interviews are important for protecting children and successfully prosecuting perpetrators, and it is also important that falsely accused individuals are exonerated.

A number of techniques are used in forensic interviews, with varying degrees of documented support. It is considered acceptable to gather information about the allegation before a forensic interview, though knowledge of allegations can increase interviewer bias and result in leading questions, and allegation-blind interviews can lead to higher rates of disclosure than allegation-informed interviews. Assessing understanding of the difference between the "truth" and a "lie," and the consequences of lying, is valuable before questioning. Open-ended questions increase the length and accuracy of responses with school-age children and adolescents. Cognitive interview techniques can also be useful, especially with older children, including recalling the event as a detailed narrative, reporting every detail of what happened, recalling the event in different sequences, and describing the event from other people's perspectives. The use of anatomically detailed dolls is controversial, with some reports of their being useful in helping children remember and describe their experience and other reports of their reducing the quality of responses and eliciting sexual play from nonabused children.

A relatively new approach to forensic interviews is the structured interview. The advantages of structured interviews are that they need limited training, use flexible and easy-to-follow protocols, and have been developed for alleged victims as well as their parents. Research has shown their utility in decreasing leading questions, increasing open-ended questions, and increasing the quality of the details elicited. Another new approach is extended forensic evaluation, in which multiple interviews are conducted to allow the child to disclose over time in a nonthreatening environment. It is recommended that interviewers be graduate-level mental health professionals with training in sexual abuse, child development, and court testimony. Stages of evaluation include gathering background information, rapport building, social and behavioral assessment, abuse-specific questioning, and review and clarification.

A promising development for improving child abuse investigations and substantiation rates is the Child Advocacy Center (CAC) model. CACs are child-friendly facilities staffed by professionals trained in forensic interviews, medical exams, and victim support and advocacy. The number of CACs has increased dramatically in recent years, with the majority of states having multiple centers.

Mandatory Reporting Statutes

All 50 states have laws that require certain professionals to report suspected child maltreatment. This commonly includes physicians, nurses, psychologists, social workers, teachers, day care workers, and law enforcement personnel. Any person may report, and many state statutes require "all persons" to report suspicions, though many individuals are unlikely to be aware of this responsibility.

Generally, mandatory reporting statutes indicate that a report is required when there is "reasonable cause" to believe that a child has been subjected to abuse or is being exposed to conditions that could result in abuse. Reports can be made via child protective services or law enforcement agencies, and 24-hour reporting is available in most states via a toll-free "hotline" phone number. Failing to report can lead to criminal penalties or civil liabilities, as well as professional ethical and malpractice complaints. The mandatory reporting requirement overrides professional confidentiality requirements.

Despite the mandatory reporting statutes, numerous studies indicate that many instances of abuse do not get reported by professionals, either because they do not recognize the situation as abusive or because they choose not to report. Research suggests that a variety of factors can influence reporting, including the perceived severity of the situation, prior success with reporting, and concerns about disrupting a therapeutic relationship.

Consequences of Sexual Abuse

A substantial amount of research has examined the potential consequences of sexual abuse. While there is no doubt that sexual abuse has serious consequences for many, the extent and nature of the impact vary considerably, and no symptom or disorder is found universally in all victims. In addition to the challenges of demonstrating experimental control, the research is faced with the presence of many potential confounding variables, such as the co-occurrence of other forms of maltreatment, domestic violence and marital dysfunction, and poverty.

Across the research on the short-term consequences, sexual abuse has been found to be associated with a number of internalizing behaviors, including anxiety, depression, suicidal ideation, problems with self-esteem, sleep disturbances, and somatic complaints. PTSD is the most commonly identified clinical syndrome found, including symptoms of reexperiencing the event, avoidance of reminders of the trauma, and arousal and hypervigilance.

Research has also demonstrated the presence of externalizing problems, including self-abusive behaviors, delinquency, and substance abuse problems. Difficulties with school performance and concentration, problems with interpersonal relationships and social competence, or increased body self-consciousness may also be found. Some children may be more interested and curious about sex and the genital areas, have heightened sexual activity, such as masturbation and precocious sexual play, or sexually act out toward adults and peers.

A substantial portion of youths may be asymptomatic following abuse. Research indicates that as many as 20% to 50% of victims do not show measurable clinical symptoms. Most of these children remain symptom free, but there is evidence of a "sleeper effect," in which symptoms do not manifest until months or years after disclosure.

A substantial amount of research has identified potential long-term effects including anxiety, depression, self-mutilation, suicidal ideation and behavior, somatization, poor self-esteem, substance abuse, sexual dysfunction, sexual deviance, and posttraumatic stress. Research has also documented less satisfaction and comfort in relationships and more maladaptive interpersonal patterns. Increased risk of sexual assault revictimization is also a problem.

The substantial variability in consequences is not surprising given the variability in the nature and extent of sexually abusive acts and the contexts in which they occur. Research has shown that factors that may influence the impact of sexual abuse on children include characteristics of the abuse (e.g., type and severity, relationship with the perpetrator), premorbid child characteristics, family functioning, and school and community support and stressors. Research indicates that parental support after disclosure is a key factor in reducing the impact of sexual abuse.

Sexual abuse can affect the entire family system, and nonoffending parents and siblings may need support for dealing with the experience. Parents report increased strain on parent-child and spousal relationships, anger, depression, and posttraumatic stress. Siblings may experience emotional distress, including fear, helplessness, shame, guilt, anger, and resentment toward the victim.

Treatment for Victims and Families

Treatment for sexual abuse is unique in that children are generally referred for services because they have experienced the event of sexual abuse, not because of specific emotional or behavioral symptoms they are exhibiting. Many children receive services because of parental concerns about damage to their child and for prevention of future difficulties and revictimization. Thus, children in treatment are a very heterogeneous group.

Interventions range from brief psychoeducation and crisis intervention, to short-term abuse-focused treatments, to more comprehensive and longer-term interventions. The general findings are that the interventions, often based on research for treating other child difficulties, are effective for treating the symptoms exhibited by sexually abused youths.

Psychological assistance at the time of disclosure is designed to assess the child and its family's needs and to provide support, psychoeducation, and short-term training in effective coping strategies. Crisis intervention services can improve parents' effectiveness in providing support and helping their child and family address the complex, abuse-related impacts and issues. Additionally, referrals for longer-term mental health services can be made if needed. It has been routine to provide asymptomatic children with treatment, especially psychoeducation, to prevent development of problems and reduce the risk of revictimization.

Abuse-specific therapy designed to decrease trauma-related symptomatology is the most extensively researched treatment and tends to use cognitive-behavioral procedures to target symptoms of posttraumatic distress. For example, anxiety and avoidance are targeted with relaxation training, desensitization and exposure, and cognitive restructuring. Behavior problems are addressed with behavior management techniques. Some young people also need intervention for sexual behavior problems to address parental supervision, education, communication, self-control, and sexual behavior rules.

Group therapy can offer opportunities not available in individual or family therapy. It provides the victims the opportunity to share experiences and feelings with other youths who have had similar experiences, helps them reduce their sense of isolation and stigma, and provides them with a safe setting to discuss and experiment with new behaviors, including social skills, and coping and problem-solving strategies. Research suggests that group interventions can be valuable for reducing problems of anxiety, depression, fear, and sexual behaviors and for increasing self-esteem.

Research indicates the importance of therapeutic services for nonoffending parents and nonabused siblings. Treatment for nonoffending parents is important to address parental distress, parental reactions, and supportive recovery of the abused child. Nonabused siblings may need services to address emotional distress involving feelings of relief, guilt, anger, and resentment, as well as for preventing future abuse and learning coping skills. Group treatments can be beneficial to parents and siblings by providing an atmosphere to give and receive support, share similar experiences, and resolve stressful issues.

Testifying in Court

Approximately half the substantiated cases result in criminal charges for the perpetrator, but only about half of those go through prosecution. Because only a small portion of cases actually proceed to trial, only a very small percentage of youths actually testify. The often long delays in court proceedings can be frustrating for families and delay recovery because of the continued need to face the situation in what can be challenging and stressful circumstances. Fortunately, participation in such legal proceedings does not appear to regularly lead to longer-term adjustment problems, and for some children and families participation has positive benefits (e.g., feelings of closure).

In response to the stressors caused by the court process, as well as the need for child witnesses to participate appropriately during proceedings, court preparation programs are increasingly available for sexually abused youths. The goals of court preparation include making the experience less stressful, helping the child understand the proceedings, improving the child's ability to participate accurately and truthfully, and increasing the likelihood that the child will be seen as a credible witness. Court preparation procedures familiarize children with court participants, processes, and terms; inform children of their rights and obligations and the arrangements of the courtroom; and teach stress management strategies, such as deep breathing and desensitization. Although not well established by research, court preparation programs are believed by prosecutors to be effective, and families and professionals working with the children find them useful.

In addition to preparation programs, courts have implemented other practices to help protect children, including "vertical prosecution," where one prosecutor deals with the case from investigation through trial and keeps in regular contact with the child and its family. Victim advocates also provide support and information throughout the often long, complicated process.

Courts have allowed modifications to make testifying less stressful and aid in gaining attention and participation. For example, some courts allow a child to hold a teddy bear or a doll while testifying to help the child feel comfortable, seat the child in a less intimidating location within the courtroom, or allow the child to testify with a screen that blocks the child's view of the defendant or via closed-circuit television (CCTV) from an adjacent room. Although many states have enacted statutes to allow CCTV testimony, it has not been widely used because of the lack of availability of the equipment in court rooms, concerns about legal challenges, and beliefs about the value of in-person testimony.

David J. Hansen and Kathryn R. Wilson

See also Child Maltreatment; Children's Testimony; False Memories; Sex Offender Treatment; Sex Offender Typologies

Further Readings

Cronch, L. E., Viljoen, J. L., & Hansen, D. J. (2006). Forensic interviewing in child sexual abuse cases: Current techniques and future directions. *Aggression and Violent Behavior, 11,* 195–207.

Finkelhor, D., & Jones, L. M. (2004, January). *Explanations for the decline in child sexual abuse cases* (*Juvenile Justice Bulletin*). Washington, DC: U.S. Department of Justice, Office of Justice, Office of Juvenile Justice and Delinquency Prevention.

Kalichman, S. C. (1999). *Mandated reporting of suspected child abuse: Ethics, law, and policy* (2nd ed.). Washington, DC: American Psychological Association.

Myers, J. E. B., Berliner, L., Briere, J., Hendrix, C. T., Jenny, C., & Reid, T. A. (Eds.). (2002). *The APSAC handbook on child maltreatment* (2nd ed.). Thousand Oaks, CA: Sage.

Saywitz, K., Mannarino, A., Berliner, L., & Cohen, J. (2000). Treatment for sexually abused children and adolescents. *The American Psychologist, 55,* 1040–1049.

Wolfe, V. V. (2006). Child sexual abuse. In E. J. Mash & R. A. Barkley (Eds.), *Treatment of childhood disorders* (3rd ed., pp. 647–727). New York: Guilford Press.

CIVIL COMMITMENT

Civil commitment is the legal process under which individuals with mental illness may be subjected to involuntary hospitalization. This entry discusses the impact and consequences of commitment, the justifications for the resulting intrusion on liberty, the statutory criteria for commitment, and the constitutional requirements that underlie them. It examines the requirement that candidates for commitment must be mentally ill or disordered and the psychiatric conditions that will qualify. It then considers the requirement of functional impairment imposed by these statutes and the Constitution, including incompetency in the case of parens patriae criteria and volitional impairment in the case of police power criteria. It also discusses the kinds of danger that may satisfy police power criteria, the degree of imminence of such danger that is required, and the methods used by clinical evaluators in predicting dangerousness. It then considers the medical appropriateness and least restrictive alternative requirements for commitment. It concludes by discussing the procedural due process hearing requirements for commitment.

The Impact and Consequences of Civil Commitment

In the past 50 years, the use of civil commitment has been reduced. The census of public mental hospitals in 1955 was around 550,000. The policy of deinstitutionalization, the shift of the locus of care from the hospital to the community, and the tightening of civil commitment criteria have reduced our reliance on involuntary hospitalization. Only about 55,000 patients are now hospitalized on any particular day. However, patients once spent long periods and sometimes an entire lifetime in the hospital, whereas most patients today are discharged after 30 days or less, and many within as few as 5 days. For many patients, civil commitment has become a revolving door, whereby they experience several periods of hospitalization each year. Civil commitment thus continues to affect a large number of patients, even if the duration of hospitalization has been dramatically reduced.

Civil commitment results in a massive curtailment of liberty. It intrudes on the fundamental interest in being free of external restraint. Patients are subjected to detailed regulation of their every activity, and they are forced to submit to various forms of intrusive treatment, including psychotropic medication, which may cause severe and unwanted side effects that are lasting. Involuntary hospitalization also imposes a severe stigma, which produces continued social and occupational disabilities long after discharge. As a result, the criteria for involuntary hospitalization have been limited, and the procedural protections required before it may be imposed have been expanded.

Justifications for Civil Commitment

There are two justifications for civil commitment. The first is the government's police power interest in protecting the community from those who are predicted to

be dangerous as a result of their mental illness. The second is the parens patriae interest in protecting the best interests of those whose illness deprives them of the ability to make rational decisions on their own behalf concerning their need for hospitalization and treatment. The Fifth and Fourteenth Amendment due process clauses place substantive and procedural limitations on governmental deprivations of liberty. At a minimum, such deprivations may not be arbitrary or purposeless. Because the liberty interest in being free of external restraint is a fundamental constitutional right, an exceedingly heavy burden of justification is placed on the government. To satisfy constitutional requirements, civil commitment thus must be justified as being necessary to accomplish one or more compelling governmental interests. The state's police power and parens patriae power interests are both compelling and in appropriate cases, therefore, will justify commitment. These two justifications are reflected in typical civil commitment statutory criteria. The individual will be entitled to a hearing at which the state must demonstrate satisfaction of the criteria and show that there is no less intrusive alternative method of achieving the government's interests in protecting the individual or the community. Then, commitment may be authorized for a limited time period.

Civil Commitment Statutory Criteria

Commitment statutes typically begin by requiring "mental illness or disability" but define these terms imprecisely or circularly. Often these illnesses or disabilities are described as "significant, severe, substantial, or gross impairments." Some conditions are expressly excluded from coverage, notably mental retardation, epilepsy, developmental disabilities, drug addiction, and alcoholism. Sometimes antisocial personality disorder is excluded. In practice, clinicians applying these definitions typically limit hospitalization to those with schizophrenia, major affective depression, or bipolar disorder. Other psychiatric diagnoses are sometimes thought of as justifying at least brief hospitalization—borderline personality disorder, narcissistic personality disorder, reactive depression, and anorexia nervosa, for example, at least when the patient is in crisis.

In addition to requiring mental illness, state civil commitment statutes typically specify some degree of functional impairment resulting from such illness. An overwhelming majority of statutes use the phrase "dangerous to self or others." The avoidance of danger to self constitutes an application of the state's parens patriae power; the avoidance of danger to others constitutes an expression of its police power in protecting the community from harm.

Parens patriae commitment is paternalistic in nature. It is based on the inability of the individual, as a result of mental illness, to understand the need for care and treatment in a hospital. The purpose is to protect the individual from harm and to improve his or her health. This form of commitment contemplates both that the individual suffers from a cognitive impairment that significantly impairs rational decision making and that hospitalization would be in his or her best interests.

An essential aspect of parens patriae commitment is the incompetency of the patient. Yet some state statutes fail to explicitly require a determination of incompetency. Because such incompetency is a historic requirement for invocation of the parens patriae power, however, courts will read this requirement into the statute to satisfy constitutional requirements. Publicly labeling an individual as incompetent is stigmatizing, and it often imposes negative self-attributional effects on the patient that may undermine performance and motivation and cause a form of depression. As a result, incompetency should be narrowly defined, and a presumption should exist in favor of competency. Many state statutes so provide. The concept of competency is rarely defined with precision. It typically requires the ability to make a decision, understand treatment information, rationally manipulate it, and appreciate the implications and consequences of alternative options. Requiring a high level of ability in these respects, however, seems unreasonable, particularly since many patients who are not mentally ill lack these abilities. Mental illness alone, even schizophrenia, does not equate with incompetence. Many patients with mental illness requiring hospitalization will possess sufficient competence to make the decision for themselves. Only if they have been determined to be so grossly impaired cognitively that their decisions are not worthy of respect should patients be found sufficiently incompetent to justify parens patriae commitment.

Commitment based on dangerousness to others constitutes an application of the state's police power interest in protecting the community. Some people suffering from mental illness may be dangerous to others. Dangerousness alone cannot justify commitment, however—many people are dangerous but not mentally ill. We typically use the criminal sanction to deal with such dangerousness, requiring an adjudication of guilt before punishment may be applied. Only rarely in our constitutional system is preventive detention permitted. Police power civil commitment is one of these rare exceptions.

In addition to dangerousness, it must be shown that the individual's mental disability significantly impairs the ability to control his or her behavior. In the context of sex offender civil commitment, the Supreme Court has required that to justify commitment, the individual's disability must make it difficult to control behavior. To justify civil commitment on police power grounds, it therefore must be shown that the individual's mental disability seriously diminishes volitional control. This requirement is not reflected in typical civil commitment statutes, but courts will mandate it as a constitutional matter.

To meet the criteria for police power commitment, the individual must be both mentally ill and predicted to be dangerous. State statutes frequently are ambiguous concerning the degree of dangerousness that must be found to exist. As a constitutional matter, such dangerousness should be predicted to be likely to occur within a reasonable time in order to justify hospitalization, and the danger to be avoided must be sufficiently serious to justify this significant intrusion on liberty. Involuntary hospitalization is not justified merely to protect the community from the inconvenience or personal offense of being confronted by someone with mental illness. The danger to be avoided must be a serious one. Certainly, the prevention of physical injury would qualify. Some state statutes permit commitment based on danger to property alone, either expressly or by leaving the term *dangerousness* undefined. Some civil commitment statutes require that the danger to be prevented be imminent, but many do not. Some courts have imposed an imminence requirement, but others have declined to do so.

When dangerousness is the basis for commitment, it must be supported by the testimony of clinical expert witnesses who have evaluated the individual. Clinical prediction of dangerousness, however, is probably accurate in no more than one out of every two cases. In recent years, risk assessment instruments have increasingly been used to supplement and anchor clinical prediction, thereby producing a higher degree of accuracy.

The Medical Appropriateness Requirement

When an individual is not mentally ill and when hospitalization is not therapeutically appropriate, hospitalization should not be permitted as a matter of due process (Winick, 2005). Even though many state civil commitment statutes may not explicitly require this determination, they often will condition commitment on its being in the "best interests" of the individual or require a finding that hospitalization is appropriate in the circumstances. In any event, this limitation would seem to be required as a matter of due process. Unless the individual suffers from a treatable mental disorder, psychiatric hospitalization should not be permitted.

The Least Restrictive Alternative Principle

Even if a police power or parens patriae power rationale justifies civil commitment, hospitalization must also be found to be the least restrictive means of accomplishing the state's interests in protecting the individual or the community. This limitation is mandated by due process, as well as by a majority of state commitment statutes. Under this principle, the court must consider whether less restrictive community placements are available for the individual that would suffice to meet his and the community's needs.

Moreover, even if hospitalization is deemed to be required, once the individual's needs can be met through community treatment, the least restrictive alternative principle would require conditional release from the hospital to such community treatment. Hospitalization should be resorted to only if it is necessary. When its purposes can be accomplished through outpatient treatment, partial hospitalization, or other forms of treatment in the community, the significant deprivation of liberty that hospitalization represents would be inappropriate.

The Civil Commitment Hearing

The commitment criteria will be applied at a hearing before a judge or a hearing examiner, where the state will have the burden of persuasion concerning satisfaction of these standards. At the hearing, the individual will be given the opportunity to cross-examine the state's clinical experts and submit his or her own expert witnesses and other evidence in rebuttal of the state's case. These and other procedural elements are constitutionally required as a matter of procedural due process. State statutes typically describe the procedures that must be followed at the hearing. These include notice and a formal hearing before involuntary hospitalization may be authorized, or shortly thereafter when commitment is sought on an emergency basis. They also include the right to have an appointed attorney, the right to have a fair and impartial judge or hearing examiner, and the right to be present. The state must bear the burden of persuasion by clear and convincing evidence.

Even though state statutes require a fairly formal adversarial judicial hearing, in practice these hearings tend to be brief and informal rituals at which the judge seems overwhelmingly to defer to the state's expert witnesses. Rather than playing the adversarial role contemplated by due process, some attorneys engage in only perfunctory advocacy, with the result that the process often appears to the patient to be a farce and a sham. This undermines the purposes of due process—to increase accuracy and allow a sense of participation. The result can be an affront to the patient's dignity, producing the feeling that he or she has been treated in bad faith, with potentially negative consequences for the efficacy of hospitalization and treatment. As a result, considerations of therapeutic jurisprudence would suggest that to the extent these practices continue to exist, they be altered in ways designed to achieve the participatory and dignitary value of due process.

Bruce J. Winick

See also Forcible Medication; Mental Health Law; Patient's Rights; Risk Assessment Approaches; Sex Offender Civil Commitment; Therapeutic Jurisprudence

Further Readings

Winick, B. J. (2005). *Civil commitment: A therapeutic jurisprudence model*. Durham, NC: Carolina Academic Press.

CLASSIFICATION OF VIOLENCE RISK (COVR)

The Classification of Violence Risk (COVR) is an interactive software program designed to estimate the risk that an acute psychiatric patient will be violent to others over the next several months. Using a laptop or a desktop computer, COVR guides the evaluator through a brief chart review and a 10-minute interview with the patient. COVR generates a report that places the patient's violence risk in one of five categories—ranging from a 1% likelihood of violence in the first category to a 76% likelihood of violence in the highest category, including the confidence interval for the given risk estimate.

The software was constructed from data generated in the MacArthur Violence Risk Assessment Study. In brief, more than 1,000 patients in acute civil psychiatric facilities were assessed on 134 potential risk factors for violent behavior. Patients were followed for 20 weeks in the community after discharge from the hospital, and their violence to others was assessed. The software is capable of assessing the 40 risk factors for violence that emerged as most predictive of violence in the MacArthur Violence Risk Assessment Study, but in any given case, it assesses only those risk factors necessary to classify the patient's violence risk.

To combine risk factors into a preliminary estimate of risk, the COVR relies on "classification tree" methodology. This approach allows many different combinations of risk factors to classify a person as high or low risk. Based on a sequence established by the classification tree, a first question is asked of all persons being assessed. Contingent on the answer to that question, one or other second question is posed, and so on. The classification tree process is repeated until each person is classified into a final risk category. This "interaction" model contrasts with the more typical "main effects" approach to structured risk assessment, such as the one used by the Violence Risk Appraisal Guide, in which a common set of questions is asked of everyone being assessed, and every answer is weighted and summed to produce a score that can be used for the purpose of obtaining an overall estimate of risk.

The authors of the COVR administered the newly developed software to independent samples of acute civil inpatients at two sites. Patients classified by the software as high or low risk for violence were followed in the community for 20 weeks after discharge. Expected rates of violence in the low- and high-risk groups were 1% and 64%, respectively. Observed rates of violence in the low- and high-risk groups were 9% and 35%, respectively, when a strict definition of violence was used and 9% and 49%, respectively, when a slightly more inclusive definition of violence was used. These results indicated that software

incorporating the multiple iterative classification tree models may be helpful to clinicians who are faced with making decisions about discharge planning for acute civil inpatients.

In the view of its authors, the COVR software is useful in informing, but not in replacing, clinical decision making regarding risk assessment. The authors recommend a two-phased violence risk assessment procedure, in which a patient is first administered the COVR and then the preliminary risk estimate generated by the COVR is reviewed by the clinician ultimately responsible for making the risk assessment in the context of additional information believed to be relevant and gathered from clinical interviews, significant others, and/or available records. Although clinical review would not revise or "adjust" the structured risk estimate produced by the COVR, and could in principle either improve or lessen predictive accuracy as compared with relying solely on an unreviewed COVR score, the authors of the COVR believed it essential to allow for such a review, for two reasons. The first reason has to do with possible limits on the generalizability of the validity of the software. For example, is the predictive validity of the COVR generalizable to Native Americans, to forensic patients, to people outside the United States, to people who are less than 18 years old, or to the emergency room assessments of persons who have not been hospitalized recently? The predictive validity of this instrument may well generalize widely. Yet there comes a point at which the sample to which a structured risk assessment instrument is applied differs so much from the sample on which the instrument was constructed and validated that legitimate questions can be raised regarding the generalizability of the validity of the instrument.

The second reason given in defense of allowing a clinician the option to review structured risk estimates is that the clinician may note the presence of rare risk or protective factors in a given case and these factors—precisely because they are rare—will not have been taken into account in the construction of the structured instrument. In the context of structured instruments for assessing violence risk, the most frequently mentioned rare risk factor is a direct threat—that is, an apparently serious statement of intention to do violence to a named victim.

John Monahan

See also HCR–20 for Violence Risk Assessment; MacArthur Violence Risk Assessment Study; Violence Risk Appraisal Guide (VRAG); Violence Risk Assessment

Further Readings

Monahan, J., Steadman, H., Appelbaum, P., Grisso, T., Mulvey, E., Roth, L., et al. (2005). *The classification of violence risk*. Lutz, FL: Psychological Assessment Resources.

Monahan, J., Steadman, H., Appelbaum, P., Grisso, T., Mulvey, E., Roth, L., et al. (2007). The classification of violence risk. *Behavioral Sciences and the Law, 24,* 721–730.

Monahan, J, Steadman, H., Robbins, P., Appelbaum, P., Banks, S., Grisso, T., et al. (2005). An actuarial model of violence risk assessment for persons with mental disorders. *Psychiatric Services, 56,* 810–815.

CLOTHING BIAS IN IDENTIFICATION PROCEDURES

A bias in an identification procedure is any factor—other than recognition—that leads witnesses to select a person. *Clothing bias* can occur whenever someone is viewed in an identification procedure wearing clothing that matches the witness's description of the clothing worn during the crime. A witness may mistakenly select the suspect based on the clothing rather than the physical appearance of the person. Although there is limited research to date, clothing bias has been demonstrated to occur with all three commonly used identification techniques: mug-shot searches, lineups, and showups (the presentation of a single suspect to an eyewitness for identification purposes). This entry will review why clothing bias is a concern for these three procedures and the ways to prevent it.

Findings to date demonstrate that for adult witnesses, clothing bias generally does not affect correct identification rates for mug-shot searches, lineups, or showups. Correct identification rates increase for children in the presence of clothing bias. As with many biases, clothing bias dramatically increases the rate of false positive choices (i.e., identifications of innocent people). This increase in false identifications has been demonstrated with adults for all three identification procedures and with children for lineups.

With mug-shot searches, innocent people may be chosen simply because they happen to be wearing clothing that matches what the perpetrator was wearing. This is problematic because people identified from mug shots are often treated as suspects in the absence of any definitive proof of their innocence (e.g., a strong alibi). Mug-shot searches are hard to protect from clothing bias because the pictures already exist. To control the clothing for future mug shots, the police could take mug shots of people dressed in standard clothing (e.g., large, loose coveralls) or take pictures from the neck up to hide the clothing worn. To control the clothing in extant mug shots, the photographs could be altered (edited) to cover up (mask) clothing or reveal only the head.

Clothing bias is of great concern in a lineup. If the suspect is the only lineup member wearing clothing similar to the perpetrator's, the suspect will stand out in the lineup—a clear source of lineup bias. Additionally, if the witness selects the suspect, the police and prosecutors may treat the identification and the match between the witness's description of the clothing and the suspect's attire as corroborating evidence of the suspect's guilt. The logic of corroboration is flawed in such cases because the identification and the clothing are not independent sources of evidence if clothing bias exists in the identification procedure.

To protect a lineup from clothing bias, the clothing of all lineup members, including the suspect, should not match the description of the perpetrator's clothing given by the witness. Ideally, the lineup would consist of only head shots, or all lineup members would be dressed alike. Corroborating evidence can be obtained by creating clothing lineups and asking witnesses to attempt to identify the clothing independently of the person. Sequential lineup presentation has been shown to reduce the size of the clothing bias effect.

Showups generally occur shortly after the crime occurs. Police investigators often will use the description provided by a witness to search the immediate area for potential suspects. Since the descriptions provided by witnesses rarely are detailed enough to ensure that only the perpetrator matches the description and because clothing information often forms a substantial and distinctive portion of the information provided in descriptions, clothing cues are likely to be an important factor in apprehending suspects who appear in showups. As a result, many suspects are likely to have been apprehended near the scene of the crime, shortly after it occurred, and because their clothing was at least a reasonable match to the witness's description of the perpetrator's clothing. This can result in witnesses viewing suspects wearing clothes that closely match the description they provided, which can in turn lead to false identifications of innocent suspects. Even when the witness's description of the clothing is incorrect, innocent suspects wearing clothing that matches the inaccurate description are at heightened risk of both apprehension and false identification. Suspects in showups wearing distinctive clothing (e.g., shirts or jackets with logos) are at greater risk of false identification due to clothing bias than those wearing common clothing (e.g., plain white T-shirts).

To protect a showup from clothing bias, the suspect should not wear clothes that match the description of the perpetrator's clothing. Sometimes it is not possible to change a suspect's clothing for showups, (e.g., when they are conducted live at the scene of a crime). In this case, the clothing of suspects could be covered in some way, such as having a blanket covering their body, so as to prevent their clothing from being a cue to the witness. However, this method has not been tested, so its effects on identification decisions are currently not known.

Conviction of innocent people for crimes can be the result of clothing bias during identification procedures. Identifications should be based on recognition of a person, not the clothing they are wearing. Clothing bias is a concern for the three commonly used methods of identification: mug shot, lineup, and showup.

Michelle I. Bertrand, Jennifer L. Beaudry,
Jamal K. Mansour, and R. C. L. Lindsay

See also Estimator and System Variables in Eyewitness
Identification; Identification Tests, Best Practices in;
Lineup Size and Bias; Mug Shots; Showups;
Simultaneous and Sequential Lineup Presentation

Further Readings

Dysart, J. E., Lindsay, R. C. L., & Dupuis, P. R. (2006).
Show-ups: The critical issue of clothing bias. *Applied
Cognitive Psychology, 20,* 1009–1023.

Lindsay, R. C. L., Nosworthy, G. J., Martin, R., &
Martynuck, C. (1994). Using mug shots to find suspects.
Journal of Applied Psychology, 79, 121–130.

Lindsay, R. C. L., Wallbridge, H., & Drennan, D. (1987). Do
the clothes make the man? An exploration of the effect of
lineup attire on eyewitness identification accuracy.
Canadian Journal of Behavioural Science, 19, 463–478.

COGNITIVE INTERVIEW

Eyewitness information is the key element in solving many crimes, yet the police are often poorly trained in conducting information-gathering interviews, and they make avoidable mistakes. To rectify this situation, Ronald Fisher and Edward Geiselman developed the Cognitive Interview (CI) procedure to collect information from cooperative witnesses. The CI techniques are based on scientific principles of cognitive and social psychology and are intended to facilitate witness memory and communication between the witness and the interviewer. Laboratory and field tests have shown that the CI increases considerably the amount of information obtained from witnesses while maintaining high accuracy. This entry describes the core elements of the CI, empirical tests to validate the procedure, and its various applications and limitations.

Police investigators depend heavily on eyewitness evidence to solve crimes, and they often bemoan the fact that witnesses do not provide as much information as the police expect. Some of this cannot be controlled, as when crimes occur quickly or under poor lighting conditions. Nevertheless, the police do have some control over witness recollection, specifically by the way they conduct interviews. Because many police investigators receive minimal training on how to conduct investigative interviews with cooperative witnesses, they conduct interviews intuitively and make avoidable errors. Studies of police interviews show that they (a) ask too many closed-ended questions (e.g., How tall was the robber?) and too few open-ended questions (e.g., Describe the robber.), (b) often interrupt witnesses in the middle of their narrative descriptions, and (c) frequently ask leading questions.

To improve police interviewing procedures, Fisher and Geiselman developed an interview procedure that is based primarily on scientific, laboratory research in cognitive psychology (hence the name *Cognitive Interview*) and social psychology. The CI attempts to enhance witness recall by addressing three integral components of the interview: (a) developing effective social dynamics between the police interviewer and the witness, (b) enhancing the witness's memory retrieval and generally facilitating the witness's and the interviewer's thought processes, and (c) facilitating communication between the witness and the interviewer. The following is a thumbnail sketch of the CI's core principles.

Social Dynamics

As in all small groups, the exchange of information depends on how psychologically comfortable the group members are with one another and each person's expectations of his or her role in the group.

Developing Rapport. Witnesses, and especially victims, are often asked to give detailed descriptions of intimate, personal experiences to police officers, who are complete strangers. If anything, the police investigator's formal appearance (badge, uniform, gun) may create a psychological barrier between the police officer and the witness. To overcome this barrier, police interviewers should invest time at the beginning of the interview to develop a meaningful, personal rapport with the witness, a feature often absent in police interviews.

Active Witness Participation. The witness has extensive first-hand information about the crime. Therefore, the witness, and not the interviewer, should be doing most of the mental work. In practice, however, police interviewers often dominate the social interaction with witnesses by asking many questions that elicit only brief answers. This relegates witnesses to a passive role, waiting for the police to ask questions. Interviewers can induce witnesses to take a more active role by (a) explicitly requesting them to do so, (b) asking open-ended questions, (c) not interrupting witnesses during their narrative responses, and (d) constructing the social dynamic so that witnesses perceive themselves to be the "experts" and therefore the dominant person in the conversation. The last point is especially important when interviewing children.

Memory and Cognition

Both the witness and the interviewer are engaged in demanding cognitive tasks: The witness is attempting to recall and describe in detail a complex event; the interviewer is listening to the witness's response, generating and testing hypotheses about the crime, formulating questions, and notating the witness's answers. Because these tasks are cognitively demanding, the witness's and the interviewer's cognitive resources must be used efficiently.

Context Reinstatement. Retrieving information from memory is most efficient when the context of the original event is re-created at the time of recall. Interviewers should therefore instruct witnesses to mentally re-create their cognitive and emotional states that existed at the time of the original event (What were your thoughts and emotions during the crime?).

Limited Mental Resources. Witnesses and interviewers have only limited mental resources to process

information. Hence, their performance suffers when they engage in other difficult tasks concurrently. Interviewers can minimize overloading witnesses by asking fewer, but more open-ended, questions. This also makes the interviewer's task easier by not having to formulate many questions. Interviewers can also promote a more efficient use of witnesses' limited mental resources by minimizing physical (extraneous noises) and psychological distractions (direct eye contact) during the interview.

Witness-Compatible Questioning. Each witness's mental record of an event is unique. Some witnesses may have focused on the perpetrator's face, whereas others may have focused on the weapon. Interviewers should tailor their questions to each witness's unique perceptions during the crime, instead of asking all witnesses the same set of questions. Interviewers often violate this rule by using a standardized checklist of questions for all witnesses.

The accessibility of event details varies during the course of the interview as the witness's mental images change. Event details will be most accessible when they are perceptually related to the witness's current mental image. Therefore, interviewers should be sensitive to the witness's currently active mental image and ask questions that are compatible with that image.

Multiple and Varied Retrieval. The more often witnesses search through their memories of the crime, the more new details they will recall. Interviewers can make use of this principle by (a) asking witnesses to describe the critical event several times during the interview and (b) interviewing witnesses on two or more occasions. If witnesses attempt to recall the target event repeatedly, they should be directed to think about the event in various ways, since different retrieval cues will activate different aspects of a complex event. For instance, interviewers might encourage witnesses to describe the crime both visually (describe what the people and objects looked like) and temporally (describe the sequence of events).

Minimizing Constructive Recall. Witnesses may construct memories of a crime by incorporating information derived from other sources—for example, the media, other witnesses, or even the interviewer. Interviewers should therefore be careful about not leaking information to witnesses either nonverbally (e.g., by smiling or paying increased attention when the witness makes a particular statement) or verbally (by asking leading or suggestive questions, e.g., Was it a red car?).

Accuracy of Response. To promote high accuracy, interviewers should explicitly instruct witnesses not to guess; rather, witnesses should indicate that they "don't know." Interviewers should also refrain from applying social pressure on witnesses or otherwise encouraging them to answer questions whose answers they are unsure of. This is particularly important when interviewing children.

Communication

For police interviews to be effective, the investigators must communicate their investigative needs to the witness. Witnesses must also communicate their knowledge of the crime to the investigator. Ineffective communication will lead witnesses to withhold valuable information or provide irrelevant, imprecise, or incorrect answers.

Promoting Extensive, Detailed Responses. Police interviews require witnesses to describe people, objects, and actions in more detail than civilians normally do in casual conversation. To promote such extraordinary descriptions, police officers should convey explicitly their need for extensive detail, which they rarely do. Sometimes witnesses withhold information because they mistakenly believe that it is not relevant for a police investigation. To minimize witnesses' withholding valuable information, interviewers should instruct witnesses to report everything they think about, whether it is trivial, whether it is out of chronological order, or even if it contradicts a statement made earlier.

Investigators often direct witnesses to provide relevant information by asking many specific, short-answer questions about investigatively relevant topics—for example, the perpetrator's age, height, or weapon. This questioning style minimizes irrelevant information, but at the cost of minimizing unsolicited information and sometimes inducing incorrect responses. Rather than asking many specific questions, interviewers should explicitly instruct witnesses to generate descriptive narratives, without waiting for the interviewer to ask questions.

Code-Compatible Output. Interviewers and respondents often exchange ideas using only the verbal medium. Some people, however, are more expressive nonverbally, and some events are better described nonverbally. Ideally, the response format should be compatible with the witness's mental record of the event. If an event is inherently spatial (e.g., the location of objects within a room), then witnesses should respond spatially—for example, by drawing a sketch of the room. In general, encouraging witnesses to sketch out the crime scene should promote more extensive recall.

Sequence of the Cognitive Interview

The CI follows a designated order intended to maximize the effectiveness of the individual techniques. The recommended sequence is common to many interviewing protocols in that it progresses from asking open-ended questions to more specific follow-up probes. The CI is divided into five sections: introduction, open-ended narration, probing for details, review, and closing the interview. The introduction establishes the appropriate psychological states and interpersonal dynamics to promote efficient memory and communication during the remainder of the interview. The open-ended narration allows the witness to provide an uninterrupted narrative of his or her recollection of the crime. The interviewer follows up by probing information-rich images, initially with framed, open-ended questions and then with more specific probes. When all the information has been collected, the interviewer reviews the witness's statement to clarify any ambiguities and to resolve any contradictions. Finally, the investigator closes the interview by collecting official information (e.g., contact information) and encouraging the witness to contact him or her in the future.

Although this is the optimal sequence, interviews invariably deviate from this plan as unexpected conditions arise. In that regard, the CI is more of a general guideline for conducting an interview rather than a fixed recipe.

Empirical Testing to Validate the Cognitive Interview

The CI has been examined in approximtely 100 laboratory tests, most of which were conducted in the United States, England, Germany, and Australia. In these tests, volunteer witnesses (typically, but not always, college students) observe either a live, nonthreatening event or a film of a simulated crime. Several hours or a few days later, the witnesses participate in a face-to-face interview, which is either the CI or a control interview. The control is either a "standard" police interview or a "structured interview," which incorporates generally accepted principles of interviewing minus those techniques unique to the CI. The interviews are usually tape-recorded, transcribed, and then scored for the number of correct statements and incorrect statements. Across these studies, the CI has typically elicited between 25% and 100% more correct statements than standard or structured interviews. This effect is extremely reliable: Of the 55 experiments examined in a recent meta-analysis, 53 experiments found that the CI elicited more information than did the comparison interview (median increase = 34%). Equally important, accuracy was as high or slightly higher in the CI interviews (accuracy rate = .85) than in the comparison interviews (.82).

All the above studies were conducted in the laboratory, with nonthreatening events. Two other studies have examined the CI with victims and witnesses of real-world crimes. In both of these studies, one conducted in Miami and one in London, some experienced police detectives received training to use the CI and other experienced detectives did not receive such training. In both studies, the CI-trained police investigators elicited considerably more information than did the untrained investigators (approximately 50% more in the U.S. study).

Although most of the empirical testing has been conducted on normal, healthy adults, several studies have examined the CI's effectiveness on unusual populations, including young children, the elderly, and those with cognitive deficits. Naturally, healthy college students remembered more than these other populations. However, the CI was equally effective with all the groups, enhancing their recollections by approximately the same amount. Some have questioned the advisability of using the CI with very young children, under the age of 5 years.

Most empirical studies have tested witness recall within a few hours or a few days of the critical event. Some studies, however, have shown the CI to enhance witness recall after several months, and one study even showed a very large benefit after 35 years.

The CI has been demonstrated to work effectively in a variety of investigative interviews in addition to criminal investigation—for example, accident or public health investigation. It has not, however, been effective in identification tasks: Witnesses given a CI prior to an identification test (e.g., lineup) were no more accurate than witnesses given a control interview.

Practical Issues

Given the success of the CI in laboratory and field experiments, how does it fare in real-world investigations? The CI has been used successfully to solve several cases, including a kidnapping, a politically motivated bombing, and child molestation. Recently, an investigator from the U.S. Bureau of Alcohol, Tobacco, and Firearms reported conducting a CI with a 38-year-old woman who had witnessed a homicide as a 5-year old child. The interview elicited scores of recollections, many of which were corroborated by police records established at the time of the crime (e.g., the location of objects and furniture at the crime scene).

Offsetting these successes, the British police reported that the complete CI was sometimes difficult to implement. They noted difficulty in communicating to witnesses some of the CI's mnemonic instructions. Other police officers have reported that using the complete CI frequently requires more time than is available, and so they often use only some of the component techniques.

Other Investigative Tasks

Although the CI was developed initially to facilitate witness memory of a crime, the technique has been shown to be effective in other interview settings. Two such applications of the CI are interviewing suspects and debriefing jurors after deliberation.

Detecting Deception. Some research shows that the CI facilitates detecting whether a suspect's testimony is truthful or deceptive. Two CI components that enhance detecting deception are asking open-ended information-gathering questions (vs. accusatory questions) and encouraging suspects to take an active role. These techniques generate longer responses from suspects, thereby permitting more opportunities to identify verbal and nonverbal cues to deception, and also allow interviewers to detect the different response strategies used by truth tellers and liars. In addition, asking suspects to describe events in different sequential orders (notably, reverse order) is particularly difficult for liars.

Debriefing Jurors. Reconstructing a jury deliberation session after a trial should assist attorneys to evaluate their trial strategies. A recent study examined the CI's efficiency in reconstructing a related decision-making task (asking a small group of people to discuss business practices that entailed ethical decisions). The CI was modified slightly to account for group decision making (considering the social dynamics of the group). Compared with the conventional method of debriefing group members, the CI elicited considerably more information and at a very high accuracy rate. Interestingly, the CI also elicited extensive information about the individual members' thought processes during the earlier decision-making task.

Componential Analysis

Although tests of the CI show that the technique, as a whole, is effective, only a few studies have isolated individual component techniques to determine which ones are effective. The results suggest that (a) each component contributes to the overall CI effect, but (b) the relative contribution of each component varies across conditions. For instance, context reinstatement is more effective when much time has passed between the original event and the interview, whereas nonverbal (code compatible) output is more effective when interviewing people with limited verbal skills.

Legal Challenges

Although the CI has been found reliably to enhance witness recollection, could it be unacceptable for forensic use? The following patterns of results suggest that the CI should be legally acceptable: (a) CI-elicited recollections are as accurate as, or slightly more accurate than, recollections from conventional interviews; (b) the CI does not render witnesses overly suggestible to leading questions—if anything, witnesses are less suggestible when interviewed with the CI; (c) witness confidence and witness credibility are not affected by the CI; (d) CI interviewers are perceived to be less manipulative than conventional interviewers; and (e) there is no carry-over effect in a preliminary interview of the type of interview conducted (CI or conventional) on the witness's later testimony.

There have been two court cases in which the CI was at issue. In a case heard by the National Court of Appeal in London (England), an earlier decision was overturned based on information collected from a witness who provided a very detailed account of the crime when interviewed with the CI. Although the Court did not mention the CI in its ruling, the ultimate decision was compatible with the information elicited by the CI. The second case entailed a pretrial hearing in California, in which the prosecution used evidence that had been elicited by a police officer trained in conducting the CI. The defense attorney claimed that the CI was similar to hypnosis and that it promoted inaccurate eyewitness testimony. (As noted earlier, accuracy is equivalent or slightly higher with the CI compared with conventional interviews, the opposite of the pattern with hypnosis.) The judge ruled against the defense's objection to the CI and permitted the CI-elicited testimony to stand.

Training in the CI

There is considerable variation across locations in the training the police receive to conduct interviews with cooperative witnesses. Several countries in Europe (England, Sweden, Norway) provide instruction in the CI as part of their basic training to all police investigators. Some regional police-training programs within the United States, Canada, and Australia also provide training in the CI, although (a) many police departments do not provide any training at all and (b) among those that do provide training in the CI, there is considerable variation in the quality. CI training is more standardized and more rigorous among some of the federal investigative agencies in the United States (e.g., FBI, National Transportation Safety Board [NTSB]). Adequate training in the CI requires, in addition to lectures and demonstration, ample opportunity for trainees to practice the techniques and receive critical feedback. Feedback from investigators has been very encouraging, especially with major, complex crimes and accidents, where the investigator has the luxury of time and resources to conduct thorough interviews.

Ronald Fisher and Nathalie Castano

See also Detection of Deception: Cognitive Load; Eyewitness Memory; Hypnosis and Eyewitness Memory; Identification Tests, Best Practices in; Instructions to the Witness; Jury Deliberation

Further Readings

Fisher, R. P., & Geiselman, R. E. (1992). Memory-enhancing techniques in investigative interviewing: The cognitive interview. Springfield, IL: Charles C Thomas.

Fisher, R. P., Geiselman, R. E., & Amador, M. (1989). Field test of the cognitive interview: Enhancing the recollection of actual victims and witnesses of crime. *Journal of Applied Psychology, 74,* 722–727.

Fisher, R. P., & Schreiber, N. (2007). Interviewing protocols to improve eyewitness memory. In M. Toglia, R. Lindsay, D. Ross, & J. Reed (Eds.), *The handbook of eyewitness psychology: Vol. 1. Memory for events* (pp. 53–80). Mahwah, NJ: Lawrence Erlbaum.

Geiselman, R. E., & Fisher, R. P. (1997). Ten years of cognitive interviewing. In D. G. Payne & R. G. Conrad (Eds.), *A synthesis of basic and applied approaches to human memory* (pp. 291–310). Hillsdale, NJ: Lawrence Erlbaum.

Kebbell, M.-R., Milne, R., & Wagstaff, G.-F. (1999). The cognitive interview: A survey of its forensic effectiveness. *Psychology, Crime and Law, 5*(1–2), 101–115.

Koehnken, G., Milne, R., Memon, A., & Bull, R. (1999). The cognitive interview: A meta-analysis. *Psychology, Crime and Law, 5,* 3–27.

COMMUNITY CORRECTIONS

Over the past 15 years, the number of people under correctional supervision in the United States has more than doubled. Most of this growth is attributable to the rapidly expanding probation population, which recently reached an all-time high of more than 4 million offenders. In fact, the vast majority of all offenders under correctional supervision are supervised in the community on probation (58%) or parole (11%). Despite their rehabilitative roots, community corrections have been heavily oriented toward surveillance over the past quarter-century. However, high rates of recidivism among supervisees have prompted calls for accountability and use of evidence-based supervision. Substantial evidence indicates that surveillance models that focus exclusively on offender control are less effective than hybrid models that focus on both offender control and offender rehabilitation. For the at-risk population of supervisees with mental disorder, evidence suggests that specialty caseloads are a promising practice. Despite these clearly defined contours of evidence-based practice, most agencies are merely at the cusp of reintroducing rehabilitation in supervision. The process of doing so is likely to be slow but will be facilitated by (a) the use of new risk management technology and (b) gradual shifts in organizational values, hiring practices, and training, to create a significant cadre of officers with hybrid orientations. Officers influence outcomes more powerfully than the programs they ostensibly apply.

Developing Community Corrections and Questioning Its Performance

The roots of probation and parole lie more in social casework than law enforcement. Probation began in 1841, when John Augustus posted bail to release a "drunkard" from a Boston jail, worked with the man for 3 weeks toward rehabilitation, and convinced a judge that the man had reformed his ways and should be set free. He went on to bail more than 2,000 offenders and assist them with employment, housing, and other issues. Parole began in 1840, when Alexander Maconochie developed a "mark system" by which prisoners at Norfolk Island could earn early release for good behavior. By the 1860s, this precursor to modern parole had been adopted in the United States. Over the past 150 years, community corrections have traveled a great distance from their rehabilitative roots to embrace the "tough on crime" stance that prevails today.

In modern probation and parole, an officer is tasked with (a) protecting community safety by monitoring and enforcing an offender's compliance with the rules of conditional release from incarceration and, often to a lesser extent, (b) promoting the offender's rehabilitation with social service referrals such as substance abuse counseling and vocational support. Despite this commonality, probation and parole differ in terms of *who* is supervised. A probationer is an offender who, on conviction, is typically sentenced directly to a term of community supervision (although a minority of probationers are granted a conditional suspended sentence to incarceration). In contrast, a parolee is convicted of a relatively serious offense, serves a portion of his or her sentence in prison, and is then granted conditional early release to serve the remainder of his or her sentence in the community. Although probation is applied in the federal system and all 50 states, the federal system and at least 15 states have abolished parole in favor of determinant sentencing.

The assumption underpinning both probation and parole is that some offenders can be safely maintained in the community and will respond well to the available services. Community supervision is viewed as a cost-effective alternative to incarceration for these offenders. Probation or parole can be revoked if an offender commits a *new offense* or a *technical violation* of the conditions governing release (e.g., reporting to one's officer, paying restitution, maintaining employment).

Although the type of supervision approach can strongly affect the rate of success (see below), the general success of modern community supervision in preventing crime and facilitating offenders' reentry into the community is modest. For example, the rates of rearrest over a 2-year period among prisoners released on parole and prisoners released unconditionally are comparable (approximately 60%) once the differences between the two groups in characteristics such as criminal history are controlled. Perhaps given their lower level of risk for re-offense, probationers (59%) are somewhat more likely to successfully complete their term of community supervision than parolees (45%). Nevertheless, many probationers and parolees fail supervision. Among policymakers, such figures have prompted many to issue a call for accountability in community corrections and some to question whether probation and parole should continue to exist in their current form.

Responding to Contemporary Challenges

The business of community corrections is challenging. Management has become results driven. Generally, inadequate budgets have tightened. Workloads have grown astronomically in size and complexity. Many offenders have substance dependence disorders and serious mental disorders, which complicates supervision. Others have been convicted of sex offenses and other violent offenses that demand close oversight. The monumental challenge is to cope with a large, complicated workload while improving the effectiveness of supervision—to do "more with less."

Given the staggering diversity across states in the organization and oversight of community supervision, there is no well-defined and homogeneous response to this challenge. Probation and parole are practitioner-led enterprises, with supervision philosophies and practices that vary considerably across agencies and officers. Despite this diversity, a few innovative responses have gained enough traction across agencies to be viewed by William Burrell as "strategic trends." These trends include creating formal partnerships with community agencies (e.g., drug courts, school-based probation) and

developing specialized caseloads (e.g., for mentally ill offenders, sex offenders). They are underpinned by a larger drive toward reintroducing rehabilitation in supervision and implementing evidence-based risk assessment, risk management, and supervision strategies.

Promoting Evidence-Based Risk Assessment and Risk Management

Although many agencies have adopted a standardized assessment of offenders' risk of criminal recidivism over the past decade, relatively few use these assessments to inform supervision. Nevertheless, several progressive agencies have begun using well-validated measures to (a) inform decisions about whether to release an offender to community supervision, (b) identify an offender's changeable risk factors for recidivism (e.g., substance abuse) to target in intervention, and (c) monitor changes in an offender's risk state over time. These measures include the Levels of Services/Case Management Inventory (LS/CMI) and the Classification Assessment and Intervention System (CAIS). The accuracy of the LS/CMI in predicting general recidivism and violent recidivism rivals that of tools that are better known in forensic circles (e.g., the Psychopathy Checklist–Revised). Unlike most forensic tools, both the LS/CMI and the CAIS assess both risk status (interindividual risk compared with other offenders) and risk state (intraindividual risk compared with oneself over time) and guide community supervision from intake to case closure. Moreover, use of the CAIS has been shown to improve outcomes for probationers and parolees. For example, in a study of approximately 44,000 offenders assigned to either CAIS-supported supervision or regular supervision, the rate of revocation for CAIS supervisees was 29% lower than that for traditional supervisees.

Reintroducing Rehabilitation Efforts to Improve Outcomes

Increasing empirical support for the "risk-needs-responsivity" (RNR) principle is largely responsible for agencies' adoption of risk assessment tools and their recognition that rehabilitation should be reintroduced in supervision. Meta-analytic studies show that offenders are considerably (24–54%) less likely to recidivate when programs match the intensity of supervision and treatment services to their level of risk for recidivism (risk principle), match modes of service to their abilities and motivation (responsivity principle), and target their criminogenic needs or changeable risk factors for recidivism (need principle). Indeed, the effectiveness of programs is positively associated with the number of criminogenic needs (e.g., attitudes supportive of crime) they target relative to noncriminogenic needs (i.e., disturbances that impinge on functioning in society, such as anxiety).

Although the *surveillance* model of supervision still dominates community corrections, empirical support for the RNR principle is helping a *hybrid* model of supervision gain ascendance in some progressive agencies. There here has long been tension in community corrections between the goals of protecting community safety ("control") and promoting offender rehabilitation ("care"). The surveillance model focuses exclusively on control, whereas hybrid models blend control and care. A growing body of research demonstrates the effectiveness of hybrid models relative to surveillance models. For example, a recent meta-analysis indicated that RNR programs significantly reduced recidivism risk ($r = .25$), whereas surveillance programs that applied sanctions without attending to risk or needs did not ($r = -.03$).

Studies of intensive supervision programs (ISPs) also suggest that rehabilitative efforts should be included in supervision. ISPs were created to reduce prison and jail crowding by having officers with reduced caseloads closely supervise relatively serious offenders in the community with prison-like controls. Traditional ISPs emphasize monitoring virtually to the exclusion of services for offenders. Evaluations of these ISPs robustly indicate that they do not reduce recidivism and sometimes exacerbate (rather than alleviate) prison crowding. For example, in an experiment that involved 14 diverse jurisdictions, offenders were randomly assigned to either traditional supervision or ISP supervision. A meta-analysis of these data indicates that, after excluding the one site in which ISP had a positive effect, ISP increased the likelihood of offenders' rearrest by 94%. Offenders in ISP were particularly likely to return to prison on technical violations. One might argue that detecting and sanctioning technical violations is an index of the surveillance model's success in preventing crime. However, there was no evidence that sanctioning technical offenses prevented new arrests.

Unlike traditional ISPs, hybrid ISPs yield positive effects. One meta-analysis indicated that ISPs that incorporated treatment (hybrids) reduced recidivism by 22%, whereas ISPs that did not (surveillance) had no effect on recidivism. Based on a matched sample

of 480 parolees, Mario Paparozzi and Paul Gendreau found that those supervised in a hybrid ISP program received significantly more social services (e.g., public assistance) than those in a traditional parole program. Hybrid ISP parolees were substantially less likely to have new convictions (19% vs. 48%) and revocations (38% vs. 59%) than traditional parolees.

There is increasing recognition that the manner in which officers implement supervision has powerful effects. For example, Paparozzi and Gendreau classified 12 ISP officers' supervisory orientation into surveillance, treatment, and hybrid categories. Within ISP, parolees with hybrid officers (19%) were remarkably less likely to have their probation revoked than those with both surveillance (59%) and treatment (38%) officers. In fact, officers' orientations toward supervision affected parolees' outcomes more strongly than the particular supervision program applied (i.e., ISP vs. traditional).

Tailoring Responses to Supervisees With Mental Disorder

The process of supervision may be especially important for probationers and parolees with mental disorders (PMDs). Both PMDs and their officers describe the quality of their relationship as coloring every interaction and strongly affecting outcomes. There is some support for this notion. In a study of 90 PMDs, Jennifer Skeem and colleagues developed and validated the revised Dual Role Relationship Inventory (DRI–R) to capture relationship dimensions such as caring, fairness, and trust. DRI–R scores related coherently to observers' codes of officer-probationer interactions during a supervision session and significantly predicted violations and revocation over a 1-year follow-up period.

PMDs constitute a large and at-risk population. The prevalence of major mental disorders is 4 to 8 times higher in corrections populations than in the general population. Relative to their nondisordered counterparts, PMDs are twice as likely to fail on probation or parole. PMDs are particularly likely to have supervision revoked for technical violations, perhaps because their reduced level of functioning makes it more difficult for them to comply with standard conditions such as maintaining employment. The vast majority of PMDs have a co-occurring substance abuse disorder, which elevates their risk of rearrest. PMDs present a number of unique challenges to supervising officers, given their pronounced need for social services (e.g., housing, social security income) and the mandate that they take psychotropic medication and participate in psychosocial treatment as a special condition of supervision.

A number of agencies have responded to these challenges by developing specialty caseloads for PMDs. These caseloads are reduced in size ($M = 48$), composed exclusively of PMDs, and supervised by an officer interested in mental health. In prototypic specialty agencies, officers advocate for services, participate in the treatment team, and tend to address noncompliance with problem-solving approaches rather than threats of incarceration. Specialty caseloads are a promising if not evidence-based practice. To date, only one relevant randomized controlled trial (RCT) has been conducted: A large matched trial is currently under way. In the RCT, PMDs in specialty probation obtained significantly more mental health services than PMDs in traditional probation, but these increased services did not translate into a reduced risk of jail rebookings during a 1-year follow-up. This echoes other studies suggesting that increased mental health services fail to reduce police contacts and rearrests. This could be because (a) the quality of the mental health services received is poor or (b) mental disorder is not the sole, or even primary, reason for PMDs' involvement in the crime. The latter notion enjoys some support. Based on a sample of 113 jail detainees with mental disorder, John Junginger and colleagues found that less than 4% had been booked for a crime directly related to their mental disorder. Given that PMDs share risk factors for crime with other offenders, hybrid models for PMDs probably will not meaningfully reduce recidivism unless they go beyond providing mental health services to target these individuals' criminogenic needs.

Looking to the Future

Evidence robustly indicates that supervision is most effective when it blends care with control. Despite increasing endorsement of rehabilitation efforts, there is little evidence that the hybrid model of supervision is being widely implemented. Surveys indicate that the vast majority of correctional treatment programs do not apply RNR and other principles of evidence-based practice. Similarly, less than 5% of probation agencies have developed specialty mental health caseloads for PMDs, and a significant number of these have pushed caseload size beyond the capacity that can conform to the prototypic hybrid model. Relatively few agencies have moved from a surveillance to a hybrid model.

The paths toward better achieving this goal include (a) use of a new generation of risk/needs assessment tools such as the LS/CMI and CAIS to direct supervision from intake through case closure, (b) extension of RNR principles to PMDs, and (c) gradual shifts in organizational values, hiring practices, and officer training to produce a larger pool of officers with hybrid orientations. The most meaningful gains likely will be made at the officer level. These gains will be gradual because a generation of officers has grown up with the law enforcement model, without exposure to rehabilitative principles. In the midst of debates about branded programs, we often lose sight of the fact that officers' orientation toward supervision and their relationships with probationers influence outcomes more strongly than the specific program they ostensibly apply.

Jennifer Skeem, Sarah Manchak,
and Jennifer Eno Louden

See also Conditional Release Programs; Prison Overcrowding; Probation Decisions; Sentencing Decisions; Sentencing Diversion Programs

Further Readings

Andrews, D., Bonta, J., & Wormith, S. (2006). The recent past and near future of risk and/or need assessment. *Crime and Delinquency, 52*(1), 7–27.

Burrell, W. (2005). *Trends in probation and parole in the states.* Washington, DC: Council of State Governments. Retrieved February 16, 2007, from http://www.appa-net.org/ccheadlines/docs/Trends_Probation_Parole.pdf

Skeem, J. L., & Manchak, S. (in press). Back to the future: From Klockars' model of effective supervision to evidence-based practice in probation. *Journal of Offender Rehabilitation.*

COMPETENCE ASSESSMENT FOR STANDING TRIAL FOR DEFENDANTS WITH MENTAL RETARDATION (CAST*MR)

The Competence Assessment for Standing Trial for Defendants With Mental Retardation (CAST*MR) consists of 50 questions and was designed to assess defendants' understanding of basic legal concepts, ability to assist their attorneys, and ability to relate important information regarding their own legal circumstances. Its purpose is to assist forensic evaluators in determining competency in defendants with mental retardation. The CAST*MR demonstrated test-retest reliability and validity in several studies prior to its publication.

Competence to stand trial is critical for ensuring due process rights for defendants in the criminal justice system. The doctrine of competence to stand trial has its origins in early English common law and relates to the accepted belief that a defendant cannot be tried in absentia. It is thought that trying an incompetent defendant who cannot understand and participate in the proceedings is equivalent to trying someone in absentia. Hence, competency is essential for due process and fundamental fairness.

The criteria for judging competence to stand trial was articulated in the 1960 Supreme Court decision *Dusky v. United States. Dusky* states that to be competent to stand trial, a defendant must have a "rational and factual understanding of the proceedings" and be able to consult with his or her attorney with a "reasonable degree of rational understanding" (p. 402).

Application of the doctrine of competence to stand trial to defendants with mental retardation requires special consideration because of the unique nature of the disability. According to the American Association on Intellectual and Developmental Disabilities (previously AAMR), "mental retardation is a disability characterized by significant limitations both in intellectual functioning and in adaptive behavior as expressed in conceptual, social, and practical adaptive skills. This disability originates before age 18" (p. 1). Because of the high risk that intellectual and adaptive behavior limitations may negatively affect the necessary elements of competence to stand trial, particular care must be taken to conduct an authentic assessment in order to preserve fairness.

Description of the CAST*MR

The CAST*MR was developed by Caroline Everington and Ruth Luckasson to assist forensic evaluators in determining competency in defendants with mental retardation. The first two sections of the CAST*MR consist of 40 multiple-choice questions. This format was chosen as it provides a quick and reliable means of assessing defendants' understanding. Many persons with mental retardation have difficulty with expressive language and exhibit acquiescence in assessment situations. This format helps correct for those problems. As will be discussed later, CAST*MR results should be supplemented with additional information relevant to the defendant's competency and necessary for clinical judgment.

The first section, Basic Legal Concepts, contains 25 multiple-choice items and addresses understanding of the roles of key players in the process—for example, judge, attorney, prosecutor, witness—and important procedures such as a plea bargain and trial. In the second section, Skills to Assist in Defense, the defendants are presented with 15 scenarios that involve the choices they must make about their case or when working with their attorneys. This section is also presented in a multiple-choice format. In the final section, Understanding Case Events, the defendants must answer a series of key questions about the circumstances of their arrest and the charges.

CAST*MR Validity and Reliability

An expert appraisal process was used to develop items for the instrument. The first versions were field tested with individuals with mental retardation as well as college students. Validation studies were conducted before publication.

There have been two primary validation studies conducted on the CAST*MR. Caroline Everington conducted the first study with defendants with and without mental retardation at the pretrial level. In the first study, it was determined that the instrument successfully discriminated between groups of defendants and had an acceptable classification rate. Test-retest reliability and internal consistency analyses yielded acceptable results as well.

A second validation study was conducted by Caroline Everington and Charles Dunn using defendants with mental retardation who were referred for evaluations of competence to stand trial. The second study replicated the results of the Everington study.

Caroline Everington, Katherine DeBerge, and Daria Mauer, studying adults with mental retardation, found that CAST*MR scores were significantly correlated with language subtests on the Woodcock-Johnson Tests of Cognitive Ability and these language tests were good predictors of CAST*MR performance. This finding supports the use of assessments of language ability in competence evaluations involving persons with mental retardation.

While there are no findings regarding malingering on the CAST*MR, Caroline Everington, Heidi Notario-Smull, and Mel Horton found that individuals in the higher-IQ range of mental retardation could alter their performance when asked to do poorly. These individuals scored lower than a group of defendants with mental retardation who had been evaluated as incompetent to stand trial and the control group of defendants with mental retardation who took the test under standard conditions. This reaffirms the need to supplement scores with additional information.

Appropriate Use of the CAST*MR

It is important that competency evaluations of persons with mental retardation include multiple sources of information. A single test score should not be the sole determinant of defendant competency. An evaluation test battery for persons with mental retardation should include an individually administered global test of intelligence and assessments of expressive and receptive language, academic skills, and adaptive behavior. Social history provides additional information on cognitive and academic skills and previous diagnoses. Interviews with key individuals who have known the defendant over time provides information relevant to competency, such as the defendant's problem-solving and decision-making skills. These sources provide corroborative information that can assist in the interpretation of CAST*MR results.

Finally, CAST*MR results should be supported with additional information on the defendant's pscholegal abilities. Other sources include information gained through questioning in the clinical interview and can include an additional assessment of competence to stand trial. It is important to check for understanding by having the defendant explain concepts in his or her own words. Decisional competency is a critical area for individuals with mental retardation. It is important to query the individual on his or her understanding of the defense strategy and his or her legal options.

The CAST*MR is published by IDS in Columbus, Ohio, and is used by evaluators throughout the United States.

Caroline Everington and Ruth Luckasson

See also Competency, Foundational and Decisional; Competency to Stand Trial; Mental Retardation and the Death Penalty

Further Readings

Dusky v. United States, 362 U.S. 402 (1960).

Everington, C., DeBerge, K., & Mauer, D. (2001). The relationship between language skills and competence to stand trial abilities in persons with mental retardation. *Journal of Psychiatry and Law, 28,* 475–492.

Everington, C., & Dunn, C. (1995). A second validation study of the competence assessment for standing trial for defendants with mental retardation. *Criminal Justice and Behavior, 22,* 44–59.

Everington, C., & Luckasson, R. (1992). *The competence assessment for standing trial for defendants with mental retardation (CAST*MR).* Worthington, OH: IDS.

Everington, C., Notario-Small, H., & Horton, M. (in press). Can defendants with mental retardation successfully fake their performance on a test of competence to stand trial? *Behavioral Sciences and the Law.*

COMPETENCY, FOUNDATIONAL AND DECISIONAL

The law in the United States requires that criminal defendants be competent to participate in the adjudicatory proceedings against them. Legal competence is a complex construct that includes both the fundamental capacities needed to participate in the process (adjudicative competence) and a degree of autonomy in making important case decisions (decisional competence). This entry examines the legal criteria for competence as well as the societal values that underlie the requirements concerning the ability of those accused of crime to participate in proceedings against them.

Criteria for Adjudicative Competence

In the United States, individuals accused of crimes are afforded certain constitutional rights and protections during the adjudicatory process. The Fifth Amendment, for example, protects defendants from being compelled by the state to testify against themselves. The Sixth Amendment provides defendants with the right to the assistance of legal counsel, the right to confront their accusers and the evidence against them, and the right to a trial by jury. To benefit from these rights, defendants must be mentally able to assert them. It is not enough that defendants be physically present during adjudicatory proceedings; they must also have the mental capacity to exercise their rights—that is, they must be "competent."

When questions are raised about a defendant's competence, it is the responsibility of the trial judge to make an inquiry and determine whether he or she has the requisite abilities to go forward to adjudication. The broad criteria for adjudicative competence were articulated by the U.S. Supreme Court in the case of *Dusky v. United States* (1960). The trial judge must determine "whether the defendant has sufficient present ability to consult with his lawyer with a reasonable degree of rational understanding, and whether he has a rational as well as factual understanding of the proceedings against him."

Careful scrutiny of this "test" for legal competence reveals several important features:

1. A defendant does not have to be completely competent. Only *sufficient* abilities are required (and these may vary with the complexity and demands of the case).

2. Adjudicative competence is concerned with *present* mental capacities. It is arguably irrelevant that a defendant had significant mental impairment at some point in the past or may again experience such difficulties in the distant future (the current inquiry does assume that present capacities are likely to be maintained in the near future during the course of the pending proceedings). In particular, adjudicative competence is distinguished from inquiries related to legal insanity, a retrospective judgment as to the defendant's mental state at the time of the offense.

3. Adjudicative competence is about *ability* or *capacity*. A defendant who is ignorant (e.g., lacks present *factual* understanding of the legal proceedings) may still be competent if it is determined that he or she is intellectually able to assimilate the relevant information (e.g., through education by or consultation with the attorney). Similarly, a voluntary unwillingness or reluctance (e.g., due to bad character or attitude) to perform the required legal tasks (e.g., to consult with one's attorney) is not a basis for a finding of incompetence.

4. The criteria are *functional legal abilities*. The mere presence of symptoms of mental disorder, even if substantial in nature, is not sufficient to render a defendant legally incompetent. There must be a further showing that the mental disorder adversely affects the abilities articulated in *Dusky* (i.e., to assist counsel, to factually or rationally understand the proceedings).

Societal Values and Competency

For the state to proceed against a defendant who is incompetent affronts important societal values that the constitutional rights were intended to protect. One important value is the dignity of the process; it offends the moral dignity of society for the state to proceed against an individual, whose liberty (and in capital cases, life) is at stake, when that individual is not capable of competent participation in the adversary proceedings. Proceeding against an individual who is "defenseless" due to mental incapacity conjures notions of a "kangaroo court" and conflicts with fundamental notions of fairness.

A second and perhaps more obvious value is *accuracy*. A variety of forms of mental incapacity impair basic cognitive abilities such as attention and memory. Attentional capacity is needed, for example, to hear, process, and heed advice from one's attorney or to attend to testimony by witnesses in order to identify erroneous or false statements. Intact memory is needed to recall and relate legally relevant, and potentially exculpatory, information to the attorney. Perceptual, emotional, or cognitive distortions regarding others' attitudes or intentions—for example, delusional beliefs that one's attorney is secretly working for the state—may impair the development of a cooperative working relationship, which is necessary for the preparation of a legal defense. Such impairments may result in inaccurate verdicts (i.e., wrongful convictions) and unjust punishments, with innocent individuals being incarcerated while criminals go free.

A third societal value implicated in the competence construct is *individual autonomy*. Respect for the individual and an individual's right to self-determination demands that a defendant be capable of at least a minimal degree of autonomous participation in the adjudicatory process. Although the Sixth Amendment provides for the assistance of counsel, respect for individual autonomy limits the extent to which an attorney can act independently of the defendant. It is, after all, the defendant's case. In recognition of this important value, the legal system precludes attorneys from making independent decisions regarding the waiver of constitutional rights; for a defendant to be competent, he or she must be capable of a minimal degree of autonomous participation in decisions such as whether to waive the right to trial and enter into a plea agreement, waive the protection against self-incrimination and testify as a witness, or waive the right to legal counsel and represent oneself in the proceedings.

Foundational and Decisional Competence

A theory of legal competence that reflects these societal values and encompasses the constitutional requirements has been articulated by the University of Virginia law professor Richard Bonnie. This theory distinguishes between two aspects of legal competence: a foundational competence to assist counsel and decisional competence. Foundational competence captures the minimal conditions necessary for a defendant to participate, in a general way, in his or her defense. These conditions include (a) understanding the allegations and the basic elements of the adversary system, (b) recognizing one's own role as the accused individual whose liberty interests are at risk, and (c) having the ability to provide relevant factual information to the lawyer in order to facilitate the development of a defense. These specific functional abilities reflect the capacities articulated by the U.S. Supreme Court in *Dusky v. United States* as fundamental to competence: the ability to assist one's attorney, and the capacity to understand, both factually and rationally, the proceedings that lead to adjudication. According to Bonnie, these baseline, or fundamental, legal capacities serve the dignity and accuracy concerns that underpin the adjudicatory process.

Decisional competence, as noted above, is more specific than the foundational competence construct. It derives from the underlying value of individual *autonomy* and implicates the functional abilities needed to demonstrate a minimal degree of independence in making decisions, specifically decisions to waive constitutional protections. Defense attorneys retain autonomy for a wide variety of case-related decisions, such as the general defense theory/strategy to pursue, which witnesses to call and what questions to ask, and so forth. However, the law does not permit attorneys to independently waive their clients' constitutional rights, and the rationale for this limit on their authority is clear—all citizens, whether wrongfully accused or otherwise, would ultimately have no protection in a system that allowed any third party to sign away those rights.

When questions arise concerning a defendant's competence to proceed, the courts routinely turn to mental health professionals for assistance in determining whether, and to what extent, mental problems (often cast as "mental disease or defect") impair competence. As noted above, the Supreme Court's language in *Dusky v. United States* provided broad descriptions of the functional legal abilities relevant to foundational competence, and these have served to guide forensic examiners' evaluations about foundational competence issues. Unfortunately, there has been no parallel case that has attempted to articulate or operationalize the functional abilities related to decisional competence.

A number of lower courts have required that a defendant's waiver of constitutional rights must be "knowing," "intelligent," and "voluntary," and these concerns underpin the colloquies that judges routinely conduct, for example, with defendants who decide to waive their constitutional rights (e.g., to a trial, to not testify against themselves) and accept a plea offer from the state.

Although explicit legal guidance is lacking regarding the functional abilities relevant to decisional competence, legal scholars and mental health professionals informed by Bonnie's theory have considered this issue. Approaches to assessing decisional competence abilities, some of which have been incorporated into contemporary competence assessment measures (e.g., the MacArthur Competence Assessment Tool–Criminal Adjudication), include evaluating (a) the defendant's ability to articulate the advantages and disadvantages of alternative courses of action (e.g., going to trial vs. accepting a plea agreement), (b) the defendant's ability to articulate a risks-and-benefits analysis of a proposed course of action, and (c) the plausibility of the defendant's reasons for a choice that the defendant considers most appropriate in his or her own case. Articulating these clinical strategies for assessing the functional abilities related to decisional competence makes explicit the basis for the clinical opinions that mental health experts may offer in the absence of clear legal definitions and guidelines with respect to decisional competence.

To date, Bonnie's distinction between foundational and decisional competence has had minimal impact in the highest legal circles. In *Godinez v. Moran* (1993), the Supreme Court addressed the issue of decisional competence and endorsed some of the lower courts' language requiring that a defendant's waiver of constitutional rights be "knowing" (intelligent) and "voluntary." However, the Court declined to articulate a separate criterion or standard for decisional competence and held that, generally, the standard for competency to waive constitutional rights is encompassed within the *Dusky* standard.

The Court's holding in *Godinez* notwithstanding, it is likely that Bonnie's theory of foundational and decisional competence has had an important impact on the field. It has raised awareness of the complexities of the adjudicative competence construct and encouraged forensic evaluators, whose reports and testimony inform the courts regarding defendants' competence-related abilities, to assess decision-making capacities as part of their evaluations.

Historically, pretrial competency evaluations for the courts were often captured under the rubric "competency to stand trial," and many of the interview guides and competency assessment instruments developed for forensic examiners focused on defendants' comprehension of trial proceedings. In a sense, this emphasis was misplaced because in reality, few defendants ever go to trial. Upward of 90% of criminal cases are resolved by some form of plea bargain or plea agreement, each of which entails the waiver of one or more of the constitutional protections discussed above. Thus, Bonnie's elaboration of the decisional competence construct has stimulated clinical thinking about the mental abilities needed to intelligently weigh decisional alternatives (e.g., to be able to describe the potential risks and benefits of alternative courses of action) and ways to craft new measures for the systematic assessment of those abilities. Through careful consultation with defense attorneys about the likely case decision points, particularly those that involve the waiver of rights, psychiatric and psychological examiners may better tailor their evaluations to provide information to the courts about defendants' foundational and decisional competence abilities.

Norman G. Poythress

See also Adjudicative Competence of Youth; Capacity to Waive Rights; Competency to Stand Trial

Further Readings

Bonnie, R. (1990). The competence of criminal defendants with mental retardation to participate in their own defense. *Journal of Criminal Law and Criminology, 81,* 419–446.

Bonnie, R. (1992). The competence of criminal defendants: A theoretical reformulation. *Behavioral Sciences and the Law, 10,* 291–316.

Bonnie, R. (1993). The competence of criminal defendants: Beyond *Dusky* and *Drope. University of Miami Law Review, 46,* 539–601.

Dusky v. United States, 362 U.S. 402 (1960).

Godinez v. Moran, 509 U.S. 389 (1993).

Melton, G. B., Petrila, J., Poythress, N. G., & Slobogin, C. (in press). *Psychological evaluations for the courts: A handbook for mental health professionals and lawyers* (3rd ed.). New York: Guilford Press.

COMPETENCY, RESTORATION OF

Evaluations of competency to stand trial are the most common source of referrals to forensic mental health practitioners. While the clear majority of those examined are viewed as competent to proceed, those found incompetent to stand trial (IST) may be subjected to treatment and training to enable them to proceed to trial, typically referred to as competency restoration. These individuals constitute the largest group referred for mental health treatment under the auspices of the criminal justice system, with several thousand persons hospitalized in the United States at any given time. Despite the significant variability in treatment and education efforts, as many as 9 in 10 persons originally found unfit are eventually adjudicated competent and proceed to disposition of the charges against them. There is a dearth of systematic research on the methods used to accomplish this result. Restoration efforts typically require no more than 4 months, and an increasing number of jurisdictions allow for outpatient treatment and training to minimize pretrial deprivation of liberty. Medication is often a key component of treatment for defendants with psychiatric illness. Prognosis is more guarded for restoration of cognitively impaired defendants.

Some commentators have questioned the propriety of the competency restoration programs provided by mental health practitioners. An alternative view holds that enabling impaired defendants to develop or regain the ability to participate in the resolution of their legal predicaments is ethically justified. This entry summarizes the legal and ethical context of competency restoration efforts, the presenting problems that are typically the focus of treatment, treatment methods and programs, and the outcomes of restoration efforts.

Legal and Ethical Context

All U.S. jurisdictions provide for treatment of individuals found IST. Traditionally, this was presumed to involve commitment to a government-run facility for inpatient care. In *Jackson v. Indiana* (1972), the Supreme Court clarified that such commitment must be reasonably related, in duration and circumstances, to the purpose of restoring the individual to competency. Those found not restorable within the reasonably foreseeable future may be subjected to civil commitment. Surveys suggest that nearly half the defendants referred for restoration are placed in state hospitals and receive services typical for a civil patient population. Most of the remainder are confined in high-security facilities. In view of the significant deprivation of liberty entailed in inpatient restoration, a small number of jurisdictions have created provisions for outpatient competency restoration treatment. This innovation is also politically attractive, as the services are much less costly.

The majority of IST defendants appear to accept restoration treatment voluntarily, but significant legal and ethical conflicts arise regarding those who refuse court-mandated treatment. In *Sell v. United States* (2003), the Supreme Court considered the circumstances under which psychiatric medication could be administered against defendants' objections, for the purpose of restoring competency. The court emphasized that alternative bases for involuntary treatment should be considered first, including treatment justified by danger to self or others or treatment through guardianship procedures. In the absence of these alternative justifications, the government could seek involuntary treatment solely to restore competency in limited circumstances—namely, if the proposed treatment was medically appropriate, substantially unlikely to have competency-impairing side effects, and necessary vis-à-vis less intrusive alternatives to accomplish an important governmental interest in bringing the defendant to trial. Nonmedication treatments have been viewed as less intrusive or objectionable and have not been a source of significant litigation.

Some have argued that mental health practitioners play an ethically conflicting role as treater and evaluator in the restoration process. This view has not gained wide acceptance. Those involved in competency restoration efforts note the importance of full disclosure to the defendant of the purpose of treatment and the procedural protections afforded by judicial hearings authorizing the treatment. They also note that it is in the defendant's interest to regain competency in order to avoid potentially lengthy commitment and benefit from the panoply of procedural rights guaranteed a defendant proceeding to trial. Despite occasional negative commentary on the ethical propriety of mental health professionals' participation in the restoration process, this role remains important in the administration of justice.

Focus of Restoration Treatment

Competency restoration is often implemented on an individualized basis, though some inpatient centers offer highly structured programs. The most common model combines these elements and involves individual treatment of any underlying mental illness combined with group education and practice modules and individual coaching. There is consistent evidence that defendants referred for non-restoration-specific, general psychiatric hospital care are significantly less likely to regain competency than those receiving care in a formal restoration program, either inpatient or community based.

Defendants referred for restoration can be broadly divided into those with primarily Axis I disorders and those with mainly cognitive limitations. In practice, many incompetent defendants exhibit multiple diagnoses, particularly involving personality disorders and substance abuse. While the latter factors are rarely priorities for immediate treatment, they may complicate restoration efforts. Given the overrepresentation of linguistic and cultural minorities among the defendant population, acculturation issues and language barriers can also be significant complicating factors. Individualized treatment planning is required to manage these varied needs.

Defendants with a major mental illness are typically treated with the implicit assumption that but for their psychiatric symptoms, they would be competent. Schizophrenic-spectrum illnesses are most commonly a focus of treatment—and less frequently, mood disorders. Symptoms including delusions, hallucinations, disorganized thought or behavior, and agitation often impair defendants' understanding of their case and proceedings or their ability to collaborate with counsel, rendering them incompetent. Medication treatment to reduce these symptoms is often the mainstay of restoration efforts and may be seen as a prerequisite to other interventions that require greater cooperation and active participation by the defendant/patient. In affective disorders, increased attention and concentration and improved morale may be targets for pharmacological intervention. Consistent with case law focusing on "medical appropriateness," any proposed treatment should comport with general standards of care for the diagnosis at hand and take into account the unique psychological, medical, and other needs and limitations of the incompetent defendant. Complete remission of symptoms is typically not required to meet the practical requirements for competency.

Educational programs appear more tailored to the needs of mentally retarded or otherwise cognitively impaired defendants. These programs typically involve formal testing and retesting to assess the defendants' baseline functioning and progress. Most programs use one or more specific adjudicative competence measures and may structure a curriculum in accord with the theoretical underpinnings of that measure. Group format educational efforts are typically offered once or more per week, up to daily in some programs. These may entail lecture-like presentations, video-recorded demonstrations, role-playing, written exercises, and handouts. Group format training offers the advantage of not only efficient service delivery but also social learning of appropriate behavior for a courtroom setting and the opportunity to assess each defendant's response to the increased stimulation of a small group setting.

Some commentators have expressed concern that mentally retarded individuals may appear to benefit from educational efforts while still lacking a more nuanced understanding of the charges and proceedings against them. This view holds that while even very limited individuals can be taught to repeat basic facts, they may yet lack the understanding and reasoning required to be a meaningful participant in the adjudication process. Practitioners should avoid "teaching to the test" used to measure progress. Alternative forms of assessment, such as open-ended questions and role-play may help differentiate those defendants who have learned basic facts from those who can apply that information in a meaningful way to the case at hand.

Restoration Success Versus Failure

The clear majority of those referred for restoration are ultimately adjudicated competent, with some centers reporting success rates of 80% to 90%. Success appears most likely for individuals with functional psychiatric illnesses that are responsive to medication treatment. Not surprisingly, individuals who show clinically significant improvement in general psychopathology are more likely to be perceived as restored to competency. There is no consensus about the factors that are predictive of restorability in primarily mentally ill defendants, and attempts to derive predictions from clinical samples have failed to generalize adequately given the rarity of nonrestorability. Half or more than half the individuals with mental retardation or acquired cognitive deficits are not restored, consistent with the intractable nature of these disorders.

It is well settled that defendants must be competent at each stage of adjudication, from arraignment through imposition of sentence. "Recidivism," which consists of a decline in functioning that warrants a return for additional restoration treatment before either trial or sentencing, is of concern in a minority of cases. These may involve the defendant's refusal of medication after discharge from a treatment program. Anecdotal evidence suggests that other causes include medication being unavailable in a jail or during transportation to court, defendants being subjected to other conditions of confinement that undermine their prior progress, or substance abuse while on bail that results in an exacerbation of symptoms. It is generally assumed that a renewal of appropriate treatment will again result in restoration or competency.

Few state statutes provide specific time limits for commitment to either inpatient or outpatient restoration treatment. Federal law provides for a 4-month inpatient commitment, with possible extensions for cause, while some states tie duration of treatment to the potential maximum sentence for the underlying charges. Many jurisdictions set no limit. With or without formal limits, the typical successful restoration occurs in 2 to 6 months. While circumstances may warrant more extended efforts in some cases, the likelihood of success beyond 3 to 4 months appears diminished.

The minority of individuals who are persistently incompetent may be subjected to civil or "quasi-criminal" commitment in lieu of further criminal proceedings. While in some jurisdictions the procedures are identical to those in the regular civil commitment statute, in the majority of states and in federal courts, special commitment procedures apply, though these must provide due process protections similar in kind to those in the regular commitment statute. Some of these are narrowly drawn to focus on danger to others or property and frequently lack provisions for commitment based on danger to self or "grave disability." The possibility of long-term commitment may discourage malingering about incompetency, particularly in jurisdictions where charges could be reinstated when the former defendant "recovers" sufficiently to warrant consideration for release.

Edward E. Landis

See also Capacity to Consent to Treatment; Civil Commitment; Competency to Stand Trial

Further Readings

Anderson, S. D., & Hewitt, J. (2002). The effect of competency restoration training on defendants with mental retardation found not competent to proceed. *Law and Human Behavior, 26*(3), 343–351.

Bertman, L. J., Thompson, J. W., Waters, W. F., Estupanian-Kane, L., Martin, J. A., & Russell, L. (2003). Effect of an individualized treatment program on restoration of competency to stand trial in pretrial forensic patients. *Journal of the American Academy of Psychiatry and the Law, 31*(1), 27–35.

Jackson v. Indiana, 406 U.S. 715 (1972).

Miller, R. D. (2003). Hospitalization of criminal defendants for evaluation of competence to stand trial or for restoration of competence: Clinical and legal issues. *Behavioral Sciences and the Law, 21*, 369–391.

Mumley, D. L., Tillbrook, C. E., & Grisso, T. (2003). Five year research update (1996–2000): Evaluations for competence to stand trial (adjudicative competence). *Behavioral Sciences and the Law, 21*, 329–350.

Noffsinger, S. G. (2001). Restoration to competency practice guidelines. *International Journal of Offender Therapy and Comparative Criminology, 45*(3), 356–362.

Sell v. United States, 539 U.S. 166 (2003).

COMPETENCY ASSESSMENT INSTRUMENT (CAI)

The Competence to Stand Trial Assessment Instrument, often called the Competency Assessment Instrument (CAI), was developed in 1973 as a companion instrument to the Competency Screening Test (CST) and sought to standardize as well as quantify the criteria for competence to stand trial. The instrument was created by an interdisciplinary team of psychologists, psychiatrists, and lawyers at Harvard's Laboratory of Community Psychiatry during a project funded by a research grant from the Center for Studies of Crime and Delinquency, National Institute of Mental Health. The CAI addresses 13 functions related to the defendant's "ability to cope with the trial process in an adequately self-protective fashion."

Although the concept that a defendant must be competent to proceed in the trial process has been generally accepted in Western jurisprudence since the late 1700s, the current standard for competence to stand trial in the United States was laid out by the U.S. Supreme Court in *Dusky v. United States* in 1960. In *Dusky*, the Court held that for a defendant to be deemed competent to stand trial, he or she must have "sufficient present ability to consult with his lawyer with a reasonable degree of rational understanding" and "a rational as well as factual understanding of the proceedings against him."

On the basis of the standard as set forth in *Dusky* as well as reviews of appellate cases and legal literature, observations of pretrial competence hearings, and interviews of attorneys and judges, the interdisciplinary team conceptualized the standard of competence to stand trial as having three parts: the ability to cooperate with one's attorney in one's own defense, awareness and understanding of the nature and object of the legal proceedings, and understanding of the consequences of the proceedings.

As one of the first semistructured measures of trial competency, the CAI influenced the development of nearly every other instrument that has been created for competence to stand trial evaluations. The administration time of the CAI is approximately 1 hour with relatively high functioning defendants. The 13 areas of functioning addressed by the CAI are the following:

1. Appraisal of available legal defenses

2. Unmanageable behavior

3. Quality of relating to attorney

4. Planning of legal strategy, including guilty pleas to lesser charges where pertinent

5. Appraisal of the role of persons involved in a trial

6. Understanding of court procedure

7. Appreciation of charges

8. Appreciation of the range and nature of possible penalties

9. Appraisal of the likely outcome

10. Capacity to disclose to attorney the available pertinent facts surrounding the offense

11. Capacity to realistically challenge prosecution witnesses

12. Capacity to testify relevantly

13. Self-defeating versus self-serving motivation (legal sense)

In the manual, the 13 functions are conceptually defined with statements, and two or three sample questions accompany each function.

Each functional item on the CAI is to be rated on a five-point Likert-type scale, wherein a score of 1 relates to a total lack of capacity to function and a score of 5 relates to no impairment, or adequate capacity to function. A score of 6 is given when there is insufficient information to score the respective item. The item scores are neither weighted nor summed, but rather are intended to stand alone and assist the evaluator in the formation of his or her subsequent report and potential testimony. The authors of the CAI explicitly set forth the caveat that the CAI is not meant to serve as a predictor of future trial-related abilities, since scores on the instrument may fluctuate over time. The scoring process functions under the assumptions that the defendant will be afforded adequate counsel and the forensic examiner using the CAI possesses a fundamental understanding of the realities of the criminal justice system.

Little is known about the psychometric properties of the CAI. The scoring of the CAI is not standardized, and there are no norms available for the instrument. Interrater reliability coefficients for the instrument have been found to range from .84 to .97 among experienced raters and from .43 to .96 among inexperienced raters. The CAI has been found to correlate with other instruments intended to measure the same abilities as the CAI (i.e., the Competence Screening Test and Interdisciplinary Fitness Interview), lending exiguous evidence in support of its construct validity. Research on the utility of the CAI as a classification or predictive tool is scant as well, but the research that was conducted found that many evaluators used the CAI as a conceptual tool—forgoing the quantification of the items.

Controversies that surrounded the CAI on its publication regarded biases that may be inherent in the scoring of the instrument. Specifically, bias against individuals who do not have confidence in the criminal adjudication process or bias as a result of an evaluator's assumptions about the dynamics of the circumstances surrounding a trial and attorney performances have been cited. Rebuttal of these criticisms has referred to the fact that the authors have clearly indicated that the scoring of the CAI operates under the presumptions of adequate legal counsel and a trial characterized by a legal standard of fairness. Although the CAI does not include a methodical evaluation of the defendant's specific trial circumstances, three items (Items 1, 4, and 9) evaluate the defendant's capacities or perceptions regarding his or her circumstances. However, the CAI manual does not provide any guidelines for characterizing the trial circumstances. The major contribution of the CAI was the delineation of

13 legally pertinent concepts and functional areas, a contribution that continues to influence the development of instruments created to evaluate defendants' competence to stand trial.

Gianni Pirelli and Patricia A. Zapf

See also Competency Screening Test (CST); Competency to Stand Trial; Forensic Assessment; Interdisciplinary Fitness Interview (IFI)

Further Readings

Dusky v. United States, 362 U.S. 402 (1960).

Grisso, T. (2003). *Evaluating competencies: Forensic assessments and instruments*. New York: Kluwer Academic/Plenum.

Harvard Medical School, Laboratory of Community Psychiatry. (1973). *Competence to stand trial and mental illness* (DHEW Publication No. [ADM] 77-103). Rockville, MD: NIMH, Department of Health, Education, and Welfare.

COMPETENCY FOR EXECUTION

The Eighth Amendment to the U.S. Constitution prohibits cruel and unusual punishment, which, according to the U.S. Supreme Court decision in *Ford v. Wainwright* (1986), includes the execution of the insane. Thus, it is unconstitutional to execute condemned inmates who become incompetent while on death row while they remain in an incompetent state. Statutes set forth by those states that permit the death penalty often do not include specific guidelines for evaluating competency for execution, and when guidelines do exist, they vary widely. When the issue of an inmate's competency for execution arises, mental health professionals are called on to assist the court in the evaluation of competency for execution and for restoring competency in those found incompetent. Given the nature of the consequences involved, these practices often present ethical challenges and are controversial in nature.

Competency for execution, called by some commentators the "last competency" for its temporal proximity to the final resolution of an inmate's legal proceedings, is raised as an issue far less often than competency to stand trial but is no less important. The legal system in the United States and many other countries has as one of its bases the presumption of competence. That is, all defendants are presumed competent unless this issue is called into question by one of the parties to a legal proceeding. The competence of a criminal defendant may arise as an issue at any point in the legal proceedings, from as early as initial arrest and interrogation, throughout the entire legal process, and finally to the time of sentencing or, for those who have been sentenced to the ultimate penalty of death, the time of execution. Just as an incompetent defendant is not allowed to proceed to trial, so too an incompetent defendant/inmate is prohibited from being sentenced or executed. The rationale against executing incompetent individuals is that, among other things, it is inhumane, neither deterrence nor retribution is accomplished, and incompetent individuals are unable to assist in appealing their sentence.

Legal Standards

The issue of the constitutionality of executing incompetent individuals was heard by the U.S. Supreme Court in 1986 in *Ford v. Wainwright*. The Court in *Ford* held that the Eighth Amendment, which bans cruel and unusual punishment, prohibits the execution of an "insane" (mentally incompetent) person. The Court reasoned that (a) execution of the insane would offend humanity, (b) executing the insane would not serve to set an example and would not reaffirm the deterrence value believed to exist in capital punishment, (c) any individual who is believed to be insane is also believed unable to prepare "spiritually" for death, (d) madness itself is punishment and, therefore, negates the punishment value of execution, and (e) no retributive value is believed to be served by executing the mentally incompetent.

The Court in *Ford* also ruled that when questions of competency for execution were raised, due process entitled a defendant to an evidentiary hearing. Furthermore, the Court stated that this evidentiary hearing is required only when defendants make a "high threshold showing" that their competency to be executed is in question. The justices, however, did not define the precise nature of the "high threshold." Moreover, the justices could not agree on the specific fact-finding procedures to be used in case such a threshold is met: Some agreed that a full "panoply" of trial-type procedures was required, others argued that a more relaxed hearing was acceptable if due process was ensured,

and still others argued that the most minimal "pro forma" procedures were acceptable.

In addition to being divided on the fact-finding procedures, the Court also failed to specify a proper legal test of incompetence within the execution context. Only Justice Powell, in his concurring opinion, addressed the issue of the legal test for competency for execution, stating that the Eighth Amendment "forbids the execution only of those who are unaware of the punishment they are about to suffer and why they are to suffer it" (p. 2608). Furthermore, he concluded that the proper test of competency should be whether defendants can comprehend the nature, pendency, and purpose of their execution. Justice Powell argued that the retributive goal of criminal law is satisfied only when defendants are aware of the connection between their crime and its punishment and defendants can only prepare for death if they are aware that it is pending shortly. Furthermore, Justice Powell asserted that the states were free to adopt "a more expansive view of sanity" that included the "requirement that the defendant be able to assist in his own defense" (p. 2608).

Despite the charge given to individual states to develop procedures to ensure that the insane would not be executed, many states do not provide specific guidelines for evaluating competency for execution, and those guidelines that do exist vary widely. The decision in *Ford* established that it was unconstitutional to execute the insane and set the stage for psychological evaluations of death row inmates whose mental status for execution is questionable; however, the *Ford* Court left open two critical issues. First, the Court did not specify the necessary fact-finding procedures to enforce the *Ford* decision. Second, the Court failed to specify the proper legal test to be implemented in cases of competency for execution.

Although it is not legally binding, the American Bar Association, in the *ABA Criminal Justice Mental Health Standards* (1989), has also provided a legal test for determining competency for execution. This test reads as follows:

> A convict is incompetent to be executed if, as a result of mental illness or mental retardation, the convict cannot understand the nature of the pending proceedings, what he or she was tried for, the reasons for the punishment, or the nature of the punishment. A convict is also incompetent if, as a result of mental illness or mental retardation, the convict lacks sufficient capacity to recognize or understand any fact which

might exist which would make the punishment unjust or unlawful, or lacks the ability to convey such information to the court. (p. 290)

Assessment of Competency for Execution

Competency for execution, more than any other area within the field of forensic assessment, has been fraught with controversy and debate regarding whether, and to what extent, mental health professionals should become involved in this type of evaluation. Indeed, the personal outcome for the inmate who serves as the evaluee in this type of evaluation weighs heavily in this debate.

Standards for competency for execution evaluations should parallel those that apply to other types of forensic evaluations. That is, the standardized procedures that are used during the evaluation should be described to the subject of the evaluation as well as in the examiner's report, assessment measures should be relevant to the referral issue(s), and the examiner should have a sound and sophisticated conceptualization of the relevant criteria for being not competent for execution. In addition, the knowledge base of examiners should cover three domains: general legal competencies, forensic assessment methodologies, and execution-related substantive content. Finally, collateral information should be gathered. This might include (but would not be limited to) information regarding life history, psychological history and disorders, deterioration-related data, previous and current written reports, and interviews with persons who have had extensive opportunities to observe the evaluee.

Detailed information on conducting evaluations of competency for execution is beyond the scope of this entry, but the interested reader is referred to the references suggested below for further information on this topic.

Given the low base rate of incompetence for execution, there is less opportunity to conduct this type of evaluation and, therefore, even less opportunity to conduct research using a sample of inmates found incompetent to be executed or even referred for evaluations of competency for execution. As a result, the literature and commentary in this area are less well developed than they are with respect to other types of competencies (such as competency to stand trial). As was the case in the context of assessing competency to stand trial, the first assessment instruments to assist evaluators in the evaluation of competency for execution have taken the form of checklists of items that serve to structure the evaluation. While the first checklists for evaluating competency to stand trial were developed in the mid-1960s, the first checklists for evaluating competency for execution have only recently been developed. The interested reader is referred to the checklists developed by Kimberley Ackerson, Bruce Ebert, and Patricia Zapf (all cited below).

Treatment for Restoration to Competency

Given the amount of debate and controversy surrounding the role of mental health professionals in the assessment of competency for execution, it is obvious that even more controversy surrounds the role of the mental health professional in the treatment of those inmates found incompetent, for the purpose of restoring their competence to be executed. This is a complex issue about which commentators have written on both sides. Some believe that it is never permissible to provide treatment for the purpose of restoring an individual to competence when the result is execution, whereas others have indicated that this may be permissible if the incompetent inmate had expressed a desire to be restored to competence at an earlier time when the inmate was competent. In addition, others have provided further commentary regarding the situation where an inmate has indicated a preference for death by electing to undergo treatment to restore competence for the purpose of execution, calling into question the rationality of that individual. What complicates matters further is that some professional bodies, such as the American Medical Association, have put forth statements indicating that providing such treatment is considered ethically unacceptable, thus putting physicians and psychiatrists who work for the prison and correctional systems, and who are expected to treat incompetent inmates for the purpose of restoring them to competence, in the difficult situation of having to reconcile how to perform the duties required by their employers while upholding the ethical requirements of their profession. Obviously, there is no easy answer.

Research on Competency for Execution

There has been a dearth of empirical research on competency to be executed. Part of the explanation for this may be the fact that only a handful of individuals have made successful claims of incompetency to be executed. In addition, this particular type of competency tends to evoke strong emotion in individuals, which in turn may affect the motivation of involved professionals to conduct research in this area. The limited amount of empirical research that has been conducted has been confined to surveys. No research to date has examined the issue of competency to be executed in a sample of offenders sentenced to death.

Patricia A. Zapf

See also Checklist for Competency for Execution Evaluations

Further Readings

Ackerson, K. S., Brodsky, S. L., & Zapf, P. A. (2005). Judges' and psychologists' assessments of legal and clinical factors in competence for execution. *Psychology, Public Policy, and Law, 11,* 164–193.

American Bar Association. (1989). *Criminal justice mental health standards.* Washington, DC: Author.

Brodsky, S. L., Zapf, P. A., & Boccaccini, M. T. (2005). Competency for execution assessments: Ethical continuities and professional tasks. *Journal of Forensic Psychology Practice, 5,* 65–74.

Ebert, B. (2001). Competency to be executed: A proposed instrument to evaluate an inmate's level of competency in light of the Eighth Amendment prohibition against the execution of the presently insane. *Law and Psychology Review, 25,* 29–57.

Ford v. Wainwright, 477 U.S. 399 (1986).

Heilbrun, K. S. (1987). The assessment of competency for execution: An overview. *Behavioral Sciences and the Law, 5,* 383–396.

Zapf, P. A., Boccaccini, M. T., & Brodsky, S. L. (2003). Assessment of competency for execution: Professional guidelines and an evaluation checklist. *Behavioral Sciences and the Law, 21,* 103–120.

COMPETENCY SCREENING TEST (CST)

The Competency Screening Test (CST) was developed to address the unnecessary pretrial detention and commitment of individuals charged with crimes but likely to be judged fit to stand trial. This forensic instrument was designed and tested to provide objective measures based on the legal criteria for determination of a defendant's capacity to participate in his or her own defense against criminal charges. Psychological diagnoses of mental illness or mental retardation may indicate incompetency for trial but may not be sufficient for such a finding by a court. Therefore, this test was developed to reduce the risk of inappropriate findings based on mental state alone.

The right of a person to be mentally as well as physically present to face his or her accusers was recognized as early as 1764 in British Common Law. In 1960, for the first time, the U.S. Supreme Court enunciated the constitutional requirement of competency to stand trial in *Dusky v. United States* (1960) and spelled out the legal standard that the defendant must have "sufficient present ability to consult with his lawyer with a reasonable degree of rational understanding" and "a rational as well as a factual understanding of the proceedings against him."

Description and Development

The CST consists of 22 items in a sentence-completion format designed as a self-reporting paper-and-pencil instrument.

The content of each item relates to some aspect of the task of a defendant preparing for and going to trial as a result of criminal charges. Each item is based on a factor within the legal definition of fitness for trial and the psychological conditions that may contribute to significant impairment of that ability.

Scores on the 22 items were subjected to a factor analysis using a varimax orthogonal rotation. Six factors emerged that were consistent with the defendant's ability to stand trial:

1. Relationship to one's attorney in establishing a defense

2. Understanding and awareness of the nature of the court proceedings

3. Affective response to the court process in dealing with accusations and feelings of guilt

4. Judgmental qualities in engaging in the strategy and evaluation of the trial

5. Trust and confidence in the attorney

6. Recognition of the seriousness of the situation

Each of the 22 items is scored on a 3-point scale, from 0 to 2, based on one or more of these factors.

A response that clearly relates to one of the legal criteria receives a score of 2. Responses characterized as redundant, circular, or impoverished but not clearly inappropriate are scored 1. A zero score would be given for an answer that reveals characteristics such as self-defeating behavior, substantial disorganization, or a thought disorder that would interfere with the ability to contribute to one's defense. For example, on Item 2, "When I go to court, the lawyer will . . .," an appropriate response is "defend me" and would be scored a 2, reflecting the nature of the proceedings and the role of the attorney. A contrasting response, "put me away," would receive a zero score. This item addresses the legal criterion of a defendant's ability to assist an attorney in his or her own defense. The psychological referent focuses on trust and the ability to engage with another, in this case the lawyer. Understanding of the role of legal representation is also an element in this item.

Scores are summated and can total in a range from 0 to 44. Qualitative differences were found at about 20; thus, a score of 20 or below is judged as incompetency for trial. Reliability by trained researchers was .93, significant at the .001 level.

As a screening instrument, the purpose of the CST is to avoid hospitalization of those defendants who may be tested in the court and most likely deemed to be competent, rather than delay the trial of those individuals. The test results of the CST and judges' decisions on return to trial were generally consistent. Focusing on the criteria for competency to stand trial also offered specific guidelines for making a judgment that could avoid pretrial detention. Several validation studies have followed the original test construction and research and have supported the efficacy of the CST.

Further Research

Additional research has been undertaken by psychologists to aid the courts in the assessment of fitness for trial. John Monahan and his colleagues at the University of Virginia have constructed an instrument based on the parameters of understanding, reasoning, and appreciation, consistent with the psychological underpinnings of the legal criteria for competency to stand trial.

Paul D. Lipsitt

See also Competency, Restoration of; Competency to Stand Trial; Georgia Court Competence Test (GCCT)

Further Readings

Dusky v. United States, 362 U.S. 402 (1960).

Lipsitt, P. D., Lelos, D., & McGarry, A. L. (1971). Competency for trial: A screening instrument. *American Journal of Psychiatry, 128*(1), 105–109.

Nottingham, E. J., IV, & Mattson, R. E. (1981). A validation study of the Competency Screening Test. *Law and Human Behavior, 5,* 329–335.

Otto, R. K., Poythress, N. G., Nicholson, R. A., Edens, J. E., Monahan, J., Bonnie, R.J., et al. (1998). Psychometric properties of the MacArthur Competence Tool–Criminal Adjudication. *Psychological Assessment, 10,* 435–443.

Randolph, J. J., Hicks, T., Mason, D. J. (1982). The Competency Screening Test: A validation study in Cook County, Illinois. *Criminal Justice and Behavior, 9,* 495–500.

COMPETENCY TO BE SENTENCED

The question of whether an individual is competent to be sentenced hinges on the broader question "What is competence?" In general, competence is defined within the legal arena as the mental ability to play an active role in legal proceedings. Competence to be sentenced is a specific form of legal competence that addresses an individual's ability to participate in the sentencing stage of trial and to both understand and appreciate the ramifications of the sentence that is imposed. The term *competence to be sentenced* has been used interchangeably with *competence to be executed*, but the former expression is more inclusive than the latter. Psychologists assist the courts by providing evaluations of competency to be sentenced, although there are minimal assessment guidelines and no accepted measures to guide their assessments.

The general standard for competency was defined by the Supreme Court in *Dusky v. United States* (1960) as the defendant's "sufficient present ability to consult with his lawyer with a reasonable degree of rational understanding" and "a rational as well as factual understanding of the proceedings against him." This protection has been deemed to include the stages from the time of arrest through the end of the trial. However, sentencing is separate from trial, and jurisdictions differ on whether the *Dusky* standard extends to the sentencing phase. In some jurisdictions, defendants need only have a minimal level of competency to be sentenced (e.g., a defendant need only understand why he or she is being sentenced). Other jurisdictions hold that sentencing is part of the trial, therefore the defendant must meet the more exacting *Dusky* standard before he or she may be sentenced. Overall, the literature suggests that the competency to be sentenced standard is less stringent than the competence to stand trial standard.

The purposes behind the guarantee of competency to be sentenced are generally argued to be threefold. First, defendants are guaranteed competency to protect their individual rights. For example, in some cases, the defendant has the right to allocution at sentencing. The right of allocution refers to a defendant's right to speak before the sentence is pronounced in order to address any legal cause why the sentence should not be pronounced or provide mitigating information that may reduce the sentence. Without the mental ability to participate in the proceedings, this right would be meaningless. Second, society has an interest in guaranteeing fair results and the dignity of the trial process. If a defendant does not appear to be a lucid participant in his or her trial and sentencing, the process loses these qualities. Third, to be competent to be sentenced, defendants should comprehend the duration and severity of the sentence. This understanding is a prerequisite for the sentence to meet its goals of punishment and deterrence from future crime. If defendants cannot rationally comprehend the reason why they have been sentenced, the punishment cannot have its desired effect on the psyche or act as a deterrent.

If a genuine doubt concerning the defendant's competency to be sentenced arises, the defense, the prosecution, or the judge may raise the issue. If there is sufficient evidence that the defendant's competency is questionable, the judge may order an examination by a mental health professional, such as a psychologist or a psychiatrist. When the evaluation is completed, the expert provides an opinion to the court in the form of a report and, possibly, testimony. The judge makes a decision regarding the competency of the defendant. If the defendant is found to be competent, the sentencing proceeds. If the defendant is found to be not competent, he or she is sent for treatment to restore competency before sentencing.

Psychologists have researched the issue of competency to stand trial, developed assessment strategies, and implemented treatment approaches to restore individuals' overall competence. The defendant's cognitive functioning is of central importance in evaluating any

form of competence. Similarly, a defendant's ability to communicate mitigating factors effectively to his or her attorney is essential. Many measures have aided in the evaluation of an individual's overall competency. These include the Competency Screening Test (CST), the Competency Assessment Instrument (CAI), the Georgia Court Competency Test (GCCT–MSH), the Interdisciplinary Fitness Interview (IFI), the Fitness Interview Test (FIT–R), the MacArthur Competence Assessment Tool–Criminal Adjudication (MacCAT–CA), and the Evaluation of Competence to Stand Trial–Revised (ECST–R). These measures provide a clinician with information relevant to an individual's competence to stand trial; however, there are minimal assessment guidelines and no accepted measures to evaluate competence to be sentenced. A comprehensive evaluation should be conducted to assess a defendant's intellect, his or her personality, and any underlying psychopathology, in addition to the basic competency criteria. As mentioned above, if a defendant is found not competent to be sentenced, the question of possible restoration to competence must be dealt with. Restoration to competence may achieved by the use of psycho-education, medication, or individual therapy.

Individuals with mental retardation or metal illness, juveniles, and people suffering from dementia are at higher risk of being found incompetent to be sentenced. These groups are identified as "at risk" due to limitations in rational understanding and abstract thinking. By definition, individuals with mental retardation have below-average intellectual abilities and impaired adaptive behavior, which affect all aspects of competency. Juveniles are labeled at risk because they are considered developmentally and psychosocially immature. Children typically develop higher-order processing and reasoning abilities as they mature. Although there is no exact age at which children develop this reasoning ability, the idea that juvenile offenders should be treated differently from adult offenders has long been an accepted legal premise. Research has focused on determining whether a juvenile possesses the minimal reasoning ability required to be found legally competent. The findings indicate that juveniles who lack developmental and psychosocial maturity (a) may not fully appreciate the long-term consequences of their decisions, (b) may yield to peer influence, and (c) may minimize the ramifications and risk of being found guilty. These limitations would lead to impaired decision making. People with mental illness and/or dementia, on the other hand, sometimes lose their ability to reason abstractly and to understand legal processes.

Kimberly A. Larson, Michael P. Griffin,
and J. Gregory Olley

See also Competence Assessment for Standing Trial for Defendants With Mental Retardation (CAST*MR); Competency, Restoration of; Competency Assessment Instrument (CAI); Competency for Execution; Competency Screening Test (CST); Competency to Stand Trial; Competency to Waive Appeals; Competency to Waive Counsel (Proceed Pro Se)

Further Readings

Cunningham, M. D., & Goldstein, A. M. (2003). Sentencing determinations in death penalty cases. In A. M. Goldstein (Ed.), *Handbook of psychology: Vol. 11. Forensic psychology* (pp. 407–436.). Hoboken, NJ: Wiley.

Dusky v. United States, 362 U.S. 402 (1960).

Melton, G. G., Petrila, J., Poythress, N. G., & Slobogin, C. (1997). *Psychological evaluations for the courts: A handbook for mental health professionals and lawyers* (2nd ed.). New York: Guilford Press.

COMPETENCY TO CONFESS

Competency to confess refers to a suspect's ability to make a knowing, intelligent, and voluntary waiver of the *Miranda* warnings at the time of police questioning. Confessions that are given after a suspect waives his or her *Miranda* rights are sometimes challenged on the basis that the suspect was not competent to confess, meaning that the suspect was not capable of making a knowing, intelligent, and voluntary waiver of the *Miranda* rights and therefore could not have understood, appreciated, and willingly waived those rights. A confession that is successfully challenged cannot be used in court against the defendant. Assessment of competency is therefore performed after the confession is given. This assessment is performed by a mental health professional (often a forensic psychologist) and takes into account the defendant's ability at the time of the interrogation to understand the warnings and make intelligent use of them and the psychological factors that could be relevant to the court in assessing the voluntariness of the waiver.

In the 1966 *Miranda v. Arizona* case, the U.S. Supreme Court ruled that any statement arising from the custodial interrogation of a suspect would be presumed involuntary and thus inadmissible unless the police provide the suspect with four warnings: (1) the suspect has the right to remain silent, (2) any statements made by the suspect can be used in court against him or her, (3) the suspect has the right to the presence of an attorney before and during the interrogation, and (4) an attorney will be provided free of charge if the suspect does not have the ability to pay for one. Many jurisdictions have added a fifth prong, that these rights can be invoked at any time during the interrogation process and that once they are invoked, the questioning must cease until an attorney is present. The U.S. Supreme Court in the *Miranda* decision opined that these rights must be waived *knowingly, intelligently*, and *voluntarily*. Case law has clarified the meaning of these three prongs.

The term *competency to confess* is a misnomer because it explicitly refers to one's ability to understand and appreciate the significance of the *Miranda* rights at the time of police questioning. It also refers to the psychological characteristics of a defendant that have an impact on the voluntariness of the *Miranda* waiver. Thus, this competency differs from other competencies (e.g., competency to stand trial, competency to consent to treatment) in that the mental health professional must examine the individual's competence at some point in the past. The court is not concerned with current or future competency with respect to *Miranda* warnings; rather, the court is concerned about whether the defendant was able to make a knowing and intelligent waiver at the time he or she was questioned by the police.

Also, not all three prongs needed to effectuate a valid *Miranda* waiver can be addressed completely by the mental health professional. Case law clearly indicates that for a waiver of rights to be deemed involuntary, there must be a showing of police misconduct. It has to be shown that the police were unduly coercive and overstepped their bounds in extracting a *Miranda* waiver. It is beyond the scope of a mental health expert's expertise to determine whether and how that threshold was crossed. Yet psychological expertise can be useful to the court in determining whether a suspect possesses psychological characteristics that increase his or her susceptibility to the effects of police conduct. Such characteristics include interrogative suggestibility, compliance, intellectual functioning, anxiety, memory, and sleep deprivation. There are a number of specialized tests that can assist the clinician in evaluating the psychological factors relevant to the voluntary prong of the *Miranda* waiver.

It is within the realm of the mental health professional's expertise to opine directly on the knowing and intelligent prongs of the *Miranda* waiver. A knowing waiver of rights is defined as the individual's understanding or comprehension of the rights combined with the manner in which the rights were administered by law enforcement. For example, one would expect different levels of understanding in illiterate suspects if they were required to read the rights on their own versus having the rights read to them. An intelligent waiver of rights is different from a knowing waiver of rights. The former involves knowledge of the rights, decision-making capacity, and appreciation of the significance of the rights based on one's knowledge of how the legal system works. Thus, while suspects may understand that they have a right to defense counsel, an intelligent waiver of the right to counsel cannot be made if they erroneously believe that a defense attorney would only work on behalf of innocent defendants.

Evaluation of a defendant's competency to confess requires a comprehensive forensic evaluation. An extensive clinical history, examination of mental status, and record review are generally combined with psychological testing to assess a defendant's cognitive and emotional functioning. The focus is directly on the psychological functioning that would have been displayed at the time of the police questioning. Given that the evaluation must be functionally based—that is, clinically relevant data should be integrated with the appropriate legal criteria (i.e., knowing, intelligent, and voluntary), the mental health professional must specifically assess behavior relevant to the legal criteria. Thomas Grisso developed four psychological tests to aid in the assessment of a juvenile's or an adult's ability to make a knowing and intelligent waiver of rights. Although these tests (like any other test) are subject to misuse, if used properly as part of a comprehensive competency assessment, they can provide useful data to the clinician and, ultimately, to the trier of fact.

The assessment of competency to confess must also take into consideration the complexity of the wording of the rights. In general, the *Miranda* warnings are written at approximately the seventh-grade level of reading comprehension. Yet the complexity of the wording of the rights varies greatly within and between jurisdictions.

Research has shown that 23% of adults do not understand at least one of the four *Miranda* rights.

Moreover, 70% of adult nonoffenders and 43% of adult offenders erroneously believe that the right to remain silent is revokable by the judge. Juveniles aged 14 years and below do not understand their rights as well as older juveniles and adults. With juveniles and adults, intelligence is positively correlated with *Miranda* comprehension.

I. Bruce Frumkin

See also Capacity to Waive Rights; Confession Evidence; Grisso's Instruments for Assessing Understanding and Appreciation of *Miranda* Rights; Reid Technique for Interrogations

Further Readings

Cloud, M., Shepherd, G., Barkoff, A., & Shur, J. (2002). Words without meaning: The constitution, confessions, and mentally retarded suspects. *University of Chicago Law Review, 69,* 495–624.

Frumkin, I. B. (2007). Psychological evaluation in *Miranda* waiver and confession cases. In R. Denny & J. Sullivan (Eds.), *Clinical neuropsychology in the criminal forensic setting.* New York: Guilford Press.

Grisso, T. (2003). *Evaluating competencies: Forensic assessment and instruments* (2nd ed.). New York: Kluwer Academic.

Miranda v. Arizona, 384 U.S. 436 (1966).

COMPETENCY TO STAND TRIAL

The legal standard for competency to stand trial in the United States was articulated by the U.S. Supreme Court in *Dusky v. United States* (1960), wherein the Court determined that a defendant must have "sufficient present ability to consult with his lawyer with a reasonable degree of rational understanding" and a "rational as well as factual understanding of the proceedings against him" (p. 402). Mental health professionals are called on to assist the courts by evaluating defendants' competency to stand trial, often aided by assessment tools designed specifically for this purpose, and by providing treatment for the restoration of competency in incompetent defendants. Psychological research in this area has examined the reliability of competency assessments, the characteristics of defendants deemed incompetent to stand trial, and the characteristics associated with restorability.

Competency to stand trial is the most common type of criminal forensic evaluation, with approximately 60,000 evaluations conducted annually in the United States. That is, between 2% and 8% of all felony defendants are referred for evaluations of competency to stand trial each year. The issue at stake in an evaluation of competency to stand trial is the defendant's *current* mental functioning; this is often confused with criminal responsibility (insanity), wherein the issue at stake is the defendant's mental state at the time of the offense. The prohibition against trying an incompetent defendant dates back to at least the 17th century and serves the dual purpose of ensuring a fair trial for the defendant and preserving the dignity of the adversarial process.

Competency to stand trial is but one type of competency that falls under the larger, more encompassing headings of adjudicative competence or competency to proceed. The issue of a defendant's competence may be raised at any point in the proceedings before a verdict is rendered; thus, competency to confess (waive *Miranda* rights), competency to plead guilty, competency to waive the right to counsel, and competency to stand trial all fall under the umbrella of adjudicative competence or competency to proceed. Furthermore, the U.S. Supreme Court in *Godinez v. Moran* (1993) indicated that the standards for the various types of criminal competencies (pleading guilty, waiving counsel, and standing trial) were to be the same. Thus, in light of the decision in *Godinez* as well as the fact that upward of 90% of criminal cases are resolved through the plea bargaining process rather than by going to trial per se, evaluations of competency to stand trial necessarily include evaluation of the defendant's ability to plead guilty and to engage in the plea bargaining process. The term *competency to stand trial* has begun to be replaced by the term *competency to proceed* in some states, but for the purpose of remaining true to the literature and commentary that have developed up to this point, the term *competency to stand trial* is used in this entry.

Legal Standard and Procedures

Since 1960, every state has adopted the *Dusky* standard either verbatim or with minor variations in the wording. In addition, some states have elaborated their competency statutes to include articulated standards wherein various specific factors that must be addressed by evaluators in a competency evaluation are set out.

The issue of a defendant's competency to stand trial may be raised by any party to the proceedings (the defense, the prosecution, or the court more generally), although in the vast majority of cases the issue is raised by the defense. A formal inquiry into a defendant's competency to stand trial must take place if a "bona fide doubt" about his or her competency exists, as all defendants are presumed competent.

Competency evaluations historically occurred in inpatient settings; however, the majority of competency evaluations now occur in community-based settings, including mental health centers, private practice offices, and jails. Research has indicated that approximately 20% (although this varies by jurisdiction) of all defendants referred for competency evaluation are deemed incompetent; thus, the vast majority of referred defendants are competent to stand trial. Various explanations for the high rate of competence have been put forth, including defense attorneys using the referrals as "fishing expeditions" to attempt to gather information that may be helpful in their defense or to investigate the feasibility of a later insanity plea. Others suggest that these referrals are made to prolong the amount of time it takes to get to trial, thus giving the defense (or perhaps the prosecution) more time to prepare the case; to have a mentally ill defendant hospitalized or treated when he or she will not voluntarily undergo hospitalization or treatment; or so that prosecutors and/or defense attorneys may guard against the possibility of a later appeal on the grounds that an individual with a known history of mental illness was allowed to proceed to trial under the presumption of competence. It is unclear how often the aforementioned reasons serve as the primary rationale for requesting a competency evaluation. In addition, it is important to acknowledge that the procedures used in various jurisdictions may account for the differing rates of incompetence. For example, in jurisdictions that use a screening process to eliminate those who are clearly competent from further evaluation, a higher rate of incompetence would be expected among defendants who undergo a formal evaluation of competency to stand trial.

Depending on the jurisdiction, one or more mental health professionals will evaluate a defendant's competency to stand trial and submit the results of this evaluation to the court in the form of a written report. A hearing on the issue of competency may take place; however, in most instances, this does not occur. Instead, the court usually renders a decision regarding the defendant's competency on the basis of the mental health professional's report. Although the determination of a defendant's competency status is a legal decision, research has shown that the courts typically concur with the opinion of mental health professionals. In fact, some research has indicated rates of agreement between the court and the evaluator to be greater than 95%.

Defendants who are found competent by the court will proceed with their case, whereas those who are found incompetent will, in most instances, be ordered by the court to undergo treatment for the purpose of restoration of competency. Treatment for restoring a defendant's competency to stand trial most often occurs on an inpatient basis, although some states have moved toward a "least-restrictive" alternative, which allows for the possibility of outpatient treatment. Generally, most defendants are restored to competency within a 1-year period. Once restored, the defendant resumes with his or her legal proceedings. Those defendants who cannot be restored to competency will generally have their charges dismissed or nolle processed.

Until the 1970s, incompetent defendants were often committed to lengthy periods of confinement in state maximum-security units, even though they were neither tried nor convicted of a crime. In 1972, the U.S. Supreme Court in the case of *Jackson v. Indiana* decided that incompetent individuals could not be held for "more than a reasonable period of time necessary to determine whether there is a substantial probability" that they will regain competency in the foreseeable future (p. 738). The Court, however, did not give any indication as to what might be considered a "reasonable" period of time. As a result of the *Jackson* decision, many states amended their statutes to include either language similar to *Jackson* or specific timelines for determining whether someone might be restored to competency.

With respect to the issue of medication, the U.S. Supreme Court in a series of decisions has indicated that a defendant may be forcibly medicated to restore competency under certain conditions, including an "overriding justification and a determination of medical appropriateness" (*Riggins v. Nevada*, 1992); its being essential to the safety of the defendant or the safety of others (*Riggins v. Nevada*, 1992; *Washington v. Harper*, 1990); or a finding that the medication is likely to restore competency and will not result in side effects that might affect a defendant's ability to assist counsel and alternative and less intrusive methods are not available (*Sell v. United States*, 2003). Thus, for the purpose of restoring competency, it seems that the right of a defendant to refuse medication is significantly limited. In this instance, it appears that the government's interest in trying a competent defendant carries more weight than a defendant's right to refuse medication.

Competency Evaluation

At its most basic, the evaluation of a defendant's competency to stand trial involves an assessment of the psycholegal abilities required of the defendant (as per the relevant legal statutes of the jurisdiction), an assessment of the current mental status of the defendant, and a determination of whether a linkage exists between any psycholegal deficits that may be evident and any mental disease or defect that may exist. Thus, a mental disease or defect serves as a prerequisite for a determination of incompetency, and any deficits in the relevant psycholegal abilities must be linked to this mental disease or defect. In addition, the evaluation of these components must occur within the specific context of the defendant's particular case. That is, the complexities of the particular case must be considered as well as, and in conjunction with, the specific abilities of the particular defendant.

Numerous forensic assessment instruments have been developed to aid in the evaluation of competency to stand trial. A full review of these instruments is beyond the scope of this entry, but the interested reader is referred to the cross-references listed below for more information. The instruments that have been developed range from simple checklists with little to no empirical support to detailed measures that have been developed and investigated with the highest level of scientific rigor. Some tools, such as the Fitness Interview Test–Revised, can be used either as a screen to help systematically identify individuals in need of further evaluation or as a means of structuring a more detailed competency evaluation. Others, such as the MacArthur Competence Assessment Tool–Criminal Adjudication or the Evaluation of Competence to Stand Trial–Revised, provide for a detailed assessment of competency-related abilities, to be used in conjunction with additional assessment with respect to the defendant's particular case. In addition, other instruments have been developed for use with specific populations of defendants, such as the Competence Assessment for Standing Trial for Defendants With Mental Retardation.

Research has demonstrated that there is generally good agreement among evaluators with respect to overall decisions regarding competency; however, examiner agreement falls significantly when specific psycholegal deficits are examined. Research has indicated that examiner agreement reaches 80% or higher for overall decisions regarding competency but that it falls to about 25% across a series of competency domains. Of course, it is the more difficult cases, the gray-area cases in which competency is truly a serious question, that are of the greatest concern and for which no research is available.

Given the low base rate of incompetence, high levels of agreement among examiners on the issue of a defendant's overall competence are to be expected; however, high levels of reliability do not ensure that valid decisions are being made. Validity is difficult to assess because of the criterion problem; that is, there is no true criterion for competency and thus no way to determine whether decisions that have been made about a defendant's competency are accurate. It is impossible to fully assess predictive validity as only those defendants who are considered competent are allowed to proceed; thus, we have no way of knowing whether a defendant who was considered incompetent was actually unable to perform the abilities required of him or her.

Characteristics of Incompetent Defendants

The vast majority of the research that has been conducted on competency to stand trial has examined the characteristics of and differences between competent and incompetent defendants. The constellation of characteristics held in common by defendants referred for evaluations of competency include being male, single, or unemployed; living alone; having a history of contact with both the criminal justice and the mental health systems; and being diagnosed with a major mental disorder.

The individuals who are found incompetent to stand trial generally show the following characteristics: poor performance on psychological tests that measure a defendant's legally relevant functional capacities, a diagnosis of psychosis, and psychiatric symptoms indicative of severe psychopathology. In addition, diagnoses of schizophrenia, mental retardation, mood disorders, and organic brain disorders have all been found to be strong predictors of incompetency.

Direct comparisons of competent and incompetent defendants reveal that incompetent defendants are significantly more likely to be single, unemployed, charged with a minor offense, and diagnosed with a psychotic disorder and significantly less likely to be charged with a violent crime and to have substance use disorders than are competent defendants.

Competency Restoration

In light of the Supreme Court's decision in *Jackson* (discussed above), most jurisdictions now require evaluators to provide an opinion regarding the restorability of a defendant who is considered incompetent to stand trial. In general, evaluators are usually required to provide information to the court on whether the defendant can be restored to competency (or the probability of restoration occurring) and what the available treatment options are for the defendant. In addition, some jurisdictions require the evaluator to provide an estimate of the time frame required for restoration. Generally, many defendants are restored to competency within 6 months, and the vast majority are restored within a 1-year period.

Although a full discussion of competency restoration is beyond the scope of this entry, some research has examined the characteristics of restorable and nonrestorable incompetent defendants. In general, this research has indicated that those defendants considered to be restorable tend to be younger and are more likely to have a previous criminal history and a nonpsychotic diagnosis than their unrestorable counterparts.

Patricia A. Zapf and Virginia G. Cooper

See also Competency, Foundational and Decisional; Competency, Restoration of; Competency Assessment Instrument (CAI); Competency Screening Test (CST); Competency to Waive Counsel (Proceed Pro Se); Evaluation of Competence to Stand Trial–Revised (ECST–R); Fitness Interview Test–Revised (FIT–R); Georgia Court Competence Test (GCCT); Interdisciplinary Fitness Interview (IFI); MacArthur Competence Assessment Tool for Criminal Adjudication (MacCAT–CA)

Further Readings

Dusky v. United States, 362 U.S. 402 (1960).

Godinez v. Moran, 509, U.S. 389 (1993).

Grisso, T. (2003). *Evaluating competencies: Forensic assessments and instruments* (2nd ed.). New York: Kluwer Academic/Plenum.

Jackson v. Indiana, 406 U.S. 715 (1972).

Melton, G. B., Petrila, J., Poythress, N. G., & Slogobin, C. (1997). *Psychological valuations for the courts: A handbook for mental health professionals and lawyers* (2nd ed.). New York: Guilford Press.

Riggins v. Nevada, 504 U.S. 127 (1992).

Roesch, R., & Golding, S. L. (1980). *Competency to stand trial.* Chicago: University of Illinois Press.

Roesch, R., Zapf, P. A., Golding, S. L., & Skeem, J. L. (1999). Defining and assessing competency to stand trial. In A. K. Hess & I. B Weiner (Eds.), *The handbook of forensic psychology* (2nd ed., pp. 327–349). New York: Wiley.

Sell v. United States, 539 U.S. 166 (2003).

Washington v. Harper, 494 U.S. 210 (1990).

Zapf, P. A., & Roesch, R. (2006). Competency to stand trial: A guide for evaluators. In I. B. Weiner & A. K. Hess (Eds.), *The handbook of forensic psychology* (3rd ed., pp. 305–331). New York: Wiley.

Zapf, P. A., Viljoen, J. L., Whittemore, K. E., Poythress, N. G., & Roesch, R. (2002). Competency: Past, present, and future. In J. R. P. Ogloff (Ed.), *Taking psychology and law into the twenty first century* (pp. 171–198). Kluwer Academic/Plenum.

COMPETENCY TO WAIVE APPEALS

Appellate review of a felony conviction is a constitutional right. The validity of a relinquishment of this or any other constitutional right rests on whether the waiver is made knowingly, intelligently, and voluntarily. There are two distinct arenas where waivers of appeals are encountered: plea bargains in criminal cases and death-sentenced inmates "volunteering" for execution. Though waivers of appellate review in plea bargains are legally complex, they are not philosophically, ethically, or forensically problematic. This is largely because the defendant makes an election that, viewed from both subjective and external perspectives, is in his self-interest. A waiver of appellate review by a death-sentenced inmate, however, is fraught with philosophical and ethical dilemmas, as well as forensic evaluation ambiguities. This situation is compounded because the U.S. Supreme Court has not articulated clear standards or procedures for evaluation of the competency of death-sentenced inmates to waive appellate review. Accordingly, forensic evaluations of this issue by mental health professionals are at best comprehensive and highly descriptive in nature.

Waiver of Appeals in Plea Bargains

Depending on the jurisdiction, a waiver of the right to appellate review may be required of a defendant as a condition for a plea bargain. A waiver under these circumstances can be viewed as analogous to the defendant entering into a contract that is perceived to be most beneficial (or least onerous) to the defendant, as well as contributing to a more efficient administration of justice. Critics, however, note that a waiver of appeals as a precondition for securing a plea bargain is inherently coercive. Furthermore, such a waiver is invariably unknowing, as at the time of the waiver, the defendant may not yet have been sentenced or may not recognize limitations in the effectiveness of counsel, sentencing in excess of the statutory maximum, racially based sentencing, and so forth.

Though these opposing considerations result in a complex legal analysis, waivers of appeals in a plea bargain are not forensically, philosophically, or ethically problematic. Forensic evaluations of the competency to make such a waiver are routinely subsumed within the broader consideration of competency to stand trial. There is little philosophical tension, as the defendant making this election is typically acting in rational self-interest—that is, to secure a less severe sentence. Furthermore, this plea bargain and the associated waiver of appeals are usually accomplished with the advice, participation, and assistance of defense counsel, whose role of facilitating the most advantageous outcome for the defendant is ethically straightforward.

Complexities in Waiver of Appeals Among Death-Sentenced Inmates

Waivers of appellate review among death-sentenced inmates are notably different from those routinely encountered at plea bargaining. Whereas the defendant in a plea bargain may quite rationally waive appeals as part of obtaining a more favorable sentence, such a waiver by a death-sentenced inmate represents an acceleration of the arguably more onerous punishment of execution. This volunteering, as it were, for death cuts against basic expectations of self-preservation and, accordingly, immediately raises questions regarding the rationality and motivations of such a determination. Equally problematic, the volunteering death-sentenced inmate is at cross-purposes with appellate counsel, who are likely to regard that they are ethically bound to delay or seek relief from the death sentence. Not uncommonly, the desire of the death-sentenced volunteer to accelerate execution is not shared by his or her family, who may seek standing to intervene as a "next friend" and continue with the appellate review.

A decision by a death-sentenced inmate to functionally accelerate execution by forgoing appeals creates significant tension between competing rights and imperatives. On the one hand, competent adults (including death-sentenced inmates) are accorded some self-determination regarding their own mortality. For example, an individual can elect to forgo or discontinue medically indicated treatment even if death is the predictable result but is barred from committing suicide or seeking physician-assisted death. There is an analogous conundrum of determining where a rational determination that solitary confinement awaiting an inevitable death is more onerous than death stops and state-assisted suicide begins.

Counterbalancing the right to self-determination among death-sentenced inmates, Justice John Marshall expressed in his dissenting opinion in *Whitmore v. Arkansas* (1990) that society has an interest in preserving the integrity of the criminal justice system and safeguarding the reliability of the application of capital punishment. Meaningful appellate review was made central to the reliable administration of the death penalty in *Gregg v. Georgia* (1976). How is the death penalty as a legitimate sanction preserved if a death-sentenced inmate who is innocent or who has been sentenced in a constitutionally flawed trial is allowed to "volunteer" in order to escape the travails of confinement?

Finally, there is tension between the complexity of appellate review and the limited literacy and legal sophistication of most capital offenders. Both direct appeals and postconviction review are extended, complicated, and tortured processes. Capital offenders may have difficulty in fully comprehending the associated legal issues or realistically evaluating their potential for success, rendering the "knowing and intelligent" condition illusory. Similarly, the concrete and rigid thinking associated with limited intelligence or neuropsychological deficits may interfere with effective problem solving and a realistic appraisal of available options, even while making "logical" arguments.

The "voluntary" factor is also a complex consideration among death-sentenced inmates who seek to waive their appeals. This complexity is a function of both internal and external experience. A history of

family dysfunction, substance dependence, and neuropsychological insults and findings as well as limited intelligence and literacy deficits are common among death-sentenced inmates. Such a background would be expected to reduce resilience. Not surprisingly, rates of depression and other psychological disorders among death-sentenced inmates are relatively high. Furthermore, the chronic stress of being under a sentence of death is not insignificant. These psychological experiences leave logic intact but significantly intrude on the death-sentenced inmate's "free will."

These internal reactions may be aggravated by the arduous conditions of confinement on death row. Quite simply, many death-sentenced inmates who seek to end their appeals do so because they find the conditions on death row to be intolerable. This is not a surprising reaction. In most jurisdictions in the United States, death-sentenced inmates are held in solitary confinement in cramped cells, in death-segregated units, with severe restriction of activities or interaction with others. These conditions have been identified as both psychologically destabilizing and inherently coercive. The coercive implications of death row confinement in waivers of appeal have gained additional salience from research by Cunningham and colleagues demonstrating that death-sentenced inmates who were mainstreamed in the Missouri Department of Corrections with non-death-sentenced inmates were not a disproportionate source of violence. The combined effects of premorbid psychological vulnerability, depression, chronic stress, and extraordinarily restrictive confinement have been identified by international courts (e.g., *Soering v. United Kingdom*, 1989) as giving rise to "death row syndrome," a legal rather than psychological classification intended to reflect the coercive totality of circumstances impinging on death-sentenced inmates.

Supreme Court Guidance on Competence to Waive Death Sentence Appeals

The U.S. Supreme Court has not provided a clear standard for determining the competence of death-sentenced inmates to waive their appeals. In *Rees v. Peyton* (1966), the Court opined that the inquiry should be directed to

> whether he has capacity to appreciate his position and make a rational choice with respect to continuing or abandoning further litigation or on the other hand

whether he is suffering from a mental disease, disorder, or defect which may substantially affect his capacity in the premises.

Unfortunately, the Court did not define "rational choice" or specify the procedures the lower court should use to determine if this standard has been met. Subsequently, in *Gilmore v. Utah* (1976), the Court did not reference the *Rees* decision, instead simply concluding that Gary Gilmore had made a knowing and intelligent waiver. Though the knowing and intelligent factors implicated an inherent autonomous decision-making consideration, an explicit "voluntary" factor was incorporated by the Supreme Court in 1990 in *Whitmore v. Arkansas*. Some additional guidance is available from *Rumbaugh v. Procunier*, a 1985 U.S. Court of Appeals for the Fifth Circuit decision that the U.S. Supreme Court let stand by denying the petition for a writ of certiorari. *Rumbaugh* sought to structure the *Rees* criteria with the following questions:

- Is the person suffering from a mental disease or defect?
- If the person is suffering from a mental disease or defect, does that disease or defect prevent him from understanding his legal position and the options available to him?
- If the person is suffering from a mental disease or defect that does not prevent him from understanding his legal position and the options available to him, does that disease or defect, nevertheless, prevent him from making a rational choice among his options?

Although these questions are helpful in providing a decision tree, they do not define the critical terms. Furthermore, they do not specify the procedures that should be employed to elicit answers to these questions.

Evaluations of Death-Sentenced Inmates for Competence to Waive Appeals

As is the case with most forensic evaluations, assessments by mental health professionals of competence to waive appeals by a death-sentenced "volunteer" are mostly descriptive rather than conclusionary. This is particularly important in light of the absence of a clear definition of many of the critical elements of competence. A descriptive approach also acknowledges that determinations of incompetence by the courts have significant variability in the nature and severity of the

qualifying psychological disorder, as well as the relationship of that disorder to rational decision making. Such a highly descriptive narrative should provide a careful analysis of the motivations for waiving appeals. The motivations underlying such a waiver may be far more complex and less obvious than the stated rationale of the volunteer. Thus, it is important not only to engage the capital inmate in discussion regarding the available options but also to gather information on any current or historical psychological disorders. Depressive symptoms and associated suicidal ideation are a particularly important focus, as is any paranoia. Many of the considerations explored in a competency-for-execution evaluation are also relevant to a waiver assessment, as these illuminate the capital inmate's understanding of his or her own impending death. Specific attention should be paid to the conditions of confinement on the respective death row and how these affect mood, future perspective, and waiver decision making. Throughout this extensive interview with the volunteering inmate, careful attention should be directed to rationality, logic, insight, and coherence of thought.

Interviews should also be held with appellate counsel, as well as prison staff, family members, and other relevant third parties. Psychological testing, including personality and cognitive assessment, may be helpful in some cases to assess aspects of the inmate's functioning that contribute to his or her understanding and motivations with respect to the waiver.

Mark Douglas Cunningham

See also Checklist for Competency for Execution Evaluations; Competency for Execution; Competency to Stand Trial

Further Readings

Blank, S. (2006). Killing time: The process of waiving appeal in the Michael Ross death penalty cases. *Journal of Law and Policy, 14,* 735.

Cunningham, M. D., & Vigen, M. P. (2002). Death row inmate characteristics, adjustment, and confinement: A critical review of the literature. *Behavioral Sciences & the Law, 20,* 191–210.

Gilmore v. Utah, 429 U.S. 1012 (1976).

Gregg v. Georgia, 428 U.S. 153 (1976).

Lyon, A. D., & Cunningham, M. D. (2006). Reason not the need: Does the lack of compelling state interest in maintaining a separate death row make it unlawful? *American Journal of Criminal Law, 33,* 1–30.

Norman, M. T. (1998). Standards and procedures for determining whether a defendant is competent to make the ultimate choice—death; Ohio's new precedent for death row "volunteers." *Journal of Law and Heath, 13,* 103.

Rees v. Peyton, 384 U.S. 312 (1966).

Rumbaugh v. Procunier, 753 F. 395 (2d 5th Cir. 1985).

Soering v United Kingdom, 11 E.H.R.R. 439 (1989).

Whitmore v. Arkansas, 495 U.S. 149 (1990).

COMPETENCY TO WAIVE COUNSEL (PROCEED PRO SE)

In the United States, it is permissible, with the approval of the judge, for a criminal defendant to act as his or her own attorney when the case goes to court. Legal and clinical issues related to the defendant's being competent to waive the right to legal representation are discussed in this entry.

In the United States, defendants accused of criminal charges are entitled to rights and protections by the Constitution. One important right articulated in the Sixth Amendment is that every accused person is entitled to representation by a legal counsel. Like other constitutional rights, the right to counsel is guaranteed—that is, no one, including even the judge, can deprive the defendant of this right. However, a defendant may request a waiver of the Sixth Amendment right to legal representation and permission of the court to represent himself or herself—in legal parlance, to proceed pro se.

Waiving some constitutional rights is a common occurrence. The overwhelming majority of criminal cases (more than 90%) are resolved through a plea agreement between the defendant and the state, and to enter a guilty plea, a defendant must waive the constitutional rights to a trial and to confront the evidence. When it is required that the defendant provide a factual basis or justification for the plea, he or she may further have to waive the Fifth Amendment right against self-incrimination.

In the context of entering a guilty plea, defendants' waiver requests typically occur after consultation with, and with the advice and consent of, their attorneys. Furthermore, by their nature, plea agreements are about disposition of the case; thus, defendants are commonly well-informed about the personal consequences of these waivers. In contrast, the request to waive the right to counsel more often marks a rift between the client and the attorney, and the potential impact on case outcome is usually not known. However, it is almost universally agreed that the likely impact is not good, as reflected in the adage that a defendant who proceeds pro se "has a fool for a client and an idiot for a lawyer." But in the most exceptional cases, criminal defendants likely disadvantage themselves because they might lack the litigation skills needed to present their cases most effectively. Nevertheless, the judge may approve a request if he or she determines that the defendant is competent to waive counsel.

Case law has articulated the qualities that must be present with respect to *competent* waivers of constitutional rights. Although there are minor variations in language across cases, generally, the judge must determine that the waiver is made *knowingly, intelligently*, and *voluntarily*. One court stated that the judge must determine whether the waiver was "made with full awareness of both the nature of the right being abandoned and the consequences of the decision to abandon it." The courts have not further articulated the specific functional abilities (i.e., behavioral indicators) that are required for a defendant to demonstrate that his or her request meets these qualitative criteria. However, the case law is clear as to what is *not* required: It is not required that the judge deem the defendant's decision to be a prudent one, nor does the competence determination hinge in any way on a demonstration that the defendant has litigation skills.

When a defendant expresses the desire to waive the right to counsel, the court, either on its own motion or on the motion of the defense attorney, may order a clinical evaluation of the defendant's mental competence. Presently, there are no standardized methods for psychiatrists or psychologists to use to evaluate competence to waive counsel, and most such evaluations will be based on unstructured interviews, the substance and process of which may vary widely across examiners. An interviewing strategy used in evaluating competence to plead guilty is embedded in the MacArthur Competence Assessment Tool–Criminal Adjudication and may offer some guidance for evaluations of competence to proceed pro se. Briefly, this strategy involves having the defendant articulate what the choices are—in this instance, proceeding with an attorney in charge of presenting the defense or proceeding pro se. The defendant is then asked to describe both the potential advantages and the potential disadvantages of each alternative. Subsequent queries require that the alternatives be compared and contrasted (e.g., "Explain why Alternative a might be better than Alternative b. Are there some ways in which Alternative b might be better than Alternative a?"). A query as to the final choice and the reasons for that choice solicits the defendant's beliefs about his or her case and situation, enabling the clinician to formulate a judgment of the plausibility or rationality and coherence of the defendant's thinking.

Ultimately, it is the judge's decision whether to permit the waiver of the right to counsel. Even if the request to waive representation by counsel is granted and the case proceeds with the accused having primary responsibility for the defense, the judge may still order that a lawyer be present during subsequent proceedings and available as a consultant to the defendant. Providing for such consultation, whether or not the defendants makes use of it, is a positive gesture by the court that attempts to ensure fairness and preserve the dignity of the adjudicatory process.

Norman G. Poythress

See also Adjudicative Competence of Youth; Capacity to Waive Rights; Competency, Foundational and Decisional; Competency to Stand Trial

Further Readings

Litwack, T. R. (2003). The competency of criminal defendants to refuse, for delusional reasons, a viable insanity defense recommended by counsel. *Behavioral Sciences and the Law, 21,* 135–156.

Mossman, D., & Dunseith, N. W., Jr. (2001). "A fool for a client": Print portrayal of 49 pro se criminal defendants. *Journal of the American Academy of Psychiatry and the Law, 29,* 408–419.

Perlin, M. (1996). "Dignity was the first to leave": *Godinez v. Moran,* Colin Ferguson, and the trial of mentally disabled criminal defendants. *Behavioral Sciences and the Law, 14,* 61–81.

Skeem, J., Golding, S. L., & Emke-Francis, P. (2003). Assessing adjudicative competency: Using legal and empirical principles to inform practice. In W. T. O'Donohue & E. R. Levensky (Eds.), *Handbook of forensic psychology: Resource for mental health and legal professionals* (pp. 175–211). Amsterdam: Elsevier.

COMPLEX EVIDENCE IN LITIGATION

Complex litigation tends to get framed as a problem for the jury system, but it is more properly viewed as a problem for any fact finder—juror, judge, arbitrator, expert panel—and for the litigants and their attorneys.

Still, the jury framing is useful because it brings into focus some of the resources a fact finder needs to tackle the problem: attention, memory storage and retrieval, education and training, and life experience. In these respects, groups are advantaged over individuals, and experts are advantaged over nonexperts. Since judges have greater average expertise but juries act as groups, it is difficult to identify a net advantage either way. And, of course, accuracy is only one criterion by which we evaluate legal judgment; a full assessment requires considerations of efficiency, fairness, legitimacy, and community representation.

The task of studying the topic of complex litigation recapitulates the key features of the problem. Complex litigation produces a vast and gnarly multidimensional search space, yet legal fact finders and jury researchers alike attempt to draw inferences from only fragmentary glimpses of isolated regions of that space. As a result, legal fact finders and jury researchers each combine sparse data with inferences that go beyond the data given. Theory is always important in sociolegal research, but for this topic, it is essential if we are to say much at all.

This entry presents a theoretical framework for evaluating expertise and collective decision making and describes the research done in this area. It also examines the types of complexity with respect to the number of parties and issues in a dispute and the amount and complexity of the evidence presented in the trial.

Theoretical Issues

Expertise

The typical jury is obviously far less expert than the judge in one key respect—expertise on the law as it pertains to the case. But because juries do not provide a rationale for their verdict, we only rarely know that a jury has made a "mistake" on the law, and juries may not feel particularly hindered by their lack of legal expertise. What may matter far more is expertise with respect to the technical issues that may arise at the trial, involving the economic analysis of market power, the engineering of heavy machinery, the etiology of a disease, or the epidemiology of toxic exposure. Here, judges may outperform the average juror; judges are above average in education and intelligence, and they may have relevant experience from past trials. But we shouldn't overestimate either intelligence or experience. Studies of expertise show that it can take a decade or more of concerted effort to develop true mastery of a technical skill. Graduate students are highly intelligent and still struggle for months to successfully complete their more technical graduate courses. And today's judges are likely to have far less actual trial experience than their predecessors of earlier generations. As a sample of the community, the jury may collectively have more relevant expertise in nonlegal issues than the relevant judge.

Groups as Information Processors

In the 1950s, Irving Lorge and Herbert Solomon deduced that, ceteris paribus, groups are better situated than their individual members to find correct answers. If p is the probability that any given individual will find the "correct" answer, then the predicted probability P that a collectivity of size r will find the answer is $P = 1 - (1 - p)^r$. More recently, Lu Hong and Scott Page have derived theorems proving that cognitively diverse groups—defined with respect to the perspectives and schemas they use to tackle a problem—can outperform even their best members. But this model, like that of Lorge and Solomon, proves group competence, not group performance. Empirically, we know that performance often falls short of competence.

Both models hinge on a key premise: If at least one member finds the answer, it will be accepted as the collectivity's solution—in short, "truth wins." This can occur only if group members recognize the "correctness" of a solution once it is voiced. Unfortunately, there are two problems with this assumption. First, Garold Stasser and his collaborators have shown that not all relevant facts get voiced; group discussion tends to focus on shared rather than unshared information. Second, even when voiced, correct answers are not always recognized as such. At best, "truth supported wins"—at least some social support is needed for a solution to gain momentum, indicating that truth seeking is a social as well as an intellective process. But even that occurs only for some tasks. One such task appears to be recognition memory; research has shown that groups outperform their members on memory tasks. But for more complex inferential tasks, members need a shared conceptual scheme for identifying and verifying solutions. When they lack such a scheme, the more typical influence pattern is *majority amplification*, in which a majority faction's influence is disproportionate to its size, irrespective of the truth value of its position. In other words, strength in numbers trumps strength in arguments.

In theory, collective decision making (or the statistical aggregation of individual judgments) is well suited for reducing *random error* in individual judgments. But *bias* is a different story. Biases can be produced by content—inadmissible evidence or extralegal factors such as race and gender—or by process, as when jurors rely on an availability heuristic (overweighting what comes most readily to the mind), an anchoring heuristic (insufficiently adjusting away from an arbitrary starting value), confirmatory bias, or hindsight bias. Analyses by Norbert Kerr, Robert MacCoun, and Geoffrey Kramer suggest that under a wide variety of circumstances, collective decision making will *amplify* individual bias rather than attenuate it. The collective will tend to amplify individual bias when there is "strength in numbers," such that large factions have an influence disproportionate to their size, as will occur explicitly in a "majority rules" system and when the case at hand is "close" rather than lopsided. A case can be close for several reasons, and each may pose different challenges for the fact finder. Facts can be ambiguous and vague; they can be clear but may contradict each other; or they can seem clear to each perceiver, but the perceivers may disagree on which side the "clear" facts support. The latter is particularly likely in an adversarial setting, where jury factions may form favoring each side of a dispute.

Defining Complexity

In 1987, Robert MacCoun postulated a preliminary taxonomy of three basic categories of complexity: dispute complexity (the number of parties and number of issues in a dispute), evidence complexity (the quantity, consistency, and technical content of evidence), and decision complexity (the complexity of the law and the complexity of the inferential steps and linkages required to render a verdict). In the 1990s, Heuer and Penrod conducted the first systematic statistical analysis of trial complexity in a field study of 160 criminal and civil trials. Judges were asked to rate the trials on a wide array of attributes. Factor analyses suggested three underlying dimensions, roughly overlapping MacCoun's categories: evidence complexity, legal complexity, and the quantity of information presented at trial. As in earlier work, it was found that judge ratings of complexity were unrelated to judge-jury agreement rates.

Both analyses treated quantity as a problem for the fact finder. On reflection, that doesn't necessarily follow. Large trials are extended over long time periods. Citizens who are able to track the plot complexities of soap operas such as *All My Children* or the team lineups of the NBA clearly have the resources to track large arrays of factual data. Indeed, inductive inference often gets easier with additional data, not harder. What probably matters more is the internal structure of the evidence—the inconsistencies and contingencies and interdependencies.

Evidence Complexity

We know very little about evidence complexity in the trial context, but there are much larger bodies of research on deductive and inductive inference in nonlegal tasks. In approaching this literature, it is useful to keep two distinctions in mind. One is between the two criteria for validity: correspondence versus coherence. Correspondence considers whether our inferences match the empirical facts; coherence considers whether our inferences "hang together" in a manner consistent with the normative standards of deductive logic, Bayesian updating, and the like. The second distinction is between competence and performance. Competence describes what we are capable of achieving; performance describes what we actually achieve. A disproportionate amount of work has been done in the "coherence/performance" cell. We know that people routinely violate normative inference standards for even fairly simple tasks, and they do so systematically rather than randomly, through the use of heuristics. But various lines of evidence from the other three cells suggest that people—and honeybees, birds, and other organisms—are competent to perform inferences of remarkable complexity and sophistication in some settings. This work suggests that competence may exceed the performance we often observe and that the structure and sampling of evidence (and the match of data to our specific competencies) may be what closes that gap. So the applied challenge is to discover ways of restructuring fact-finding procedures to bring performance closer to competence.

David Schum (using a Bayesian perspective) and Nancy Pennington and Reid Hastie (using narrative schemas or "stories") have done much to elucidate how the internal structure of evidence gets cognitively represented and analyzed by fact finders. (Much of this work has been collected in Hastie's edited volume *Inside the Juror.*) Schum's work shows that people can sometimes perform better when tackling small, piecemeal inferences rather than larger, more global inferences. Pennington and Hastie show how the temporal ordering of evidence at trial can facilitate (or interfere with) fact finders' ability to form coherent narratives. Unfortunately, the adversarial setting poses difficulties very different from those one might encounter when mastering skills such as reading or learning to use a computer program. Evidence structures aren't neutral; some favor one litigant at the expense of another. Indeed, lawyers with weak cases may even seek to undermine clarity.

Highly technical evidence involving statistics, chemistry, engineering, or economics poses additional problems. The amount of time experts spend in explaining highly technical concepts at trial falls well short of the time one spends learning in a semester-long course (without prerequisites!), though it still greatly exceeds what we can usually simulate in a mock jury experiment. Nevertheless, it seems likely that fact finders rely heavily on heuristic cues ("lots of charts," "sure looked smart") to compensate for their limited understanding of the material. Thus, Joel Cooper and his colleagues found that jurors were influenced by the content of expert testimony on the medical effects of polychlorobiphenyls (PCBs) when it was relatively simple but relied on the witness's credentials when the testimony was complex.

Dispute Complexity

Much of what we know about how juries handle dispute complexity comes from an important program of research by Irwin Horowitz and his collaborators. They found that mock jury verdicts are systematically influenced by the size and configuration of the plaintiff population. Aggregating multiple plaintiffs into a single trial appears to increase the likelihood that the defendant will be found liable, but each plaintiff's award may be smaller than in a consolidated trial. There are similar trade-offs involved in trying all the issues together versus bifurcating (or trifurcating) the trial into segments addressing causation and liability versus compensatory versus punitive damages—unitary trials may increase liability but lower damages. These effects are not neutral with respect to the parties, but bifurcation may be justified on procedural grounds because it appears to improve the quality of the decision process.

Conclusions

If judges clearly outperformed juries as legal fact finders in complex cases, we would face a dilemma. But we don't. Neither theory nor research indicates that judges are superior to juries in complex cases; it is safe to say that both need all the cognitive help we can give them to cope with an increasingly complex world.

Research on complexity suggests that jurors may be better able to cope with complexity if they are encouraged to use the same strategies used by students who take notes and ask questions in class. Although the cognitive advantages of treating fact finders like active information processors may seem obvious, some attorneys and judges are reluctant to cede control over the case, in whatever small measure. But research shows that while these innovations help only modestly, they also do little or no observable harm.

Robert MacCoun

See also Jury Competence; Jury Decisions Versus Judges' Decisions; Jury Deliberation; Jury Reforms; Statistical Information, Impact on Juries

Further Readings

Cooper, J., Bennett, E. A., & Sukel, H. L. (1996). Complex scientific testimony: How do jurors make decisions? *Law & Human Behavior, 20,* 379–394.

ForsterLee, L., Horowitz, I. A., & Bourgeois, M. (1994). Effects of notetaking on verdicts and evidence processing in a civil trial. *Law & Human Behavior, 18,* 567–578.

Hastie, R. (Ed.). (1993). *Inside the juror.* Cambridge, UK: Cambridge University Press.

Heuer, L., & Penrod, S. (1994). Trial complexity: A field investigation of its meaning and its effects. *Law & Human Behavior, 18,* 29–51.

Horowitz, I., & Bordens, K. S. (2002). The effects of jury size, evidence complexity, and note taking on jury process and performance in a civil trial. *Journal of Applied Psychology, 87,* 121–130.

Kerr, N., MacCoun, R. J., & Kramer, G. (1996). Bias in judgment: Comparing individuals and groups. *Psychological Review, 103,* 687–719.

Lempert, R. O. (1981). Civil juries and complex cases: Let's not rush to judgment. *Michigan Law Review, 80,* 68–132.

MacCoun, R. J. (1987). *Getting inside the black box: Toward a better understanding of civil jury behavior.* Santa Monica, CA: RAND.

Computer-Assisted Lineups

Many people are familiar with the live lineups and photo lineups shown in television crime dramas.

Increasingly, however, police departments are making use of computer technology to construct lineups and administer them to witnesses. Computer technology can be used to build better lineups by tapping into larger databases of faces to provide better choices to witnesses as well as to provide flexibility and efficiency to officers in the office or the field. Computer-assisted lineups can be administered either simultaneously or sequentially, and they have the added benefits of being programmed exactly to department policy and preserving lineup administration procedures and choices.

Lineup Construction

Researchers at the University of Northern Iowa have developed a Web-based program that allows officers to construct a lineup in the office or in the field. Internet capability (via modem, cable, wireless, or cell phone) allows the computer to link to a central database of faces that can be searched on the basis of a description of the perpetrator. The officer can then construct the lineup. Researchers use a method to evaluate lineups in order to determine if nonsuspect lineup members are serving as adequate fillers. This is referred to as a mock witness evaluation, and it involves providing a person who is not the actual witness with a description of the suspect. The mock witness is then given a lineup and asked to pick out the suspect. If mock witnesses can pick out the suspect at a greater than chance rate, the lineup is said to be biased. Typically, the realization that a lineup is biased occurs well after the lineup administration procedure, usually at the criminal trial. However, the computerized method allows for a mock witness test to be conducted during the course of the investigation, and in the event that the lineup is biased, new lineup members can be selected, thereby avoiding biased lineups being shown to witnesses. The police can accomplish this by sending the lineup and the description of the suspect to officers not associated with the case (across the hall or the state), providing for the lineup to be evaluated prior to administering it.

Lineup Presentation

Police lineups in the United States have traditionally been administered by presenting the witness a photo array, typically arranged six photos to a page. (These are sometimes referred to as "6-packs.") In this type of lineup, photos are presented simultaneously, and the witness chooses a photo by pointing at or stating the position number of the lineup member. There has been a recent movement toward administering lineups sequentially, so that witnesses see only one photo at a time. Unlike the simultaneous lineup, in which there is only one lineup decision, witnesses make a decision for each photo in the sequential lineup ("yes" or "no"). One benefit of the sequential lineup is that it has been demonstrated to reduce false identifications of innocent individuals.

Administrator Bias

An additional benefit of the sequential method is that the photos can be randomized so that the administrator does not know which photo the witness is looking at, reducing the likelihood of administrator bias. Administrator bias occurs when the administrator inadvertently gives cues to which photo belongs to the suspect. When neither the administrator nor the witness knows who the suspect is, the procedure is referred to as "double-blind" administration. Computer-assisted lineups provide for reduced interaction between administrator and witness, which greatly reduces the unintentional cues that can pass from the administrator to the witness.

Policy and Procedures

Law enforcement agencies typically have procedures for how lineups should be administered. However, deviations in procedure can easily occur when using traditional hard-copy lineup administration. Not only do computers have the capability to monitor and collect an enormous amount of information, they can also be programmed to administer the lineup exactly in accordance with policy and procedures. The administrator needs only to start the program and then can minimize his or her presence. Computers have the additional benefit of providing both written and audio instructions in any language. Lineups can be administered either simultaneously or sequentially. Lineup members can be randomly assigned to new positions each time the lineup is presented, with the administrator keeping accurate track of the position of each lineup member while recording the time taken to make each lineup decision. Many computers are equipped with condenser microphones and video cameras, thus enabling recording of the exact cursor location as well as audio and video of the event. Depending on the procedures, confidence can be measured for each lineup decision or after the lineup is complete.

Lineup Preservation

Once a lineup decision has been made, the identification information must be recorded and preserved. A multitude of problems can occur in the preservation of hard-copy lineup information: Information about where the photos were gathered from and who the photos represent, along with administration information (who administered the lineup, the date and time, etc.), can easily get lost or not be recorded at all. Evidence obtained using computers can be better preserved than evidence from traditional hard-copy lineups. Lineup evidence in the form of data, photos, audio, and video (including a replay of the entire identification event) can be stored on the computer and automatically copied to a DVD, and it can be uploaded to a departmental server and stored on backup drives for later review by researchers, law enforcement personnel, attorneys, or jurors.

Showups

Many identifications occur shortly after the commission of a crime because law enforcement officers often apprehend suspects in the vicinity of the crime. When this occurs, the law enforcement personnel will either bring the witness to the location where the suspect was apprehended or take the suspect to the witness. Either way, this is referred to as a showup. Showups are problematic because both the law enforcement officer and the witness know who the suspect is. Researchers at the University of Northern Iowa have begun experimenting with using handheld personal digital assistants (PDAs) in lieu of showups. PDAs have the ability to take a photo of the suspect and send the photo to a centralized location, either by phone or by WiFi. Technicians at the centralized location can then construct a lineup around the photo and transmit the lineup back to the PDA, allowing the officer to administer a sequential lineup to the witness. One added benefit is that the lineup can be transferred from the suspect's location to the witness's location, involving less physical transfer of people and PDAs. The handheld PDA has many of the capabilities of desktop or laptop computers, including playing sound instructions, audio recording the witness's identification, and transferring the evidence back to a centralized location for preservation.

Otto H. MacLin

See also Lineup Filler Selection; Showups; Simultaneous and Sequential Lineup Presentation

Further Readings

MacLin, O. H., Meissner, C. A., & Zimmerman, L. A. (2005). PC_Eyewitness: Administration and applications for research in eyewitness identification psychology. *Behavior Research Methods, 37,* 324–334.

MacLin, O. H., & Phelan, C. (in press). PC_Eyewitness: Evaluating the New Jersey method. *Behavior Research Methods.*

MacLin, O. H., Zimmerman, L. A., & Malpass, R. S. (2005). PC_Eyewitness and the sequential superiority effect: Computer based lineup administration. *Law & Human Behavior, 29*(3), 303–321.

CONDITIONAL RELEASE PROGRAMS

Conditional release programs for persons acquitted by reason of insanity (not guilty by reason of insanity or NGRI) are designed to maximize public safety while meeting the courts' mandate that some individual liberties be protected. These programs developed as a result of the state and federal court decisions in the 1960s, which required that this population be provided with commitment procedures similar to civil commitment. Prior to these decisions, persons found NGRI were given an automatic, indefinite "life sentence" to maximum-security state psychiatric hospitals for crimes ranging from shoplifting to murder. Under the new laws, persons committed as NGRI had to meet the commitment requirements of civil patients—that is, mental illness and dangerousness. Their continued commitment had to be periodically reviewed, and if they no longer met the commitment standards, they were to be released. Concerned with releasing what were believed to be "dangerous" offenders with mental illness into the community, states created a new category of posthospitalization supervision—conditional release. Research suggests that both goals were met in that insanity acquittees no longer languished in hospitals with no hope of being released and those who remained dangerous and mentally ill remained in a secure facility.

The other major watershed event that affected the insanity defense, especially release procedures, was the NGRI acquittal of John Hinckley from the charge of attempting to assassinate President Ronald Reagan in 1981. Following Hinckley's 1982 acquittal, the most common type of legal change in this area of law was in postacquittal procedures. Most states responded by providing shared responsibility between the trial court and the clinicians responsible for the day-to-day inpatient treatment of the committed population. Until then, hospital clinicians or the county court where the hospital was located had made the release decisions. Hinckley's acquittal further decreased the already declining popularity of the insanity defense among the public. He eventually received a number of 1-day conditional releases under the supervision of his parents in 2003, more than 22 years after his actions. His release was widely opposed by the victims' families, the Justice Department, and many others.

Conditional release programs are often referred to as "mental health parole or probation," but they significantly differ from traditional criminal justice aftercare supervision. The major differences between the two types of programs are in the length of the supervision period, the due process requirements for revocation, and the agency responsible for supervision. In most states, conditional release can be extended for any number of reasons, including clinical concerns, such as medication compliance; safety concerns; and lack of adequate community placement. For most parolees or probationers, their supervision time is finite. A few states limit the duration of conditional release to the maximum sentence that would have been given by the court had the defendant been convicted, reducing the utility of conditional release for less serious offenders. More often, conditional release is a relatively unrestrained and extensive period of community supervision and consequently makes the insanity defense a lesser plea and outcome.

Revocation of conditional release is less difficult than in the criminal justice system. Few states require a formal due process hearing to revoke conditional release, unlike criminal justice postrelease programs. Typically, conditional release can be revoked if the individual simply violates any term of the release. While some states have in place more procedural safeguards, they are still minimal compared with other aftercare programs. A final difference that highlights the special circumstances of the population acquitted NGRI is in the agency responsible for supervision. These programs often bisect the mental health and criminal justice systems due to the legal status of persons acquitted NGRI. Because an insanity plea is an affirmative defense, defendants admit to factual guilt but are legally not responsible due to lack of mens rea. Consequently, while their treatment and confinement are provided within the mental health system across all states, their release might be controlled to some extent by the criminal justice system, in particular the county's criminal court of commitment. This dual responsibility can cause professional conflict and confusion, making the release of insanity acquittees a complex legal and procedural process. None of this confusion surrounds parole or probation.

While in most states an NGRI finding leads to an automatic inpatient evaluation, this is not the case in all states. A few states allow the judge discretion in bypassing an order for hospitalization. Following an NGRI commitment, periodic reviews are conducted at intervals designated by state law: commonly 30 days, 60 days, 90 days, 1 year, and then annually. At this review, the treating psychiatrist or patient advocate can recommend or request conditional release. This application sets in motion the state's conditional release procedures, which range from a simple approval by a judge in the county where the acquittal was recorded to a complex, multilayered process in which hospital, state, and court officials are required to approve the petition. In some states, the county judge and/or district attorney have to approve even internal security changes, such as from closed to open unit, or grounds privileges. The complexity of the release procedures has an impact on the likelihood of release, who is released, and the length of time between approval and actual release. An important component of conditional release is the availability of community programs to provide services to this forensic population.

An innovative program developed in Oregon in 1978 and established in Connecticut in 1985 sought to gain greater control over persons found NGRI. The Psychiatric Security Review Board (PSRB) is a multidisciplinary independent board with full responsibilities for persons found NGRI. Decision making is highly centralized, and this board grants and revokes conditional release and sets the terms of release. This model has never been attempted in states with large populations.

Most persons found NGRI and subsequently placed on conditional release draw little, if any, public attention, and the petitions are usually supported by the courts. Who supervises the persons on conditional release programs varies from state to state. Many states, in particular larger states with larger NGRI populations, have special intensive case managers who have experience or special training with forensic clients. Their caseload is often smaller than in traditional aftercare programs. This common model for conditional release leads to decentralized supervision

and decision making once the person is released. In addition to possible revocation, conditional release can be extended by the court, or the person can be discharged from all supervision.

Lisa Callahan

See also Treatment and Release of Insanity Acquittees

Further Readings

Appelbaum, P. S. (1994). *Almost a revolution: Mental health law and the limits of change.* New York: Oxford University Press.

Callahan, L. A., & Silver, E. (1998). Factors associated with the conditional release of persons acquitted by reason of insanity: A decision tree approach. *Law & Human Behavior, 22,* 147–163.

Steadman, H. J., McGreevy, M. A., Morrissey, J. P., Callahan, L. A., Robbins, P. C., & Cirincione, C. (1993). *Before and after Hinckley: Evaluating insanity defense reform.* New York: Guilford Press.

CONDUCT DISORDER

Conduct disorder (CD) is a repetitive and persistent pattern of behavior that violates the rights of others or age-appropriate norms and causes significant impairments in various domains of functioning. CD accounts for a substantial number of youths who enter into mental health facilities in the United States and Canada, and for this reason it is an important disorder for researchers to investigate and for clinicians to treat. Although CD continues to be problematic for the individual and society, remarkable progress has been made in our understanding of CD. Subtyping approaches have helped reduce some of the heterogeneity of the disorder and provide a better understanding of the potential etiologies associated with various types of CD. In addition, intervention programs have been developed that have been shown to be effective. These treatment programs tend to be intensive and multimodal, focusing on working with the youth to reduce CD symptoms but also providing parent training to improve attachment as well as parental monitoring and supervision practices. It is hoped that future research focusing on further refining the subtypes of CD and determining interventions that are most effective with specific subtypes of youth will assist mental health professionals in reducing CD symptoms and the concomitant costs to society.

Definition and Subtypes

According to the *Diagnostic and Statistical Manual of Mental Disorders* (fourth edition, text revision; *DSM-IV-TR*), CD is a repetitive and persistent pattern of behavior that violates others' rights or age-appropriate norms and causes clinically significant impairments in various domains of functioning. For example, symptoms of CD may include aggression, damaging property, and lying. For a diagnosis of CD, the youth must have evidenced 3 of the 15 symptoms within the past 12 months, with at least 1 symptom being present for the past 6 months.

Because youths with CD are a heterogeneous group, various attempts have been made to identify subtypes of CD for informing etiology and intervention strategies. Earlier versions of the *DSM* differentiated between socialized versus undersocialized and aggressive versus nonaggressive dimensions. The socialized subtype was characterized by covert and overt antisocial behavior committed within the context of groups, whereas the undersocialized subtype was characterized by assaultive behavior that was carried out alone.

The current version of the *DSM* in part incorporates Terrie Moffitt's taxonomy and differentiates subtypes based on the age of onset: The childhood-onset and adolescence-onset subtypes are defined by characteristics of the disorder being present before and after the age of 10, respectively. This classification is intended to distinguish the life-course-persistent antisocial youth from the adolescence-limited antisocial youth, a potentially less serious subtype of CD. In support of this distinction, research by Paul Frick and Jeffrey Burke and colleagues has found that childhood-onset CD is associated with temperament and family dysfunction, whereas adolescence-onset CD is associated with delinquent peer affiliation. Furthermore, early onset is associated with the persistence of CD and an increased likelihood of violent and criminal behavior.

Two other classification systems include differentiating CD into overt and covert subtypes and on the basis of two common co-occurring disorders, attention deficit hyperactivity disorder (ADHD) and anxiety. Research by Jeffrey Burke and colleagues and Paul Frick and colleagues suggests that there is some evidence for the utility of these distinctions. The presence of covert symptoms is associated with the persistence

of CD, and youths with both CD and ADHD engage in a greater variety of delinquent behaviors and are more violent. In contrast, youths with both CD and anxiety display fewer impairments in peer relationships and have fewer police contacts.

Prevalence and Impact

According to the *DSM-IV-TR*, the prevalence of CD ranges from 1% to more than 10% in the general population. Large-scale population studies report prevalence rates ranging from 3% to 10% in nonclinical samples. Prevalence rates by gender are reported to range from 2% to 16% in boys and 1% to 9% in girls. The differences in prevalence rates are likely due to differences in the age of the youths sampled, CD criteria, time frame, and method of assessment.

The negative consequences associated with CD affect a variety of domains, including education (e.g., poor academic performance), employment (e.g., increased likelihood of the need for financial assistance), relationships (e.g., peer rejection), mental health (e.g., substance abuse), and criminality. Second, a diagnosis of CD can increase one's risk for other psychiatric and emotional disorders. The most well-established outcome is the link between CD and antisocial personality disorder (APD) in adulthood, on the assumption that there is a developmental progression between the disorders. Research by Lee Robins suggests that between 25% and 40% of children with CD will meet the diagnostic criteria for APD.

Finally, CD is one of the most costly diagnoses in terms of involvement with mental health services and the criminal justice system. Youths with CD use a variety of services, including additional school resources, social services, general health services, inpatient and outpatient mental health services, and juvenile justice services. Research by Michael Foster and Damon Jones indicates that the cost of services used by the average youth with CD exceeds $14,000 per youth by the end of adolescence and the cost of total expenditures across adolescence is approximately $70,000 more than for youths without any behavioral disorders. Research by Stephen Scott and colleagues indicates, in more general terms, that children with CD cost 10 times more than those without CD.

Conduct Disorder and Psychopathy

Research by Paul Frick and Donald Lynam suggests that psychopathy and a callous and unemotional interpersonal style may identify a subtype of childhood-onset CD. More important, the presence of callous-unemotional traits may provide the necessary developmental link between CD and psychopathy. Cross-sectional studies have found that antisocial youths with callous-unemotional traits exhibit a greater number, variety, and severity of conduct problems and more severe forms of aggression. Children with CD and callous-unemotional traits also evidence a preference for thrill-seeking activities, possess a reward-dominant response style, and demonstrate less anxiety. Further support for this distinction is the finding that genetic factors appear to play a larger role in those with callous-unemotional traits. Finally, callous-unemotional traits are predictive of a number of negative outcomes, including a greater number and variety of conduct problems, higher levels of proactive aggression and self-reported delinquency, more police contacts, and a diagnosis of APD in adulthood.

Prevention and Intervention

CD is typically regarded as a disorder that is not very amenable to treatment efforts. In fact, earlier research suggested that the majority of early treatment efforts have been found to be largely ineffective. Second, treatment of CD is difficult owing to noncompliance. Finally, certain interventions, such as peer group strategies, can have iatrogenic effects and increase the level and severity of antisocial behavior. Despite these generally negative early findings with respect to the treatment of CD, a number of interventions have been found to be effective, including medication and various psychosocial treatments.

For very severe cases of CD, some have suggested that psychopharmacology may be indicated. Jeffrey Burke and colleagues suggest that drugs such as lithium, risperidone, and methylphenidate may be effective for youths with severe CD. More specifically, LeAdelle Phelps and colleagues suggest that haloperidol, clonidine, methylphenidate, and risperidone may be effective in reducing severe aggression in youths with CD. However, psychopharmacology is not recommended as the primary treatment for CD because there is a lack of evidence that medication can alter the symptoms of CD per se and the medications do not have a prophylactic effect on CD symptoms. Rather, it appears that medication is most effective in reducing severe conduct problems in difficult cases. Although we note these recommendations for severe CD, we do so with caution given the lack of sound

methodological studies on the effectiveness of psychopharmacological treatments for youths with CD. Mental health professionals should carefully weigh the costs and benefits of administering drugs in the treatment of CD.

A number of effective behavioral and psychosocial interventions for treating CD have been reviewed by Alan Kazdin and Paul Frick. One of the most effective interventions is parent management training (PMT). The focus of PMT is to reduce problem behaviors and increase prosocial behaviors by educating parents in techniques such as positive reinforcement, consistent discipline, and effective supervision. There is evidence suggesting that PMT is effective in the short term in clinical populations, reduces deviant behavior across multiple domains, and is able to reduce problematic behaviors to within the levels of normative youth, with benefits evident 1 to 3 years after treatment. Similarly, intervention strategies that use appropriate parenting strategies and attachment principles have also proved effective in terms of decreasing externalizing and internalizing problems in adolescents with CD. However, it can be difficult to motivate parents to complete treatment programs, and there is evidence that parent training is not always effective with severely dysfunctional families.

Another effective treatment strategy adopts a cognitive-behavioral approach, which targets deficits in social cognition and problem solving, largely through inhibiting impulsive or angry responding by altering the processing of social information. A variant of this approach is child social skills training, which focuses on addressing interpersonal problems through techniques such as anger control and coping skills. There is some evidence for the effectiveness of social skills training in terms of decreases in aggression and antisocial behavior, increases in prosocial behavior in the short term, and improved interactions with peers. However, it can be difficult to maintain the skills over long periods and in domains outside the therapeutic setting. Therefore, some researchers recommend booster sessions to maintain the effects of treatment.

A promising approach is that of multimodal interventions such as multisystemic therapy (MST), which addresses risk at the individual, family, peer, school, and neighborhood levels. MST involves a comprehensive assessment to determine how the various levels influence the youth's problem behavior, and this information is then used to develop an individualized, intensive treatment plan. For example, parents may be educated in how to improve communication, and youths may be encouraged to increase their association with prosocial peers. There is some evidence of the effectiveness of MST in terms of reduction in aggressive behavior, lower rearrest rates, and fewer days of incarceration, with the benefits maintained for as long as 5 years posttreatment.

As noted by Paul Frick and Eva Kimonis, the general conclusions regarding intervention for CD are that treatment is more effective with younger children, who exhibit less severe conduct problems; treatment effects do not generalize across settings; and it is difficult to sustain improvements over time. Bearing in mind these concerns, future efforts should be directed toward determining which treatments are the most effective at different developmental stages and for specific subtypes of youth.

In addition to developing and administering appropriate intervention strategies, efforts should also be directed toward the prevention of CD symptoms. Interventions focus on mental illness with the goal of reducing or ameliorating impairment, whereas prevention focuses on mental health with the goal of developing adaptive, prosocial functioning. Generally, prevention programs do not address CD directly but address the risk factors related to CD and target youths identified as being at high risk for developing CD. Promising prevention programs include early family-based interventions that provide support and services to women during and after pregnancy, school-based interventions that provide additional intensive classroom programs, and community-based interventions that provide programs and activities in the community to promote prosocial behavior. Some examples include the Triple-P positive parenting program, the Fast Track program, and the Incredible Years parenting program. Follow-up studies with youths who received these types of interventions found that they resulted in less aggression, fewer acting-out behaviors, lower arrest and recidivism rates, and less severe criminal offenses.

Zina Lee and Randall T. Salekin

See also Juvenile Offenders; Juvenile Offenders, Risk Factors; Juvenile Psychopathy; Mental Health Needs of Juvenile Offenders

Further Readings

American Psychiatric Association. (2000). *Diagnostic and statistical manual of mental disorders* (4th ed., text revision). Washington, DC: Author.

Kazdin, A. E. (1995). *Conduct disorders in childhood and adolescence* (2nd ed.). Thousand Oaks, CA: Sage.

Kazdin, A. E. (2002). Psychosocial treatments for conduct disorder in children and adolescents. In P. E. Nathan & J. M. Gorman (Eds.), *A guide to treatments that work* (2nd ed., pp. 57–85). New York: Oxford University Press.

Lynam, D. R. (1996). Early identification of chronic offenders: Who is the fledgling psychopath? *Psychological Bulletin, 120,* 209–234.

Moretti, M. M., Emmrys, C., Grizenko, N., Holland, R., Moore, K., Shamsie, J., et al. (1997). The treatment of conduct disorder: Perspectives from across Canada. *Canadian Journal of Psychiatry, 42,* 637–648.

Salekin, R. T., & Frick, P. J. (2005). Psychopathy in children and adolescence: The need for a developmental perspective. *Journal of Abnormal Child Psychology, 33,* 403–409.

CONFESSION EVIDENCE

Confession evidence is highly potent, and its incriminating effects are difficult to erase. This entry describes the impact of confessions on jury verdicts, examines three concerns about the way in which juries evaluate confession evidence, and considers the steps that can be taken to ensure that jurors assess such evidence appropriately.

In cases where a confession is disputed, a judge determines the voluntariness and admissibility of the confession during a preliminary hearing. In the American criminal justice system, if a confession is deemed voluntary, it is then submitted for consideration to the jury. In some states, the jury is specially instructed to make an independent judgment of voluntariness and to disregard statements found to be coerced; in other states, the jury receives no such instruction. Either way, it is clear that jurors faced with evidence of a confession, and the defendant's claim that it was false, must determine the credibility and weight of that evidence in reaching a verdict.

Mock jury studies have shown that confession evidence has a greater impact on jury decision making than other forms of human evidence, such as eyewitness identification and character testimony. Confessions are so difficult to overcome that mock jurors tend to trust them even when it is not legally and logically appropriate to do so. In a study that illustrates this point, Saul Kassin and his colleague presented mock jurors with one of three versions of a murder trial. In the low-pressure version, the defendant had confessed to the police immediately on questioning. In the high-pressure version, he was interrogated aggressively by a detective who waved his gun in a menacing manner at him. In the control version, there was no confession in evidence. Faced with the high-pressure confession, participants reasonably judged the statement to be involuntary and self-reported that it did not influence their decisions. Yet when it came to verdicts, this confession significantly boosted the conviction rate. This pattern appeared even in a situation in which subjects were specifically admonished by the judge to disregard confessions that they found to be coerced.

Criminal justice statistics reinforce the point that confessions tend to overwhelm other exculpatory evidence, resulting in a chain of negative legal consequences—from arrest through prosecution, conviction, and incarceration. Archival analyses of actual cases that contained confessions that were later proved false innocent have thus shown that when innocent confessors plead not guilty and proceed to trial, jury conviction rates range from 73% to 81%.

There are three bases for concern about the way in which juries can be expected to evaluate confession evidence in support of conviction. First, common-sense leads people to trust behaviors that do not appear to serve a person's self-interest, such as confessions. Most people believe that they would never confess to a crime that they did not commit and do not expect that others would either. Indeed, in a wide range of contexts, social psychologists have found that in perceiving the behaviors of others, people tend to overestimate the influence of dispositions and underestimate the influence of situational factors—a phenomenon known as fundamental attribution error.

A second basis for concern is that people, including professional lie catchers, are not typically adept at distinguishing between truth and deception. For example, although it is common to assume that "I'd know a false confession if I saw one," a recent study has shown that neither college students nor police investigators were able to differentiate between true and false confessions made by male prisoners. Hence, there is reason to believe that lay jurors would have difficulty in distinguishing between true and false confessions when presented as evidence.

Third, jurors do not typically see the corruptive process of interrogation by which confessions are elicited. In many cases of proven false confessions, the statements that were presented in court often contained accurate details about the crime, statements of motivation, apologies and expressions of remorse, and even corrections to errors that the suspects had supposedly identified. Typically presented with an oral, written, or taped confession but not the questioning that preceded it, however, jurors are not in a position to evaluate the source of these details. False confessions thus tend to appear voluntary and the product of personal knowledge, masking the coercive processes through which they were produced.

It is clear that additional safeguards are needed when confession evidence is presented in court. There are two possibilities in this regard. One is for trial courts to permit psychologists to testify as experts—a practice that is common but not uniform across states. The purpose of this testimony is to assist juries by informing them about the processes of interviewing and interrogation, the phenomenon of false confessions, the psychological factors that increase the risk of a defendant making a false confession, and other general principles (the purpose in these cases is not for the expert to render an opinion about a particular confession, a judgment that juries are supposed to make).

A second important mechanism is to ensure that judges and juries can observe the process by which confessions are produced by videotaping entire interrogations. A videotaping policy would have many advantages: The presence of a camera would deter interrogators from using highly coercive tactics, prevent frivolous defense claims of coercion, provide a full and accurate record of how the statement was produced, and perhaps even increase the fact-finding accuracy of judges, who must rule on voluntariness (they will observe for themselves the suspect's physical and mental state, the conditions of custody, and the interrogation tactics that were used), and juries, who must render a verdict (they will see how the statement was taken and from whom the crime details originated).

Importantly, interrogations should be videotaped with an "equal focus" visual perspective, showing both the accused and the interrogators. In numerous studies, Daniel Lassiter and colleagues have found that lay people, juries, and even trial judges are more attuned to the situational factors that draw confessions when the interrogator is on camera than when the sole focus is on the suspect.

Julia C. Busso and Saul M. Kassin

See also False Confessions; Interrogation of Suspects; Videotaping Confessions

Further Readings

Kassin, S. M., & Sukel, H. (1997). Coerced confessions and the jury: An experimental test of the "harmless error" rule. *Law and Human Behavior, 21,* 27–46.

Lassiter, G. D., Geers, A. L., Handley, I. M., Weiland, P. E., & Munhall, P. J. (2002). Videotaped confessions and interrogations: A change in camera perspective alters verdicts in simulated trials. *Journal of Applied Psychology, 87,* 867–874.

CONFIDENCE IN IDENTIFICATIONS

The confidence that eyewitnesses express in their decision at an identification test or lineup has long been recognized within the criminal justice system as an indicator of the likely reliability or accuracy of the witness. In contrast, psychology researchers have downplayed the diagnostic value of eyewitness identification confidence. Although only a relatively small proportion of the variance in identification accuracy is associated with variance in confidence, recent research using what is known as a confidence-accuracy (CA) calibration procedure suggests that confidence—measured immediately after the identification decision—can provide a useful (but not infallible) pointer for crime investigators to the likely accuracy of positive but not negative (i.e., lineup rejections) lineup decisions. This conclusion definitely does not apply, however, to confidence judgments expressed in the courtroom as, by this time, there has been an opportunity for postidentification influences (such as feedback from lineup administrators or other witnesses) to shape any subsequent confidence judgments. Nor is the conclusion applicable to judgments expressed by witnesses prior to having viewed a lineup. A major challenge for future research in this area will be to define the boundary conditions for obtaining robust CA calibration, which, in turn, will enhance the capacity to diagnose the likely accuracy of identification decisions.

Eyewitnesses will often provide some sort of expression of confidence in their memory when they examine a police lineup or photo spread or when they testify in court about the identity of the offender. Their degree of confidence is known to exert a strong influence on assessments made by the police, lawyers, and jurors about the likely reliability of their testimony. Yet it is known that eyewitness confidence is sometimes an extremely misleading cue to the likely accuracy of an identification. The following sections examine when identification confidence is informative about the offender's identity and when it is likely to mislead.

Eyewitness confidence has been of major interest because confidence is an easily obtainable index that could potentially provide a guide for the criminal justice sector as to the likely reliability of an eyewitness identification response. Given the crucial role that identifications can play in some investigations and trials, together with the overwhelming evidence of eyewitness fallibility provided by DNA exoneration cases and experimental simulations of identification tests, knowing how much weight should be attached to witnesses' confidence estimates is an important forensic issue.

Even prior to attending an identification test, witnesses may express a particular degree of confidence in their capacity to identify the offender, with the confident witness likely to impress police investigators. These assessments are likely to be influenced by a variety of factors such as witnesses' evaluations of the strength of the memorial image for the offender, their recollections of the quality of view they had of the offender at the time of the crime, their perceptions of how good a recall they displayed when interviewed by the police, and so on. To date, there is no evidence to indicate that such preidentification test confidence assessments should be considered as a guide to the likely accuracy of an identification.

Factors for and Against a Confidence-Accuracy Relationship

There is now a sizable literature on the relationship between confidence, when expressed after an identification decision, and identification accuracy. Researchers have mounted compelling arguments both for and against expecting a strong relationship between identification confidence and accuracy. For example, in recognition memory theories and research, the strong link between memory signal strength and recognition accuracy and confidence provides firm grounds for expecting a meaningful CA relationship. Furthermore, witnesses with very strong memories of the offender are likely to make a rapid identification, with the apparent ease or speed of the identification providing a potentially reliable cue to confidence. Other support comes from research on psychophysical discrimination, indicating that confidence may well regulate, rather than be a result of, the decision process.

Arguments against a strong CA relationship have, however, been much more consistently advanced, with these views reinforced by demonstrations of overconfidence in various domains of human judgment. Some of the grounds for questioning a meaningful CA relationship include our (a) inability to review all factors that should shape confidence; (b) tendency to focus too heavily on confirmatory evidence for a decision; (c) problems with translating subjective judgments of confidence into some kind of numerical confidence value; (d) reliance on cues to confidence that, while sometimes veridical, may also be misleading (e.g., a face in a lineup may seem very familiar not because it is that of the offender but because it had been seen in the context of the event previously, or witnesses may infer that the face in the lineup that seems most familiar must be the offender because they got an excellent view of the offender at the crime); and (e) almost inevitable exposure to postidentification social influences that produce malleable confidence judgments.

Confidence-Accuracy Correlation

For some time the dominant view among eyewitness memory researchers has been that postidentification confidence does not provide a particularly informative guide to the likely accuracy of an identification decision. It has been generally accepted that the CA relationship is best described as lying between weak (at worst) to modest (at best) for witnesses who make a positive identification (i.e., choosers) from either a culprit-present lineup or a culprit-absent lineup—indicated by CA correlations that seldom exceed 0.3—and virtually nonexistent (correlations around 0) for witnesses who reject either of these lineups (nonchoosers). Note, however, that the correlations for choosers have been shown to be higher when, for example, (a) the encoding and test stimuli have been allowed to vary as they do in the real world, (b) stimulus encoding conditions were optimal, and (c) witnesses were encouraged to be self-aware with respect to their preidentification decision behaviors by being asked to view a video of their own identification decision before giving a confidence assessment.

Although the finding of a modest CA correlation is clearly a reliable one, it does not provide the complete picture regarding the CA relationship. This requires supplementing the correlation between confidence and the identification decision outcome (accurate, inaccurate) with an examination of other characteristics of the CA relation—specifically, an examination of CA calibration and patterns of overconfidence/underconfidence. The correlation coefficient reflects the variance in decision accuracy associated with variations in confidence. For the eyewitness identification paradigm, which typically involves a witness making a single identification decision, this therefore reflects variance explained at the level of the group but is not informative about the likely accuracy of a witness's decision accompanied by a specific level of confidence (e.g., 70% confident or 90% confident). Information about the latter is, however, obtainable by applying the calibration approach to the examination of the CA relationship and, since the late 1990s, a number of studies of the CA relationship in eyewitness identification have used this approach.

Confidence-Accuracy Calibration

At a conceptual level, the procedure is quite simple, with the proportion of accurate identification decisions determined for each level of identification confidence (10%, 20%, etc.). This provides the basis for plotting a calibration curve and the derivation of calibration, overconfidence/underconfidence, and resolution statistics. Inspection of the calibration curve provides a direct indication of the levels of identification accuracy expected in association with varying degrees of confidence; for example, judgments made with 100% confidence might be characterized by 85% accuracy. Perfect calibration is, of course, characterized by 0% accuracy at 0% confidence, 10% accuracy at 10% confidence, right through to 100% accuracy at 100% confidence. Any departure from perfect calibration is not only illustrated by comparing the obtained and ideal calibration curves but can also be captured in a calibration statistic (varying from 0 to 1, with 0 indicating perfect calibration) and an overconfidence/underconfidence statistic (varying from 0 ± 1, with increasing positive and negative departures from 0 denoting increasing overconfidence and underconfidence, respectively). In addition to the guide provided by the calibration procedure to the likely accuracy of identification decisions made with particular levels of confidence, it also provides a resolution statistic that (like the correlation coefficient) indicates variance in decision accuracy associated with confidence.

A number of studies have now applied the calibration approach to the study of the CA relation within the eyewitness identification paradigm. While these studies have sampled only a limited range of forensically relevant variables and, indeed, a limited array of levels on each of those variables, they have at least used several different sets of stimulus materials and events (including both central and peripheral targets) that have given rise to different rates of correct and false identifications, different retention intervals between encoding and test (with the longest being 1 week); varied the similarity of lineup targets and foils; and varied the lineup instructions.

Studies with adult participants have presented calibration curves, for positive identification responses (or choosers), that roughly parallel the ideal calibration curve. In other words, as confidence increases so too does accuracy in a systematic manner, a pattern not suggested by the typically modest CA correlations reported in these same studies. Generally, however, the curves indicate some degree of overconfidence, with accuracy rates at the high end of the confidence scale (i.e., 90% to 100% confident) typically around the 75% to 90% level. In contrast, no such systematic patterns have been detected for participants who rejected the lineup (i.e., nonchoosers). Three other findings are also noteworthy. First, in association with confidence estimates of 90% to 100%, diagnosticity ratios— indicating the ratio of hits to false alarms—were substantially higher than for lower confidence estimates. Second, participants whose identification responses were very fast were better calibrated than those whose identifications were slow. The latter finding is to be expected given that participants with an exceptionally strong memory for the culprit should not only identify the culprit when present in the lineup, and be appropriately confident, but should also be less likely to falsely identify an innocent suspect, thereby reducing the likelihood of confident, incorrect responses. Third, there is some evidence that interventions designed to improve adults' scaling of confidence judgments (by causing them to reflect carefully on the encoding and identification test conditions or the possibility that their identification decision could be mistaken) can reduce overconfidence and improve CA calibration.

It is encouraging that similar patterns of CA calibration findings have also been reported in a number of studies using various forms of a face recognition paradigm, the basic requirement of which is to judge whether or not faces presented at test had been among an array of faces that had previously been presented in a study phase. Specifically, these studies have demonstrated robust CA calibration for positive (but not negative) decisions in both absolute and relative

judgment versions of the face recognition paradigm, but with overconfidence more pronounced as task difficulty increased (e.g., shorter stimulus exposure durations at either study or test).

One feature of the calibration studies that must be highlighted is that the confidence judgments from participant witnesses were obtained immediately after the identification response, thereby ensuring that they were not affected by any postidentification influences (e.g., from the lineup administrator or other witnesses) that are known to exert a profound influence on confidence judgments quite independent of the accuracy of the identification response. Thus, while the calibration studies illustrate meaningful CA relations, eyewitness researchers are in strong agreement that confidence assessments provided after some delay (e.g., in the courtroom) are potentially highly misleading about the likely accuracy of an identification.

Not all the evidence on the CA relation obtained with the calibration approach is positive about the CA relation. For example, research done with samples of children aged 10 to 13 years highlights poor CA calibration and extreme overconfidence, illustrated by accuracy rates sometimes as low as 30% in association with confidence judgments of 90% to 100%. Furthermore, children's overconfidence in their identifications has, thus far, proven resistant to interventions designed to reduce it.

Applied Implications

While there is still much to be done in terms of testing the generality of findings obtained via the calibration approach across a variety of forensically relevant conditions, the present findings are, nevertheless, important from an applied perspective. As indicated earlier, while the CA correlation addresses the group-level variance in accuracy explained by confidence, the calibration approach provides the additional insight into the likely accuracy of particular identifications made with some specific level of confidence. The available data strongly suggest that police investigators should pay close attention to witnesses' confidence estimates solicited at the time of the identification and, hence, not subject to any social influence. Specifically, extremely confident (and rapid) identifications of the suspect in the lineup, while by no means guaranteed to be accurate, should signal to police investigators that there is a very real chance that the suspect is the culprit and, thus, stimulate a closer search for supportive evidence. When, however, the identification of the suspect is not made with extremely high confidence, and is perhaps made in a ponderous manner, it should signal real doubts about whether the suspect is the culprit and act as a reminder to investigators that they should strongly consider alternative hypotheses about the culprit's identity. In contrast, investigators should not attempt to interpret the likely accuracy of witnesses' rejections of a lineup based on the associated confidence levels. Although lineup rejections have diagnostic value with respect to the guilt or innocence of the suspects, the witnesses' confidence levels do not assist in that diagnosis.

Encouragingly consistent with these conclusions that are based on experimental simulations are some analyses of findings from real criminal cases. In this archival work, when there was strong incriminating (nonidentification) evidence against a suspect (which admittedly does not prove that the suspect was the culprit), very confident witness identifications much more strongly pointed to the police suspect than to the innocent lineup foils.

Barriers to the Use of the Calibration Approach

Application of the calibration approach to the study of the CA relation in eyewitness identification has clearly been valuable. Unfortunately, there is one major obstacle to the more widespread application of the approach. As the published work shows, use of this approach in the eyewitness identification context requires extremely large sample sizes. The typical eyewitness identification task simulates the real-world investigation: The witness observes a crime, views a lineup, and either makes a positive identification or rejects the lineup. In other words, only one data point is provided by each participant witness. However, stable calibration curves and statistics (for choosers or nonchoosers) require approximately 200 to 300 data points for each experimental condition examined. Thus, the existing published studies with an identification paradigm are characterized by sample sizes considerably in excess of what many laboratories find practical to achieve. In contrast, an old-new face recognition paradigm allows for a large number of repeated measures and, in turn, derivation of calibration statistics for each participant. One consequence of this sample size problem is that future research into how calibration varies over forensically relevant conditions is likely to proceed quite slowly.

Confidence Malleability

The issue of social influences on identification confidence and the malleability of confidence have already been mentioned—and these issues are also discussed specifically elsewhere. Some further discussion of these issues is required here, however, to round out the discussion of identification confidence.

As has been indicated, the empirical evidence shows that witness confidence judgments are informative about the likely accuracy of positive identification decisions if they are solicited at the time of the identification. But from the time of the identification through to the end of a trial, witnesses may have a variety of further interactions with the police, other witnesses, and lawyers, culminating often in a courtroom appearance. Although none of these interactions can have any bearing on the accuracy of the decision that was indicated at the identification test, they do have the potential to influence significantly any subsequent expression of confidence in that decision. This may mean, for example, that any confidence judgment expressed in the courtroom may be quite different from the one that was made at the time of the actual identification test. In turn, whereas confidence at the time of the identification decision may be informative about identification accuracy, these subsequent expressions of confidence may not be.

Some of the key variables that have been shown to influence postidentification judgments of confidence include confirming and disconfirming feedback about the accuracy of the identification provided, for example, by a lineup administrator or another witness. This feedback may be in the form of explicit verbal feedback from one of these sources or may involve more subtle verbal or nonverbal cues. Regardless of when and how the feedback is delivered, its impact will be to make a witness appear more credible or believable if it is confirming feedback and thus inflates confidence or less credible if it disconfirms and deflates confidence. In other words, cues that can affect confidence judgments but not the underlying judgmental accuracy can render a witness more or less believable to jurors. Thus, a witness who falsely identifies an innocent police suspect may not be particularly confident at the time of making an identification but may be exceptionally confident at some later stage in a courtroom. It is for these reasons that eyewitness researchers have strongly endorsed the collection of any assessments of confidence at the time of the identification—for it is then that the confidence judgments are maximally informative about accuracy—and have little faith in the probative value of identification confidence judgments that witnesses may express in the courtroom.

Neil Brewer

See also Confidence in Identifications, Malleability; Optimality Hypothesis in Eyewitness Identification; Response Latency in Eyewitness Identification

Further Readings

Brewer, N. (2006). Uses and abuses of eyewitness identification confidence. *Legal and Criminological Psychology, 11,* 3–24.

Brewer, N., & Wells, G. L. (2006). The confidence-accuracy relationship in eyewitness identification: Effects of lineup instructions, foil similarity and target-absent base rates. *Journal of Experimental Psychology: Applied, 12,* 11–30.

Cutler, B. L., & Penrod, S. D. (1989). Forensically relevant moderators of the relation between eyewitness identification accuracy and confidence. *Journal of Applied Psychology, 74,* 650–652.

Juslin, P., Olsson, N., & Winman, A. (1996). Calibration and diagnosticity of confidence in eyewitness identification: Comments on what can be inferred from the low confidence-accuracy correlation. *Journal of Experimental Psychology: Learning, Memory, and Cognition, 22,* 1304–1316.

Kassin, S. M., Tubb, V. A., Hosch, H. M., & Memon, A. (2001). On the "general acceptance" of eyewitness testimony research: A new survey of the experts. *American Psychologist, 56,* 405–416.

Keast, A., Brewer, N., & Wells, G. L. (in press). Children's metacognitive judgments in an eyewitness identification task. *Journal of Experimental Child Psychology*.

Lindsay, D. S., Read, J. D., & Sharma, K. (1998). Accuracy and confidence in person identification: The relationship is strong when witnessing conditions vary widely. *Psychological Science, 9,* 215–218.

Sporer, S. L., Penrod, S. D., Read, J. D., & Cutler, B. L. (1995). Choosing, confidence, and accuracy: A meta-analysis of the confidence-accuracy relation in eyewitness identification studies. *Psychological Bulletin, 118,* 315–327.

CONFIDENCE IN IDENTIFICATIONS, MALLEABILITY

Eyewitnesses are often asked to indicate how confident they are in the accuracy of their identification and other testimony-relevant judgments. These reports are highly influential in evaluations of identification accuracy. Unfortunately, eyewitnesses' confidence reports are highly malleable, easily influenced by myriad variables. The solution is to record witnesses' confidence in their identification and report of crime details immediately, so as to preserve whatever useful information confidence provides.

A witness's confidence in the accuracy of his or her identification is perhaps the most studied of all variables related to eyewitness decision making—for good reason. Eyewitness confidence is the most intuitively appealing variable for use in assessments of accuracy. Indeed, it is specially highlighted by the U.S. Supreme Court for use in such evaluations. This recommendation is consistent with lay assumptions of what variables predict identification accuracy: People believe that a confident witness is an accurate one. This assumption does have empirical support. Under certain circumstances, there is a strong, positive correlation between confidence and accuracy. For example, when viewing conditions are disparate, a strong confidence-accuracy relationship emerges: Witnesses who see a culprit under difficult viewing conditions are less confident compared with those who see a culprit under optimal viewing conditions. Other research confirms the existence of a useful relationship between confidence and accuracy. One meta-analysis determined that the confidence-accuracy correlation for witnesses who made choices from lineups or photo spreads was moderate ($r = .41$). These investigations are highly valuable in clarifying the maximum possible utility of confidence reports in assessing accuracy.

These investigations capture confidence reports under the best possible circumstances. Because no external variables have been introduced (e.g., photo-spread administrator influence), they are, in some sense, pure measures of the extent to which confidence is related to accuracy. Therefore, it is possible to think of these confidence reports as the *estimator* versions of this variable because they derive from factors outside the control of the justice system. For example, the system cannot ensure that a witness has a good view of the culprit. Therefore, to the extent that the quality of the witness's view determines how confident he or she is, the justice system has no hand in a witness's confidence.

In other ways, the justice system has a substantial role in the level of confidence an eyewitness expresses in his or her identification. This influence is driven by system variables—those variables the justice system can control. Many system variables have been implicated in confidence inflation. This influence has been demonstrated across three different categories of confidence reports: current confidence in the identification decision (e.g., How confident are you in the accuracy of your identification right now?), retrospective confidence in the identification decision (e.g., How confident *were* you when you made your identification?), and reports about details of the witnessed event (e.g., What kind of disguise was the culprit wearing?). As described below, the malleability of confidence in each of these three categories can be attributed to system variables.

Confidence in Reports of Crime Details

Although confidence malleability is most prominently studied in relation to identification accuracy, some researchers have focused on its malleability in the context of crime detail recollections. In one investigation, eyewitnesses questioned over the course of 5 weeks reported significantly elevated confidence levels at the end of that period, without any corresponding increase in the accuracy of their reports. The same elevation occurred when eyewitnesses were questioned over the course of 5 days. In addition, a manipulation as simple as the context in which a confidence report is given can influence the magnitude of an eyewitness's certainty. Witnesses who give reports about crime details in public provide significantly lower confidence ratings than do those witnesses who give reports privately, even though the accuracy in both groups is equivalent. The number of times a witness is interviewed and the context of the interview are both variables under the control of the investigating officers to a certain extent.

Current Confidence in Identification Accuracy

In many crimes, many people witness the same event. Some of the crimes for which innocent people were wrongfully convicted include up to five individuals all identifying the same person. In one of the most elaborate empirical examinations of the effect of cowitnesses, witnesses saw a live staged crime in pairs. Witnesses were then separated for the identification attempt and confidence report. Finally, witnesses were randomly assigned to learn one of four types of information about their cowitness's decision. Those who

learned that their cowitness identified the same person they did or identified an implausible other reported the highest levels of confidence. Those who learned that their cowitness either identified someone else or did not make an identification all had confidence levels that were significantly lower than witnesses in a control (no cowitness information) condition. Information from a cowitness can also alter confidence in reports of crime details. In one study, witnesses' confidence in whether an accomplice was present at the scene of a crime changed depending on their partner's report of whether that accomplice was present. The justice system has limited control of whether cowitnesses speak to one another. At the very least, cowitnesses should be separated until each has provided an identification decision, complete report of crime details, and indicated the confidence in each judgment.

Cowitnesses are not the only source of contamination for current confidence reports. Photospread administrators have long been targeted as a potential source of influence in eyewitnesses' decisions. Initially, concerns centered on the ability of a photospread administrator to affect an eyewitness's choices; research does suggest this is a worthy concern. Recently, however, concerns have expanded to include the problem of administrators influencing an eyewitness's confidence. In one demonstration of this problem, eyewitnesses attempted identifications in two conditions. In one condition, the photospread administrator knew who the suspect was. In the other condition, the photospread administrator did not know who the suspect was. Eyewitnesses who made identifications under the first condition reported higher confidence in their accuracy than did eyewitnesses who made identifications in the second condition. The influence inherent in this situation is easily solved by ensuring that the person administering a set of photos to an eyewitness does not know who the suspect it; the system can control whether this safeguard is adopted.

Retrospective Confidence in Identification Accuracy

Malleability in retrospective confidence reports is perhaps the most problematic of the three categories, in part because this category is specifically highlighted by the U.S. Supreme Court for use in determining accuracy. The Court indicates that the relevant confidence report is from the "confrontation," suggesting that they recognized the possibility for confidence to increase over time. Unfortunately, profound distortions in witnesses' memories of how confident they were at the time of the identification are easy to create with postidentification feedback. Witnesses who hear that their identification was correct report remembering with greater certainty at the time of the identification compared with witnesses who heard nothing about their accuracy. Because this effect occurs for eyewitnesses who have made false identifications, the manipulation produces a set of highly confident, but wrong, eyewitnesses. As with the other system variables described above, this one has an easy solution. If confidence reports are collected immediately after an identification is made, eyewitnesses' confidence reports will not be vulnerable to influence by the photospread administrator.

Implications of Confidence Malleability

As noted above, there is a nontrivial, positive relationship between confidence and accuracy under certain circumstances. However, because confidence is malleable, the significant relationship between the two variables can easily be compromised or even eliminated. One way in which the confidence-accuracy correlation is eliminated is by suggesting to witnesses that they prepare for cross-examination. In such a situation, witnesses who have made inaccurate identifications often inflate their confidence to the point where their confidence is indistinguishable from that of accurate witnesses. Postidentification feedback has a similarly devastating effect on the confidence-accuracy correlation: Witnesses who hear that their identification was correct report equivalent levels of confidence, regardless of whether their actual identification was accurate or inaccurate.

The implications of confidence inflation are profound because a witness's confidence in the accuracy of his or her identification carries enormous weight in judgments of accuracy, often trumping other variables. In one set of studies, mock jurors were provided with information about 10 variables, all of which influence identification accuracy (e.g., the culprit's disguise). None of the 10 variables influenced mock jurors' assessments except confidence. In another experiment, jurors who participated disregarded the quality of a witness's view, evaluating him or her positively as long as confidence was high. This reliance on confidence is unproblematic except that eyewitnesses routinely produce highly confident reports about identifications that are incorrect. Ample real-world evidence suggests that this is a significant problem. Many individuals exonerated by DNA evidence were convicted on the basis of confident eyewitness identifications.

Future Research on Confidence Malleability

Even though confidence malleability is a well-studied phenomenon, there are many unanswered questions. For example, researchers do not yet know for how long confidence is malleable. Some research suggests that postidentification feedback still influences retrospective certainty reports even when it is given 48 hours after an event is witnessed. These results are provocative—suggesting that confidence may be malleable for extended periods of time. However, because few studies include manipulations of time, the extent to which confidence is malleable is not well understood. The reason for the susceptibility of confidence to external influences is also not well understood. One contributing factor may be that confidence reports are derived from many sources. One other factor is undoubtedly the extent to which the stimulus matches the witness's memory (i.e., ecphoric similarity). Another factor is the desire of witnesses to determine whether their judgment is correct (i.e., the desire for informational influence). In at least one study, the tendency to conform eyewitness decisions to others was highest when the witnessing conditions made identification difficult (i.e., the stimulus was in view for a very short time) and the task was important.

Remedies for Confidence Malleability

The most obvious remedy for confidence inflation is to record witnesses' reports immediately after an identification is made or a crime is reported. This solution is appealing for three reasons. First, providing a confidence report may in fact inoculate witnesses against future inflations. In one study, witnesses who provided a private retrospective confidence report were less affected by postidentification feedback than were witnesses who did not. Second, records of confidence reports would allow defense attorneys to challenge subsequent inflation through cross-examination at trial. This is likely to be difficult, as one study demonstrated that mock jurors are resistant to attempts to undermine a witness's confidence report by providing evidence that it has inflated over time. Finally, recording confidence is easy. It does not require specialized equipment or training. It can easily be incorporated into interviews with witnesses. Should immediate confidence reports not be recorded, another common suggestion is to introduce expert testimony on the malleability of confidence. This solution is less appealing because research has demonstrated that mock jurors are relatively insensitive to testimony impugning the correlation between confidence and accuracy. In some studies, jurors persist in using confidence reports even after being told that they are only minimally useful in assessing accuracy. Therefore, the most reasonable solution is to prevent eyewitnesses' confidence from inflating in the first place. The best way to do this is to collect immediate records of confidence reports in both identification accuracy and crime details.

Amy Bradfield Douglass

See also Confidence in Identifications; Estimator and System Variables in Eyewitness Identification; Expert Psychological Testimony on Eyewitness Identification; Eyewitness Memory; Identification Tests, Best Practices in; Juries and Eyewitnesses; *Neil v. Biggers* Criteria for Evaluating Eyewitness Identification; Postevent Information and Eyewitness Memory; Wrongful Conviction

Further Readings

Baron, R. S., Vandello, J. A., & Brunsman, B. (1996). The forgotten variable in conformity research: Impact of task importance on social influence. *Journal of Personality and Social Psychology, 71*(5), 915–927.

Bradfield, A., & McQuiston, D. E. (2002). When does evidence of eyewitness confidence inflation affect judgments in a criminal trial? *Law and Human Behavior, 28*(4), 369–387.

Bradfield, A. L., Wells, G. L., & Olson, E. A. (2002). The damaging effect of confirming feedback on the relation between eyewitness certainty and identification accuracy. *Journal of Applied Psychology, 87*(1), 112–120.

Lindsay, S. D., Read, J. D., & Sharma, K. (1998). Accuracy and confidence in person identification: The relationship is strong when witnessing conditions vary widely. *Psychological Science, 9*(3), 215–218.

Luus, C. A. E., & Wells, G. L. (1994). The malleability of eyewitness confidence: Co-witness and perseverance effects. *Journal of Applied Psychology, 79,* 714–724.

Sporer, S., Penrod, S., Read, D., & Cutler, B. L. (1995). Choosing, confidence, and accuracy: A meta-analysis of the confidence-accuracy relation in eyewitness identification studies. *Psychological Bulletin, 118,* 315–327.

CONFLICT TACTICS SCALE (CTS)

Two general types of incidence surveys exist: the Conflict Tactics Scale (CTS) and the Crime Victim Surveys (CVS). The former requires people to indicate what actions they have taken to resolve family conflicts; the latter requires people to indicate by what crimes they have been victimized. The CVS find the rates of reporting wife assault to the police comparable with the reporting rates for other assaults. However, these surveys have a filtering problem such that people who do not consider their abuse victimization to be a crime do not respond in the affirmative. Hence, incidence rates of reported spousal abuse, which are not defined as criminal by the victim, are low. To circumvent this filtering problem, Straus, Gelles, and Steinmetz devised the CTS, which asks respondents to report modes of conflict resolution in the family. This avoids the problem of whether the respondent defines the action as criminal or not and, therefore, attempts to obtain more accurate estimates of the frequency and incidence of domestic assault in a general population. Straus found violence incidence rates with the CTS were 16 times greater than with the CVS. Presenting the CTS in the context of normal conflict rather than a criminal act reduces filters against reporting.

Surveys of Incidence: Conflict Tactics Surveys

Several surveys using the CTS have been completed. They include (a) a nationally representative U.S. sample of 2,143 interviewed in 1974 by Response Analysis Corporation; (b) a survey of spousal violence against women in the state of Kentucky, which interviewed 1,793 women; (c) a second national survey completed by Straus and Gelles in 1985; and (d) a sample of 1,045 for the Province of Alberta, Canada. These were each obtained by a survey that interviews a representative sample drawn from a general population about experiences of being victimized by violence during family conflicts and the type of actions used to resolve these conflicts. These rates refer to the use of violence at any time in the marriage and may include both unilateral and reciprocal violence. Straus reported approximately equal perpetration rates by gender. This common measure enables some direct comparison between these surveys.

Kennedy and Dutton used a combination of face-to-face meeting and random-digit dialing techniques to survey 1,045 residents in Alberta, Canada, leading to a comparison of American and Canadian rates of wife assault. The "minor" violence rates for the two countries are virtually identical, but the American "severe violence" rates were higher than the Canadian rates. By way of comparison with these North American data, Kim and Cho reported that the Korean intimate partner violence rate was 37.5% for wife assault (any violence) in the preceding year versus 11.6% reported by Straus et al. In 1985, Fumagai and Straus found a lifetime incidence of wife assault in Japan of 58.7% versus 22% in the United States.

Fals-Stewart, Birchler, and Kelley asked 104 men in a spousal violence treatment program and their partners to keep a weekly diary identifying days of physical aggression and a daily CTS checklist for violence. Male-to-female agreement on "violence days" was better after treatment than before, perhaps because couples were aware of tracking. Interestingly, the women were violent on more days than the men, regardless of whose report was read.

Moffitt et al. confirmed Straus's point in one of the best methodological studies of intimate violence to date, the Dunedin study. When asked about "assault victimization," they found that respondents reported rates of male violence that were much higher than the rates of female violence, and both rates were quite low. When they asked the same respondents about "relationships with partners," the rates reported by both genders were much higher and equivalent.

Criticisms

Some criticisms have been made about the CTS: (a) the CTS ignores the context in which the violence occurred, (b) differences in gender size between men and women make acts scored the same on the CTS quite different in reality, (c) impression management or social desirability factors may preclude people from answering the CTS accurately, and (d) the CTS queries violence occurring in a conflict and may miss "out of the blue" violence.

Straus's rejoinders to these criticisms are as follows. First, the assessment of context should be done separately because there are so many context variables that they could not all be included on the CTS. The CTS is designed in such a way that any special set of context questions can be easily added. Second, a similar problem, Straus notes, is that repeated slapping is highly abusive and dangerous but gets counted as Minor Violence on the CTS. Straus argues that while it is possible to weight actions by differences in size between perpetrator and victim, or to construct an upper limit after which slapping gets counted as Severe Violence, such weightings have rarely led to changes in research results. Third, the social desirability criticism was answered, in part, by a study by Dutton and Hemphill, which correlated scores on two measures of social desirability (the tendency to present a "perfect image" on self-report tests) and scores on the CTS. Social desirability is measured by a test called the Marlowe-Crowne test (MC), which assesses the tendency to present the self in a socially acceptable manner. MC scores did correlate significantly; the higher their social desirability score, the lower their reported rates of verbal abuse. However, it did not correlate with their reports of physical abuse, nor with any reports of abuse (verbal or physical) made against them by their wives. Hence, it seems that reports of physical abuse are largely uncontaminated by socially desirable responding. This means that the incidence survey rates are probably fairly accurate as far as image management is concerned. Finally, the vast majority of violent acts are perceived as emanating from conflict. While the CTS may miss an out-of-the-blue attack, it more than makes up for this with its increased sensitivity over crime victim surveys.

Donald G. Dutton, Jessica Broderick,
and Makenzie Chilton

See also Domestic Violence Screening Instrument (DVSI); Intimate Partner Violence; Spousal Assault Risk Assessment (SARA)

Further Readings

Browning, J., & Dutton, D. G. (1986). Assessment of wife assault with the Conflict Tactics Scale: Using couple data to quantify the differential reporting effect. *Journal of Marriage and the Family, 48,* 375–379.

Straus, M. A., & Gelles, R. J. (Eds.). (1990). *Physical violence in American families.* New Brunswick, NJ: Transaction.

Straus, M. A., Hamby, S. L., & Boney-McCoy, S. (1996). The revised Conflict Tactics Scales (CTS2): Development and preliminary psychometric data. *Journal of Family Issues, 17,* 283–316.

CONFORMITY IN EYEWITNESS REPORTS

Eyewitness research has repeatedly shown that exposure to postevent information can affect a witness's ability to accurately report details of an originally encoded event. In everyday life, postevent information might be encountered when individuals who have shared the same experience discuss this with one another. Even when each person has witnessed the same event, their memories are likely to differ because of naturally occurring differences in the details attended to at the time, as well as differences in each person's ability to accurately remember those details. Despite initial differences in recollections of an event, when people talk about their memories they can influence each other such that their subsequent individual memory reports become similar. The phenomenon of people's memory reports becoming similar to one another's following a discussion has been referred to as "memory conformity." This entry discusses the ways in which researchers have investigated conformity in eyewitness reports, typical research findings, and current theoretical explanations for the memory conformity effect.

When memory conformity occurs in the context of a forensic investigation, there can be serious implications. For example, it might be assumed that seemingly corroborative witness statements are a product of independent witnesses with consistent versions of events, when in fact memory conformity might be responsible for the similarities if there has been some form of interaction between cowitnesses. Therefore, it is important that the police take care not to give undue weight to the consistency of statements from witnesses who may have talked when judging the accuracy of an eyewitness account.

A typical paradigm used to investigate memory conformity in eyewitness reports involves pairs of participants being led to believe that they have encoded the same stimuli (often a simulated crime event shown on video or slides), when in reality they are shown stimuli that bear a similarity but differ in critical ways. These critical differences can take the form of added items (where one dyad member sees an item that his or her partner did not and vice versa) or contradicting items (where both dyad members see the same item, but details of this item differ in terms of color or product). This manipulation allows different features of the encoded stimuli to be observed by each participant. Dyad members are then given time to discuss what they have seen. An individual recall test for the originally encoded stimuli is then administered to examine the effects of cowitness discussion on memory. The dependent variable of interest is whether, and how often, witnesses report an item at test that they have encountered from a cowitness as opposed to seeing with their own eyes.

Alternative procedures to investigate memory conformity include using a confederate to act as a cowitness and purposefully introduce items of misleading postevent information into the discussion. Other experiments have presented cowitness information indirectly by incorporating it into a recall questionnaire, or the experimenter reveals responses that have purportedly been given by other witnesses.

A common finding for memory conformity research, regardless of procedure or stimuli used, is that social influences encountered in the form of postevent information from a cowitness can mediate accuracy in joint recall and recognition tasks, with individuals often exhibiting conformity to the suggestions and judgments of others. Significant conformity effects are also evident following a delay in postdiscussion memory tests that are performed alone.

Theoretical explanations for conformity in eyewitness reports share strong parallels with those accounting for the effects of postevent information on memory. For example, research has shown that source misattributions account in part for conformity in eyewitness reports, as individuals sometimes claim to remember seeing items of information that have actually been encountered from a cowitness. Informational motivations to report accurate information at test are also thought to play a role. Here, individuals choose to report the postevent information encountered from a cowitness at test if it is accepted as veridical. Informational motivations to conform are often evident in situations where individuals doubt the accuracy of their own memory or when the information encountered from another individual convinces them that their initial judgment was erroneous. In support of this, research has found that the influence exerted by one person on another's memory judgments can be modulated by person perception factors. For example, tendencies to conform can be increased (or decreased) by manipulating the perceptions of each individual regarding the relative knowledge each has of stimuli they encoded together as a dyad. Similar effects can be obtained by manipulating the perceived relative competence of each individual or the overt confidence with which individuals make their assertions to each other.

Research continues to explore which factors can increase, decrease, and possibly eliminate the longer-term effects of conformity on memory. However, progress in addressing such issues has been hampered by the complexity of the phenomenon itself, due to the inherently dynamic and variable nature of realistic interactions between individuals. Despite this, new paradigms to investigate conformity in eyewitness reports are being developed and refined so that the effects of naturalistic interactions on subsequent memory reports can be investigated with full experimental control.

Fiona Gabbert

See also Eyewitness Memory; False Memories; Postevent Information and Eyewitness Memory; Source Monitoring and Eyewitness Memory

Further Readings

Gabbert, F., Memon, A., & Allan, K. (2003). Memory conformity: Can eyewitnesses influence each other's memories for an event? *Applied Cognitive Psychology, 17,* 533–543.

Roediger, H. L., Meade, M. L., & Bergman, E. T. (2001). Social contagion of memory. *Psychonomic Bulletin & Review, 8,* 365–371.

Shaw, J. S., Garven, S., & Wood, J. M. (1997). Co-witness information can have immediate effects on eyewitness memory reports. *Law and Human Behavior, 21,* 503–523.

Wright, D. B., Self, G., & Justice, C. (2000). Memory conformity: Exploring misinformation effects when presented by another person. *British Journal of Psychology, 91,* 189–202.

CONSENT TO CLINICAL RESEARCH

Informed consent practices have evolved over time after instances were documented in which research participants were not treated fairly or respectfully, were not informed, or were subjected to unnecessary harm. Current federal regulations support the ethical treatment of persons in the research setting in that the participation is voluntary, that the risks outweigh the benefits, and that all people are given an equal chance to participate. When a researcher invites a participant into the research setting, the researcher is required to provide the necessary information, to ensure that the participant fully understands the information, and to stop the research if it is felt that these standards have not been met. Prior to enrollment in a research study, that candidate must provide valid consent for participation. That is, the participant must be fully informed about the research purposes, risks, benefits, freedom to withdraw consent, and other relevant information; must enter voluntarily into the research; and must be capable of making an informed decision. Informed consent to clinical research is important in the field of psychology and law, because psychological researchers must be aware of the requirements of conducting research and must protect themselves and also their research participants from any ethical breaches. Clinical research refers to studies conducted in a setting where clinical conditions, either medical or psychiatric, are diagnosed and treated. This entry provides a historical basis for the evolution of informed consent, the requirements of informed consent, and will end with a brief discussion of the capacities of potentially vulnerable individuals who may have compromised ability to give a valid consent by virtue of impaired capacity or lack of voluntariness.

Historical Perspective

In research settings, individuals are protected by the doctrine of informed consent, which has evolved through policies, regulations, and professional codes. In the 1940s, unspeakable acts were committed when medical experiments on human subjects were conducted in concentration camps in Nazi Germany. In response to the atrocious experiments, the first formal document for conveying the ideas of protection of persons as human subjects and informed consent was developed. The Nuremberg Code set forth 10 guidelines for the ethical treatment of persons involved in research. The first statement of the Nuremberg Code states that the voluntary consent of the human subject is absolutely essential. Before an affirmative decision by the person can be made, one must know the nature, duration, and purpose of the experiment; the method and means in which it is conducted; and the reasonable inconveniences expected, which may possibly come from participation. The Nuremberg Code further states that experiments should only be conducted by scientifically qualified persons, that the results should yield fruitful results for the good of society, that all harm to the participant should be avoided, and that the participant may end the experiment at any time. The Nuremberg Code was expanded when the World Medical Association adopted the Declaration of Helsinki in 1964. The Code established independent ethical review committees to oversee all experimental procedures, which set the stage for the later development of institutional review boards (IRBs).

Although the Nuremburg Code helped to identify basic ethical principles of research, there were still instances in which egregious ethical breaches continued. The Tuskegee Syphilis Study, which began in 1932 and ultimately ended in 1972, was a research study in which medically ill patients were not offered effective medical treatment, which became available during the course of the research. In 1972, the unethical manner of the research project was made public and this ultimately led to the 1974 Research Act. The National Research Act was signed into law, thereby creating the National Commission for the Protection of Human Subjects of Biomedical and Behavioral Research. The charge of the commission was to identify the basic ethical principles that should underlie research involving human subjects and to develop guidelines that should be followed in accordance with the described principles. The 1979 Belmont Report emerged as a product of this work group and mandated that all researchers gain approval from an IRB before proceeding with any type of experimentation.

Principles of Beneficence, Justice, and Respect

The Belmont Report specified the three basic ethical principles governing scientific research. These include respect for persons, beneficence, and justice. Respect for persons specifies that individuals should be treated as autonomous persons, and those whose decision making is compromised should be given special protections and safeguards. Furthermore, participants must enter into a research setting voluntarily and with adequate information. Beneficence is applied in the research setting in that persons are entitled to participation that is free from harm and that maximizes possible benefits and minimizes possible harm. The principle of justice dictates that individuals should be treated fairly and equally in the research setting,

according to their need, effort, contribution, and merit, and that all persons must share the responsibility of research.

The three principles of the Belmont Report are translated into informed consent by maintaining that persons are participating of their own free will and that the benefits to the person outweigh the risks. The Belmont Report served as the basis for the Code of Federal Regulations, which was approved in 1978. In addition, in 1993, the International Ethical Guidelines for Biomedical Research Involving Human Subjects were developed. In 2005, the Department of Health and Human Services released a revised edition of the Federal Code of Regulations on the Protection of Human Subjects. Title 45, part 46 of the U.S. Code of Federal Regulations upholds the application of the Belmont Report principles and is now generally accepted as the uniform policy for the protection of research participants. Outlined are specific definitions and statements as they apply to both federally and nonfederally funded research projects.

Requirements of Informed Consent

The theory of informed consent to research is that a research participant is both voluntary and fully informed about the nature and consequences of an experimental situation before giving consent to participate. There are three essential elements to the doctrine of informed consent: voluntariness, information, and competency. The first element is that the person voluntarily consents to the procedure, in that the individual chooses freely to participate. To be voluntary, the person must consent without the presence of coercion, fraud, or duress, which may hinder the person's decision-making ability. Stanley and Guido further elaborate that when an individual is consenting to participate in psychological research, one must consider the environment to ensure that the participant's voluntary status is not compromised by the setting (e.g., prison, hospital, school).

Second, an individual must be fully informed of the proposed research setting to which he or she is consenting. The disclosure of information, which is provided in a formal informed consent document to the research participant, should include a description of the proposed procedures, its purpose, duration of the research procedure, the risks and benefits of participation, alternatives to participation, and the voluntariness of participation. Other issues that should be disclosed are that the individual has the opportunity to withdraw from the research setting at any time, issues of confidentiality, and any other pertinent information such as how to contact the main investigator.

The final element required to obtain informed consent is competency, which refers to the functional capacity to give valid consent to participate in research. Grisso and Appelbaum note that those persons who cannot use the disclosed information because of a lack of certain cognitive abilities are not capable of participating in an informed consent procedure. When the impairment reaches a certain level of severity, a determination can be made of incompetence. In legal terms, a de facto incompetence determination is made when inquiries into the person's actual capacities reveal a sufficient lack in cognitive functionality.

When making a judgment about one's decision-making capacities, three types of information are usually required as delineated by Grisso and Appelbaum: (1) the person's clinical condition, (2) the person's degree of functioning in tasks involving decision-making abilities, and (3) the situation-specific demands. There are four legal standards for assessing decision-making competence, which include the ability to communicate a choice, the ability to understand relevant information, the ability to appreciate the circumstances and likely outcome, and the ability to rationally manipulate the information. Grisso and Appelbaum also note that although four standards have been proposed, not all courts and jurisdictions apply all concepts in a determination of competency. Also of importance is that a person's status on the four abilities is not all-or-none. A person usually possesses all the abilities but in varying degrees and one must consider the complexity of the decision being made in relation to the condition of the person making that decision.

For researchers it is important to provide all the necessary information to the potential participant so that he or she is able to make an informed decision. The information of the purposes, procedures, benefits, risks, and voluntary nature of participation must be outlined in a written document and signed by both parties. It is the responsibility of the researcher to ensure that the participant understands the information and is not being coerced in any way to participate.

Competency of Special Populations

When conducting research with normal healthy populations, researchers tend to presume that the participant is capable of understanding the material in the informed consent document and capable of making an autonomous decision of whether to participate or not. However, when conducting research with potentially vulnerable populations, the same assumption cannot necessarily be made. Potentially vulnerable populations include children and adolescents, who are vulnerable because of their developmental level and their susceptibility to coercion; prisoners and other institutionalized individuals by virtue of their lack of voluntary status; medical patients who may have impaired cognitive function ranging from being comatose to some memory impairment; and psychiatric patients as a result of possible compromised capacity to consent. Several empirical studies have examined the ability of psychiatric patients to provide informed consent; a brief summary of the findings follows. In persons with schizophrenia and psychotic disorders, mixed results have been produced. The consensus is that these types of patients, on the whole, perform more poorly than their non-ill counterparts on tests of competency. Several studies, however, have further noted that even with this divide, there is much heterogeneity among the schizophrenic patients and many are able to perform at a level similar to non-ill persons. Research on persons with affective disorders is somewhat more promising, with this group performing at a level similar to non-ill persons in most of the published studies. Finally, elderly patients with Alzheimer's disease seem to be the population at the greatest risk for having impaired levels of cognitive processing and thus a diminished ability to provide informed consent.

Elizabeth Arias and Barbara Stanley

See also Capacity to Consent to Treatment; Capacity to Consent to Treatment Instrument (CCTI); MacArthur Competence Assessment Tool for Clinical Research (MacCAT–CR)

Further Readings

Appelbaum, P., Lidz, C., & Meisel, A. (1987). *Informed consent.* New York: Oxford University Press.

Meisel, L., & Lidz, C. (1977). Toward a model of the legal doctrine of informed consent. *American Journal of Psychiatry, 134*(3), 285–289.

Stanley, B., & Galietta, M. (2006). Informed consent in treatment and research. In I. Weiner & A. Hess (Eds.), *The handbook of forensic psychology* (3rd ed., pp. 211–239). Hoboken, NJ: Wiley.

Stanley, B., & Guido, J. (1996). Informed consent: Psychological and empirical issues. In B. H. Stanley, J. E. Sieber, & G. B. Melton (Eds.), *Research ethics: A psychological approach* (pp. 105–128). Lincoln: University of Nebraska Press.

Government Printing Office. (1949). *Trials of war criminals before the Nuremberg Military Tribunals under Control Council Law* (No. 10, Vol. 2, pp. 181–182). Washington, DC: Author.

Coping Strategies of Adult Sexual Assault Victims

Coping strategies of adult rape victims refers to the ways in which rape victims respond to an assault. Most of this research focuses on female victims because most sexual assault victims are women. Although the term *coping* implies that someone is adjusting well, coping strategies can actually be either helpful or unhelpful. Less helpful strategies include avoiding dealing with the assault, withdrawing from others, using drugs and alcohol to self-medicate, blaming one's self, and focusing on the past and on why the assault occurred. Among the more helpful strategies reported are seeing the assault in a more positive light, relying on one's religious beliefs, and focusing on what currently is controllable. Disclosing the assault can lead to either positive or negative reactions from others. Positive reactions are more common, although negative reactions have a greater impact.

Knowledge about the strategies victims use to deal with an assault is relevant to several kinds of professionals who work with victims. For example, knowledge about which strategies have been helpful or unhelpful is useful to those who provide direct services to victims (e.g., psychologists, social workers, advocates). This information also might be used by a psychological expert in a sexual assault case to help explain the effects of the rape on a victim to a judge or jury. It is important, however, to keep in mind that most rapes are not reported and, of those that are reported, many are not charged and few go to trial.

Specific Coping Strategies

In the general research literature on coping, nine primary forms of coping have been identified: cognitive restructuring, problem solving, support seeking, distraction, avoidance, social withdrawal, emotional regulation/expressing emotions, rumination, and helplessness. Several studies have assessed the frequency with which rape victims use these strategies and the relationship between the use of the strategy and the postrape symptoms of distress. Typical symptoms of distress among rape victims include those associated with posttraumatic stress disorder (PTSD), depression, and anxiety. Of the studies that have assessed one of these forms of coping among rape victims, avoidance and social withdrawal are generally associated with greater distress. Avoidance involves trying not to think about or deal with the assault (e.g., trying to block it out), and social withdrawal, of course, involves withdrawing from others. The strategies associated with better adjustment fall mainly within the category of cognitive restructuring, which refers to trying to see the assault in a different or more positive light. Although this might seem unlikely, many victims do actually report positive changes in their lives following an assault, such as that they appreciate life more. Teaching coping skills such as cognitive restructuring also has been found to reduce symptoms in experimental studies. The results of studies assessing emotional regulation/expressing emotions are mixed, partly because of methodological problems with the studies. However, the general research literature on coping suggests that expressing emotions is associated with better adjustment. Another coping strategy not included in this categorization scheme is religious coping, which generally is associated with lower distress levels among victims.

Another way in which victims may try to cope with the assault is by drinking or using drugs. Several studies indicate that victims report more alcohol and drug abuse and dependence than do nonvictims. Because drinking and drug use are risk factors for sexual assault, it is important to try to determine if the substance use came before or after the assault. Studies that attempt to assess the timing of the substance abuse relative to the sexual assault generally indicate that the substance abuse started after the assault. Alcohol and drug use by victims is related to higher distress levels; thus, victims may be using substances to self-medicate their distress.

Social Support

Although support seeking is considered one of the primary forms of coping, research on support processes in rape victims goes beyond the examination of support seeking as a coping process. For example, one issue for rape victims is whether and to whom to disclose the assault. Although disclosing the assault may not necessarily be for the purpose of seeking support, unlike other events that are more public (e.g., bereavement), victims only receive supportive or unsupportive reactions from others if they disclose the assault to them. The act of disclosing the assault or of seeking support also should be distinguished from the supportive or unsupportive reactions of others to the victim regarding the assault. Thus, research in this area has focused on whether and to whom victims disclose, what kinds of reactions they receive, and how those reactions are related to victims' distress levels. This research suggests that although most rape victims do not report the assault to the police, most disclose to someone, such as friends or family members. In general, victims indicate that they received mostly positive and supportive reactions from others. However, negative reactions, such as being blamed or treated differently, also occur and appear to be more common from formal (e.g., the police, physicians) than from informal (e.g., friends, family) support providers. Negative social reactions tend to be more associated with distress than positive social reactions are associated with well-being. Nonetheless, being believed and being listened to by others, especially friends and family, is associated with better adjustment among rape victims. Many friends and victims report that the assault had a positive effect on their relationships (e.g., it brought them closer).

Attributions About the Cause of the Rape

Individuals who have been sexually assaulted often struggle to regain a sense of control over their lives. One way to do this is to try to identify the cause of the assault (i.e., make a causal attribution) and thus recognize how the assault could have been prevented. For rape victims, this may involve trying to identify what they could have done differently to avoid being raped. Much of the research on the relations among attributions and posttrauma distress has been guided by the theory that behavioral self-blame, which involves attributing the assault to one's past behavior, is an adaptive response to rape because it is associated with the belief that future rapes can be avoided. In contrast, characterological self-blame, which involves attributing the rape to some stable aspect of one's self that

cannot be changed, is thought to be maladaptive because it is not associated with a sense of future control. This theory has been described as dominating research on attributions and adjustment for more than two decades and as being widely accepted as having implications for interventions with trauma survivors.

Although this theory suggests that behavioral self-blame is adaptive, behavioral self-blame consistently is associated with more, rather than less, distress among survivors of rape. In addition, behavioral self-blame generally is unrelated to perceived future control among victims of rape. In other words, behavioral self-blame does not appear to foster the belief that future rapes can be avoided, which was the proposed mechanism for its adaptive value. Characterological self-blame is also consistently related to higher distress levels. Indeed, the two types of self-blame are highly correlated with each other. Experimental studies suggest that reductions in self-blame in treatment are associated with reductions in PTSD symptoms.

Research on attributions has tended to focus on self-blame, perhaps because of the predominance of the aforementioned theory. However, other kinds of blame, such as blaming the rapist or other external factors, tend to be more common than self-blame. These other types of blame also are associated with more distress. It appears that focusing on the past and on why the assault occurred is associated with higher distress levels. It is less adaptive to focus on the past and on why the assault occurred, or even on how future assaults can be avoided, than to focus on aspects of the assault that are currently controllable, such as the recovery process.

Patricia A. Frazier

See also Child Sexual Abuse; Rape Trauma Syndrome; Victimization

Further Readings

Filipas, H., & Ullman, S. (2001). Social reactions to sexual assault victims from various support sources. *Violence and Victims, 16,* 673–692.

Frazier, P. (2003). Perceived control and distress following sexual assault: A longitudinal test of a new model. *Journal of Personality and Social Psychology, 84,* 1257–1269.

Frazier, P., Mortensen, H., & Steward, J. (2005). Coping strategies as mediators of the relations among perceived control and distress in sexual assault survivors. *Journal of Counseling Psychology, 52,* 267–278.

Ullman, S. (2000). Psychometric characteristics of the Social Reactions Questionnaire: A measure of reactions to sexual assault victims. *Psychology of Women Quarterly, 24,* 257–271.

Ullman, S., Filipas, H., Townsend, S., & Starzynski, L. (2005). Trauma exposure, posttraumatic stress disorder and problem drinking in sexual assault survivors. *Journal of Studies on Alcohol, 66,* 610–619.

CRIMINAL BEHAVIOR, THEORIES OF

When crime is truly the product of rational choice, the offender commits the act for reasons of personal gain or gratification. His or her behavior is under his or her complete control. How and to what degree, however, might other factors intrude on and compromise his or her ability to exercise free will? The response to this question has come in the form of innumerable theories, each purporting to explain criminal behavior in terms of specific factors. Broadly speaking, these theories involve three categories of factors: psychological, biological, and social. In fact, human behavior is the product of complex interactions among many factors. Rather than providing a summary of myriad theories, this entry focuses on the main factors involved in the expression and suppression of criminal behaviors.

Social Factors

There is a vast criminological literature that identifies a wide range of environmental factors as causally linked to criminal behavior. These include developmental, social, and economic factors. For example, poverty is often cited as a socioeconomic condition linked to crime. The stress, strain, and frustration experienced by those lacking the financial resources to meet their needs and fulfill their desires through legitimate means renders them more inclined to commit crime than affluent individuals with ready access to legitimate means. Poor nutrition is an especially troubling aspect of poverty. Nutritional deficiencies can result in or exacerbate problems such as learning disabilities and poor impulse control. Such cognitive dysfunctions have been identified as precursors to delinquency and adult criminality. Thus, one's position in the social structure of society—as operationalized by variables such as level of income—can be a significant contributing factor in the criminal

activities of some individuals by virtue of its impact on brain function.

Growing up in a household where parental displays of violence are commonplace can shape the behavior of children so as to make them more likely to respond to their own problems with violent means. While aggression and violence are not synonymous, that they are correlated is undeniable. Psychologist Albert Bandura demonstrated the importance of social learning in the development of aggressive behavior. Exposure to a violent role model may operate as a trigger of preexisting psychological and biological factors that predispose that individual to aggressive behavior. This may explain why only one of the two sons whose father assaults their mother grows up to beat his own wife—there were additional factors that rendered him more readily influenced by the violent model; or, conversely, the nonviolent son was resistant to the influence by virtue of individual "protective" factors, such as high IQ.

There is a substantial literature on a "cycle of violence" whereby victims of childhood abuse and neglect are predisposed to engage in violent behavior in adulthood, thus passing the violence from one generation to the next. Other research has examined the effects of being bullied during formative years, finding that the victims in turn become victimizers. In animal experiments, exposure to conditions of inescapable threat has been found to alter specific chemicals in the brain involved in aggression and the inhibition of aggression, with the result that formerly docile animals go on to display inappropriate and excessive aggression, attacking smaller, weaker animals whenever presented with them. In essence, they become the "playground bully." Thus, a change in the environment—exposure to inescapable threat—leads to changes in biology, which lead to the changes in behavior. Empirical studies on the effects of child maltreatment reveal that in addition to psychological problems actual structural and functional damage to the developing brain may occur. These neurobiological effects may be an adaptive mechanism for living in that dangerous environment. Regardless, they also tend to predispose the individual to a range of psychiatric conditions, aggressive behaviors, and stress-related illnesses. Resilient children, so called because of their ability to thrive under high-risk conditions, appear to have cognitive capabilities (notably higher verbal intelligence) that enable them to adapt to their stressful environment. Understanding the mechanisms that underlie resilience may reveal deficits in those who succumb to the harmful effects of their disadvantaged or abusive childhood—often becoming delinquent and criminal as a result.

Of course, the majority of poor people are not criminals, and the majority of those growing up in abusive homes or who are bullied do not go on to become criminals, raising the question: What it is about those who commit crime that distinguishes them from others who experience similar circumstances but are law abiding? Furthermore, why would individuals who do not experience such adversity commit crime? The answer to these questions is that social factors affect different people differently. By and large it is the psychological and biological makeup of an individual that determines how and to what extent external forces affect his behavior. Psychological and biological factors interact to render an individual more or less vulnerable to adverse social conditions. This should not be taken to diminish the influence of social factors on criminal behavior, for indeed they have a significant role, but rather to highlight the fact that the effect they have depends on the psychological and biological makeup of the individual. Ultimately, it is the individual who acts—criminally or otherwise.

Psychological Factors

By virtue of the requirement of mens rea, criminal courts are concerned with the psychological elements that underlie criminal behavior. Research teaches, however, that the psychology of the offender emanates from a biological substrate. And, one's psychological states affect various aspects of his or her biology. Mind and brain have an indelible connection. An individual's psychological state or mental status—whether at the scene of a crime or in a courtroom—involves biological mechanisms.

Psychopathology—the study of diseases/disorders of the mind—constitutes a major area of preparation for the forensic psychologist. While the vast majority of individuals with mental disorder do not commit crimes, it is estimated that rates of serious mental disorder among prison inmates are three to four times greater than they are for members of the general population. Although this cannot blindly be taken to mean that the crimes of mentally disordered inmates were due to their psychopathology, or that mental disorder predated their incarceration, their disproportionate numbers relative to the general population nonetheless confer significance to mental disorder as a contributing factor in criminal behavior.

The relationship between criminal behavior and mental disorder is complex. Individuals who experience false perceptions (i.e., have hallucinations such as hearing voices that have no basis in objective reality) and/or hold false beliefs (i.e., have delusions such as "people are out to kill me") are considered to have a major mental disorder, or psychosis. Recent research has linked schizophrenia, a psychosis, to an increased risk of committing violent crime—usually against significant others in their lives (not the randomly encountered strangers portrayed in popular media). While it is understandable how someone who is out of touch with reality can harm another as a result (e.g., by having a delusion that he has a divine mission to cleanse the streets of vermin—say, by killing homeless people), the majority of psychotic individuals do not commit crimes.

Research on hallucinations in schizophrenics reveals that the basis for their false perceptions is brain dysfunction. For example, the occurrence of auditory hallucinations coincides with the firing of neurons in brain regions normally involved in processing sound—but in this case in the absence of sound. Instead of asking the nebulous question, "Why does a schizophrenic hear voices?" we are now positioned to ask why neurons in particular regions of the brain misfire in the absence of external stimuli. Thus, the impetus for violence in a schizophrenic individual—when he attacks because the voices say the other person intends harm—appears to arise out of aberrant neural activity.

Of the mental disorders currently recognized by clinicians and researchers, most are not deemed psychoses. Rather, they are disorders of personality, impulse control, and the like. Psychopathy, a form of personality disorder, is exhibited as a cluster of specific affective, interpersonal, and socially deviant behaviors. Although psychopaths make up only about 1% of the general population, they are estimated to comprise approximately 25% of prison populations. The nature of their disorder—lacking remorse for their antisocial actions and emotional empathy for those whose rights they violate—makes them especially well suited for criminal activity. While most psychopaths are not criminal (nonetheless behaving in ways that disregard consideration for others), of those who are, recidivism rates tend to be significantly higher than for nonpsychopathic offenders.

Although psychopaths are not psychotic, the neurobiological mechanisms that normally impart emotion to cognitions, thoughts, and attitudes appear to be dysfunctional in the psychopath. The psychologist Robert Hare suggests that whereas genetic (and other biological) factors determine the aberrant personality structure, the environment may shape how the disorder is expressed as behavior. Positron emission tomography and single-photon-emission computed tomography scans have identified a number of specific regions in the brains of violent psychopaths that do not function normally. In particular, the prefrontal cortex—part of the frontal lobes of the brain largely responsible for rational decision making and impulse control—appears to be underaroused, rendering it incapable of effectively managing emotional urges. Impulsive behaviors, including crimes, are the result.

However cognitive abilities are defined, certainly they have a major role in criminal behavior. Where research has used IQ as a measure of intelligence, by and large offenders have lower scores than nonoffenders. Typically, individuals with low intellectual ability have difficulty delaying gratification, curbing their impulses, and appreciating the alternative means to get what they want. With substantial intellectual impairment, they tend to be less inhibited from doing harm because they lack the appreciation for the wrongfulness of their conduct. Although environment can facilitate or suppress the development and expression of one's cognitive abilities, research indicates that these have a substantial heritable component.

The concept of emotional intelligence holds considerable promise for a more comprehensive understanding of chronic criminality. Those with low emotional intelligence—people who lack insight into their own behavior and empathy toward others—are less inhibited about violating the rights of others. Injury to the (ventromedial) prefrontal cortex has been linked to the onset of reckless and antisocial behavior (including violence) without remorse, suggesting our moral compass is rooted in specific frontal lobe functions that for the chronic offender are defective.

Much neglected in the mainstream literature on criminal behavior are the effects of traumatic events in early childhood from a psychoanalytic perspective. Twenty-first century technology provides for—should we choose—a recasting of Freudian constructs as specific neurobiological factors. The id, responsible for generating unconscious and primitive urges, may correspond with the limbic system—which includes brain structures involved in basic emotions, motivation, and memory. The aspect of the personality Sigmund Freud referred to as the ego mediates the self-centered demands of the id. The ego develops in childhood and grounds the individual in reality. It would be this rational aspect of personality that negotiates with the emotional and impulsive id. Read frontal lobes here. As for Freud's superego, the moral aspect of personality may well "reside," at least partially, in the ventromedial prefrontal cortex. Remorseless antisocial behavior follows damage to this area of the brain. Reconceptualizing Freudian constructs in this manner need not negate their validity, for the basic tenet—relating defects of personality to early trauma—remains intact. Rather, a neurobiological interpretation of psychoanalytic processes affords them something they heretofore lacked—the ability to be empirically validated.

While we refer to disordered mental states or diseased mind, frequently understated or unstated are the neurobiological processes that underlie them. Whatever the psychological problem, we can no longer speak of the psychological factors associated with criminal behavior without also discussing biological factors—virtually in the same sentence.

Biological Factors

The numerous and varied social and psychological factors that increase the risk of criminal behavior are mediated by biological processes.

Proper diet is essential to optimal brain function. For example, complex carbohydrates are broken down to make glucose—the basic fuel for the brain. Many nutrients are involved in converting that glucose into energy. A deficiency in any one of these essential nutrients compromises brain function by lowering the available energy. The frontal lobes of the brain, responsible for rational thinking, organizing behavior, and moderating emotional impulses, require approximately twice the energy as the more primitive regions. If energy levels are depleted, higher functions become impaired leaving lower brain activity uninhibited. Effectively, our emotions will have their way with us. Beyond basic energy needs, specific nutrients are required for the synthesis of neurotransmitters. It is, therefore, understandable how malnutrition compromises cognitive function and, in so doing, facilitates antisocial and aggressive behaviors.

Of the diagnosed illnesses associated with violent behavior, substance abuse ranks highest. The disinhibiting effects of alcohol are evident in police reports—replete as they are with accounts of domestic violence, aggravated assault, murder, and rape under its influence. Substance abuse has a particularly deleterious effect on individuals with preexisting mental disorder, exacerbating their dysfunction. It is not that alcohol causes violent behavior; rather, it appears to trigger violence in those already prone to behave violently by virtue of other factors.

Exposure to toxic agents in the environment such as pesticides and lead can delay or impair an individual's intellectual development and thus affect behavior and its regulation. In this regard, teratogens—factors that interfere with normal embryonic development—have a particularly important role in predisposing some individuals to a life of crime. The legacy of cognitive deficits and behavioral sequelae due to, for example, prenatal exposure to drugs and alcohol, are well documented in the literature.

Neurotransmitters are responsible for conducting electrochemical impulses within and across regions of the brain (as well as throughout the body). Many psychiatric disorders have been linked to imbalances in neurotransmitter systems. Serotonin is involved in a number of brain functions, including regulation of emotional states. In laboratory experiments, lowering the serotonin levels results in the onset of impulsive and aggressive behavior. That abuse and neglect in childhood can result in permanently reduced levels of serotonin is therefore an important observation for our understanding of the etiology of violence.

Hormones function in much the same way as neurotransmitters except they are released into the bloodstream rather than between neurons. Abnormally high levels of circulating testosterone—a sex hormone associated with the drive to dominate and compete—have been linked to excessive aggression. The phenomenon of "roid rage" in body builders who use anabolic steroids and exhibit extreme and uncontrollable violence attests to this effect. Such observations, as well as research on stress hormones correlating, for example, low levels of salivary cortisol with severe and persistent aggression, show the importance of hormonal contributions to criminal behavior.

Research on skin conductance, heart rate, and brainwave activity has linked low arousal to criminal behavior. In fact, in young children, these psychophysiological conditions have been reported to portend later delinquency with a high degree of accuracy. What these and the aforementioned studies suggest is that the brains of chronic offenders work differently. As we proceed to identify more of the factors linked to criminal behavior, we will take with us one particular question, the answer to which will have implications that at once generate fear and optimism: To what extent are the factors genetically determined?

A variety of methodologies—examining twins and adoptees, chromosomal abnormalities, and DNA polymorphisms—have been applied to evaluate the role of genetic factors in criminal behavior and aggression. Although it is not anticipated that a "crime gene" will ever be discovered, it is clear there are genes that code for specific neurochemicals linked to different kinds of behavior. To illustrate, a specific—albeit rare—mutation has been identified in a gene that holds the recipe for a particular enzyme known to affect the level of certain neurotransmitters in the brain. This defect has been linked to a propensity toward impulsive and excessive aggression and violence in each of the men of the family who has this mutation.

Studies in behavioral genetics support the contention that aggressive behavior is moderately heritable. Aggressive behaviors confer advantage to the males of a species as they compete for territory and access to females. Evolutionary psychology holds that aggressive traits that increase reproductive success will be selected and carried across successive generations. Primatologist Ronald Nadler contends that sexual aggression is inherent in the behavioral repertoires of great apes—animals that are among our closest biological affiliates. Human males, as a function of their drive to procreate, would be naturally inclined to have sex with as many different partners as possible, maximizing the probability that the species will survive and also that their own genes will be transmitted to the next generation. The fact that most males do not rape is in large measure due to their socialization; rapists are males who have not been effectively socialized in this regard. We can appreciate through this example how specific psychosocial risk factors (e.g., low intelligence) can increase the probability of criminal and violent behavior—in this case, rape.

The long tradition of assuming crime to be the product of volition, unencumbered by aberrant psychological or biological processes, is under attack. In the end, we may find it is psychologist Adrian Raine's bold conceptualization of criminality as a clinical disorder that best fits what we learn. To embrace this position, however, would require us to revisit our notions of crime and punishment—and treatment. If criminal behavior, at least impulsive violent criminal behavior, is inherently pathological, the implications are legion. In their determinations of culpability, the courts are thus wise to proceed with caution. As behavioral science research and technology advance, it is likely that the critical mass of the data will, ultimately, persuade.

Candice A. Skrapec

See also Criminal Responsibility, Assessment of; Forensic Assessment; Mens Rea and Actus Reus; Psychopathy; Psychotic Disorders

Further Readings

Hare, R. D. (1993). *Without conscience: The disturbing world of the psychopaths among us.* New York: Pocket Books.

Raine, A. (1993). *The psychopathology of crime: Criminal behavior as a clinical disorder.* New York: Academic Press.

Salovey, P., & Mayer, J. (1990). Emotional intelligence. *Imagination, Cognition, and Personality, 9*(3), 185–211.

Strueber, D., Lueck, M., & Roth, G. (2006, December). The violent brain. *Scientific American,* pp. 20–27.

Teicher, M. H. (2002, March). Scars that won't heal: The neurobiology of child abuse. *Scientific American,* pp. 68–75.

Widom, C. S. (1989). The cycle of violence. *Science, 244,* 160–166.

CRIMINAL RESPONSIBILITY, ASSESSMENT OF

Mental health professionals are frequently asked to evaluate criminal defendants to assist the courts in determining whether those individuals may have been legally insane (i.e., not criminally responsible) at the time of their crimes. This entry discusses the legal concept of and criteria for insanity, as well as the challenges that forensic experts face in conducting these evaluations.

In contemporary Western society, prohibited behaviors are typically codified in the criminal law, and most citizens are held to be responsible to obey these laws. Individuals who violate the law may be prosecuted and, if convicted, punished for their behavior. Such individuals are said to be "criminally responsible," a label that reflects the moral and legal judgment that the person had neither a justification nor an excuse for his or her

behavior, should have known better, and must endure the punishment as a corrective mechanism intended to discourage the recurrence of such behavior.

As the last sentence indicates, behavior that on its face appears to be criminal may in some circumstances not warrant the legal and moral conclusion that the actor is "guilty" or "criminally responsible." For example, under most circumstances, it is unlawful to take the life of another person, yet doing so in "self-defense" (the victim was threatening the life of the actor) may constitute a justification that precludes a finding of guilt. Similarly, taking money from another person (robbery), when performed under duress (a third-party threatens to kill the actor's child unless the money is taken), may be seen as justified because of the greater harm (death of the child) that was avoided by robbing the victim.

There are other individuals, or classes of individuals, who may be exempt or excused from judgments of "criminally responsible," not because of extraordinary or justifying circumstances, but because of individual characteristics or features that render them, in society's eyes, incapable of making the appropriate moral and legal judgments required to behave appropriately and (perhaps also) incapable from benefiting from punishment as a corrective measure. For our purposes, two such classes of individuals will be mentioned, both of which have been recognized in Western cultures, literally for centuries, as inappropriate targets for judgments of moral and legal culpability.

The first class of individuals is children, who, because of youthful age, lack of life experience, and mental or emotional immaturity, are considered not accountable as moral actors in the way that adults are held accountable for their behavior. Although exceptional cases may be found, the law has generally considered it an *unrebuttable assumption* that children at the age of 7 years and younger may not be held to adult standards of criminal responsibility, whereas there is a *rebuttable assumption* that children between the ages of 7 and 14 years are not moral agents to be held to adult standards of criminal responsibility.

The second group or class of individuals, and the one of primary focus here, comprises individuals with significant mental disorders whose symptomatology contributes to their "criminal behavior" in specific ways that society deems excuses them from moral culpability (criminal responsibility). In more common legal parlance, these individuals are considered "legally insane" or "not guilty by reason of insanity."

The insanity defense is generally unpopular in public opinion because of misperceptions about how it is used. Survey studies reveal public beliefs that the insanity defense is both frequently used and often successful. Such beliefs are likely distortions that result from the high degree of publicity surrounding notorious cases such as those of Patty Hearst, David Berkowitz ("Son of Sam"), Jeffrey Dahmer (none of whom was judged legally insane), and John Hinckley (who was found insane). However, neither belief is correct. Research shows that the insanity defense is asserted in less than half of 1% of criminal cases and more often than not it fails. Furthermore, when the insanity defense is successful, it is not the result of clever lawyers pulling the wool over the eyes of naive jurors. Most successful insanity defenses are not seriously challenged by the prosecution; more often it is clear to all parties that the defendant was insane at the time of the offense (according to criteria discussed below) and should not be held legally and morally responsible for his or her actions. Thus, many successful insanity defenses result, in effect, from plea agreements.

The following sections discuss (a) the criteria for legal insanity, (b) the legal calculus for determining when a defendant meets these criteria, and (c) the methods used by mental health professionals to gather evidence and formulate opinions about the mental state of a defendant at the time of an offense.

Criteria for Legal Insanity

Historians of Western law point to the influence of Henry de Bracton, whose writings on English law in the 13th century introduced notions of mental capacity and intent into deliberations about guilt and moral culpability. Early language referenced notions such as "infancy" or reasoning capacity not far removed from that of a "wild beast" as potentially exculpating mental states. The most influential English case was the *M'Naghten* case (1843), which established as the test for insanity that the accused

> was laboring under such defect of reason, from disease of the mind, as not to know the nature and quality of the act he was doing; or, if he did know it, that he did not know he was doing what was wrong.

The emphasis in *M'Naghten* on impairment in the ability to "reason" or to "know" clearly made judgments about a defendant's *cognitive* capacities central to the legal determination of insanity. This emphasis has survived in modern formulations that reference a defendant's "ability to appreciate the wrongfulness of his conduct." However, over the course of time modern psychiatry has influenced the law to consider *volitional* as well as cognitive impairments as potential bases for legal insanity. Thus, formulations in some jurisdictions refer to insanity resulting from criminal behavior that was due to an "irresistible impulse" or impaired capacity "to conform one's conduct to the requirements of the law" irrespective of the presence of cognitive impairment.

Finally, some formulations specify quantitative, albeit imprecise, levels of impairment for the insanity test to be met. Thus, it may be that not merely "impaired capacity" but "*substantially* impaired capacity" must be established to excuse the defendant from being criminally responsible for his or her behavior.

The Calculus of Legal Tests for Insanity

In jurisdictions that allow the insanity defense, judges and juries must apply the relevant legal test. The structure of all such tests requires three findings by the trier of fact. First, there is a predicate mental condition from which the defendant must have been suffering at the time of the offense. In the M'Naghten formulation above, the requisite condition is a "disease of the mind." More modern formulations reference the presence of "mental disease or defect" or similar language. It is important to note that in virtually all formulations, the legal definition for the predicate mental condition is neither highly precise nor tied explicitly to clinically recognized categories of mental illness or other mental impairments. (It is the case, however, that in many jurisdictions certain clinical conditions are explicitly barred by law as a basis for an insanity defense, most commonly (a) states of intoxication due to voluntarily consumed drugs or alcohol and (b) "disorders" defined almost exclusively on the basis of a history of antisocial behavior, such as antisocial personality disorder or sociopathy.)

The second component in the legal test is that the criminal act was affected by (loosely, "caused" by) the predicate mental condition. In other words, merely having a "disease of the mind" or a "mental disease or defect" alone is not sufficient to excuse the defendant from being criminally responsible. Mentally ill people may commit crimes for all the noncrazy reasons that other people do; they may steal because they are greedy, fight because they are angry, or drive poorly because they are intoxicated. To sustain an insanity defense, the mental impairment must have contributed to the occurrence of the criminal behavior.

Finally, the link between the predicate mental impairment and the criminal behavior must specifically be of the type prescribed in the legal test. As noted above, depending on the legal jurisdiction, the test for insanity may reference either cognitive or volitional impairments. Imagine a scenario in which a person with a well-established diagnosis of generalized anxiety disorder ("mental disease") suddenly felt extremely anxious in a situation where the only means of escaping was to take another person's car and drive away. He is not confused as to the ownership of the car (i.e., he "knows" that it belongs to another person), does not think that he has that person's permission to take the car (i.e., has no illness-related delusion that he has the authority or approval to take the car), and is aware of, and maybe even consciously anxious about, the possibility that he could be arrested for taking the car. Under a purely cognitive insanity formulation that focuses on "knowing" or "appreciating" the wrongfulness of his behavior, there is little to suggest that the actor's illness (acute anxiety symptoms)—although it motivated his decision to take the car—impaired his cognitive abilities in the way prescribed by the legal test. Alternatively, under a volitional formulation that referenced impaired control of impulses or capacity to conform conduct, the sudden strong urge to flee, arguably animated by his anxiety disorder, might support a finding of insanity.

Clinical Assessment of Criminal Responsibility

When the defense decides to pursue a defense of insanity, mental health professionals, commonly psychiatrists or psychologists, are hired by the prosecution and defense and/or appointed by the court to evaluate the defendant's mental condition and to provide reports and/or testimony as to the defendant's criminal responsibility. This is one of the most challenging types of evaluation for mental health professionals in their roles as forensic examiners because it is different, in so many ways, from the ordinary evaluations that they conduct in clinical (nonlegal) settings.

Clinical diagnostic assessments are imperfect even under optimal conditions—that is, when the clinician is working with a voluntary, candid, and willing client and the focus is on present mental functioning and treatment planning. Such conditions are almost never present when evaluations for criminal responsibility are being conducted. Because the insanity evaluation focuses narrowly on a specific point in time in the past, this inevitably diminishes the utility of commonly used clinical measures, such as psychological tests or other diagnostic procedures. Instead, insanity evaluations rely to a large extent on reviews of investigative evidence collected by the police, interviews with defendants, and information collected from third parties who may have knowledge relevant to the defendant's behavior and functioning at or near the time of the offense. Thus, investigative reporting, rather than traditional clinical assessment, is perhaps a better conceptual model for criminal responsibility evaluations.

The challenges faced in conducting criminal responsibility evaluations include the following:

The Evaluation Is Retrospective. It is not uncommon for insanity evaluations to be conducted weeks or months after the defendant's arrest. Furthermore, the time window between the crime and the clinical evaluation may be extended considerably if the arrest is made only after a prolonged investigation. Much can happen during this interval to distort the reconstructed picture of the defendant's prior mental state, including the following:

1. The defendant has a mental illness that has deteriorated over time; the clinician interviews the defendant in this more disturbed state and may attribute more psychopathology at the time of the offense than was actually present.

2. The defendant has a mental illness that improves either spontaneously, due to the cyclical nature of the disorder, or to treatment received (e.g., in jail); the clinician interviews the defendant in this less disturbed state and may attribute less psychopathology at the time of the offense than was actually present.

3. Although not symptomatic at the time of the offense, the defendant may have developed symptoms subsequent to the offense (e.g., a reaction to the nature of the crime itself, to events that occurred at arrest or in the jail, or in anticipation of serious consequences); the clinician may attribute some of this symptomatology as being present at the time of the offense.

4. Information obtained by interviewing the defendant or third-party sources (e.g., witnesses, family members), even if offered "honestly," may be less accurate due to deterioration of memory over time.

Concerns About Information Validity. Most people who provide information to the forensic examiner have a personal or professional interest in the opinions and findings that the examiner will reach. Thus, concerns about the validity of information are greater in insanity evaluations (and other forensic assessments) than with evaluations conducted for standard clinical and therapeutic purposes.

A defendant may view a successful insanity defense as his or her only hope for avoiding a lengthy prison sentence and thus be motivated to exaggerate or fabricate symptoms of mental disorder in describing behavior and motivations at the time of the offense. Family members sympathetic to the defendant's plight may distort information in ways that they believe are helpful to the case. The attorney(s) may be selective in the investigative information made available to the clinician, withholding that which they believe might lead the clinician to an unfavorable opinion. Evidence may be gathered and provided by the police in ways that provide a misleading picture of the defendant's prior mental functioning. For example, a defendant who is mentally confused and verbally incoherent may be cajoled into signing a "confession," drafted in perfectly organized and sensible language by an arresting officer, that belies the extent of psychopathology present at the time of arrest.

Translating Clinical Findings for Legal Consumers. Based on information gathered from the defendant, the police, and available third-party sources, the forensic examiner attempts to reconstruct an account of the defendant's mental state at the time of the offense that considers whether, and the extent to which, symptoms of mental disorder may have contributed to the alleged crime. However, as noted above there is no direct translation of clinically recognized mental disorders, which can vary from relatively benign (e.g., nicotine use disorder) to severely incapacitating conditions (e.g., schizophrenia, manic disorder), into legal terms such as *disease of the mind* or *mental disease or defect.*

Similarly, various formulations of the legal criteria for insanity require qualitative or quantitative determinations of either the nature of the functional legal impairment (e.g., ability to "know" or to "appreciate" wrongfulness of conduct) or the extent of impairment (e.g., categorically *"did not* know" vs. *"lacked substantial capacity* to know") for which there is no clinical or scientific technology.

That there is no scientific basis for translating clinical findings into specific legal conclusions poses a challenge to forensic examiners who are often pressured by the attorneys, if not also the courts, to give conclusory opinions under the mantra of "reasonable medical (or scientific) certainty." Mental health professionals have no "capacimeters" for determining whether the specific nature or extent of impairment in a given case is sufficient to excuse the defendant from his or her moral obligation to obey the rules. These constructs are legal terms of art that, in any individual case, have meaning only as expressed in the eventual social and moral judgment of the judge or jury when the verdict is reached. The status of an individual *being legally insane* (i.e., "not criminally responsible") is a social construction that has no meaning prior to, or independent of, the jury's pronouncement.

This is not to say that clinical evaluations of criminal responsibility cannot be helpful to legal decision makers. Rather, the challenge for forensic examiners is to collect information relevant to a defendant's legal functioning and to describe it to the triers of fact in ways that facilitates *their* ultimate judgments, but without offering moral judgments of their own under the guise of scientific expertise.

To illustrate with an example, one defendant who had a long and well-documented history of mental disorder experienced a recurrence of symptoms that included the delusional belief that he had been appointed to the position of deputy director of the FBI (in reality, the individual had worked in a factory for 20 years). On the basis of this belief, and the further notion that he was urgently needed in Washington, D.C., on matters of national security, he boarded a Greyhound bus and, without license or permission, drove it away from the bus depot. He was arrested and charged with unlawfully driving away a motor vehicle.

In this case, a forensic examiner might report that at the time of the offense the defendant experienced symptoms (i.e., delusions—strongly held but erroneous beliefs) of a well-recognized mental disorder (schizophrenia) with which he had been diagnosed for a number of years. Although the objective evidence is that the defendant is a factory worker, the manifestation of his illness at the time of the offense included a set of beliefs that distorted his perceptions of reality with respect to his occupation (i.e., objectively he was not an FBI official) and his rights and duties associated with his occupation (i.e., objectively he did not have the authority to commandeer a public transportation vehicle in the interest of national security). The nature of these distortions impaired his ability to judge correctly with respect to the action of taking control over the bus.

This formulation lacks a conclusive opinion as to whether or not the defendant's symptoms at the time of the offense satisfy the required predicate condition ("he suffered from a mental disease"). Also absent is any conclusory opinion that the symptoms categorically did, or did not, relate to the criminal act in the prescribed way (i.e., "he did not know that what he was doing was wrong"). However, the formulation does provide a plausible accounting of the relationship between the defendant's symptoms and the criminal behavior, but leaves it to the jury to "connect the dots," so to speak, in a fashion congruent with their collective social and moral intuitions as to whether or not an individual so disturbed should be held criminally responsible.

Norman G. Poythress

See also Automatism; Criminal Responsibility, Defenses and Standards; Forensic Assessment

Further Readings

De Pauw, K. W., & Szulecka, T. K. (1988). Dangerous delusions: Violence and misidentification syndromes. *British Journal of Psychiatry, 152,* 91–96.

Dreher, R. H. (1967). Origin, development and present status of insanity as a defense to criminal responsibility in the common law. *Journal of the History of the Behavioral Sciences, 3,* 47–57.

Goldstein, A. M., Morse, S. J., & Shapiro, D. L. (2003). Evaluation of criminal responsibility. In A. M. Goldstein (Ed.), *Handbook of psychology: Vol. 11. Forensic psychology* (pp. 381–406). Hoboken, NJ: Wiley.

Morse, S. J. (1994). Causation, compulsion, and involuntariness. *Bulletin of the American Academy of Psychiatry and the Law, 22,* 159–180.

Morse, S. J. (1994). Culpability and control. *University of Pennsylvania Law Review, 142,* 1587–1655.

Poythress, N. G. (2004). "Reasonable medical certainty": Can we meet *Daubert* standards in insanity cases? [Editorial]. *Journal of the American Academy of Psychiatry and the Law, 32,* 228–230.

Slobogin, C. (2007). *Proving the unprovable: The role of law, science, and speculation in adjudicating culpability and dangerousness.* New York: Oxford University Press.

Criminal Responsibility, Defenses and Standards

Although the insanity defense is numerically insignificant, it remains profoundly important to the criminal justice system as the focal point of the ongoing debate on the relationship between legal responsibility, free will, mental illness, and punishment. The insanity defense has substantially survived in spite of persistent philosophical and political criticism. Its history reflects a balance and tension between changes in attitudes toward developments in psychiatry and psychology and changes in attitudes toward criminal justice, incapacitation, and the desire to punish. Probably no other area of criminal law and procedure reflects a jurisprudence that is so driven by myths as that of the insanity defense. Yet only a handful of American jurisdictions have legislatively abolished it.

Insanity defense issues have concerned the courts and legislative bodies for hundreds (perhaps thousands) of years. As the various tests have developed— M'Naghten, irresistible impulse; Durham, the test proposed in the American Law Institute's Model Penal Code (ALI-MPC); the federal Insanity Defense Reform Act, diminished capacity—and as efforts are made to limit the scope and use of the defense, either by use of a "guilty but mentally ill" verdict or by outright abolition, it is clear that the symbolic values of the insanity defense must be considered carefully at all times. No area of our legal system has engendered a more intense level of debate than the role of the insanity defense in the criminal justice process. On the one hand, this difficult subject is seen as a reflection of the fundamental moral principles of the criminal law, resting on beliefs about human rationality, deterrability (i.e., whether the punishment of a person whose profound mental illness leads him to commit what would otherwise be a criminal act would serve as a deterrent to others), and free will, and as a bulwark of the law's moorings of condemnation for moral failure. On the other hand, it is castigated by a former attorney general of the United States as the major stumbling block in the restoration of "the effectiveness of Federal law enforcement" and as tilting the "balance between the forces of law and the forces of lawlessness." Yet the percentage of insanity defenses pled is small (at the most 1%), the percentage of those successful is smaller (1/4 of 1%), and the percentage of those successful in *contested* cases is minuscule (1/10 of 1/4 of 1%).

Notwithstanding the defense's relative *numerical insignificance,* it touches—philosophically, culturally, and psychologically—on our ultimate social values and beliefs; it is rooted in moral principles of excuse that are accepted in both ordinary human interaction and criminal law; and it continues to serve as a surrogate for resolution of the most profound issues in criminal justice. Although the defense has been significantly narrowed in many jurisdictions in the past 25 years—a condition intensified by the verdict in the John Hinckley case (which involved the attempted assassination of President Ronald Reagan) as well as several other unpopular or "wrong" jury verdicts in cases involving sensationalized crimes or public figure victims—reports of its demise are, to a great extent, exaggerated and, in spite of public outrage, the doctrine has remained alive in most jurisdictions.

The insanity defense has been a major component of the Anglo-American common law for more than 700 years. Rooted in Talmudic, Greek, and Roman history, its forerunners actually can be traced back to more than 3,000 years. The sixth-century Code of Justinian explicitly recognized that the insane were not responsible for their acts and also articulated the early roots of the temporary insanity and diminished capacity doctrines. By the ninth century, the "Dooms of Alfred" (a code of laws compiled by Alfred the Great) acknowledged that an impaired individual—who could not acknowledge or confess his offenses—was absolved from personally making restitution. In pre-Norman England, the law similarly shifted reparations responsibility in the event that a "man fall out of his senses or wits, . . . and kill someone."

The defense's "modern" roots can be traced at least as far back as 1505, the first recorded jury verdict of insanity, but it is clear that even prior to that case, juries considered "acquittal to be the appropriate result" in certain insanity defense cases. Furthermore, William Lambard's late-16th-century text on criminal responsibility (*The Eirenarcha*) suggested that the insanity defense was already well settled in England, and Sir Edward Coke's 1628 treatise, *Institutes of the Laws of England,* gave the law the familiar maxim that the " madman is only punished by his madness."

Early Developments

In the early 18th century, English judges began the process of attempting to define for juries that condition of the mind which would excuse, as a matter of law, otherwise criminal behavior. In *Rex v. Arnold* (1724), the first of the historically significant insanity defense trials, Judge Tracy charged the jury in the following manner:

> That is the question, whether this man hath the use of his reason and sense? If he . . . could not distinguish between good and evil, and did not know what he did . . . he could not be guilty of any offence against any law whatsoever. . . . On the other side . . . it is not every kind of frantic humour or something unaccountable in a man's actions, that points him out to be such a madman as is to be exempted from punishment: *it must be a man that is totally deprived of his understanding and memory, and doth not know what he is doing, no more than an infant, than a brute, or a wild beast, such a one is never the object of punishment.*

The law of criminal responsibility evolved further in 1800, in the case of James Hadfield, which envisioned insanity in the following manner:

> That a man could know right from wrong, could understand the nature of the act he was about to commit, could manifest a clear design and foresight and cunning in planning and executing it, but if his mental condition produced or was the cause of a criminal act he should not be held legally responsible for it.

This trend toward a more liberal defense continued in the case of *Regina v. Oxford* (1840), which concerned the attempted assassination of Queen Victoria, in which the jury charge combined portions of what would later be known as the "irresistible impulse" test and the "product" test.

M'Naghten Case

The most significant case in the history of the insanity defense in England (and perhaps in all common-law jurisdictions) arose out of the shooting by Daniel M'Naghten of Edward Drummond, the secretary of the man he mistook for his intended victim, Prime Minister Robert Peel (as with all the other cases already discussed, the victim was a major political figure). Enraged by the jury's insanity verdict, Queen Victoria questioned why the law was of no avail, since "everybody is morally convinced that [the] malefactor . . . [was] perfectly conscious and aware of what he did," and demanded that the legislature "lay down the rule" so as to protect the public "from the wrath of madmen who they feared could now kill with impunity."

In response to the Queen's demand, the House of Lords asked the Supreme Court of Judicature to answer five questions regarding the insanity law; the judges' answers to two of these five became the M'Naghten test (1843):

> The jurors ought to be told in all cases that every man is presumed to be sane, and to possess a sufficient degree of reason to be responsible for his crimes, until the contrary be proved to their satisfaction; and that to establish a defence on the ground of insanity, it must be clearly proved that, at the time of the committing of the act, the party accused was labouring under such a defect of reason, from disease of the mind, as not to know the nature and quality of the act he was doing; or, if he did know it, that he did not know he was doing what was wrong.

There are three main features of this formulation: First, it is predicated on proof that the defendant was suffering from a "defect of reason, from disease of the mind." From the time of *M'Naghten* until today some finding of "mental disease or defect" has been a necessary predicate for the insanity defense. Second, once such a "disease" is shown, the inquiry focuses on what the defendant was able to "know." That is, the interest of the law under this test is in the ability of the defendant to "know" certain things. It is for this reason that the inquiry is sometimes referred to as a "cognitive" formula. Third, the M'Naghten test focuses on two things the defendant must be able to "know" to be guilty of a crime. One is "the nature and quality" of the act that was committed. The other is that the act "was wrong." In both instances, the question is whether the defendant was "capable" of knowing these things, that is, whether the mental illness had robbed the defendant of the capacity to know what "normal" people are able to know about their behavior. The idea, in sum, is that people who are unable to know the nature of their conduct or who are unable to know that their conduct is wrong are not proper subjects for criminal punishment. In commonsense terms, such persons should not be regarded as morally responsible for their behavior.

This test has been severely criticized as rigid and inflexible, based on outmoded views of the human psyche, of little relation to the truths of mental life, reflecting antiquated and outworn medical and ethical concepts. Furthermore, the use of language such as "know" and "wrong" was criticized as "ambiguous, obscure, unintelligible, and too narrow." Donald Hermann and a colleague have argued, by way of example, that the cognitive aspect of one's personality cannot be seen as the sole determinant of one's subsequent behavior (and the basis of one's ultimate criminal guilt) because the psyche is an integrated entity.

Critics also maintain that the narrow scope of the expert testimony required by the M'Naghten test deprives the jury of a complete picture of the psychological profile of the defendant as the test ignores issues of affect and control.

Nevertheless, American courts readily adopted the M'Naghten formulation and codified it as the standard test, "with little modification," in virtually all jurisdictions until the middle of the 20th century.

Irresistible Impulse

In a partial response to criticisms of the M'Naghten test, several courts developed an alternative test that later became known as the "irresistible impulse" test, adapted from a test first formulated in 1883 by Lord Stephen:

> If it is not, it ought to be the law of England that no act is a crime if the person who does it is at the time . . . prevented either by defective mental power or by any disease affecting his mind from controlling his own conduct, unless the absence of the power of control has been produced by his own default.

This rule allowed for the acquittal of a defendant if his mental disorder caused him to experience an "irresistible and uncontrollable impulse to commit the offense, even if he remained able to understand the nature of the offense and its wrongfulness." It was based, in the words of Abraham Goldstein, one of the leading legal scholars on the history of the insanity defense, on four assumptions:

> First, that there are mental diseases which impair volition or self-control, even while cognition remains relatively unimpaired; second, that the use of M'Naghten alone results in findings that persons suffering from such diseases are not insane; third, that the law should

make the insanity defense available to persons who are unable to control their actions, just as it does to those who fit M'Naghten; fourth, no matter how broadly M'Naghten is construed, there will remain areas of serious disorder which it will not reach. (p. 67)

At its high-water mark, this test had been adopted in 18 jurisdictions, but today, far fewer states follow its teachings.

The Product Test

Charles Doe, a mid-19th-century New Hampshire State Supreme Court judge, first crafted what became known as the *product test*: "If the [crime] was the off-spring or product of mental disease in the defendant, he was not guilty by reason of insanity" (*State v. Pike*, 1870). This test first entered the legal public's consciousness in 1954, when it was adopted by the District of Columbia in *Durham v. United States*, rejecting both the M'Naghten and the irresistible impulse tests as based on "an entirely obsolete and misleading conception of the nature of insanity," one that ignored the reality that "the science of psychiatry now recognizes that a man is an integrated personality and that reason, which is only one element in that personality, is not the sole determinant of his conduct" (p. 871) and that a far broader test would be appropriate.

Durham held that an accused would not be criminally responsible if his "unlawful act was the product of mental disease or mental defect" (pp. 874–875). This test would provide for the broadest range of psychiatric expert testimony, "unbound by narrow or psychologically inapposite legal questions" (Weiner, 1985, p. 710). The case was the first modern, major break from the M'Naghten approach and created a feeling of intellectual and legal ferment. It was adopted, however, in fewer than a handful of jurisdictions and became the topic of fairly rigorous criticism, that it allegedly failed to provide helpful guidelines to the jury and that it was—at its core—a "nonrule," providing the jury with no standard by which to judge the evidence; that it misidentified the moral issue of responsibility with the scientific issues of diagnosis and causation; and that it was too heavily dependent on expertise, leading to the usurpation of jury decision making by psychiatrists. Within a few years after the *Durham* decision, the court began to modify and—ultimately—dismantle it, culminating in its decision in *United States v. Brawner* (1973), the most important of

the many federal cases that had rejected M'Naghten and adopted instead the ALI-MPC test.

American Law Institute's Model Penal Code Test

In an effort to avoid the major criticisms of M'Naghten, the irresistible impulse test, and Durham, the ALI couched the substantive insanity defense standard of its MPC in language that focused on volitional issues as well as cognitive ones. According to the ALI-MPC standard, a defendant is not responsible for his criminal conduct if, as a result of mental disease or defect, he "lacks substantial capacity either to appreciate the criminality of his conduct or to conform his conduct to the requirements of law" (§ 4.01(1)). Under this formulation, the term mental disease or defect specifically excluded "an abnormality manifested only by repeated criminal or otherwise antisocial conduct" (§ 4.01(2)).

Although the ALI-MPC test was rooted in the M'Naghten standard, there were several significant differences. First, its use of the word *substantial* was meant to respond to case law developments that had required a showing of total impairment for exculpation from criminal responsibility. Second, the substitution of the word *appreciate* for the word *know* showed that a sane offender must be emotionally as well as intellectually aware of the significance of his or her conduct and that mere intellectual awareness that the conduct is wrongful when divorced from an appreciation or understanding of the moral or legal import of behavior can have little significance. Third, by using a broader language of mental impairment than had M'Naghten, the test captured both the cognitive and affective aspects of impaired mental understanding. Fourth, its substitution in the final proposed official draft of the word *wrongfulness* for *criminality* reflected the position that the insanity defense dealt with an impaired moral sense rather than an impaired sense of legal wrong.

Although there were some immediate criticisms of the ALI-MPC test, principally due to the attempt to bar "psychopaths" or "sociopaths" from successfully using the defense, the test was generally applauded as encouraging adjudication based on reality and the practical experience of psychiatrists by recognizing that both the volitional and the cognitive processes of an individual may be impaired. The test was subsequently adopted by more than half of the states and, in some form, by all but one of the federal circuits. Perhaps most significant, the District of Columbia Court of

Appeals, in overruling its "product" test of *Durham v. United States* in *United States v. Brawner*, adopted the ALI-MPC test.

Insanity Defense Reform Act

Slightly more than a decade after *Brawner*, in the wake of John Hinckley's failed attempt to assassinate U.S. President Ronald Reagan, Congress enacted the federal Insanity Defense Reform Act. This law had the effect of returning the insanity defense in federal jurisdictions to status quo ante 1843: the year of *M'Naghten*. The bill changed the federal law in several material ways:

1. It shifted the burden of proof to defendants, by a quantum of clear and convincing evidence.

2. It articulated, for the first time, a substantive insanity test, adopting a more restrictive version of M'Naghten, thus discarding the ALI-MPC test previously in place in all federal circuits.

3. It established strict procedures for the hospitalization and release of defendants found not guilty by reason of insanity.

4. It severely limited the scope of expert testimony in insanity cases.

Diminished Capacity

One of the most difficult concepts in substantive insanity defense formulation is that of diminished capacity, a doctrine that holds that evidence of reduced mental capacity tending to show the absence of any mental state essential to the alleged crime should be accepted by the trial court, whether or not an insanity plea was entered (*People v. Wells*, 1949, pp. 63–70). There seems little question that the diminished capacity doctrine was developed to be used in murder cases to mitigate the harshness of a potential death penalty by raising the question of whether the defendant could sufficiently appreciate the nature of his or her act so as to sustain a first-degree murder conviction. In addition, use of the doctrine has been justified as a means to ameliorate defects in a jurisdiction's substantive insanity defense test criteria and as a means of permitting juries to make more accurate individualized culpability judgments.

This doctrine, however, has been routinely criticized for its difficulty and arbitrariness in application,

leading to uneven and inequitable outcomes, and while it had been endorsed in some form in nearly 25 jurisdictions, it has failed to capture major support and has even lost the support it previously enjoyed.

"Guilty but Mentally Ill"

Perhaps the most significant development in substantive insanity defense formulations in the past 20 years has been the adoption in more than a dozen jurisdictions of the hybrid "guilty but mentally ill" (GBMI) verdict. It received its initial impetus in Michigan, as a reflection of legislative dissatisfaction with and public outcry over a state Supreme Court decision that had prohibited automatic commitment of insanity acquittees. There, legislation was enacted that provided for a GBMI verdict—as an alternative to the not guilty by reason of insanity (NGRI) verdict—if the following were found by the trier of fact beyond a reasonable doubt:

1. That the defendant is guilty of an offense

2. That the defendant was mentally ill at the time of the commission of the offense

3. That the defendant was not legally insane at the time of the commission of the offense

The rationale for the passage of the GBMI legislation was that the implementation of such a verdict would decrease the number of persons acquitted by reason of insanity and ensure treatment of those who were GBMI within a correctional setting. It was conceived that once a defendant were to be found GBMI, he or she would be evaluated on entry to the correctional system and provided appropriate mental health services either on an inpatient basis as part of a definite prison term or, in specific cases, as a parolee or as an element of probation. This model was followed—in large part—in most of the other states that have adopted the GBMI test.

Most academic analyses have been far more critical, rejecting it as conceptually flawed and procedurally problematic and as not only superfluous but also dangerous. By way of example, in practice, the GBMI defendant is not ensured treatment beyond that available to other offenders. Thus, Christopher Slobogin (one of the leading current scholars in this area of the law) suggests, it is "not only misleading but dangerous to characterize the [GBMI] verdict either as a humane advance in the treatment of mentally ill offenders or as a more effective way of identifying offenders in need of treatment." The GBMI verdict, he concludes, is "a verdict in name only" (p. 515).

Insanity Defense Myths

The empirical research has revealed that at least half a dozen myths about the insanity defense had arisen and have been regularly perpetuated but were all disproven by the facts. The research showed that the insanity defense opens only a small window of nonculpability, that defendants found that NGRI does not "beat the rap," and, perhaps most important, that the tenacity of these misbeliefs in the face of contrary data is profound.

Myth 1: The insanity defense is overused. All empirical analyses have been consistent: the public, legal profession, and, specifically, legislators dramatically and grossly overestimate both the frequency and the success rate of the insanity plea. This error undoubtedly is abetted by media distortions in presenting information on persons with mental illness charged with crimes.

Myth 2: The use of the insanity defense is limited to murder cases. In one jurisdiction where the data have been closely studied, slightly less than one third of the successful insanity pleas entered over an 8-year period were reached in cases involving a victim's death. Furthermore, individuals who plead insanity in murder cases are no more successful in being found NGRI than persons charged with other crimes.

Myth 3: There is no risk to the defendant who pleads insanity. Defendants who asserted an insanity defense at trial and who were ultimately found guilty of their charges served significantly longer sentences than defendants tried on similar charges but did not assert the insanity defense. The same ratio is found when exclusively homicide cases are considered.

Myth 4: NGRI acquittees are quickly released from custody. Of all the individuals found NGRI over an 8-year period in one jurisdiction, only 15% had been released from all restraints, 35% remained in institutional custody, and 47% were under partial court restraint following conditional release.

Myth 5: NGRI acquittees spend much less time in custody than do defendants convicted of the same offenses. Contrary to this myth, NGRI acquittees actually spend almost double the amount of time that defendants convicted of similar charges spend in prison settings and often face a lifetime of postrelease judicial oversight.

Myth 6: Criminal defendants who plead insanity are usually faking. This is perhaps the oldest of the insanity defense myths and is one that has bedeviled American jurisprudence since the mid-19th century. Of 141 individuals found NGRI in one jurisdiction over an 8-year period, there was no dispute that 115 were schizophrenic (including 38 of the 46 cases involving a victim's death), and in only three cases was the diagnostician unable to specify the nature of the patient's mental illness.

Abolition and Limitation Proposals

In the past two decades, state legislatures in Idaho, Montana, Kansas, and Utah have abolished the insanity defense, and in those jurisdictions, state supreme courts have subsequently held that abolition of the defense did not violate due process. Arizona stopped barely short of abolishing the insanity defense by creating a "guilty except insane" verdict that eliminates the "nature and quality of the act" prong from the M'Naghten test. In one instance (Nevada), such abolition was struck down as unconstitutional in *Finger v. State of Nevada* (2001), with the majority of the sharply divided court finding that legal insanity was a "fundamental principle" entitled to due process protections. The court reasoned as follows:

> Mens rea is a fundamental aspect of criminal law. Thus it follows that the concept of legal insanity, that a person is not culpable for a criminal act because he or she cannot form the necessary mens rea, is also a fundamental principle. (p. 80)

The U.S. Supreme Court recently addressed questions raised in Arizona's insanity defense:

> Whether due process prohibits Arizona's use of an insanity test stated solely in terms of the capacity to tell whether an act charged as a crime was right or wrong; and whether Arizona violates due process in restricting consideration of defense evidence of mental illness and incapacity to its bearing on a claim of insanity, thus eliminating its significance directly on the issue of the mental element of the crime charged (known in legal shorthand as the mens rea, or guilty mind). (*Clark v. Arizona*, 2006)

In both instances, the Court held there was no violation of due process.

Michael L. Perlin

See also Criminal Responsibility, Assessment of; Guilty but Mentally Ill Verdict; Insanity Defense, Juries and; Insanity Defense Reform Act (IDRA); Mental Health Law; Treatment and Release of Insanity Acquittees

This entry is largely adapted from Perlin, M. L. (2002). *Mental disability law: Civil and criminal* (2nd ed., chap. 9). Newark, NJ: Matthew Bender.

Further Readings

American Law Institute. (1962). *Model penal code.* Philadelphia: Author.

Clark v. Arizona, 548 U.S. _____ 126 S. Ct. 2709 (2006).

Durham v. United States, 214 F.2d 862 (D.C. Cir. 1954) (overruled in *United States v. Brawner*, 471 F. 2d 969 (D.C. Cir. 1972).

Finger v. State of Nevada, 27 P.3d 66 (Nev. 2001).

Goldstein, A. S. (1967). *The insanity defense.* New Haven, CT: Yale University Press.

Low, P. W., Jeffries, J. C., & Bonnie, R. J. (2000). *The trial of John W. Hinckley, Jr.: A case study in the insanity defense* (2nd ed.). New York: Foundation Press.

Morris, N. (1984). *Madness and the criminal law.* Chicago: University of Chicago Press.

People v. Wells, 202 P. 2d 63 (Cal. 1949).

Perlin, M. L. (1989/1990). Unpacking the myths: The symbolism mythology of insanity defense jurisprudence. *Case Western Reserve Law Review, 40,* 599–731.

Perlin, M. L. (1994). *The jurisprudence of the insanity defense.* Durham, NC: Carolina Academic Press.

Perlin, M. L. (1997). "The borderline which separated you from me": The insanity defense, the authoritarian spirit, the fear of faking, and the culture of punishment. *Iowa Law Review, 82,* 1375–1426.

Perlin, M. L. (2002). *Mental disability law: Civil and criminal* (2nd ed., Vol. 4). Newark, NJ: Matthew Bender.

Regina v. Oxford, 173 Eng. Rep. 941 (1840).

Rex v. Arnold, 16 How. St. Tr. 695 (1724).

Slobogin, C. (1985). The guilty but mentally ill verdict: An idea whose time should not have come. *George Washington Law Review, 53,* 494–527.

State v. Pike, 49 N.H. 399, 442 (1870).

United States v. Brawner, 471 F.2d 969 (1973).

Weiner, B. A. (1985). Mental disability and criminal law. In S. J. Brakel, J. Parry, & B. A. Weiner (Eds.), *The mentally disabled and the law* (3rd ed., pp. 693–773). Chicago: American Bar Association.

CRISIS AND HOSTAGE NEGOTIATION

Since the 1970s, some clinical psychologists (often referred to as operational psychologists) have become more actively involved in the resolution of critical incident situations, which are classified as either hostage situations or crisis intervention situations. Police psychologists are valuable contributors to the training of tactical and crisis/hostage negotiators. On-scene responsibilities for operational psychologists include providing professional consultation on the potential behavioral effects of psychopathology and psychopharmacology, selection of primary and backup negotiators, suggestions and input regarding the actual negotiation process, and operational consultation to the tactical commander. Research shows that police departments that employ psychologists during special operation responses have significantly fewer casualties of both hostages and hostage takers and more incidents that are peacefully resolved via a negotiated surrender than by a tactical entry or violent confrontation. Police psychologists, in providing cogent consultation and robust training dynamics to specialized police crisis response teams, have made a dramatic contribution to reducing the risk of injury and death for all participants in these critical events.

Hostage and Crisis Negotiation

Within both federal and local law enforcement environments, a hostage situation has become defined as any situation in which individuals are being held via active coercion by another person or people and demands are being made by the hostage taker(s). These demands are by design established by the hostage taker(s) to gain compliance as well as establish an inherent power by the hostage taker(s) over the responding law enforcement agency. Typically, a hostage situation results from the interruption of a criminal act in which the perpetrators take hostages with an ultimate goal of forcing law enforcement to comply with their demands for escape. At the other end of the continuum are hostage situations initiated by a terrorist group whose goal is to communicate their political agenda via media exposure. The terrorists attempt to actualize this confrontation by using the hostages as political pawns, as the terrorists have the option of choosing martyrdom for themselves and/or death to the hostages if their demands are not met.

As hostage negotiation developed over the decades of the 1970s and 1980s, it was observed that the majority of negotiator incidents were either initiated by an individual or within some family dyad. As such, the typical negotiator intervention entailed interaction with a barricaded subject, a suicidal individual, or a couple who were engaged in a violent domestic confrontation. These incidents required the application of crisis-intervention techniques and active listening skills. The overall principle in crisis negotiation is that time is on the side of the negotiator in that the passage of time will provide a "cooling off" period for the individual who is seen as a victim rather than as a perpetrator. Over time, the emotional lability of the individual will dissipate, which allows for the introduction of active listening techniques by the negotiator. This system of communication provides a spectrum of responses that facilitate viable, objective problem-solving options to the individual in crisis.

Team Composition and Tactics

A hostage/crisis negotiation event is a complicated and potentially dangerous undertaking for any law enforcement agency. Almost all these situations demand the response of a two-pronged team, the special weapons and tactics team (SWAT). The SWAT team consists of a heavily armed and specially trained group of police officers, while the second component of the team is the group of police negotiators. The primary function of the tactical team is for the protection of the SWAT team, especially the negotiators, the victims of the event, the general public, hostages (if any), and, lastly, the subject(s). The tactical team is also responsible for initiating any proactive or reactive options during the progression of the event. The negotiator team is responsible for the acquisition of any on-scene information deemed relevant to both the tactical and negotiator teams. The second primary function of the negotiators is, obviously, the active negotiation process.

On the arrival of the SWAT team, the tactical members will diligently establish an inner perimeter that allows for the establishment of a safe (within the constraints of the actual situation) environment for the tactical operations center (TOC). The TOC is the central decision and command area for the supervisory personnel. The TOC consists of the tactical commander, typically a lieutenant; a tactical team leader (sergeant); a negotiator team leader (lieutenant or sergeant); and the police psychologist. These individuals have been trained in the dynamics of critical events and usually are certified tactical commanders, with the police psychologist having received at least 80 hours in specialized courses in hostage and crisis negotiation. In major metropolitan police departments, such command and supervisory personnel have responded to more than 300 to 1,200 of these SWAT callouts to date. The responsibility of the TOC is to initially determine if the presence of the SWAT team at the specific scene is legal and/or necessary. A second task is to develop an initial action plan. Third, the TOC is responsible for maintaining an ongoing acceptable and risk-effective course of action. Within this action plan are typically four options: immediate assault on the location, selected sniper fire (an exigent situation to prevent the loss of life to innocent participants), introduction of chemical agents, and a negotiation process. It should be noted that these four options are fluid in nature and can be used in combination and in no specific order. The decision process to use any option is predicated on the anticipated *outcome* following the initiation of any one or more of these actions.

Most negotiation teams consist of a lead and backup negotiator, an electronics technician/negotiator, several support negotiators, a team leader, and a mental health consultant. Unless there is an exigent situation, the mental health consultant is never the lead negotiator (for ethical reasons), nor does just one negotiator initiate and maintain the negotiation process (for safety reasons). The lead negotiator is the police officer responsible for speaking directly to the subject and for developing and maintaining active listening skills and verbal tactics that will increase the likelihood for a successful resolution of the crisis. The most effective negotiators are those who are the best *listeners*, for it is only through listening that the negotiator will begin to understand and emotionally connect with the subject. The secondary negotiator is responsible for physically protecting (typically by preventing the lead negotiator from gradually placing his body and head in the line of fire while distracted by the negotiation process) the lead negotiator, monitoring the radio frequency, and listening to the negotiation process and relaying information and suggestions (typically made by the mental health professional) back to the lead negotiator. If necessary, during a protracted negotiation process, the backup negotiator may relieve the primary negotiator. The electronics technician/negotiator is responsible for maintaining all negotiator equipment, setting up all the required equipment at the scene, and interfacing with local telephone companies and national cellular companies, as well as coordinating the dispatch and arrival of the local power/utility company crew (in the event the tactical commander decides to cut the electrical power in the subject dwelling). The support negotiators are responsible for gathering all relevant information regarding the subjects (e.g., physical description, clothing, weapons, prescription/nonprescription medications, contact phone numbers, and arrest and psychiatric history). This is done via records checks and interviewing on-scene family members, friends, and witnesses. The support negotiators also maintain a running log of times and relevant events during the SWAT callout. A final responsibility of the support negotiators is to interview/debrief any hostages who are released during a hostage situation. The negotiator team leader assists the mental health consultant in the assignment of team responsibilities for the specific callout as well as providing consultation at the TOC. The mental health consultant provides assistance to the negotiator team leader in negotiator assignments, provides psychological personality assessment, psychotropic consultation, monitors negotiator team performance and stress reactions, and provides dispositional consultation to the TOC.

Once the team responsibilities are determined, the TOC commander, tactical and negotiator team leaders, and the mental health consultant determine the communication mode by which the primary negotiator will attempt to make contact with the subject. This decision is predicated on officer safety first and the type of crisis situation. There are four means by which to communicate with the subject: police vehicle public address (PA) system, parabolic PA, telephone (landline, cell phone, throw phone), or voice to voice. If the situation is a criminal, barricaded subject with no hostages, then either PA system is typically used for officer safety as well as the commanding tone of the PA. For all other situations, it is preferable to use some form of phone system and optimally establish tactical presence to support the use of voice to voice (the negotiator and subject are close enough to one another to communicate by simply speaking in a conversational tone to one another) for the resolution phase.

The Effects of Time and the Stockholm Syndrome

Hostage and crisis negotiation is an extremely complicated process incorporating three basic principles. First is the concept of time, in which, during most critical events, the extension of time invariably works in favor of successful resolution. During this so-called 60- to 90-minute rule, the passage of time allows for the ventilation of extreme emotional responses (for the subjects, hostages, and police officers). This dissipation of emotion allows for the introduction of more logical and rational problem solving, the influence of physiological needs, as well as, in the hostage situation, the opportunity for the hostages to escape.

However, it should never be assumed that hostages, if given the opportunity, will proactively initiate an escape or will assist the SWAT team in the successful resolution of the crisis. The underlying process, which is extremely powerful in most hostage situations, has become known as the Stockholm syndrome. This gradually occurs as a natural process of the passage of time (typically over hours and days); however, if there is significant violence at the onset of the taking of hostages, this syndrome compels an immediate and powerful influence. This syndrome compels one of the following behaviors: The hostages will begin to have positive feelings toward the hostage takers, the hostages will begin to develop negative feelings toward law enforcement, and the hostage takers will begin to develop positive feelings toward their hostages. The effect of the Stockholm syndrome on the negotiation process is rather consistent for the hostage takers and the hostages. The positive dynamic is that as time elapses, and if the hostage takers have begun to develop positive feelings toward their hostages, they are actually less likely to harm, much less kill, their hostages, whom they now begin to see as humans and not just objects for barter. However, negative aspects include the hostages' inability to self-initiate their escape, communication by hostages of unreliable information to the negotiators either on release or during captivity, or hostages' interference with the rescue operation. In rare cases, if the Stockholm syndrome is not severe, some hostages have been known to exaggerate the motives and weaponry of the hostage takers to the negotiators, with the intent of having the SWAT team conclude the hostage takers were more dangerous than in fact they were, and the tactical team eventually would feel compelled to initiate an active entry and perhaps kill the hostage takers.

The Influence of Power Tactics and Face-Saving

The second component in the negotiation process is incremental display of power, in the hope of avoiding its actual use during the negotiation process. A highly visible tactical containment combined with the third component, the presentation of face-saving issues, becomes the most integral component of the negotiation process. The process of negotiation and active listening assumes that the interchange among individuals even within a crisis situation possesses rewards and costs for both factions. The goal is to maximize mutual benefits while concurrently minimizing costs—an interaction in which the lead negotiator emphasizes a process of quid pro quo (something for something). Face-saving techniques allow both law enforcement and the subjects to maintain some semblance of control while agreeing on options of mutual gain. For example, a barricaded subject may have agreed to resolve the crisis by meeting the tactical officers outside his home, but the media have positioned their cameras where he will easily be videotaped being taken into custody. A face-saving negotiation is for both the TOC personnel and the subject to agree that he or she will be taken into custody at the back of his or her home to avoid the humiliation of his or her arrest being filmed by the local media.

Active Listening and the Resolution Process

The successful negotiator is highly skilled in active listening, the ability to focus on what the subject is speaking and to accurately process not only what the subject is saying but also the accurate emotional content that is actually being communicated. In other words, active listening is a technique to maximize an empathic exchange between the negotiator and the subject. There are 14 identified communications techniques within the active listening process. Experience has established that the most effective techniques are those of clarification and paraphrasing, primary-level empathy, and especially self-disclosure. Clarification and paraphrasing are most typically used during the initial contacts with the subject so that during these more emotionally laden contacts, the likelihood of miscommunication and misunderstanding is minimized. For example,

Negotiator: By "old lady," do you mean your wife?

Subject: Yeah, that's right, her.

Negotiator: So, it sounds like things have been going very badly between you two today.

Now, over time, the negotiator will begin to insert primary-level empathy and self-disclosure:

Negotiator: Boy, it sure sounds like everything appears to be falling apart, and you're pretty angry and scared.

Subject: Yeah, but you really don't know what it's like for me now!

Negotiator: Maybe, maybe not, but I know that I was feeling really hurt and scared when I was going through my divorce a few years ago.

The relatively long process of establishing an empathic rapport between the lead negotiator and the subject is known as the "hook." The hook is the point at which the negotiator has established a position of trust with the subject and is now able to lead the subject through the concrete process of either releasing hostages and/or being taken into custody. In all situations, once the subject is taken into custody by the SWAT team, the individual is arrested and taken to jail or, in the case of a crisis situation (suicidal subject), he or she is transported to the nearest crisis response unit.

The negotiation process for hostage and barricade incidents is the responsibility of highly trained and experienced SWAT teams. Communication, a clearly articulated and flexible plan, creativity, and patience are the key components predictive of a successful outcome. The negotiator's application of active listening skills and the demonstration of empathic communication are critical skills for the successful resolution of critical incidents.

Scott W. Allen

See also Critical Incidents; Police Psychologists; Police Psychology

Further Readings

Allen, S. W. (1991). Assessment of personality characteristics related successful hostage negotiators and their resistance to post-traumatic stress disorder. In J. T. Reese, J. M. Horn, & C. Dunning (Eds.), *Critical incidents in policing* (Rev. ed., pp. 1–16). Washington, DC: U.S. Dept. of Justice, Federal Bureau of Investigation.

Butler, W. M., Leitenberg, H., & Fuselier, G. D. (1993). The use of mental health professional consultants to police hostage negotiation teams. *Behavioral Sciences and the Law, 11,* 213–221.

Fuselier, G. D. (1988). Hostage negotiation consultant: Emerging role for the clinical psychologist. *Professional Psychology: Research and Practice, 19*, 175–179.

Hatcher, C., Mahondie, K., Turner, J., & Gelles, M. G. (1998). The role of the psychologist in crisis/hostage negotiations. *Behavioral Sciences and the Law, 16*, 455–472.

Lancely, F. J. (1999). *On-scene guide for crisis negotiators.* Boca Raton, FL: CRC Press.

McMains, M. J., & Mullins, W. C. (2000). *Crisis negotiations: Managing critical incidents and hostage situations in law enforcement and corrections.* Cincinnati, OH: Anderson.

CRITICAL INCIDENTS

This entry examines the causes of critical incident stress in law enforcement officers. It discusses how, by identifying critical incident stressors and the personal, team, and organizational factors that render them meaningful, law enforcement agencies can proactively influence officers' critical incident stress outcomes. To appreciate how this can be accomplished, it is necessary to understand the role of mental models in the etiology of critical incident stress.

Through their training and operational experiences, officers develop mental models that determine their ability to adapt to and impose meaning on the incidents they attend. Furthermore, officers respond to incidents as members of law enforcement organizations whose culture (through interaction with colleagues, senior officers, and organizational procedures) influences the development and maintenance of mental models and thus how challenging critical incident experiences are made sense of. An incident becomes critical when its characteristics fall outside expected operational parameters and officers' mental models are unable to make sense of and adapt to the novel, challenging circumstances that ensue.

Law enforcement officers experience critical incidents regularly. These can range from multivehicle traffic accidents and mass homicides to natural disasters and acts of terrorism. While traditionally viewed as a precursor to posttraumatic pathology (e.g., posttraumatic stress disorder [PTSD]), growing recognition of a link with positive outcomes (e.g., posttraumatic growth) have implications for how critical incident stress in law enforcement is conceptualized and managed.

Conceptualizations of critical incident stress must encompass how officers' mental models can either increase vulnerability to adverse stress reactions or increase their resilience and their capacity to experience posttraumatic growth, with each outcome being influenced by prevailing approaches to critical incident stress management. With regard to the latter, the dominant approach has involved critical incident stress management or debriefing. In addition to issues regarding the efficacy of debriefing, growing evidence for significant team and organizational influence on posttrauma outcomes calls for more comprehensive and proactive approaches to critical incident stress management.

Two approaches to managing critical incident stress are discussed here. The first involves developing officers' mental models to increase the range of circumstances they can adapt to. Because officers will continue to experience challenging incidents, the second involves developing their capacity to render novel experiences meaningful.

Developing Mental Models

Incidents become critical when their circumstances (e.g., deliberately flying a passenger aircraft into a building) and associated levels of uncertainty (e.g., regarding the nature and duration of a threat, length of involvement), personal danger (e.g., being secondary targets of terrorist attacks, exposure to biological or radiation hazards), or operational demands (e.g., performance expectations, crisis decision making, interagency role stress) fall outside the expected parameters of officers' operational mental models.

By incorporating these characteristics into training programs, it is possible to increase the range of critical experiences officers can render meaningful, reduce levels of posttrauma pathology, and contribute to officers realizing a sense of personal and professional growth from critical incident work. Training can also increase officers' knowledge of stress reactions and how to use support mechanisms to create positive emotions.

Although training can reduce critical incident stress risk, a need to prepare for the unexpected means that critical incident stress management must also proactively develop officers' capacity to adapt to critical circumstances and reduce their vulnerability to adverse reactions (e.g., PTSD). Research has identified several personal and team and organizational factors that inform how these goals can be accomplished.

Personal Factors

Vulnerability to adverse critical incident stress outcomes has been linked to, for example, preexisting psychopathology (which increases vulnerability directly) and social skills and problem-solving deficits that have an indirect effect by reducing officers' ability to develop solutions to novel problems or limiting their ability to effectively use available social support. In contrast, officers characterized by their relatively high levels of extraversion, hardiness, and self-efficacy are more resilient and better able to render novel, challenging experiences meaningful. Training not only plays an important role in developing hardiness and self-efficacy but it also helps socialize officers into the fabric of the organizational culture, introducing a need to consider how sense making occurs in teams and in relationships with senior officers.

Team Factors

Although generally considered to ameliorate stress reactions, if demands on a social network occur at a time when all its members have support needs, social support mechanisms can increase officers' vulnerability to experiencing posttrauma stress reactions. This problem can be managed by developing a supportive team culture. Renee Lyons and colleagues coined the term communal coping to describe how cohesive teams contribute to stress resilience through, for example, facilitating cooperative action and collective efficacy to resolve problems associated with responding to critical incidents. Realizing the full benefits of personal and team resources, however, is a function of the quality of the organizational culture in which officers work.

Organizational Factors

The severity of stress reactions is greater if officers experience them in an organizational culture that discourages emotional disclosure and that attributes blame for response problems to officers. Similarly, cultures characterized by poor consultation and communication and excessive paperwork increase vulnerability to posttrauma pathology. In contrast, police organizations that delegate responsibility to and empower officers, and encourage senior staff to work with officers to identify the strengths that helped them deal with an incident and to use this knowledge to develop future capabilities, increase officers' stress resilience.

Finally, predicting all the eventualities that law enforcement officers could encounter is impossible. Consequently, support procedures must be in place to manage any residual posttrauma reactions. This can include counseling strategies designed to facilitate positive resolution and coworker and peer support provided within a supportive team and organizational culture.

Exposure to critical incidents will remain a reality for law enforcement officers. Critical incident stress management involves both reducing vulnerability (e.g., enhancing problem-solving skills, reducing inappropriate operational procedures) and increasing resilience (e.g., increasing hardiness, developing team mental models, delegating operational responsibility). By developing personal and team competencies and support resources and ensuring they are enacted within a supportive organizational culture, law enforcement agencies can act proactively to positively influence the critical incident outcomes officers will experience.

Douglas Paton

See also Police Occupational Socialization; Police Stress; Police Training and Evaluation; Posttraumatic Stress Disorder (PTSD); Terrorism

Further Readings

Paton, D., Violanti, J. M., & Smith, L. M. (2003). *Promoting capabilities to manage posttraumatic stress: Perspectives on resilience.* Springfield, IL: Charles C Thomas.

Violanti, J. M., & Paton, D. (2006). *Who gets PTSD? Issues of vulnerability to posttraumatic stress.* Springfield, IL: Charles C Thomas.

Cross-Race Effect in Eyewitness Identification

The *cross-race effect* (CRE, also referred to as the *own-race bias* or *other-race effect*) is a facial recognition phenomenon in which individuals show superior performance in identifying faces of their own race when compared with memory for faces of another, less familiar race. Over three decades of research on the CRE suggests a rather robust phenomenon that carries practical implications for cases of mistaken eyewitness identification, particularly in situations that involve a poor opportunity to encode other-race faces and when a significant amount of time occurs between observation of the perpetrator and a test of the witness's memory. While the CRE has not generally been observed in the accuracy of descriptions for own-race versus other-race faces, research has found that individuals often attend to facial features that are diagnostic for own-race faces and misapply these feature sets when attempting to identify and describe other-race faces. As such, theorists have proposed that encoding and representational processes are largely responsible for the CRE, including the role of interracial contact and perceptual categorization processes. This entry summarizes this research on the CRE, including how it operates in eyewitness identification and person descriptions, the influence of certain social and cognitive psychological mechanisms that may underlie the effect, and the potential role of training programs for improving other-race face identification.

Laboratory Studies of the CRE

Research in cognitive and social psychology over a span of three decades has examined the CRE, providing a substantial body of work demonstrating the reliability and robustness of the effect. The vast majority of the research has focused on individuals' attempts to identify both own-race and other-race faces. Across studies, a "mirror effect" pattern is generally observed, such that individuals demonstrate both significantly greater correct identifications of own-race faces (referred to as "hits") and significantly fewer false identifications of own-race faces (referred to as "false alarms"). Overall, participants are 1.40 times more likely to correctly identify an own-race face, while they are 1.56 times more likely to falsely identify an other-race face. Composite signal detection measures of discrimination accuracy (i.e., the ability to distinguish between faces seen previously and novel faces) and response criterion (i.e., the tendency for responding "yes" versus "no" to faces regardless of whether they have been seen before or not) have also been used to describe the CRE. As might be expected, discrimination accuracy is better for own-race faces, and individuals generally demonstrate a more liberal response criterion for other-race faces (indicating that they are more likely to say "seen before" to such faces).

Several factors have been shown to moderate the CRE. For example, studies have shown that shorter viewing times are more likely to produce the effect such that under brief encoding conditions performance is superior on own-race faces. As viewing time increases, however, the CRE reduces in size such that performance can become equivalent on own-race and other-race faces with a sufficient opportunity for encoding. Retention interval, or the time between stimulus presentation and test, has also been shown to moderate the effect. Studies indicate that as the retention interval increases, participants' response criterion becomes more liberal for other-race faces, thereby producing a CRE on measures of response criterion. As such, participants are more willing to identify other-race faces (i.e., to respond "seen before") when a lengthy delay occurs between study and test phases.

Studies have evidenced the CRE across a wide variety of ethnic and racial groups. While the original research in this area dealt primarily with Whites and Blacks in the United States, more recent studies have included samples from Canada, Great Britain, Germany, Turkey, South Africa, and parts of the Middle East and Asia. Whites, Blacks, Asians, Hispanics, Natives/Indians, Jews, and Arabs, among others, have been included in these studies with each demonstrating a CRE in face identification performance. Research has shown that, in general, Whites demonstrate a larger CRE than Blacks with respect to measures of discrimination accuracy and that "majority-group" individuals demonstrate a more robust CRE than do "minority-group" individuals.

The CRE in Eyewitness Identification and Person Descriptions

Laboratory research on the CRE has suggested a rather robust phenomenon with some practical implications, particularly with regard to witnesses in real cases who may be confronted by an assailant of a different race or ethnicity. The question naturally arises whether such situations could lead to an increased risk of mistaken identification and/or failures to identify the perpetrator. Studies that have investigated eyewitness identification suggest that the CRE occurs just as frequently in laboratory "facial recognition" paradigms as they do in simulated "eyewitness identification" paradigms involving a single "perpetrator" at study and a six- or eight-person "lineup" presented at test. As such, researchers have suggested that the CRE is likely to be seen in real cases of eyewitness identification, especially when the opportunity to view the perpetrator is limited and when a significant amount of time passes between the crime event and the attempted lineup identification (consistent with the moderating factors discussed above). Along these lines, researchers have examined whether mistaken eyewitness identification, and the CRE in particular, may play a critical role in cases of wrongful conviction. Data from these studies indicate that nearly 40% of cases involving mistaken identification result from the CRE. Archival studies of real cases have also indicated that the likelihood of identifying an own-race suspect is significantly greater than that of an other-race suspect, particularly when there is strong evidence to suggest his or her culpability.

Witnesses to a crime are frequently asked to provide a verbal description of the perpetrator they viewed. These descriptions are then used by investigators in attempting to identify a suspect in the immediate vicinity. Given the robustness of the CRE in face identification, researchers have also investigated whether a similar effect might be evidenced in person descriptions. To date, only a handful of studies have examined this possibility, with the majority concluding that no differences exist in the *accuracy* of descriptions provided for own-race versus other-race faces. However, researchers have found that individuals of different races/ethnicities often report different features when differentiating faces and further that these features are most useful for characterizing faces of their own race. For example, caucasians frequently use hair color, hair texture, and eye color to distinguish faces, whereas African Americans rely on face outline, eye size, eyebrows, chin, and ears. While it is clear that we try to distinguish faces of other races by the facial features that are distinguishable within our own race, the problem appears to lie in that those same features are generally less useful when applied to other-race faces.

Theoretical Underpinnings of the CRE

Several theoretical mechanisms have been identified with regard to the CRE, including interracial contact and social attitudes, encoding and representational processes, perceptual-memory expertise, and perceptual categorization. First, racial contact and attitudes have been implicated as moderators of the CRE. Across studies, interracial contact has been shown to account for a small, but significant, amount of variance in performance on other-race faces such that greater interracial contact tends to reduce the size of the observed CRE. Furthermore, studies have suggested that the form of interracial contact may be important to

its influence on face identification such that individuals must be motivated to individuate other-race members through contact (i.e., social utility). The properties of natural social environments that foster the development of high performance levels with other-race faces are presently unknown. While social attitudes have not been shown to directly moderate the CRE, an indirect relationship appears to exist such that social attitudes may account for the amount of interracial contact one engages in and thereby influence the CRE. For example, individuals who profess prejudiced attitudes toward other-race groups are less likely to have significant amounts of contact with such individuals and, as a result, appear more likely to demonstrate the CRE. However, the causal direction of the contact-attitude relationship is more difficult to identify and could work in either direction.

A great deal of research suggests that encoding and representational processes may be responsible for recognition differences in the CRE. As noted above, individuals of different races/ethnicities appear to rely on different feature sets when encoding faces, and these feature sets appear to be most useful when encoding faces of one's own race. In addition, individuals have been shown to attend to greater numbers of features for own-race faces and to group or "chunk" these features when representing the face. As a result, own-race faces are better differentiated in memory based on these feature sets, while other-race faces appear to be more clustered and less differentiated. This encoding and representational advantage allows individuals the ability to better "recollect" own-race faces at test based on those features identified and selected at encoding. In contrast, the clustering of other-race faces in memory leads to poorer recognition performance at test and, prominently, a greater likelihood of falsely identifying a novel other-race face.

Studies that have validated the role of encoding and representational processes in the CRE also suggest that individuals' processing of own-race faces might be likened to that of an "expert" perceptual-memory skill. One such theory proposes that faces may be encoded with respect to individual features or isolated aspects (i.e., "featural" processing) and with regard to configural or relational aspects among features (i.e., "configural" processing). Studies suggest that "experts" encode objects (such as faces) in a more configural manner, while "novices" encode objects on a more featural basis. Using a variety of paradigms, researchers have demonstrated that own-race faces appear to be processed in a more configural manner (consistent with expert-level processing), while other-race faces are processed with respect to individual features (consistent with novice-level processing).

Research studies have also noted that the CRE may be due to a process of racial categorization. In particular, individuals appear to process other-race faces at a superficial level that is consumed with a focus toward racial categorization. As a result of these categorization processes, other-race faces are coded with an emphasis on category-related information (stereotypes) and less with regard to individuating information. Researchers have demonstrated that such categorization processes can both influence our perception of a face (i.e., stereotype consistent) and lead to deficits in performance consistent with the CRE.

Improving the Recognition of Other-Race Faces

Given the bulk of research suggesting that the CRE may be a product of interracial contact and the role of encoding-based mechanisms (e.g., perceptual learning), researchers have attempted to develop a variety of training programs over the years to improve participants' recognition of other-race faces. While some of these studies included forms of positive and negative feedback, others have focused on improving participants' ability to distinguish between other-race faces and teaching participants to identify "critical" feature sets that are useful for discriminating such faces. Taken together, these studies have generally met with some success in producing short-term improvements in recognition performance; however, when participants are tested at longer posttraining retention intervals, this improvement in performance tends to diminish. Nevertheless, these studies suggest that individuals may be trained to improve their face recognition performance to a certain extent, and researchers continue to develop training protocols that might be employed by government agents or business professionals who may be sent abroad.

Jessica L. Marcon, Christian A. Meissner, and Roy S. Malpass

See also Estimator and System Variables in Eyewitness Identification; Expert Psychological Testimony on Eyewitness Identification; Exposure Time and Eyewitness Memory; Eyewitness Descriptions, Accuracy of; Eyewitness Identification: Field Studies; Eyewitness Memory; Training of Eyewitnesses

Further Readings

Brigham, J. C., Bennett, L. B., Meissner, C. A., & Mitchell, T. L. (2006). The influence of race on eyewitness memory. In R. Lindsay, D. Ross, J. Read, & M. Toglia (Eds.), *Handbook of eyewitness psychology: Memory for people* (pp. 257–281). Mahwah, NJ: Lawrence Erlbaum.

Meissner, C. A., & Brigham, J. C. (2001). Thirty years of investigating the own-race bias in memory for faces: A meta-analytic review. *Psychology, Public Policy, & Law, 7*, 3–35.

Sporer, S. L. (2001). Recognizing faces of other ethnic groups: An integration of theories. *Psychology, Public Policy, & Law, 7*, 36–97.

CSI EFFECT

The *CSI* effect refers to the belief that jurors' expectations about forensic evidence at trial are changing due to the popularity of crime investigation programming such as CBS's *CSI: Crime Scene Investigation*. Much of the support for this effect comes from anecdotal evidence. The limited empirical evidence on this topic indicates that *CSI* may influence some of jurors' case perceptions but has no effect on verdict decisions.

CSI is one of the most popular shows on network television, consistently ranking high in the Nielsen ratings and spawning several spin-off shows. These shows depict crime scene investigators using highly technical procedures to recover microscopic evidence that ultimately reveals the details of the crime, including the perpetrator. Criminal investigations in real life differ markedly from this representation. In actuality, forensic evidence such as DNA and fingerprints are not always available from a crime scene, and when they are available, they may only be analyzed in important cases or in larger departments due to the expense. Furthermore, forensic laboratories may take weeks to return results that are less than conclusive. According to attorneys and the media, inaccurate portrayals put forth by programs such as *CSI* are causing jurors to expect more, and stronger, forensic evidence at trial. The concern is that when prosecutors fail to present this evidence, jurors are being more lenient, providing fewer convictions.

Belief in the *CSI* effect is pervasive among the legal and media communities. According to news reports, evidence of the *CSI* effect has been found in courtrooms around the country. For instance, in Phoenix,

Arizona, jurors in a murder trial voiced concern that a bloody coat introduced as evidence had not been tested for DNA, even though tests were not considered necessary because the defendant had admitted being at the murder scene. Some observers have attributed the 2005 acquittal of actor Robert Blake, charged with murdering his wife, Bonnie Bakley, to the *CSI* effect. Even though the prosecutor presented more than 70 witnesses against Blake in this case, it is believed that the jury wanted to see forensic evidence such as blood splatter or gunpowder residue and found Blake not guilty when such evidence was not presented. Attorneys have even begun questioning potential jurors about their viewing habits during voir dire and warning jurors about the fictional nature of *CSI*.

The *CSI* effect is most commonly defined as leading to a prodefense bias, as the above examples illustrate. In this sense, exposure to crime investigation programming serves to raise jurors' conviction threshold, requiring more incriminating evidence to find guilt. However, this effect can also be conceptualized in another way. Some commentators note that crime investigation programming enforces the belief that forensic science is infallible and can provide definitive evidence of guilt. Adherence to this belief would actually work *for* the prosecution, leading to more convictions when any type of forensic evidence is presented, regardless of quality. In this way, crime investigation programming may actually lower jurors' conviction threshold, requiring less incriminating evidence to find guilt.

To date, little empirical research has examined the impact of crime investigation programming on jurors' verdicts and case perceptions. The little research that does exist, consisting of a few law reviews and conference presentations, typically examines this effect by measuring mock jurors' exposure to crime investigative programming (e.g., hours per week) and having them read through a case summary and answer various questions about the case, including verdict.

The results of these preliminary studies are mixed, but most suggest that watching crime investigation programming does not influence verdict. In three studies, mock jurors who report watching *CSI* a lot were no less (or more) likely to find a defendant guilty than are mock jurors who watch little or no *CSI*. However, one study did find the predicted prodefense effect, such that more hours of TV watching was related to a perception of less strength in the prosecution's case, which was related to more acquittals. Also, most studies have found that the more a mock

juror finds the shows to be believable and realistic, the more likely the juror is to favor the prosecution and find the defendant guilty. Thus, whether jurors believe the shows are realistic may be a better predictor of decisions than how much the juror watches the shows. Finally, there is also some suggestion that prosecution's warning against *CSI*-caliber evidence may produce a backfire effect, weakening the prosecution's case among jurors who do not watch *CSI*.

Why is there no direct relationship between *CSI* and verdict? Intuitively, it seems like such programming should have an effect on jurors' expectations for evidence. There is a large body of research identifying the media as an important source of knowledge and expectations, particularly for events for which people have little experience, such as a trial. Should a relationship between exposure to criminal investigation programming and juror behavior truly exist, there are a variety of possible reasons a clear effect has not emerged in research. As already noted, there are at least two possible effects viewing *CSI* can have on juror behavior: It can make jurors expect high-quality forensic evidence and therefore raise the conviction threshold, or it can lead jurors to believe that all forensic evidence is infallible, thereby lowering the conviction threshold when forensic evidence is present. It is plausible that both effects may be occurring simultaneously, such that jurors are coming to require forensic evidence at trial but at the same time are finding any forensic evidence sufficient for guilt. These two effects may therefore be working against each other, leading to no noticeable change in verdict.

Another possibility is that *CSI* programming may only influence the behavior of certain types of people. It has been suggested by Tom Tyler that the overvaluing of forensic evidence caused by exposure to *CSI* may be strengthened among those greatly in need of closure or belief in a just world. Similarly, jurors who do not have much need for cognition may be more likely to rely on expectations generated by crime investigation programming as a cognitive heuristic.

In conclusion, empirical research has yet to identify a clear *CSI* effect, at least as conceptualized by the legal community and the media. Research efforts continue in an attempt to ascertain what influence, if any, such programming has on juror expectations and behavior.

Margaret C. Reardon and Kevin M. O'Neil

See also Jury Competence; Pretrial Publicity, Impact on Juries; Statistical Information, Impact on Juries

Further Readings

Tyler, T. R. (2006). Viewing *CSI* and the threshold of guilt: Managing truth and justice in reality and fiction. *Yale Law Journal, 115,* 1050–1085.

CYBERCRIME

There is no agreed precise definition of the term *cybercrime*, but in a general sense, it has been used to describe any illegal activities conducted through the use of a computer or network of computers. Some researchers have emphasized that it is crime that takes place on the Internet, which has led to a more comprehensive definition of illegal computer-mediated activities that often take place in global electronic networks. Such crime includes computer hacking, Internet fraud, identity theft, and the illegal transfer of technologies. Increasingly, psychological research in this area also makes reference to cyberstalking, cyberterrorism, and Internet child pornography as examples of cybercrime.

Much of what is referred to as cybercrime might be thought of as traditional crime that is committed through the use of new tools. If we think of cybercrime in this way, we can see that many traditional crimes can be conducted with the Internet as a source of communication—for example, the sharing of pedophile information. The Internet has also opened up new opportunities for other traditional crimes, such as fraud and deception. In both these instances, the criminal activity is not dependent on the new technologies but is certainly aided and possibly transformed by them. There are many newer crimes that can only be perpetrated within cyberspace, among which are intellectual property theft, identity theft, and spamming. As new technologies occupy an increasingly large space in our lives, criminals are increasingly using them to engage in criminal activities. It may also be the case that the nature of the technologies, in particular the Internet, is a catalyst for the emergence of some criminal behaviors that might otherwise not have been evidenced.

Although there is lack of agreement as to what precisely constitutes a cybercrime, one element common to most definitions is that it involves the use of a computer. The computer may be the focus, or target, of the crime—for example, hacking or the use of a virus to infect a computer network. It may also be the tool used to commit the crime, such as downloading or distributing child pornography, or fraud. It may also be a medium for the use of materials gained through criminal activity, such as copyright theft of DVDs, where the person using the computer did not commit the original illegal act but subsequently engages in illegal activity. In this way, the computer might also be a source of invaluable forensic evidence.

The emergence of cybercrime has mirrored the development of the new technologies. A survey conducted in 2002 by the U.S. Federal Bureau of Investigation and the Computer Security Institute suggested that in the previous 12 months, 90% of business respondents had detected security breaches, from which 80% had suffered financial loss. It is of concern that a substantial number of these breaches were from people within the organization, and this has become a focus for some of the emerging research. What is it about the new technologies that increases the likelihood of people taking risks, breaching moral or ethical codes, and committing crimes? Such is the concern about the potential for widespread criminal activity that in 2001, 30 countries, including the United States, signed the Council of Europe Cybercrime Convention, which was the first multilateral instrument drafted to address the problems posed by the spread of criminal activity on computer networks. This Convention requires parties to establish laws against cybercrime, ensure that law enforcement agencies have the necessary procedural authority to investigate and prosecute cybercrime offenses, and provide international cooperation to other parties in the fight against computer-related crime.

Major Types of Cybercrime

Cybercrime has been broadly divided into two types, which might lie at opposite ends of a spectrum. The first type of cybercrime is often experienced as a discrete event by the victim and is facilitated by the introduction of crimeware programs, such as viruses or Trojan horses, into the user's computer. Examples of this type of cybercrime might include identity theft and bank or credit card fraud based on stolen credentials. The second type of cybercrime, which lies at the other end of the spectrum, includes activities such as cyberstalking, child solicitation, blackmail, and corporate espionage. Viewed in this way, cybercrime represents a continuum ranging from crime that is almost entirely technological in nature to crime that is largely related to people. Sarah Gordon and Richard Ford divide cybercrime into two distinct categories: Type I cybercrime, which is mostly technological in nature, and Type II cybercrime, which has a more pronounced human element. The following is a brief description of some of the major types of cybercrime.

Computer hacking refers to the unauthorized access to a computer or computer network, which may or may not result in financial gain. For example, hackers may attack a network solely to protest against political actions or policies or simply to show that they can do it, but equally, it can be used to access bank accounts or data banks. The level of disruption caused may be localized within a given organization or may, for example, in extremis, potentially disrupt the availability of power to a large geographical area. Were this to occur, it would result in widespread social disruption, which may be motivated by ideology and which traditionally may have been seen as terrorist activity.

The illegal transfer of technology, or piracy, includes industrial espionage and the piracy of software, logo, and hardware designs. The perpetrator may be an individual (a young person sharing a program with a friend) or a network (a company installing software on multiple computers for which it owns a restricted license), and it may be enabled by others (such as a government). Its intended use may be financial, recreational, or for military or terrorist activities, and it may be motivated by a complex array of factors. The theft can breach contracts, trade secrets, and national and international laws involving copyrights.

Identity theft is broadly defined as the unlawful use of another's personal identifying information (name, address, social security number, date of birth, registration number, taxpayer identification number, passport number, driver's license information, or biometric information such as fingerprint, voiceprint, or retinal image). Such information is obtained in a variety of ways. Low-technology routes include theft of wallets or handbags or sifting through garbage to look for bank statements, utility bills, and so on. High-technology methods include skimming, where offenders use computers to read and store information encoded on the magnetic strip of an ATM or credit card. This information can be re-encoded onto another card with a magnetic strip. Identity thieves steal identities to commit an array of crimes, such as taking out loans, cash advances, and credit card applications, which may include large-scale operations such as taking control of entire financial accounts.

Spamming has also been identified as a cybercrime, although most of us would not generally consider it to be so. Spamming is the distribution of unsolicited bulk e-mails that contain an array of messages, including invitations to win money; obtain free products or services; win lottery prizes; and obtain drugs to improve health, well-being, or sexual prowess. David Wall has argued that spamming embodies all the characteristics of cybercrime in its global reach: networking capabilities; empowerment of the single agent through the (re)organization of criminal labor; and use of surveillant technologies, which creates small-impact bulk victimizations. Currently, over half of all e-mails are spam, and this constitutes a major obstacle to effective use of the Internet and its further development.

Cyberstalking generally refers to using the new technologies to harass or menace another person by engaging in behavior that persists in spite of another's distress or requests that it should stop. It can take many forms, such as unsolicited hate mail, e-mail whose content is obscene or threatening, malicious messages posted in newsgroups, e-mail viruses, and electronic junk mail or spam. It is analogous to other forms of stalking but uses technology to achieve its aims and is motivated by a desire to gain control over the victim.

Online pornography is considered a cybercrime only when its content is illegal (such as abusive images of children). Criminal activity may relate to downloading, trading, and producing such images, although the criminality of the act will depend on the geographical location of both the material and the person accessing or distributing it. Some countries do not have laws that criminalize child pornography, and therefore an individual producing such images within that jurisdiction would not be seen to engage in cybercrime, but another individual in a country where such laws exist may access the images and thereby commit a criminal act. This highlights one of the difficulties in relation to cybercrime, in that while the Internet has no boundaries, legislation does. This has probably been the main impetus for the European Convention on Cybercrime.

Cybercriminals

It has been suggested that cyberspace opens up infinitely new possibilities and that with the right equipment, technical know-how, and inclination, you can go on a global shopping spree with someone else's credit card, break into a bank's security system, plan a demonstration in another country, and hack into the Pentagon—all on the same day. As Yvonne Jewkes and Keith Sharp note, going online undermines the traditional relationship between physical context and social situations, and this is coupled with perceived anonymity, access, and affordability. As a consequence, this increases disinhibition and risk taking, in part because through the new technologies we can constantly re-create ourselves. The Internet has also changed the boundaries of what constitutes acceptable, problematic, or deviant behavior.

Cybercriminals are not a homogeneous group, and while some criminal activities (such as stalking and engagement with child pornography) are more likely to be carried out by males, psychologists have noted that students, terrorists, amateurs, and members of organized crime have also been identified as being involved in cybercrime. The motivations for such criminal activities include revenge, a desire for notoriety, the technical challenge, monetary gain, or the promotion of ideology. As previously noted, the largest proportion of cybercrime is perpetrated by a company's own employees and includes people with highly sophisticated technical skills and those who are relative novices.

Attempts to generate profiles or taxonomies of computer criminals have been limited in their scope. There is little empirical research in this area, but analyses of cybercrime subjects suggest that the majority are male, have at least a high school education, commit their crimes alone, and are students within the 18- to 23-year age range.

Responses to Cybercrime

The emergence of cybercrime has resulted in changes in legislation within and between jurisdictions, mirroring the fact that the new technologies are not limited by geographical boundaries. Indeed, the location of the offender in relation to the scene of the crime is an important characteristic. In traditional crime, such as burglary, the criminal is physically present at the scene of the crime. This is very different from cybercrimes, in which offenders not only are often not present but also may be located in another country. Cybercrime has also opened up many gray areas in terms of what constitutes a crime. For example, many people may engage in activities that they do not even realize are criminal, such as pirating software from a friend.

There are many challenges for the future in relation to cybercrime. Criminal activities on the Internet are not analogous to similar behavior in the physical world. The Internet enhances the potential for criminal and deviant behavior in several ways. The first of these relates to the dramatic increase in access to the Internet worldwide, providing limitless opportunities for criminal behavior and a vast marketplace for such activities. The Internet also provides a sense of anonymity or disconnectedness for the offender, lowering the risk of detention and reducing the level of physical risk normally associated with criminal activity. It also challenges traditional concepts of time and space.

Ethel Quayle

See also Pornography, Effects of Exposure to; Stalking; Terrorism; Victimization

Further Readings

Gordon, S., & Ford, R. (2006). On the definition and classification of cybercrime. *Journal in Computer Virology, 2*(1), 13–20.

Jewkes, Y., & Sharp, K. (2002). Crime, deviance and the disembodied self: Transcending the dangers of corporeality. In Y. Jewkes (Ed.), *Dot.cons: Criminal and deviant identities on the Internet* (pp. 1–14). Cullompton, UK: Willan.

Speer, D. L. (2000). Redefining borders: The challenges of cybercrime. *Crime, Law & Social Change, 34,* 259–273.

Taylor, M., & Quayle, E. (2003). *Child pornography: An Internet crime.* Brighton, UK: Routledge.

Wall, D. S. (2004). Digital realism and the governance of spam as cybercrime. *European Journal on Criminal Policy and Research, 10,* 309–335.

D

DAMAGE AWARDS

Damage awards function as a remedy for wrongdoing in civil lawsuits; they constitute money awarded to an injured party as compensation for injuries or other losses ("compensatory" damages). They can also serve as punishment for the wrongdoer ("punitive" damages). These awards are made mostly by juries and occasionally by judges who previously determined that a wrongdoer was liable for damages. Determining damages—especially for intangible injuries such as pain and suffering—can be difficult, and juries have been criticized for issuing awards that seem extravagant and unpredictable. Although some of the criticisms are unfounded (e.g., jurors are not especially sympathetic toward plaintiffs), jurors occasionally do experience difficulty in applying jury instructions and following procedures that blindfold them to the consequences of their verdicts. Reforms intended to address these issues should be based on empirical analysis, and psychologists are well-positioned to provide the relevant data.

Various Kinds of Damage Awards

Damage awards are of two general types, compensatory and punitive, and they serve different functions. Compensatory awards are intended to return an injured person or entity (e.g., a business, agency, or corporation) to pre-injury levels of functioning—that is, to restore that party to the position it was in prior to the injury or harm. For example, a person injured in an automobile accident may receive a compensatory damage award to cover any medical costs, lost wages, and pain and suffering related to the injuries sustained in the accident. As another example, a business may receive a compensatory damage award to cover any revenues lost to competitors involved in price-fixing, trademark infringement, or sharing of trade secrets.

Compensatory damage awards are themselves of two sorts: economic and noneconomic. Economic damages are intended to cover the financial or economic costs incurred by the injured party. These can include past and future lost wages, past and future expenses related to medical care and rehabilitation, past and future lost profits, and loss of reputation or business opportunity. In theory, these awards should be relatively easy to gauge because they are generally tied to objective data such as hospital bills, costs of property repairs, and amount of time away from work. In fact, even these losses are difficult to assess because they require jurors to make predictions about the future and then to discount their awards to present value (i.e., the injured party is given an economic damage award now that will, over time, grow to equal the amount that the jury has deemed appropriate). In addition, they may require a jury to agree on economic uncertainties such as future interest rates, the likelihood that injured persons would have been promoted or received raises or that businesses would have been profitable had they not been harmed, and projected life expectancies for persons who require lifelong care.

Determining noneconomic damages can be even more problematic. Their function is to compensate the injured party for "pain and suffering," including bodily harm; emotional distress, such as fear, depression, and anxiety; loss of enjoyment of life; and pain and disfigurement. For example, after the drug manufacturer Merck was found liable for the death of a Houston man who had been taking the painkiller Vioxx, it was required to pay millions of dollars to the man's widow to compensate her for pain and suffering. Noneconomic damages are especially difficult to assess because they have no obvious metric: There is no cost accounting of one's pain and suffering. Juries have sometimes been criticized for being capricious and unpredictable in determining damages (as described below), and criticism often focuses on an unexpected award for pain and suffering.

Punitive damage awards are intended not to compensate for injuries but rather to punish wrongdoers for malicious and egregious behavior or gross negligence and to deter that party and others from similar conduct in the future. For example, juries have assessed large punitive damage awards against tobacco companies after finding that the companies knew about the health risks of cigarette smoking long before they made those risks known to the public. As another example, juries have awarded billions of dollars in punitive damages in cases stemming from the 1989 grounding of an Exxon oil tanker in Prince William Sound, Alaska, which devastated miles of shoreline, destroyed wildlife habitats, and financially ruined the local fishing industry. Punitive awards are usually not made in the absence of compensatory awards, and appellate court decisions require some reasonable relationship between the two.

Size of Damage Awards

The examples provided above were of large damage awards in high-profile cases; jurors have often been criticized for assessing damages of these magnitudes. In fact, though, multimillion dollar awards are atypical. According to data compiled by the Bureau of Justice Statistics from the 75 most populous counties in the United States in 2001, the median damages awarded to plaintiffs who prevailed at trial (only approximately half of all plaintiffs who went to trial) was a modest $27,000. Awards varied considerably by type of case. For example, the median awards in automobile negligence and medical malpractice cases were $16,000 and $422,000, respectively. Awards in excess of $1 million were rare, given in only 8% of cases in which plaintiffs prevailed.

Punitive damage awards were also rare and, when provided, were modest. According to the Bureau of Justice data, only 6% of winning plaintiffs were awarded punitive damages, and these awards were given only in certain kinds of cases: tort cases involving slander/libel or intentional wrongdoing and contract cases involving partnership disputes, employment discrimination, and fraud. Punitive damages are rare in personal injury cases. The median punitive damages awarded in jury trials in 2001 was $50,000 ($83,000 in contract trials and $25,000 in tort trials), and only 12% of plaintiff winners who received punitive damages were awarded $1 million or more.

Despite the fact that the median damage award is modest, some damage awards—particularly punitive damage awards—are indeed very large and contribute to the perception that juries are erratic and capricious in the manner in which they assess damages. Indeed, this perception has gelled into significant criticism of jurors' ability to be fair and impartial in the awarding of damages, and on several occasions the U.S. Supreme Court has considered appeals based on the apparent excessiveness of a punitive damage award.

Controversy Surrounding Decisions About Damages

Criticism regarding damage award decision making has centered on two concerns: first, that juries are overly sympathetic to plaintiffs in awarding excessive sums of money, especially for punitive damages, and second, that they are biased against wealthy or deep-pocketed defendants. Valerie Hans and colleagues have examined both of these assumptions empirically by interviewing jurors who served in civil cases and by conducting laboratory-based research studies. Their data indicate that rather than favoring plaintiffs, most jurors tend to be skeptical of their motives. For example, the majority of jurors agreed that there are far too many frivolous lawsuits and that people are too quick to sue. When questioned about their own deliberations, jurors indicated that they questioned the legitimacy of plaintiffs' complaints and scrutinized their motives. Jurors said they looked unfavorably on plaintiffs who did not seem as badly injured as they claimed or who had preexisting medical conditions. Jurors also scrutinized whether plaintiffs might have contributed to their own injuries and were unsympathetic to those who did little to mitigate their injuries. In fact, some jurors described themselves as acting as a defense against illegitimate grievances and frivolous lawsuits. So, far from being overly sympathetic to plaintiffs, jurors apparently tend to be skeptical of their claims.

The second concern is that juries are biased against wealthy defendants, including large corporations, and act as a sort of "equalizer" in transferring monies from wealthy defendants to poor or needy plaintiffs. There is some evidence that awards tend to be higher in cases that involve corporate defendants than in cases with individual defendants. Other data suggest, however, that this finding may not be the result of the defendant's financial well-being. Rather, juries apparently treat corporations differently than individual defendants because they hold the former to a higher standard than the latter (a "reasonable corporation" standard) and reason that corporations are better positioned than individuals to anticipate harms and to work to minimize or prevent them.

In general, these concerns may be related to the fact that jurors have relatively little guidance from their jury instructions about how to assess damages or translate their judgments onto a monetary scale. The laws of damages are relatively vague, leading some critics to suggest that this situation allows jurors' biases to operate freely and that extravagant and unpredictable awards are the result. The problem is especially acute in areas of the law that are still developing or that lack precision: sexual harassment claims, libel actions, and cases involving intentional infliction of emotional distress.

Some commentators have suggested that a solution to the unbounded nature of jury decisions on damages is to make judges responsible for determining punitive damages. Judges already have occasion to award damages in bench trials and can control damage awards in jury trials through the mechanisms of additur and remittitur, which allow them to add to or reduce damage awards to the levels that they deem appropriate. In some states, only judges can assess punitive damages. An obvious question, then, is how punitive awards issued by judges compare with those assessed by juries. Data suggest that in most cases (particularly in cases with modest punitive awards), juries' and judges' awards are of similar size and variability and that both are based on the actual and potential severity of harm to the plaintiff.

Determining Jury Damage Awards

Psychologists have been especially interested in analyzing the factors that influence jurors' decisions about damage awards. In part, this reflects an objective of much psycholegal research conducted to assess the validity of legal assumptions about human behavior. In the context of damage awards, the law assumes that particular factors will be considered by jurors in their decisions about compensatory damages and that different factors will be considered in decisions about punitive damages. Psychologists have asked whether jurors are able to compartmentalize their decision making in this way.

The data on this topic are mixed; many studies suggest that jury awards are influenced by variations in legally relevant evidence, yet simulation studies show that jurors occasionally consider information that is theoretically unrelated to the decision at hand. For example, though most studies show that evidence of a defendant's egregious conduct appropriately influences punitive but not compensatory damage awards, a few studies have found that it is sometimes considered (inappropriately) by jurors in assessing compensation. Similarly, though most studies have found that the severity of the plaintiff's injuries appropriately influences compensatory but not punitive damage awards, a few studies have shown that jurors inappropriately factor injury severity into their judgments of punitive damages, at least in cases involving medical defendants.

Interestingly, jurors' intuitions about what normally or typically occurs in various injury-producing situations also influence their awards. Injuries that are perceived as atypical (e.g., suffering a whiplash after a fall) evoke greater sympathy in jurors than do typical injuries (e.g., suffering a broken bone in a fall) and result in greater compensation.

There are many ways in which damages can be assessed; some data suggest that jurors assimilate their awards to the monetary figures provided by the attorneys during the trial. The *ad damnum* is the amount of money requested by the plaintiff; defense attorneys sometimes counter this with their own suggested amounts. These suggested figures (sometimes referred to as "anchors") are likely to influence jurors because people tend to doubt their abilities to attach monetary values to unquantifiable injuries. According to the pioneering jury researcher David Broeder, the *ad damnum* does "yeoman service as a kind of damage jumping-off place for jurors" (Broeder, 1959, p. 756). More recent studies have shown that, in general, the higher the *ad damnum,* the larger the award. There is an upper limit to this effect, however; damage awards boomerang if the request is wildly excessive and out of line with the evidence.

Another way in which jurors assess damages involves evaluating separate components of a plaintiff's request (e.g., lost wages, loss of future earning capacity, loss of life's pleasures), attaching monetary values to each of these components, and then summing them to arrive at a total compensatory damage award. Jurors are forced to perform a componential analysis in courts that use special verdict forms that require them to answer specific questions about the facts of the case and to calculate awards related to each set of facts.

Finally, some data suggest that rather than analyzing the components of an injury, jurors reason more holistically by agreeing on a general figure that "seems" right. Interviews with jurors who served in tort and contract cases revealed that approximately one third of juries determined damages by picking a number that seemed fair and just.

A peculiar aspect of some civil jury trials is the application of "blindfold rules," which prohibit disclosure to jurors of the implications of their verdicts. Judges sometimes blindfold the jury regarding information such as attorneys' fees, the tax consequences of damage awards, the insurance carried by the parties, and the possibility of additions to or reductions in damage awards by appellate courts. The rationale for these rules is that with blindfolds in place, jurors will not become confused by complex evidence or influenced by evidence that is lacking in probative value.

In fact, there is substantial evidence that blindfolding rules may result in, rather than prevent, verdicts based on misinformation. Jurors are naturally inclined to consider information to which they are blindfolded even when this information is not presented in court. On occasion, these discussions involve explicit reference to these so-called "silent topics." A large percentage of jurors interviewed about their deliberations report that their juries discussed factors such as attorneys' fees and the defendant's insurance. Even if these factors are not explicitly talked about, jurors' implicit beliefs (not always correct) can influence their verdicts on damages. As a result, awards are sometimes unpredictable and inconsistent. Research suggests that it may be preferable to treat jurors like the careful and thoughtful arbiters they usually are and to provide them with clear and complete instructions, at least about those facets of damage awards on which all parties agree.

Reforming Jury Damage Awards

Given the controversial nature of some jury damage awards, it is not surprising that proposals for changing the system have been offered, primarily by groups interested in tort reform. In fact, during the 1980s and 1990s, a majority of state legislatures implemented laws aimed at reducing jurors' discretion and reining in large awards. Among the reforms are laws that cap damage awards at some specified amount (primarily for noneconomic and punitive damages) or eliminate them altogether (for punitive damages), clarify the elements of damage award decisions, bifurcate the trial into two segments so that jurors are presented with discrete questions and sets of evidence in each segment and cannot consider irrelevant evidence, require some portion of a damage award to be paid to a governmental or charitable organization rather than to the injured party, and (as previously mentioned) move punitive damage assessments from the jury to the judge.

Importantly, many of these reforms were instituted without empirical backing; as a result, their implications are only now being understood. But recently conducted studies have brought into focus some unintended consequences, at least in terms of caps on damages. For example, mock jury research has shown that in cases with injuries of low to moderate severity, limits on awards for pain and suffering actually increased both the size and the variability of the awards. Other research has shown that although caps on punitive damage awards certainly reduce the size of punitive awards, they also increase the size and variability of compensatory awards. Similarly, caps on noneconomic damages result in larger economic damages, which are unbounded. Further research suggests that if jurors are altogether prevented from awarding punitive damages, the compensatory award may be augmented as a way to punish the defendant. These findings reflect the holistic reasoning notion described previously. Sometimes, jurors have a sense of "total justice"—an idea of what they think is fair in terms of compensation for the injured party and payment by the injurer—and, lacking clear guidance on the complementary functions of various kinds of damage awards, do what they can to deliver it.

Psychologists have much to offer in this realm, particularly by conducting sophisticated psycholegal research that mirrors jurors' actual task demands and that can illuminate the effects of these reform laws on jurors' judgments. Carefully conducted empirical research studies can show how jurors manage the difficult task of awarding damages and what procedural changes can help them function more effectively.

Edith Greene

See also Jury Competence; Jury Decisions Versus Judges' Decisions; Jury Reforms

Further Readings

Broeder, D. (1959). The University of Chicago jury project. *Nebraska Law Review, 38,* 744–760.

Diamond, S., Saks, M., & Landsman, S. (1998). Juror judgments about liability and damages: Sources of variability and ways to increase consistency. *DePaul Law Review, 48,* 301–325.

Greene, E., & Bornstein, B. (2003). *Determining damages: The psychology of jury awards.* Washington, DC: American Psychological Association.

Hans, V. (2000). *Business on trial: The civil jury and corporate responsibility.* New Haven, CT: Yale University Press.

Vidmar, N. (1998). The performance of the American civil jury: An empirical perspective. *Arizona Law Review, 40,* 849–899.

DANGER ASSESSMENT INSTRUMENT (DA)

The Danger Assessment Instrument (DA), in its current form, is a 20-item actuarial test designed to assess the risk of serious or lethal intimate partner violence. It is intended for use with adult women who have suffered physical abuse at the hands of men who are their current or former intimate partners. Although originally developed to assist in safety planning conducted by people delivering services to victims, the DA more recently has been used by some law enforcement agencies to help manage the risks posed by perpetrators. Systematic review of the DA is complicated by the fact that it has been used in several different forms for a variety of different purposes and by the lack of a formal test manual.

Description and Development

Development of the DA began in the early 1980s. The DA differs from other tests designed to assess the risk of intimate partner violence—such as the Spousal Assault Risk Assessment Guide (SARA) and the Domestic Violence Screening Instrument (DVSI)—in that its development focused specifically on risk of serious or lethal violence. In its original form, it comprised 15 risk factors that were identified in retrospective studies of intimate partner homicide—cases in which battered women killed or seriously injured their abusive partners or in which battered women were killed or seriously injured by their abuser partners. In 2004, the DA item pool was revised and expanded to 20 items, based on the findings of a multisite study that compared

risk factors for life-threatening (lethal or near lethal) versus less serious intimate partner violence. Some of the items reflect the nature or severity of intimate partner violence in the victim's relationship with the perpetrator, such as a history of threats to kill, forced sex, or strangulation; some reflect characteristics of the victim, such as whether she has children from a previous relationship or has a history of suicidal threats or attempts; and others reflect characteristics of the perpetrator, such as whether he has a history of problems with employment or substance use.

The DA can be completed independently or in collaboration with a service provider. Administration of the DA begins with a calendar assessment, in which the victim reviews a calendar to determine the nature of frequency of intimate partner violence experienced by the victim in the previous year. The victim identifies the approximate dates of any abuse and rates the seriousness of each incident using a 5-point scale (1 = slapping, pushing; no injuries and/or lasting pain to 5 = use of weapon; wounds from weapon). This history taking gathers information that is useful when rating the 20 risk factors, but it also is intended to decrease the extent to which victims minimize the intimate partner violence that they have experienced.

Next, victims are asked to rate the presence of the 20 risk factors on a 2-point scale (0 = no, 1 = yes). Some are rated on the basis of lifetime presence, whereas others are rated on their presence in the past year. Items ratings are then summed using a simple unit-weighting procedure to yield total scores that range from 0 to 20; alternatively, a more complex differential weighting procedure can be used that yields total scores ranging from −3 to 37. Total scores can be classified into four categories that reflect the risk of life-threatening violence: <7 = variable danger, 8 to 13 = increased danger, 14 to 17 = severe danger, and >18 = extreme danger. The risk categories are associated with suggested intervention strategies and directions regarding what should be communicated to the victim. For example, if a victim's DA score falls in the severe danger category, the service provider is advised to inform the victim that she is in severe danger, engage in assertive safety planning with her, and recommend a high level of supervision for the perpetrator.

Psychometric Evaluation

The psychometric properties of different versions of the DA have been evaluated only to a limit extent and solely within the framework of classical test theory.

Evaluations of structural reliability have reported Cronbach's alpha averaging about .75 to .80, and evaluations of short-term test-retest reliability have reported correlations averaging about .90. Given that the DA is an actuarial test of violence risk, these findings are actually somewhat disappointing: First, they indicate that the risk factors included in the test are at least moderately correlated, which suggests that they are likely to be substantially redundant as predictors of intimate partner violence. Second, they indicate that the DA is apparently insensitive to short-term changes or fluctuations in violence risk.

Little or no information is available concerning the interrater reliability of the DA—that is, agreement between victims and evaluators or agreement among evaluators with respect to the item or total scores.

There have been no studies evaluating the psychometric properties of the DA within the framework of modern test theory.

Validity

Some support for the validity of the DA comes from retrospective studies that found a significant association between total scores and measures of the seriousness of past intimate partner violence. Some research has attempted to determine whether the DA can discriminate between victims of lethal (or life threatening) versus nonlethal intimate partner violence, with disappointing results; but this may be because the DA must be scored on the basis of information provided by collateral informants (e.g., relatives, friends) when victims are deceased, possibly resulting in decreased validity of test scores.

There is also some research supporting the predictive validity of the DA with respect to intimate partner violence. First, indirect evidence comes from studies that found moderate to high correlations, typically between .55 and .75, between DA total scores and scores on other measures related to risk of intimate partner violence, such as the Conflict Tactics Scale and the Index of Spouse Abuse. Second, direct evidence comes from prospective studies that have found a moderate association between DA total scores and repeated intimate partner violence. Although there have been few direct comparisons, the predictive validity of the DA appears to be about the same as that of other procedures for assessing risk of intimate partner violence. To date, there has been no investigation of the predictive validity of the DA specifically with

respect to life-threatening violence, the purpose for which it was originally developed.

Recommendations

The DA can be useful as part of a comprehensive assessment of risk of intimate partner violence. It has two important strengths: It systematically gathers information from victims, who can provide a unique perspective on the history of violence in the relationship and on the perpetrator's background and psychosocial adjustment, and it considers victim vulnerability factors that are relevant to safety planning.

The DA also has some important limitations. There is no formal manual to guide proper administration, scoring, and interpretation or that provides the technical information necessary to undertake a comprehensive review of the test. There is a lack of information concerning the interrater reliability of DA item and total scores. There is a lack of systematic research on the predictive validity of the DA with respect to intimate partner violence in general and no research with respect to life-threatening intimate partner violence. At the present time, then, it may be best to use the DA as structured professional guidelines for risk assessment rather than as a quantitative or actuarial test.

Stephen D. Hart and Kelly A. Watt

See also Domestic Violence Screening Instrument (DVSI); Intimate Partner Violence; Spousal Assault Risk Assessment (SARA); Violence Risk Assessment

Further Readings

Campbell, J. C. (1995). *Assessing dangerousness.* Thousand Oaks, CA: Sage.

Campbell, J. C., Webster, D., Koziol-McLain, J., Block, C., Campbell, D., Curry, M., et al. (2003). Risk factors for femicide in abusive relationships: Results from a multisite case control study. *American Journal of Public Health, 93,* 1089–1097.

DEATH PENALTY

Most countries have abolished the death penalty. The United States retains the death penalty, although it has attempted to make executions more humane. The

Supreme Court has restricted use of the death penalty based on the type of crime and the characteristics of the criminal. Psychologists and other social scientists have conducted research on issues such as whether the death penalty serves as a deterrent, what drives public support for capital punishment, how jurors decide whether to sentence a defendant to life in prison or death by execution, and the possibility of wrongful convictions and executions.

The International Context

Killing is one of the oldest forms of punishment for criminal behavior, and even today, executions are widespread. Worldwide, shooting, hanging, beheading, lethal injection, and stoning are the most frequently used methods of execution. According to Amnesty International, China currently leads the world in the annual number of executions, followed by Iran, Saudi Arabia, the United States, and Pakistan. The United States and Japan are the only industrialized democracies that still execute criminals. There is a clear international trend toward abolition—between 1985 and 1995, 37 counties abolished the death penalty; and between 1995 and 2005, another 22 countries did so. More than half the countries in the world have now eliminated capital punishment or have ceased to carry out executions. Once abolished, capital punishment is rarely reinstated. Only four countries have reinstated the death penalty (Gambia, Nepal, Papua New Guinea, and the Philippines) after abolishing it, and of those, two have since abolished it again.

American Methods of Execution

The three "modern" methods of execution practiced in the United States—electrocution, poisonous gas, and lethal injection—were developed in an effort to make executions more civilized. Prior to the first electrocution in 1890, hanging was the dominant means of execution in the United States. Hangings were often botched, resulting in gruesome spectacles. Government officials wanted not only to end such spectacles but also to put an end to hangings, which were strongly associated in the public mind with lynching and vigilante justice. Each time a new method of execution was developed—first the electric chair, then the gas chamber, then lethal injection—the main argument was that the new method would be more humane and reliable than its predecessor. Of course, no method of killing is completely humane or reliable. Lethal injection, the method now used in 37 of the 38 states that impose the death penalty, has been challenged on the grounds that it can cause great pain, although the condemned prisoner's suffering is masked by the paralyzing drugs that are part of the execution process. As some commentators have noted, discussions of whether the death penalty is humane must take into account not only the actual killing of the prisoner but also the long process preceding an execution, including the years spent waiting on death row and the rituals leading up to the execution.

The Supreme Court and the Death Penalty

The constitutionality of capital punishment has been challenged on the grounds that it violates the Eighth Amendment's prohibition against "cruel and unusual punishment" or the Fourteenth Amendment's guarantee of "equal protection" under the law. In the 1972 case of *Furman v. Georgia,* in a 5:4 decision, the Supreme Court held that because of the "uncontrolled discretion of judges or juries," the death penalty was being "wantonly and freakishly" applied. Capital punishment—as administered at the time—was ruled unconstitutional. However, by 1976, the Court had approved a series of reforms aimed at controlling the discretion of judges and jurors (*Gregg v. Georgia*). The most important reforms included bifurcated capital trials, where guilt is decided in the first phase and, if the defendant is found guilty, a second "penalty phase" is conducted to determine whether the person found guilty should be sentenced to death or life in prison. More recent decisions by the Supreme Court have placed further restrictions on the penalty of death. The Court has held that mentally retarded murderers cannot be put to death (*Atkins v. Virginia,* 2002), only juries (not judges) can decide whether a convicted murderer should be sentenced to death, and those who commit their crimes as juveniles cannot be sentenced to death (*Roper v. Simmons,* 2005). In states that authorize the death penalty, only "aggravated" murder or murder with "special circumstances" is eligible for the death penalty. State laws vary, but examples of capital crimes include murder for hire, murder during the commission of a robbery or rape, murder of a police officer, or kidnapping and murder. The federal crimes of espionage and treason can also result in a death sentence.

The Capital Murder Trial

Many researchers have explored how the unique features of capital murder trials affect guilt and sentencing. One such unique feature is the death qualification process. During jury selection, potential jurors in capital cases are asked whether they would be willing to consider imposing a sentence of death if the defendant is eventually found guilty of capital murder. Prospective jurors who say they would be unwilling to vote for a sentence of death are not permitted to serve on capital juries. Research has shown that the process of death qualification results in a less demographically representative jury (e.g., fewer females and fewer non-White jurors) as well as a jury that is more receptive to the prosecution and more likely to impose a sentence of death. A second distinctive feature of capital trials concerns the penalty phase instructions to jurors. In most states, jurors are instructed to weigh or balance aggravating factors that support a sentence of death against mitigating factors that support a sentence of life. Based on postverdict interviews with hundreds of capital jurors, the Capital Jury Project has found that jurors have great difficulty in understanding both the concept of "mitigation" and the concept of "weighing." In addition, many jurors often wrongly assume that unless they vote for a death sentence, the defendant will be eligible for parole and may eventually be released from prison. Like the death qualification process, the ambiguity of penalty phase instructions tends to increase the probability of a death sentence.

Deterrence

Deterrence—the theory that the existence of the death penalty will prevent potential murderers from actually committing murder—was one the earliest justifications for executing criminals. Barbarous forms of execution such as breaking at the wheel, burning at the stake, decapitation, and disemboweling were thought to be especially effective at creating the fear necessary to deter those who might consider committing a capital crime. Despite the intuitive appeal of this theory, research does not support a deterrent effect for the death penalty. The introduction of the death penalty does not suppress murder rates, and its abolition does not cause murder rates to rise. Scores of studies have investigated whether capital punishment has a deterrent effect. These studies have looked at homicide rates in jurisdictions with and without the death penalty

(e.g., adjacent states) or examined homicide rates over time when the death penalty is abandoned or reinstated. In examining the possibility of a deterrence effect, social scientists have attempted to control statistically for factors that are known to contribute to rates of violence—for example, size of the police force, number of young males in the population, and unemployment rates. Specific analyses have also been conducted to determine whether only crimes punishable by death (e.g., aggravated murder) are deterred, and studies have been conducted to determine whether it is the actual number of executions (as opposed to whether the death penalty is an available punishment) that deters. The overall finding of more than 40 years of research is that the death penalty does not deter murderers. Although some researchers have found a deterrent effect for some jurisdictions over a specific period of time, other researchers have found what has been called the "brutalization effect"—a small but consistent increase in the number of murders in the weeks following an execution.

Research on deterrence tends to rely on large data sets collected over long periods of time. But the theory of deterrence also relies on a psychological explanation of what happens in the minds of potential killers. For capital punishment to effectively deter, potential murderers would need to believe that there is a high probability of being caught, convicted, sentenced to death, and eventually executed for their crimes. And if the availability of the death penalty is to have a deterrent effect beyond that provided by life in prison, the potential killer would also need to judge the possibility of eventual execution as substantially more frightening than the prospect of spending the rest of his or her life in prison. Even a rational analysis of these probabilities would not necessarily deter a potential killer, and because most murders are committed under the influence of drugs or powerful emotions, it seems implausible that murderers rationally weigh out alternatives.

Public Opinion

Media coverage often emphasizes that a majority of Americans support capital punishment. It is true that when Americans are asked the general question, "Do you favor or oppose the death penalty for persons convicted of murder?" approximately 66% of respondents indicate their support. This support has fluctuated over time. In 1966, support for capital punishment dropped to 42%, but by 1988, support had risen to 79% of the public. Overall, males are significantly more supportive than females, Whites are more supportive than Blacks, and Republicans are more supportive than Democrats. While responses to a broad question about support for or opposition to the death penalty may give a rough indication of American attitudes at a particular time, such general responses can be misleading. More detailed survey research reveals that support often rests on mistaken assumptions about issues such as cost, fairness of application, or deterrence. In addition, support falls when alternative punishments are mentioned. The public is about evenly divided if respondents are asked to choose between the option of "the death penalty" or "life in prison without the possibility of parole" for "persons convicted of murder." When the punishment of "life without parole plus restitution" is offered as an alternative to the death penalty, a majority of Americans endorse it.

Wrongful Conviction and Execution

Decisions about who is guilty of capital murder and who should be executed are entrusted to a fallible legal system. The possibility of wrongful conviction and execution of an innocent defendant has always been part of the public debate over capital punishment, but the emergence of DNA as a means of criminal identification has made this argument much more prominent. During the past 30 years, more than 120 people have been released from death row because of new evidence or reanalysis of existing evidence. It is important to note that the number of wrongful convictions exposed by DNA analysis is only a fraction of the total. Such DNA-based exonerations are only possible if biological evidence (e.g., blood, semen, skin cells) has been collected at the crime scene and preserved for later testing. It is impossible to know how many prisoners currently on death row are actually innocent. For most death row inmates, there is clear evidence of guilt. And many who claim to be innocent could be lying. But it is likely that there are also cases where wrongfully convicted death row inmates are unable to prove their innocence because of lack of evidence or lack of resources.

More than 1,000 condemned prisoners have been executed since the reinstatement of the death penalty in 1976. It is impossible to know exactly how many of these prisoners were actually innocent. Once a prisoner has been killed, courts rarely entertain claims of innocence, and lawyers, investigators, and journalists turn their attention to cases where possibly innocent prisoners can still be saved. Despite the difficulty of conclusively proving wrongful executions, there are a handful of cases where there is persuasive evidence that the wrong man was executed (e.g., Ruben Cantu, Gary Graham, Larry Griffin, James O'Dell, Leo Jones). The reality of wrongful conviction and wrongful execution raises the issue whether retention of the death penalty is so valuable that it justifies occasionally sending an innocent person to death row and perhaps to the execution chamber.

If the decision to retain or abandon capital punishment was based solely on research findings, it would have been abolished long ago. However, like many important social policies, the decision is driven by emotional and political as well as empirical considerations.

Mark Costanzo

See also Aggravating and Mitigating Circumstances, Evaluation of in Capital Cases; Aggravating and Mitigating Circumstances in Capital Trials, Effects on Jurors; American Bar Association Resolution on Mental Disability and the Death Penalty; Competency for Execution; Death Qualification of Juries; Juveniles and the Death Penalty; Mental Illness and the Death Penalty; Mental Retardation and the Death Penalty; Moral Disengagement and Execution; Racial Bias and the Death Penalty

Further Readings

Atkins v. Virginia, 536 U.S. 304 (2002).

Bedau, H. A. (2004). *Killing as punishment.* Boston: Northeastern University Press.

Costanzo, M. (1987). *Just revenge: Costs and consequences of the death penalty.* New York: St. Martin's Press.

Dow, D. R. (2005). *Executed on a technicality.* Boston: Beacon Press.

Furman v. Georgia, 408 U.S. 238 (1972).

Gregg v. Georgia, 428 U.S. 153 (1976).

Myers, B., & Greene, E. (2004). The prejudicial nature of victim impact statements: Implications for capital sentencing policy. *Psychology, Public Policy, and Law, 10,* 492–515.

O'Neil, K. M., Patry, M. W., & Penrod, S. D. (2004). Exploring the effects of attitudes toward the death penalty on capital sentencing verdicts. *Psychology, Public Policy, and Law, 10,* 443–470.

Osofsky, M. J., Bandura, A., & Zimbardo, P. G. (2005). The role of moral disengagement in the execution process. *Law and Human Behavior, 29,* 371–393.

Roper v. Simmons, 543 U.S. 551 (2005).

Zimring, F. E. (2003). *The contradictions of American capital punishment.* New York: Oxford University Press.

Web Sites

Death Penalty Information Center:
http://www.deathpenaltyinfo.org

DEATH QUALIFICATION OF JURIES

Death qualification is a unique form of jury selection that is used only in capital cases. Potential jurors are screened beforehand on the basis of their attitudes toward death penalty, and persons holding "disqualifying" attitudes or beliefs about capital punishment are dismissed from further participation. In the late 1960s, the U.S. Supreme Court established the standard by which prospective jurors could be constitutionally excluded from service on a capital jury as one of "unequivocal opposition" (i.e., if the prospective juror said that he or she could never impose the death penalty no matter what the facts or circumstances of the case). Since then, the process of death qualification has been the subject of extensive legal commentary and social science research, as well as the focus of a number of constitutional challenges and revisions in the legal standard of exclusion itself.

The Nature and Effect of Death Qualification

In modern death penalty jurisprudence, all capital trials are bifurcated. If a capital defendant is convicted of a crime for which the death penalty is a possible punishment (first-degree murder plus some special circumstance or feature that is found to be present in the case), a second sentencing or penalty phase of the trial is held. In this phase, the capital jury decides whether to sentence the defendant to death or some lesser punishment (typically life in prison without possibility of parole). To accommodate the state's interest in having only those jurors serve who can consider imposing the death penalty in the second part of the capital trial, should one occur, the law permits the screening of all potential jurors on the basis of their death penalty views. However, this selection or screening process transpires at the very outset of the trial, before any evidence has been presented and, perforce, before the actual jury has decided whether the defendant is guilty or not. Because it occurs so early in the trial, death qualification may have a significant impact on all of the jury's subsequent decision making.

In fact, social science research has established the fact that death-qualified juries are significantly different from non-death-qualified juries in a number of important ways. For one, death qualification produces juries that are less representative than non-death-qualified juries. That is, because women and minorities (especially African Americans) are more likely to oppose the death penalty, they are more likely to be excluded from death-qualified juries. Also, because attitudes toward the death penalty tend to be correlated with other attitudes about the criminal justice system, researchers have found that death qualification produces juries that hold a more homogeneous perspective than other juries, where attitudinal diversity would be more likely to occur. Among other things, death-qualified juries are generally more favorable to the perspectives of prosecutors and law enforcement, more susceptible to things such as potentially prejudicial pretrial publicity and aggravating evidence that may be introduced at trial, and simultaneously more oriented toward "crime control" goals and less committed to "due process" values.

Perhaps not surprisingly—given the way death qualification skews the composition of the group deemed eligible to serve, death-qualified juries also tend to be "conviction prone." That is, based on the same set of case facts and circumstances, research shows that they are more likely to find a defendant guilty than are non-death-qualified juries. Of course, because they are selected precisely on the basis of their willingness to impose the death penalty, they also are "death prone"—that is, they are more likely to render death verdicts than a non-death-qualified jury would be.

In addition, research has shown that the process of death qualification itself produces biasing effects among persons exposed to it. That is, because it requires jurors to consider the issues that would be germane only after they had found the defendant guilty (e.g., whether they actually could impose the death penalty) and to commit themselves to a course of action that would occur only in the sentencing phase of the trial (i.e., pledge to consider all punishment options, including the death penalty)—before any evidence has been presented, the process of death qualification itself appears to increase prospective jurors' belief in the defendant's likely guilt. The nature of the questioning that occurs during death qualification also has the potential to desensitize jurors to the issue of imposing the death penalty, to lead some jurors to believe that they have committed themselves to actually imposing the death penalty if they find the defendant guilty, and to imply that death penalty imposition is the legally approved sanction in the penalty trial of their case. Obviously, these process-related biases occur in addition to the effects that death qualification has on the composition of the capital jury.

There is one additional aspect of death qualification that continues to have legal and social scientific significance. The process of excluding potential jurors from participation in capital trials solely on the basis of their feelings about the death penalty has implications for an important legal judgment that courts make about the scope of death penalty support in the United States. In particular, as Justice John Paul Stevens and others have acknowledged, one of the key "societal factors" that the U.S. Supreme Court has continued to look to "in determining the acceptability of capital punishment to the American sensibility is the behavior of juries" (*Thompson v. Oklahoma*, 1988, p. 831). Thus, the behavior of capital juries, each one of which has been created through a process that includes death qualification, continues to serve as a measure of the "national consensus" on the death penalty and an important index of the extent to which certain death penalty laws offend evolving standards of decency, the hallmark of an Eighth Amendment analysis. However, because death-qualified juries are selected precisely on the basis of their willingness to actually impose the death penalty, and therefore differ from non-death-qualified jurors on this dimension (as well as many others), their death-sentencing behavior is unlikely to be representative or reflective of the true "American sensibility" with respect to capital punishment.

Legal Challenges to Death Qualification

Social science research documenting the range of biasing effects produced by death qualification has served as the basis for a number of constitutional challenges arguing that the unrepresentative and conviction-prone nature of the capital jury compromises the fair trial rights of capital defendants. In one of the first of these cases, the U.S. Supreme Court raised the threshold of legal exclusion from one of mere

"scruples" against the death penalty (which had been the operative death qualification standard for more than 100 years) to "unequivocal opposition"—a belief strong enough to preclude the juror from ever returning a death verdict. (See *Witherspoon v. Illinois*, 1968.) However, the social science data offered in support of the petitioner's claim that death qualification was unconstitutional were deemed too "tentative and fragmentary" to support such a ruling.

A little more than a decade later, a major challenge to death qualification was lodged in California. It relied on a large body of more recently assembled social science data and was based on state constitutional grounds. Although the state Supreme Court cited and discussed the numerous social scientific studies that were introduced in an evidentiary hearing in the case, the court stopped short of prohibiting death qualification, at least as it was practiced in California. However, the court did seek to minimize the biasing effects of the process of death qualification itself by requiring that it be conducted on an individual, sequestered basis (to minimize the extent to which any one juror was repeatedly exposed to it; see *Hovey v. Superior Court*, 1980).

In *Lockhart v. McCree* (1986), the U.S. Supreme Court rejected a federal constitutional challenge that was based on many of the same studies that had been introduced in the California case. The Court questioned the validity of the relevant social science research, noting that none of the studies was methodologically perfect and, of course, could entirely recreate the "felt responsibility" of an actual capital jury. In addition, however, the Court ruled that, even if valid, the research was not dispositive since juries biased in the ways that death-qualified juries appeared to be could have arisen by chance. Specifically, Justice Rehnquist wrote for the majority that "it is hard for us to understand the logic of the argument that a given jury is unconstitutionally partial when it results from a State-ordained process, yet impartial when exactly the same jury results from mere chance" (p. 178).

Changes in the Legal Standard of Exclusion

The legal standard that is used in the death qualification process has changed several times. As noted earlier, in 1968, the U.S. Supreme Court modified the operative standard that had been in use for more than a century. In addition, however, some 17 years after this decision, the Supreme Court again revised the threshold for excluding jurors from participation in capital cases—this time broadening it from unequivocal opposition to merely holding death penalty attitudes that would "prevent or substantially impair the performance of his [or her] duties as a juror in accordance with his [or her] instructions and oath" (*Wainwright v. Witt*, 1985, p. 852). The significance of the *Witt* opinion was acknowledged by legal practitioners and scholars alike, who suggested that the less precise language and seemingly broader scope of the *Witt* formulation would result in a substantial increase in the size of the excludable group as well as complicate the precise application of the legal standard of exclusion.

Finally, the death qualification standard underwent yet another doctrinal change in 1992, when the U.S. Supreme Court ruled that persons whose *support* of the death penalty is so strong that it would "prevent or substantially impair" the performance of their duties (sometimes called "automatic death penalty" or "ADP" jurors) also should be legally disqualified from serving in capital cases. (See *Morgan v. Illinois*, 1992.) Thus, "modern" death qualification now operates to exclude persons whose death penalty attitudes would merely "impair" the performance of their functions in a capital trial, and it eliminates persons on the basis of both support for as well as opposition to extreme death penalty. In practical terms, the intended "balancing" of the standard of exclusion (by including extreme death penalty supporters as well as opponents) does not seem to have significantly altered the biasing effects brought about by death qualification. Scholars and practitioners acknowledge that extreme death penalty supporters are not as readily identified as the comparable group of death penalty opponents. As a result, death-qualified juries continue to suffer from many of the biases identified in the earlier research and relied on as the basis for constitutional challenges (albeit, in some jurisdictions, on an attenuated basis).

Craig Haney

See also Death Penalty; Jury Selection; Voir Dire

Further Readings

Allen, M., Mabry, E., & McKelton, D. (2004). The impact of juror attitudes about the death penalty on juror evaluations of guilt and punishment. *Law and Human Behavior, 22,* 715–731.

Bersoff, D. (1987). Social science data and the Supreme Court: *Lockhart* as a case in point. *The American Psychologist, 42,* 52–58.

Haney, C. (Ed.). (1984). Death qualification [Special issue]. *Law and Human Behavior, 8.*

Haney, C., Hurtado, A., & Vega, L. (1994). "Modern" death qualification: New data on its biasing effects. *Law and Human Behavior, 18,* 619–633.

Hovey v. Superior Court, 28 Cal. 3d 1 (1980).

Lockhart v. McCree, 476 U.S. 162 (1986).

Morgan v. Illinois, 504 U.S. 719 (1992).

Thompson, W. (1989). Death qualification after *Wainwright v. Witt* and *Lockhart v. McCree. Law and Human Behavior, 13,* 185–215.

Thompson v. Oklahoma, 487 U.S. 815 (1988).

Wainwright v. Witt, 469 U.S. 412 (1985).

Witherspoon v. Illinois, 389 U.S. 1035 (1968).

DELUSIONS

Delusions are firmly held false beliefs. They are associated with numerous disorders, including schizophrenia and delusional disorder, but can also be found in patients with affective disorders and dementia. Several different types of delusions are recognized, including erotomanic delusions, grandiose delusions, jealous delusions, persecutory delusions, delusions of control, nihilistic delusions, delusions of guilt or sin, somatic delusions, and delusions of reference. Assessment of delusions involves determination of the etiology as well as the severity and tenacity of symptom presentation. Treatment is dependent on the etiology of the symptoms and can include antipsychotic, antidepressant, or mood-stabilizing medications as well as cognitive therapy.

Definition of Delusions

Delusions are fixed beliefs that are false and have no basis in reality. Delusions can be either bizarre, such as thinking that aliens are controlling your thoughts and behaviors, or nonbizarre, such as believing that one is being watched or spied on. In addition, delusions can be mood congruent, in which the delusion is consistent with the emotional state—such as depression or mania, or mood incongruent, whereby the delusion is not consistent with the emotional state. An example of a mood-congruent delusion would be believing oneself to be God during the height of a manic episode; an example of a mood-incongruent delusion would be a depressed person's belief that his or her thoughts are being controlled by the Central Intelligence Agency. For a belief to be considered a delusion, it must be pathological in nature.

Disorders Associated With Delusions

Delusions are symptoms of several psychological disorders and are indicative of a psychotic mental illness. Along with hallucinations, delusions are the most recognizable symptoms of schizophrenia. However, the presence of delusions alone is not sufficient to warrant a diagnosis of schizophrenia. In schizophrenia, the delusions can be either bizarre or nonbizarre.

Delusions are the predominant symptom of delusional disorder, which is a mental disorder in which the person holds one or more nonbizarre delusions in the absence of any other psychopathology. In addition, the person must not have ever met any of the diagnostic criteria of schizophrenia. In many instances, a person with delusional disorder can function normally in most aspects of life, and the only indication of mental illness is the behavior that results directly from the delusional belief. For example, a person could believe that he or she is being spied on through the electrical outlets in his or her house, so that person covers all the outlets with electric tape. With the exception of this behavior, which is directly related to the delusional thought, the person is able to maintain a job and relationships. Historically, delusional disorder was referred to as paranoia.

Delusions have also been associated with dementia, severe depression, and the manic phase of bipolar disorder.

Types of Delusions

There are several different types of delusions, such as erotomanic delusions, delusions of grandiosity, jealous delusions, persecutory delusions, delusions of control, nihilistic delusions, delusions of guilt or sin, somatic delusions, and delusions of reference.

Erotomanic Delusions

An erotomanic delusion is a delusion in which the individual believes that he or she has a special, loving relationship with another person, who is usually a famous individual or someone of high standing. The subjects of delusions are often popular media figures such as politicians, actors, and singers. In certain instances, the delusional individuals believe that the subject of their delusion is communicating secret love messages to them through signals such as gestures and body posture. As part of the delusion, the delusional individuals believe that their feelings are reciprocated by the subject of their delusion. In the case of celebrities, these gesture are usually transmitted to the delusional individual through the radio or television. In most cases, the subject of the delusion has no contact with, or awareness of, the delusional individual. Erotomanic delusions are most often found in individuals diagnosed with schizophrenia or delusional disorder.

Erotomanic delusions can lead to stalking or other potentially dangerous behaviors. In some extreme cases, the delusional individual has broken into the house of the subject of the delusion and even killed the person. A number of widely reported crimes have been associated with erotomanic delusions: in 1989, Rebecca Schaeffer, a young actress, was shot and killed at her home by an individual who had an erotomanic delusion about her. Also, it was reported that the assassination attempt on the former U.S. president Ronald Reagan was driven by an erotomanic delusion: John Hinckley Jr. shot Reagan in the deluded belief that this action would cause the actress Jodie Foster to publicly declare her love for him.

There is some controversy about the prognosis for those who are diagnosed with erotomanic delusions. According to some researchers, such individuals respond poorly to treatment, while other researchers view the delusions as symptomatic of an underlying psychotic disorder that generally will respond to antipsychotic medications and supportive psychotherapy. There is some evidence that individuals with delusional disorder have poor compliance with treatment, as they are often so enthralled with the subject of their delusion that they cannot be persuaded to take medications that may diminish the symptoms.

Grandiose Delusions

Individuals who have delusions of grandiosity often have an exaggerated sense of self-importance or inflated worth. They may be convinced that they possess superior knowledge or skills or that they have a special relationship to a deity or a celebrity. In certain cases, the delusional individuals may actually believe that they themselves are a deity (such as Jesus Christ) or a famous person. More commonly, those with delusions of grandiosity may believe that they have achieved a great accomplishment for which they have not received sufficient appreciation and respect.

Some theorists believe that delusions of grandiosity result as a consequence of low self-esteem and negative emotions. This is known as the delusion-as-defense hypothesis. Other researchers argue that the delusions of grandiosity are an exaggerated manifestation of the individual's true emotions and belief. This is known as the emotion-consistent hypothesis. One study investigated both hypotheses in a sample of 20 patients with grandiose delusions and found that there were no differences between covert and overt self-esteem in the sample. The authors of the study concluded that the grandiose delusions may be exaggerations of the emotional state of individuals. Grandiose delusions can be associated with schizophrenia or delusional disorder and are a common symptom of the manic phase of bipolar disorder.

Jealous Delusions

Jealous delusions, or delusions of infidelity, involve the false belief that the delusional individual's spouse or sexual partner is unfaithful or having an affair. Delusional jealousy can involve stalking or spying on the spouse/lover as the delusional individual seeks evidence to confirm the existence of the affair. This type of delusion often stems from pathological jealousy and can seriously affect romantic relationships, and in certain cases the delusional individual's jealousy can escalate into violence and even murder.

Persecutory Delusions

Individuals with persecutory delusions believe that specific individuals, or people in general, are "out to get them." Individuals with delusions of persecution suspect that others are participating in intricate plots to persecute them. In some cases, they may believe that they are being spied on, drugged, or poisoned. In more extreme cases, the individuals may believe that they are the subject of a conspiracy and someone (often a government agency) wants them dead. Some delusions of persecution are vaguer and more general, such as the false belief that one's coworkers are giving one a hard time. In other cases, the delusions can be a network of numerous well-formed false beliefs that are highly intricate and involved, such as an elaborate

governmental conspiracy that can explain every aspect of the individual's life.

Persecutory delusions are a hallmark symptom of several disorders, including paranoid schizophrenia; delusion disorder, paranoid type; and paranoid personality disorder. Paranoid delusions have also been noted in cases of severe depression and dementia.

Other Delusions

Other types of delusions include delusions of control, nihilistic delusions, delusions of guilt or sin, somatic delusions, and delusions of reference. Those with delusions of control have the false belief that someone else is controlling their thoughts, emotions, and behaviors. This can include the belief that outside forces are inserting or removing thoughts from their mind, that their thoughts are being broadcast out loud, or that someone is controlling their bodily movements. Nihilistic delusions refer to false beliefs that the world is coming to an end. Delusions of sin or guilt refer to intense feelings of guilt or sin for something the person has not done; for example, individuals with such delusions may falsely believe that they have committed a horrible crime for which they should be punished or that they are somehow responsible for natural disasters, even though this is impossible. Somatic delusions usually involve the false belief that the individual has a medical disorder or a physical deformity. These beliefs differ from hypochondriasis, as somatic delusions are often very specific and in some cases quite strange. Finally, individuals who experience delusions of reference believe that they may be receiving special messages from the television, newspaper, radio, or the way things are arranged around them. Individuals with this disorder may believe that people are talking about them or taking special notice of them even when that is not the case.

Delusions of control, nihilistic delusions, and delusions of reference are considered bizarre delusions. However, persecutory delusions, somatic delusions, grandiose delusions, as well as most delusions of jealousy and guilt are generally considered nonbizarre.

Assessment of Delusions

If a delusional disorder is suspected, an individual should be evaluated by a physician to rule out any organic etiology (such as dementia). This may include a thorough medical history, a review of the medications the patient is taking, blood workup, and possibly brain scans. If the delusions do not appear to be related to an organic cause, then the patient should undergo an evaluation by a psychiatrist or a psychologist. This evaluation will generally involve an interview and psychological assessment. There are several instruments that are used by psychologists to assess delusions. These include the MacArthur-Maudsley Delusions Assessment Schedule, the Brown Assessment of Beliefs Scale, the Positive and Negative Syndrome Scale, and the Scale for the Assessment of Positive Symptoms.

Treatment of Delusions

Delusions that are symptoms of schizophrenia will generally respond to treatment with antipsychotic medications such as thioridazine, clozapine, haloperidol, or risperidone. Delusions that are not associated with schizophrenia may not respond to antipsychotic medications, and in those cases, medications other than, or in addition to, antipsychotic medications should be used. Delusions that are symptoms of a mood disorder should be treated with antipsychotic medications as well as antidepressants or mood stabilizers. If the etiology of the delusions is medical, then resolution of the medical disorder should alleviate the delusional symptoms. Additionally, cognitive therapy has been recommended as an adjunctive therapy for individuals who experience delusions.

Elizabeth L. Jeglic

See also Hallucinations; Mental Health Courts; Police Interaction With Mentally Ill Individuals; Violence Risk Assessment

Further Readings

American Psychiatric Association. (2000). *Diagnostic and Statistical Manual of Mental Disorders* (4th ed., text revision). Washington, DC: Author.

Appelbaum, P. S., Robbins, P. C., & Monahan, J. (2000). Violence and delusions: Data from the MacArthur Violence Risk Assessment Study. *American Journal of Psychiatry, 157,* 566–572.

Eisen, J. L., Phillips, K. A., Baer, L., Beer, D. A., Atala, K. D., & Rasmussen, S. A. (1998). The Brown Assessment of Beliefs Scale: Reliability and validity. *American Journal of Psychiatry, 155*(1), 102–108.

Leeser, J., & O'Donohue, W. (1999). What is a delusion? Epistemological dimensions. *Journal of Abnormal Psychology, 108,* 687–694.

Mullen, P. E., & Pathe, M. (1994). The pathological extensions of love. *British Journal of Psychiatry, 165,* 614–623.

Smith, N., Freeman, D., & Kuipers, E. (2005). Grandiose delusions: An experimental investigation of the delusion as defense. *Journal of Mental Disorders, 193*(7), 480–487.

DETECTION OF DECEPTION: COGNITIVE LOAD

Cognitive load interview protocols are designed to make interviews more demanding for suspects. This increased demand has a greater effect on liars than on truth tellers because liars already find being interviewed more mentally taxing than do truth tellers. The result is that cognitive load interview protocols facilitate discrimination between liars and truth tellers.

Lying in an interview setting is often more cognitively demanding than truth telling. First, formulating the lie itself is cognitively taxing. Liars need to make up their stories while monitoring their fabrications so that they are plausible and adhere to everything the observer knows or might find out. In addition, liars must remember their earlier statements and know what they told to whom, so that they appear consistent when retelling their story. Liars should also avoid making slips of the tongue and should refrain from providing new leads to investigators. Second, liars are typically less likely than truth tellers to take their own credibility for granted, in part because truth tellers typically assume that their innocence will shine through. As such, liars will be more inclined than truth tellers to be conscious of, and hence monitor and control, their demeanor so that they will appear honest to the lie detector. Monitoring and controlling one's own demeanor are cognitively demanding. Third, because liars do not take their credibility for granted, they may monitor the interviewer's reactions more carefully to assess whether they are getting away with their lie. Carefully monitoring the interviewer also requires cognitive resources. Fourth, liars may be preoccupied with the task of reminding themselves to act and role-play, which requires extra cognitive effort. Fifth, liars have to suppress the truth while they are lying, and this is also cognitively demanding. Finally, whereas activating the truth often happens automatically, activating a lie is more intentional and deliberate and thus requires mental effort.

Many sources support the premise that lying is cognitively demanding. First, in police interviews with real-life suspects, lies are accompanied by increased pauses, decreased blinking, and decreased hand/finger movements, all of which are signs of cognitive load. Second, police officers who saw videotapes of suspect interviews reported that the suspects appeared to be thinking harder when they lied than when they told the truth. Third, participants in mock-suspect experiments directly assessed their own cognitive load during interviews and reported that lying is more cognitively demanding than truth telling. Finally, deceiving is associated with activating executive, "higher" brain centers (such as the prefrontal cortex), which are typically activated when high cognitive load is experienced.

By using protocols that introduce additional cognitive load, investigators can exploit liars' higher cognitive demand to facilitate discrimination between liars and truth tellers. For example, interviewees could be asked to recall their stories in reverse order. This task is cognitively more demanding than recalling a story in chronological order. Liars, whose cognitive resources are depleted by the more demanding act of lying, find reverse order recall more debilitating than do truth tellers because liars have fewer cognitive resources left over than truth tellers. Indeed, research has demonstrated that liars and truth tellers differ more from each other in terms of displaying signs of cognitive load when they recall their stories in reverse order than in chronological order. The occurrence of more noticeable differences between liars and truth tellers should facilitate lie detection. Indeed, investigators were more accurate in discriminating between liars and truth tellers when the interviewees told their stories in reverse order than in chronological order.

An alternative technique to induce additional cognitive load is to require interviewees to perform a concurrent secondary task (time-sharing) while being interviewed. Again, liars, whose cognitive resources are already partially depleted by the act of lying, find this additional, concurrent task particularly debilitating. An experiment revealed that this showed up as poorer performance on the primary task (e.g., providing a statement during the interview) and also on the secondary task (e.g., determining whether each figure presented on a screen was similar to the target figure presented earlier).

Investigators sometimes have evidence available, such as fingerprints and closed-circuit TV footage, that may link a suspect to a crime. They can then present this incriminating evidence against a suspect in a strategic fashion to increase cognitive load by limiting the number of acceptable explanations suspects can offer to account for the current situation. Suppose that the suspect's car was noticed near the crime scene just after the crime had taken place but that the suspect did not refer to the car in his or her alibi. After being confronted with this piece of evidence, the suspect may reply that he or she had simply failed to mention previously that he or she had used the car on that particular day, thereby adapting his or her story to match the evidence. However, suppose that the police officer does not reveal at this stage that the car was noticed near the crime scene but asks some questions about the car instead (e.g., "Did you use your car that day?"). When confronted with the evidence after these questions, the suspect has fewer opportunities to provide acceptable solutions if he or she has already told the interviewer that he or she did not use the car on that particular day. The number of acceptable solutions would be reduced even further if the suspect indicated that he or she did not lend the car to anyone else and that nobody else had the car keys.

In sum, investigators using cognitively based interview protocols increase their ability to discriminate between liars and truth tellers by making the interview situation more taxing for interviewees.

Aldert Vrij, Ronald Fisher,
Samantha Mann, and Sharon Leal

See also Detection of Deception: Magnetic Resonance Imaging (MRI); Detection of Deception: Use of Evidence in; Detection of Deception in High-Stakes Liars

Further Readings

Hartwig, M., Granhag, P. A., Strömwall, L., & Kronkvist, O. (2006). Strategic use of evidence during police interrogations: When training to detect deception works. *Law and Human Behavior.*

Vrij, A., Fisher, R., Mann, S., & Leal, S. (2006). Detecting deception by manipulating cognitive load. *Trends in Cognitive Sciences, 10,* 141–142.

Vrij, A., Fisher, R., Mann, S., & Leal, S. (in press). Increasing cognitive load in interviews to detect deceit [Invited chapter]. In B. Milne, S. Savage, & T. Williamson (Ed.), *International developments in investigative interviewing.* Uffculme, UK: Willan.

DETECTION OF DECEPTION: EVENT-RELATED POTENTIALS

P300 is a brain wave derived from the electroencephalogram (EEG), which has recently been used as a novel information channel in the detection of deception. The traditional channels are recorded from the autonomic nervous system and include physiological activity such as respiration pattern, blood pressure, and skin conductance. In contrast, the EEG is a record of sequential, spontaneously changing voltages as a function of time, recorded from the scalp surface in humans. It reflects the spontaneous activity from the underlying cerebral cortex. If as these changing voltages occur, a discrete stimulus event (such as a light flash) occurs, the EEG breaks into a series of somewhat larger peaks and troughs, called components. This series of waves is called an event-related potential (ERP).

These early peaks and troughs represent sensory activity (exogenous ERP components), and the later (endogenous) components may represent the psychological reaction to the sensory events. P300 is the name of one heavily researched ERP. It is elicited by stimulus events that are rare and meaningful to subjects. For example, if a stimulus series consists of a set of randomly occurring first names, each presented singly on a display screen about every 3 s, and the subject's own first name is one of the stimuli presented about 15% of the time, with the remaining 85% of the presentations being of other, unfamiliar names, the P300 will be elicited by the rare, meaningful (subject's own) name. P300 is named in respect of its positive (P) polarity and its occurrence at about 300 to 800 ms after the stimulus onset. Simple stimuli such as brief sounds elicit early P300 peaks (300–400 ms), whereas more complex stimuli such as words elicit later peaks (500–800 ms).

It occurred to Dr. J. Peter Rosenfeld and colleagues in the early 1980s that P300 might be used in deception detection situations to index recognition of the presentation of crime scene details known only to perpetrators (and the authorities) and not to innocent suspects. The protocol would involve presentation (usually on a display screen) of items of information, such as possible murder weapons (e.g., pistol, rifle, knife, axe). The guilty party, but not the innocent subject, would react with a P300 to the actual murder weapon (e.g., the pistol), called the *probe* stimulus. Neither guilty nor innocent subjects would react to the other,

irrelevant items from the weapons category, which were not actually used in the crime, as the guilty party would know. Thus, the difference in P300 amplitude between the probe-evoked ERP and the irrelevant-evoked ERP indicates guilt. This protocol was closely related to the Guilty Knowledge Test (GKT) invented by David Lykken in 1959, which used autonomic nervous system responses to stimuli. One difference was that in the P300 protocol, there was usually a third stimulus type used, also rarely presented, called the *target*. This was typically one other irrelevant item but one to which the subject is told to respond by pressing a unique button. In one version of the protocol, the subject is told to press a "No" button (for "No, I don't recognize this") in response to both probes and irrelevant items and "Yes" ("I do recognize this") in response to targets. Of course, in saying "No" to the probe, the guilty subject lies, but it is hoped that his P300 ERP reveals his guilty recognition all the same. The target stimulus is used to force attention onto the display screen, since the three stimulus types are presented unpredictably in random sequence, and if the subject neglects to respond to the target stimulus as instructed, the operator knows that the subject is not paying attention and will report this to the authorities. But if the subject is always paying attention, he or she cannot avoid seeing the probe stimuli, which evoke P300s in guilty subjects.

Early reports in the 1990s (by J. Peter Rosenfeld and colleagues and by John J. B. Allen and Emanuel Donchin and their respective coworkers) with this protocol reported high overall accuracy (80–95% correct classification of guilty and innocent subjects), and they were received with considerable enthusiasm; it was naively believed that because the P300s occurred with such short reaction times (fractions of a second post-stimulus) relative to the slow autonomic reaction times in the GKT, the P300-based protocols would resist *countermeasures* (CMs), intentional covert responses subjects can learn to make that can defeat the GKT. Unfortunately, J. Peter Rosenfeld and colleagues showed in 2004 that P300-based GKTs were also vulnerable to CMs. The guilty subjects were simply trained to covertly respond (e.g., with secret toe wiggles) systematically to irrelevant stimuli, thus turning them into P300-evoking targets. It then became impossible to distinguish between probe and irrelevant P300s, whose typical difference without CMs indexed guilt. Reports from John J. B. Allen's lab showed similar results.

However, in 2006, J. Peter Rosenfeld and colleagues reported that a second-generation P300-based deception test using a wholly novel protocol was accurate and highly resistant to CMs. More than 100 subjects have been studied to date, and the accuracy rates have been 90% to 100% in many experiments, dropping by only 0% to 10% with CM use. Moreover, a new feature built into this new protocol alerts operators about CM use. In the new protocol—called the Complex Trial Protocol (CTP), two stimuli are presented on each trial, and there are four possible trial types. The first stimulus is either a probe or an irrelevant, and the subject responds with one simple behavioral acknowledgment that the stimulus has been seen. About 1 to 1.5 s later, a second stimulus is presented, which is either a redefined target or not one. The subject here signals target or nontarget. The subject's absolute behavioral reaction time to the first stimulus is significantly increased if a CM is being used, and the reaction time to irrelevants, which without a CM is less than or the same as that to probes, is usually increased to much greater than probe reaction time if a CM accompanies the irrelevant. Thus, occasionally successful CM use or attempted but unsuccessful CM use has always been detected. The probe P300 amplitude actually *increases* during CM use (unlike what is seen with the older protocol based on three trial types—probe, irrelevant, or target). Such an increase means that the CTP is still likely to see a probe-irrelevant difference even if the irrelevant P300 increases, as expected, during CM use. It appears that this new protocol is powerful because its multiple demands made on the subject force attention on the key stimuli, thus enhancing P300 responses to them.

Other brain-activity-based dependent indices of deception have been suggested and researched in preliminary ways. These approaches have different theoretical foundations. Dr. J. Peter Rosenfeld and colleagues have also examined the P300 amplitude *distribution* (not simple amplitude) across the scalp (a kind of "brain map") as a promising new index of deception. The motivation for pursuing this new approach is, again, the possibility of removing CMs. It was simple to develop CMs for the earlier P300-amplitude-based protocols because the antecedents of P300 amplitude—rareness and meaningfulness—are relatively well-known. If one knows the antecedents of P300, then one knows how to manipulate it. On the other hand, very little is known about how to manipulate the amplitude distribution across the scalp, thus facilitating the creation of a CM method.

J. Peter Rosenfeld

See also Detection of Deception in Adults; Polygraph and Polygraph Techniques

Further Readings

Allen, J., Iacono, W. G., & Danielson, K. D. (1992). The identification of concealed memories using the event-related potential and implicit behavioral measures: A methodology for prediction in the face of individual differences. *Psychophysiology, 29,* 504–522.

Farwell, L. A., & Donchin, E. (1991). The truth will out: Interrogative polygraphy ("lie detection") with event-related potentials. *Psychophysiology, 28,* 531–547.

Johnson, R., Jr., Barnhardt, J., & Zhu, J. (2004). The contribution of executive processes to deceptive responding. *Neuropsychologia, 42,* 878–901.

Lykken, D. T. (1998). *A tremor in the blood.* Reading, MA: Perseus Books.

Rosenfeld, J. P. (2006). The Complex Trial (CT) Protocol: A new, countermeasure-resistant protocol for deception detection [Abstract]. *International Journal of Psychophysiology, 61,* 300.

Rosenfeld, J. P., Angell, A., Johnson, M., & Qian, J. (1991). An ERP-based, control-question lie detector analog: Algorithms for discriminating effects within individuals' average waveforms. *Psychophysiology, 38,* 319–335.

Rosenfeld, J. P., Cantwell, G., Nasman, V. T., Wojdac, V., Ivanov, S., & Mazzeri, L. (1988). A modified, event-related potential-based guilty knowledge test. *International Journal of Neuroscience, 24,* 157–161.

Rosenfeld, J. P., Ellwanger, J. W., Nolan, K., Wu, S., Bermann, R. G., & Sweet, J. J. (1999). P300 scalp amplitude distribution as an index of deception in a simulated cognitive deficit model. *International Journal of Psychophysiology, 33,* 3–19.

Rosenfeld, J. P., Soskins, M., Bosh, G., & Ryan, A. (2004). Simple effective countermeasures to P300-based tests of detection of concealed information. *Psychophysiology, 41,* 205–219.

Tardif, H. P., Barry, R. J., Fox, A. M., & Johnstone, S. J. (2000). Detection of feigned recognition memory impairment using the old/new effect of the event-related potential. *International Journal of Psychophysiology, 36,* 1–9.

DETECTION OF DECEPTION: MAGNETIC RESONANCE IMAGING (MRI)

Traditional means of lie detection, such as the polygraph, rely on measurements of peripheral nervous system (PNS) activity. Recent advances in noninvasive brain imaging techniques, such as functional magnetic resonance imaging (fMRI), have aroused public and academic interest in developing a viable alternative. This entry briefly explains the technique of MRI and its application in the detection of deception.

How MRI Works

An MRI scanner is a powerful superconducting electromagnet with a central bore large enough to accommodate a human body. This magnet generates a magnetic field perpendicular to the plane of the central bore. It is equipped with electromagnetic gradient coils that produce weaker, rapidly changing magnetic fields. These magnetic "pulses" cause the hydrogen nuclei in the body to resonate and emit radiofrequency signals used to create tomographic images with a spatial resolution of less than a millimeter that can be reconstructed into a three-dimensional image. Blood oxygenation level–dependent (BOLD) fMRI is an enhanced technology that measures regional changes in the levels of oxygenated hemoglobin and reflects regional brain activity with a time resolution of seconds. The small effect size of the BOLD fMRI signal associated with most cognitive phenomena (<2%) requires a scanner field strength of at least 1.5 T and multiple repetitions of each stimulus class to achieve a meaningful signal-to-noise ratio. Compared with psychophysiological recordings, fMRI measures of lie detection have theoretical advantages of proximity to the source of deception (central nervous system, CNS). Although fMRI is a less direct measure of CNS activity than electroencephalography, the significantly better spatial resolution of fMRI may lead to higher test specificity.

Use of MRI in Detecting Deception

Initial fMRI studies demonstrated prefrontal- and parietal-lobe differences between lies and truth on a multisubject average level. These data linked the classic Augustinian definition of lying ("To have a thought, and, by words or other means of expression, to convey another one") with the concept of deception as a cognitive process involving working memory and behavioral control and led to a moral conclusion that truth is the basic state of the human mind. Second-generation studies, using 3-T scanners and sophisticated logistic regression and machine-learning methods of data analysis, showed the feasibility of discriminating lies and truth in single subjects. These studies support the critical role of the inferior frontal and posterior parietal cortex in deception and estimate the potential accuracy of the approach to be 76% to 90%. An important conclusion of these studies is that lie and truth patterns are, at least partially, task specific. These findings paved the road for clinical trials of the technique and spurred an increasingly emotional debate on the ethical, legal, and procedural issues surrounding the future applications of this technology. Critics emphasize both insufficient data and potential privacy violations, the latter leading to the term *cognitive freedom* and a new discipline of "neuroethics." Proponents of fMRI advocate its noninvasive nature, the objectivity of fMRI data analysis, and the fact that fMRI requires a fully cooperative and conscious subject, making coercive use impossible. Potential forensic and medical applications of this technology differ in the degree of accuracy they would require, as well as in ethical and practical dimensions. For example, an fMRI test requested by a criminal defendant to create a "reasonable doubt" in a criminal trial may require a lower accuracy threshold than routine screening of thousands of suspects, most of whom are unlikely to be the perpetrator of an offense of interest. Diagnosing malingering is the most immediate potential medical application, but other applications, such as the differentiation of denial and deception during psychotherapy, are conceivable.

Further studies are necessary to determine the clinical utility of fMRI for forensic and medical lie detection. Myriad questions related to the effects of risk, medications, medical and psychiatric disorders, CMs, age, gender, and language remain to be answered. Performance of the technology in "real-life" situations needs to be examined in clinical trials. Furthermore, both experimental and applied lie detection should not be confused with attempts to use fMRI for "mind reading." Whereas lie detection is focused on the brief and singular act of deception, mind reading would capitalize on the patterns of brain activity in response to sensory probes. Such probes could invoke highly variable sequential and parallel cascades of memory retrieval and language preparation. Harnessing such probes to applied information gathering would pose a computational and validation hurdle far beyond those faced by fMRI-based lie detection. Finally, a controlled clinical comparison between the polygraph and fMRI characterization of deception is unavailable at the time of this writing. The development of a technology using both PNS and CNS measures, either simultaneously or sequentially, may have clinical utility. To avoid unreliable data and inappropriate application, it is imperative that the multidisciplinary research on the neurobiology of deception is funded, conducted, and published by peer-reviewed public and academic organizations that adhere to the standards of responsible research practices.

Although one cannot predict which combination of behavioral probe and brain-imaging technology will ultimately become the method of choice in applied lie-and-truth discrimination, the prevailing demand and scientific progress are likely to produce a clinical application of fMRI-based studies of deception in the near future.

Daniel D. Langleben and Melissa Y. De Jesus

See also Detection of Deception: Cognitive Load; Detection of Deception: Event-Related Potentials; Detection of Deception in Adults; Detection of Deception in High-Stakes Liars; Malingering; Polygraph and Polygraph Techniques; Psychotic Disorders

Further Readings

Langleben, D. D., Loughead, J. W., Bilker, W. B., Ruparel, K., Childress, A. R., Busch, S. I., et al. (2005). Telling truth from lie in individual subjects with fast event-related fMRI. *Human Brain Mapping, 26*(4), 262–272.

Spence, S. A., Hunter, M. D., Farrow, T. F., Green, R. D., Leung, D. H., Hughes, C. J., et al. (2004). A cognitive neurobiological account of deception: Evidence from functional neuroimaging. *Philosophical Transactions of the Royal Society of London. Series B, Biological Sciences, 359*(1451), 1755–1762.

Vrij, A. (2001). *Detecting lies and deceit: The psychology of lying and the implications for professional practice.* Chichester, UK: Wiley.

DETECTION OF DECEPTION: NONVERBAL CUES

Trying to find a tell-tale sign of deceit (a "Pinocchio's nose") in human nonverbal behavior has been the subject of much effort, and many suggestions have been put forward. In lay people's thinking and in police interrogation manuals alike, one can find numerous ideas about detecting deceit from nonverbal behaviors such as eye contact or gestures. The scientific research shows, however, that overall only a few nonverbal behaviors are associated with deception. Under certain conditions, such as time to prepare the lie, special motivation to convincingly tell a lie, and when the lie is about concealing a transgression, there seem to be some nonverbal behaviors that may distinguish liars from truth tellers.

Research on beliefs about deception shows that presumed experts (e.g., police officers) and lay people (e.g., college students) have very similar beliefs. They mostly indicate nonverbal signs of deception, especially a decrease in eye contact, when lying. Furthermore, presumed experts and lay people alike believe that an association exists between deception and an increase in body movements.

Scientific Study of Nonverbal Behaviors

To find out about potential nonverbal correlates of deception, psychologists and other researchers conduct experiments. They instruct some people to lie and/or tell the truth (the lies are most often "constructed" for the sake of the experiment) and videotape the telling of truths and lies in interviews or mock interrogations. (If the focus is on the speech-related variables, audiotapes are of course sufficient.) Then, these videotapes are closely analyzed, and the frequency and/or duration of a list of nonverbal behaviors are scored. The scored behaviors are then summarized for truths and lies separately, and if statistical comparisons show significant differences, researchers conclude that there are systematic nonverbal signs of deceit and truthfulness. A great number of such studies have been published. In this entry, findings from several meta-analyses and research overviews are summarized.

Included in the concept *nonverbal behavior* are body movements (e.g., gestures and leg movement), facial indicators (e.g., eye contact, smiling), and speech behaviors (sometimes called paraverbal behaviors; e.g., response latency and pitch of voice).

Theoretical Approaches

Why would the nonverbal behavior of a liar give him or her away? Scientists usually suggest three different processes (or approaches) that might answer that question. According to the *emotional approach* (sometimes called the affective approach), the three most common types of emotion associated with deception are guilt, fear, and excitement. A liar might feel guilty because he or she is lying, might be afraid of getting caught, or might be excited about the possibility of fooling someone ("duping delight").

According to the *cognitive complexity approach* (sometimes called *cognitive load* or *working memory model*), the lie should be possible to detect from the liars' nonverbal behavior because it is more difficult to lie than to tell the truth. The liars have to come up with believable answers, avoid contradicting themselves, and tell a lie consistent with what the interviewer knows or might find out. Additionally, they have to remember what they have said, in order to declare the same things again if asked to repeat their statement.

The *attempted control approach* emphasizes that liars may be concerned that their lies will be detected by, for example, nonverbal behaviors and will therefore try to suppress such behaviors. In other words, they will try to make a convincing impression by, for example, suppressing their nervousness and masking evidence of thinking hard. However, when controlling their body language, liars may overcontrol their behavior, therefore exhibiting body language that will appear planned, rehearsed, and lacking in spontaneity. For example, liars may believe that bodily movements will give their lies away and will consequently avoid any movements not strictly essential, resulting in rigidity.

All three processes may occur simultaneously. That is, liars could—at the same time—be nervous, have to think hard, and try to control themselves. Which of these processes is most prevalent depends on the situation. In high-stake lies, nervous responses are more likely to occur. In complicated lies, indicators of increased cognitive load are more likely to occur. Attempts to control behavior, voice, and speech may especially occur in motivated liars.

Before turning to the outcomes of reviews about nonverbal behavior, it should be emphasized that the approaches only suggest that the presence of signs of emotions, content complexity, and impression management may be indicative of deceit. None of these approaches claim that the occurrence of these signs necessarily indicates deception. Truth tellers might experience exactly the same processes. For example, innocent (truthful) suspects might very well be anxious if they worry about not being believed in a police interview. Because of that fear, they may show the same

nervous reactions as liars who are afraid of being caught. The lie catcher is then put in a difficult position: Should the nonverbal behaviors be interpreted as signs of guilt or of innocence? The behavior does not provide the answer. The false accusation of a truth teller on the basis of the emotional reactions displayed has been labeled the *Othello error*, after Shakespeare's play.

Nonverbal Behavior and Deception in General

The most notable result of research to date is that nonverbal behaviors generally do not correlate strongly with either deception or truthfulness; very few reliable nonverbal cues to deception have been found.

There is evidence that liars tend to speak in a *higher-pitched voice,* which might be the result of experienced arousal. However, differences in pitch between liars and truth tellers are usually small and detectable only with technical equipment. Furthermore, sometimes liars' *voices sound tenser* than truth tellers' voices, another result of arousal. S*peech errors* (e.g., word and/or sentence repetition, sentence incompletion, slips of the tongue) occur more often during deception, and *response latency* is longer before giving deceptive answers. There is also evidence of *message duration* being shorter for liars, who also tend to make *fewer illustrators* (hand and arm movements modifying what is said verbally). The decrease in movements might be the result of lie complexity or overcontrol of behavior. Moreover, compared with truth tellers, liars tend to sound vocally *less expressive, more passive,* and *more uncertain.* This might all be the result of overcontrol of behavior. Liars also sound *less involved* and come across as being *less cooperative* and tending to make *more negative statements.* This might be caused by a negative emotion felt by the liar.

Perhaps the most remarkable outcome of the literature reviews is the finding that several signs of nervousness, such as *gaze aversion* (*avoidance of eye contact*) and *fidgeting,* are generally unrelated to deception. One reason why nervous behaviors do not seem to be systematically related to deception is that truth tellers could be nervous as well. Another reason could be that in most deception studies, people are requested to lie or tell the truth for the sake of the experiment, and in such studies, liars might not be aroused enough to show cues of nervousness.

Summarizing the literature, there seem to be a greater number of reliable verbal cues to deception than nonverbal cues. This contradicts most police interrogation manuals, which typically emphasize nonverbal cues to deception, and contradicts presumed experts' and lay people's beliefs about what gives a liar away as well.

The results presented so far are at the most general level—across all available studies without taking into account differences in the experimental designs. There are, however, a few presumably moderating factors that have been studied often enough to allow for interesting conclusions; three of these are discussed below.

Transgressions

An important factor, and most relevant to the forensic context, is the distinction between lies that are about transgressions and those that are not. Lies about transgressions are told to hide and/or deny acts such as cheating, stealing, and committing other crimes, small and large. In other studies, participants, for example, pretended to experience another emotion that they did not in fact experience or lied about their opinions. The question is whether differences between liars' and truth tellers' nonverbal behavior emerge when they are interviewed about transgressions they have or have not committed.

The literature describing the lies that were not about transgressions shows only one behavior that separates the liars from the truth-tellers, and that is *fidgeting*. When participants were talking about their likes or dislikes, their opinions and emotions, or anything else that did not involve a bad behavior, they fidgeted more when lying than when telling the truth. The cues to lies about transgressions are more important in legal contexts. People lying about transgressions *look more nervous* than do truth tellers; they also *blink more* and have a *faster speech rate*. Additionally, they are more inhibited than truth tellers in the sense that they *move their feet and legs* less often.

Motivation

In many studies, the liars did not have any special motivation to tell a convincing lie. Many simply participated as part of a study, with no special rewards for succeeding or punishments for failing. It is of importance to separate those studies in which participants had some special motivation to do well and those in which they did not. The question is this: If people are motivated to get away with their lies, will that show up in the form of fewer cues to deception because they

are trying harder to tell a good lie or will their lies become more obvious as the stakes are raised?

Research has shown that when participants had no special incentives, there were no obvious nonverbal cues to deception. When people do not have that much invested in their lies, others will have a very hard time knowing when they are lying. However, when liars do care about getting away with their lies, then several behaviors may betray them. It is only when participants are motivated to do well that they speak in a *higher pitch* when lying than when telling the truth. Although liars also seem *tenser* than truth tellers regardless of motivation, the difference is pronounced for those who are highly motivated to get away with their lies. In the previous section, in which results were summarized for all studies, there were no differences whatsoever in how often liars looked at the other person and how often truth tellers did. But when participants are motivated to do well, then one stereotype about liars becomes a reality: They make *less eye contact* than truth tellers do. There was also some evidence, under high motivational conditions, that liars made *fewer foot and leg movements* than truth tellers.

Preparation

Sometimes suspects know beforehand that they are going to be interviewed, which gives them a chance to prepare their answers. Presumably, liars should manage to appear more like truth tellers when they can plan their answers in advance than when they cannot. The available research indicates that when having time to plan, liars have *shorter response latency* than truth tellers. When there is no time to prepare, the opposite pattern is found. There is also some evidence that liars show *shorter message duration* than truth tellers when they have time to prepare their responses.

Limitations and Conclusions

Although researchers have in some studies tried to raise the motivation of and the stakes for the lying participants, the question still remains how the results from laboratory-based studies reflect what may happen in real-life high-stakes situations such as police interviews.

In a few studies, the behavior of real-life suspects, interviewed about serious crimes such as murder, rape, and arson and facing long prison sentences if found guilty, has been examined. Results revealed that these suspects did not show the nervous behaviors typically believed to be associated with lying, such as gaze aversion and fidgeting. In fact, they exhibited an *increase in pauses*; a *decrease in eye blinks*; and (for male suspects) a *decrease in finger, hand, and arm movements*. This is more in line with the content complexity and attempted control approaches than with the emotional approach.

In summary, under certain conditions, there seem to be a few differences between truth tellers and liars in their nonverbal behavior. However, it is of great importance to realize that these differences, albeit significant in meta-analyses, are not large. Since the observed effect sizes are small, the *practical* value may be quite low. None of the behaviors discussed here can be used as a fail-safe decision rule. The available research thus indicates that there is no nonverbal indicator of deception that always works—there is no "Pinocchio's nose."

Leif A. Strömwall and Pär Anders Granhag

See also Detection of Deception: Reality Monitoring; Detection of Deception in Adults; Statement Validity Assessment (SVA)

Further Readings

DePaulo, B. M., Lindsay, J. J., Malone, B. E., Muhlenbruck, L., Charlton, K., & Cooper, H. (2003). Cues to deception. *Psychological Bulletin, 129,* 74–118.

Granhag, P. A., & Vrij, A. (2005). Deception detection. In N. Brewer & K. D. Williams (Eds.), *Psychology and law. An empirical perspective* (pp. 43–92). New York: Guilford Press.

Sporer, S. L., & Schwandt, B. (2006). Paraverbal indicators of deception: A meta-analytic synthesis. *Applied Cognitive Psychology, 20,* 421–446.

Vrij, A. (2000). *Detecting lies and deceit: The psychology of lying and the implications for professional practice.* Chichester, UK: Wiley.

Zuckerman, M., DePaulo, B. M., & Rosenthal, R. (1981). Verbal and nonverbal communication of deception. In L. Berkowitz (Ed.), *Advances in experimental social psychology* (Vol. 14, pp. 1–60). New York: Academic Press.

DETECTION OF DECEPTION: REALITY MONITORING

People sometimes try to determine whether they have actually experienced an event they have in mind, or whether this memory is based on imagination. The processes by which a person attributes a memory to an actual experience (external source) or imagination (internal source) is called reality monitoring (RM). Although the RM concept is not related to deception, scholars believe that the concept has this application and can be used as a lie detection tool. Much of the RM deception research is concerned with testing the assumption that RM assessments can be used to discriminate between liars and truth tellers.

The core of RM is that memories based on real experiences differ in quality from memories based on fiction. In their seminal work on memory characteristics, Marcia Johnson and Carol Raye argued that memories of real experiences are obtained through perceptual processes. They are therefore likely to contain *sensory information*: details of smell, taste, or touch, visual details, and details of sound; *contextual information*: spatial details (details about where the event took place and details about how objects and people were situated in relation to each other) and temporal details (details about the time order of events and the duration of events); and *affective information*: details about people's feelings throughout the event. These memories are usually clear, sharp, and vivid. In contrast, memories about imagined events are derived from an internal source and are therefore likely to contain *cognitive operations*, such as thoughts and reasonings ("I must have had my coat on as it was very cold that night"). They are usually vaguer and less concrete.

From 1990 onward, scholars have examined whether RM analyses can be used to discriminate between truths and lies. The assumption those scholars make is that truths are recollections of experienced events, whereas lies are recollections of imagined events. Obviously not all lies are descriptions of events that a person did not experience. Many lies are not about events but are about people's feelings, opinions, or attitudes. And even when people lie about events (about their actions and whereabouts), they can sometimes describe events that they actually have experienced. For example, a burglar who denies having committed a burglary last night can claim that he went to the gym instead. He then can describe an actual visit he had made to the gym (but on another occasion).

Researchers have examined whether deceptive statements that are based on events that the liar imagined differ in terms of RM criteria from truthful statements about experienced events. The typical procedure is that liars and truth tellers are interviewed, and these interviews are taped and transcribed.

RM experts check for the presence of RM criteria in these transcripts. To date, a standardized set of RM deception criteria has not been developed. Different researchers use different criteria and sometimes use different definitions for the same criterion.

Most researchers include the following criteria in their RM veracity assessment tool:

Clarity and vividness of the statement: This criterion is present if the report is clear, sharp, and vivid instead of dim and vague.

Perceptual information: This criterion refers to the presence of sensory information in a statement, such as sounds ("He really shouted at me"), smells ("It had a smell of rotten fish"), tastes ("The chips were very salty"), physical sensations ("It really hurt"), and visual details ("I saw the nurse entering the ward").

Spatial information: This criterion refers to information about locations ("It was in a park") or the spatial arrangement of people and/or objects ("The man was sitting to the left of his wife").

Temporal information: This criterion refers to information about when the event happened ("It was early in the morning") or explicitly describes a sequence of events ("When he heard all that noise, the visitor became nervous and left")

Cognitive operations: This criterion refers to descriptions of inferences made by the participant at the time of the event ("It appeared to me that she didn't know the layout of the building") or inferences/opinions made when describing the event ("She looked smart").

All criteria are thought to be more present in truthful than in deceptive accounts, except the cognitive operations criterion, which is thought to be present more in deceptive than in truthful accounts. Research has shown general support for these assumptions, although the support for some criteria, such as temporal and spatial details, is stronger than the support for other criteria, such as cognitive operations. Moreover, truths and lies can be detected above the level of chance with the RM tool, with average truth and lies accuracy scores being just below 70%.

There are restrictions in using an RM veracity assessment tool. For example, the tool cannot be used with young children. In some circumstances, children do not differentiate between fact and fantasy as clearly as adults do, for several reasons, including the fact that children have a richer imagination than adults. Children may therefore be better than adults at imagining

themselves performing acts. It is probably also difficult to use the RM tool when people talk about events that had happened a long time ago. Over time, cognitive operations may develop in memories of experienced events because they facilitate the remembering of events. Someone who drove fast in a foreign country may try to remember this by remembering the actual speed the speedometer indicated; alternatively, the person could remember this by logical reasoning and by deducing that he or she must have driven fast because he or she was driving on the motorway. Imagined memories, on the other hand, can become more vivid and concrete over time if people try to visualize what might have happened.

Aldert Vrij

See also Eyewitness Memory; False Memories; Repressed and Recovered Memories; Statement Validity Assessment (SVA)

Further Readings

DePaulo, B. M., Lindsay, J. L., Malone, B. E., Muhlenbruck, L., Charlton, K., & Cooper, H. (2003). Cues to deception. *Psychological Bulletin, 129,* 74–118.

Johnson, M. K., & Raye, C. L. (1981). Reality monitoring. *Psychological Review, 88,* 67–85.

Lindsay, D. S. (2002). Children's source monitoring. In H. L. Westcott, G. M. Davies, & R. H. C. Bull (Eds.), *Children's testimony: A handbook of psychological research and forensic practice* (pp. 83–98). Chichester, UK: Wiley.

Masip, J., Sporer, S., Garrido, E., & Herrero, C. (2005). The detection of deception with the reality monitoring approach: A review of the empirical evidence. *Psychology, Crime, & Law, 11,* 99–122.

Vrij, A. (2000). *Detecting lies and deceit: The psychology of lying and its implications for professional practice.* Chichester, UK: Wiley.

Detection of Deception: Use of Evidence in

The paradigmatic finding from research on deception detection is that people are poor at discriminating between liars and truth tellers. This entry shows, however, that deception detection performance can be significantly improved if the investigator is allowed to interview the suspect, is given background information about the case and the suspect, and knows how to strategically use this background information (evidence) when conducting the interview. This entry contains a description of the psychological basis for the so-called Strategic Use of Evidence (SUE) technique and also explains what it means to strategically use evidence during an interview.

The research conducted to date on the issue of strategic use of evidence to detect deception shares two important features. First, it is based on a mock-crime paradigm, where half the participants commit a mock crime and the other half commit a noncriminal act. Second, for each suspect there is some potentially incriminating information indicating his or her guilt, but this information does not preclude that the suspect is in fact innocent. The interviewers were different for different studies: experienced police officers, police trainees, and trained experimenters.

This line of research is primarily motivated by three facts. First, there is often some information (evidence) pointing to the guilt of the person who becomes a suspect in a criminal investigation. Second, the so-called interview and interrogation manuals have very little to offer in advising how to best use this potentially incriminating information when interviewing a suspect. Third, both archival and field experiments show that many investigators tend to use the potentially incriminating evidence in a nonstrategic manner.

The SUE technique rests on the *psychology of guilt and innocence*. It has been found that it is significantly more common among guilty than innocent suspects to bring a strategy to the interview room. Research further shows that with respect to the strategies used during an interview, guilty and innocent suspects differ markedly. Specifically, guilty suspects will—if given the opportunity—avoid mentioning possibly incriminating information during an interview and—if deprived of the avoidance alternative—deny that they hold incriminating knowledge. Both these findings fit neatly with what is known of some of the most basic forms of human behavior—namely, aversive conditioning. That is, research on aversive conditioning has found an *avoidance response* (so as to try to prevent confrontation with a threatening stimulus) and an *escape response* (so as to try to terminate a direct threat).

In sharp contrast, research on the behavior and cognition of innocent suspects shows that they do not tend to avoid and escape the potentially incriminating information. Instead, their main strategies seem to be "to keep the story real" and "to tell the truth like it happened." In short, they trust the truth to shine through. This is in accord with well-established cognitive biases such as the *belief in a just world* (i.e., people will get what they deserve and deserve what they get) and the *illusion of transparency* (one's inner feelings will manifest themselves on the outside).

The fact that guilty and innocent suspects employ different strategies can be very useful for the investigator who needs to assess the veracity of the statement offered by a particular suspect, if he or she knows how to use the existing evidence strategically. In essence, the investigator should first use the case file to identify pieces of potentially incriminating information, place extra weight on information that the suspect will not know for certain that the investigator possesses, and then prepare questions addressing the potentially incriminating information. In its most basic form, the SUE technique proposes that when conducting the actual interview, the investigator should encourage the suspect to give a free recall—without disclosing any of the potentially incriminating information to the suspect—and then ask questions, of which some address the potentially incriminating information, still without revealing what the investigator knows.

If the potentially incriminating information is used in a strategic manner, as suggested by the SUE-technique, then two predictions can be made: First, guilty suspects will deliver a statement that, on one or several occasions, contradicts what the interviewer knows. That is, it will be possible to identify statement-evidence inconsistencies. Second, innocent suspects can be expected to tell a story consistent with what the interviewer knows. That is, there will be a high degree of statement-evidence consistency. Importantly, both these predictions have received empirical support.

A training study using highly motivated police trainees showed that the ones who received training in how to use the evidence strategically during an interview achieved a significantly higher deception detection accuracy (85%) than did the ones who received no such training (56%). By interviewing in accordance with the SUE technique, the trained interviewers managed to both create and use a diagnostic cue to deception—namely, statement-evidence inconsistency. In addition, for trained interviewers it was found that innocent suspects experienced much less cognitive demand than guilty suspects (which is a positive finding), whereas for untrained interviewers it was found that innocent and guilty suspects did not differ in terms of cognitive demand (which is a negative finding).

In sum, if interviewers learn to strategically use potentially incriminating information, they will enhance their ability to detect deception and truth. In essence, the SUE technique works because it draws on the psychology of guilt and innocence and, particularly, the striking heterogeneity in guilty and innocent suspects' strategies. The SUE technique is not a confrontational interrogation technique; it instead belongs to the information-gathering techniques. However, the key factor is not the amount of information gathered as such but to draw on the differences in information that innocent suspects volunteer and guilty suspects avoid and escape from providing.

Pär Anders Granhag and Leif A. Strömwall

See also Detection of Deception: Cognitive Load; Detection of Deception in Adults; Interrogation of Suspects

Further Readings

Hartwig, M, Granhag, P. A., Strömwall, L. A., & Kronkvist, O. (2006). Strategic use of evidence during police interviews: When training to detect deception works. *Law and Human Behavior, 30,* 603–619.

Hartwig, M., Granhag, P. A., Strömwall, L. A., & Vrij, A. (2005). Detecting deception via strategic disclosure of evidence. *Law and Human Behavior, 29,* 469–484.

Kassin, S. M. (2005). On the psychology of confessions: Does innocence put innocent at risk? *The American Psychologist, 60,* 215–228.

DETECTION OF DECEPTION BY DETECTION "WIZARDS"

Wizards of deception detection are rare individuals who achieve scores of 80% or higher on at least two of three videotaped lie detection tests. Most people's accuracy on these tests is about 50%, as would be expected by chance alone. Of more than 15,000 people tested, only 47 have been so classified. Although these individuals are termed "wizards," their accuracy is not due to magic but to a particular kind of social-emotional cognition coupled with a strong motivation to discern the truthfulness of others.

Although the exact distribution of the ability to detect deception is not known, increasing evidence suggests that it is distributed mesokurtically (normally), like many psychological and physical variables. Among a hundred randomly selected people, most will be average in height. Only a very few will be exceptionally short or exceptionally tall. So, too, with lie detection. Most people are average in lie detection ability, but a very few (i.e., truth wizards) will be highly accurate.

Much of the research on lie detection has focused on identifying behaviors that differentiate between honest and deceptive behaviors. Implied but not stated in such research is the belief (or hope) that such behaviors can be used to detect automatically whether someone is lying or not. Certainly, there is evidence that some behaviors are more or less likely to occur in deception than in honesty. To date, however, no single behavior has been identified that always or usually occurs when someone is lying. Although some people have "tells"—behaviors they exhibit when they are lying, such tells vary from person to person, and not everyone has them. Another complication is that verbal and nonverbal behaviors related to deception do not occur in isolation. They are part of an expressive system that communicates a variety of information, such as emotions, thoughts, feelings, habits, social class, health, age, and many other aspects of individuality. The behaviors of liars and truth tellers must be evaluated in terms of their appropriateness for the individual, the situation, the statement being made, the relationship with the person discussing the veracity of the information, the stakes in the situation, and the rewards or punishments involved. Consistency among behaviors and the authenticity of any given behavior must also be evaluated. Thus, the task of detecting deception shares many characteristics with other judgments under uncertainty, including those involved in social cognition and social-emotional intelligence.

Most truth wizards are exceptionally sensitive to verbal and nonverbal clues to emotion and cognition. They notice facial expressions, including micro expressions, which most people do not. They are sensitive to nuances of language. They are aware of vocal clues—pitch, resonance, and respiration. They do not use just one of these cue domains but several of them. Average lie detectors attend to a more limited array of behaviors. Expert lie detectors are also more sensitive to baselines—whether the baseline is the person's usual behavior or the person's personality, social class, gender, or ethnicity. Wizards use these baselines to evaluate the behavioral clues they have perceived. On the other hand, no wizard uses all the available deception clues, and no single wizard is 100% accurate. Wizard accuracy, like that of most people, is affected by emotional disruption (e.g., someone looks like an ex-girlfriend) or lack of familiarity with a particular kind of lie.

A defining characteristic of almost all truth wizards is the motivation to know whether someone is lying or not, coupled with extensive experience in observing many kinds of people and obtaining feedback about their behavior. Most people are not highly motivated to know the truth. In fact, most people have a truthfulness bias, a tendency to call a higher percentage of people truthful than the base rate would suggest. But some people, including most wizards, because of their profession or because of events in their personal life, report a drive to know the truth. They do not show the cognitive laziness that most people exhibit when making social judgments.

Wizards range in age from 25 to 75, although most are middle aged. They include extroverts and introverts, liberals and conservatives, believers and atheists, heterosexuals and homosexuals, men and women, and people of many ethnic groups. Some are intellectuals with advanced degrees; others are high school graduates.

Truth wizards were identified after testing thousands of college students as well as professional groups with an interest in accurate lie detection. Among such unselected groups only one in a thousand qualified as a wizard. The discovery of several highly accurate groups (e.g., Secret Service agents, federal judges) suggested that focused testing of such professions would produce a much higher percentage of truth wizards. In such preselected targeted groups, the yield of wizards ranged from 5% to 20%.

The ability to predict the professional groups within which wizards are more likely to occur is one demonstration of the construct validity of the identification method used. Like all measurement methods, however, this method has limitations. Few expert lie detectors are equally good at detecting every kind of lie, even with the small sample of lie types used in the wizard research. In addition, there are many individuals who are good at lie detection in real life whose talent will not be assessed accurately by watching a videotape of someone else's interview. So a videotape-test method will be subject to false negatives. But

some people's ability (including that of truth wizards) can be measured accurately in this way. The construct validity of the procedure used is bolstered by the professional achievements of many of the wizards (some of them have been featured in books and TV shows for their lie detection abilities and "people sense") as well as the increasing efficiency in identifying the groups in which they are located.

Intense examination of the processes used by truth wizards in evaluating truthfulness has uncovered behavioral and attributional clues that have not yet been studied in other research on lie detection. The methods of person perception used in real life by truth wizards can be used to test the theories of interpersonal sensitivity and social cognition developed in the laboratory and to develop better methods for training lie detection professionals.

Maureen O'Sullivan

See also Detection of Deception: Cognitive Load; Detection of Deception: Nonverbal Cues; Detection of Deception in Adults; Detection of Deception in High-Stakes Liars; Statement Validity Assessment (SVA)

Further Readings

Ekman, P. (2001). *Telling lies* (3rd ed.). New York: Norton.

Ekman, P., O'Sullivan, M., & Frank, M. (1999). A few can catch a liar. *Psychological Science, 10*(3), 263–265.

O'Sullivan, M. (2003). The fundamental attribution error in detecting deceit: The boy-who-cried-wolf effect. *Personality and Social Psychology Bulletin, 29*(10), 1316–1327.

O'Sullivan, M. (2005). Emotional intelligence and detecting deception. Why most people can't "read" others, but a few can. In R. Riggio & R. Feldman (Eds.), *Applications of nonverbal communication* (pp. 215–253). Mahwah, NJ: Lawrence Erlbaum.

O'Sullivan, M. (2007). Unicorns or Tiger Woods? Are expert lie detectors myths or rarities? A response to: On lie detection "wizards" by Bond and Uysal. *Law and Human Behavior, 31,* 117–123.

DETECTION OF DECEPTION IN ADULTS

Deception is defined, for the purposes of this entry, as a successful or unsuccessful deliberate attempt to create in another a belief that the sender of the message considers to be untrue. Although it is hard to think of a context in which *no* deception transpires, the study of deception and how to detect it is especially crucial in the forensic setting. Most law enforcement professionals, who must assess veracity on a daily basis, know that deception is quite frequent in forensic contexts and that making mistakes when assessing veracity can have severe consequences—the innocent may be sentenced to punishment, the guilty may be freed to commit more crimes. To be able to correctly detect deception is therefore of utmost importance. Yet comprehensive study over the past 40 years has shown that the human ability to detect deception is just above the level of chance. The consistency of this finding is striking, although there are factors moderating the rate of correct judgments. For example, accuracy is somewhat higher when listening to rather than watching the liar, when one has access to baseline information about the liar's behavior, and when detecting unprepared rather than prepared messages.

How to Study Deception Detection

To gain insight into deception, psychologists and other researchers conduct experiments. They instruct some people either to lie or to tell the truth and instruct others to judge the veracity of the resulting statements. Those who lie or tell the truth in these experiments are referred to as *senders*, the truthful and deceptive statements as *messages,* and those who judge the messages as *receivers.* In this entry, the accuracy of these receivers is at focus, more specifically the accuracy of human judgments made without any specialized tools or aids in detecting deception on the basis of verbal content and the liar's behavior. The receivers are typically given videotaped or audiotaped statements, and ordinarily, half the messages a receiver encounters are truths and half are lies; hence, the chance level of correct judgments a receiver could expect is 50%. Lie detection ability is most often expressed as percent correct, but other indices of deception detection accuracy, such as standardized differences between truth and lie detection accuracy, are also calculated.

The standard lie detection experiment contains several factors that have been examined through experimental manipulation. For example, the senders of the message can be adults, adolescents, or children, or they can be persons with or without special skills at lying, such as experienced criminals. Furthermore, the content of the lies (and truths) have been varied: People have lied about their personal feelings, about their committing of transgressions such as adultery or sanctioned crimes, or in placing the blame on someone other than the culprit. Lie detection through different media has also been tested: Are people better lie detectors when having access to video or audio or written transcripts? In addition, characteristics of the receivers have been varied: Are certain groups of people, such as police officers, better lie detectors? These are only some of the factors that have been scientifically examined.

Overall Results

Overall accuracy of lie detection has been analyzed in several meta-analyses and reviews. The results are unanimous in terms of the mean percentage of accuracy: In the typical research setting, lies are discriminated from truths at levels that are only slightly better than would be attained by flipping a coin. The mean percentage of accuracy is just under 54. This effect is small, but since it is based on thousands of veracity judgments, it is significantly better than the level of chance. Typically, studies report an accuracy rate between 50% and 60%.

In calculating the just presented overall percentage of accuracy, some exclusion criteria have been applied. Studies in which training to detect deception is provided are not included, nor are studies on adults' ability to detect children's deception. Also excluded are studies on implicit lie detection and studies not in the English language.

Because deception judgments can have severe consequences whether or not they are correct, it is important to understand the factors that may bias the judgments in one direction or another. The research literature has evidenced a truth bias—receivers' tendency to make systematic mistakes in the direction of judging messages as truthful, with a mean percentage of around 56% (which is significantly greater than 50%). One consequence of this truth bias is that people on average correctly identify truthful messages (mean percent correct just above 61%) more often than they correctly identify deceptive messages (mean percent correct just below 48%).

Using percent correct as a measure of accuracy has been criticized, and other measures have been suggested. However, analyses of log-odds ratios or signal detection measures, among others, also indicate an overall accuracy rate of about 54%. The different deception detection measures are highly inter-correlated.

A deception detection accuracy (sometimes referred to as lie/truth discrimination) of 54% is the typical result over a variety of receiver samples, sender samples, deception media, types of lies, and contexts. Conceivably, there might be certain conditions under which judges will show different accuracy rates. To evaluate these possibilities, an inspection of various subsets of the research literature on deception judgments is needed. In the following section, a number of factors that may moderate deception detection accuracy are discussed.

Deception Medium

Lies and truths can be evaluated over different media. It is of interest to compare detection rates for lies that can be seen, heard, or read. For example, the video medium might encourage the use of a liar stereotype. Having access to verbal content only may give the receiver the chance to analyze the messages more thoroughly.

Results have shown that lie/truth discrimination accuracy is lower if judgments are made in the video-only medium (rather than audiovisual and audio-only, as well as written transcripts). Further results show that messages are perceived as most truthful if judged from audiovisual or audio presentations, followed by written transcripts and video presentations.

The medium in which deception is attempted thus affects its likelihood of detection—lies being more evident when they can be heard. Given that the stereotype of a liar is largely visual (eye contact, fidgeting, gestures), this stereotype is most strongly brought to mind by the video medium. Those senders who appear nervous, tormented, or distressed are then judged to be lying; but these expressions may be the result of factors other than deceit.

Preparation

Sometimes people have anticipated that they have to lie and are therefore prepared in their attempted deceit. On other occasions, the lie is told in response to an unanticipated need, and people are then unprepared for the task of lying. Being prepared or not should, in principle, affect the sender's believability. The available research suggests that receivers achieve higher deception detection accuracy when judging unprepared than prepared messages. It has been found

that it is easier to discriminate between unprepared lies and truths than between prepared lies and truths. Furthermore, prepared messages appear more truthful than messages that were unprepared.

However, differences in experimental design have been shown to lead to differences in accuracy rates. Studies in which the senders produced both prepared and unprepared messages yielded the result just described. Studies in which the preparation factor was examined by having messages from unprepared participants compared with those from prepared participants did not show any reliable difference in receivers' ability to detect deception and truth. Here, the unprepared messages were more often judged as truthful. Further research on this issue is certainly needed.

Baseline Familiarity

Common sense would predict that a receiver should more correctly pinpoint the lies of a sender he or she has some familiarity with ("baseline exposure"). If one has more knowledge of someone's behavior than one gets from just watching a few minutes on a videotape, one should be able to detect deviations from that behavior *if* telling a lie causes deviations in behavior.

Results indicate that baseline exposure does indeed improve lie/truth discrimination: Receivers achieve a higher accuracy when given a baseline exposure. However, one should be aware that senders who are familiar to the receiver are more likely to be judged as truthful. People seem unwilling to infer that someone familiar to them is lying.

Motivation

Sometimes deception studies are criticized because the research participants do not have any incentive to be believed, and this lack of motivation in the task could influence participants' believability. Deception research has, however, addressed this issue and investigated the effects of different levels of sender motivation. Furthermore, the influential deception scholar Bella DePaulo has hypothesized that senders are undermined by their efforts to get away with lying. According to her *motivational impairment hypothesis,* the truths and lies of highly motivated senders will be more easily discriminated than those of unmotivated senders. Experimental studies show that lies are easier to discriminate from truths if they are told by motivated rather than unmotivated senders, in accordance with the hypothesis.

However, this result has been found for within-study comparisons and has generally not been found when comparing between studies. Here, the reliable difference found is that motivated participants appear less truthful than those with no motivation to succeed. It matters little if a highly motivated speaker is lying or not; what matters is the fear of not being believed. Research further indicates that motivation in itself affects how the sender is perceived differently for different media: Motivation reduces senders' video and audiovisual appearance of truthfulness but has no effect on how truthful a sender *sounds*. Is seems as if motivation makes people resemble a visible stereotype of a liar. If so, motivational effects on credibility might be most apparent in video-based judgments.

In conclusion, the accumulated evidence suggests that people who are motivated to be believed appear deceptive, whether or not they are lying.

Interaction

In some studies, the deceptive and truthful senders are alone, talking to a camera. In other studies, an experimenter, blind to the veracity of the person in front, asks a standardized set of questions. Sometimes, the interaction partner is attempting to judge the veracity (such as in a mock police interview or interrogation); on other occasions, an observer may be making this judgment. The latter occurs, for example, when the interaction partner is the experimenter and the observer is the receiver assessing veracity on the basis of the videotaped interaction. In principle, social interaction might influence the receiver's veracity judgments and/or the receiver's success at detecting deception.

The literature produces clear evidence that receivers are inclined to judge their interaction partners as truthful much more often than observers do. The overall pattern in the literature further suggests that observers are better than interaction partners at discriminating lies from truths. It seems as if people do not want to believe that someone has just lied to them without their spotting it. Alternatively, the reluctance to attribute deception to interaction partners could be the result of not wanting to insinuate that the partner is a liar.

In summary, research suggests that lies told in social interactions are better detected by observers than interaction partners.

Expertise

Usually, those making veracity judgments in deception research are college students. They have no special training and may have no interest in or reason for succeeding in the task. Reasonably, people with more experience would be better at judging deceit, and to assess this possibility, researchers have also tested presumed deception detection experts. These are individuals whose occupations expose them to lies, and they include law enforcement personnel, judges, psychiatrists, job interviewers, and customs officials.

The results are clear-cut. The "experts" are not experts at lie detection—there is no reliable difference in deception detection accuracy compared with novices. The accumulated research further suggests that experts are more skeptical than nonexperts, meaning that they are less inclined to believe that people are truthful. Having been targets of deceit in their professional roles, these experts may have overcome the usual unwillingness to infer that certain people are liars. However, it should be noted that the experimental setting that the experts have been tested in may not make possible a fair representation of their expertise. For example, police officers very rarely assess veracity on the basis of one, short videotaped interview and without having access to evidence. Therefore, the conclusion that experts are not better than laypeople at detecting deception may be premature. Future research is needed to shed light on experts using their expertise in a more ecologically valid setting.

Beliefs About Deception

The most often stated reason for the low accuracy rates found in deception research is that there is a disparity between what actually is indicative of deception and what people *believe* to be indicative of deception. As hinted at earlier, there is a stereotypical belief concerning a liar's behavior. A belief is a feeling that something is true or real; it can be strong or weak, correct or incorrect. The beliefs that a person holds are often reflected in his or her behavioral dispositions; that is, beliefs guide action. Hence, if one wants to learn about deception detection, it is important to study people's beliefs about deception.

Two different methods have been used to investigate people's beliefs about cues to deception: surveys and laboratory-based studies. In the surveys, participants have typically been asked to work through a list of prespecified verbal and nonverbal behaviors and for each particular behavior (e.g., gaze aversion and head movements), rate the extent to which they believe that this behavior is indicative of deception. The second method is used in studies where participants first watch videotapes of deceptive and truth-telling senders and then judge these in terms of veracity. Most studies on beliefs about deception have employed college students as participants, but there is also research on experts' beliefs about deception (e.g., police officers, customs officers, prison guards, prosecutors, and judges).

The available research shows that the beliefs held by experts and lay people are very similar. In terms of nonverbal cues, the evidence suggests that both experts and lay people consider nervous behaviors to indicate deception. For example, both experts and lay people believe that eye contact decreases during lying, but research on objective cues to deception has shown that this particular cue is not a reliable predictor of deception. Furthermore, both experts and lay people have indicated a strong relationship between deceptive behavior and an increase in bodily movements, which is also incorrect. In terms of verbal indicators of deception, both experts and lay people believe that truthful messages are more detailed than deceptive ones, and to some extent, research on objective cues to deception supports this belief. Researchers have in addition studied cross-cultural beliefs about deception and found that people around the world believe that deception can be spotted in the eye behaviors of the sender, such as gaze aversion. As regards accuracy in cross-cultural deception judgments, the available research shows that, as expected, deception is even harder to detect when the sender and receiver are not from the same cultural or ethnic group.

In sum, research on beliefs about deception has shown that the beliefs are similar for experts and lay people and that these beliefs to a rather large extent are misconceptions about how liars actually behave.

Training to Detect Deception

In a number of published studies, researchers and scholars have tried to train people in detecting deceit. The training programs have differed markedly in content and duration, but information about the mismatch between beliefs about deception and actual indicators of deception seems commonplace. Often, feedback on the veracity judgments made has been provided as

well. In general, training has been shown to significantly increase the accuracy of lie detection—a small but detectable increase is most often found. However, even if an increase is found, it usually is from, say, 55% to 60%, which is still of limited practical value. Furthermore, the long-term effect(s) of training is not as yet known. Unfortunately, the one group of participants that has been the hardest to train to become better in the deception detection task is police officers.

Limitations and Future Challenges

When deception detection research has been criticized, it is often the type of lies studied that has come under attack. For example, most of the lies studied have not been about transgressions, so some critics have argued that the lies told are not high-stake lies; others argue that the social aspects of lying and lie detecting are too constrained in experimental settings; and legal scholars point out aspects of the forensic world that have not been examined in research contexts. Deception researchers have tried to answer the critics by, for example, studying murderers' and other criminals' lies in police interviews, lies that could harm children, and lies to lovers. Researchers have also begun to study naturalistic deceptive interactions, jurors' credibility judgments, and police officers' assessments of veracity after conducting the interviews themselves.

In experiments, the receivers come across one brief message and must judge the veracity of that message on the spot, with no time or opportunity to collect additional information. Outside the laboratory, however, additional information is important. When asked to describe their discovery of a lie, people rarely state that the discovery was prompted by behaviors displayed at the time of the attempted deception. Rather, they say that lie detection took days, weeks, or even months and involved physical evidence or third parties. In police interviews, for example, the evidence in the case may be used as a tool to detect deception. Future studies will be needed to examine the impact on lie detection of these and other forms of extra-behavioral information. At present, across hundreds of experiments, the typical rate of deception detection in adults remains just above the level of chance.

Pär Anders Granhag and Leif A. Strömwall

See also Detection of Deception: Nonverbal Cues; Detection of Deception: Reality Monitoring; Detection of

Deception: Use of Evidence in; Detection of Deception in Children; Statement Validity Assessment (SVA)

Further Readings

Bond, C. F., Jr., & DePaulo, B. M. (2006). Accuracy of deception judgments. *Personality and Social Psychology Review, 10,* 214–234.

DePaulo, B. M., Zuckerman, M., & Rosenthal, R. (1980). Humans as lie detectors. *Journal of Communication, 30,* 129–139.

Granhag, P. A., & Strömwall, L. A. (Eds.). (2004). *The detection of deception in forensic contexts.* Cambridge, UK: Cambridge University Press.

Granhag, P. A., & Vrij, A. (2005). Deception detection. In N. Brewer & K. D. Williams (Eds.), *Psychology and law. An empirical perspective* (pp. 43–92). New York: Guilford Press.

Kraut, R. (1980). Humans as lie detectors: Some second thoughts. *Journal of Communication, 30,* 209–216.

Vrij, A. (2000). *Detecting lies and deceit: The psychology of lying and the implications for professional practice.* Chichester, UK: Wiley.

DETECTION OF DECEPTION IN CHILDREN

The credibility and reliability of children's testimony are particularly important in instances where children are called on as primary witnesses in legal proceedings, such as sexual abuse or child custody cases. Although it is expected for children to provide truthful statements about given events, children may also give false reports in these situations for a variety of reasons, and research suggests that adults are relatively poor at detecting such lies. Consequently, despite younger children's difficulties in concealing their verbal and nonverbal deceptive behaviors effectively, these may not be easily detected by adults. Only with extensive training are adults able to differentiate the verbal statements of a lie or a truth teller at a rate above the chance level. Adults' ability to detect children's lies is affected by the developmental level of the child, with younger children having difficulties in maintaining the truthfulness of their statements during follow-up questioning. Although subtle differences are noted in children's nonverbal behavioral expressions when in a lie- or a truth-telling situation, these discrepancies are small

and hard to detect, even for professionals whose job it is to detect a liar. A credible assessment system to detect the lies of young children, especially in light of related factors such as coaching and truth induction, is needed. As more research is undertaken to detect children's deception, the complexity of the relationships between children's developmental age, adult biases, and cognitive control of one's verbal and nonverbal expressive behaviors will delineate a pathway in the direction of accurate detection of children's lies by professionals and laypersons alike.

Children's Deception

Considerable research has been done on children's unintentional false reports due to repeated or suggestive questioning, children's memory of events, and children's ability to distinguish fact from fantasy. Less attention, however, has been given to children's intentional and deliberate false reports—that is, reports that the individual knows are untrue yet are made with the deliberate purpose of deceiving others. Children may conceal or fabricate a report about an alleged event at the behest of an adult or because they are fearful of the effects their truthful testimony might have, such as upsetting or disappointing loved ones.

Generally, children lie for the same reasons as adults: to avoid punishment or negative consequences, for personal gain, to protect one's self-esteem, to conform to social conventions of politeness, or to spare another's feelings. Children's lie-telling behavior emerges in the preschool years, with lies to escape punishment among the first types of lies children tell. Nevertheless, young children's ability to deceive is not very good. Their first lies tend to be false denials or short verbal responses (e.g., "No, I didn't do it"). In the school-age years, children become better able to elaborate and maintain their lies over extended periods. Some evidence exists to suggest that children's lie-telling abilities are related to their increased cognitive understanding of others' mental states and their inhibitory control. Furthermore, as children become older, they may naturally lie for a range of motivations. Deciding to lie requires an analysis of the costs and benefits of telling the truth versus lying. School-age children will lie for another (e.g., a parent) when they perceive there are negative consequences for the other and low costs to their self-interest. In circumstances where the consequences of telling the truth might be very negative, children may be more inclined to lie as a tactical strategy in order to avoid those consequences. Moreover, some research suggests that when children are in hostile environments, where they perceive that there are similar negative outcomes whether they are caught in a lie or telling the truth, children are more likely to lie and to be convincing liars, even at a young age.

When telling a lie, it is important to be a convincing liar so as to avoid detection. Thus, it is important to control one's verbal and nonverbal expressive behaviors. Liars must ensure that what they say and how they present themselves do not contradict. If they are lying about some misdeed, they do not want to appear nervous or shifty so as to raise suspicions in their interrogator or others. Similarly, they will want to make sure that all their verbal statements made after their initial lie do not contradict or reveal information that may make others disbelieve their claims. Thus, lie tellers have to control both their verbal and their nonverbal expressive behaviors, lest they be detected by others. According to studies that examine the detection of children's false statements, adults make use of such verbal and nonverbal cues to discriminate between the truthful and deceptive statements of children. There are two measurement techniques used for detection of children's deception: Either adults are asked to detect lies by observing video clips of lie and truth tellers' reports and to provide judgments regarding the veracity of each report or the occurrences and frequencies of honest and dishonest behaviors are compared with the scores of lie and truth tellers.

Detecting Deception

Research on detecting children's truth- and lie-telling behaviors has been conducted in both laboratory and field studies. Laboratory studies have usually used one of two methodologies to detect deception. In the first, children are told to make a false report about an event. These reports are examined using one or both of the following measurement techniques: Trained coders observe the reports for behavioral markers, or video clips of the children's reports are shown to adults, who are asked to discriminate between the truth and lie tellers. This methodology allows examination of children's false reports about specifically designed events that may be analogous to legally relevant settings, such as children reporting about a medical examination. However, such reports may be unnatural due to children being instructed to lie or

"pretend," making the act of lying in these cases of very low perceived consequences and thereby unlike certain real-life situations. In the second commonly used laboratory-based methodology, naturalistic situations are created in which children can choose to lie spontaneously about an event, such as committing a transgression (e.g., peeking at a forbidden toy). Video clips of children's behaviors in these situations are used for detecting the truthfulness of their claims. In these naturalistic lie-telling situations, children may have greater motivation to lie due to the perceived increased risk of consequences of the situation (e.g., getting caught), and thus, they have greater ecological validity. However, current laboratory procedures tend to create situations where children produce only short verbal reports, and the situations created are not necessarily similar to the types of reports given in the legal system. Field study reports, another methodology, use children's actual reports of events (e.g., sexual abuse) to analyze statements for markers of deception. This methodology has the advantage of being realistic and having ecological validity because actual forensic reports are used. However, unlike the other methodologies where it is known for certain that the child is lying, it is impossible to know for certain which reports are fabricated and which are true.

Children's Nonverbal Deception Cues

Research has found that when children lie, they reveal subtle signs of their deception in their nonverbal expressive behavior when compared with truth tellers. For instance, in some cases, children will have bigger smiles. However, in other circumstances, lie tellers have been found to display more negative expressive behaviors than do truth tellers. Other behavioral markers of a liar include nonfacial cues such as hand and arm movements, leg and foot movements, and more pauses in speech. Depending on the situation, children may show different behavioral cues to their deception owing to feelings of guilt, fear, or excitement. While these behavioral cues are noted, there are no typical markers of deception across all situations, and any differences found between the nonverbal expressive behaviors of liars and truth tellers are subtle and only detected by trained coders looking for such differences.

Age differences in children's abilities to control their nonverbal expressive behaviors while in a potentially deceiving situation have been revealed from some studies using adult observers of these behaviors.

In particular, evidence is provided in the research literature to suggest that the lies of younger preschool and early-elementary-school children are easier to detect than those of older children or adults. As children become older, they have more muscular control and may be better able to control and suppress nonverbal behavioral cues to their deceit. In other types of studies, however, observers have been found to be at chance level at detecting even young children's deception. Studies where young children's deceit has been detected have tended to use methodologies where children were instructed to lie about an event. In studies where children lied spontaneously, adult observers were unable to detect even preschool children's deceit on the basis of their nonverbal expressive behavior. In addition, studies that have placed children in simulated courtroom settings have found that mock jurors were unable to discriminate between children's truthful and fabricated reports. In those studies, discriminating markers of children's deception compared with truth tellers may be masked by the nature of these anxiety-provoking situations. Both laypersons and professionals whose career is centered on detecting deception (e.g., the police, customs officers, social workers, judges) have been found to have difficulties distinguishing child truth tellers from lie tellers. Therefore, in general, children's deception in naturalistic lie-telling situations is not easily detected on the basis of their nonverbal behaviors.

Children's Verbal Deception Cues

By and large, research has found that adults may have more success in analyzing children's verbal cues than their nonverbal cues of deception to detect a liar. Studies that have examined children's spontaneous lies have found that below 8 years of age, children are not very skilled at maintaining their lies in their subsequent verbal statements. When asked follow-up questions, children tend to reveal information that implicates them in their deception. As a consequence, studies have found that adults can detect young children's lies based on children's inability to maintain their lies in their verbal statements. As children become older, in the later elementary school age years, their ability to maintain their lies over extended verbal interchanges and statements increases. As a result, older children's verbal deception is harder to detect than younger children's, and adults have difficulty distinguishing deceptive statements from truthful ones.

The ability to verbally deceive may be related to the increased cognitive load that is required to maintain a lie beyond the initial verbal statement. This requires assessing the knowledge of the lie recipient and strategically adapting one's message to be convincing while simultaneously remembering what one has previously said. Thus, it appears that with increased cognitive sophistication, older children are better at maintaining their lies by employing verbal-leakage control.

The most popular technique for measuring the veracity of children's verbal statements analyzes components of speech content for certain discriminating features. The Criteria-Based Content Analysis (CBCA) technique was designed to determine the credibility of child sexual abuse reports. CBCA is a systematic assessment technique using transcripts of children's reports. Coders indicate the presence or absence of 19 criteria assumed to be present in reports of actual events. The method is based on the Undeutsch hypothesis (formulated by the German psychologist Udo Undeutsch) that a statement derived from memory of an actual experience will differ in content and quality from a statement based on the imagination. Field research using CBCA assessment has found that children's truthful sexual abuse reports received higher scores than those believed to be fabricated. Laboratory studies using CBCA have also found differences between lie and truth tellers. For instance, truth tellers included more details in their reports than lie tellers. Despite only small differences being found, and differences in the criteria that discriminated between children's true and false reports, CBCA studies received higher accuracy rates at detecting true and fabricated reports than nonverbal studies. Although in general, accuracy rates vary for CBCA analysis, this method has been found to be the most successful in detecting children's fabricated reports, with most of the rates well above chance level.

There are several caveats of the CBCA technique, especially for use with young children's statements. First, it is not clear if the CBCA can accurately discriminate very young children's true and fabricated reports. Some criteria may not be included in very young children's fabricated reports owing to either cognitive complexity or their having less command of language, potentially making the reports of younger children difficult to classify. Furthermore, using the CBCA criteria, accounts of events familiar to the child are more likely to be considered as true statements than are accounts of events that are unfamiliar.

Therefore, truthful reports of unfamiliar events may not produce high CBCA scores when compared with accounts that are familiarized to children due to repeated experience or talking about the situation, regardless of whether or not the stated events actually occurred. Finally, this technique requires trained coders to detect differences in children's true and false reports. Studies that have trained laypersons to use CBCA have found mixed results with regard to improved lie detection accuracy. Accordingly, noted differences are not easily detected by laypersons, and use of the CBCA technique may require extensive training before accurate detection is achieved.

Other Factors

A number of other factors can either help or hinder the detection of children's deception, and as more research is conducted in the area, more factors may be revealed. Children's lies may be more sophisticated when an adult coaches the child to lie and helps prepare their false statements. Coaching may help children tell more convincing lies as well as maintain their lies over repeated questioning. Inconsistent statements that are revealed through the use of follow-up questions are less likely to be exposed when children are coached on what to say. Coaching is of particular importance in legal cases, because when children lie in court, the possibility exists that they may have been coached by an adult close to them to conceal or fabricate certain information. The handful of studies that have examined this issue have found that children who receive coaching to deceive are not easily detected. Even more, children below 7 years of age who have had coaching in preparing their lies are able to maintain consistency in their verbal deceptive reports.

Another factor that may help adults detect children's deception is interviewer instructions about the importance of telling the truth (sometimes referred to as "truth induction"). Research has found that asking children about their understanding of truth and lies, as well as having children promise to tell the truth before they are asked about a critical event, helps adults detect children's lies and truth with an accuracy that is above chance level. It may be that under these circumstances, adults are better able to detect children's nonverbal deception cues, which may be made more salient due to children's guilt, or contradictory emotions, after promising to tell the truth and then lying.

Adults' biases are another factor that may contribute to their perception of a given child as a liar and thus play a role in adults' overall accuracy of detection. For instance, boys are more likely to be perceived by adults as lie tellers than girls. Conversely, adults tend to have a truth bias, believing in general that children are truthful. In particular, women are more likely to perceive children as truthful than male adult detectors. Finally, some evidence suggests that those who have experience dealing with children in their daily lives (e.g., parents, educators, child care workers, etc.) are better at detecting children's lies than those who have comparatively little experience with children.

There has been no real examination of children's lying in high-stakes situations, where the consequences of being caught are serious, thus making them similar to real-life cases. Most studies have had no consequences at all for the child (i.e., when the child is instructed to lie). The most serious high-stakes situations in which children's lie-telling behavior has been examined have been in relation to denying a transgression that is relatively minor in real life, such as peeking at a forbidden toy or having the child or his or her parent break a toy after its being touched. It may be that in situations where the consequences are perceived as very grave to the child (e.g., being taken away from a close relative), the motivation to lie convincingly may be greater, thus making children's lies harder to detect.

Victoria Talwar and Mina Popliger

See also Children's Testimony; Detection of Deception: Nonverbal Cues; Detection of Deception in Adults; Detection of Deception in High-Stakes Liars; Statement Validity Assessment (SVA)

Further Readings

Akehurst, L., Bull, R., Vrij, A., & Kohnken, G. (2004). The effects of training professional groups of lay persons to use criteria-based content analysis to detect deception. *Applied Cognitive Psychology, 18,* 877–891.

Goodman, G. S., Myers, J. E. B., Qin, J., Quas, J. A., Castelli, P., Redlich, A. D., et al. (2006). Hearsay versus children's testimony: Effects of truthful and deceptive statements on jurors' decisions. *Law and Human Behavior, 30,* 363–401.

Granhag, P. A., & Stromwall, L. A. (Eds.). (2004). *The detection of deception in forensic contexts.* New York: Cambridge University Press.

Leach, A.-M., Talwar, V., Lee, K., Bala, N., & Lindsay, R. C. L. (2004). "Intuitive" lie detection of children's deception by law enforcement officials and university students. *Law and Human Behavior, 28,* 661–685.

Talwar, V., & Lee, K. (2002). Development of lying to conceal a transgression: Children's control of expressive behaviour during verbal deception. *International Journal of Behavioral Development, 26,* 436–444.

Talwar, V., Lee, K., Bala, N., & Lindsay, R. C. L. (2006). Adults' judgments of children's coached reports. *Law and Human Behavior, 30,* 561–570.

DETECTION OF DECEPTION IN HIGH-STAKES LIARS

High-stakes lies occur where there are large positive consequences of getting away with the lie or large negative consequences of getting caught. Because the outcome of the lie is of considerable concern to the liar, it follows that he or she will probably experience more guilt and/or detection anxiety than when telling low-stakes lies. In addition, the liar will probably try particularly hard in such situations to avoid getting caught. This increased effort will be cognitively demanding, and therefore liars probably experience more cognitive load when telling high-stakes lies than when telling low-stakes lies. Accordingly, scholars believe that detecting high-stakes lies should be easier than detecting low-stakes lies. Most lies told in daily life are of the low-stakes variety; these lies are easier to replicate and hence are most commonly researched in laboratory situations. Studies of high-stakes liars have revealed, however, that their behavior is similar to that of low-stakes liars insofar as it typically reveals signs of increased cognitive load and behavioral control. Observers can make use of such signs of increased cognitive load when attempting to detect these high-stakes lies.

For practical reasons, most deception detection research has focused on low-stakes lies; a participant will be asked to lie about a fairly trivial matter for the sake of the experiment. The stakes may be raised slightly, by informing the participant either that his or her behavior will be scrutinized for sincerity by an observer or that being a good liar is an important indicator of being successful in a future career (many careers require the ability to hide one's true feelings or intentions). Sometimes participants are motivated by the offer of a reward for a convincing performance.

Laboratory experiments, however, cannot ethically re-create a high-stakes lie scenario. It is true that the majority of lies told by most people are low-stakes, trivial, day-to-day lies. However, what of the suspects in police interviews, smugglers at airports, speech-delivering corrupt politicians, and adulterous spouses? Some have attempted to create examples of such lies by raising the stakes further in laboratory studies—for example, by giving participants the opportunity to "steal" U.S.$50 and allowing them to keep the money if they are able to convince experimenters. Moreover, some participants have faced an additional punishment if found to be lying—for example, sitting in a cramped, dark room listening to blasts of white noise. Studies such as these raise ethical concerns and yet still fail to compete with the stakes in many real-life situations.

Another way to examine the behavior of the high-stakes liar is to look at instances where people have been caught on video telling lies and truths in real life. Such field research is more difficult than laboratory studies in that in real life it can be difficult to establish the ground truth. Therefore, it is imperative that it be known for sure when the communicator is telling the truth and when he or she is lying. In some situations, researchers have looked at suspects in their video-taped police interviews; then, through reviewing case files containing solid evidence (forensic evidence, reliable witness statements, etc.), elements of suspect interviews were established where it was known that the suspects had told the truth or lied. Treated in this fashion, similar clips can be examined for behavioral information and shown to observers to see if they are able to detect such lies.

Deception research in general has demonstrated that behavioral differences between liars and truth tellers are subtle at best and often inconsistent. They are the result of conflicting mechanisms in the liar. The liar may experience emotional arousal, which makes him or her nervous, resulting in behaviors that are stereotypically associated with lying, such as increased fidgeting, gaze avoidance, and so on. Simultaneously, the liar might try to control his or her behavior to avoid displaying such stereotypical deceptive behavior, which would result in exhibiting fewer fidgety moves and maintaining eye gaze. Finally, because lying is often (though not always) more cognitively complex than truth telling, the liar might experience behaviors associated with increased cognitive load (e.g., decreased blinking and body movements and increased pauses in speech). Laboratory research has more or less consistently revealed that, despite people's stereotypes of lying behavior, liars are stiller than truth tellers and able to maintain eye gaze. This indicates that behavioral control and cognitive load may be more overpowering mechanisms than emotional arousal in the low-stakes liar. One would expect then that in a higher-stakes lying situation, emotions are likely to run higher. Although this might be the case, it would appear that the desire to appear credible (controlling behavior) and the cognitive load associated with telling a higher-stakes lie increase even more so, since research into the behavior of high-stakes liars such as suspects in police interviews reveals similar patterns in behavior to laboratory research subjects, with the addition of a decrease in blinking and an increase in speech pauses.

If high-stakes liars behave similarly as low-stakes liars (in that, on the whole, they display signs of increased cognitive load and increased control rather than nervousness), then could their lies be any easier to detect? As mentioned earlier, people expect certain behaviors of a liar, yet these behaviors often fail to be displayed. This is one reason why most people do not score above the level of chance when trying to detect people's lies in experiments. In contrast, in experiments where police officers were shown clips of real-life liars and truth tellers (suspects in police interviews) and asked to make veracity judgments, the overall accuracy was more than 65%. Why it is higher is unclear. It could be that the situation that observers were being asked to judge was more contextually relevant to them than, for example, watching students who have been asked to lie or tell the truth about trivial matters. It could be that observers were able to make use of the signs of increased cognitive load that the suspects did reveal (increased pauses in speech, bodily rigidity, etc.) or perhaps that they were able to pick up on something less tangible.

Samantha Mann and Aldert Vrij

Further Readings

DePaulo, B. M., Lindsay, J. L., Malone, B. E., Muhlenbruck, L., Charlton, K., & Cooper, H. (2003). Cues to deception. *Psychological Bulletin, 129,* 74–118.

Mann, S., Vrij, A., & Bull, R. (2002). Suspects, lies and videotape: An analysis of authentic high-stakes liars. *Law and Human Behavior, 26,* 365–376.

Mann, S., Vrij, A., & Bull, R. (2004). Detecting true lies: Police officers' ability to detect deceit. *Journal of Applied Psychology, 89,* 137–149.

DEVELOPING COMPREHENSIVE THEORIES OF EYEWITNESS IDENTIFICATION

See WITNESS MODEL

DIMINISHED CAPACITY

Diminished capacity refers to two distinct doctrines. The first, known as the *mens rea variant,* refers to the use of evidence of mental abnormality to negate a mens rea—a mental state such as intent, required by the definition of the crime charged (the mens rea variant). The second, known as the *partial responsibility variant,* refers to the use of mental abnormality evidence to establish some type of partial affirmative defense of excuse. Courts have used various other terms, such as *diminished responsibility*, to refer to one or both of these distinct doctrines, but the term used is unimportant. Confusion arises, however, when the two types of doctrine are not clearly distinguished. Neither entails the other, and distinct legal and policy concerns apply to each.

The Mens Rea Variant

Mental abnormality can negate mens rea, primarily in cases in which the disorder is quite severe and produces a cognitive mistake. For example, in *Clark v. Arizona* (2006), a recent case that reached the Supreme Court of the United States, the defendant claimed that he believed that the police officer he killed was really a space alien impersonating a police officer. If this was true, the defendant did not *intend* to kill a human being with the *knowledge* that the victim was a police officer. Historically, the legal objection to using mental abnormality to negate mens rea was that traditional doctrine required that mistakes had to be objectively reasonable and a mistake that mental abnormality produces is definitionally unreasonable. Thus, evidence of such mistakes was excluded, even though it is logically relevant to whether a requisite mens rea was in fact present.

The logic of the mens rea variant is impeccable. Crimes are defined by their elements, and the prosecution must prove all these elements beyond a reasonable doubt. If the prosecution is unable to prove an element, then the defendant should be acquitted of a crime requiring that element. The defendant using the mens rea variant of diminished capacity seeks simply to use evidence of mental abnormality to cast reasonable doubt on the presence of a mental state element that is part of the definition of the crime charged. Such use of mental abnormality evidence is not a full or a partial affirmative defense. It is functionally and doctrinally indistinguishable from the use of any other kind of evidence for the same purpose, and it thus does not warrant a special name as if it were a unique doctrine.

Justice or fairness seems to require permitting a criminal defendant to use relevant evidence to cast reasonable doubt on the prosecution's case when criminal punishment and stigma are at stake. Nonetheless, a criminal defendant's right to introduce relevant evidence may be denied for good reason, and the U.S. Supreme Court recently held that the Constitution does not require the admission of most kinds of mental abnormality evidence offered to negate mens rea, even if such evidence is logically relevant and probative. About half the American jurisdictions exclude mental abnormality evidence altogether when it is offered to negate mens rea, and the other half permit its introduction but typically place substantial restrictions on the use of the evidence.

Total Exclusion of Mental Abnormality Evidence

The most common justifications for exclusion of mental abnormality evidence to negate mens rea are that courts and legislatures confuse the mens rea claim with a partial or complete affirmative defense, that mental abnormality evidence is considered particularly unreliable in general or for this purpose, and that permitting the use of such evidence would compromise public safety. If mens rea negation is wrongly thought to be an affirmative defense, it may appear redundant with the defense of legal insanity or a court might believe that creating a new affirmative defense is the legislature's prerogative. If mens rea negation were an affirmative defense, these might be good reasons to reject the admission of mental abnormality

evidence, but these reasons are unpersuasive because they rest on a confused doctrinal foundation.

The unreliability rationale for exclusion is stronger in principle because courts are always free to reject unreliable evidence. The difficulty with this rationale is that mental abnormality evidence is routinely considered sufficiently reliable and probative to be admitted in a wide array of criminal and civil law contexts, including competence to stand trial, legal insanity, competence to contract, and others. Criminal defendants are afforded special protections in our adversary system because the defendant's liberty and reputation are threatened by the power of the State. For the same reason, there is also a powerful motivation to provide defendants special latitude to admit potentially exculpatory evidence, especially when evidence of the same type is admitted in other contexts where much less is at stake. It seems especially unfair to exclude evidence of mental abnormality, which is rarely, if ever, the defendant's fault, when most jurisdictions in some circumstances routinely admit evidence of voluntary intoxication to negate mens rea.

The public safety rationale is also sound in principle. If a mentally abnormal and dangerous defendant uses abnormality evidence successfully to negate all mens rea, outright acquittal and release of a dangerous agent will result. Virtually automatic involuntary civil commitment follows a successful affirmative defense of legal insanity, but the State has less effective means to preventively confine dangerous defendants acquitted outright.

The problem with the public safety rationale is practical rather than theoretical. Mental disorders may cause agents to have profoundly irrational reasons for action, but they seldom prevent people from forming intentions to act, from having the narrow types of knowledge required by legal mens rea, and the like. Moreover, the mens rea termed *negligence*—unreasonable failure to be aware of an unjustifiable risk that one has created—cannot be negated by mental abnormality because such failure is per se objectively unreasonable. Consequently, very few defendants with mental disorder will be able to gain outright acquittal by negating all mens rea or will even be able to reduce their conviction by negating some mens rea. Public safety would not be compromised by the mens rea variant.

The only possible exception to the observation that mental abnormality seldom negates mens rea is the mental state of premeditation required by many jurisdictions for conviction for intentional murder in the first degree. On occasion, a person with a disorder may kill on the spur of the moment, motivated by a command hallucination or a delusional belief. Such people are capable of premeditating, but the mental abnormality evidence simply tends to show that they did not premeditate in fact on this occasion. And even if premeditation is negated, the intent to kill is not.

Limited Admission of Mental Abnormality Evidence

If the rationale for the mens rea variant is accepted, as a logical matter, the evidence should be admitted to negate *any* mens rea that might have been negated in fact. Indeed, this is the Model Penal Code position. Nonetheless, virtually all jurisdictions that have permitted using mental abnormality evidence to negate mens rea have placed substantial limitations on doing so, largely because they incorrectly fear large numbers of outright acquittals that could result from following the pure logical relevance standard for admission. Limited admission is thus based on a policy compromise between considerations of fairness and public safety: A defendant is able to negate some but not all mens rea, which typically results in conviction for a lesser offense. The effect of mental abnormality on culpability is thus considered, albeit partially, *and* a potentially dangerous defendant does not go free entirely, albeit the sentence is abbreviated.

Partial Responsibility Variant

Some criminal defendants who acted with the mens rea required by the definition of the crime charged and who cannot succeed with the insanity defense nonetheless have mental abnormalities that substantially compromise their capacity for rationality. The logic of the partial responsibility variant flows from this observation. In general, the capacity for rationality, the capacity to grasp and be guided by reason, is the touchstone of moral and legal responsibility. Mental abnormality potentially compromises moral and legal responsibility because in some cases it renders the defendant so irrational that the defendant is not a responsible agent. The capacity for rationality is a continuum, however, and in principle, responsibility should also be a continuum, allowing for a partial defense. Nonetheless, no generic partial excuse for diminished rationality arising from mental abnormality

exists in any jurisdiction in the United States or in English law. Thus, for example, a mentally abnormal defendant who killed intentionally and with premeditation has no doctrinal tool to avoid conviction and punishment for the most culpable degree of crime—first degree murder—even if the killing was highly irrationally motivated as a result of substantial mental abnormality.

Courts are unwilling to create a generic excuse for many reasons, including the belief that they do not have the power to create new excuses, the fear that they will be inundated with potentially confusing or unjustified cases, and the fear that dangerous defendants might go free too quickly and endanger the public. Furthermore, courts believe that creating a genuine partial excuse is a "legislative act" that exceeds judicial prerogative. In a few jurisdictions, courts tried to develop a partial excuse in the guise of adopting the mens rea variant, but these attempts used extremely problematic mens rea concepts, were confusing, and have largely been abandoned. Legislatures appear unwilling to enact a generic partial excuse because, in general, legislatures are not responsive to claims that are to the advantage of wrongdoers and because legislators, too, fear the consequences for public safety.

Partial Responsibility Doctrines and Practices

Despite their reluctance to adopt a generic partial responsibility doctrine, courts and legislatures have adopted various doctrines or practices that are in fact forms of partial excuse. Most prominent are (a) the Model Penal Code's "extreme emotional disturbance" doctrine (Sec. 210.3.1(b)) and English "diminished responsibility," both of which reduce a conviction of murder to the lesser crime of manslaughter; (b) one interpretation of the common-law provocation/passion doctrine, which reduces an intentional killing from murder to voluntary manslaughter; and (c) the use of mental abnormality evidence as a mitigating factor at sentencing hearings.

The extreme emotional disturbance doctrine, promulgated by the Model Penal Code and adopted in a small minority of American states, reduces murder to manslaughter if the killing occurred when the defendant was in a state of extreme mental or emotional disturbance for which there was reasonable explanation or excuse. Mental abnormality evidence is admissible in most jurisdictions to establish that such disturbance existed. English diminished responsibility permits the reduction of the charge to manslaughter if the defendant killed in a state of substantially impaired mental responsibility arising from mental abnormality. Neither doctrine negates the lack of intent or conscious awareness of a very great risk of death that is required for the prosecution to prove murder. Both simply reduce the degree of conviction and, thus, punishment and stigma because mental abnormality diminishes culpability. These partial responsibility doctrines exist only within the law of homicide, but in principle, both operate and could be formally treated as generic affirmative defenses of partial excuse, because nothing in the language of either doctrine entails that it applies only to homicide.

Many jurisdictions in the United States and in English law also contain the provocation/passion doctrine, which reduces a murder to manslaughter if the defendant killed subjectively in the "heat of passion" in immediate response to a "legally adequate" or "objective" provocation—that is, a provoking event, such as finding one's spouse in the act of adultery, that would create an inflamed psychological state in a reasonable person. The defendant kills intentionally and is criminally responsible, but the provocation/passion doctrine reduces the degree of blame and punishment. The rationale supporting this mitigating doctrine is controversial, but one interpretation is that psychological states such as "heat of passion" diminish rationality and responsibility and the defendant is not fully at fault for being in such a diminished condition because the provocation was sufficient to put even a reasonable person in such a state. In this interpretation, the provocation/passion doctrine is a form of partial excuse related to but narrower than extreme emotional disturbance and diminished responsibility.

In jurisdictions that give judges unguided or guided sentencing discretion, mental abnormality is a factor traditionally used to argue for a reduced sentence. Many capital sentencing statutes explicitly mention mental abnormality as a mitigating condition, and some even use the language of the insanity defense or the extreme emotional disturbance doctrine as the mitigation standard. The partial excuse logic of such sentencing practices is conceded and is straightforward. A criminally responsible defendant whose behavior satisfied all the elements of the offense charged, including the mens rea, and who has no affirmative defense may nonetheless be less responsible because mental abnormality substantially impaired the defendant's rationality.

Stephen J. Morse

See also Criminal Responsibility, Defenses and Standards; Mens Rea and Actus Reus

Further Readings

American Law Institute. (1962). *Model Penal Code.* Philadelphia: Author.

Arenella, P. (1977). The diminished capacity and diminished responsibility defenses: Two children of a doomed marriage. *Columbia Law Review, 77,* 827–865.

Clark v. Arizona, 548 U.S. ____ 126 S. Ct. 2709 (2006).

Fingarette, H., & Hasse, A. F. (1979). *Mental disabilities and criminal responsibility.* Berkeley: University of California Press.

Horder, J. (1992). *Provocation and responsibility.* Oxford, UK: Clarendon Press.

Mackay, R. D. (1995). *Mental condition defenses in the criminal law.* Oxford, UK: Clarendon Press.

Morse, S. J. (1984). Undiminished confusion in diminished capacity. *Journal of Criminal Law and Criminology, 75,* 1–55.

Morse, S. J. (1993). Diminished capacity. In S. Shute, J. Gardner, & J. Horder (Eds.), *Action and value in criminal law* (pp. 239–278). Oxford, UK: Clarendon Press.

DIPLOMATES IN FORENSIC PSYCHOLOGY

Diplomates in forensic psychology are dually certified by the American Board of Forensic Psychology (ABFP) and its parent organization, the American Board of Professional Psychology (ABPP), as experts in applying the science and profession of psychology to U.S. law and the U.S. legal system.

The certification process consists of four distinct phases: initial application, written examination, practice sample review, and oral examination. The applicant must possess a doctoral degree in psychology from a program acceptable to the ABPP. A program is automatically deemed acceptable if accredited by the American Psychological Association (APA) or the Canadian Psychological Association or if listed by the Association of State and Provincial Psychology Boards (ASPPB). Acceptability is also presumed if the applicant holds the Certificate of Professional Qualification issued by the ASPPB or if the applicant is registered with the National Register of Health Service Providers in Psychology.

The applicant must have accumulated at least 1,000 hours of qualifying experience in forensic psychology over a minimum of 4 years of practice. An earned law degree may be substituted for 2 of these 4 years, and successful completion of a qualifying formal postdoctoral fellowship may be substituted for 3 of these 4 years, as long as the 1,000-hour experience requirement has been met. The applicant also must have received 100 hours of qualifying specialized training in forensic psychology. This training may consist of direct supervision by a qualified forensic professional, continuing education attendance, or relevant classroom activities at the graduate or postgraduate level.

The written examination consists of 200 multiple-choice questions that focus primarily on the following eight areas of forensic psychological research and practice: (1) ethics, guidelines, and professional issues; (2) law, precedents, court rules, and civil and criminal procedure; (3) testing and assessment, judgment and bias, and examination issues; (4) individual rights and liberties, civil competence; (5) juvenile, parenting, and family/matrimonial matters; (6) personal injury, civil damages, disability, and workers' compensation; (7) criminal competence; and (8) criminal responsibility. The ABFP provides the applicant with a periodically updated reading list that identifies key legal cases, books, and book chapters for each topic area.

The applicant who passes the written examination is admitted to formal candidacy and is invited to submit two practice samples of his or her forensic psychological work. These practice samples must represent two distinct and separate areas of forensic endeavor; for example, one acceptable practice sample could address mental state at the time of the offense, while the other could address trial competency; however, it would not be acceptable for one practice sample to address parenting capacity involving a relocation issue if the other addressed parenting capacity involving allegations of sexual abuse. To ensure a sufficiently current professional review, the forensic work forming the basis of each practice sample must have been generated no more than 2 years prior to the date on which the candidate's original application was accepted.

Typically, practice samples consist primarily of evaluative reports; however, with prior agreement of the ABFP, and for good cause, an alternative submission, solely authored by the candidate, may be substituted for one of the two practice samples. Examples of potentially acceptable alternative submissions include a forensic psychological book chapter, a forensic psychological article accepted for publication in a peer-reviewed journal, a forensic psychological test manual, or a forensic psychological treatment program or treatment protocol. Practice samples are reviewed by an appointed faculty of Diplomates in Forensic Psychology. The purpose of this review is to ensure that the candidate possesses a high level of professional competence and maturity, with the ability to articulate a coherent rationale for his or her work in forensic psychology.

The submission of two acceptable practice samples qualifies the candidate to proceed to the oral examination, which is designed to determine the quality of his or her practice and forensic knowledge in areas exemplified by the practice samples as well as to determine the candidate's understanding and application of ethical standards, in particular the current version of the APA's *Ethical Principles of Psychologists and Code of Conduct* and the *Specialty Guidelines for Forensic Psychologists*, promulgated in part by the American Psychology-Law Society. The oral examination lasts for approximately 3 hours, conducted by a panel of three diplomates in forensic psychology. Panelists are instructed to bear in mind that one implication of their recommendation to award certification is that they would also feel comfortable in referring the candidate to persons soliciting the expertise in question. The panel's recommendation is reviewed and voted on by the ABFP, after which the ABPP informs the candidate of the results.

Currently, there are approximately 240 diplomates in forensic psychology, serving in a wide variety of treatment, assessment, teaching, and research settings. All diplomates in forensic psychology are also designated as fellows of the American Academy of Forensic Psychology, a member organization that maintains an online directory and a Listserv on professional issues, operates a continuing education program in forensic psychology, and confers awards in recognition of outstanding professional contributions and promising graduate student research.

Eric York Drogin

See also Doctoral Programs in Psychology and Law; Ethical Guidelines and Principles; Expert Psychological Testimony; Postdoctoral Residencies in Forensic Psychology; Trial Consulting

Further Readings

Dattilio, F. M. (2002). Board certification in psychology: Is it really necessary? *Professional Psychology: Research and Practice, 33,* 54–57.

Dattilio, F. M., & Sadoff, R. L. (2003). *Mental health experts: Roles and qualifications.* Mechanicsburg, PA: Pennsylvania Bar Institute.

Dattilio, F. M., Sadoff, R. L., & Gutheil, T. G. (2003). Board certification in forensic psychiatry and psychology: Separating the chaff from the wheat. *Journal of Psychiatry and Law, 31,* 5–19.

Drogin, E. Y. (in press). Expert qualifications and credibility. In D. Faust & M. Ziskin (Eds.), *Coping with psychiatric and psychological testimony* (6th ed.). Los Angeles: Law & Psychology Press.

Parry, J. W., & Drogin, E. Y. (2007). *Mental disability law, evidence, and testimony: A comprehensive reference manual for lawyers, judges, and mental disability professionals.* Washington, DC: American Bar Association.

Disability and Workers' Compensation Claims, Assessment of

Disability insurance and workers' compensation both concern illness or injury in the context of work. These terms are sometimes (erroneously) used interchangeably, but in actuality they refer to very different concepts. Disability insurance provides benefits to an eligible claimant whose ability to work is compromised by injury or illness. The cause of the injury or illness need not be related directly or indirectly to the work setting. In contrast, workers' compensation is designed to provide financial relief to an employee who is injured or becomes ill as a direct result of work-related factors. Thus, the key issue in disability evaluations is functional capacity, while the key issue in workers' compensation evaluations is causality.

When assessing disability or workers' compensation claimants, it is critical for the evaluator to use a variety of data sources. Psychological and/or neuropsychological tests are usually considered an integral component of the evaluation, and test selection should be determined by the specific referral questions and the nature of the claimed impairment. Owing to the possibility of secondary gain on the part of the claimant, all disability and workers' compensation evaluations should include an assessment of symptom validity to rule out exaggeration or other forms of dissimulation. Conclusions expressed by the evaluator should focus on the specific referral questions, and statements regarding ultimate issue determinations should be avoided.

Disability Claims

Disability, used in the context of disability claims, is a legal rather than a psychological or medical term. Its definition is determined by the terms of the policy, contract, or entitlement program under which the claimant has applied for benefits. Sources of disability benefits include private disability insurance policies, public and private sector employee benefits, and federal entitlement programs (Social Security Disability). Each of these sources of benefits is subject to different federal, state, and local laws. For example, Social Security Disability and private sector employee benefits are regulated by federal law (the Social Security Act and the Employee Retirement Income Security Act of 1974, ERISA). Private disability policies are usually governed by the laws of the state in which the policyholder resides. State and local government employee benefits are exempt from ERISA regulation and are defined by state statutes, local ordinances, and (when applicable) collective-bargaining agreements.

Although policies and entitlement programs vary, there are some concepts common among all disability sources. Disability refers to functional capacity, not diagnosis. To be eligible for benefits, the claimant must meet the specific definition of disability determined by the policy or program under which benefits are sought. Regardless of the source, most definitions of disability include two prongs: (1) The claimant must have sustained an injury or illness that (2) renders him or her unable to perform the substantial and material duties of his or her occupation (or, in some cases, to be able to perform any work at all). Thus, a valid disability claim requires both the substantiation of the presence of a condition as well as proof that this condition creates impairment in the claimant's functional abilities to perform his or her occupation. It also must be established that the absence from work is, in fact, due to the illness or injury and not to circumstantial factors (e.g., being laid off) or choice (e.g., job dissatisfaction, the desire to relocate).

When a policyholder files a claim for disability benefits, the insurance company initiates an evaluation of the claim to determine if the policyholder is entitled to benefits. Mental health claims are particularly difficult to adjudicate as they are based on subjective symptoms. During the course of the claim investigation, psychologists and psychiatrists are often called on to perform independent medical examinations (IMEs) to assist the insurance company in assessing the objective basis of the claim. If the claim is denied or terminated, the claimant may request an appeal of the decision by the company. If this decision is unfavorable to the claimant, the claimant may initiate legal proceedings against the company.

In the assessment of disability claims, the key issue is functionality; specifically, has the claimant's ability to function in his or her occupation been impaired? Thus, in the IME, three questions must be addressed: (1) Does the claimant have a psychiatric condition? (2) Are there functional impairments related to this condition? (3) Do these functional impairments affect work capacity?

It is important that the concepts of diagnosis, symptoms, and functional capacity not be confused. Diagnosis refers to the presence of a specific psychiatric condition (e.g., bipolar disorder, panic disorder with agoraphobia). Symptoms refer to the subjective experience of the condition (e.g., loss of interest, anxiety). Functional capacity, however, refers to the ability to perform specific tasks or activities—for example, interacting appropriately with the public, remembering pertinent information, adding a column of numbers.

It is the loss of functional capacity that is critical in the evaluation of a disability claim. Thus, it is necessary for the evaluator to draw logical connections between diagnosis, symptoms, and functional impairment, for example, establishing how depression—manifested by symptoms such as insomnia, diminished concentration, and feelings of fatigue—leads to a reduced capacity to stay alert and focused over the course of an 8-hour workday, compromising the claimant's ability to do his or her job.

Workers' Compensation Claims

Workers' compensation is essentially a no-fault system of compensating employees for losses due to accidental injury or illness sustained in the course of employment. Whether the injury is due to the employer's negligence or the employee's, the compensation is the same. This reduces the need for protracted litigation, allowing employers to contain costs

and employees to obtain the needed benefits in a timely manner. The benefits provided by workers' compensation include both lost wages and medical care to treat the injury or illness.

The laws governing workers' compensation differ in each state. In all states, employees are compensated for physical injuries, such as a knee injury caused by lifting a heavy piece of equipment. Employees in most states are also compensated for physical injuries originating out of mental stimuli (e.g., ulcers attributed to job stress) and mental injuries that accompany a physical injury (e.g., posttraumatic stress disorder following the loss of an eye). In only a few states are employees compensated for purely mental injuries, such as panic attacks resulting from a stressful work environment.

Unlike disability, in workers' compensation, the key issue is causality. To be compensable, the claimant's injury or illness must be the result of his or her employment. From the standpoint of assessment, this requires both establishing the existence of an illness or injury and ruling out non-work-related causes of the employee's difficulties. In the workers' compensation system, independent evaluations are referred to as qualified medical examinations (QMEs). The questions the QME is typically asked to address include the following:

1. Did work cause or contribute to the illness or injury?

2. Are there preexisting conditions contributing to the disability?

3. Is there a need for current or future medical care?

4. Is the condition stable and not likely to improve?

5. Is there permanent impairment?

6. Can the claimant return to his or her regular job?

Evaluation of Disability and Workers' Compensation Claims

Given the subjective nature of psychological conditions, it is critical for the evaluator, when assessing disability or workers' compensation claimants, to use a variety of data sources in forming opinions. These sources may include (a) a review of relevant medical, psychological, educational, and occupational records; (b) collateral information obtained directly from third parties, such as treating providers, family members, or coworkers; (c) information obtained from the claimant during the clinical interview; (d) information obtained during the claim investigation; and (e) psychological and/or neuropsychological test data. It is important that the evaluator not rely solely on the claimant's self-report but view it as one, among many, of the sources of evaluation data.

Psychological and/or neuropsychological tests are usually considered an integral component of a disability or workers' compensation evaluation. Test selection should be determined by the specific referral questions and the nature of the claimed impairment. Although most disability and/or workers' compensation disputes are resolved without litigation, as with any forensic evaluation admissibility issues should be a consideration in test selection. Depending on the jurisdiction, *Frye* (general acceptance) or *Daubert* (testable, peer-reviewed, known error rate, and general acceptance) standards should be taken into account. Therefore, the best practice is to use tests that are standardized, objective, valid, and reliable.

Evaluators are typically asked to rule in or rule out symptom exaggeration or malingering, as claims for disability and workers' compensation benefits present the possibility of secondary gain in terms of financial remuneration and/or avoidance of work. Although base rates are difficult to establish, it has been estimated that malingering occurs in 7.5% to 33% of all disability claims. Methods for assessing symptom validity include using multiple sources of data, analyzing patterns of psychological and neuropsychological test performance, employing the validity scales included in standardized psychological tests (e.g., the F scale on the Minnesota Multiphasic Personality Inventory–2 [MMPI–2]), administering specifically designed measures of symptom validity (e.g., the Test of Memory Malingering, Validity Indicator Profile), and using structured interviews (e.g., Structured Inventory of Reported Symptoms, Miller Forensic Assessment of Symptoms Test). The use of multiple methods is preferable.

It is important to fully respond to the referral questions and not add information that is unrelated to or goes beyond the scope of these questions. Ultimate issue decisions—such as whether the claimant meets the policy definition of disability or has a compensable workers' compensation claim—should not to be made by the evaluator. The evaluator's role is to provide the referral source with information related to the functional capacity of the claimant or the causality of the claimant's condition. Conclusive statements such as "The claimant is disabled" or "This is a compensable claim" should be avoided in favor of statements such as "The claimant's inability to follow multistep directions would significantly limit her ability to perform complex surgical procedures" or "The claimant's acute distress disorder was likely precipitated by the armed robbery that occurred in the workplace."

At the conclusion of the evaluation, a written report should be provided to the referral source. This report should be well organized with data sources clearly identified. It is helpful to have separate sections summarizing the materials reviewed, the self-reported history provided by the claimant, information obtained from collateral sources, behavioral observations, psychological test data, and any other data used by the evaluator. This should be followed by a discussion of the evaluator's impressions and interpretation of the data. Inconsistencies and gaps in the data should be noted. Finally, the evaluator should explicitly respond to each referral question.

It is important to keep in mind that the consumers of the IME or QME report are insurance company personnel and attorneys, not mental health professionals. Professional jargon, acronyms, and undefined scientific or medical terms should be avoided. Clear, concise language should be used, so that the report is useful to the reader and not subject to misinterpretation.

Lisa D. Piechowski

See also Detection of Deception in Adults; Expert Psychological Testimony, Admissibility Standards; Forensic Assessment; Malingering

Further Readings

Hadjistavropoulos, T., & Bieling, P. (2001). File review consultation in the adjudication of mental health and chronic pain disability claims. *Consulting Psychology Journal: Practice and Research, 53*(1), 52–63.

Piechowski, L. D. (2006). Forensic consultation in disability insurance matters. *Journal of Psychiatry & Law, 34*(2), 151–167.

Samuel, R., & Mittenberg, W. (2005). Determination of malingering in disability evaluations. *Primary Psychiatry, 12*(12), 60–68.

Vore, D. A. (2007). The disability psychological independent medical evaluation: Case law, ethical issues, and procedures. In A. M. Goldstein (Ed.), *Forensic psychology: Emerging topics and expanding roles* (pp. 489–510). Hoboken, NJ: Wiley.

DISPARATE TREATMENT AND DISPARATE IMPACT EVALUATIONS

Disparate treatment and disparate impact cases involve actions on the part of an employer that a plaintiff worker claims are based on the worker's race, gender, color, national origin, religion, disability, or age. Determining damages in these cases should follow the same practices as those used in tort, sexual harassment, or ADA (Americans with Disabilities Act, 1990) cases, with special focus on the employee's work history.

In civil rights cases, forensic psychologists' concern is most often focused on emotional damages in lawsuits brought in relation to claims of sexual harassment or work environments made hostile by racial prejudice or sexual bias. This entry, however, focuses on how forensic psychologists may function in cases involving an employer's work policies that affect individuals of a particular class. That is, these are cases involving the psychological impact of decisions that employers make about hiring or firing employees or setting the conditions, terms, compensation, or privileges that employees enjoy. For these decisions to trigger a lawsuit, they must have differential effects on individuals of distinct protected classes. The policy or decision must place one group at a relative advantage or disadvantage as compared with the other groups. This entry first provides a context for understanding how and why these issues may be brought to court. Next, it considers *disparate treatment* and *disparate impact* as patterns of employer activities. The entry concludes with a discussion of evaluation issues for forensic psychologists in these cases.

Historical and Legal Context

Dating back to the Reconstruction period immediately following the Civil War, the Fourteenth Amendment to the U.S. Constitution provided for *due process* and equal protection under the law for all individuals. Although this amendment was intended to provide civil rights protection to African Americans, a series of subsequent Supreme Court decisions prevented this amendment from providing substantive change in civil rights protection for people of color.

It was not until the passage of the Civil Rights Act of 1964 that race and color, along with national origin, sex, and religion, became truly protected classes. Although

other sections of the act provide for civil rights protection in arenas such as voting and public accommodations, Title VII applies to employment and forbids employers having more than 15 employees from discriminating on the basis of race, color, national origin, religion, or sex. The relevant portion of the act reads as follows:

> Sec. 2000e-2. Unlawful employment practices
>   (a) Employer practices
>   It shall be an unlawful employment practice for an employer–
>   (1) to fail or refuse to hire or to discharge any individual, or otherwise to discriminate against any individual with respect to his compensation, terms, conditions, or privileges of employment, because of such individual's race, color, religion, sex, or national origin; or,
>   (2) to limit, segregate, or classify his employees or applicants for employment in any way which would deprive or tend to deprive any individual of employment opportunities or otherwise adversely affect his status as an employee, because of such individual's race, color, religion, sex, or national origin.

Title VII prohibits retaliation against an employee for engaging in protected conduct, such as filing a complaint with the Equal Employment Opportunities Commission or a lawsuit. It also provides for protection against discrimination. This protection is best conceptualized as a conjunction between two things: (1) membership of the plaintiff in a protected class, as indicated by that person's race, color, sex, national origin, or religion, and (2) actions of the employer to hire, fire, or alter the conditions, terms, compensation, or privileges of the worker's employment. That is, discrimination occurs when the employer does something to a worker because the employee is, for example, a woman, an African American, a Sikh, or of Mauritanian ethnicity.

Other federal laws, including the Age Discrimination in Employment Act of 1967 (ADEA) (8 U.S.C. § 1324) and the ADA (42 U.S.C. § 12101) include similar provisions. These laws provide protection against discrimination based on age and disability, respectively.

Disparate Treatment

An employer may make decisions that directly disadvantage individuals from a particular protected class.

This is intentional discrimination based on the employer's belief, perhaps based on prejudice, that one group of workers will not perform well in a particular job. For example, for many years, employers would not consider women for many hazardous or physically arduous tasks, such as firefighting, police work, or working as roustabouts on oil rigs. People of color were not considered by some employers to embody the "front-office look," which would allow them to work as receptionists or in public relations jobs. In these settings, employees possessing particular characteristics were not hired or promoted into particular jobs.

In disparate treatment cases, the plaintiff must establish two elements: (1) that the employee has suffered adverse action by the employer in the form of being fired, not being hired, or not being promoted and (2) a similarly situated employee not in that class was treated more favorably. An alternative legal theory may be proven by evidence indicating employer conduct revealing bias against employees of a particular class. For example, if an employer used a derogatory epithet in relation to employees of a particular race, a presumption of disparate treatment may be made.

However, employers have an opportunity to prove that the employment actions were decided on a legitimate, nondiscriminatory basis. That is, there may be a valid reason for individuals of a particular class to be excluded from a job. For example, religious organizations may exclude individuals not of that faith from a particular job. People of one gender may not be chosen for a specific job, such as bathroom attendant or undergarment fitter.

In situations in which the employer is claiming that there is a legitimate reason for excluding a particular group of employees from a job, the employee filing suit must prove that the supposed legitimate basis offered by the employer is in fact a *pretext* for discrimination. That is, although the employer claims a real-life justification for excluding employees from a position, the real reason is that the excluded employees are, for example, male, Jewish, or Korean.

Disparate Impact

In other situations, employers may not clearly intend to discriminate against a class of employees. Employees may be placed at a disadvantage because of an employer policy that, on the face of it, should have no differential effect on individuals in particular groups. For example, an employer may have a minimum height requirement for employees working in an auto parts depot. Although this requirement would be considered *facially neutral*, it would eliminate more women than men from consideration for the job because women are typically shorter than men. In another example, a position may require individuals to work on Friday nights. Again, although this job requirement may appear to be fair, it would disadvantage observant Jews and would constitute discrimination on the basis of religion. Disparate impact claims have been brought in cases in which written tests, such as the Minnesota Multiphasic Personality Inventory–2 (MMPI–2), or subjective interviews were used as a basis for employee selection.

Employers may defend these cases by claiming "business necessity." That is, the employer may claim that the practice is "job-related for the position in question and consistent with business necessity" (42 U.S.C. § 2000e-2(k)(1)(A)(i)). Courts have been friendly to these defenses, especially in cases involving the ADEA, because in age discrimination cases, salary level often correlates highly with the age of employees.

Psychological Consultation

In cases of disparate treatment or disparate impact, the effects of job actions resulting from the alleged discrimination are the focus of the forensic psychologist's attention. For example, if an employee is fired from a job because of disparate treatment, the psychologist would focus on the emotional impact of forcible unemployment. Research indicates that being fired may have an impact beyond the economic implications. One's job is often considered the same as one's identity, and a fired worker may feel as though not only a source of income has been lost but also a source of self-esteem. In losing the job, the employee may suffer the loss of a social network, which may have been based on relationships with coworkers. Work provides structure for time, and the loss of that structure may leave a worker with little to do with his or her day. Unemployment brings with it a host of changes on the home front, sometimes necessitating the spouse to go to work, or changes in the family dynamics because of the loss of one parent's bread-winning role. Similar changes may be expected in situations involving failure to promote or failure to hire.

In all these cases, the psychologist may employ evaluation techniques commonly used in evaluations of individuals who have suffered other losses. A review of the plaintiff's vocational history is particularly important, along with an assessment of the place of the job in the person's life. Collateral interviews are especially important in these evaluations because family members and friends may provide information concerning changes in self-esteem and lifestyle that may not be obvious to the plaintiff.

William E. Foote

See also Americans with Disabilities Act (ADA); Forensic Assessment; Personal Injury and Emotional Distress; Sexual Harassment

Further Readings

Civil Rights Act of 1964, Title VII, 42 U.S.C. § 2000e-2. Retrieved June 18, 2007, from http://www.eeoc.gov/policy/vii.html

Foote, W. E. (2003). Forensic evaluation in Americans with Disabilities Act cases. In I. B. Weiner (Series Ed.) & A. D. Goldstein (Vol. Ed.), *Handbook of Psychology: Vol. 11. Forensic Psychology* (pp. 279–300). New York: Wiley.

Foote, W. E., & Goodman-Delahunty, J. (2005). *Evaluating sexual harassment: Psychological, social, and legal considerations in forensic examinations*. Washington, DC: American Psychological Association Press.

Parry, J. W. (1996). *Regulation, litigation and dispute resolution under the Americans with Disabilities Act: A practitioner's guide to implementation*. Washington, DC: American Bar Association Commission on Mental and Physical Disability Law.

DISSOCIATIVE IDENTITY DISORDER

Dissociative identity disorder (DID), formerly known as multiple-personality disorder, is one of the more controversial diagnoses in the *Diagnostic and Statistical Manual of Mental Disorders* (fourth edition; *DSM-IV*), with there being considerable disagreement over the validity and etiology of the disorder. Amnesia between identities is central to a diagnosis of DID. While explicit memory tests often result in amnesic responding in DID patients, more objective memory tests often fail to corroborate self-reports of amnesia between identities. Two perspectives dominate the debate on the cause of DID, with the traditional view proposing that DID manifests as a mechanism for coping with childhood trauma and

an alternative sociocognitive perspective suggesting that DID is a response to social demands, with an iatrogenic etiology. The rise in prevalence rates of DID has led to the increased importance of this diagnosis in the court of law. Given the controversy surrounding the validity of the disorder, care should be taken when considering subjective claims of amnesia, as these self-reports are not guaranteed to be substantiated by objective laboratory evidence.

The Diagnosis of DID

To meet the criteria for a *DSM-IV* diagnosis of DID, two or more distinct identities must be present who recurrently take control of an individual's behavior. These alter identities may have distinct personal histories, names, and abilities (e.g., computer proficiency, literacy) and can even vary in professed sex and age. This fractionation of identity must also be accompanied by an inability to recall important personal information, beyond that of ordinary forgetfulness. This memory loss, termed inter-identity amnesia, is thought to result from the compartmentalization of memory within identities and can manifest in many ways, such as gaps in time or the discovery of unfamiliar items in one's possession.

The properties of inter-identity amnesia can vary. In a one-way amnesia, communication is asymmetrical, as one identity may be omniscient for the experiences of the other but not vice versa. In a two-way amnesia, both identities are unaware of each other's experiences, memories, and sometimes even existence. A diagnosis of DID cannot be made if the symptoms are due to substance use or a general medical condition. DID is diagnosed more commonly in females than males (from three to nine times more often) and is often diagnosed in individuals with a history of other psychiatric diagnoses. Symptom onset varies, although many individuals report dissociative symptoms dating back to as early as childhood.

As with most other diagnoses, clinicians rely on the self-report of patients when diagnosing DID. This is typically done using either unstructured questioning or a structured interview such as the Structured Clinical Interview for *DSM-IV* Dissociative Disorders (SCID–D). The Dissociative Experiences Scale (DES) is another common self-report measure of dissociative symptoms, which requires individuals to rate their symptoms on a Likert-type scale, although the DES cannot confirm the diagnosis of DID.

Given the centrality of amnesia to DID, evidence of inter-identity amnesia is essential to a diagnosis. Caution is warranted when interpreting self-reported symptoms of amnesia, however, as research using objective measures of memory reveals an inconsistent picture that does not consistently corroborate the subjective symptoms reported by patients. Studies that have examined memory transfer across identities have provided mixed results, typically finding that some memories are shared between reportedly amnesic identities while other memories are not. It has been proposed that these differences in memory transfer depend on whether the memories are explicit versus implicit. Explicit memory tests require conscious recollection and typically produce amnesia between identities. For example, an amnesic identity may deny any memory of words presented to another identity when asked to recall them. In contrast, implicit memory tasks rely on the premise that prior experiences can influence subsequent behavior independent of conscious awareness—such tasks often show memory transfer. Although the amnesic identity may claim to not recognize the words, given an implicit test, such as a word-stem completion task, he or she may perform in a manner that suggests memory of the words on some level, typically assumed to be implicit and unconscious.

This pattern of amnesia on explicit but not implicit tasks is not unlike that found in organic amnesia. This pattern has alternatively been interpreted as a response to situational expectations, where individuals modify their response patterns in conformance with their expectations about how a person with inter-identity amnesia should respond. Explicit memory tests, unlike implicit tests, are typically obvious assessments of memory, and amnesic responding on explicit tests could result from motivated compliance with expectations. Implicit memory tests, in contrast, tend to be less transparent measures of memory and are less susceptible to manipulation.

Given the inconsistent findings of memory transfer, and also the controversy surrounding the disorder, inter-identity amnesia should ideally be verified by objective tests of inter-identity amnesia that do not rely solely on self-report. Some investigators have attempted to objectively assess memory by using psychophysiological measures such as brain electrical recordings or by creating paradigms where amnesia is difficult to simulate. These methods have typically demonstrated that memories transfer across identities despite self-reports of amnesia. Moreover, one study

has suggested that this memory transfer is conscious and explicit. Therefore, although a phenomenological experience of memory loss may be reported by DID patients, this amnesia cannot always be verified by objective memory tests. Given the centrality of inter-identity amnesia to a DID diagnosis and the current reliance on uncorroborated self-report measures, increasing importance needs to be placed on using objective tests of memory to make an accurate diagnosis of DID.

The Controversy

Controversy surrounds DID, as many skeptics question the validity of the disorder. Research on the properties of inter-identity amnesia has led to conflicting findings, as detailed above. In addition, critics of the disorder highlight the many changes that have occurred in prevalence rates and symptom presentation over time. Historically, DID has been an infrequently diagnosed disorder, with only a handful of cases being reported until the 1900s. However, rates of diagnosis skyrocketed in the 1980s, with prevalence rates numbering in the thousands. DID was popularized in the media around this same time by movies such as *The Three Faces of Eve* and *Sybil*. It has been suggested that this exponential increase in diagnoses is mostly circumscribed to specific cultures such as North America, with the majority of diagnoses believed to be attributable to a small percentage of psychologists.

In addition to the increasing prevalence rates, the nature of symptoms has evolved. Earlier DID patients commonly reported only a few identities and often needed a period of transient sleep to switch between identities. In contrast, present-day DID patients typically report approximately 15 alters and the ability to voluntarily switch among identities. These diagnostic, cultural, and symptomatological inconsistencies have incited an ongoing debate about the validity of reported symptoms, resulting in two competing etiological interpretations.

Perspectives on Causal Mechanisms

Two perspectives dominate the debate on the cause of DID. The posttraumatic interpretation of DID, also termed the disease model, conceptualizes the disorder as a posttraumatic condition resulting from childhood abuse, as the majority of DID patients report a history of child abuse. This perspective suggests that the generation and compartmentalization of multiple identities is manifested as an adaptive strategy that allows the individual to cope with trauma. Consonant with this theory, some DID patients report symptoms similar to those found in posttraumatic stress disorder, such as nightmares, flashbacks, and increased startle responses. The disease theory attributes the rise in prevalence of DID to more accurate diagnoses by clinicians as a result of increased awareness of childhood abuse and its psychiatric sequelae, greater acceptance of the disorder, and a more in-depth focus on previously overlooked symptoms. According to this explanation, certain physicians in specific cultures are becoming sufficiently familiar with the disease to accurately diagnose those symptoms of DID that previously went undiagnosed or misdiagnosed.

Critics of this disease model question the fidelity of memories of abuse reported by DID patients. Such reports are almost exclusively retrospective, and it has been firmly established that childhood memories are susceptible to distortion. In addition, critics suggest that a belief in the disease model may lead clinicians to specifically search for dissociative symptoms in clients with a known history of abuse or for memories of abuse in a client presenting dissociative symptoms, inflating the correlation between DID and memories of abuse. Techniques known to facilitate memory distortion, such as hypnosis, have been used by some clinicians, resulting in questions about the validity of uncovered memories of abuse and the existence of alter identities. Often, memories of abuse are uncovered in therapy, leading many to challenge the veridicality of these memories and point to a theory of a therapist-induced iatrogenic etiology.

An alternative perspective to the disease model, termed the sociocognitive model, proposes that DID is a socially influenced construction that is legitimized and maintained through social interactions. According to this theory, as the disorder has become more widely accepted, DID patients have learned how to present themselves as having multiple identities. Patients form a belief as to how others expect them to act and behave accordingly. This theory suggests that therapists play a large role in the generation and maintenance of this disorder through the use of suggestive questioning, the provision of information about how patients with the disorder should act, and the legitimization of the disorder. This sociocognitive perspective suggests an iatrogenic etiology, proposing that the disorder is generated by the client in response to the suggestive questioning

and expectations of the therapist. This view does not assume that a DID patient is consciously faking symptoms but instead speculates that dissociative symptoms are manifested as a way for individuals to view themselves in a way that is congruent with what they believe is expected of them. Often a patient seeks therapy to deal with unspecified psychological distress, and the expression of dissociative symptoms can result in a DID diagnosis, which may bring relief, explanations, and the potential for treatment. Thus, symptoms can be created and experienced by the patient as veridical in that DID patients interpret their normal life experiences from the viewpoint of a fractionated self. According to the sociocognitive model, an increase in the popularity and social acceptance of the disorder has led to greater manifestations of DID symptoms by highly suggestible individuals. Supporting the sociocognitive model, studies have found that alternate personalities can be generated and maintained by individuals with no psychiatric history when undergoing suggestive questioning.

Forensic Implications

Given the rising numbers of individuals diagnosed with DID, it is no surprise that the controversy surrounding DID has carried over into the courtroom. DID diagnoses have been used as a defense for individuals charged with crimes including kidnapping, forgery, drunk driving, and rape, with varying outcomes. Defendants with DID have pleaded innocent for crimes that they do not remember, purportedly committed by other identities. These defense pleas raise the question as to whether an individual can be held legally responsible for a crime committed by another alter not under the control of the dominant identity. The validity of the DID diagnosis is central to the debate over whether a DID patient should be considered as one unitary individual or as a conglomerate of multiple identities and, in the latter case, whether these distinct identities can be individually and dissociably culpable of a crime. Inter-identity amnesia is another important aspect of this debate, raising the question of whether an individual can be held criminally responsible for a crime committed by another identity of which he or she has no memory or awareness. As demonstrated by the inconsistency in the courtroom verdicts, this debate has not been resolved.

A DID diagnosis has additional ramifications for the legal system. Legal suits have been brought against clinicians for either falsely diagnosing or failing to diagnose the disorder. Alter identities have asked for separate legal representation and have been asked to give sworn testimony. The age of the accused alter identity has also been used as an argument to determine whether the patient is tried in a juvenile or an adult court, and a DID diagnosis can affect decisions about competency to stand trial.

Taking into account the exponential increase in diagnosis rates, it may be that veridical cases of DID are interspersed among many others that do not completely fit the diagnosis and that are the iatrogenic result of misdiagnoses, suggestive therapy, or demand characteristics. Intentional malingering or exaggeration of deficits should also be a consideration, especially in situations with important consequences, as in the case of litigation. Given the controversy over the validity of the disorder, care needs to be taken when making a diagnosis of DID. Self-report measures of memory loss, commonly used for diagnosis, have not always been corroborated by more objective measures of memory, suggesting that the subjective amnesia experienced by the individual may not correspond with the objective experience of amnesia. Thus, caution should be used in evaluating or admitting claims of amnesia in cases of DID, especially in the courtroom where the ramifications of a faulty diagnosis are high. Since inter-identity amnesia is a necessary criterion for a diagnosis of DID and can play an important role in the courtroom, an objective determination of such amnesia is critical and should be necessary to confirm a diagnosis of DID.

Lauren L. Kong and John J. B. Allen

See also Criminal Responsibility, Assessment of; False Memories; Forensic Assessment; Malingering

Further Readings

Allen, J., & Iacono, W. (2001). Assessing the validity of amnesia in dissociative identity disorder: A dilemma for the *DSM* and the courts. *Psychology, Public Policy, and Law, 7*(2), 311–344.

Gleaves, D. (1996). The sociocognitive model of dissociative identity disorder: A reexamination of the evidence. *Psychological Bulletin, 120*(1), 42–59.

Spanos, N. (1994). Multiple identity enactments and multiple personality disorder: A sociocognitive perspective. *Psychological Bulletin, 116*(1), 143–165.

DIVORCE AND CHILD CUSTODY

Divorce is exceedingly common in the United States, and it can have long-ranging effects on all parties involved, particularly children. In those relatively rare circumstances in which child custody issues cannot be resolved by the parents, the process can become even more contentious and emotional and ultimately end up in the court system. To inform its decision making in these contested cases, courts may appoint mental health examiners to evaluate families and either recommend a specific custody decision or provide detailed information about the factors affecting a child's development within potential custody environments. Custody evaluations are thought to be perhaps the most complex and acrimonious referral questions addressed by forensic examiners. Research has begun to identify those areas that most affect children's adjustment following divorce, so that psychologists may focus their evaluations on these areas in the future. Many questions remain, however, concerning how best to characterize, quantify, and predict what constitutes the best outcome for children in relation to custody.

Divorce and Its Aftermath

Of children from married parents in the United States, more than 40% will experience the effects of divorce. An untold, but likely larger, percentage of children who are born to cohabitating but unmarried parents also will experience the separation of their parents. Evidence suggests that at least a quarter of separating parents will experience substantial conflict concerning child custody. Despite this, the majority of custody decisions are resolved by parents without resorting to litigation. The use of alternative resolution techniques, such as divorce mediation, appears to be increasing as a means of resolving contested cases, rather than resorting to judicial determinations.

The courts typically may choose from a variety of different forms of custody that are thought to best serve the child. Most states differentiate between *physical custody*, which relates to the time spent with parents, and *legal custody*, which refers to rights regarding decision-making capacities (e.g., schooling, medical care). The majority of children appear to live primarily with their mothers, although there is some evidence of increasing residence with single fathers. Joint physical custody, the effects of which have been widely debated since the 1980s, appears to be relatively uncommon. Of note, custody arrangements appear to evolve over time, with actual living situations not necessarily corresponding with the initial legal agreements.

Legal Standards

All U.S. jurisdictions determine custody using the "best interests" standard, wherein custody is granted in accordance with the promotion of circumstances that ostensibly are in the best interests of the children. In practice, this standard has been found to be vague and difficult to apply. Some states have begun to operationalize the term *best interests* by identifying specific factors that have an impact on a child's welfare. In turn, these factors become the specific focus of the custody evaluation process.

Custody standards for many states are informed by the Uniform Marriage and Divorce Act (1979), which specifies various factors on which the best interests standard for a specific child should be based (e.g., the interaction and interrelation of the children and their parents). Although the specific standard differs from state to state, some evidence of standardization has begun to emerge. For example, state codes typically require an evaluation of each parent's current status (e.g., employment, parenting skills), history (e.g., in terms of caretaking, substance abuse, spousal abuse), and psychological health (e.g., ability to be flexible, general mental health). The courts also are to consider the wishes of the child concerning placement if the child is developmentally able to express such wishes. In addition, the courts may flexibly consider any other factors found to be relevant. Of note, some authorities have questioned the heavy emphasis on what are ostensibly in a child's best "psychological" interests rather than on factors such as economic, educational, or medical well-being.

Although the states have attempted to identify important types of information on which to base custody decisions, they do not limit the methods through which this information is gathered. For example, examiners typically are not constrained in their choice of evaluation approaches or tests. Likewise, courts do not have standard formulae for weighting the evidence provided. Such plasticity in the actual application of the law prevents courts from being locked into a formula that inadequately reflects the complexity and variety of the custody situations that they encounter, but it also

has raised criticisms concerning the lack of direction provided and the potential for subjective biases to enter into the decision-making process.

Professional Standards of Practice

Mental health experts are involved in custody cases in various roles, such as mediators, examiners, and therapists. The role of the examiner has been argued to be exceedingly difficult and one fraught with disproportionately high rates of malpractice claims. In recognition of the importance and difficulty of the examiner's role, several organizations have published professional guidelines to inform and direct the various participants in the divorce and custody process. For example, the American Psychological Association (APA) has published guidelines for psychologists to apply in child custody evaluations during divorce proceedings. These guidelines are primarily an extension of the professional ethics code to custody matters. They delineate the examiner's responsibility in terms of disclosing the forensic (rather than therapeutic) role to the participants in the evaluation, representing the child regardless of who engaged the examiner's services, and using current best practices when carrying out the evaluation.

The Association of Family and Conciliation Courts has also published standards of practice for child custody evaluations. More extensive than the APA guidelines, this document recommends specific areas that the examiner should evaluate. The American Academy of Child and Adolescent Psychiatry has provided the most detailed guidelines for both the process to be used and the content to be addressed by the custody examiner.

The Process of Conducting Child Custody Evaluations

Custody evaluations may involve a variety of data collection techniques, including psychological testing, interviews, and direct observation of the parties. Procedures vary across jurisdictions and according to the examiner's preferences. Although examiners may be retained by one party in the dispute, more commonly the court appoints a mental health professional to develop an impartial evaluation of all parties. The examiner frequently begins by gathering collateral information about the history of the case, as well as about the parent's financial and employment history, medical records, and school records.

Most evaluations by psychologists include the use of psychological tests, although there is no standardization in the field concerning which tests to use or how to interpret and apply the data derived from them. Surveys of examiners indicate that most include the Minnesota Multiphasic Personality Inventory–2 (MMPI–2) in their assessment of adults. Measures of intelligence are frequently given to both adults and children. A significant proportion of examiners also use projective tests with adults and children, some of which have been designed specifically for use in child custody evaluations. The conceptual/theoretical basis and psychometric adequacy of these instruments, particularly those designed solely for use in custody cases, have been questioned by various authorities. More generally, the use of standard "objective" tests such as the MMPI–2 and intelligence tests has been questioned, in that the connection between the test results and the legal question (e.g., what is in a child's best interests) may be unclear or, at best, indirect.

Examiners usually interview the parents and the children, and they may interview others who are close to the family or who have specific, meaningful information to provide. Information of interest includes the behavioral patterns of the parent, his or her parenting strengths and weaknesses, and his or her current emotional state. The examiner gauges the degree of commitment and groundwork evidenced with regard to realistically preparing for custody. In-depth information is sought regarding the parent's relationship with each child, as well as how he or she currently interacts with the other parent. When interviewing children, the examiner assesses their relationship with each parent, their current emotional and behavioral functioning, and their social/educational history. Although young children usually are not asked to express custody preferences, older children may be asked to describe what living situations they would most prefer.

Direct observation often is valued for providing more data about how the child and parent interact together. For example, the examiner may have the child and parent perform a structured task and evaluate how well they interact together. Some examiners use naturalistic observations, wherein they visit the home and see how the parent-child dyad interacts in that setting.

Research on Divorce and Child Custody Outcomes

Custody evaluations can be informed by research from multiple domains. Examiners should be familiar with a wide variety of research findings and incorporate the best data in the evaluation process. Relevant areas of research include the influence of parents on their children's development, mental disorders and parenting, mental disorders and children, the impact of specific parenting practices on child development, the impact of divorce on parents and children, the impact of parental conflict on children's adjustment, parenting after divorce, economics and remarriage, the impact of access to the noncustodial parent, and the impact of the type of custody arrangement on children's development.

A voluminous literature exists concerning how children respond to parental separation and divorce. Unfortunately, clear and unequivocal conclusions (which might lead to straightforward recommendations in contested custody cases) typically are the exception rather than the rule. As such, this summary highlights trends in this literature, with the qualification that these general trends belie considerable variability at the individual level.

At the most basic level, divorce appears to be associated with modest increases in an array of short- and long-term negative outcomes for children, including externalizing behavior problems, depression, school difficulties, poorer relationships with parents (particularly fathers), and subsequent romantic relationship dysfunction. Of considerable importance, the causal effect of divorce per se on these outcomes is not well understood, with various other factors possibly explaining these negative outcomes. For example, research suggests that the level of parental conflict exhibited may be more important in terms of predicting children's adjustment than is the experience of divorce itself. Also of note, some recent research suggests that divorce may actually result in improved functioning, at least among children from "high-conflict" families. Children whose families are cordial following the divorce tend to be psychologically healthier than those from high-conflict families.

To promote better outcomes for children, many states now encourage families to use mediation and other nonadversarial methods of working through the divorce and custody arrangements. Some evidence suggests that the use of mediation helps families emerge from the process in a healthier manner. For example, postdivorce conflict tends to be lower in families using mediation than in control groups. Likewise, noncustodial parents appear to be more likely to maintain regular contact with their children after divorces that employ mediation.

Researchers are currently investigating the impact of the amount of contact with the noncustodial parent on the adjustment of the children. Early findings suggest that economic support is more important than the amount of contact between the parent and children. Although the amount of contact does not appear to predict children's future well-being, the consistent payment of child support does.

Further complicating our understanding of the causal role of divorce on subsequent negative outcomes, research has suggested that there is a "nonrandom selection" into divorce, such that many of the problems identified in children of divorce were present prior to the separation. Some evidence even has suggested that genetic effects may play a role, although genetic factors do not explain all of the variance in these outcomes. Finally, some authorities have highlighted the importance of distinguishing between the high levels of emotional distress caused by divorce and the relatively lower levels of psychological disorder that seem to be attributable specifically to divorce. Although serious psychological impairment is a relatively infrequent outcome, painful memories, emotional turmoil, and negative appraisals of the experience are quite common.

M. Catherine Dodson and John F. Edens

See also Child Custody Evaluations; Forensic Assessment

Further Readings

American Psychological Association. (1994). Guidelines for child custody evaluations in divorce proceedings. *American Psychologist, 49,* 677–682.

Emery, R. E., Otto, R. K., & O'Donohue, W. T. (2005). A critical assessment of child custody evaluations: Limited science and a flawed system. *Psychological Science in the Public Interest, 6,* 1–29.

Grisso, T. (2003). *Evaluating competencies: Forensic assessments and instruments* (2nd ed.). New York: Kluwer Academic/Plenum.

Otto, R. K., Buffington-Vollum, J. K., & Edens, J. F. (2003). Child custody evaluation: Research and practice. In I. B. Weiner (Series Ed.) & A. Goldstein (Vol. Ed.), *Handbook of psychology: Vol. 11. Forensic psychology* (pp. 179–208). New York: Wiley.

Doctoral Programs in Psychology and Law

Doctoral programs are the most prominent educational path for training scholars in psychology and law, providing training for many students interested in the core areas of these disciplines. There are a variety of training models aimed at educating students in both disciplines, but there is lack of agreement about the best model. However, recommendations have been made for the core objectives that should be present in any doctoral program. Regardless of the training model, there are a variety of employment opportunities available for graduates of these select programs, and students applying to them should be aware that admission can be very competitive.

Psychology and law is one of the fastest growing areas in all of psychology. This tremendous growth is obvious in the continued expansion of psychology into the courts, the establishment of professional organizations such as the American Psychology-Law Society (AP-LS), the number of professional journals devoted specifically to psychology and law or publishing psychology and law–related articles, and the increasing number of graduate programs designed to train students. Doctoral programs award the highest degrees possible in psychology and law, the Ph.D or the Psy.D. The Ph.D. is typically seen as a research-based degree, and the Psy.D. is seen as a practice-oriented degree with less emphasis on students conducting independent research and more emphasis on issues such as assessing and treating mental illness. Although doctoral degrees are not necessary to work in psychology and law, they are frequently preferred for employment in many areas. This entry focuses on describing some of the specialty areas available in doctoral programs, evaluating the different training models and training areas of these programs, suggesting some of the employment opportunities, and briefly describing the admission process for those individuals interested in obtaining a doctorate in psychology and law.

Doctoral Program Specialty Areas

A marked increase in the number of doctoral programs in psychology and law over the past 30 years is a clear indication of the tremendous recent growth in this specialty area. The University of Nebraska is typically credited with establishing the first doctoral program in psychology and law in the early 1970s. However, since then, more than 20 doctoral programs with a significant emphasis on psychology and law have been established across Canada and the United States. AP-LS publishes a comprehensive list of these programs on its Web site. The list of doctoral programs in psychology and law is as extensive and varied as the available specialty areas and their models for training students.

There are typically five predominant specialty areas of psychology represented in doctoral programs: cognitive, developmental, social, community, and clinical. The cognitive, developmental, and social are considered as nonclinical areas of psychology. Programs in these areas do not train students to assess or treat mental illness but instead focus on research and teaching. Clinical doctoral programs examine the role of mental health on different aspects of the law, and community psychology programs may have a clinical or a nonclinical focus. Whatever the broad training differences, there may be overlap between the topics studied by nonclinical and clinical psychologists.

Cognitive psychologists focus on human perception and memory. Cognitive psychologists who work in psychology and law focus on topics such as eyewitness identification, repressed memories, and the detection of deception. A cognitive psychologist may be interested in the different factors that influence eyewitnesses' ability to accurately recall the events surrounding a crime, such as their level of stress, the racial identity of the perpetrator, the presence of a weapon, or the way a police lineup is conducted.

Developmental psychologists examine the issues that normally affect children or adolescents but are increasingly focusing on the entire developmental process, including old age. Developmental psychologists trained in psychology and law may study topics involving the suggestibility of juveniles when interviewed or testifying, the ability of juveniles to make legal decisions, or the impact of divorce and separation. For example, a developmental psychologist may study whether adolescents have the same ability as adults to understand the criminal charges they are facing and whether their comprehension influences their ability to assist in their legal defense.

Social psychologists examine the influence of others or groups on the decisions people make. Social psychologists are interesting in topics such as jury decision making, jury selection, and the credibility of witnesses. Social psychologists have found that certain characteristics of a jury alter the likelihood of a legal verdict. For example, the size of a jury may vary, depending on the nature of the trial and the jurisdiction. Social psychologists have discovered that the smaller the jury, the less those jurors will deliberate and the poorer their accurate recall of trial related information.

Community psychologists are interested in the way society interacts with the individual. Community psychologists interested in psychology and the law focus on the manner in which the law affects the people it is designed to protect or help. A community psychologist may examine the effects of a change in a specific law—for instance, whether decreasing the blood alcohol limit for driving under the influence of alcohol increases or decreases the number of alcohol-related deaths—or the general impact of health care programs on the people they intend to target.

Clinical psychologists assess and treat individuals who are mentally ill or have psychological difficulties. Clinical psychologists interested in psychology and law focus on the mental health aspects of criminal and civil law. Clinical forensic psychologists may conduct risk assessments of violent offenders, evaluate defendants for competency to stand trial or insanity, assess whether someone involved in a lawsuit over an automobile accident suffers from posttraumatic stress disorder, or be involved in a child custody dispute after a marital separation. A student attending a doctoral program in psychology and law is typically interested in at least one of these areas, but there are a variety of models or ways by which a doctoral student may be educated in any of them.

Training Models in Psychology and Law Doctoral Programs

No matter what the specialty area, the ways in which a student is trained in these doctoral programs are significant. Doctoral programs in psychology and law are joint-degree programs or specialty programs in psychology and law or provide a minor or emphasis in psychology and law. There is no agreement about the superiority of any of these training models. Each approach presents unique advantages and disadvantages that any student should consider.

Joint-degree programs enable the student to receive both a degree in psychology, typically a doctoral degree (Ph.D. or Psy.D.), and a law degree, typically a J.D. Although the doctoral degree and the J.D. are the standard degrees awarded in joint-degree programs, the oldest joint-degree program, at the University of Nebraska, also offers a master's degree in psychology (M.A.) and a master's degree in legal studies (M.L.S.) in combination, corresponding to Ph.D and J.D. There has been an increase in joint-degree programs, so that several universities now offer them. The joint-degree programs tend to be extremely competitive because a student must have the ability to complete advanced degrees in two very different and demanding disciplines. The goal of these joint-degree programs is not to simply train someone in both law and psychology but to integrate that training. This approach means that students alternate their formal coursework between psychology and law to better understand the interaction between the two fields.

The benefit of this training model is that it allows for the true integration of the divergent disciplines. This integration may better allow the graduates to identify aspects of the law that could benefit from a sophisticated psychological investigation. The simultaneous exposure also may increase the familiarity an individual feels in examining issues from both perspectives. The joint degree may open up a variety of different employment possibilities that training in one field does not offer. A graduate of a joint-degree program may be able to work as an attorney for a law firm, as a clinical psychologist, or as an academic in a law school or psychology department. However, there are several disadvantages to joint-degree programs. There is the additional time and financial expense required for attending these programs because one has to complete two rigorous advanced degrees without being employed full-time. In addition, simply obtaining two advanced degrees in two different disciplines does not automatically mean additional employment opportunities. Graduates of these programs often struggle with the question of whether they are psychologists or attorneys and with proving one or the other to a prospective employer.

Specialty programs in psychology and law offer only doctorate degrees in psychology but typically have the same depth of training in psychology and law as joint-degree programs. Students in these programs still take specially designed courses in psychology and law, maybe even take some law classes, participate in research on different psycholegal topics, or participate in clinical practicums in prisons or forensic hospitals. Students in specialty programs are allowed more flexibility in designing their program of study than those in joint-degree programs but are still considerably immersed in psychology and law. They also are able to do so while spending less time in school. However, students in these programs may not have the same flexibility in terms of employment or understand all the areas in which psychology and law interact, because of their more narrowly focused training. As a result, they

may lack some sophistication in applying psychology to legally relevant issues.

The third model for training in psychology and law is the psychology and law minor. These programs do not offer the same depth or breadth that the other two training models offer. Students in these doctoral programs usually work with a professor in one of the five specialty areas and conduct research on a psychology and law–related topic or engage in some forensic clinical work. These students may take specialty courses related to psychology and law, but their primary training is in their specialty area (e.g., cognitive). These programs offer some experience in psychology and law but do not allow the interested student to become an expert in the interdisciplinary field.

Training Areas and Objectives in Doctoral Programs

By 1995, the field of psychology and law recognized that there was a great deal of diversity in the training models for psychology and law programs, and there was some concern about future training. As a result, the National Invitational Conference on Education and Training in Law and Psychology was held at the Villanova Law School. The conference attendees worked in several different areas related to both undergraduate and graduate training in psychology and law. One of those groups focused on the specific objectives doctoral programs in psychology and law should have in training psycholegal scholars. The conference did not endorse any of the training models previously identified but did identify five areas that they believed were crucial in the development of psycholegal scholars.

First, doctoral programs should train students in *substantive psychology.* Substantive psychology encompasses the foundational areas of psychology, such as biological, cognitive, developmental, personality, and social psychology. It also includes an awareness of the professional and ethical issues that arise when working in psychology. In addition to these foundational topics, doctoral programs should encourage awareness of the cultural and social forces that work to shape our view, especially since many graduates of these programs will shape social policy.

Second, these programs should emphasize training in *research design and statistics.* The conference attendees suggested that because one of the strengths of graduates of psychology and law programs was their ability to apply different psychological methods to legal issues, it was important for students to have a foundational knowledge in the area. Students should get experience in performing research both in the laboratory and in a real-world setting. They should also be familiar with rudimentary and sophisticated statistical techniques.

Third, doctoral programs should encourage the acquisition of *legal knowledge.* Acquiring legal knowledge does not simply mean that students should be familiar with the law but that they should be comfortable and able to act as active participants in an interdisciplinary field with psychologists, lawyers, and judges. Doctoral programs that offer this type of training will allow their graduates to better address legal questions in ways that are psychologically meaningful and legally relevant.

Fourth, doctoral programs training psycholegal scholars should train them in *substantive legal psychology.* An education in substantive legal psychology should comprise coursework across a variety of different topics and domains. This approach should give students an understanding of the integration of the two disciplines by encouraging them to read empirical and nonempirical work in the area, examine some of the historical underpinnings of the application of psychology to the legal arena, and become familiar with the role of specific statutes and case law in social science.

Finally, the conference recommended that one of the crucial objectives in training doctoral students should be immersion in *scholarship and training.* Doctoral programs should educate students in conducting their own original research and scholarship. Students should present at scholarly conferences and publish in professional journals. This experience should culminate with their doctoral dissertation in an area of interest to them. Training should not be confined to production of scholarship but should also take place in real-world settings.

Employment Opportunities for Graduates of Doctoral Programs

There are a host of different employment opportunities for students who graduate from psychology and law doctoral programs. However, the employment opportunities depend on the specialty area, the training model, and the available opportunities in the doctoral programs. One of the most common areas of employment for graduates of doctoral programs in psychology and law is academia. Many graduates of

these programs become professors in undergraduate and graduate departments. They continue to teach and conduct research and scholarship with students who have similar interests. Because of the interdisciplinary nature of psychology and law, graduates may teach in psychology departments, law schools, criminal justice departments, or a variety of other social science related areas.

Clinically trained graduates may be employed as forensic clinicians. They may work in prisons, forensic hospitals, or private practice, conducting evaluations and providing treatment for individuals with mental health issues. For example, a forensic clinician may run a group for individuals who have been convicted of sexual assault to reduce the likelihood that they will sexually re-offend when they are released from prison. The clinician also may conduct an evaluation to assist the court in determining whether a defendant is competent to stand trial or is not responsible by reason of insanity. Forensic clinicians are routinely called on to testify in court as expert witnesses in order to explain their findings to judges and juries.

Some graduates of doctoral programs in psychology and law work as trial consultants. Trial consulting includes a wide range of activities, such as preparing witnesses to present themselves in the best possible manner, educating attorneys on presentation of their evidence, and selecting juries. Trial consultation involves the direct application of psychological knowledge to the practice of law. Trial consultants may work for one of the many large trial consulting firms, work internally for a large law firm, or have a primary position as an academic while providing trial consultation as a secondary part of their job.

Other graduates of doctoral programs in psychology and law solely conduct research in the area. Some researchers function primarily as policy evaluators and work for state agencies, where they may assess the ongoing effectiveness of sex offender treatment, evaluate the impact of a child welfare program, determine whether the detention of juveniles in a juvenile-only facility is more effective than their detention along with adult offenders, or identify psychological research that is relevant when a state or the federal government is proposing new legislation. Researchers also may work for federal agencies such as the Secret Service or the Federal Judicial Center to assist law enforcement and the courts by conducting research on violence prediction or various issues relevant to the federal courts.

Applying for Admission to Doctoral Programs

Applying for admission to doctoral programs in psychology and law does not require special qualifications above those required for admission to a doctoral program in any area of psychology. Psychology and law doctoral programs are looking for applicants with outstanding undergraduate grades, impressive Graduate Record Exam (GRE) scores, excellent letters of recommendation, experience in conducting research, and demonstration of a genuine interest in the field of psychology and law. However, applicants to doctoral programs in psychology and law should be aware that the process is extremely competitive for the most established programs. For example, for the most competitive programs in psychology, clinical Ph.D. programs, the acceptance rate typically is around 10%. There is no reason to believe that the acceptance rates at the most competitive programs are any lower for forensic clinical students, and in fact, they may even be more competitive because of the increased interest in the area and fewer available spots. Furthermore, because there are only a few joint-degree programs and students must possess the motivation and intellectual ability to complete two advanced degrees, they are likely to be extremely competitive. There are also doctoral programs that are less competitive or even master's programs that may be viable options for individuals who do not possess the qualifications or ability to gain admission to the well-established doctoral programs in psychology and law.

Matthew T. Huss

See also Master's Programs in Psychology and Law; Trial Consulting

Further Readings

Bersoff, D. N., Goodman-Delahunty, J., Grisso, J. T., Hans, V. P., Poythress, N. G., & Roesch, R. G. (1997). Training in law and psychology: Models from the Villanova conference. *The American Psychologist, 52,* 1301–1310.

Bottoms, B., Costanzo, M., Greene, E., Redlich, A., Woolard, J., & Zapf, P. (2004). Careers in psychology and the law: A guide for prospective students. Retrieved from http://www.ap-ls.org/students/careers%20in%20psychology.pdf

Huss, M. T. (2001). What is forensic psychology? It's not *Silence of the Lambs! Eye on Psi Chi, 5,* 25–27.

Melton, G. B., Huss, M. T., & Tomkins, A. J. (1999). Training in forensic psychology and law. In I. B. Weiner & A. K. Hess (Eds.), *Handbook of forensic psychology* (2nd ed., pp. 700–720). New York: Wiley.

Ogloff, J. R. P., Tomkins, A. J., & Bersoff, D. N. (1996). Education and training in psychology and law/criminal justice: Historical foundations, present structures, and future developments. *Criminal Justice and Behavior, 23,* 200–235.

Packer, I. K., & Borum, R. (2003). Forensic training and practice. In I. B. Weiner (Series Ed.) & A. D. Goldstein (Vol. Ed.), *Handbook of psychology: Vol. 11. Forensic psychology* (pp. 21–32). Hoboken, NJ: Wiley.

DOMESTIC VIOLENCE

See INTIMATE PARTNER VIOLENCE

DOMESTIC VIOLENCE COURTS

Domestic violence courts (DVCs) are specialized court settings that deal predominantly with cases involving domestic violence. They have emerged in different state, regional, and national contexts, giving rise to different operational styles and models. For example, courts may sit full or part-time and deal with different levels of offense seriousness and all or various aspects of case progression (pretrial review hearings, trials, sentencing and/or monitoring of offenders). Regardless of the operational style, the philosophy guiding these courts is that domestic violence is a crime that poses particular difficulties for both the victim and the criminal justice system; therefore, a specialized method of dealing with these cases is necessary. This entry describes the operation of DVCs in the United States, Canada, and the United Kingdom. It establishes the defining features of these courts and reviews the research relating to how specialization has changed their processes, outcomes, and overall effectiveness.

Domestic Violence Courts in the United States

Court specialization in the United States is grounded in "problem-solving" or "therapeutic" approaches to domestic violence. The problem-solving approach provided impetus for the development of the first specialist courts in Florida. The courts were believed to increase efficiency, and most criminal justice practitioners felt that the judicial and prosecutorial expertise resulting from specialization had a positive effect on the system for handling cases and helped reduce recidivism. Specialist courts also began to be developed in New York, initially based on the criminal "cluster court" model, whereby criminal cases involving domestic violence matters are assigned to a dedicated session for domestic violence cases only. The dedicated listing of cases facilitates the allocation of specialist judges and prosecutors and independent advocacy support for victims. The involvement of advocates was found to enhance the quality of information available to the prosecution and increase the likelihood of victims remaining committed to the prosecution. Some courts in New York progressed from the criminal cluster court model to a combined civil/criminal model, realizing the benefits of the latter, in particular for ensuring judicial consistency in relation to all orders. For example, having a divorce proceeding and a criminal assault case heard in a combined court would promote the ideal of "one family, one judge." While the development of DVCs can be driven primarily by system needs such as effective case management and efficient use of resources, other key objectives include increasing victim safety and perpetrator accountability. Practitioners feel that these courts are more responsive to victims' needs and provide improved enforcement and better services for perpetrators.

By the late 1990s, a plethora of DVCs were in operation in the United States, and various attempts were made to compare them with a view to identifying good practice. One such review was undertaken by the National Center for State Courts, which estimated that there were more than 300 courts with some specialized court structures, processes, or practices distinct to domestic violence in the United States; however, the review found much variation in court processes and a lack of systematic evidence of their benefits. The report identified cultural and organizational problems that hindered the development of DVCs. Other concerns included the views that the pursuit of efficiency may result in "assembly-line justice" and that the promotion of information sharing may be detrimental to victims in some cases (e.g., where custody issues were involved). But the benefits of specialization were clear, in terms of increased judicial understanding of domestic violence issues,

perpetrator accountability, and more comprehensive support provided to victims.

The core "components" of effective DVCs were identified from the review. These include advocacy services for information exchange between the victim and the court, the coordination of partner agencies, environments that offer security and comfort to victims and children, specialist court personnel who receive ongoing training, evenhanded treatment of both parties and a serious tone to indicate that domestic violence is being treated seriously, integrated information systems for sharing and accessing information, evaluation and accountability of court processes and outcomes, protocols for risk assessment compliance, monitoring of defendants with court orders, and sentencing that is consistent and promotes the accountability of domestic violence offenders.

Domestic Violence Courts in Canada

In Canada, a number of multi-agency approaches to domestic violence have been promoted. In Ontario, the impetus for an improved judicial response to domestic violence came from a domestic homicide review following the killing in 1996 of Arlene May, a mother of five, by her former boyfriend. The new court that was subsequently established was evaluated by the Woman Abuse Council of Toronto, which concluded that specialized courts do make a difference. For example, men sent to the perpetrator program from the DVC had a lower breach rate than men sent via other routes. The court, established in Winnipeg in 1990, deals with intimate partner violence as well as other forms of abuse. Evaluations of this court demonstrated that it was successful in reducing the time taken to process cases and bringing about more appropriate sentencing. Prior to specialization, the most frequent sentences were conditional discharge, suspended sentences, and probation: Imprisonment was rare. In the 2 years after specialization, the most frequent sentences were probation, suspended sentences, and imprisonment. The review of Canadian initiatives to challenge violence against women concluded that "specialization has become the key to effective system reform."

Domestic Violence Courts in the United Kingdom

The introduction of specialist courts in the United Kingdom has been relatively recent, as the first was established in Leeds in 1999. The basic features of DVCs operating in England and Wales include focusing on criminal (not civil) matters heard in Magistrates' Courts, dealing mainly with pretrial hearings rather than trials, identifying domestic violence cases and thereafter either "clustering" or "fast-tracking" them, having an advocate present to support victims, having a specialist police officer present to provide information to the court, and relying on multi-agency partnerships. These courts attempt to achieve a variety of aims: increase the effectiveness of court systems in providing protection and support to victims and imposing appropriate sanctions on offenders; enhance the coordination of criminal justice, public, voluntary, and community sector agencies in working with victims and offenders; reduce delays in the processing of cases; and reduce the rates of revictimization.

In 2006, the Home Office announced its national domestic violence plan, which has a tripartite structure, including "one-stop-shops" to provide a range of advocacy and support services for victims, specialized courts, and multi-agency responses for very-high-risk victims. This plan capitalizes on local innovation and documented evidence that such approaches can make a positive difference in the lives of victims and their children. Other recent national developments include new guidance for the police in investigating domestic violence, a revised prosecution policy published by the Crown Prosecution Service, and a joint national training program for the police and prosecutors. In addition, the government provided £2 million to underpin a new national training and accreditation program for independent domestic violence advisors (IDVAs), beginning in 2005. The support, information, and advocacy provided by IDVAs to victims were found to be crucial in the success of DVCs. The Home Office plans to have 50 DVCs operational by the end of 2007. Documented benefits include reducing the number of cases lost before trial, increasing the number of defendants pleading guilty or being convicted after trial, and providing advocacy for and increasing the confidence of victims.

To summarize, research on DVCs in England and Wales has found that these courts act as a beacon of good practice in terms of victim-centered justice, enhance victim satisfaction, send a message to the victim that she is being heard, send a message to the offender that domestic violence will not be tolerated and that the offense is taken seriously, increase public confidence in the criminal justice system, provide a catalyst for multi-agency working, and promote the coordination of efforts to support the victim.

Case Progression in Domestic Violence Courts

Understanding the strengths and limitations of DVCs needs to be set not only in the local and national contexts within which these courts are embedded but also in the context of the dynamics of domestic violence itself, which is multi-faceted (incorporating emotional and psychological abuse as well as crimes of violence and/or sexual abuse). Research has shown that, understandably, victims are often reluctant to be witnesses in court for a range of reasons: fear and intimidation; frustration with the complexity and lengthiness of the court process; concerns over housing, welfare, and immigration status; and their own relationship with the defendant and his with any of their children. It is therefore important to remember what a difficult decision a victim faces when determining whether to participate in a criminal justice case against someone with whom she has been, or may continue to be, in an intimate relationship.

Research shows that domestic violence cases tend to progress through the criminal justice system differently than comparable cases without a domestic context. In an early study on British prosecution practices, compared with non-domestic-violence cases, more domestic violence cases were not prosecuted, and when they were, more defendants were found not guilty. The impetus for developing DVCs emerged from these failures. Therefore, one of the main aims of DVCs is to reduce attrition of domestic violence cases, and the available evidence suggests that case progression *is* different when it occurs in DVCs. For example, a study of more than 4,000 defendants processed by a DVC in Memphis concluded that "prosecution was the norm rather than the exception" as prosecutors proceeded in 80% of cases and more than two thirds of the defendants pleaded guilty, were found guilty, or were placed on diversion. British statistics show that conviction rates in DVCs are higher than in other courts: 71% compared with 59%.

Case progression in domestic violence cases is problematic because of the important role ascribed to victim participation: There is a well-documented and pronounced relationship between victim participation and the successful resolution of these cases. Even within DVCs, victim participation remains a crucial determinant of case outcomes. A recent study of a DVC in Toronto found that prosecutors were seven times more likely to prosecute a case when victims were perceived to be cooperative. In a study of five British DVCs, it was found that even with the support provided to victims by advocates, half the victims still chose to retract. Thus, case progression in DVCs still depends in large part on the perceived wishes or credibility of the victim as a prosecution witness.

Sentencing in Domestic Violence Courts

In the United States, the most common sanction for convicted domestic violence offenders is probation with all or part of a jail sentence suspended. In the United Kingdom, a recent report on several demonstration projects aimed at reducing domestic violence found that sentencing practices varied considerably. For example, the use of custodial sentences for convicted defendants ranged from 11% to 50%.

Sentencing practices are expected to differ when courts are specialized. An evaluation of six U.S. sites found the benefit to be more consistent sentencing, with the added value of incorporating advocacy for victims into the court process. The specialization of drug and domestic violence courts in West Yorkshire (where the first domestic violence court was established in Leeds) was noted to offer the possibility of providing justice with a greater focus on rehabilitation and integration of the offender into the community.

Although the aim of sentencing in DVCs is to "promote accountability from domestic violence offenders," it is unclear what specific penalties might best achieve this. A short prison sentence might be the best deterrent for one offender, but a long period of probation may be the most effective for another. Furthermore, research suggests that victims often desire the rehabilitation rather than punishment of offenders, yet perpetrator programs are not uniformly available as sentencing options. It is also unclear what effects specific penalties might have on victims' levels of satisfaction and safety. In conclusion, more evidence is needed about sentencing in DVCs and the long-term impacts on offenders, victims, and the wider community.

Amanda L. Robinson

See also Bail-Setting Decisions; Battered Woman Syndrome; Children's Testimony; Expert Psychological Testimony; Intimate Partner Violence; Police Decision Making and Domestic Violence; Sentencing Decisions; Spousal Assault Risk Assessment (SARA); Substance Abuse and Intimate Partner Violence; Victim Impact Statements; Victim Participation in the Criminal Justice System

Further Readings

Cook, D., Burton, M., Robinson, A., & Vallely, C. (2004). *Evaluation of specialist domestic violence courts/fast track systems.* London: Crown Prosecution Service and Department of Constitutional Affairs. Retrieved from http://www.cps.gov.uk/publications/docs/specialistdvcourts.pdf

Hague, G., Kelly, L., & Mullender, A. (2001). *Challenging violence against women: The Canadian experience.* Bristol, UK: Policy Press.

Kelitz, S. (2001). *Specialization of domestic violence case management in the courts: A national survey.* Williamsburg, VA: National Center for State Courts. Retrieved from http://www.ncjrs.gov/pdffiles1/nij/grants/186192.pdf

Sacks, E. (2002). *Creating a domestic violence court: Guidelines and best practices.* San Francisco: Family Violence Prevention Fund. Retrieved from http://fvpfstore.stores.yahoo.net/creatdomviol.html

DOMESTIC VIOLENCE SCREENING INSTRUMENT (DVSI)

The Domestic Violence Screening Instrument (DVSI and DVSI–R versions) was designed to assess the risk of repeated domestic violence in the future on the basis of information available at the time of use. The DVSI was originally created by the Division of Probation Services in Colorado. It was crafted as a short, easy criminal records review and made available to prosecutors, judges, and probation officers soon after a suspect's arrest. The original instrument included 12 items related to past criminal and social history, completed by a review of official records, with the 12 items summed to calculate risk scores ranging from 0 to 30. It was substantially revised in Connecticut between 2002 and 2003, involving modification and consolidation of the items (now 11), along with corresponding coding instructions. Besides the 11 structured items, two additional mechanisms were added for assessing the imminent risk of violence to the victim or other persons based on an assessor's subjective professional judgment.

The original DVSI was validated using two samples of subjects drawn from four pilot judicial districts of the 22 in Colorado: 1,465 male suspects arrested for domestic violence offenses committed against female partners between July 1997 and March 1998 and 125 female partners of the men arrested. These women were offered financial compensation to participate in the study, but locating them and soliciting their willingness to participate was difficult, resulting in a relatively small sample.

Concurrent validity was determined by comparing the DVSI with an alternative risk assessment instrument, the Spouse Assault Risk Assessment (SARA) guide, to determine the level of agreement in classifying cases into the high-risk and low-to-moderate-risk categories using both instruments. The greater the agreement in classification, the greater is the concurrent validity of the DVSI. Cross-classifying the high-risk and low-to-moderate-risk distributions on the DVSI and the SARA showed high levels of agreement between the two instruments. The SARA also includes two summary risk ratings in which the assessor estimates imminent risk of violence to the partner and imminent risk of violence to others. Perceived risk of violence to the partner was highly correlated with the DVSI risk classification. Discriminant validation involved comparing the DVSI with the perceived risk of violence to others on the assumption that the DVSI assesses the risk of repeated intimate partner violence, not violence toward others. An association, therefore, is not expected. The association was weak and not statistically significant.

Predictive validity was determined by estimating the association between the DVSI and repeated violence during an 18-month follow-up period, using official records to measure three behavioral outcomes: arrests for violations of domestic violence restraining orders, domestic violence re-arrests, and general criminal perpetration arrests. The perpetrators classified as high risk were re-arrested more than those classified as low to moderate risk on the DVSI. Violations of domestic violence restraining orders were higher for high-risk than lower-risk suspects, as was the case for domestic violence re-arrests. Predictive validity was also evaluated by making comparisons between DVSI risk scores and forms of controlling, intimidating, threatening, or physically violent behaviors reported by the 125 women victims during a 6-month follow-up period. No significant relations were found between the DVSI risk scores and controlling behaviors or less

serious forms of intimidating, threatening, or physically violent behaviors. However, high-risk classification on the DVSI was significantly associated with more severe forms of these behaviors: destruction of property; threatening to hit, attack, or harm the victim; and the use of threats to obtain sex from the victim. The DVSI was also significantly associated with more severe forms of physically violent behavior: choked or tried to drown the victim, used physical force to obtain sex, or tried to kill the victim.

Implementing and Modifying the DVSI in Connecticut

The DVSI was adopted as a risk assessment instrument in Connecticut in May 2002 because of the promising findings of the Colorado study and the suitability of the instrument for risk assessments in this state, which must be done by family relations counselors (FRCs) within an approximately 24-hour period after arrest. After initial training sessions on the administration of the DVSI, a pilot phase was implemented that resulted in modifications of item definitions, coding rules, inclusion of professional judgment of imminent risk categories, clarification of confusing items, and consolidation of seemingly redundant items. Revisions were finalized in January 2003.

The DVSI–R includes 11 items and the two summary risk ratings. The 11 items are statistical or actuarial in nature, referring to previous involvement in nonfamily as well as family violence, prior family violence intervention or treatment, violation of protective orders or other forms of court supervision, prior or current verbal or emotional abuse, the frequency and escalation of family violence in the past 6 months, the use of objects as weapons, substance abuse, the presence of children during such incidents, and employment status. The instrument captures two primary components of risk assessment (statistical/actuarial and structured professional judgment), yet it remains brief and efficient to administer. The DVSI–R is informed by five sources of data: police reports, criminal history review, protective order registry review, perpetrator interviews, and victim interviews.

An initial validation study of the DVSI–R was conducted using 14,970 risk assessments by FRCs from September 1, 2004, through May 2, 2005, and covering Connecticut's 23 judicial geographic areas. Preliminary evidence shows that the DVSI–R has promising concurrent and predictive validity. Further validation is currently under way using 18-month recidivism data on 3,797 defendants.

Kirk R. Williams

See also Forensic Assessment; Intimate Partner Violence; Violence Risk Assessment

Further Readings

Campbell, J. C., O'Sullivan, C., Roehl, J., & Webster, D. (2005). *Intimate partner violence risk assessment validation study: The RAVE study* (Final report). Washington DC: National Institute of Justice.

Kropp, P. R., & Hart, S. D. (2000). The Spousal Assault Risk Assessment (SARA) guide: Reliability and validity in adult male offenders. *Law and Human Behavior, 24,* 101–118.

Skilling, N. (2002). *Validation study for the use of the Domestic Violence Screening Instrument (DVSI) and the Spousal Assault Risk Assessment (SARA) for evaluating probation clients.* Minneapolis, MN: Research and Systems Technology, Department of Community Corrections, Hennepin County.

Williams, K. R., & Houghton, A. B. (2004). Assessing the risk of domestic violence re-offending: A validation study. *Law and Human Behavior, 28,* 437–455.

Williams, K. R., & Grant, S. R. (2000). Empirically examining the risk of intimate partner violence: The Revised Domestic Violence Screening Instrument (DVSI-R). *Public Health Reports, 121,* 400–408.

DOUBLE-BLIND LINEUP ADMINISTRATION

A double-blind lineup refers to a lineup procedure in which both the witness and the lineup administrator are unaware of which lineup member is the suspect under investigation. Scholars began recommending this procedure, in contrast to the typical procedure in which the lineup administrator knows which lineup member is the suspect, because of concerns that a nonblind administrator would unintentionally communicate to the witness the identity of the suspect, increasing the rate of mistaken identifications when the suspect is not the perpetrator. Laboratory research suggests that the use of double-blind lineups may decrease the rate of mistaken identifications, especially when other lineup procedures lead to an increase in identification rates.

Definition

When a photo or live lineup is administered to an eyewitness, it is common for the police officer administering the lineup to be aware of the suspect's identity. This type of lineup procedure is referred to as a *single-blind lineup*, because although the witness is blind to the suspect's identity, the administrator of the lineup is not. Psycholegal researchers have expressed concern that when lineups are implemented in this fashion, the administrator may consciously or unconsciously emit cues to the witness and influence the witness's choice. This possibility is problematic when the suspect in question is actually innocent, as the witness could be led to misidentify an innocent person. Therefore, researchers have suggested that the police implement a double-blind procedure, meaning that both the witness and the police officer administering the lineup are unaware of which lineup member is the suspect.

Origins of the Recommendation for Double-Blind Lineups

In 1996, the American Psychology-Law Society (AP-LS; Division 41 of the American Psychological Association) selected a group of eyewitness experts to review the scientific literature on eyewitnesses and make recommendations regarding the best procedures for constructing and conducting lineups and photo spreads. In this paper, the authors argue that lineups can be viewed as a research experiment in which the lineup administrator is akin to the experimenter. In this lineup-as-experiment analogy, the police have a hypothesis that they are testing (i.e., that the suspect is the perpetrator), and they create materials (lineups) with which to test their hypothesis. The lineup administrator then collects data to test the hypothesis by administering the lineup to the witness, finally interpreting the results obtained from the witness to see whether they support the hypothesis that the suspect is the perpetrator. This panel noted that as in other types of experiments, lineups in which the lineup administrator knows which lineup member is the suspect produce a test of the hypothesis that is susceptible to bias.

Although these potential biases may not occur in a conscious or deliberate manner, social-psychological research suggests that when experimenters knew the hypotheses of their studies they unconsciously influenced the participants' behavior. The earliest of these experiments, conducted by Rosenthal and colleagues, demonstrated that experimenters influenced the ability of rats that they thought were "maze smart" to maneuver a maze faster than rats that they thought were "maze stupid," even though there were no intellectual differences between the two groups of rats. In a similar experiment conducted with students attending a public school, Rosenthal and colleagues administered an intelligence test to students and informed the teachers that not only would this test determine a child's IQ but it would also pinpoint students who had the potential to make above-average intellectual progress throughout the year. Before the next school year began, teachers were given the names of the "gifted" students. In reality, their test had no such predictive ability, and the names had been drawn randomly. The students were tested again, and those who had been identified as being able to achieve above-average development showed a larger gain in IQ points, and teachers' ratings of these students stated that they were better behaved, more interested in learning, and friendlier than their peers.

This research has obvious implications for conducting lineups to test eyewitness memory. If a lineup administrator knows which lineup member is the suspect, he or she may consciously or unconsciously give verbal or behavioral cues to the witness that would influence the witness to choose the photo of the suspect. If the lineup administrator were blind to the suspect's identity, however, it would eliminate these expectancy effects and result in an unbiased lineup administration. Furthermore, the use of double-blind lineup procedures could also eliminate the influence of postidentification feedback on witnesses' ratings of their confidence in the accuracy of their identification decision.

At about the same time that the AP-LS group recommended double-blind lineups as a best practice in conducting lineups, the then U.S. attorney general Janet Reno convened a task force comprising psychologists, lawyers, judges, and police officers to create a manual of recommended best practices for police stations to follow when conducting an investigation. Although many of the practices suggested by the AP-LS group were also recommended in the manual, the task force did not include double-blind procedures in the guidelines for collecting eyewitness evidence. Instead, administrator knowledge of the suspect's identity was addressed in the introduction to the manual, where police officers were instructed on the possible dangers of single-blind lineups. However, the authors stated that they had refrained from including double-blind procedures in the recommendations because police officers had expressed concerns about the logistics of implementation. For example, many police stations with small police forces might find it difficult to locate a police officer who was not aware of the suspect's identity.

Empirical Support for the Use of Double-Blind Lineups

Psychological research specifically testing the influence of administrator knowledge has not produced a definitive answer as to whether single-blind lineups are more likely to result in mistaken identifications than are double-blind lineups. Early research seemed to indicate that when single-blind administrators presented a sequential lineup to a witness, the witness identified the innocent suspect in a target-absent lineup more often than when double-blind procedures were used, but only when there was a third party observing the lineup administration; there was no effect of investigator knowledge of the suspect's identity for simultaneous lineups. Other research that manipulated administrator contact with an eyewitness found that administrators who were aware of the suspect's identity and presented simultaneous lineups to an eyewitness produced more mistaken identifications than did administrators who were not allowed direct contact with a witness (instead presenting the witnesses with a folder containing the photographs and sitting behind the witnesses while they viewed the lineup photos). Several other studies have failed to find an effect of administrator influence at all. The most recent research on administrator influence has found that other biasing factors, such as biased instructions, need to be present for single-blind administrators to influence witnesses' decisions. It has been hypothesized that these other biasing factors serve to lower witnesses' criterion levels necessary to make an identification and, therefore, allow more opportunities for knowledgeable administrators to influence a witness.

Sarah Greathouse, Ryan Copple,
and Margaret Bull Kovera

See also Eyewitness Memory; Identification Tests, Best
   Practices in; Instructions to the Witness; Simultaneous and
   Sequential Lineup Presentation; Wrongful Conviction

Further Readings

Phillips, M. R., McAuliff, B. D., Kovera, M. B., & Cutler, B. L. (1999). Double-blind photoarray administration as a safeguard against investigator bias. *Journal of Applied Psychology, 84,* 940–951.

Rosenthal, R. (1966). *Experimenter effects in behavioral research.* New York: Appleton-Century-Crofts.

Russano, M. B., Dickinson, J. J., Greathouse, S. M., & Kovera, M. B. (2006). Why don't you take another look at number three: Investigator knowledge and its effects on eyewitness confidence and identification decisions. *Cardozo Public Law, Policy, and Ethics Journal, 4,* 355–379.

Technical Working Group for Eyewitness Evidence. (2003). *Eyewitness evidence: A trainer's manual for law enforcement* (NCJ 188678). Washington, DC: U.S. Department of Justice, National Institute of Justice.

Wells, G. L., Small, M., Penrod, S., Malpass, R. S., Fulero, S. M., & Brimacombe, C. A. E. (1998). Eyewitness identification procedures: Recommendations for lineups and photospreads. *Law and Human Behavior, 22,* 603–647.

DRUG COURTS

Drug courts are therapeutically oriented courts that attempt to reduce drug-related crime through a mixture of treatment and judicial oversight. Dade County, Florida, established the first drug court in 1989. By mid-2006, there were 1,563 drug courts in the United States, including 411 juvenile drug courts. Single- and multisite studies of drug courts, as well as meta-analyses, suggest that drug courts are more effective than traditional criminal courts in reducing recidivism, though this finding does not apply to all drug courts, nor does it apply to all defendants who appear before drug courts.

In the 1980s, the federal government and many states enacted stricter drug laws, which increased the number of defendants charged with drug-related offenses. In addition, it is estimated that between one fourth and one half of adult arrestees and one half of female arrestees are at risk of drug dependence. Drug courts were set up as a vehicle for diverting at least some of these defendants to treatment on the assumption that successful treatment would reduce the risk of future offending. The emergence of drug courts, and their rapid growth, was also stimulated by significant funding by the federal government, as well as other types of local and state funding.

Drug courts do not adhere to a single, rigid model. For example, they may differ on target populations, the types of treatment that are available, and program completion and retention rates. Despite these differences, most of them share several defining characteristics. First, they focus on providing early assessment and diversion to treatment. Some courts do this prior to adjudication of the charge, while others require the person to plead to the charge as a condition for receiving treatment rather than criminal sanctions. Second, drug courts monitor the person's adherence to treatment and other conditions established by the court, through regular oversight by probation and treatment staff and through status hearings conducted at regular intervals by the court. As part of monitoring, the defendant is subjected to frequent drug testing. Third, drug courts use a mix of incentives and sanctions in an effort to shape behavior. Incentives may include gift certificates, praise of the defendant's efforts in public judicial hearings, and graduation ceremonies on successful completion of the treatment program. Punishment for infractions, such as a failed drug test or a missed court date, often relies on graduated sanctions, including incarceration. Fourth, if the person successfully completes the treatment program, the charge may be dropped (in jurisdictions that use a preplea model) or expunged from the person's record (in jurisdictions using a postplea model).

There are other differences between drug courts and traditional criminal courts. The creation of a drug court in a jurisdiction affects the way in which criminal cases are assigned to various judges. In the absence of a drug court, there is usually little effort to assign drug-related cases to a particular judge; rather, these cases are assigned for disposition in the same way that other criminal cases are assigned. In contrast, drug courts are specialty courts, and one of the characteristics of specialty courts is that cases involving defendants eligible for the court are typically consolidated before one judge. Drug courts are also therapeutically oriented, which has an impact on the role of the judge and attorneys. The adversarial process is at the heart of the traditional criminal court. However, in a drug court (as with other therapeutically oriented courts) the adversarial process is de-emphasized, on the ground that it may be an obstacle to a therapeutic outcome. Instead, the judge, the defense attorney, and the prosecuting attorney are supposed to be united in working for the outcome that best enhances the defendant's therapeutic prospects while not placing public safety at risk.

The judge plays a dual role; on the one hand, the judge seeks to create a relationship with the defendant that increases the likelihood that the defendant will comply with treatment, while on the other, the judge retains the authority to punish the individual for behavior that deviates from the dispositional plan. Drug courts, like other therapeutically oriented courts, also are likely to spend more time on an individual case and emphasize the opportunity for the defendant to participate in the design of the treatment plan and other conditions that the defendant will be required to meet.

There have been many studies of drug courts, including single-site, multisite, and meta-analyses. While many of these studies reportedly rely on different methods and/or have methodological flaws (e.g., few are random-assignment studies) and comparison across studies is difficult because of the lack of uniformity in what is being measured, the most recent meta-analysis concluded that drug courts are more effective than traditional criminal courts in reducing recidivism and in enabling defendants to reduce substance use. It has been suggested that a number of factors may influence the effectiveness of a specific drug court, including the characteristics of the offenders eligible for the drug court program, the characteristics of the drug court program itself, the available treatment services, and community contextual issues. Studies to date do not provide conclusive evidence on the effect of any of these discrete variables, though research suggests that drug courts relying on a single treatment provider and drug courts using a single preplea or postplea model (rather than a mixed model) achieved better outcomes.

Drug courts and therapeutic courts are not without controversy. Some commentators question whether a therapeutic orientation dilutes defendant rights. Others debate whether the use of coercion is effective and ethical in mandating treatment compliance. Despite these continuing debates, the number of drug courts continues to grow, and at this point, they have become part of the judicial mainstream.

John Petrila

See also Mental Health Courts; Procedural Justice; Substance Abuse Treatment; Substance Use Disorders; Therapeutic Jurisprudence

Further Readings

Goldkamp, J. S. (1994). *Justice and treatment innovation: The drug court movement* (National Institute of Justice Update, NCJRS Document Reproduction Service No. NCJ 149 260). Washington, DC: U.S. Department of Justice, Office of Justice Programs.

U.S. General Accounting Office. (1997). *Drug courts: Overview of growth, characteristics, and results.* Washington, DC: Author.

U.S. General Accounting Office. (2005). *Adult drug courts: Evidence indicates recidivism reductions and mixed results for other outcomes.* Washington, DC: Author.

Wilson, D. B., Mitchell, O., & Mackenzie, D. L. (2006). A systematic review of drug court effects on recidivism. *Journal of Experimental Criminology, 2,* 459–487.

"DYNAMITE CHARGE"

In a majority of U.S. courts, particularly criminal courts, jury verdicts are required to be unanimous. Occasionally, however, juries are unable to reach a consensus. In such instances, judges will sometimes prompt juries to reach a decision by issuing an instruction that is often referred to as the "dynamite charge." The dynamite charge stresses the importance of reaching a unanimous verdict and puts particular pressure on jurors who hold the minority opinion to reconsider their position. Researchers have begun to explore the effects of this controversial instruction.

During jury deliberations, jurors are expected to engage in a process of social influence. Ideally, juries are supposed to come to a unanimous decision by engaging in reasoned discussion designed to convince one another that a particular decision is the correct one. By the end of the deliberations, if a unanimous verdict is reached, each juror should privately believe that the jury verdict is in fact the correct verdict. This type of influence, in which a person adopts a position because he or she has been convinced that it is truly the correct position, has been termed *informational social influence*. Another type of influence, *normative social influence*, may also play a role in jury decision making. Normative social influence occurs when a juror outwardly agrees with the jury verdict (i.e., he or she goes along with the majority's position) but privately disagrees with the decision. The juror only acquiesces due to perceived or real pressure to go along with the group decision. This, ideally, should *not* occur during jury deliberation.

If a jury deadlocks (i.e., members are unable to reach a consensus), the jury is considered to be "hung." A hung jury results in a mistrial, and a retrial may be held. Most courts view a hung jury as an outcome to be avoided because the time and resources devoted to the case do not lead to a verdict. If a jury indicates to the judge that it is unable to reach a unanimous verdict, in an effort to avoid a mistrial, the judge may order continued deliberation after issuing a supplemental instruction known as the dynamite charge. The U.S. Supreme Court first sanctioned the use of the dynamite charge (also known as the *Allen* charge) in 1896 in *Allen v. United States*. The exact wording of the dynamite charge can vary, but in its typical form, it reminds the jurors of their duty to reach a unanimous decision, and it suggests to jurors holding the minority position that they reconsider their position in light of the majority's opinion.

Proponents of the dynamite charge point out that it appears to be an effective means of encouraging verdicts. There are numerous case examples in which the dynamite charge seemed to "blast" deadlocked juries into returning unanimous verdicts soon after the charge was delivered (earning it its nickname). On the other hand, critics of the dynamite charge argue that it unfairly pressures minority jurors into changing their votes by suggesting that it is primarily their responsibility, and not the duty of majority jurors, to reconsider their position. Critics worry that the charge encourages minority jurors to acquiesce to the majority because of normative social influence (i.e., conforming due to social pressure) rather than informational social influence (i.e., a true change in opinion). In addition, there is concern that the charge incorrectly suggests to jurors that they must reach a verdict and that the jury is not permitted to hang. As a result of these concerns, some courts have ruled against the use of the dynamite charge, while others have attempted to create modified versions of it. Notably, the American Bar Association (ABA) developed guidelines for an alternate version of the dynamite charge, which reminds jurors of their duty to deliberate but does not single out minority jurors; in fact, the ABA recommends that the instruction include an admonition that specifically instructs jurors *not* to simply acquiesce to pressure from other jurors.

The criticisms and proposed reforms of the dynamite charge assume that the charge affects jurors in a particular way; however, only a few studies have attempted to directly assess the effect of the dynamite charge on jury decision making. In the first study on this topic, Saul Kassin and his colleagues recruited undergraduates to participate as mock jurors, and after reading a summary of a trial, the participants engaged in what they thought were deliberations with other jurors via written notes (in reality, there were no other jurors). The researchers manipulated whether the participants were part of the majority or minority group during deliberation and whether they received the dynamite charge or no supplementary charge after deadlocking. Consistent with critics' fears, the results indicated that minority jurors who received the dynamite charge were more likely to feel pressurized to change their votes and more likely to actually change their votes than majority jurors who received the dynamite charge. Minority jurors were no more likely to change their votes than majority jurors in the no-instruction condition. In addition, majority jurors exerted more normative pressure after receiving the dynamite charge, suggesting perhaps that the dynamite charge encourages the use of normative social pressure.

In another study, Vicki Smith and her colleague continued to explore the effect of the dynamite charge by having participants read a trial transcript and then engage in face-to-face deliberations in groups of six. They manipulated the type of supplemental charge deadlocked juries received, and they varied whether the participants were a part of the majority or minority. Consistent with the results from the first study, minority jurors who received the dynamite charge felt more pressure and were more likely to change their votes than majority jurors who received the dynamite charge. Surprisingly, there was no corresponding increase in the amount of normative pressure exerted by majority jurors who received the dynamite charge, indicating that the increased pressure felt by minority jurors was directly due to the dynamite instruction.

The published research in this area suggests that critics' concerns that the dynamite charge may selectively coerce minority jurors to capitulate to the majority are warranted. A number of pressing questions remain, including the effects of modified versions of the dynamite charge and variations in how and when the dynamite charge is delivered. In a more recent exploration, Ludmyla Washula compared the traditional dynamite charge with a version consistent with the ABA's recommendations. The results indicated that the ABA version attenuated the majority's influence under certain conditions and jurors who received the ABA version were less likely to misunderstand the law regarding hung juries than those who received the traditional dynamite charge. More research is needed to understand the full effects and parameters of the dynamite charge as well as to explore alternatives in the event that the dynamite charge is found to unfairly pressure minority jurors.

Melissa B. Russano

See also Juries and Judges' Instructions; Jury Deliberation; Jury Size and Decision Rule

Further Readings

Allen v. United States, 164 U.S. 492 (1896).

Kassin, S. M., Smith, V. L., & Tulloch, W. F. (1990). The dynamite charge: Effects on perceptions and deliberation behavior of mock jurors. *Law and Human Behavior, 14,* 537–550.

Smith, V. L., & Kassin, S. M. (1993). Effects of the dynamite charge on the deliberations of deadlocked mock juries. *Law and Human Behavior, 17,* 625–643.

ELDER ABUSE

Although elder abuse is a pervasive and growing problem, much about this topic remains unknown, and inconsistency in definitions has hampered research and practice. Both the lack of clarity of definition and the underreporting of cases have prevented a clear picture of prevalence. Notwithstanding, it is estimated that between 1 and 2 million Americans over age 65 have experienced some type of abuse. Elder abuse occurs in both institutional and domestic settings. Currently six types of abuse are generally agreed on. Profiles of victims have found no gender differences, but likelihood of abuse is higher in elders with low income and in those who are depressed or who have experienced earlier domestic abuse. Abusers are most often children and other family members of victims. Regarding treatment and prevention, collaborative approaches have been shown to be best suited for elder abuse victims; psychologists play an important role on these teams. Finally, additional funding has been noted as critical for improving prevention and treatment services, but equally important is the need for additional research.

Definitions and Prevalence

Early attempts to compile statistics on elder abuse suffered from a lack of consistency in definition. While there is still some disagreement among the various interested professional groups, a generally accepted definition of elder abuse now exists. *Elder abuse* is the umbrella term used to refer to any act that causes harm or risk of harm to a vulnerable adult. The acts can occur to elders living in domestic settings (private homes, apartments, etc.) and to elders in institutional or residential facilities. Regardless of site, six different types of abuse have been identified. For all types, acts are considered abuse whether they are intentional or not and whether they include verbal or nonverbal behavior. *Physical abuse* includes inflicting pain or injury or depriving a basic need. *Sexual abuse* includes nonconsensual sexual contact of any kind. *Emotional or psychological abuse* is the infliction of emotional anguish or distress. *Financial or material exploitation* involves funds, property, and assets. *Neglect* is the loss of food, shelter, health care, or protection and is the most common type in domestic settings. *Self-neglect* is any act by the elder himself or herself that threatens health or safety. Finally, *abandonment* is the desertion of an elder by anyone who has assumed responsibility for care.

An accurate picture of the incidence and prevalence of elder abuse is elusive for a number of reasons. First, not all states use the preceding definitions. Second, there are no uniform reporting standards or systems. This has prevented the collection of comprehensive national data. Third, only a portion of elder abuse cases is ever reported. Vulnerable elders are even less able or willing, and thus less likely, than are victims of other domestic abuse to report abuse or neglect. Current estimates suggest that only 1 out of every 5 cases in all settings is reported and only 1 in every 14 cases in domestic settings. Consequently, statistics suffer from underreporting. The National Center on Elder Abuse estimates that between 1 and 2 million Americans aged 65 and over, a frequency of 2% to 10%, have been injured, exploited, or otherwise mistreated. Specific studies indicated that in 1996, nearly 450,000 adults aged 65 and over were abused and/or neglected in domestic settings, and in 2003, the Long Term Care Ombudsmen programs reported 20,673 complaints from institutional residents. A survey of State Adult Protective Services (the agencies responsible for collecting and investigating reports of elder abuse) by the Administration on Aging, in 2004, found an increase of 19.7% in reports from 2000 to 2004 and an increase of 15.6% in substantiated cases. In considering these data, it should be remembered that the population of elders and of vulnerable elders is increasing. Furthermore, improvements in reporting and investigating may also underlie some of the increase in the number of cases reported and certainly in the substantiation of those cases. As evidence for this, states with mandatory reporting and tracking have higher rates of investigation.

Profiles of Victims and Perpetrators

Research has examined both who is most likely to be abused or neglected and who is most likely to perpetrate these crimes. The median age of abuse victims in 1996 was 77.9. In 2004, more than two in five of the cases reported involved elders aged 80 or over. In 1996, 66.4% of the victims of domestic elder abuse were White, while 18.7% were Black; Hispanic elders accounted for 10% of the domestic elder abuse cases. Minority elders may be even less likely than majority elders to report abuse, for doing so would bring shame on the family. Men and women are equally likely to be abused; men may be more likely to be victims of self-neglect. Elder abuse is more likely in situations where the husband has a lower level of education (wife's education does not seem to play a role), when family income is low, when depression is present, and when abuse occurred earlier in the household. Again, reporting problems hamper accurate data.

Perpetrators of abuse and neglect are most often children of the victim (32.6%), followed by other family members (21.5%), and then spouses and intimate partners (11.3%). Early data indicated that men were more likely to be abusers, but more recent research suggests that both men and women are equally likely to perpetrate elder abuse and neglect crimes. This may be a reflection of better reporting, better definitions, or both. Furthermore, earlier studies focused primarily on physical and sexual abuse. More

recent data on the abuser may reflect the incorporation of emotional and financial abuse and neglect. Research has yet to clarify the profile of perpetrators based on type of abuse.

Prevention and Treatment Approaches

In addition to profiling victims and abusers, a significant proportion of the research has focused on identifying best practices to improve programs and services for victims, help prevent abuse and neglect, and inform policy and law. State adult protective services are charged with screening and investigating reports and coordinating with local service providers to care for victims and with the local police to detain perpetrators. Research on the benefits of collaborative approaches has shown that elder victims are cared for more quickly and efficiently, and prevention of recurrence of abuse is greater over the long term when multiple agencies work in partnership. The greatest potential benefit, however, is in the detection and prevention of abuse. Several models have been suggested and some efficacy data have emerged suggesting that a multi-agency, interdisciplinary approach in each community has the potential to greatly reduce the incidence of elder abuse. Much more evaluation research is needed to identify the critical components of collaborative programs.

Finally, with regard to prevention, several experts in the field have implicated the widespread ageism present in society that allows elder abuse and neglect to flourish. Studies have shown that the same services available for victims of child or domestic abuse (e.g., foster homes, women's shelters) are not available for elders. Funds devoted to prevention and treatment of elder abuse are significantly less than that devoted to other types of crimes. Even the paucity of law on the federal level and the inconsistency of state laws (although all 50 states and most territories do have laws regarding elder abuse) are indicative of the poor view of elders. There is substantial literature on the negative view of elders in society and the potential for maltreatment as a result of these stereotypes. Specific to elder abuse is the literature on perception of abuse. One example is a study that presented six different scenarios to college students and asked them to rate whether abuse was present in the scenario, whether the caregiver or the older adult was the abuser, and how justified the abuse was. Scenarios included those in which a daughter throws a frying pan at her mother, a daughter threatens to poison her mother's food, a daughter withholds money belonging to her mother, and a daughter refuses to take her mother to a doctor's appointment. Students also answered questions about their relationships with their grandparents. Results showed that students found caregiver abuse to be more justifiable when the older adult was portrayed as being agitated or senile but less so when the older adult was helpless. Students who reported closer contact with their own grandparents found more instances of abuse to be unjustifiable than those students who did not maintain close ties with grandparents.

Psychologists have increasingly been part of interdisciplinary teams of professionals involved in the prevention and treatment of victims of elder abuse. Important to the definition of elder abuse and to the design of services and care programs, psychologists have helped improve prevention and treatment efforts. Those with psychology and law training have the potential to make the greatest impact. In addition to the need for more funding and staff, state adult protective agencies reported in a 2004 survey that they had a pressing need for training. Specifically, they cited that forensic interviewing, cross-training with professionals in the legal system, and improved law enforcement were critical to improving services for their clients. Clearly, increased and continuing funding and research are needed in all areas of elder abuse to help ensure the health and well-being of vulnerable elders.

M. Cherie Clark and Paul W. Foos

See also Financial Capacity; Guardianship; Proxy Decision Making

Further Readings

American Bar Association Commission on Law and Aging. (2005). *Information about laws related to elder abuse.* Available at http://www.ncea.aoa.gov

Lachs, M. S., & Pillemer, K. (2004). Elder abuse. *Lancet, 364,* 1192–1263.

National Center on Elder Abuse. (2005). *Fact sheet: elder abuse prevalence and incidence.* Available at http://www.ncea.aoa.gov

U.S. Administration on Aging. (2006). *Elders rights and resources.* Retrieved July 17, 2007, from http://www.aoa.gov/eldfam/Elder_Rights/Elder_Rights.asp

ELDERLY DEFENDANTS

As the average life span increases, the population of elders involved in the court system grows. Thus, there has been some concern about how elders are treated when in court, in prison, and on death row.

Elders on Trial

Although research is limited, some studies have shown that elders are perceived to be less credible as witnesses, perhaps because the accuracy of their memory is in doubt. There is also scant research as to how elders are treated when they are defendants. Anecdotal evidence suggests that age may affect the decisions of some jurors and judges. In 2006, 89-year-old George Weller was on trial for driving his car through a farmers' market and killing 10 people. The jury found him guilty of manslaughter, which was the most severe of their verdict options. Several members of the jury told the media that the jury had decided that the defendant's age should not affect their verdict. The judge sentenced him to probation, noting that Weller's frail health would pose difficulties for the prison system. Furthermore, the judge feared that Weller's health would suffer if he was sent to prison. Thus, both jurors and the judge commented on the defendant's age when discussing their decisions. In a second case, 86-year-old Edgar Killen was on trial in 2005 for killing three men in 1964. During voir dire, the prosecutor asked potential jurors whether the defendant's age or health would affect their decisions. The jury rejected the murder charges and, instead, found the defendant guilty of manslaughter. The judge awarded Killen the maximum sentence of 60 years. In his official opinion, the judge recognized that the lengthy sentence was essentially a life sentence but noted that age is not a factor in sentencing. As these cases illustrate, age could be influential in determining the outcome of a trial in some cases. Research is needed to determine if age has a statistically significant effect on trial outcomes.

Elders in Prisons

In recent years, the number of elderly prisoners has grown. This has led to concern that prisons are ill equipped to meet the special needs of elders, such as special dietary needs and those arising from physical limitations. Prisons have implemented a variety of solutions. Some prisons have released nonviolent elderly prisoners; others have released prisoners who are very ill and deemed to be at low risk of recidivating. Some prisons have developed programs that release prisoners with ankle bracelets that monitor their movement. Finally, some prisons have created separate geriatric units for elder prisoners. These units are tailored to the needs of the elderly. Most of these options are implemented because prisons are not physically or financially able to meet the needs of elder prisoners.

Elders on Death Row

The approximately 100 elders who are on death row present a different kind of challenge; in recent years, several court cases have challenged the constitutionality of executing elders. One case involved 76-year-old Clarence Allen, a wheelchair-bound death row prisoner, who suffered from many ailments, including blindness. Before his 2006 execution, he claimed that his execution would violate the Eighth Amendment prohibition on cruel and unusual punishment.

While the U.S. Supreme Court has determined that it is unconstitutional to execute juveniles, the mentally ill, and the mentally retarded, the Court has refused to consider cases concerning the execution of elders. The Court determined that these other groups do not have the mental capacity that makes someone deserving of the death penalty. For instance, psychological research has indicated that juveniles are immature and are sometimes unable to logically consider the outcomes of their actions. Similarly, the limited mental abilities of the mentally ill and the mentally retarded make the death penalty inappropriate for such prisoners. Most elders are not likely to receive the same leniency from the Court, unless they can show some mental deficit (e.g., Alzheimer's disease or dementia) that would make their conditions similar to that of the mentally ill or mentally retarded.

In determining whether the death penalty violates the Eighth Amendment, courts often also consider whether such punishment violates the community's "evolving standards of decency." For example, the Supreme Court determined that the community was opposed to executing the mentally ill. It is difficult to determine the public's opinion about the execution of the elderly because researchers have not studied this issue as thoroughly as they studied opinion about executing members of the other groups. There is anecdotal evidence that the public may not support execution of elders in some cases. Before 74-year-old James Hubbard was executed in 2004, his friends and community members started a petition asking the governor to convert his death sentence to life in prison. Hubbard suffered from cancer and dementia; he no longer understood why he was on death row awaiting execution. Thus, his supporters felt that he did not deserve to be put to death. Despite the public support for Hubbard, the courts and governor refused to stop the execution.

Psychologists have much to learn about how elders are treated in the legal system. Research is needed to determine how age affects verdicts and sentences, how prisons can best meet the needs of elder prisoners, how age-related mental problems affect the capacity to understand one's situation, and whether the public supports the execution of elders.

Monica K. Miller and
L. Beth Gaydon

See also Death Penalty; Elderly Witnesses; Juveniles and the Death Penalty; Mental Illness and the Death Penalty; Mental Retardation and the Death Penalty

Further Readings

Bornstein, B. H. (1995). Memory processes in elderly eyewitnesses: What we know and what we don't. *Behavioral Sciences and the Law, 13,* 337–348.

Elgit, H. C. (2005). *Ageism and the American Legal System.* Gainseville: University Press of Florida.

Gaydon, L. B., & Miller, M. K. (2007). Elders in the justice system: How the system treats elders in trials, during imprisonment, and on death row. *Behavioral Sciences & the Law, 25*(5), 677–699.

Lemieux, C. M., Dyeson, T. B., & Castiglione, B. (2002). Revisiting the literature on prisoners who are older: Are we wiser? *Prison Journal, 82,* 440–458.

ELDERLY EYEWITNESSES

As the potential pool of elder witnesses continues to expand with the aging U.S. population, the age group referred to in the literature as older adults or seniors has become of greater interest to researchers. The group typically comprises healthy, active members of the community falling into the 60- to 80-year age band. Older eyewitnesses tend to provide less detailed and less accurate descriptions of actions and persons than younger witnesses when their processing resources are depleted, but they can provide as much information as younger witnesses under some conditions. With regard to face recognition, a number of recent studies suggest that older adults are more prone to what are referred to as false recognitions.

Recall of Persons, Actions, and Events

Where comparisons have been made between different age groups, young adults have been found to be superior to older adults in some eyewitness skills. For example, Dan Yarmey in his studies reports that young adults are more accurate in their recall of perpetrator characteristics, environmental details, and details of actions than older adults. This applies to both free recall (where the witness provides a narrative account from his or her own perspective) and cued recall (where the witness responds to interviewer questions). Older adult witnesses tend to provide fewer descriptions of the perpetrator (physical and clothing characteristics) than younger witnesses. Differences between young and older adults in the amount and accuracy of recall may be even greater over long retention intervals (such as a month) and when conditions at the time of witnessing are poor, reducing the resources that are available to attend to what is happening. This may mean that there are fewer cues available at the time a witness tries to retrieve the information. Fergus Craik's classic work on memory processes indicates that older adults benefit from "environmental support" during questioning (the retrieval phase). This could take the form of an interview that provides the witness with some instruction on how to recreate, during retrieval, the personal, physical, and emotional context at the time of witnessing. For example, when older adults are questioned with a Cognitive Interview, a procedure that can aid memory search and retrieval, they can recall as much and sometimes even more information than younger adults. One qualification should be borne in mind, however. The educational level and verbal intelligence of the adult (young and old) appear to be important factors in boosting his or her recall performance, as compared with younger adults. While further research is needed on this issue, police officers and jurors should note that although verbal recall can be reduced in old age, a verbally skilled and well-educated senior can be just as reliable a witness as a young adult.

Susceptibility to Misinformation

Several recent studies have shown that older adults may experience difficulty in distinguishing between what they have witnessed themselves as opposed to what they may have heard from someone else (i.e., a problem identifying the precise source of the information). A typical consequence is that any misleading information that may be encountered subsequent to witnessing an event is erroneously reported as if it were part of the original event. However, older adults are not always more susceptible to misinformation. The contradictory findings are likely due to the fact that older adults are remembering less information overall, and this may also mean that they may pay less attention to misleading details. Additionally, there are differential rates of memory declines in older adults depending on educational level, verbal intelligence, intellectual pursuits, expertise in different skill domains, and level of physical activity. Finally, the conditions under which older adults are tested in laboratory studies (e.g., video presentation of event, short retention interval, and single interview) may obscure differences in performance that might arise under more realistic test conditions.

Recognition and Identification

The typical finding in laboratory studies of unfamiliar face recognition (the recognition of faces seen only once before) is that older adults are more likely to "false alarm" to new faces. In other words, they are more likely to falsely "recognize" a face they had not seen previously. Of particular concern are the higher rates of false identifications when seniors view lineups that do not contain the culprit. As indicated earlier, aging is typically associated with a reduction in cognitive resources and an increased reliance on nonanalytic strategies such as familiarity. It is the recollection of contextual information that is critical in an eyewitness situation that older adults might have particular difficulty with.

Field studies of actual eyewitnesses also provide us with some information on the identification ability of older adult witnesses. Tim Valentine collected data from 640 witnesses who attempted to identify suspects in 314 lineups; data were obtained from four identification suites in London in September 2000. Broadly classified by age, 48% of those below 20 years of age had made a suspect identification as compared with only 28% of the older age group (aged 40 years plus). There were no differences in the rates of identifications of the stand-ins or foils (innocent persons. in a police lineup). In most cases, the suspects were young adults, and there is some evidence that older adults do less well with younger faces (as compared with older faces), at least in situations where the perpetrator is not present in the lineup. In other words, older adults might have some advantage when recognizing faces that are closer in age to themselves.

Finally, stereotypes of elderly witnesses have been examined in simulated jury studies conducted by Liz Brimacombe in Canada. Participant jurors were presented with the videotaped testimony of young and older witnesses. In one study, older seniors were less accurate in their responses to direct and cross-examination questions but were not rated as less credible than younger seniors or younger adults. A later study confirmed that senior witnesses (70-year-olds) did provide less accurate testimony than younger adults (20-year-olds). Jurors were able to spot this and hence rated the seniors as less credible. However, age stereotypes did not bias the judgments of jurors. Further analysis showed that the witnesses (young and old) who were rated as most credible had provided fewer negative qualifiers (e.g., "I think, but I am not sure . . ."). Thus, what a witness actually says and their confidence, rather than their age, may be more important determinants of credibility.

Amina Memon

See also Cognitive Interview; Exposure Time and Eyewitness Memory; False Memories; Identification Tests, Best Practices in; Juries and Eyewitnesses; Mug Shots; Retention Interval and Eyewitness Memory; Source Monitoring and Eyewitness Memory; Unconscious Transference

Further Readings

Balota, D. A., Dolan, P., & Duchek, J. (2000). Memory changes in healthy older adults. In E. Tulving & F. I. M. Craik (Eds.), *The Oxford handbook of memory* (pp. 395–425). New York: Oxford University Press.

Brimacombe, C. A., Quinton, N., Nance, N., & Garrioch, L. (1997). Is age irrelevant? Perceptions on young and old adult witnesses. *Law and Human Behavior, 21,* 619–634.

Memon, A., Bartlett, J. C., Rose, R., & Gray, C. (2003). The aging eyewitness: The effects of face-age and delay upon younger and older observers. *Journal of Gerontology: Psychological Sciences and Social Sciences, 58,* 338–345.

END-OF-LIFE ISSUES

As the range of options for extending life and for hastening death continues to expand, so the range of issues faced by clinical evaluators also has grown. Among the most complex are those surrounding requests for assisted suicide, euthanasia, or the withdrawal or refusal of life-sustaining interventions. The availability of some of these alternatives varies by jurisdiction and medical condition, although all persons are afforded the right to refuse life-sustaining treatment. However, like all treatment decisions, requests to hasten death depend on the patient's decision-making competence. Forensic evaluators have increasingly been asked to participate in competency evaluations, particularly around end-of-life treatment decisions. For the patient who is incompetent to make treatment decisions, advance directives can help determine the course of end-of-life treatment and help preserve the patient's autonomy. But advance directives often raise a new set of questions regarding exactly when the directive should be implemented and, if a health care proxy has not been appointed, who should make treatment decisions. As public debates regarding legalized suicide or euthanasia progress, these issues will likely become even more important.

Defining Clinical/Legal Issues at the End of Life

This following section defines key terms and concepts pertaining to end-of-life decision making, including physician-assisted suicide (PAS), euthanasia, do-not-resuscitate (DNR) orders, and advance directives. Perhaps the most controversial of these issues are PAS and euthanasia. Both these interventions involve actions that directly lead to a hastened death in a seriously ill person; however, they vary in the nature of the clinician's involvement. In PAS, the clinician provides assistance and guidance, typically in the form of a prescription for medication that the patient can use if he or she chooses to commit suicide. Of key importance, it is the patient and not the physician who ultimately administers a lethal dose of medication. In 1997, this practice was legalized in Oregon, resulting in fierce public debate. Euthanasia, on the other hand, involves the intentional administration of a lethal medication *by the clinician* (presumably in response to a patient's request) for the sole purpose of ending life. In 1998, one of the leading proponents of euthanasia, Dr. Jack Kevorkian, provided a lethal injection (i.e., euthanasia) to a patient suffering from amyotrophic lateral sclerosis (ALS, also known as Lou Gehrig's disease) on national television. He was subsequently convicted of second-degree murder and sentenced to 10 to 25 years in prison. Although euthanasia is now legal in the Netherlands and Belgium, it remains illegal in the United States.

Both PAS and euthanasia are distinguished from the clinical practice of administering high doses of pain medication in an effort to control severe pain, often with the awareness that death is likely to occur. This practice, referred to as "the law of double effect," differs because the express purpose of the medication is to control pain, not to end life.

In addition to interventions that have the direct effect of ending life immediately, there are a number of other death-hastening procedures that are often the source of controversy and psycholegal inquiry. For example, death can be hastened by withdrawing or refusing life-sustaining medical care, sometimes referred to as "passive euthanasia." This includes decisions to remove mechanical ventilation (i.e., a machine to keep a comatose patient breathing), refuse needed renal dialysis, or refuse or terminate artificial nutrition and hydration. In such cases, the rejection of needed medical interventions can hasten a death that might otherwise be delayed for weeks, months, or even years. Yet while legal debate and controversy surrounds more direct interventions such as PAS and euthanasia, the right of a mentally competent adult to refuse life-sustaining interventions is uncontested.

Refusal of life-sustaining interventions becomes more complex and controversial when the patient no longer has the capacity to make or articulate a competent decision. In patients with life-threatening or terminal illness, such situations are often anticipated, and patients provide their consent *in advance*. There are two legal mechanisms to accomplish this goal: Advance Directives (ADs, sometimes called "Living Wills") and the Durable Power of Attorney or Health Care Proxy (although different jurisdictions have used slightly different labels to describe these two types of legal instruments). Regardless of the term used, both alternatives enable the patient to influence treatment decisions that may arise after he or she has lost the capacity to provide informed consent.

ADs are broad in range and encompass highly specific interventions and situations such as the DNR order (a refusal of CPR if the patient's heart stops) to very broad documents that specify multiple scenarios in which different treatments are desired or rejected. The broadest mechanism of all is the health care proxy or durable power of attorney, where the medically ill or elderly person appoints another individual to make treatment decisions on his or her behalf in the event that he or she becomes incapacitated. Each of these ADs provides a mechanism for individuals to protect their autonomy and influence treatment decisions, although both ultimately rely on another person's willingness or ability to carry out the patient's wishes. Moreover, while these instruments remain dormant until the patient loses the capacity to make treatment decisions, controversies often arise as to whether the situation described in an AD exists (e.g., if the patient has specified that treatment should be withheld if no chance of recovery exists). In such cases, medical, mental health, and forensic specialists are often asked to provide input to determine appropriate directions.

Legal History of the "Right to Die"

Although case law regarding the right to determine what medical treatments are implemented is long-standing, end-of-life treatment decisions were rarely addressed before the seminal New Jersey Supreme Court decision *In re Quinlan* (1976). Although this case never reached the Supreme Court, the request by Karen Quinlan's parents to terminate the mechanical respirator that was keeping their daughter alive was widely recognized as the first significant challenge to the medical profession's practice of extending life as long as possible.

The right-to-die issue first reached the U.S. Supreme Court roughly 15 years later, in *Cruzan v. Director, Missouri Department of Health* (1990). Like *Quinlan,* this case also involved a young woman, Nancy Cruzan, who fell into a persistent vegetative state (i.e., comatose with no evidence of brain activity) that required the insertion of a feeding tube. After 4 years, her parents requested the removal of the feeding tube to allow their daughter to die. The hospital refused to comply, and the Cruzans subsequently sued the Missouri Department of Health. Although the Court ruled in favor of the state, the decision affirmed the right of competent persons to refuse life-sustaining medical intervention, whether through their own decision making or through ADs. However, the Court left standards for determining decision-making competency and guidelines for decision making to the states.

The Supreme Court addressed hastened death even more directly in a pair of 1997 cases that challenged existing prohibitions against PAS. In *Washington v. Glucksberg* (1997) and *Vacco v. Quill* (1997), the Court considered the question of whether permitting some terminally ill patients to discontinue life-sustaining treatment (e.g., the Cruzan decision), while denying other terminally ill individuals the right to hasten death (i.e., those who do not require such interventions) violated the Due Process and Equal Protection clauses of the Fourteenth Amendment. Although the Court rejected this assertion by distinguishing between active and passive methods for hastening death, the Court opined that decisions about PAS could be determined by the individual states, essentially clearing the way for legalized PAS.

The Court's opinion was not accidental; 3 years earlier, Oregon voters had approved a ballot referendum authorizing the Death with Dignity Act, legalizing PAS in that state (a number of other states have held referendums on this issue before and since Oregon's, but voters have rejected these proposals). In October of 1997, shortly after the *Washington v. Glucksberg* (1997) and *Vacco v. Quill* (1997) rulings, Oregon's referendum took effect, making this the first and only state in the United States to legalize PAS. Under the guidelines of the Oregon's Death with Dignity Act (or ODDA), an Oregon resident may request a prescription for a medication that will result in death. The individual must be 18 years of age or older, with a terminal illness and a life expectancy of less than 6 months. Additionally, the individual must be capable of making a "reasoned judgment" (described further below). Request for PAS must be made at least twice, of which one request must be written, and the physician is required to solicit a second opinion regarding the patient's diagnosis. Finally, the physician is responsible for determining if a mental disorder has impaired the patient's judgment (i.e., rendered him or her incompetent) and, if so, whether mental health consultation and/or treatment is required. This latter requirement has engendered considerable controversy, largely because of concerns that patients with significant depression may not be accurately identified. However, data from Oregon indicate that requests for PAS are relatively rare, accounting for roughly 1 in 10,000 Oregon deaths (.01%) or 40 to 50 requests per year. Of those patients who qualify for PAS and fulfill all the requirements, approximately two thirds ultimately die by ingesting the prescribed medication. This rate is substantially lower than data from the Netherlands, where euthanasia accounts for roughly 3% of all deaths.

Treatment Decision Making

A critical element of end-of-life decision making is the ability of the patient to make a rational, informed choice. The term *competence* refers to a determination as to whether one is legally authorized to make decisions for himself or herself. However, it can be difficult to determine competence in terminally ill patients, in part because impairments are often subtle, like dementia or depression (vs. psychosis, which is a common basis for incompetence among psychiatric patients). Even when "rational thinking" appears intact, symptoms such as depression can affect end-of-life decisions. For example, depression can increase a patient's skepticism about the efficacy of pain or symptom control and contribute toward a feeling of hopelessness, at times leading to requests for PAS or refusals of life-sustaining interventions despite long-standing moral or personal objections to hastened death. Later, once symptoms have been treated, these patients may be thankful that their request for euthanasia was not fulfilled. On the other hand, denying terminally ill patients the right to refuse life-sustaining treatment may inflict undue pain and distress, essentially ignoring the patient's autonomy. Thus, accurate evaluations of a patient's decision-making capacity, once this ability has been called into question, is critical and requires considerable expertise, both in the legal issues (i.e., evaluating decision-making capacity in general) as well as the specific context (severe or life-threatening illness).

Once a patient has been found incompetent to make treatment decisions, the mechanism for deciding among treatment options hinges on the particular jurisdiction. This process is, in theory, greatly simplified when ADs exist to document the patient's wishes. However, in actuality, ADs are often less helpful than patients assume. These instruments often present information in vague terms (e.g., "when the prognosis for recovery or posttreatment quality of life is extremely poor") that make it difficult to determine exactly when to apply the directive. Furthermore, physicians may be reluctant to carry out the patient's wishes, even when no dispute as to applicability of the directive exists (particularly if they disagree with the decision). In the absence of a designated health care proxy, families may debate about whom to appoint to make treatment decisions on the patient's behalf or disagree about which course of action is best. Although a mental health evaluator may participate in helping clarify issues such as decision-making capacity, determining who acts as the surrogate decision maker and establishing guidelines for decision making are usually left to the treating physician, hospital ethics committees, or even the courts.

Barry Rosenfeld and Lia Amakawa

See also Proxy Decision Making; Psychiatric Advance Directives

Further Readings

American Medical Association Council on Ethical and Judicial Affairs. (1998). Optimal use of orders not to intervene and advance directives. *Psychology, Public Policy, and Law, 4,* 668–675.

Cruzan v. Director, Missouri Department of Health, 497 U.S. 261 (1990).

Emanuel, L. L. (1988). *Regulating how we die: The ethical, medical, and legal issues surrounding physician-assisted suicide.* Cambridge, MA: Harvard University Press.

In re Quinlan, cert. denied, 429 U.S. 92 (1976).

Rosenfeld, B. (2004). *Physician-assisted suicide, euthanasia, and the right to die: The interface of social science, public policy, and medical ethics.* Washington, DC: American Psychological Association Press.

Vacco v. Quill, 521 U.S. 793 (1997).

Washington v. Glucksberg, 521 U.S. 702 (1997).

Werth, J., Benjamin, G., & Farrenkopf, T. (2000). Requests for physician-assisted deaths: Guidelines for assessing mental capacity and impaired judgment. *Psychology, Public Policy, and Law, 6*(2), 348–372.

ESTIMATOR AND SYSTEM VARIABLES IN EYEWITNESS IDENTIFICATION

A distinction between estimator and system variables is made in the eyewitness research literature between two categories or types of variables that influence the accuracy of eyewitness accounts. System variables are those that are (or can be) under the control of the justice system, whereas estimator variables cannot be controlled by the justice system. Examples of system variables include factors such as the instructions given to eyewitnesses prior to their viewing a lineup or the number of people who are used in a lineup. Examples of estimator variables include factors such as how good a view the eyewitness had of the perpetrator during the crime or whether the witness and perpetrator were of the same or different race. The estimator versus system variable distinction tends to be tied to a temporal unfolding of events, in the sense that events that occur before or during the witnessing experience are necessarily relegated to estimator variable status whereas system variables begin to come into play later, once the investigation is under way. There is no presumption in the estimator variable versus system variable distinction that one category of variables has more impact on eyewitness accuracy than the other. Nevertheless, this distinction, first articulated in 1978 by Gary L. Wells, has tended to result in a higher premium being placed on system variables because these can be used to help minimize eyewitness errors in actual cases, whereas estimator variables can only be used to postdict how the variables might have influenced the eyewitness.

The study of system variables has generally been tied to policy-related recommendations on ways to improve how crime investigators interview eyewitnesses and on ways to improve how lineups are constructed and conducted. The study of estimator variables, in contrast, has more often been tied to the development of expert testimony that can assist triers of fact (e.g., judges, juries) in deciding whether to accept the testimony of an eyewitness as having been accurate or mistaken. In fact, however, system variables are as relevant to expert testimony as are estimator variables, and in recent years, it has become more apparent that estimator variables and system variables are not independent. In general, the impact of system variables is likely to depend somewhat on the levels of the estimator variables. An obvious example of this dependence is when the estimator variables are highly favorable to the existence of an extremely deep, solid memory. If memory is strong enough, system variables would not likely have much impact. For instance, system variable research shows that it is critical for eyewitnesses to be warned prior to viewing a lineup that the actual perpetrator might not be present, because the absence of such a warning leads eyewitnesses to select someone from a lineup even if the actual perpetrator is not present. However, if the eyewitness's memory is strong enough (e.g., attempting to pick one's own mother from a lineup), the presence or absence of this warning is of little consequence. Hence, a complete understanding of eyewitness performance clearly requires research on both system and estimator variables.

Generally, system variables can also serve the function of being estimator variables, but estimator variables cannot be system variables. In some cases, however, variables that traditionally have been considered estimator variables have taken on system-variable-like properties. The confidence of an eyewitness, for instance, has traditionally been considered an estimator variable because it was presumed to be beyond the control of the justice system, and the emphasis of the estimator variable research on eyewitness confidence was to find out how well or poorly it postdicted the accuracy of the eyewitness. Now, however, there is a great deal of research showing that procedures that are under the control of the justice system affect the confidence of the eyewitness and the magnitude of the confidence-accuracy relation. In this sense, eyewitness confidence, traditionally an estimator variable, has taken on some of the properties of a system variable.

In eyewitness identification research, system and estimator variables have been further subdivided in recent years into two types—namely, suspect-bias variables and general-impairment variables. Suspect-bias variables are those that influence the eyewitness specifically toward identifying the suspect from a lineup, whereas general-impairment variables simply reduce the overall performance of the eyewitness. An example of a general-impairment system variable is when the lineup administrator fails to instruct the eyewitness that the perpetrator might not be in the lineup. In this case, the instruction failure impairs the eyewitness's performance (by making the eyewitness insensitive to the possibility that the correct answer might be "not there") but does not specifically bias the eyewitness toward the suspect any more than it biases the eyewitness toward the nonsuspects in the lineup. An example of a suspect-bias system variable is when a lineup is structured in such a way that the suspect stands out as the obvious choice (e.g., as the only one who fits the description of the culprit). An example of a general-impairment estimator variable is poor viewing conditions at the time of witnessing. Poor viewing conditions might impair the eyewitness's performance on the lineup, but poor viewing conditions do not specifically bias the eyewitness toward the suspect

any more than they bias the eyewitness toward the nonsuspects in the lineup. An example of a suspect-bias estimator variable is when the eyewitness has source confusion, such as when an innocent suspect is picked out of a lineup because he was familiar; but he was familiar because he had been a customer, not because he was the person who robbed the clerk.

Gary L. Wells

See also Expert Psychological Testimony; Identification Tests, Best Practices in

Further Readings

Wells, G. L., Memon, A., & Penrod, S. (2006). Eyewitness evidence: Improving its probative value. *Psychological Science in the Public Interest, 7,* 45–75.
Wells, G. L., & Olson, E. (2003). Eyewitness identification. *Annual Review of Psychology, 54,* 277–295.

ETHICAL GUIDELINES AND PRINCIPLES

Ethics is a term used to describe the guiding philosophies and/or moral values of a group or an individual. Although ethics are by definition theoretical in nature, they are the underlying principles that help guide the conduct of any given society, profession, or individual.

This entry reviews important concepts for understanding the application of ethical principles to the practice of forensic psychology. It addresses issues such as identifying the intended beneficiary of forensic services, the application of the principle of beneficence/nonmalfeasance, and the relevance of existing professional standards and guidelines. It then summarizes four of the major elements of ethical forensic psychological practice: competency, judgment, responsibility, and accountability.

Intended Beneficiary of the Forensic Product or Service

A critical aspect of ethical practice is the clarification of the forensic task(s) to be provided and the acquisition of informed consent from the intended recipient(s) of those services, which should occur prior to providing forensic services. This includes clarification of at least the following areas:

- What is the forensic psychological service being requested?
- What is the *risk-benefit analysis* for any recipient or client receiving or not receiving the service?
- What is the *product* of this service?
- Who is the *direct recipient* of provision of this service?
- Who is the *retaining client* for this service?
- Who is the *ultimate beneficiary* of this service?

Forensic psychological service most commonly refers to any service that is undertaken for the purpose of, or with the anticipation of, assisting a third-party decision maker or trier of fact. This may refer to services provided at the request of an attorney, judge, or court order, as well as other third parties such as an insurance company, licensing board, employer, parole board, or other administrative body, or pursuant to applicable law, statute, or contract. Forensic psychological services may include multiple elements, such as a record review, psychological testing, clinical interviews, collateral interviews, and a review of current professional literature. Or such services may be narrower in scope, such as providing consultation to an attorney by reviewing relevant records and summarizing applicable professional literature. What usually defines a service as forensic is the fact that it is undertaken for the purpose of providing psychological information about a party to a third party, generally in the context of an adjudicative decision-making process.

It is important to note that a service that was not originally intended for the purpose of assisting a third-party decision maker is *not* usually considered a forensic psychological service, even if it is eventually used as evidence in a decision-making process. For example, a psychologist who has provided treatment to a criminal offender may be called on to testify at the parole board hearing; but in doing so, the psychologist is not providing a forensic service (as the primary purpose of therapy is to help the offender and not to assist a third-party decision maker), and the psychological testimony would be provided within the role of therapist-expert as opposed to a forensic expert. Whether or not such information is ultimately of use to a third-party decision maker is a separate issue from whether the work was undertaken for that purpose.

Unlike other types of psychological services, the *beneficiary of forensic psychological services* is not the party who is being evaluated. On the contrary, the services undertaken by the forensic practitioner may be harmful to the offender, either directly (e.g., if the

evaluation portrays the examinee in a negative light) or indirectly (e.g., if the evaluation harms the examinee's legal case). Similarly, although psychologists are traditionally regarded as serving in a helping capacity, the product of a forensic psychologist may be seen as directly or indirectly harmful to other parties involved in the legal matter (e.g., providing consultation to an attorney that helps exonerate an alleged perpetrator may be perceived by some as harming the alleged victim). Therefore, in the forensic context, psychologists are still "helping professionals," but the role of the forensic psychologist is to be helpful to the *court* and only incidentally to any other party or counsel.

What each of these scenarios has in common is the fact that the direct beneficiary of the forensic psychological service is not any one individual but, rather, the court or other tribunal in which the forensic psychological service is being used. That is, the forensic practitioner is trying to help the third-party decision maker by applying his or her scientific, technical, expert knowledge to the psycholegal issue. Regardless of the outcome of the matter, the forensic psychologist has helped by participating in the process. Accordingly, the indirect beneficiary of forensic psychological services is society itself, as we all benefit from the appropriate use of expert knowledge to facilitate a fair and accurate judicial process.

A separate issue from who is the beneficiary of forensic psychological services is the question of *who is the client* of the forensic psychologist on any particular matter. Typically, the client is the referring party; that is, the party requesting forensic psychological services—usually an attorney, judge, or administrative body. The client may also be another individual professional, such as when a psychologist is asked by a forensic psychiatrist or master's-level forensic examiner to conduct psychological testing. In most cases, the client of the forensic practitioner is someone other than the party who is being examined.

Beneficence and Nonmalfeasance

For all psychologists, a governing ethical standard is "to produce good" (beneficence) and "to do no harm" (nonmalfeasance). This is a critical aspect of forensic psychological practice as well. However, unlike most psychological practice, the commitment of beneficence/nonmalfeasance is not to the party who is being examined by the forensic practitioner but, rather, to the client of the forensic services. Indeed, the party being examined may very well be harmed by the outcome of the forensic psychological examination (consider the losing party in a custody dispute), but the court benefits from the "good" produced by the forensic psychologist (whose purpose in a custody dispute is to serve the best interests of the child). Even in a case where the client of the forensic services is an individual attorney (who has, e.g., retained a forensic psychological consultant to review records and examine his or her client in a personal injury matter) and the result of the forensic services is not favorable to the attorney's client (e.g., the opinion of the forensic psychologist is that the client's psychological problems are primarily a result of factors other than the claimed acts), the forensic practitioner has nonetheless helped the attorney by providing him or her with important psychological information about his or her client and/or case prior to entering a courtroom. This information provides the attorney with possible strategies for structuring the case, approaching settlement, and presenting evidence at trial. Furthermore, the psychological information directly benefits the court by potentially expediting the judicial process (e.g., if the case settles rather than moving to a full-blown trial) and indirectly benefits society as a whole (i.e., by facilitating due process). In these ways, the forensic practitioner has fulfilled a commitment to beneficence/nonmalfeasance regardless of the content of the opinion provided to the attorney.

Guidance: Standard of Care (EPPCC) and Aspirational (SGFP)

In considering the application of ethics to a profession, it is important to distinguish between standards of care and aspirational guidelines. A *standard of care* is a required and enforceable mandate that directs professional conduct and decision making. The goal of a standard is to provide the minimum expectations for a particular profession. When a professional has violated such a code of conduct, a governing body may seek recourse and enforce consequences to that professional. With regard to the practice of forensic psychology, standards of care are defined and enforced by the American Psychological Association's Ethical Principles of Psychologists and Code of Conduct (EPPCC). However, these standards are designed primarily to govern the profession of psychology in general and not designed specifically for the practice of forensic psychology.

An *aspirational guideline*, or principle, is similar to a standard in that it provides professionals with information to help guide their conduct and professional

judgment. Unlike a standard, however, an aspirational guideline is not a mandate; nor is it enforceable. Accordingly, aspirational guidelines are expected to be integrated with other relevant sources of information to help guide professional decision making. For forensic practitioners, aspirational guidelines have been provided by the American Psychology-Law Society's Specialty Guidelines for Forensic Psychologists (SGFP). The goal of these guidelines is to help inform forensic practitioners and guide professional judgment in the practice of psychology and the law. Four major themes of professional guidelines to be reviewed here include competence, judgment, responsibility, and accountability.

Technical and Substantive Competence

In forensic psychological practice, one can conceptualize two major types of competence: technical and substantive. *Technical* competence refers to the parties and the experts having met the deadlines and other technical requirements to be "legally qualified" to testify on a particular issue. These competencies are mostly identified in Civil Rules 26 and 35 and to a lesser extent in the Rules of Evidence. For example, a court may decide that an expert is technically not "qualified" to testify if the subject matter of the expert's preferred testimony was not adequately disclosed or if a written report signed by the expert was not provided in a timely manner.

Substantive competence refers to whether the forensic practitioner has the requisite expertise, scientific knowledge, and experience to be helpful to the trier of fact. The court must be satisfied that the psychologist is adequately qualified to testify by virtue of the psychologist's education, training, and/or experience; that the preferred testimony is sufficiently based on reliable facts or data; that it is the product of reliable principles and methods; and that the psychologist has applied the principles and methods reliably to the facts of the case. These competencies are mostly identified in the Rules of Evidence and are elaborated on in *Frye v. United States* (1923) and *Daubert v. Merrell Dow Pharmaceuticals* (1993).

Professional Competence

A forensic psychologist may have substantive competence in some areas (e.g., child development, psychometrics) but not in others (e.g., competency to stand trial, sex-offender risk assessment). Substantive competence should be maintained through ongoing experience, acquisition of knowledge (e.g., reading, continuing education), and/or professional consultation. When expanding one's expertise by undertaking a new type of forensic service, the ethical forensic practitioner seeks supervision and/or consultation with another forensic psychological practitioner who has established expertise in that area. The ethical forensic practitioner *does not misrepresent his or her competence* in communications to potential clients, either verbally (e.g., on accepting a referral, during expert qualification) or in writing (e.g., in one's curriculum vita).

An ethical forensic practitioner should also have some degree of substantive competence with regard to his or her *knowledge of the legal system.* Although it is not necessary to have competence as an attorney, it is important that a forensic practitioner be aware of the legal aspects of the particular forensic service he or she is providing, such as the elements of the psycholegal question, the examinees' rights in participating in the examination, and the rules of evidence for providing an expert opinion to the court.

Finally, an ethical forensic practitioner demonstrates an *appreciation of individual and contextual differences.* Specifically, the forensic practitioner is able to effectively balance his or her knowledge of general psychological principles with his or her understanding of the individual being examined, as well as the context in which an examination is occurring. For example, an individual's test-taking style may reflect cultural differences rather than clinical psychopathology (e.g., "healthy paranoia" vs. clinical paranoia). Similarly, an individual's response style may vary greatly from one context to another (e.g., self-disclosure of problems in a personal injury examination may be greater than self-disclosure of problems in a child custody examination) that is consistent with the demand characteristics of that setting and not necessarily evidence of a deliberate effort to distort one's self-presentation.

Judgment

The judgment of the ethical forensic practitioner should be guided by at least four basic principles: relevance, accuracy, equitable perspective, and candor.

With regard to *relevance,* the ethical and competent forensic practitioner focuses the scope of his or her examination on the legally relevant factors that are subject to psychological inquiry. For example, when examining an individual's competency to stand trial, forensic psychological practitioners limit the scope of

their examination to assessing whether the individual has an impaired ability to understand the nature of the proceedings against him or her and/or the ability to cooperate with his or her attorney. For any given aspect of an individual's history to be relevant to the examination (e.g., that the individual was sexually abused as a child), it must be relevant to the psycholegal issue (e.g., does his history of child sexual abuse impair his current functioning?).

An ethical forensic psychologist should also *present his or her findings accurately*—in other words, with objectivity, impartiality, and nonpartisanship. The role of the forensic psychologist is not to advocate for one "side" or another but, rather, to provide the court with all relevant psychological information so that the court can render its decision.

To maintain accuracy and objectivity, the ethical forensic practitioner should maintain an *equitable perspective* of the various "sides" of the psycholegal issue and test plausible rival hypotheses for each formulated opinion. For example, a forensic practitioner conducting a personal injury examination should consider all potential causes of an examinee's psychological damage before rendering an opinion about the damage caused by the alleged tortuous acts.

As part of formulating an equitable perspective, the ethical forensic practitioner should *assign fair weight to the data* on which the opinion was founded and not be unfairly or unduly prejudicial in presenting the data. For example, a father may have used cocaine on one or two occasions since the birth of a child, but this fact does not, in and of itself, provide evidence of cocaine abuse or dependence—and more important, it does not directly speak to his parenting capacity. Rather, past cocaine use is one data point that must be integrated with other information about the father and weighed against data known about the mother.

Unlike many other types of psychological services, forensic psychology involves the integration of multiple sources of data, including the use of collateral informants. These collateral sources of data may be useful in obtaining information about an examinee that the examinee is unwilling or unable to provide on his or her own. However, in integrating collateral sources of data, the forensic practitioner should be aware of the nature of the relationship between the collateral informant and the examinee and the potential bias inherent in such a relationship. Accordingly, the forensic practitioner should not rely on such data in isolation but, rather, integrate this information with other data to corroborate or disconfirm hypotheses.

And it goes almost without saying, that unless the practitioner is candid about all of the above and the entire examination process, the examiner is putting the desires of the client ahead of the needs of the court. Only by being candid can the expert be most helpful to the court's understanding of the data collected and opinion formed.

Responsibility

The ethical forensic practitioner has a responsibility to maintain the *integrity* of the profession. Specifically, they provide services in a manner that is respectful to all parties involved, impartial, accurate, and well documented. It is important that the ethical practitioner recognizes the distinct role of the forensic psychologist and clarifies this role with all parties prior to undertaking forensic psychological services.

Forensic psychological experts are expected to *refrain from engaging in role conflicts.* They should not provide forensic psychological services when past, present, or future interests or relationships are likely to impair their objectivity (albeit unwittingly). Among the most important role conflicts to avoid is serving in both a therapeutic and forensic role.

Forensic practitioners *document all relevant data* in the course of their examination, beginning from the moment they can reasonably anticipate that their services may be relied on by a trier of fact. Documentation includes, but is not limited to, letters, handwritten notes, e-mail correspondence, facsimile, recordings, test data, and interpretive reports. When provided with appropriate subpoenas and court orders, all relevant records are made available to the requesting party.

Accountability and Informed Consent

As soon as is feasible, forensic psychological experts obtain *informed consent* from all parties involved in the provision of forensic psychological services. Informed consent refers to an exchange between the provider of services and the person being examined. The ethical forensic practitioner provides the examinee (as well as the examinee's attorney) and other recipients of forensic services (e.g., collaterals, nonparty examinees) with as much information as possible about the examination process to help the examinee make an informed decision about whether or not to participate. This information typically should include, but is not limited to, the purpose, nature, and anticipated use of the examination and report, the impartial nature of the examiner's role, the anticipated methods and procedure for addressing the psycholegal issue, the limitations of scientific knowledge to address that issue, any potential risks of participation, the nonconfidential nature of the examination, the voluntariness of the examination (if not court ordered), relevant fee agreements, and the examinee's rights and responsibilities.

The Big Picture

The ultimate conceptual goal of good forensic practice is surprisingly easy to identify. As reflected in Evidence Rule 702, expert witnesses are in the unique position among witnesses of being the only witnesses who are allowed to offer opinions if, among other things, their opinion testimony "will assist the trier of fact." Being misled, having relevant information omitted, hearing opinions that are weighted unfairly, or in any other way being presented information by an expert witness that is distorted rather than trustworthy does not assist the trier of fact in better understanding the evidence. The goal is for the court to be able to trust what experts say and to be able to trust that whatever an expert does say in offering an opinion adequately reflects all that is relevant regarding that opinion, including all reasonable perspectives on that opinion.

Jennifer Wheeler

See also Expert Psychological Testimony, Admissibility Standards; Expert Testimony, Qualifications of Experts; Forensic Assessment; Mental Health Law; Therapeutic Jurisprudence

Further Readings

Committee on Ethical Guidelines for Forensic Psychologists. (1991). Specialty guidelines for forensic psychologists. *Law and Human Behavior, 15,* 655–665 (revision draft in preparation).

Covell, C. N., & Wheeler, J. G. (2006). Revisiting the irreconcilable conflict between therapeutic and forensic: Implications for sex offender specialists. *American Psychology-Law Society Newsletter, 26,* 6–8.

Daubert v. Merrell Dow Pharmaceuticals, 509 U.S. 579 (1993).

Frye v. United States, 293 F. 1013 (D.C. Cir. 1923).

Greenberg, S. A., & Shuman, D. W. (2007). When worlds collide: Therapeutic and forensic roles. *Professional Psychology: Research and Practice, 38,* 129–132.

Greenberg, S. A., Shuman, D. W., & Meyer, R. (2004). Unmasking forensic diagnosis. *International Journal of Law and Psychiatry, 27,* 1–15.

Heilbrun, K. (2001). *Principles of forensic mental health assessment.* New York: Kluwer Academic/Plenum.

Melton, G. B., Petrila, J., Poythress, N. G., & Slogobin, C. (1997). *Psychological evaluations for the courts: A handbook for mental health professionals and the courts.* New York: Guilford Press.

ETHNIC DIFFERENCES IN PSYCHOPATHY

Psychopathic personality disorder comprises a distinct collection of deviant affective, interpersonal, and behavioral features. Results of psychopathy testing can sway life-altering decisions for the examinee, including granting of parole, outcome in sexually violent predator civil commitment trials, gaining access to treatment, and even being sentenced to death. Because the disorder is strongly predictive of violent and general criminal recidivism, it has had an impact on correctional theory, public policy, and legal decision making on an international scale. Although psychopathy is one of the most researched disorders within the field of psychology and law, until recently most empirical investigations involved White male prisoners and forensic psychiatric patients in North America. Given that assessments of psychopathy occur regularly and as a matter of law in many contexts, it is crucial to ascertain the extent to which the primarily White male research base generalizes to other relevant populations, such as individuals of other ethnic backgrounds. Research indicates that the Psychopathy Checklist–Revised (PCL–R) measures the disorder in an unbiased way across ethnocultural groups within a single culture (White vs. Black within North America, Scottish vs. English and Welsh within the United Kingdom). However, there is some evidence of cross-national metric invariance: That is, North Americans obtain PCL–R scores that are 2 to 3 points higher than those of Europeans, given equivalent levels on the underlying trait of psychopathy. Moreover, whereas there is little cross-cultural bias in ratings of affective symptoms of psychopathy, bias does exist for ratings of the interpersonal and behavioral symptoms. In light of the substantial weight placed on PCL–R results when important decisions about individual liberties are made, it is crucial that cross-cultural research continue, preferably using more culturally informed classifications of ethnic status and with varied samples, including women and girls and individuals outside of Europe and North America. Such research may also shed light on the etiological bases underpinning the divergent manifestations of psychopathy.

Ethnicity refers to differences in culture and ancestry. In social sciences research, the term *race* is often used interchangeably with *ethnicity*, although the former term generally denotes more fine-grained genetic differences. In psychopathy research, race typically is based on self-identification rather than biological or genetic classification. In this entry, the term ethnicity is used to refer to ethnic, cultural, and racial groups as conceptualized within the relevant research literature on ethnicity and psychopathy. Three key issues have been addressed within this research base: (a) the degree to which similar patterns of associations between external correlates of psychopathy are observed across groups, (b) measurement generalization across groups, and (c) mean levels of psychopathic traits across groups.

External Correlates of Psychopathy Across Ethnic Groups

For psychopathy to be construed as a universal syndrome, the correlates of psychopathy should be similar across ethnic groups. The correlates that, perhaps, are of greatest interest include antisocial behavior and violence. Results of studies on adult criminal offending in the community conducted outside North America and with non-Whites in North America are similar in that psychopathy is inversely related to age of onset of criminal behavior and that individuals scoring high on psychopathic traits commit more violent and nonviolent crime and are more versatile in their crime patterns. Meta-analytic evidence indicates, however, that psychopathy is a weaker correlate of violent recidivism among more ethnically diverse samples of juvenile offenders relative to primarily White samples. Pertaining to institutional aggression, meta-analytic results indicate that the country under study matters: Although the predictive utility of psychopathy for broad categories of institutional misbehavior is good, its relation to violent infractions in the United States is substantially smaller than in non-U.S. institutions. One explanation for this disparity is the potentially greater ethnic heterogeneity in U.S. samples.

Another class of external correlates of psychopathy comprises psychophysiological and behavioral variables that exhibit reliable patterns in North American samples. The few cross-cultural studies investigating such variables offer inconsistent findings. Additionally, studies of performance on laboratory tasks that assess cognitive and emotional processing in North America suggest that Whites and Blacks high on psychopathic traits may process information differently.

Studies conducted in North America and abroad on the association between psychopathy and major mental illness and personality disorders indicate similar patterns for comorbid psychiatric diagnoses and self-report personality traits. However, research investigating White and Black U.S. offenders suggests that members of these groups do not manifest the same patterns of correlations between psychopathy and self-report personality measures. Whereas the association between psychopathy and self-reported negative affect is similar for Blacks and Whites, associations between impulsivity and psychoticism are less consistent. The observed discrepancies suggest that mechanisms underlying psychopathy may differ for Blacks and Whites and may be influenced by genetic and sociocultural factors that vary across ethnic groups.

Measurement Generalization Across Ethnic Groups

In contemporary research, psychopathy most often is operationalized vis-à-vis the PCL family of measures. Traditional psychometric evaluations indicate adequate reliability for the PCL–R among non-White adults as well as for adolescents of various ethnicities assessed with the youth version of the measure. To demonstrate cross-cultural equivalence of the PCL–R, it is also necessary to demonstrate that the factor structure of the measure is the same across ethnic groups (i.e., that the same items or symptoms cluster together). There is clear evidence of a replicable factor structure(s) among White and Black adult men in U.S. prisons; among White, Black, and Latino boys in the United States; and among European men (including men from Scotland and several continental European countries).

Cross-cultural equivalence in the case of the PCL–R also requires that the association between test scores and the latent trait of psychopathy be invariant across ethnic groups (metric invariance), which may be examined using item response theory (IRT). IRT confers several distinct advantages to investigations of

cross-cultural disparities: Representative samples are not required, more detailed analysis of individual ratings can be provided, and a determination can be made regarding whether scores are measured on the same scale with different ethnic groups. An often-cited analogy that involves the measurement of temperature using Fahrenheit and Celsius degrees may help clarify the last point: Although both scales measure the same construct, comparisons are meaningless because they differ in zero points and scale increments. In the case of the PCL–R, metric variance across groups is problematic because different scores could express the same level of the latent trait of psychopathy (or, conversely, the same PCL–R score obtained by two groups would not represent the same underlying level of the disorder). In general, research using IRT methods indicates that the PCL–R may be used in an unbiased way with Blacks. However, there does appear to be evidence of metric invariance between North America and Europe (both in the United Kingdom and continental countries). Compared with North Americans, Europeans tend to obtain lower PCL–R total, factor, and item scores for the same level of the underlying trait of the disorder, thereby prompting some experts to recommend adjusting the diagnostic threshold of a total PCL–R score of 30 used in North America to 28 when used in Europe. The symptoms tapping the deficient affective experience seem to be the most diagnostic of psychopathy and are thought to be more stable across cultures compared with the interpersonal and behavioral features of the disorder. However, at extreme levels of psychopathy, the interpersonal symptoms may provide more diagnostic information (especially in the United Kingdom). Research indicates that these cross-national differences in psychopathy reflect genuine differences in the expression of the disorder, rather than raters' perceptions of the psychopathic symptoms.

Differences in Levels of Psychopathic Traits

Because the generalizability of the measurement of PCL–R total scores across Blacks and Whites has been demonstrated, it is appropriate to use this instrument to investigate whether these groups differ in the extent to which they display psychopathic characteristics. Two large-scale meta-analyses have examined this issue for adults and adolescents. When differences between PCL–R total scores of Black and

White adults from 21 studies were examined in the aggregate (with an overall sample size of 8,890 individuals), no reliable, meaningful differences in scores between the two groups were observed. When differences between total scores on the youth version of the measure of Black and White adolescents from 16 studies were averaged (with an overall sample size of 2,199), ratings of psychopathic characteristics were significantly higher among Black youth. Importantly, however, the overall magnitude of this effect was small and corresponded to about 1.5 points on the 40-point psychopathy scale. There was considerable heterogeneity in the effect sizes (associations between scores and ethnicity) in both studies, but no clear moderators of the relation between ethnicity and psychopathy scores were identified.

Explaining Cross-Group Differences in Psychopathy

Experts agree that a host of biological, psychological, and social factors likely contribute to the etiology of personality disorders. A major weakness in the psychopathy research in this area is that ethnic/racial categories are fairly simplistic, created on the basis of self-identification in the absence of a consideration of relevant variables (including biological, genetic, psychological, and social) that influence group membership. Substantial within-group heterogeneity exists regarding important dimensions such as acculturation, ethnic identity, socioeconomic status, and neighborhood characteristics, and these sources of heterogeneity present obstacles to pinpointing the etiological factors underlying any group differences that may be observed. Pertaining to psychopathy research, relying on simplistic classifications of ethnicity such as Black and White severely constrains the potential to identify more proximal causes of observed disparities in psychopathy. As but one example of the importance of considering how contextual factors that vary across ethnic groups may be critical in explaining socially deviant behavior, consider the example of living in a "bad" neighborhood. In a large-scale study in which more than 900 civil psychiatric patients were administered the screening version of the PCL–R and followed in the community for 1 year, the degree to which an individual's neighborhood was disadvantaged (indexed by rates of public assistance, poverty, unemployment, managerial employment, vacant dwellings, female-headed households, and

average household wage) was strongly associated with race (i.e., being Black was associated with living in a more disadvantaged neighborhood). Race retained little relation to psychopathy once neighborhood disadvantage was taken into account by statistical methods. In this study, of the 100+ risk factors for violence that were studied, psychopathy was the strongest predictor of community violence. Importantly, even after statistically taking into account factors such as psychopathy and race, the amount of concentrated poverty in participants' neighborhoods still significantly predicted violence. Whereas race did predict violence when considered on its own, the effect of race alone in predicting violence disappeared after statistically controlling for neighborhood disadvantage. That is, regardless of whether participants were Black or White, those who lived in highly disadvantaged neighborhoods were more likely to be violent. Although further investigation clearly is needed, these results highlight the importance of investigating cultural and social processes that may influence psychopathic traits.

Laura S. Guy

See also Forensic Assessment; Hare Psychopathy Checklist–Revised (2nd edition) (PCL–R); Psychopathy; Psychopathy Checklist: Screening Version; Psychopathy Checklist: Youth Version

Further Readings

Cooke, D. J., Kosson, D. S., & Michie, C. (2001). Psychopathy and ethnicity: Structural, item, and test generalizability of the Psychopathy Checklist–Revised (PCL–R) in Caucasian and African American participants. *Psychological Assessment, 13,* 531–542.

Cooke, D. J., & Michie, C. (1999). Psychopathy across cultures: North America and Scotland compared. *Journal of Abnormal Psychology, 108,* 58–68.

Cooke, D. J., Michie, C., Hart, S. D., & Clark, D. (2005). Searching for the pan-cultural core of psychopathic personality disorder. *Personality and Individual Differences, 39,* 283–295.

McCoy, W. K., & Edens, J. F. (2006). Do Black and White youths differ in levels of psychopathic traits? A meta-analysis of the Psychopathy Checklist measures. *Journal of Consulting and Clinical Psychology, 74,* 386–392.

Okazaki, S., & Sue, S. (1995). Methodological issues in assessment research with ethnic minorities. *Psychological Assessment, 7,* 367–375.

Skeem, J. L., Edens, J. F., Camp, J., & Colwell, L. H. (2004). Are there ethnic differences in levels of psychopathy? A meta-analysis. *Law and Human Behavior, 28,* 505–527.

Skeem, J. L., Edens, J. F., Sanford, G. M., & Colwell, L. H. (2003). Psychopathic personality and racial/ethnic differences reconsidered: A reply to Lynn (2002). *Personality and Individual Differences, 35,* 1439–1462.

EVALUATION OF COMPETENCE TO STAND TRIAL–REVISED (ECST–R)

Evaluation of Competency to Stand Trial–Revised (ECST–R) is a semistructured interview that is designed to assess criminal defendants' capacities as they relate to courtroom proceedings. In *Dusky v. United States* (1960), the U.S. Supreme Court established the three basic prongs required for competency to stand trial: (1) factual understanding of the proceedings, (2) rational understanding of the proceedings, and (3) rational ability to consult with counsel. The ECST–R was developed and validated for assessment of the *Dusky* prongs. In addition, the ECST–R includes a specific screen for feigned incompetency.

Description and Development

Prototypical analysis with competency experts identified core representative items for three ECST–R competency scales: Factual Understanding of the Courtroom Proceedings (FAC), Rational Understanding of the Courtroom Proceedings (RAC), and Consult with Counsel (CWC). Prototypical items were also evaluated by trial judges and highly experienced forensic psychiatrists. In addition to competency scales, the ECST–R uses multiple detection strategies for validating its four Atypical Presentation (ATP) Scales: Psychotic (ATP–P), Nonpsychotic (ATP–N), Both (ATP–B; sum of ATP–P and ATP–N), and Impairment (ATP–I). A fifth ATP scale is not used to assess feigning, but masks the intent of the other ATP scales: Realistic (ATP–R).

Samples from four major studies were combined for normative data and test validation. Three samples consisted of mentally disordered offenders: (1) 100 detainees on a psychiatric unit of a large metropolitan jail, (2) competency cases including 28 pretrial evaluations and 42 inpatients in competency restoration, and (3) 56 inpatients in competency restoration. They were supplemented with 95 jail inmates and 89 additional competency referrals.

Reliability

Internal consistencies (alpha coefficients) were high for overall competency (.93) and the individual competency scales: FAC (.87), RAC (.89), and CWC (.83). Interrater reliabilities were exceptional for these competency scales: FAC (.96), RAC (.91), and CWC (.91). Even when focusing on individual competency items, interrater reliabilities remained strong ($Mr = .77$). In addition, most individual competency ratings remained stable across a 1-week interval with more than 90% of the ratings remaining identical. ATP scales had moderate to high internal consistencies (alphas from .70 to .87) with the exception of ATP–R (.63), which serves a different purpose. ATP scales have outstanding interrater reliabilities (rs from .98 to 1.00)

Validity

The previously described prototypical analysis provided strong evidence of content validity. For construct validity, confirmatory factor analyses were used to test various models of the *Dusky* prongs for the ECST–R competency items. With one cross-loading, the confirmatory factor analyses confirmed a three-factor model with high loadings ($M = .72$) for competency items on their designated scales.

For criterion-related validity, ECST–R competency scales demonstrated a high concordance with independent opinions of experienced forensic experts and legal outcomes. It also evidenced moderate correlations with the MacCAT–CA, despite major conceptual differences between the two competency measures. In addition, very large effect sizes were found between defendants with and without impairment on ECST–R competency scales for both the severity of psychotic symptoms (Cohen's ds from 1.95 to 2.98) and overall functioning (ds from 1.60 to 1.75).

The ATP scales were validated using a combination of known-group comparisons and simulation designs. Both suspected malingerers and simulators produced much higher scores than genuine inpatients on the ATP scales with the logical exception of ATP–R. Very large effect sizes were found for both suspected malingerers ($Md = 1.99$) and simulators ($Md = 1.74$).

Forensic Applications

The ECST–R is a second-generation competency measure that was carefully constructed and validated to evaluate the *Dusky* prongs, which applies to competency evaluations across the United States. Some jurisdictions have augmented the *Dusky* standard with additional criteria. In these instances, forensic psychologists may use the ECST–R to evaluate core issues that can be supplemented by interview-based methods and collateral sources.

ECST–R conclusions are based on both normative data and case-specific deficits. Normative-based interpretations compare a defendant's ECST–R score with that of 356 impaired but genuine pretrial defendants. Nomothetic interpretations for competency are provided for individual ECST–R scales based on T-score transformations for moderate (60T to 69T), severe (70T to 79T), extreme (80T to 89T), and very extreme (90T and above) elevations. Because the Supreme Court in *Daubert v. Merrell Dow Pharmaceuticals* (1993) and subsequent cases required an examination of error rates, the ECST–R became one of the first forensic measures to evaluate error rates in the context of standard error of measurement. For example, at a "very probable" level of certitude, the estimated error rate is <5.0%.

Not all competency-related abilities will be captured by the ECST–R or by any other competency measure. Therefore, the nomothetic interpretations are supplemented with case-specific deficits. Based on the ECST–R and other data sources, focal deficits are sometimes observed that are germane to competency determinations. The ECST–R provides an opportunity to document these case-specific deficits.

A crucial issue in competency evaluations is the genuineness of the defendant's efforts in describing his or her psychological impairment and competency-related abilities. Unlike alternative measures, the ECST–R provides a direct method to screen for possible malingering. If malingering is established by independent measures such as the Structured Interview for Reported Symptoms (SIRS), the ECST-R provides explicit guidelines for assessing the relationship of feigned impairment to the issue of competency to stand trial.

Richard Rogers

See also Forensic Assessment; Malingering

Further Readings

Daubert v. Merrell Dow Pharmaceuticals, 509 U.S. 579 (1993).

Dusky v. United States, 362 U.S. 402 (1960).

Rogers, R., Jackson, R. L., Sewell, K. W., & Harrison, K. S. (2004). An examination of the ECST-R as a screen for feigned incompetency to stand trial. *Psychological Assessment, 16,* 139–145.

Rogers, R., Jackson, R. L., Sewell, K. W., Tillbrook, C. E., & Martin, M. A. (2003). Assessing dimensions of competency to stand trial: Construct validation of the ECST-R. *Assessment, 10,* 344–351.

Rogers, R., & Shuman, D. W. (2005). *Fundamentals of forensic practice: Mental health and criminal law.* New York: Springer.

Rogers, R., Tillbrook, C. E., & Sewell, K. W. (2004). *Evaluation of Competency to Stand Trial-Revised (ECST-R) and professional manual.* Odessa, FL: Psychological Assessment Resources.

EXPERT PSYCHOLOGICAL TESTIMONY

Expert testimony in psychology comes in many types and concerns a vast array of subjects. Psychological expertise ranges widely both in scientific subject areas and the breadth of the legal landscape covered. Indeed, there are few, if any, legal contexts in which expert testimony on psychology does not sometimes have an impact. This is not surprising, because law shares with psychology an abiding interest in human behavior. Because of the large number of areas in which psychology and law intersect, any summary will be somewhat incomplete. This entry, therefore, is intended to illustrate the range of expertise and the legal contexts in which it is put to use. It first reviews expert testimony according to its subject, with sections on testimony concerning past mental states, past behavior, future behavior, and current mental states. The entry concludes with a discussion of the probative value of other evidence. Many of these categories of evidence appear in both civil and criminal cases, and the basic admissibility standards in these two legal domains are the same. Hence, for example, predictions of future violence might be used in civil cases (e.g., civil liability for failing to predict violence), civil cases that are quasi-criminal (e.g., sexually violent predator commitments), and criminal cases (e.g., capital sentencing). Also, many subjects of expert psychological testimony are used by both prosecutors and criminal defendants (e.g., the battered-woman syndrome [BWS]) and by plaintiffs and civil defendants (e.g., polygraphs).

Past Mental States

In the popular imagination, the principal use of psychological expertise occurs in the context of discerning past mental states in criminal cases. The central legal context in which this subject arises is insanity. Insanity in the law is a construct that relates to responsibility or what might be termed moral culpability. The law presumes that behavior is freely willed and the product of a rational mind. A person might be excused under the law if these presuppositions are demonstrated not to be so in a particular case. Most jurisdictions employ an insanity defense based on the 19th-century case of Daniel M'Naghten, who attempted to assassinate Sir Robert Peel, the British Prime Minister, but shot and killed Peel's assistant, Edward Drummond, by mistake. Under the test, a defendant should be acquitted if he "was under such a defect of reason, from disease of the mind, as not to know the nature and quality of the act he was doing, or, if he did know it, that he did not know he was doing what was wrong."

As a practical matter, the subject of past mental states is complicated by the very different vocabularies that lawyers and scientists bring to the subject. Lawyers speak in terms of insanity and diminished capacity, whereas psychologists employ an expansive vocabulary designed to account for the wide variation in behaviors observed. The law, therefore, presumes, and has constructed, a world in which mental capacity to reason exists largely in two-dimensional space: A person was sane or insane when he or she committed a particular act. Psychology, in contrast, presumes, and has constructed, a world in which mental capacity to reason varies widely in multidimensional space: A person might suffer from a disability with multiple etiologies and with varying effects on his or her capacity to reason.

Although insanity occupies much of the scholarly attention regarding past mental states, much of the syndrome literature similarly involves the effort to explain preexisting thought processes. For example, the BWS is used in many jurisdictions to demonstrate that battering victims did not behave unreasonably when they used deadly force against their batterers. Part of the factual inquiry for triers of fact in these cases, as defined by substantive law, is whether the battered woman believed that she was in imminent danger of harm at the time that she killed the batterer. Since many of these cases involve circumstances in which the defendant acted at a time when she did not confront an immediate objective harm—if, say, the killing occurred when the victim was sleeping—the psychological proof is offered to support her claim that she was reasonable in believing that harm was nonetheless imminent. According to BWS advocates, this inference follows from available research in two possible ways. First, as a general matter, the data suggest that prolonged abuse renders battered women constantly fearful, a psychological outcome that is a natural consequence of the violence. Second, advocates argue that specific clinical observations can support the individual defendant's claim that she was in constant fear and, thus, honestly and reasonably believed that harm was imminent when she killed.

A fundamental challenge for psychologists regarding past mental state concerns the inherent difficulty in assessing a phenomenon that cannot be observed even indirectly. In effect, when the law asks psychologists to assess past mental states, it puts them in the role of forensic investigator. Little research is available to suggest that psychologists can fulfill this role in a reliable fashion. Nonetheless, some scholars, most notably Christopher Slobogin, argue that the inherent difficulty of the task should lead courts to relax the usual rules of admissibility. According to this view, psychologists can still "assist the trier of fact" regarding past mental states, even if the phenomenon defies direct observation or straightforward test.

Past Behavior

Possibly the most controversial use of psychological expertise is behavioral profile evidence or psychological expertise that is offered as proof that a person committed some act, typically one that he or she is charged with a crime for having committed. Most evidence codes proscribe the use of past bad acts—referred to as "character evidence"—and thus ostensibly prohibit behavioral profiling for the purpose of proving that the defendant probably committed the alleged crime because he or she has a propensity to commit such crimes. Nonetheless, courts still often admit such evidence in one form or another. The most egregious examples of this practice involve courts' admission of evidence such as rapist profiles to prove the substantive offense.

More common, however, is court allowance of evidence that serves dual purposes: one permissible and the other not. For example, there is a growing use of BWS by states to prosecute alleged abusers. BWS would not ordinarily be allowed simply to support the inference that because the defendant abused the witness in the past, he is probably guilty of the assault for which he is on trial. This is prohibited character evidence. However, in many cases, women who were abused and filed a police complaint subsequently testify at trial that the defendant was not the source of her injuries. Prosecutors have successfully introduced BWS for the purpose of impeaching the witness's testimony and thus explaining why she changed her story. But evidence of past battering, which is symptomatic of BWS, is likely to be used by the trier of fact substantively—that is, for the prohibited purpose of proving that the defendant assaulted the witness on the occasion in question.

Future Behavior

The subject of predicting future behavior raises a host of issues involving both the reliability of the claimed expertise and the scope of the substantive and procedural rules that apply to that expertise. The most usual prediction involves a person's likelihood of behaving violently. Courts call for expert predictions of future violence in a wide assortment of legal contexts, including ordinary civil commitment hearings, capital sentencing hearings, commitment hearings following a verdict of not guilty by reason of insanity, commitment hearings following a determination of incompetency to stand trial, parole and probation hearings, and hearings under community notification laws for "sexual predators." Yet courts regularly remark that predicting future behavior is inherently difficult, and most research indicates that psychiatrists and psychologists do not do it very well. Indeed, this area of the law presents a paradox in which judges seemingly take the most lenient approach toward scientific evidence involving some of the most controversial science to enter the courtroom.

As a general procedural matter, courts ordinarily do not apply evidentiary rules of admissibility to predictions of violence. In many areas, such as capital sentencing or probation hearings, rules of evidence do not apply. In other areas, such as commitment hearings or community notification determinations, evidence rules ostensibly apply, but courts proceed, either implicitly or explicitly, on the basis that the substantive law requires psychological expert testimony. Hence, the expertise is admissible not because it is deemed relevant and reliable but because it is deemed necessary under the substantive law that applies to the case.

Although evidence rules might not apply to predictions of violence, constitutional safeguards do. The Supreme Court, however, rejected a constitutional challenge to predictions of violence in *Barefoot v.* *Estelle* (1983), the only case it has heard on the subject. The *Barefoot* Court rejected the defendant's contention, backed by an amicus brief submitted by the American Psychiatric Association (APA), that predictions of future violence were unreliable. The Court argued that "neither petitioner nor the [American Psychiatric] Association suggests that psychiatrists are always wrong with respect to future dangerousness, only most of the time."

Despite the APA's statement that psychiatrists cannot distinguish accurate from inaccurate predictions, the Court believed juries could do so. "We are unconvinced . . . that the adversary process cannot be trusted to sort out the reliable from the unreliable evidence and opinion about future dangerousness, particularly when the convicted felon has the opportunity to present his own side of the case." Yet as Justice Blackmun pointed out in dissent, this observation "misses the point completely," for "one can only wonder how juries are to separate valid from invalid expert opinion when the 'experts' themselves are so obviously unable to do so."

Current Mental State

A seemingly less daunting task for psychologists than describing past mental states, characterizing past behavior, or predicting future behavior involves assessing current mental states. The law seeks such mental assessments in a variety of contexts, including the competency of defendants to be tried and the competency of those convicted of capital offenses to be executed. In the former category, the issue involves whether a defendant is able to assist in his or her own defense and comprehends the nature of the proceedings and the charges against him or her. In the latter category, the issue involves whether the condemned person comprehends the State's reasons for executing him or her and understands what is about to occur.

Competency assessments are typically decided by judges as a matter of law. Experts usually rely on a mixture of clinical judgment and standardized tests, which may range widely in terms of reliability and construct validity. Indeed, this area has not been the subject of close or critical review by the courts, and there appear to be few guidelines for courts to ensure the receipt of relevant and valid scientific opinion. In general, evidence rules do not apply to this subject and courts do not employ evidentiary standards of reliability to expert opinion regarding current mental states. Indeed, this task, perhaps more than any other, tends to be handled by court-appointed experts.

Commentary on the Probative Value of Other Evidence

A large segment of psychological expertise is devoted to the subject of how people ordinarily respond, mentally and behaviorally, to different sets of circumstances. For example, research on domestic violence indicates that many victims of such abuse fail to leave battering relationships for a variety of psychological and sociological reasons. Similarly, research on victims of rape and sexual assault indicates that many of them do not report the crime immediately, again for a variety of reasons. In the law, this kind of research might be relevant on a couple of related issues. Specifically, it is sometimes offered to buttress the credibility of a witness. For instance, this research might suggest that an alleged victim of sexual assault is not an untruthful witness because he or she failed to report the crime in a timely fashion, since it is not unusual for sexual assault victims to delay reporting. This sort of testimony is also proffered for the more general purpose of giving triers of fact background information regarding the usual circumstances that surround similar situations. For example, triers of fact might be informed in a case involving a defendant who was battered that a large percentage of battered women do not leave abusive situations. Courts' receptivity to these uses varies.

In most jurisdictions, evidence cannot be introduced for the specific purpose of buttressing the credibility of a witness. Courts consider the use of evidence to support a witness's credibility to be an invasion of the province of the jury. Juries are entrusted with the task of assessing credibility. At the same time, however, many courts allow expert testimony regarding how people tend to respond to particular situations for the purpose of educating the jury regarding the background context confronted by the testifying witness. Three basic contexts arise with regard to this kind of evidence. In some cases, such as sexual assault cases, psychological evidence is proffered not to show that a witness is truthful but to demonstrate that, in light of how other people respond in similar situations, the witness' account is not unbelievable. In the second, the expert does not speak to the credibility of a witness but is offered to inform the jury regarding the likely accuracy of a witness's testimony. In the third group, experts are offered to speak

to credibility directly, usually through the use of a test such as a polygraph. These three contexts will be considered in turn.

In many cases, especially including rape cases and sexual assault of children, psychological expertise is proffered to show that the alleged victim's behavior is not inconsistent with that of others who have experienced similar trauma. Evidence, for example, that an alleged rape victim failed to immediately report the crime might be put into perspective by expert testimony that many sexual assault victims behave similarly. This can be important evidence in a case in which the defendant claims consent because the witness's behavior might otherwise appear inconsistent with having been assaulted. In this view, evidence on the reporting rates of sexual assault are not offered to support the credibility of the witness but to inform the jury about how people tend to respond to similar situations. As many courts and commentators have observed, however, there is a very fine line—if any line at all—between the permitted purpose of rebutting the defendant's contention that the victim's behavior is inconsistent with having been assaulted and the prohibited purpose of supporting the prosecution's contention that the victim's behavior is consistent with having been assaulted. It is illogical to permit expert evidence to prove nonconsent but not to prove that a rape occurred (i.e., in most cases, nonconsent). But most courts adhere to this distinction.

The second group of cases is not overly controversial as regards invading the trier of fact's province to decide witness credibility, because it principally concerns the general accuracy of similarly situated witnesses. The lion's share of this type involves expert opinion on the reliability of eyewitness identification. (Expert testimony on implantation of false memories in repressed-memory cases would be another example.) Courts rarely raise the credibility objection to this evidence for a couple of reasons. First, a principled line can be drawn between credibility and accuracy, and the latter seems less invasive of the jury function. Second, eyewitness experts usually do not testify regarding the accuracy of a particular witness but, instead, only to the general factors that might interfere with eyewitness accuracy. Again, this form of testimony is less invasive. Nonetheless, courts have not been enthusiastic admirers of psychological expertise on the unreliability of eyewitnesses. Objections to this sort of expert testimony typically involve the question whether the information is "beyond the ken" of the average layperson. Under most modern evidence codes, the subject need not be entirely "beyond the ken," because expert testimony need only "assist the trier of fact" (and be reliable) to be admitted. Nonetheless, much psychological expertise has been excluded on the basis that it simply reflects common sense. Although courts have become somewhat more receptive to expert testimony regarding the unreliability of eyewitness identifications recently, it is still looked on by many courts as only marginally helpful to triers of fact and largely a waste of the court's time.

In a third group of cases, the specific import of proffered expert testimony is the credibility of a specific witness. Today, this evidence is best represented by testimony regarding the results of polygraph machines. Surprisingly, perhaps, modern courts do not object to this evidence on the ground that it invades the province of the trier of fact. Indeed, courts, including a majority of justices on the U.S. Supreme Court (*United States v. Scheffer*, 1998), have questioned whether this rationale would be sufficient to exclude a reliable lie detector. Instead, courts have focused on the lack of demonstrated reliability of these tests to support exclusion. Most courts agree that polygraphs are not admissible, at least absent stipulation of the parties prior to administration of the test. But their rationale for exclusion—lack of proven validity—leaves open the possibility that future tests, such as fMRI, might be admitted if validity is adequately demonstrated.

David L. Faigman

See also Expert Psychological Testimony; Expert Psychological Testimony, Admissibility Standards; Expert Testimony, Qualifications of Experts

Further Readings

Barefoot v. Estelle, 463 U.S. 880, 887 (1983).

Monahan, J., & Loftus, E. F. (1982). The psychology of law. *Annual Review of Psychology, 33,* 441–475.

Faigman, D. L. (1989). To have and have not: Assessing the value of social science to the law as science and policy. *Emory Law Journal, 38,* 1005–1095.

Faigman, D. L, & Monahan, J. (2004). Psychological evidence at the dawn of the law's scientific age. *Annual Review of Psychology, 56,* 631–659.

Special Theme: Expert testimony in the courts: The influence of the Daubert, Joiner, and Kumho decisions. *Psychology, Public Policy, and Law, 8,* 180.

United States v. Scheffer, 523 U.S. 303 (1998).

EXPERT PSYCHOLOGICAL TESTIMONY, ADMISSIBILITY STANDARDS

Expert psychological testimony, like any testimony, must meet certain criteria or standards for admissibility before it is allowed into court. Although the admissibility of expert evidence was initially governed by the general acceptance standard set in *Frye v. United States* (1923), more recent standards, including the Federal Rules of Evidence, have shifted focus to an evaluation of the reliability of the evidence. This entry outlines the historical changes in admissibility standards, starting with the *Frye* decision and the Federal Rules of Evidence and progressing through a trio of recent Supreme Court decisions that address the admissibility of expert evidence. These decisions include *Daubert v. Merrell Dow Pharmaceuticals* (1993), which established whether the Federal Rules of Evidence superseded the *Frye* standard when judging the admissibility of scientific evidence, and *General Electric Co. v. Joiner* (1997) and *Kumho Tire Company v. Carmichael* (1999), which established the scope of the *Daubert* decision.

Frye v. United States

Before the *Daubert* decision, most courts insisted that testimony proffered by an expert be relevant to the triers of fact and based on generally accepted principals. Specifically, this meant that the area the expert was testifying to must result from theory and technique that have been generally accepted by a scientific community. This principle was adopted from a District of Columbia (DC) Court of Appeals ruling that occurred in 1923.

In *Frye v. United States* (1923), the DC Court of Appeals issued one of the first decisions governing the admissibility of expert evidence. When James T. Frye was on trial for murder in the first degree, the defense proffered an expert who would testify about a lie detection test that was based on changes in the examinee's systolic blood pressure in response to questions. The trial court ruled that this expert testimony was inadmissible, and Frye was convicted. In an appeal of his conviction, Frye argued that the trial court's failure to allow the expert testimony was improper and resulted in his conviction. The appellate court reexamined the case and upheld the original verdict, introducing what is now referred to as the "*Frye* test" for the admissibility of expert evidence. In its decision, the court wrote that the methods used by an expert must be generally accepted within the expert's field. In the court's opinion, the lie detection test Frye wished to introduce to trial had not gained recognition among other experts in the field, and this was grounds for its exclusion.

The court established the *Frye* test to ensure that unreliable expert testimony was not admitted at trial, in part because of concerns that jurors would be unable to differentiate between good and bad science. Rather than relying on trial court judges or on jurors to make determinations about the value or reliability of expert evidence, *Frye* leaves the responsibility of evaluating the reliability of novel scientific methods to the relevant scientific community. If there is a significant dispute in the relevant scientific community over the reliability of a theory or practice, then the court could choose to exclude the evidence. Essentially, the court placed the responsibility of ensuring that valid science entered the court on the practitioners in the field.

Over time, the *Frye* test became the primary standard that the courts used to evaluate the introduction of scientific evidence. However, dissatisfaction with the *Frye* standard began to grow as opponents argued that *Frye* was too vague and that it prevented novel scientific discoveries from being admitted in trial because there had not been sufficient time for the discovery to become generally accepted. As expert testimony became increasingly common in courts, it became apparent that more structured guidelines would have to be created. Finally, 50 years after the *Frye* standard had been established, new rules governing the admissibility of expert evidence were adopted in the Federal Rules of Evidence (FRE).

Federal Rules of Evidence

In the late 1960s and early 1970s, an advisory committee convened by then Chief Justice Earl Warren drafted new rules to govern the admissibility of evidence in all federal courts. These rules, known as the FRE, were eventually adopted by the Supreme Court and, with modification, enacted into legislation by Congress in 1975. Article VII of these rules addressed the admissibility of expert testimony specifically. Rule 702 states that "if scientific, technical or other specialized knowledge will assist the trier of fact" in weighing the evidence or determining facts, and the expert proffering such testimony has been qualified as an expert based on his or her "knowledge, skill, experience, training, or education," then the jury should be allowed to hear the testimony. Thus, the rule states that experts do not

necessarily have to come from a scientific background. Experts can come from groups that have a certain skill, such as bankers or plumbers, when that skill or experience allows them to form an opinion that assists the trier of fact in understanding the evidence. Moreover, expert testimony must be helpful to the trier of fact in determining facts at issue in the trial. Although these rules were designed to apply only in federal courts, many states modeled their own rules of evidence on the federal rules, including Rule 702.

Daubert v. Merrell Dow Pharmaceuticals

As concerns grew over the admissibility of expert evidence, which began to play a larger role in many cases, questions arose about which standard should be used to determine the admissibility. Some federal courts continued to rely on the Frye standard, whereas other federal courts relied on the FRE when making determinations about the admissibility of expert evidence. The decision in *Daubert v. Merrell Dow Pharmaceuticals* (1993) addressed these concerns by clarifying specifically what standards should be used when admitting expert testimony.

The petitioners in *Daubert v. Merrell Dow Pharmaceuticals* (1993) were two children, Jason Daubert and Eric Schuller, who were born with serious birth defects, and their parents, who were appealing a trial court's ruling that excluded expert testimony supporting the position that the drug Bendectin could be a teratogen. Their initial suit alleged that the children's birth defects had been caused by their mother's use of an antinausea drug, Benedectin, manufactured by Merrell Dow, during her pregnancies. To support their position, the plaintiffs proffered eight experts who based their conclusions that Bendectin was a teratogen on both test-tube and live studies on animals that demonstrated a relationship between Bendectin and birth defects, research showing that Bendectin had a similar chemical structure to other drugs known to cause birth defects, and a meta-analysis of published epidemiological studies that examined the rate of birth defects among children born to women who had used Bendectin versus those who had not. Merrell Dow proffered a highly qualified expert who stated that he had reviewed all the literature surrounding Bendectin and human teratogens and found that there was no evidence to support its being responsible for the birth defects.

The District Court granted a summary judgment for Merrell Dow and dismissed the case, writing that the animal and chemical structure research on which the plaintiffs' experts based their opinions was irrelevant and that the results of the meta-analysis had not been generally accepted within the field of epidemiology, because it had not been peer-reviewed or published. Thus, the District Court relied on the *Frye* standard for excluding the testimony proffered by the plaintiffs. The plaintiffs appealed the District Court's decision, arguing that the court had improperly used the *Frye* standard when judging the admissibility of its expert evidence as *Frye* had been replaced by the FRE. The Supreme Court agreed to hear the case and ruled in favor of the petitioners, agreeing that the FRE had replaced *Frye* as the appropriate standard for judging the admissibility of expert testimony.

In its decision, the Supreme Court outlined a two-pronged test for the admissibility of expert testimony. One prong required that expert testimony must be relevant to an issue before the court to be admissible. The second prong required that the expert testimony be reliable. In essence, the Supreme Court ruled that judges must evaluate whether scientific evidence is based on reliable methodology rather than relying on general acceptance in the scientific community to determine whether the testimony is admissible. The court sought to help judges who lack the scientific training to make these determinations by offering suggestions for criteria that could be used to evaluate research. For one, the court suggested that judges examine whether the theory or hypothesis on which the research is based can be falsified or tested. Second, the court stated that another way to assess whether the proffered evidence is reliable is to determine if it has been peer-reviewed and published. Third, judges should evaluate whether the technique in question has a known or potential error rate. Finally, although no longer a necessary and sufficient characteristic for admissibility, the Court suggested that judges could still use general acceptance as a factor in determining whether or not to admit testimony.

The *Daubert* decision held that the admissibility of scientific evidence depends on its scientific validity. The guidelines for judging the admissibility of scientific evidence promulgated in *Daubert* shifted the focus of the admissibility decision from determining whether the evidence was accepted by other scientists to an examination of the methods of the research on which experts base their opinions. Essentially, the decision in *Daubert* transferred the role of gatekeeper from the relevant scientific community to the trial court judge.

General Electric Co. v. Joiner

Although the *Daubert* decision settled the controversy regarding the appropriate standards by which judges should evaluate the admissibility of scientific expert testimony, there was disagreement over the standard to be used when reviewing such decisions. The Supreme Court addressed this question in *General Electric Co. v. Joiner* (1997). In this case, Robert Joiner, the plaintiff, had brought suit alleging that his development of lung cancer was influenced by his exposure to dielectric fluid contaminated with polychlorinated biphenyls while on the job at General Electric. Joiner sought to introduce testimony from several experts that exposure to polychlorinated biphenyls, not his history as a smoker, caused the early onset of his lung cancer, but the District Court ruled that the experts' evidence was mere speculation and, therefore, inadmissible. On appeal, the Eleventh Circuit Court of Appeals applied a stringent standard of review when assessing this ruling and decided that the District Court had been wrong to exclude the expert testimony. They believed that the FRE showed preference for the admission of expert testimony and based on this analysis concluded that the District Court should have allowed the expert testimony.

However, the United States Supreme Court reversed the decision of the Eleventh Circuit Court, ruling that the appellate court had applied the wrong standard of review. The Court determined that the proper standard of review for decisions regarding the admissibility of expert testimony should be whether the judge abused his or her discretion by excluding the expert testimony. The Court explained that although the FRE may provide for the admission of a greater variety of scientific testimony, the trial court judge still retains his or her role as gatekeeper and must evaluate the reliability of the proffered expert evidence to approve or deny its admissibility rather than abdicating this responsibility due to the perceived liberal thrust of the FRE. The Supreme Court then ruled that the District Court had reasonable grounds to question the reliability of the expert testimony proffered by Joiner and had not abused its discretion in excluding it.

Kumho Tire Company v. Carmichael

Although *Daubert* provided trial court judges with guidance regarding the factors to be considered when determining the admissibility of scientific expert evidence, it did not address the issue of nonscientific expert testimony. A later Supreme Court case, *Kumho Tire Company v. Carmichael* (1999), answered the question of whether the *Daubert* standards should apply to nonscientific testimony as well. In this case, a tire on Patrick Carmichael's minivan failed, causing Carmichael to lose control of the car, resulting in a car accident, which resulted in serious injuries and one death. Carmichael then brought suit against Kumho Tire Co., alleging that the tire had been defective. Carmichael wished to introduce testimony from an expert in tire failure analysis to show that the blowout was due to a tire defect rather than age or overuse. The District Court refused to admit the expert testimony, citing that the testimony failed to meet the standards set forth in FRE 702 or the reliability factors put forth in *Daubert*.

The Eleventh Circuit Court reversed the decision, stating that the U.S. District Court was mistaken in its application of the *Daubert* reliability standard to non-scientific testimony. The Circuit Court ruled that the expert testimony at issue relied on experience-based rather than scientific knowledge, which was outside the scope of *Daubert*. Therefore, the Circuit Court ruled that the admissibility of the expert testimony had to be reconsidered under Rule 702 instead. However, the United States Supreme Court disagreed with the Circuit Court when it reviewed and reversed the decision. The Court decided that judges' gate-keeping responsibility outlined in Rule 702 applied to specialized and technical knowledge, in addition to the previous application to scientific knowledge. Thus judges were responsible for determining the relevance and reliability of nonscientific expert testimony as well as scientific testimony. According to the Court, the FRE 702 and 703 did not distinguish between scientific and nonscientific expert testimony and allows experts testifying on technical and specialized topics, as they do to scientific experts, the same latitude in presenting their opinions—latitude that is not granted to nonexpert witnesses. The Court also recognized the difficulty in distinguishing scientific from technical or specialized knowledge, because experts often have more than one type of knowledge to offer.

The Court then considered how judges should assess the reliability of these other types of expert knowledge, ruling that the *Daubert* factors could be used to evaluate expert testimony based on specialized and technical knowledge just as they can be used to evaluate scientific expert testimony. However, the Court reemphasized the statement in *Daubert* that the four factors outlined in that case were not an exhaustive list of criteria and reaffirmed the power of judges to consider other factors when determining admissibility. The Court noted that not all types of expert testimony can be judged solely on the basis of those four factors, as they do not always apply, but also recognized that they can apply to non-scientific knowledge, such as experientially based knowledge, as well. Therefore, they do not need to be applied exclusively, or even considered at all, in every case. The Court noted that judges have the same broad freedom in determining how to assess reliability of expert testimony as they enjoy in appellate review of their admission decisions as determined by *Joiner*. *Kumho* again reaffirmed judges' discretionary authority when evaluating expert testimony and deciding its admissibility.

Effects of Changing Standards on the Admissibility of Expert Evidence

Given the shift in standards, it was expected that rates of admissibility for scientific testimony might be affected. Some scholars argued that, under *Daubert*, it was now possible for novel scientific evidence that was based on reliable and valid methods, but had not yet had time to gain general acceptance, to be admitted. This change would result in an increase in the rates of admission for scientific testimony. Other scholars argued that some generally accepted findings were based on unreliable methods and could now be challenged, resulting in a decrease in the admissibility of some types of evidence. Research on admissibility decisions pre- and post-*Daubert* has shown that the overall rates of admission were not significantly affected by *Daubert*. In contrast, the shift in standards did have an impact on the criteria used by judges to evaluate the admissibility of scientific testimony. Judges were less likely to rely on general acceptance or the *Frye* standard after *Daubert* and more likely to rely on *Daubert* criteria (e.g., peer review, falsifiability, error rates) to justify their admissibility decisions than they were before *Daubert*. Despite this increase in the use of *Daubert* criteria to justify admissibility decisions, after the decision, the best predictor of whether judges ruled to admit expert testimony were issues related to the FRE rather than the *Daubert* criteria or general acceptance.

Research has also shown that there have been relatively few changes in the admission rates for expert testimony post-*Joiner* and *Kumho*. Admission rates remained the same for experts in both civil and criminal cases. However, research has shown that admission rates for scientific expert testimony have actually increased post-*Kumho*, which suggests that judicial review of scientific testimony became less stringent while preserving judges' previous approach to determining the admissibility of other types of expert testimony. Other research has suggested that no effect for *Kumho* was seen because judges had already started judging nonscientific expert testimony on the basis of reliability before the decision was handed down. Therefore, *Kumho* affirmed the practice of gatekeeping for nonscientific expert testimony that many judges had already assumed, without a negative impact on the admission rates for expert testimony.

Ryan W. Copple, Jennifer M. Torkildson,
and Margaret B. Kovera

See also Expert Psychological Testimony; Expert Psychological Testimony, Forms of

Further Readings

Daubert v. Merrell Dow Pharmaceuticals, 509 U.S. 579 (1993).

Dixon, L., & Gill, B. (2002). Changes in the standards for admitting expert evidence in federal civil cases since the Daubert decision. *Psychology, Public Policy, & Law, 8,* 251–308.

Faigman, D., & Monahan, J. (2005). Psychological evidence at the dawn of the law's scientific age. *Annual Reviews of Psychology, 56,* 631–659.

Frye v. United States, 293 F. 1013 (D.C. Cir. 1923).

General Electric Co. v. Joiner, 522 U.S. 136, 118 S. Ct. 512 (1997).

Groscup, J. L. (2004). Judicial decision-making about expert testimony in the aftermath of *Daubert* and *Kumho*. *Journal of Forensic Psychology Practice, 4,* 57–66.

Groscup, J. L., Penrod, S., Huss, M., Studebaker, C., & O'Neil, K. (2002). The effects of *Daubert v. Merrell Dow Pharmaceuticals* on the admissibility of expert testimony in state and federal criminal cases. *Psychology, Public Policy, & Law, 8,* 339–372.

Kumho Tire Co. v. Carmichael, 526 U.S. 137 (1999).

Youngstrom, E. A., & Busch, C. P. (2000). Expert testimony in psychology: Ramifications of Supreme Court decision in *Kumho Tire Co., Ltd. v. Carmichael. Law and Ethics, 10,* 185–193.

EXPERT PSYCHOLOGICAL TESTIMONY, FORMS OF

Expert evidence comes to court in a variety of forms and, in particular, at a couple of levels of generality. It often involves general research findings that, although relevant to a particular case, also transcend that case. General research findings will sometimes be used in the establishment of applicable law and decided by judges but, more typically, will be considered a component of the fact-finding duties of triers of fact. A large part of expert evidence, however, involves factual issues that are specific to particular cases, though they may be claimed instances of more general phenomena. Courts and scholars have proposed various models to account for the several ways in which expert evidence is manifested in court. The three most influential of these models are considered here.

To be admitted, expert opinion must be relevant to a material fact in dispute. This basic requirement ties proffered expertise to the substantive law of the case. Hence, for example, if applicable law requires that a substance be proven to have *caused* the plaintiff's injury, expert proof regarding causation will be relevant; and if this proof is reliable and valid, it will usually be admitted. But proving simple causation of this sort can be a complicated matter. The plaintiff must first prove that the substance in question sometimes *does* cause the injury and, moreover, that it *did* cause the injury in this case. As this example illustrates, the facts in dispute in a legal case can appear at a couple of levels of generality. This fact has great relevance both to how and whether experts testify and the procedural legal response to proffers of different forms of expert opinion.

The recognition that facts arrive in court in different forms has spawned several scholarly attempts to impose some schematic theme on them. Three frameworks, in particular, have received considerable attention and are discussed below. These are (1) Kenneth Culp Davis's distinction between legislative facts and adjudicative facts; (2) John T. Monahan and Laurens Walker's three-part division of social authority, social frameworks, and social facts; and (3) post-*Daubert* courts' differentiation between general causation and specific causation.

The Davis Model

In 1942, Kenneth Culp Davis identified two basic kinds of facts having evidentiary significance—what he termed *legislative facts* and *adjudicative facts*. According to Davis, legislative facts are those facts that transcend the particular dispute and have relevance to legal reasoning and the fashioning of legal rules. Although judges are responsible for deciding questions of legislative facts, they very often are the subject of expert testimony. For instance, the question of whether juveniles are as cognitively competent as adults for purposes of evaluating the constitutionality of imposing the death penalty for offenses committed before adulthood is a legislative fact. Such legislative facts are decided by judges, typically, at the trial stage and reviewed de novo on appeal. At the appellate level, legislative facts are sometimes referred to as mixed questions of law and fact.

Adjudicative facts, on the other hand, are those facts particular to the dispute. In ordinary litigation, these are the facts that drive the dispute. Examples of such facts include whether the traffic light was red or green, the presence or absence of a stop sign, or the kind of weapon allegedly brandished by the defendant. Adjudicative facts are within the province of the trier of fact (the jury or, if there is no jury, the judge) to decide. On appeal, in nonconstitutional cases, review is deferential under the abuse-of-discretion standard. The appellate standard of review for constitutional adjudicative facts is considerably more complicated, but in most instances, they are reviewed de novo.

The Monahan-Walker Model

Although the Davis dichotomy has been extremely influential in providing a nomenclature that is regularly employed by the courts, it fails to capture the complex interrelationship between different kinds of facts in actual courtroom practice. Monahan and Walker refined Davis's dichotomy in the context of social science research, though their three-part taxonomy could be applied to most forms of expert evidence. A basic difference between the Davis and the Monahan and Walker approaches concerns the respective focus each takes to the subject. Davis primarily focused on the nature of the legal question involved—legislative-like decisions or case-specific adjudications. In contrast, Monahan and Walker focused on the kinds of social science available to answer the various kinds of legal issues in dispute. In this way, the Monahan-Walker model is more finely tuned to the relevant issues raised by expert evidence. In particular, their model takes into account both the science

available on the subject and the level of fact in dispute under applicable law.

Monahan and Walker identified three levels of evidentiary convergence between social science and law: social authority, social frameworks, and social facts. *Social authority* refers to social science research relevant to the determination of legislative facts and thus the formation of legal rules. According to their proposal, social authority is analogous to legal authority and should be consulted similarly. Hence, judges would consider social science "precedent" (i.e., available research) as presented through briefs, through arguments, and *sua sponte*. The information found to be relevant would then be incorporated into the judge's conclusions of law. Alternatively, in the Monahan-Walker model, social science research might be relevant to social facts (largely equivalent to Davis's adjudicative facts), in which case, after being deemed admissible, it would be presented to the trier of fact through expert testimony. Finally, social science research might have relevance as a combination of social authority and social fact. Monahan and Walker label this concept "social frameworks." In social frameworks, some issue in the particular dispute is claimed to be an instance of a social scientific finding or theory of general import. According to the model, the judge would consider and instruct the jury on the verity of the general claim, but the jury would also hear expert testimony on how the theory applies in the case before it.

Although the Monahan and Walker model has generally received positive recognition, by far their identification of the concept of social frameworks has had the greatest influence. This impact has occurred largely because of the fact that most social science comes into the courtroom in this two-stage form. This is so even when the two levels of the framework are not explicitly set forth, as occurs perhaps too often in practice. To illustrate the power of the social framework concept, consider three examples: the battered woman syndrome (BWS), eyewitness identification, and predictions of violence.

BWS illustrates social frameworks in their conventional sense, in that courts have always expected that there is a general fact that had to be proved and an issue as to whether the case at hand was an instance of that general fact. In the traditional context in which BWS is offered as proof, the defendant is a woman who has killed her abuser under circumstances that traditionally would not have qualified as self-defense. This may be because she killed when the victim was sleeping or otherwise not attacking her and when, seemingly, she was not in "imminent harm" of "serious physical injury or death." According to proponents of BWS, however, a person who experiences chronic uncontrolled domestic violence develops certain psychological reactions to this violence. Courts have generally concluded that the psychological reactions attending BWS are relevant to the question of whether a defendant killed with the reasonable belief that she was in imminent harm. As the Monahan and Walker social frameworks concept makes clear, there are two separate social science issues that are relevant here. The first is the framework itself and concerns the question of whether social science research supports the claim that particular—legally relevant—psychological reactions develop as a result of chronic battering. If, and only if, the answer to this initial framework question is yes, a second question arises in these cases. Specifically, the social fact part of the framework requires proof that the particular defendant in the case suffers from BWS.

A second example of a social framework is the research on the unreliability of eyewitness identifications. This work nicely demonstrates how some framework research might be demonstrable at the general level but is left to the trier of fact to apply at the social fact level. Indeed, it is interesting to note that the reluctance to apply eyewitness research to particular cases appears largely to reside with the experts in this area, rather than with any specific limitations historically placed on this evidence by the courts. It appears that findings that have largely been generated by research scientists are used in court at the framework level but not applied in any case-specific way by the experts themselves. This is a use specifically contemplated by the Federal Rules of Evidence. The Advisory Committee's Note, for example, states that Rule 702 "recognizes that an expert on the stand may give a dissertation or exposition of scientific or other principles relevant to the case, leaving the trier of fact to apply them to the facts."

A third example of social frameworks is clinical predictions of violence—a form of expertise that is often offered as a social fact but without support of any social framework. Although there is a robust research literature on actuarial predictions of violence, which effectively would provide a social framework for this kind of evidence, many clinicians continue to testify based on clinical judgment alone. In effect, therefore, this evidence is being offered as social fact evidence, without any supporting research framework in which to set it. Courts have been particularly clueless as regards this sort of evidence, which should be excluded systematically. As a general matter, no applied science exists only at the social fact level. Whether explicit, implicit, or ignored, every scientific opinion regarding a particular case depends on the existence of some general theory or framework of which a particular case is a claimed instance. Courts display their scientific ignorance, and clinicians display their legerdemain, when they pretend that this is not so.

The Courts' Model of Causation: General and Specific

In many contexts, courts have seemingly begun to develop a basic sophistication regarding scientific foundations in considering the different kinds of expert opinion that might be offered. Beyond the taxonomies of Davis and Monahan and Walker, working courts have been forced to recognize the basic difference between what most scientists study and what most legal disputes are about. Scientists typically study variables at the population level, and most of their methodological and statistical tools are designed for this kind of work. The trial process, in contrast, usually concerns whether a particular case is an instance of the general phenomenon. There has been little systematic work done on the problem of reasoning from general research findings to making specific statements about individual cases.

Courts have increasingly noted the different levels of abstraction at which science comes to the law. Science comes to courts as an amalgam of general principles or theories and specific applications of those principles. Courts have recognized these two levels of abstraction most clearly in medical causation cases, in which they routinely distinguish between general causation and specific causation.

General and specific causation are merely subinstances of the inherent division between the general and the specific in applied science. Indeed, these concepts closely parallel the Monahan and Walker social frameworks idea, though the courts have primarily developed the concept outside of the context of social science. *General causation* refers to the proposition that one factor (or more) can produce certain results, and thus the finding transcends any one case. *Specific causation* considers whether those factors caused those results in the particular case at bar. Consider, for example, the complaint in *Daubert v. Merrell Dow Pharmaceuticals* (1993) itself. The plaintiffs claimed that Jason Daubert's mother's ingestion of Bendectin during pregnancy caused or contributed to his birth defects. This claim had both general and specific components. As a matter of general causation, the plaintiffs were obligated to show that Bendectin sometimes causes birth defects. This hypothesis transcends the particular dispute and is as true in California as it is in New York. In addition, the plaintiffs had to show that Jason's birth defects were attributable to his mother's ingestion of Bendectin. This proof might involve showing that she took the drug during the relevant period of gestation and that other factors did not cause the defects. This is specific causation.

Virtually all scientific evidence shares this basic dichotomy between the general and the specific. Science provides methods by which relationships or associations can be identified and, typically, quantified. Scientific theories often involve induction from the particular to the general. The law, however, needs to apply these general lessons to specific cases. Although still little appreciated among psychologists, this division between what scientists do and what the law needs is one of the areas needing the greatest attention by those interested in the psychology-and-law connection.

David L. Faigman

See also Expert Psychological Testimony; Expert Psychological Testimony, Admissibility Standards; Expert Testimony, Qualifications of Experts

Further Readings

Daubert v. Merrell Dow Pharmaceuticals, 509 U.S. 579 (1993).

Davis, K. C. (1942). An approach to problems of evidence in the administrative process. *Harvard Law Review, 55,* 364–425.

Monahan, J., & Walker, L. (1986). Social authority: Obtaining, evaluating, and establishing social science in law. *University of Pennsylvania Law Review, 134,* 477–517.

Monahan, J., & Walker, L. (2002). *Social science in law: Cases and materials* (5th ed.). Westbury, NY: Foundation Press.

Walker, L., & Monahan, J. (1987). Social frameworks: A new use of social science in law. *Virginia Law Review, 73,* 559–598.

Walker, L., & Monahan, J. (1988). Social facts: Scientific methodology as legal precedent. *California Law Review, 76,* 877–896.

EXPERT PSYCHOLOGICAL TESTIMONY ON EYEWITNESS IDENTIFICATION

Psychologists occasionally testify about the factors that influence eyewitness identification accuracy in criminal cases in which eyewitness identification is a pivotal issue. Considerable research has addressed the need for this testimony and its impact on the jury. Typically, the expert witness is trained in cognitive or social psychology and has published scholarly work about eyewitness identification accuracy. Most often, the expert witness is offered by the attorney for the defendant. In such cases, the expert undergoes "direct examination" by the defense attorney and "cross-examination" by the prosecuting attorney.

The purpose of this form of expert testimony is to educate the jury about the factors that are known from research to influence the likelihood of false identification. The content of the expert testimony typically focuses on issues such as factors affecting the likelihood of mistaken identification, the suggestiveness of lineup and photoarray procedures, and the relation between eyewitness confidence and identification accuracy. For example, with respect to witnessing factors, an expert might testify that witnesses are more likely to make false identifications when identifying a perpetrator of another race than when identifying a perpetrator of their race. Extreme stress associated with a violent crime inhibits a witness's ability to accurately encode information. The presence of a weapon creates a "weapon focus" effect and increases the likelihood of false identification. With respect to lineups, an expert witness might testify that false identifications are more likely with suggestive lineup instructions and when lineup members are presented simultaneously rather than sequentially. An expert witness might also testify that eyewitness confidence is not strongly related to identification accuracy and that eyewitness confidence levels can be inflated by information provided by cowitnesses or investigators that validates the eyewitness's selection from the lineup. Expert witnesses do not offer opinions about the accuracy of eyewitness identification in a given case.

The decision to admit expert psychological testimony about eyewitness identification into court is normally left to the discretion of the trial judge, and the likelihood of admission varies considerably from state to state and in federal courts. Typical reasons for excluding expert psychological testimony about eyewitness identification include the following. Many judges have ruled that the content of the expert testimony is merely a matter of common sense and, therefore, of little benefit to jurors. Judges have also ruled that the research is not commonly accepted within the relevant discipline. Other judges have ruled that the testimony is not helpful to jurors, because it addresses only research and does not inform the jury about the accuracy of the identification in the specific case at trial. Still other judges have ruled that the testimony will prejudice the jury by making them unnecessarily skeptical about the eyewitness identification.

Psychological research on expert testimony has taken various forms. Some research has directly examined the validity of the reasons for excluding the expert testimony. For example, as noted above, judges have ruled that the content of the testimony does not go beyond the jurors' common sense. This implies that the average juror is well-informed about the factors that influence eyewitness identification accuracy. Scholars have developed several ways of testing the degree to which jurors are so informed. Some have conducted surveys of juror knowledge by administering test questions about factors affecting eyewitness identification. Others have described eyewitness identification experiments to students and asked them to predict the outcomes of the experiments. Their predicted outcomes are then compared with the actual outcomes of the experiments. Still other scholars have developed simulated trials (transcripts or videotaped enactments of trials) in which some evidence is held constant while other evidence (e.g., the suggestiveness of lineup procedures) is systematically manipulated. This methodology enables the researcher to examine what factors influence juror decisions and whether those factors are consistent with what is known from the research on eyewitness identification. This body of research on common sense supports the conclusion that what psychologists have to offer to the jurors well exceeds their common sense. For example, contrary to conclusions from the research literature, eligible jurors lack a full understanding of the impact of cross-race recognition, high stress, and weapon focus on identification accuracy and believe that eyewitness confidence is a stronger predictor of identification accuracy than the research suggests.

Research has also examined the extent to which the content of expert testimony is generally accepted among psychologists with expertise in eyewitness identification. This research takes the form of surveys of these experts and shows that many (but not all) of the factors about which experts testify are generally accepted in the relevant scientific community.

Does expert testimony about eyewitness identification prejudice the jury? What effect does expert testimony have on juries? Some researchers have addressed these questions by conducting trial simulation experiments. In these experiments, students or jury-eligible community members serve as "mock-jurors" and either read trial transcripts or view videotaped enactments of trials. Some trials would contain expert testimony while others would not. The research findings are mixed, with many studies showing that expert testimony makes jurors more skeptical about the accuracy of eyewitness identification, meaning they are less likely to convict a defendant based on eyewitness identification after hearing expert testimony. Other studies have found that expert testimony improves juror decision making by teaching jurors to rely on factors that are known to influence the likelihood of false identification (e.g., high stress, weapon focus, suggestive lineup procedures) and to not rely on factors that do not predict identification accuracy (e.g., witness confidence).

In sum, expert psychological testimony about eyewitness identification is a relatively new safeguard developed to prevent mistaken identifications from resulting in erroneous convictions. Its effectiveness is limited by virtue of the fact that it is often not allowed in criminal cases. Some of the reasons that judges typically give for not allowing this form of expert testimony are not supported by empirical research. Research on the effectiveness of expert testimony suggests that it can be helpful but not universally so.

Brian L. Cutler

See also Expert Psychological Testimony, Admissibility Standards; Expert Psychological Testimony, Forms of; Expert Testimony, Qualifications of Experts; Eyewitness Memory

Further Readings

Benton, T. R., Ross, D. F., Bradshaw, E., Thomas, W. N., & Bradshaw, G. S. (2006). Eyewitness memory is still not common sense: Comparing jurors, judges and law enforcement to eyewitness experts. *Applied Cognitive Psychology, 20,* 115–129.

Cutler, B. L., & Penrod, S. D. (1995). *Mistaken identification: Eyewitnesses, psychology and the law.* New York: Cambridge University Press.

Cutler, B. L., Penrod, S. D., & Dexter, H. R. (1989). The eyewitness, the expert psychologist, and the jury. *Law and Human Behavior, 13,* 311–332.

Devenport, J. L., & Cutler, B. L. (2004). Impact of defense-only and opposing eyewitness experts on juror judgments. *Law and Human Behavior, 28,* 569–576.

Kassin, S. M., Tubb, V. A., & Hosch, H. M., & Memon, A. (2001). On the "general acceptance" of eyewitness testimony research: A new survey of the experts. *American Psychologist, 56,* 405–416.

Leippe, M. R. (1995). The case for expert testimony about eyewitness memory. *Psychology, Public Policy, and Law, 1,* 909–959.

Leippe, M. R., Eisenstadt, D., Rauch, S. M., & Seib, H. M. (2004). Timing of eyewitness expert testimony. Jurors' need for cognition, and case strength as determinants of trial verdicts. *Journal of Applied Psychology, 89,* 524–541.

EXPERT TESTIMONY, QUALIFICATIONS OF EXPERTS

Under the Federal Rules of Evidence and virtually all state codes, expertise is defined by the nature and scope of the proffered opinion. The basic issue with regard to a qualifications assessment is whether the witness has the background to support his or her intended testimony. An expert must be qualified to "assist the trier of fact." But no strict tests or minimum requirements apply to the assessment of qualified expertise. The level of qualifications required varies with the demands of the proffered testimony.

The Federal Rules of Evidence, for example, define qualifications broadly, encompassing "knowledge, skill, experience, training, or education." In general, courts interpret the main qualifications requirement in relation to the expert's claimed expertise and the nature of the testimony. Hence, experts on medical matters are expected to have medical degrees, appropriate certifications, and experience, but auto mechanics or real estate appraisers might only need years of experience and demonstrable skills. Professional degrees or certifications, therefore, may be considered by courts because they reflect the expert's level of skill or experience but are not formal requirements of the rules. As a practical matter, courts typically consult the experts' respective fields for guidance regarding what constitutes a "qualified" expert. Not all fields,

however, have well-articulated standards, and many subjects of interest to the law are studied by fields with widely varying professional requirements.

Because an expert's qualifications must be sufficient to support his or her intended testimony, courts regularly demand that experts possess certain minimal degree requirements or professional certifications before being allowed to testify. In a case presenting an issue of medical causation, for instance, a court is likely to require an expert to possess a medical degree. Similarly, testimony regarding structural engineering will typically be introduced through the testimony of a structural engineer. In most jurisdictions, the question of a particular expert's qualifications is within the discretion of the trial court and will not be overturned absent a finding that the lower court abused its discretion. Indeed, it is highly unusual for an appellate court to reverse a lower court's finding that a particular expert passes or fails the qualifications test.

With regard to fields with highly formalized credentialing requirements, courts tend to follow the respective field's expectations regarding what it takes to be "qualified." This usually means that the courts mirror the respective fields from which the experts hail. If, for example, a field requires certification to practice the expertise, courts tend to assume that party experts from that field will possess the requisite certification. Experts who fail to meet their own field's qualifications demands are presumed unqualified by most courts. This, however, is a rebuttable presumption. Courts use a field's certification requirements as a guidepost for judging expertise, not as a prerequisite to receiving an expert's opinion. In effect, therefore, a field's certification requirement constitutes a factor, albeit an important one, in the assessment of qualifications.

Many expert fields, however, have no formal credential requirements, and the courts similarly follow the field's lead here too. Hence, medical experts usually must have attained the M.D. degree at a minimum, but experts on psychological subjects might possess a host of degrees or even experience-based specialization. For example, courts sometimes find experts with just a B.A. degree, together with significant work experience, to be minimally qualified to testify generally on subjects such as the battered woman syndrome or child abuse accommodation syndrome.

Although courts are typically permissive regarding credentials when experts propose to testify on general subjects in psychology, there are limits to this generosity. In particular, courts might require higher educational attainment before an expert will be permitted to testify about a relevant diagnosis. For example, while a court might permit a social worker with relevant experience to testify that it is not unusual for rape victims to fail to immediately report an assault, it is likely to require clinical certification to diagnose the alleged victim as suffering from posttraumatic stress disorder. Similarly, courts usually demand a medical degree to support testimony about drug treatment or the effects of a particular drug regime on human behavior.

Perhaps the most pressing issue presented in the context of expert testimony is whether experts must demonstrate specialized knowledge of the subject of the testimony. The hallmark of contemporary science (and all expertise) is specialization. This trend leaves courts somewhat uncertain as to whether generalists should be permitted to testify about matters that are highly specialized. Courts tend to approach this matter flexibly. In practice, this means that the matter is within the trial court's discretion. Some courts require experts to have demonstrated expertise in the specific areas and topics on which they are to testify. Other courts provide that generalists may testify on specialty areas and that their lack of expertise in those areas is a matter of weight for the trier of fact.

All the general issues presented regarding the qualifications of experts to testify can be found in the many legal contexts in which training and experience in psychology might assist triers of fact. Indeed, psychology possibly illustrates better than any other field the complexities associated with measuring an expert's qualifications. Psychological expertise comes in myriad forms and is introduced for a great variety of purposes. As a general matter, as is true with other areas of substantive expertise, an expert psychologist's qualifications depend on the nature of his or her proffered testimony. A witness proposing to testify on the unreliability of eyewitnesses, for example, would be expected to be steeped in the research in this area. A witness proffered on whether a defendant suffered from posttraumatic stress disorder would be expected to have clinical expertise. These two examples roughly represent the two basic domains in which psychologists are offered to testify: research-based knowledge and clinical opinion. Each of these domains presents special difficulties with regard to qualifications, not least because there is no obvious line that divides the two.

In a number of legal contexts, psychological research is relevant to general background facts, even

if the expert cannot reliably testify regarding how those circumstances affected the particular case. Specifically, research studies can often assist the trier of fact to understand the background context regarding some matter that is relevant to the case at hand. For example, researchers might offer to testify regarding the suggestibility of young children to leading questions in a case involving sexual assault, but they may be unable to provide a reliable opinion regarding whether a particular child's testimony was influenced by the questioning that occurred in the case at hand. A witness proposing to testify regarding general research results should generally have expertise in the relevant literature as well as in statistics and research design. Very often, an expert proffered to testify regarding a particular research area will be someone who has published extensively on the subject—though this would not be a prerequisite in most jurisdictions.

In many cases, expert psychological evidence will also be proffered on an issue that is particular to the case. In theory, the proponent of such testimony has the obligation to demonstrate the admissibility of both the general framework and the framework's applicability to the particular case. With regard to expert qualifications, at least in theory, this means that an expert must be qualified on the research basis for the general framework and the clinical application of that research framework to particular cases. This will often mean that different experts will testify to these two subjects. Consider, for example, a defendant who claims that she killed in self-defense based in part on the battered woman syndrome. As an initial matter, the defendant has the burden to demonstrate the basic validity of the claimed syndrome. This is a claim that ought to be premised on the research literature and should be introduced by an expert qualified to discuss the strengths and weaknesses of that literature. Additionally, the defendant is likely to proffer an expert opinion that she suffered from the syndrome. This very often requires the introduction of an additional expert, one qualified to offer clinical expert testimony that is relevant and reliable for the particular claim.

It must be emphasized that the issue of qualifications is intrinsically bound to the associated standards for admissibility of the substantive expert testimony. In federal cases, for example, this means that the admissibility inquiry will be parallel to the determination made under Rule 702 and *Daubert v. Merrell Dow Pharmaceuticals* (1993) and its progeny. Accordingly, if an asserted expertise cannot be shown to be sound, then even the most eminent (most highly qualified) practitioner of that asserted expertise still would not be permitted to testify as an expert. In fact, courts are likely to find that the issues of qualifications, reliability, and fit are inextricably intertwined and, in practice, cannot easily be disentangled. Qualifications are relative, being more or less useful depending on the expert's familiarity with the subject that fits, or is relevant to, the matter to be decided by the trier of fact. Qualifications, therefore, cannot be evaluated in the abstract. At some point, certainly, the question of qualifications becomes a matter of weight rather than admissibility. But just as with Rule 702 validity assessments, the judge's gatekeeping obligations should extend not merely to qualifications in the abstract but qualifications to testify about the subject that is relevant to the issues in dispute.

David L. Faigman

See also Expert Psychological Testimony; Expert Psychological Testimony, Admissibility Standards; Expert Psychological Testimony, Forms of

Further Readings

Berger, M. (2002). The Supreme Court's trilogy on the admissibility of expert testimony. In Federal Judicial Center (Ed.), *Scientific evidence reference manual* (2nd ed., pp. 9–38). Washington, DC: Federal Judicial Center.

Daubert v. Merrell Dow Pharmaceuticals, 509 U.S. 579 (1993).

Faigman, D. L., Kaye, D. H., Saks, M. J., Sanders, J., & Cheng, E. K. (2007). *Modern scientific evidence: The law and science of expert testimony* (2nd ed.). St. Paul, MN: West/Thompson.

Giannelli, P. C. (2004). Expert qualifications: Who are these guys? *Criminal Justice, 19,* 70–71.

Murphy, C. P. (1994). Experts, liars, and guns for hire: A different perspective on the qualifications of technical expert witnesses. *Indiana Law Journal, 69,* 637–657.

Exposure Time and Eyewitness Memory

When assessing the potential of an eyewitness, among the first things an investigator has to decide is whether or not the witness had an opportunity to observe what

took place for a sufficient time. The decision is likely to be influenced by a witness's assessment of the length and quality of exposure to a perpetrator's face. A longer exposure can increase the ease with which details come to mind at the time of remembering and increase the likelihood that witnesses will correctly recognize a face from an identification lineup and provide a more detailed description. However, an extended exposure could make the witness more confident in their identification ability even when they are wrong. It has been recommended that investigators should not rely too heavily on witness confidence as an indicator of accuracy.

There are two points to bear in mind when examining the relationship between eyewitness memory and exposure duration. First, eyewitnesses are not very good at making estimates of the duration of a given event, and witnesses may overestimate the length of exposure to a face. Second, a longer exposure to a face can make a witness more confident in their ability to make an identification, although there are numerous other factors that could inflate (or deflate) a witness's confidence.

When witnesses are asked whether or not they could identify someone seen earlier, they will rely on various sources of information when making a judgment about the strength of their memory. One source of information that could influence their decision is "availability" or the ease with which information can be brought to mind. A longer exposure is associated with an increase in availability, and this can have interesting consequences for the accuracy of an eyewitness's identification.

Don Read was the first to examine the use of the availability heuristic in an eyewitness identification setting. He found that participants who interacted with store clerks for a longer duration (4–15 minutes as compared with 30–60 seconds) made a higher number of correct choices from lineups in which the culprit was present. However, it was found that the false identification rate in the target-absent lineups were inflated if the store clerks received additional information (cues) about the target. The latter finding fits with the hypothesis that availability of additional cues can sometimes lead a witness to believe that they have a stronger memory for the target, and in a target-absent lineup this can have potentially serious consequences.

The question of why an increase in exposure would lead witnesses to overestimate their ability to make an accurate identification from a lineup was explored by researchers at Aberdeen University using "mock" eyewitnesses (aged 17 to 81 years). The witnesses individually viewed a video reconstruction of a robbery at a savings bank. No weapons were seen in the video, although the culprit indicated to the clerk that he had a gun. The critical aspect of this video for the purposes of the study was the length of exposure to the culprit's face in the video. Two versions of the video were created. In one version, the culprit's face (full-frontal and profile view) was visible for 45 seconds, and in another version, the culprit's face (full-frontal and profile view) was visible for 12 seconds. No other details differed, and the videos were of the same duration (1 minute 40 seconds). About 35 to 40 minutes after witnessing the robbery, witnesses in the long-exposure group made more correct identifications of the robber when he was present in the lineup. They also provided more correct descriptions of the robber under the long-exposure condition. A longer exposure did not appear to inflate false identifications when the culprit was absent from the lineup in the Aberdeen study.

One additional finding from the comparison of witnesses exposed to a target for a shorter or longer duration in the Aberdeen study could be of use to investigators. Witnesses in the long-exposure condition were more confident in their identification decisions than were witnesses in the short-exposure condition. However, they were confident even when they were inaccurate. In other words, confidence was *not* a reliable indicator of accuracy under long exposure. This effect was most marked in the culprit-absent conditions. This finding becomes more meaningful when the implications for assessing witness credibility are examined. When deciding whether or not a given witness is likely to be reliable, a police officer or a juror may rely on that witness's verbal expression of their confidence. To summarize, the research suggests that the likelihood of a witness making an accurate identification is increased if he or she has seen the perpetrator's face for a longer period of time. However, an extended exposure could make witnesses more confident in their identification ability even when they are wrong. Therefore, while a longer exposure increases the chances of an accurate identification, investigators should not rely too heavily on witness confidence as an indicator of accuracy.

So far it has been proposed that the extent of time of exposure to a face could be useful information when assessing the potential of an eyewitness to aid an investigation and the administration of justice. One of the limitations of prior research on exposure duration is

that it has been assumed that a witness who is exposed to a perpetrator for a longer time will be paying more attention to the face and processing it more "deeply," thereby providing a stronger and more accessible memory trace. However, this assumes that there is nothing else at the scene of the crime to attract one's attention. This is typically not the case. For example, research has shown that when a perpetrator is holding a weapon, a witness's attention may be drawn to that, and consequently, the witness may spend less time looking at the face (referred to as the weapon-focus effect). It is important in future research to identify various situational factors that alter the relationship between degree of exposure and memory for an event.

Amina Memon

See also Confidence in Identifications; Confidence in Identifications, Malleability; Eyewitness Memory; Eyewitness Memory, Lay Beliefs About; Retention Interval and Eyewitness Memory; Weapon Focus

Further Readings

Memon, A., Hope, L., & Bull, R. H. C. (2003). Exposure duration: Effects on eyewitness accuracy and confidence. *British Journal of Psychology, 94,* 339–354.

Pedersen, A., & Wright, A. (2002). Do differences in event descriptions cause differences in duration estimates? *Applied Cognitive Psychology, 16,* 769–783.

Read, J. D. (1995). The availability heuristic in person identification: The sometimes misleading consequences of enhanced contextual information. *Applied Cognitive Psychology, 9,* 91–121.

EXTREME EMOTIONAL DISTURBANCE

A number of states in the United States provide by statute that defendants charged with murder or attempted murder may seek to mitigate the charges against them by claiming, and proving, that when they intentionally murdered or attempted to murder their victim, they did so under the influence of an extreme mental or emotional disturbance (EED) for which there was a reasonable explanation or excuse. Typically, such statutes provide that the reasonableness of such explanation or excuse shall be determined from the viewpoint of a person in the defendant's situation at the time of the crime, under the circumstances as the defendants believed them to be. If successful with the EED defense, a defendant charged with murder should be found guilty of the lesser crime of manslaughter.

The EED defense can be contrasted with the (also partial) defense of *provocation*, which exists in other states. Under the defense of provocation, if a defendant charged with murder can prove that he or she killed his or her victim in response to an objective provocation that would cause an ordinary person to suffer a loss of control—and that an adequate time for "cooling off" had not passed—the defendant should likewise be found guilty of manslaughter, rather than murder.

Unlike the provocation defense, the EED defense does not require that the defendant acted in response to certain, particular, provoking circumstances or that the defendant did not have time to cool off. However, although EED statutes typically do *not* mention "loss of control" as a requirement for an EED defense, court decisions often *do* state that the EED defense should be limited to situations in which the defendant understandably suffered a loss of control because of extreme stress and that his or her ability to reason was overwrought by emotion. However, according to court decisions, the defense also allows for a defendant to proffer a claim of EED for emotions that may have been "simmering in the unconscious."

The EED defense should also be contrasted with the *insanity defense*. The insanity defense varies from state to state but typically provides that defendants should not be considered responsible for their criminal conduct if, at the time of such conduct, the defendant could not appreciate what he or she was doing or that it was wrong. To succeed with an insanity defense, a defendant usually has to prove that, at the time of his or her crime, he or she suffered from a severe psychiatric impairment and had a very significantly impaired ability to perceive reality; and if successful with an insanity defense, the defendant will be sent to a hospital, rather than prison, until the defendant is no longer dangerous, at which time the defendant (now a patient) would be released.

A severe, diagnosable, psychiatric impairment or a severe lack of reality testing is not necessary for a successful EED defense; but if *successful* with an EED defense, the defendant may still go to prison, although for a shorter period of time than if the EED defense had not succeeded. Nevertheless, the defense often warrants a mental health evaluation of the defendant. The assessment would be conducted to evaluate the presence of any mental disorders, other mental frailties,

or any unique set of conditions that might have rendered the defendant more emotionally vulnerable to the stress than any other individual who might have been subject to the same or similar circumstances.

The EED defense is not raised very often in criminal cases. For one thing, it applies only to charges of intentional murder or attempted murder. For another, it provides a defendant with no benefit if the prosecutor is willing to offer the defendant a plea bargain, which allows the defendant, charged with murder, to plead guilty to manslaughter. On the other hand, the existence of the EED defense may make prosecutors more willing to plea bargain than would otherwise be the case.

EED statutes do not specify which extreme emotions would, or would not, justify a successful EED defense. However, even though defendants do sometimes go to trial with an EED defense based on a claim of overwhelming anger, a number of court decisions hold that acting out of extreme rage, alone, would *not* allow a defendant to qualify for, or even to raise, an EED defense. And there is evidence from a variety of sources that defendants pleading an EED defense are far more likely to succeed when they acted out of fear—even if mixed with anger—rather than out of anger alone. Clearly, however, a great deal of discretion is, intentionally, left to juries (when they are the finders of fact) in EED cases. "In the end," as the New York Court of Appeals put it, the purpose of the EED defense is "to allow the finders of fact to mitigate the penalty when presented with a situation which, under the circumstances, appears to them to have caused an understandable weakness in one of their fellows."

Yet, as previously noted, courts are reluctant to let *any* defendant charged with murder plead an EED defense (and obtain, perhaps, a mitigation of their deserved penalty). Thus, to establish an EED defense, some courts require evidence that the onset of the claimed extreme emotional disturbance was sudden, or caused by a *triggering event*, or (without requiring psychiatric testimony) evidenced a "mental infirmity not rising to the level of insanity," or led to a "loss of self control or similar disability." Judges, in their sound discretion, may preclude an EED defense before trial or, based on the evidence presented at trial, may refuse to allow the jury to consider an EED defense.

It should also be emphasized that even if an EED defense goes to a jury, to succeed with the defense, the defendant must prove not only that he or she acted under the influence of an extreme emotional disturbance but also that there was a reasonable explanation or excuse for the disturbance. As noted above, the reasonableness of such explanation or excuse should be determined, under the law, from the viewpoint of a person in the defendant's situation, under the circumstances as he or she believed them to be. It is clear, however, that having killed while in the throes of an extreme emotional disturbance does *not* necessarily merit the EED defense. If the trier of fact determines that the defendant's extreme emotions—for example, a defendant's extreme rage—were *not* reasonable under the circumstances, then the EED defense should be, and probably will be, denied.

Expert testimony supporting an EED defense is *not* required to maintain the defense. However, mental health professionals may and do testify as experts in EED cases to help the trier of fact determine the precise nature of the defendant's claimed EED at the time of the crime(s) charged. It is questionable, however, whether expert witnesses should address the issue of whether a defendant's EED was *reasonable.* Arguably, at least, whether a defendant's extreme emotional reaction was *reasonable* under the circumstances is not an issue regarding which mental health professionals have any special expertise and should best be left to the trier of fact.

In evaluating a defendant's emotional state at the time of a crime, mental health professionals should conduct the evaluation in the same manner as other types of "mental state at the time of the offense" evaluations. Subjective information gathered from the defendant and more objective, third-party sources should be considered. The clinician should attempt to identify the emotions that the defendant was experiencing at the time and whether the emotions were indeed intense. The evaluator also should assess which personality factors and/or mental conditions may have contributed to the defendant's supposedly aroused feelings and how the situation(s) which the defendant found himself or herself in may have elicited, or contributed to, his or her emotionally aroused state (if any) at the time of the charged criminal act.

Thomas R. Litwack and Stuart M. Kirschner

See also Criminal Responsibility, Assessment of; Criminal Responsibility, Defenses and Standards; Expert Psychological Testimony; Forensic Assessment; Homicide, Psychology of; Insanity Defense Reform Act (IDRA); Mental Health Law; M'Naghten Standard; Plea Bargaining

Further Readings

Baze v. Parker, 371 F.3d 310 (6th Cir. 2004).

Hall, H., Mee, C., & Bresciani, P. (2001). Extreme mental or emotional disturbance (EMED). *Hawaii Law Review, 23,* 431–477.

Kirschner, S. M., & Galperin, G. J. (2002). The defense of extreme emotional disturbance in New York County: Pleas and outcomes. *Behavioral Sciences and the Law, 20,* 47–50.

Kirschner, S. M., Litwack, T. R., & Galperin, G. J. (2004). The defense of extreme emotional disturbance: A qualitative analysis of cases in New York County. *Psychology, Public Policy, and Law*, 10, 102–132.

People v. Cassasa, 49 N.Y.2d 668, cert. denied, 449 U.S. 842 (1980).

People v. Lyttle, 408 N.Y.S.2d 578 (1976).

People v. Patterson, 39 N.Y.2d 288 (1976), aff'd, 432 U.S. 197 (1977).

People v. Roche, 98 N.Y.2d 70 (2002).

EYEWITNESS DESCRIPTIONS, ACCURACY OF

Police investigators will frequently request that a witness to a crime provide a verbal description of the alleged perpetrator. Such descriptions provide critical information that the police use throughout an investigation, from the identification of possible suspects in the vicinity of the crime, to the selection of photographs for mug books or lineup identification arrays, to the construction of sketches or composites that may be distributed to the general public. Although descriptions of persons are often accurate, they unfortunately also tend to lack sufficient detail to single out an individual suspect.

Quantity Versus Quality of Person Descriptions

Numerous archival studies have examined the quantity and quality of person descriptions provided in real cases. On average, witnesses tend to provide between 7 and 10 descriptors, and these descriptors tend to be quite consistent (or congruent) with the defendant who is subsequently identified. Unfortunately, the vast majority of descriptors provided by witnesses are general, including characteristics such as gender, race, age, height, weight, build, and complexion. Aspects of the clothing worn by the perpetrator are also frequently mentioned, but such features provide only a brief opportunity for use in identifying a suspect in the immediate aftermath of a crime. More specific facial features (such as eye color, hair color or style, and face shape) are rarely mentioned by witnesses, and those that are included tend to focus on the upper portions of the face. Taken together, witnesses appear to provide an accurate general impression of the perpetrator but often fail to include more specific facial details. Laboratory studies of witness descriptions tend to concur with studies of real witnesses, indicating that although witnesses generally provide accurate descriptions, they rarely include descriptors that might be useful for individuating a target face.

Factors That Influence Description Accuracy

Research suggests that a variety of cognitive and social psychological factors can influence the accuracy of a witness's description. First, encoding-based factors are those that occur around the time of the critical event when the witness interacts with or views the perpetrator. For example, low levels of illumination, greater distance between the witness and the perpetrator, a brief amount of time for viewing the perpetrator, the experience of stress or anxiety on the part of the witness (sometimes based on the presence of a weapon), and a witness under the influence of alcohol or drugs have all been shown to reduce the accuracy and completeness of person descriptions. Second, a subset of factors may occur between the time of encoding and retrieval of the description (i.e., during the retention interval) to influence the accuracy of a witness's description. For example, longer delays between encoding and retrieval have been shown to significantly reduce the quality of descriptions provided by witnesses, and exposure to "misinformation" (as described later in this entry) has been demonstrated to significantly impair a witness's memory and thereby his or her person description. Finally, certain characteristics of the witness can influence the quality of his or her person description. In particular, adults tend to provide more detailed descriptions than do children, though few differences in the accuracy of person descriptions have been noted between these two populations. Similarly, young adults are superior at recalling person descriptions when compared with

middle-aged and elderly adults. Interestingly, unlike the cross-race effect in face identification, few differences in accuracy have been noted when individuals attempt to describe faces of another, less familiar race or ethnicity.

Methods for Obtaining Person Descriptions

Interviewing techniques such as feature checklists, cued recall, and free-recall methods are well-established practices of investigators for eliciting person descriptions from eyewitnesses. Regardless of which technique is used, however, acquiring a complete yet accurate description has proven to be very difficult. Probably, the most common method for obtaining person descriptions is simply to ask the witness to freely describe what they remember about the perpetrator. While this free-recall technique regularly leads to highly accurate descriptions, critical details of distinguishing characteristics are often omitted from recall. Consequently, it is common practice for investigators to ask more direct, follow-up questions about specific features (e.g., "Do you remember if the man had facial hair?") or to attempt to confirm the identity of a suspect that they have identified (e.g., "Did the man have short black hair and blue eyes?"). Studies suggest that such leading questions can be very dangerous in that they can "misinform" a witness's original memory for the perpetrator and subsequently impair his or her ability to both provide an accurate description and identify the perpetrator. Research on feature checklist techniques similarly suggest that providing witnesses with numerous descriptors regarding a face can create confusion in memory and lead them to report the presence of features that they are actually unsure of. Finally, witnesses to a crime are often asked to describe the perpetrator many times over the course of an investigation. Research suggests that this process of repeated retrieval can have both positive and negative effects. On the positive side, repeatedly recalling information has been shown to lead to increases in recalled information and to offer some "protection" to the memory trace. Unfortunately, erroneous details generated during early retrieval episodes are also repeatedly recalled over time with increased confidence.

Of the attempts to develop an interviewing technique to maximize description completeness without sacrificing accuracy, the Cognitive Interview is perhaps the most well known. It has been shown to reliably improve the completeness of person descriptions in comparison with other "standard," free-recall techniques. Unfortunately, some studies have suggested that the Cognitive Interview results in a slight cost in description accuracy in the form of increased errors. This has led some researchers to suggest that warning witnesses to be cautious in providing person descriptors may ultimately produce the greatest accuracy and simultaneously protect the witness's memory from the confabulation of details.

The Description-Identification Relationship

It seems intuitive that an eyewitness who is capable of providing an accurate verbal description of a perpetrator would also be able to subsequently identify the perpetrator with greater accuracy; however, this seemingly obvious relationship between description and identification accuracy has not been demonstrated consistently in the research literature. For example, in what is known as the *verbal overshadowing effect*, researchers have demonstrated that asking participants to provide a verbal description of a face can actually impair their ability to subsequently identify that face from an array of similar photographs. In contrast, other studies have demonstrated that recognition of faces can be *facilitated* (or enhanced) by asking participants to provide a verbal description prior to test. A small body of literature has also assessed the specific relationship between verbal description and identification ability in memory for faces using a variety of measures of description quality, including indices of *accuracy* (the proportion of correct details reported), *completeness* (the total number of features reported), the frequency of *correct* and *incorrect details* that are reported, and the degree of *congruence* between the description provided and the face that is subsequently identified. Overall, there appears to be a small but reliable correlation between description accuracy and identification accuracy, and this effect appears to be particularly accounted for by the frequency of incorrect details that are generated in a description. Given the small size of the relationship between description and identification of faces, it appears possible that both memory tasks rely on a common underlying mental representation, yet also function on the basis of independent processing orientations (i.e., featural vs. holistic processing, respectively).

Kyle J. Susa and Christian A. Meissner

See also Children's Testimony; Cognitive Interview; Cross-Race Effect in Eyewitness Identification; Elderly Eyewitnesses; Exposure Time and Eyewitness Memory; Eyewitness Memory; Facial Composites; False Memories; Neil v. Biggers Criteria for Evaluating Eyewitness Identification; Postevent Information and Eyewitness Memory; Repeated Recall; Stress and Eyewitness Memory; Verbal Overshadowing and Eyewitness Identification; Weapon Focus

Further Readings

Meissner, C. A., & Brigham, J. C. (2001). A meta-analysis of the verbal overshadowing effect in face identification. *Applied Cognitive Psychology, 15,* 603–616.

Meissner, C. A., Sporer, S. L., & Schooler, J. W. (2006). Person descriptions as eyewitness evidence. In R. Lindsay, D. Ross, J. Read, & M. Toglia (Eds.), *Handbook of eyewitness psychology: Memory for people.* Mahwah, NJ: Lawrence Erlbaum.

Sporer, S. L. (1996). Describing others: Psychological issues. In S. L. Sporer, R. S. Malpass, & G. Koehnken (Eds.), *Psychological issues in eyewitness identification* (pp. 53–86). Hillsdale, NJ: Lawrence Erlbaum.

EYEWITNESS IDENTIFICATION: EFFECT OF DISGUISES AND APPEARANCE CHANGES

People who wear a disguise are attempting to conceal their appearance or change how they look. Culprits may wear any of a number of possible disguises for the commission of a crime. For example, a bank robber may wear a ski mask, or dark sunglasses and a knit cap. Changes in facial characteristics may result not only from a deliberate attempt to change one's physical appearance while committing a crime but also because, with the passage of time, a culprit naturally ages and thus may look different from when the crime took place. Research has examined the influence of several disguises and appearance alterations such as hairstyle and facial hair changes, removal or addition of eyeglasses, and the wearing of a cap. Overall, disguise and changes in appearance make accurate recognition significantly more difficult. This decrease in recognition can be dramatic depending on the degree of change. The greater the change, the greater the decrease in accuracy for witnesses, both adults and children, trying to make an identification. The hair, hairline, and upper portion of the face, if obscured, are particularly ineffective for later accurate identification. Both the simultaneous and sequential lineup procedures have been tested in laboratory settings to determine their efficacy when a culprit's appearance has changed (e.g., hairstyle, facial hair). For child and adult witnesses, both lineup procedures produced comparable and lowered accurate identification rates when an appearance change occurred compared with the case when there was no change.

Remembering Faces

How do we remember a face? Do we remember the features of a face or do we remember the whole face as a gestalt? Some debate has occurred over this issue, with a number of questions remaining unanswered. It may be that both types of encoding occur or that one strategy is more relied on depending on the developmental stage of the observer. For example, it has been suggested that adolescents and adults are more likely to use a gestalt or holistic approach to remembering faces, taking the whole face in, whereas younger children may be more likely to rely on a featural strategy, focusing on individual features.

Change of Appearance: Facial Characteristics

Regardless of the process that we use to remember a face, it becomes much more difficult to do this when facial characteristics change. Moreover, a change in one feature may make the whole face appear different. Consider the case when someone changes hairstyles or hair color or if a male shaves off his beard or grows facial hair. Changes in any of these features make it more difficult to correctly recognize that person.

The influence of three facial changes on recognition/identification accuracy has been examined across a number of studies: changes in hairstyle, facial hair, and the addition or removal of glasses. To study the influence of these changes, often participants are presented with several photographs featuring different "targets." Following some delay, participants are presented with another set of photographs, some of which are never-before-seen faces, some are of the targets as they appeared in the initial set of photographs, and others are of the targets but with some changes in appearance—for example, the target may not be wearing glasses in the first set of photos but could be wearing glasses in the new set. When an alteration or change is made, there is a significant decrease in accurate identification. Moreover, when changes to facial features are combined, the difficulty with identification can increase. Most often, changes to facial features results in an inability to correctly recognize the person seen previously.

The natural aging process can also make accurate identification more difficult. For example, a 2-year difference in time can reduce recognizability, in particular if there is a large discrepancy between the two appearances, such as when facial hair is grown. In one study examining the aging process, participants initially viewed photographs of high school students whom they would later have to recognize in a set of photos taken 2 years later. Participants had difficulty in correctly recognizing photos if there was a large discrepancy between the high school photo and the photo taken of the same person 2 years later.

Disguise

Culprits may attempt to evade identification by wearing a variety of disguises that conceal either part or most of their face during the commission of the crime. They have been known to wear ski masks revealing just the eyes and mouth, hats and sunglasses, stockings over their head, and other sorts of masks. Studies that have examined the influence of disguise often have participants watch a videotaped mock crime in which half the participants see the culprit wearing a disguise, such as a knit cap that obscures the hair and hairline. The remaining participants see the culprit without the disguise. Research indicates that participants are almost twice as likely to provide an accurate identification of the culprit when there is no disguise than when a disguise is donned. Moreover, the facial composites produced by participants who see a culprit with a cap show much greater variability than composites from those participants who saw a culprit without a cap.

Researchers have attempted to determine which features are more essential for later recognition/identification. The upper portions of the face, including the hair, hairline, and eyes, seem more critical for later accurate recognition than the lower portions. Hair in particular is a feature that many people focus on and later use as a cue for recognition. Unfortunately, hair changes are very easy to achieve and can be used to avoid eyewitness identification. Other fairly easy changes that can prove problematic for eyewitnesses include removing or adding eyeglasses and growing or shaving off of facial hair.

The degree to which a change in appearance or disguise is successful in evading later recognition/identification is determined by the extent of the change. For example, framed eyeglasses will likely have a weaker effect than tinted sunglasses; removing a partial beard will likely be less concealing than removing a full beard. It has been suggested that eyewitnesses' ability for accurate identification declines because of *cue mismatch*; that is, a witness's memory trace of the target/culprit does not match the person they are currently examining. This incongruent memory trace may lead a witness to identify an innocent person, or they may not identify the culprit.

Children

Although it is generally accepted that adults are capable of encoding faces holistically, less is known about children's encoding abilities. Some researchers believe that children encode faces featurally until approximately age 10 and then switch to a more holistic encoding strategy. Most research on children's facial recognition abilities has suggested that younger children are more likely to pay attention to (and thus encode) specific features of the face. In fact, some studies find that younger children, 6 to 7 years old, are better at identifying individual features of a face (especially the eyes) than older children, aged 9 to 10.

Certain types of changes may be more challenging for children than for adults, especially if younger children are relying more on a featural encoding strategy than a holistic one. When children below 10 years are providing descriptions of strangers seen for a brief time (e.g., 2 minutes), often only two or three descriptors are reported. (It is important to note that although children may have more descriptors to report, they may not have the language skills or verbal ability to describe the features to report them.) Descriptors provided by children often pertain to hair characteristics. If hair changed from the time of encoding to recognition, children may have difficulty in correctly identifying the stranger's face.

Research that has examined the influence of change in appearance on children's recognition abilities finds that children can be misled when paraphernalia is used. For example, a number of facial recognition studies that initially show children photos of targets wearing hats and glasses find that children are likely to misidentify others provided they are wearing the same paraphernalia worn by the targets. Moreover, if the target removes the paraphernalia, children are unlikely to identify the person as someone who was previously seen.

Identification Procedures

It has been recommended that lineup members, other than the suspect, be selected by matching the descriptors that eyewitnesses provide in their description of the culprit. For example, if the witness describes the culprit as having short, dark hair, medium build, and a fair complexion, all lineup members should fit this description. The exception to this recommendation occurs when the suspect does not match one or more descriptors provided by the witness. In such a case, the other lineup members should match the *suspect* on the particular features reported by the eyewitness. The remaining features in the eyewitness's description should match all the lineup members. This strategy allows for some variation among lineup members but also tries to ensure that the suspect does not stand out. Having the suspect stand out may lead to wrongful identification.

If a mask or another disguise is used, it may be possible for the police to construct a lineup for the mask or disguise. Similar to a person lineup, a lineup for a mask or disguise would allow the witness to view the suspected item, such as sunglasses, along with other distractors (e.g., other pairs of sunglasses). Witnesses can attempt to identify the sunglasses worn by the culprit during the crime, for example. Alternatively, the suspect and other lineup members may be requested to wear the disguise or mask for the lineup identification.

The police may choose from a number of lineup procedures when conducting an identification. In the simultaneous lineup procedure, the witness looks at the lineup members all at once. In a sequential lineup, witnesses look at lineup members one at a time. With the latter procedure, witnesses are required to make an identification decision for each lineup member without being able to look at other members. More specifically, witnesses are not able to move forward or backward in the sequence.

Both the simultaneous and sequential lineup procedures have been tested in laboratory studies when a culprit has changed appearance following the commission of a crime. Overall, when a culprit changes appearance (i.e., change in hairstyle, removal of a beard), the correct identification rate (i.e., picking out the guilty person when that person is in the lineup) decreases significantly compared with when there is no change in the culprit's appearance. This result has been found for adults as well as children.

Also, in laboratory studies, simultaneous and sequential lineup procedures were compared in terms of a witness's ability to correctly reject a lineup (i.e., saying the guilty person is not present in a lineup that does not contain him or her) when the suspect did not match the culprit's description. Correct rejection rates have been found not to differ significantly across these two lineup procedures when there is an appearance mismatch. The evidence to date does not support the use of a sequential lineup when a suspected change of appearance or disguise has been used. Although the simultaneous procedure may be recommended over the sequential, no "ideal" procedure for lineup identification can be touted when there is a suspected change in appearance or when a disguise has been used to commit the crime.

Joanna D. Pozzulo

See also Appearance-Change Instruction in Lineups; Children's Testimony; Expert Psychological Testimony on Eyewitness Identification; Eyewitness Memory; Lineup Size and Bias; Mug Shots; Simultaneous and Sequential Lineup Presentation; Wrongful Conviction

Further Readings

Memon, A., & Gabbert, F. (2003). Unravelling the effects of sequential presentation in culprit-present lineups. *Applied Cognitive Psychology, 17,* 703–714.

Pozzulo, J. D., & Balfour, J. (2006). The impact of change in appearance on children's eyewitness identification accuracy: Comparing simultaneous and elimination lineup procedures. *Legal and Criminological Psychology, 11,* 25–34.

Pozzulo, J. D., & Marciniak, S. (2006). Comparing identification procedures when the culprit has changed appearance. *Psychology, Crime, and Law, 12,* 429–438.

Eyewitness Identification: Field Studies

A substantial base of laboratory research is now available to aid our understanding of eyewitness identification processes and to support recommendations for lineup reform. However, there are also a limited number of peer-reviewed, published studies that measure eyewitness responses in real police cases. Although few, the studies include large-scale investigations involving a sizable combined sample of eyewitnesses (4000+). The traditional simultaneous lineup format in these studies produces a modal suspect identification (SI) rate of around 40% to 50% and a filler selection rate of approximately 20%.

Field studies bring unique strengths and weaknesses to research efforts, capturing eyewitness decisions in the most forensically relevant settings but under circumstances that lack the control and precision of the lab. Existing field studies—archival summaries of police reports and descriptive data from pilot research—effectively augment laboratory findings.

Each witness decision for a field lineup falls into one of three response categories: (1) an SI, (2) a filler identification, or (3) no choice from the lineup. A challenge for eyewitness field research is that an unknown percentage of real-world lineups do not include the perpetrator. Suspect selections cannot be directly equated with accurate identifications, because any false identification of an innocent suspect is contained within the SI category. Filler selections (foils [innocent persons] or false alarms) are known errors and signal investigators that the witness has a poor memory or is uncooperative, or that the filler is a better match to the offender than is the suspect. "No choice" responses (a lineup rejection) include witnesses unable or unwilling to make a lineup selection. These limitations of data interpretation must be kept in mind as the following field studies are examined.

Archival field studies provide baseline data regarding eyewitness responses under traditional lineup practice—a simultaneous display of lineup members administered by an investigator who knows the identity of the suspect. Some field information is also available for showups—a single-member lineup.

An early examination of 224 identifications made by eyewitnesses to real crimes in California revealed an SI rate of 56% and a showup SI rate of 22%. A year later, a 1994 study in Vancouver, Canada, detailed 170 identification attempts, 90% from simultaneous photo lineups. The authors reported SI rates for robbery victims (46%) and witnesses (33%) and for fraud victims (25%).

A larger sample of police files was reviewed in 2001 for 689 California identification attempts following crimes ranging from homicide to theft. Similar rates of SI were found for 284 simultaneous photo lineups (48% SI) and 58 live simultaneous lineups (50% SI). Live lineup decisions produced 24% false alarms and 26% lineup rejections. (Researchers do not always separate filler and "no choice" decisions, often because police reports do not provide this level of detail.) Showup identification rates were similar whether live (258) or photo (18)—76% and 83% SI, respectively—and significantly higher than rates for the full array. Of particular interest were 66 lineup identifications by eyewitnesses who had made an earlier identification of the same suspect. Significantly more SIs were made in later attempts (62%) compared with witnesses attempting a single identification (45%). A 2005 update of the California simultaneous lineup data, including overlap with the earlier data set, produced an SI rate of 52% for photo and 46% for live lineups; filler picks were at 15% for the overall group.

Additional archival summaries come from researchers in England. These include 2,200 witness identifications for 930 live, simultaneous identity parades. Outcome similarities across studies are evident (also including an unpublished third study of 843 witnesses and 302 lineups by the London police): When the offender was not known previously to the witness, approximately 40% of witnesses identified the suspect, 20% chose a filler, and 40% made no choice from the lineup. When the perpetrator was previously known, not surprisingly, SI was more likely.

Along with recent reforms in lineup practice, data are emerging that capture eyewitness responses under double-blind sequential lineup practice—a one-at-a-time presentation of lineup members, administered by an investigator who does not know the identity of the suspect. A 2006 Minnesota pilot project generated SI rates of 54%, fillers 8%, and "no choice" 38%. This field study also showed that repeated viewing of a lineup by the witness was associated with a reduction in SIs and rising filler selections.

Some of these descriptive studies have also attempted to examine the impact on witness decisions of crime-incident features, such as weapon presence. The researchers are careful to point out the dangers of comparing pseudo-experimental conditions. For example, weapon absence may be confounded with crime type (fraud vs. robbery) and, therefore, also with differential witness attention, quality of culprit description, and delay prior to lineup. While substantial support has been found in controlled laboratory tests for the negative impact of factors such as weapon presence, delay, and cross-race identification, field studies present inconsistent results. The difficulty of interpreting study results following nonrandom assignment is illustrated by a London research team, comparing a "lineup suite" with a standard police-station setting. The researchers noted that lineups assigned to the suite differed in important ways from those assigned to ordinary police stations: time lapsed since the crime event, race of the suspect, and crime violence. Lineup setting was confounded with other critical factors.

Finally, an ancillary line of hybrid lab-field research has developed around testing for fairness of real lineups. A *mock witness procedure* requires lab participants, who have not seen the crime and are armed only with the culprit description provided by the real witness, to identify the suspect from the lineup. This procedure is typically used to evaluate individual lineups suspected of biased structure. An emerging use of this paradigm is to analyze a sample of lineups from a jurisdiction of interest. Lineup fairness was tested in England using this procedure, demonstrating video lineups to be fairer than photos. In the Minnesota pilot of double-blind sequential lineups, a mock witness procedure confirmed fair lineup construction through a sample of field lineups.

As we look to the future, there is great potential for information gain in well-designed experimental field tests that include methodological necessities such as random assignment and double-blind administration, but data from such tests are not yet available.

Nancy K. Steblay

See also Estimator and System Variables in Eyewitness Identification; Eyewitness Memory; Showups; Simultaneous and Sequential Lineup Presentation

Further Readings

Klobuchar, A., Steblay, N., & Caligiuri, H. (2006). Improving eyewitness identifications: Hennepin County's Blind Sequential Lineup Pilot Project. *Cardozo Public Law, Policy & Ethics Journal, 4,* 381–413.

Valentine, T., Pickering, A., & Darling, S. (2003). Characteristics of eyewitness identification that predict the outcome of real lineups. *Applied Cognitive Psychology, 17,* 969–993.

EYEWITNESS IDENTIFICATION: GENERAL ACCEPTANCE IN THE SCIENTIFIC COMMUNITY

This entry focuses on the degree to which experts and others are persuaded that each of a number of factors influences the accuracy of eyewitness identifications. Supreme Court cases, among them *United States v. Amaral* (1973) and *Daubert v. Merrell Dow Pharmaceuticals* (1993), have opened avenues of research addressing how the influence of various factors on the judgments of eyewitnesses is perceived by different parties in the legal system. Reflecting their familiarity with the literature, experts substantially agree on the extent to which many variables influence identifications. Research indicates that jurors do not agree with the experts on many of these influencing factors. The use of legal processes that will help jurors make better decisions in cases that involve eyewitness identifications, such as having experts testify in these cases, is thus justifiable. Those who serve as law enforcement personnel show unexpected patterns of agreement with experts, though this tendency may change as a result of eyewitness reform at the state level.

The Rationale

The issue of whether or not to allow scientific findings into the courtroom continues to evolve in the United States. The Supreme Court established the admissibility of eyewitness research in *United States v. Amaral* (1973). The later *Daubert v. Merrell Dow Pharmaceuticals* (1993) ruling established criteria that had to be demonstrated for scientific testimony to be entered into a trial. One of these criteria was that the basis for the testimony should be generally accepted by the scientific community. The *Daubert* decision renewed interest in what eyewitness factors are in fact generally accepted by the scientific community. The first survey focusing on the acceptance of eyewitness factors was published in 1989. Research since then has greatly expanded psychologists' understanding of how members of the scientific, legal, and lay communities accept the findings reported in the eyewitness literature and how this acceptance has changed over time.

It is now common for members of the legal psychology community to distinguish between what are known as system variables and estimator variables. *System variables* are those that are under the control of the legal

system and that can potentially bias an eyewitness during the course of a criminal identification procedure. For example, bias could enter into an identification procedure through the techniques used to construct the criminal lineup or by the use of leading identification instructions given to an eyewitness. In contrast to system variables, *estimator variables* are those that encompass eyewitness and crime scene characteristics that are not under the direct control of the legal system. Examples include the length of time afforded to the eyewitness to view the crime or the presence of multiple perpetrators at the crime scene. The provision of expert testimony in a trial in which variables such as these are relevant may serve to highlight potential biases in the identification procedure that otherwise may have escaped consideration by the judge or jurors.

The Opinions of Experts

Survey research demonstrates that many phenomena experts overwhelmingly reported as being sufficiently reliable to introduce under oath in 1989 continue to be viewed as reliable influences on the accuracy of eyewitness identifications more than a decade later. There appears to be considerable consensus among experts as to the reliability of the research evidence regarding the wording of questions, the construction of lineups, and the role of witnesses' attitudes and expectations in influencing their identifications, and on the relationship between witnesses' confidence in their identification and their identification accuracy. Furthermore, experts agree on the existence of other variables that reliably influence eyewitness identifications, such as the rate at which memories decay, the impact of exposure time on memory and subsequent identifications, and the unconscious transference of the memory of a familiar face from one situation to another. Appreciable increases were observed between 1989 and 2001 in the percentage of experts who agreed that human attention is likely to be focused on a weapon rather than on a perpetrator's face (a weapon focus effect) and the impact of hypnotic suggestibility. Both changes in consensus were attributed to the respective increases in interest and scholarship on both topics in the years following the publication of the first expert survey.

Later research would investigate the general acceptance of eyewitness factors not addressed in the original 1989 survey of experts. Attesting to the expanding corpus of literature in the eyewitness field, a substantial majority of experts agreed on the malleability of eyewitness confidence, the suggestibility of the child eyewitness, and the tendency of eyewitnesses to choose suspects from a lineup previously encountered in mug shot arrays. Other factors agreed on by a majority of experts included the impact of alcohol on the eyewitness, the difficulty in making identifications of perpetrators not of the same race as the eyewitness, and the reduction in false identifications due to the use of sequential rather than simultaneous lineups. Other phenomena that were supported by at least two thirds of the experts included the inferior accuracy of the child eyewitness when compared with the adult eyewitness, the potential for misleading memories recovered from childhood, and how the use of similar foils (here foil refers to an innocent person in a police lineup) in a lineup increases eyewitness accuracy.

The Opinions of Judges

Although individual jurors are ultimately responsible for interpreting the testimony of an expert witness and applying their insight to the facts of the case at hand, judges alone determine whether the expert witness meets the *Daubert* criteria for inclusion in the trial. Judges, like jurors, may rely on common sense when interpreting eyewitness evidence in the absence of formal psychological training. Eyewitness identification errors have been cited in many cases of wrongful conviction, although a survey reported that only 43% of judges believed that such errors have been made in half of the reported cases of wrongful conviction. However, not all evidence is discouraging. Survey data on judges' knowledge and beliefs about eyewitness factors revealed that while judges may agree correctly with statements on eyewitness issues, these same individuals report that the average juror would not be likely to respond correctly. A modest correlation ($r = .30$) was reported between a judge's knowledge of eyewitness factors and the willingness of the judge to admit expert testimony.

Agreement between judges and experts was observed on less than half (40%) of 30 eyewitness factors, which included (but were not limited to) the role of attitudes and expectations, the cross-race effect, and the impact of exposure time. Judges were in agreement with experts on less than half (37%) of the listed system variables, including the malleability of an eyewitness's confidence, the biasing effects of showup lineups, and what constitutes a fair lineup. Judges were not in agreement with experts regarding the phenomenon of hypnotic suggestion. When data collected from a 2004 survey of judges were compared with the results of

experts in a previous survey, judges and experts agreed on 7 of 8 items.

The Opinions of Jurors

If a case is tried by a jury, the jurors serve as the ultimate arbiter of fact in the courtroom, and they must decide not only on whether case-relevant eyewitness factors should be taken into consideration during deliberation but also on what weight should be given when considering a verdict. The testimony of experts may serve to allay juror concerns about eyewitness phenomena. Nearly three quarters of respondents in one survey replied that their primary aim as an expert witness was to educate the jury. Thankfully, few researchers reported that they would be willing to testify in court regarding an eyewitness factor on which the published literature was "inconclusive." In contrast, approximately three quarters of those experts who regarded the evidence as "generally reliable" and a plurality of those who saw it as "very reliable" were willing to testify about these factors. Ninety-five percent of these surveyed experts believed that expert testimony on eyewitness issues had a positive impact on juries.

There was correspondence between experts and jurors on only 4 of the 30 survey statements (13%). As expected, significant differences in the rates of agreement emerged between experts and jurors on the statements focusing on factors classified as system variables, such that jurors were less in agreement about the eyewitness factor than the experts. The four eyewitness factors that experts and jurors did agree on were statements regarding the effects that violence, alcohol, and stress have on an eyewitness and the fact that trained observers are not more accurate witnesses than untrained people. The largest discrepancies observed between experts and jurors were found for statements regarding lineup instructions and hypnotic suggestibility, with jurors expressing significantly less agreement about those eyewitness factors than experts. Juror accuracy (50.7%) differed significantly from the level of accuracy seen among judges and law enforcement personnel when accuracy was defined as agreement with those statements to which at least 75% of experts agree.

Other Evidence

Understanding the general acceptance of eyewitness factors among law enforcement personnel is critical in that members of this population draw their knowledge on the subject both from empirical literature and their experiences in the field. Law enforcement personnel were in agreement with the expert community on only 12 of the 30 statements (40%), among them the role of attitudes and expectancies, the suggestibility of the child eyewitness, and the cross-race effect. Notably, they perceived the influence of only two of the eight (25%) system variables in the same manner as the experts. Experts and law enforcement personnel did not differ in their judgment of the biasing effect of showups and the importance of members of a lineup resembling the description of the suspect. Law enforcement personnel, however, had significantly lower agreement rates than experts with respect to all other system variables (e.g., the malleability of eyewitness confidence, the impact of question wording). Of interest is the fact that the most significant differences between the agreement rates for law enforcement personnel and experts were observed for statements concerning the presentation format of the lineup and the instructions administered during the lineup. When agreeing with statements endorsed by 75% of experts, judges and law enforcement personnel were equally accurate (65.9% and 63.8%, respectively).

General acceptance can be indexed not only in terms of the degree of correspondence among opinions across various participants in trial proceedings but also in terms of the decisions made by policymakers with respect to the implementation of applications derived from empirical psycholegal research. For example, a panel of legal scholars, law enforcement practitioners, and psycholegal experts made recommendations as to procedures that should be adopted by the police when they obtain eyewitness evidence. One example of this is the recommendation that witnesses and those law enforcement officers who conduct lineups both be unaware of who is a suspect and who is not (double-blind procedures) when lineups are conducted. Some states (e.g., New Jersey, North Carolina, and Wisconsin) have implemented such recommendations at the time this entry was written, and additional states are considering this and other reforms as well.

Kevin W. Jolly and Harmon M. Hosch

See also Confidence in Identifications; Cross-Race Effect in Eyewitness Identification; Estimator and System Variables in Eyewitness Identification; Expert Psychological Testimony, Admissibility Standards

Further Readings

Benton, T. R., Ross, D. F., Bradshaw, E., Thomas, W. N., & Bradshaw, G. S. (2005). Eyewitness memory is still not common sense: Comparing jurors, judges, and law enforcement to eyewitness experts. *Applied Cognitive Psychology, 20,* 115–129.

Daubert v. Merrell Dow Pharmaceuticals, 509 U.S. 579 (1993).

Kassin, S. M., Ellsworth, P. C., & Smith, V. L. (1989). On the general acceptance of eyewitness testimony research: A survey of the experts. *American Psychologist, 44,* 1089–1098.

Kassin, S. M., Tubb, V. A., Hosch, H. M., & Memon, A. (2001). On the general acceptance of eyewitness testimony research: A new survey of the experts. *American Psychologist, 56,* 405–416.

Seltzer, R., Lopes, G. M., & Vanuti, M. (1990). Juror ability to recognize the limitations of eyewitness identifications. *Forensic Reports, 3,* 121–137.

United States v. Amaral, 488 F.2d 1148 (9th Cir. 1973).

Wise, R. A., & Safer, M. A. (2004). What US judges know and believe about eyewitness testimony. *Applied Cognitive Psychology, 18,* 427–443.

Eyewitness Memory

Eyewitness memory plays a pivotal role in many criminal trials. A substantial body of psychological research on eyewitness memory has developed over the years. This research examines various types of eyewitness memory, factors that influence eyewitness memory, methods of improving eyewitness memory, and how eyewitness memory is evaluated in the course of investigations and criminal trials.

History of Research on Eyewitness Memory

The advent of psychological research related to the legal system can be traced to 1908, when Alfred Binet demonstrated that a person's response to questioning could be influenced by the way in which the question was asked. Although his work did not have a profound influence on the legal system at the time, it was the beginning of empirical research involving witness testimony. Soon thereafter, William Stern actually applied this research directly to eyewitness testimony. He was able to demonstrate that eyewitnesses are susceptible to error and that witnessing variables, such as emotions at the time of the event, can serve to affect the accuracy rate. Around the same time, Hugo Munsterberg released his book, *On the Witness Stand,* which examined problems associated with eyewitness memory as well as jurors' inability to accurately assess eyewitness testimony. Munsterberg's research was met with quick criticism from John Henry Wigmore, who stated that psychological research was not of a nature that the legal system could use. It is fair to say that Munsterberg's research was not up to present-day methodological standards, but even with this caveat, the importance of his work cannot be diminished. He was the first researcher to examine issues related to eyewitness memory in a systematic and scientific manner.

It was not until the 1970s that eyewitness research was again brought to the forefront, this time by Elizabeth Loftus. She demonstrated, using realistic stimuli such as videotaped and live events, that memory in general, including eyewitness memory, could be altered simply by the way in which the interviewer asked the question. Because of her rigorous methodological controls, she was able to both examine the quantity of eyewitness memory and assess the accuracy and quality of the remembered information. Her research spurred interest in the topic among her students and colleagues. This included Robert Buckhout, who demonstrated the prevalence of eyewitness identification errors. Although there was still some skepticism as to the use of eyewitness research in the legal field, the research gained some ground in 1978, when Gary Wells distinguished between estimator variables and system variables. Establishing this dichotomy made it possible for critics to comprehend how psychological research could contribute to the legal system and allowed researchers to focus their efforts on issues that the legal system could implement.

Types of Eyewitness Memory and Factors Affecting Eyewitness Memory

Broadly speaking, eyewitness memory can be divided into two general classes: eyewitness recall and eyewitness identification, corresponding to the traditional recall-and-recognition distinction pervasive in the cognitive psychological research on human memory. Eyewitness recall often plays an important role in the investigation of crimes. When a crime occurs, police officers responding to the crime interview the

eyewitnesses regarding their memories associated with the crime, including descriptions of the perpetrator(s) and the crime itself. The interviewee may be interviewed numerous times throughout the investigation. Some of the details recalled by the eyewitness, such as a description of a weapon or description of clothing worn by the perpetrator, may become important later in the investigation or even at trial.

Research on eyewitness recall has examined factors that influence the accuracy of eyewitness descriptions, such as levels of stress experienced by the eyewitness or the presence of a weapon. One of the most widely studied factors, witness questioning, relates to the information that is given to witnesses after they experience the event and the way in which the witnesses are questioned about the event. It has been repeatedly demonstrated that the wording and intonations of questions can lead eyewitnesses to provide incorrect information. In this research, participants who witnessed an event are questioned in a way that induces subsequent reports containing false details. For example, participant witnesses were asked either "Did you see a broken headlight?" or "Did you see the broken headlight?" Even though only one word is different between the two conditions, participants who heard the word "the," rather than the word "a," were more likely to indicate that they had seen a broken headlight. The majority of research discussed thus far has involved adults. However, research has also demonstrated sizeable effects of postevent information on both older adults and children alike. In fact, children below the age of 3 to 4 and adults over the age of 65 seem to be the groups that are most likely to fall prey to postevent suggestion.

Not only can memory of an event be altered by the way in which the witness is questioned, but the act of repeatedly questioning a witness can also have profound effects on the witness's memories of the event. For example, repeatedly asking college students to think about events that were plausible but did not occur in their childhood (e.g., knocking over a punch bowl at a party) led them to accept the events as true. The most famous example is the "Lost in the Mall" demonstration. In this demonstration, an adolescent boy was asked to remember when he was lost in a mall as a young boy. The boy, who initially indicated he did not remember the event, was asked to simply think about the event and write down his memories of the event each night. This is a therapeutic technique called journaling. After 2 weeks of journaling, not only did he remember the event, an event that in fact never occurred, but he also provided specific details of the event, such as the color of the man's shirt who found him as well as the coarseness of the man's hand. Critics of false memory research argue that lab-created false memories are plausible and fairly benign. They dispute the generalizability of the results to legal and therapeutic settings in which the memories recalled are often more traumatic and more atypical (e.g., childhood sexual abuse).

Eyewitness Recognition

Eyewitness identification of perpetrators can play a central role in the investigation of a crime and in resolving the case, whether by trial or through plea bargaining. Eyewitness identification can occur spontaneously, as is the case when a crime victim encounters her perpetrator in public and calls the police. Eyewitness identification can also occur through identification tests, such as showups, photo arrays, and live lineups. These identifications appear very persuasive and compelling to jurors.

Research on eyewitness identification has examined a large array of factors that are thought to influence identification accuracy. These factors include the conditions under which the crime occurred, exposure time to the perpetrator, stress experienced by the witness, the presence of a weapon, disguises worn by the perpetrator, and the time between the crime and the identification.

One such factor that has received a significant amount of attention in the psychological literature is the cross-race effect or own-race bias (ORB). That is, the more an eyewitness's race is congruent with the race of the perpetrator the more likely the witness will make an accurate identification. In contrast, when the witness and perpetrator are from different races, identification accuracy is impaired. Although there are some differences in false identifications (specifically, White participants demonstrate a larger ORB effect compared with Black participants), the results of accurate identifications indicate no differences in the ORB effect between participants. One theory of ORB posits that the extent to which the ORB effect occurs is dependent on how much interracial experience a person has with the target race. This theory has been supported in that those participants who live in areas that allow for more interracial experience do not demonstrate the typical ORB effect compared with those who do not have this experience.

Methods of Improving Eyewitness Memory

The aforementioned distinction between eyewitness recall and identification accuracy is useful for explaining how psychological research has been used to develop methods for improving eyewitness memory. Practical recommendations from research on eyewitness recall have focused on how to form questions that do not mislead the eyewitness and how to avoid implanting false memories. Research has also examined whether hypnosis can be used to improve eyewitness recall, but the conclusions from this research are pessimistic.

One of the great success stories from research on improving eyewitness recall is the cognitive interview. the cognitive interview was derived from three basic processes: memory/cognition, social dynamics, and communication. The process begins by directing the eyewitness to close his or her eyes and mentally reconstruct the event. Although not always feasible, this can also be done by having the eyewitness revisit the crime scene. The interviewer should not interrupt the witness and should only ask open-ended questions. Witnesses should be encouraged to describe the event from multiple perspectives and should be asked to respond, "I don't know" rather than guess when unsure. The interviewer should establish a rapport with the witness to balance issues of authority and encourage active participation on the part of the witness. After the eyewitness describes the event, the interviewer should use probing questions to exhaust the memory. Research has demonstrated that careful and thorough use of this procedure can lead to an increase in memory for the event without causing increases in incorrect information.

Research on improving eyewitness identification has likewise yielded impressive gains. There are various tests that are used to identify a suspect. Two of the most common of these tests are the lineup and the showup. A lineup can be conducted either live (the witness views actual people) or by using a photo spread (the witness views a series of photos). In general, a lineup usually contains several fillers, people in the lineup that are known to be innocent, and one suspect. Lineups can contain more than one suspect, but for a variety of reasons, it is not recommended.

The various aspects of lineup administration have been researched extensively. For example, the instructions that are given before the administration of a lineup can affect the likelihood of the witness choosing from the lineup; this effect occurs independently of whether or not the lineup contains the perpetrator. Furthermore, it is recommended that the witness be told that the perpetrator may not be present in the lineup, which therefore encourages the witness not to pick from a lineup that they feel does not contain the culprit. Equally important in the lineup instruction and administration are the fillers that accompany the suspect. The fillers serve as a control for guessing, and if chosen, the administrator will be aware that the eyewitness has made a mistaken identification. It is equally important that the fillers are also picked with some consideration for the description of the suspect given by the witness. To the extent that the fillers are similar in appearance to the witness's description of the culprit, it is ensured that the witness's subject choice was not based solely on logical deduction. The presentation of the lineup has also been researched. The two most researched presentation types are the simultaneous lineup, in which the witness views all lineup members at once, and the sequential lineup, in which only one lineup member is shown at a time. Research has repeatedly demonstrated that sequential lineup presentations produce fewer false identifications than simultaneous lineups when the culprit is not actually present in the lineup. However, correct identification rates do not differ between the two lineup presentation modes when the culprit is present in the lineup. If at all possible, a double-blind lineup procedure should always be used. The double-blind procedure refers to a lineup in which the administrator does not know the identity of the suspect. If the lineup administer is unaware of the identity of the suspect, then he or she cannot unwittingly relay information about the identity of the suspect to the witness.

The improvement in identification accuracy gained by these procedures, coupled with large numbers of DNA exonerations in recent years, has led many states to implement these reforms to ensure the fairest and most unbiased lineup identification procedures. For example, in New Jersey and North Carolina, police departments and prosecutor offices are now required to conduct sequential lineups. Similarly, Santa Ana, California, and several counties in Minnesota have opted for sequential lineups. In Clinton, Iowa, the arresting officer is not permitted in the room during the identification procedure. Many cities, such as New York and Seattle, have started using computerized programs to present photo arrays. In Chicago, as well as parts of Wisconsin and Minnesota, committees have been developed for the purpose of investigating identification procedures to reduce false identifications.

Evaluating Eyewitness Memory

In some sense, all estimator variables could be considered postdictors of eyewitness accuracy. Although research has focused on eyewitness recall, testimony, and identification, research on the postdictors has almost exclusively been limited to eyewitness identification. One of the most widely studied postdictor variables is eyewitness confidence. This is most likely the case because jurors seem to find confident eyewitnesses extremely persuasive and believable. This perception of confident eyewitnesses is understandable; intuitively, it seems as though there should be a strong positive relationship between witness confidence and accuracy. This belief is underscored by the fact that the court has suggested that jurors may employ witness confidence as an indicator of the accuracy of the witness. Unfortunately, psychological research has found unequivocally and repeatedly that the relationship between confidence and eyewitness accuracy is, at best, a weak one. Furthermore, this weak relationship deteriorates as the time interval between the event and the confidence statement increases. The reason for the lack of relationship between confidence and accuracy may be that witnesses often rely on misleading information as the basis for their confidence estimates. For example, it has been shown that confirmatory feedback increases participants' confidence in their eyewitness identification. Simply telling a witness that they have chosen correctly increases the witness's confidence in the accuracy of his or her identification relative to participants who are not given any feedback. This confidence inflation is especially prominent when the participants are inaccurate.

Just as eyewitness confidence serves an important function in the prosecution phase, eyewitness descriptions of the perpetrator serve an extremely important function in the investigation process. Investigators may use the descriptions to locate the suspect. The problem is that descriptions are generally incomplete and nondescript, such as "White male, 5 feet 9 inches to 6 feet, about 18 to 24 years old." It should be noted that while the descriptions are generally incomplete, the information that is collected is usually accurate. This is especially the case when witnesses are simply asked to describe the assailant without any prompts from the investigator. The key question is whether description accuracy and length of description correlate with eyewitness identification accuracy. It could be assumed that witnesses who give more complete and detailed descriptions of the culprit would be more accurate in their identification. In fact, the U.S. Supreme Court has employed the witness description accuracy as an indicator of the witness's reliability. However, it has generally been found that the quality and quantity of the witness descriptions are not related to identification accuracy.

Not only do witness descriptions poorly predict accurate identifications, but they may also in fact harm later identification accuracy. This is what happens in the case of verbal overshadowing. Verbal overshadowing refers to the impairment in lineup identification accuracy when the witness is asked to describe the suspect's face prior to the lineup administration. Although witness descriptions and identifications are weakly correlated, two factors are inconsistent with this finding. First, witnesses who are particularly adept at describing faces are likely to benefit from the description. Second, the correlation between witness description and identification accuracy is improved when the culprit's face is especially easy to describe, such as when there is a tattoo on the face or a facial disfigurement.

One estimator variable that is thought to be predictive of identification accuracy is the speed of the identification. The rationale is that witnesses with a good view of the culprit and a vivid memory of the crime should identify the witness quickly and without hesitation. For the most part, the research on speed of identification has been consistent with this logic. Furthermore, it has been noted that witnesses who indicate that the face "popped out" at them when viewing the lineup tend to be more accurate in their identification than witnesses who indicated that they had to take more time to make their decisions. Thus, there is a strong relationship between accuracy and speed of identification, with faster identification resulting in more accurate identification.

Eyewitnesses in the Courtroom

Considerable research has addressed how jurors evaluate eyewitness memory and whether their evaluations can be improved. Using trial simulation methods, research demonstrates that jurors are often insensitive to the factors that are known to influence eyewitness memory: stress experienced by the witness, weapon focus, and the influence of suggestive identification procedures. Furthermore, jurors tend to rely on factors that are known not to strongly predict identification accuracy. Witness confidence, for example, has a strong impact on jurors' evaluations of eyewitness identifications. In these studies, highly confident witnesses are persuasive, and jurors tend to convict perpetrators on the basis of testimony by highly confident witnesses.

The apparent inability of jurors to evaluate eyewitness identification procedures in a manner consistent with the research on eyewitness identification has led some psychologists to conclude that knowledgeable psychologists should testify in court as expert witnesses. The purpose of the expert testimony is not to make a judgment as to the accuracy of the identification but rather to provide all the relevant information so that the jury can make an informed decision when assessing the reliability of the witness. Not all those in the legal system agree on the efficacy or use of eyewitness testimony during trials. Some argue that the testimony may bias the witness; others indicate that the testimony is superfluous because issues of memory are of common knowledge (a conclusion that is inconsistent with research findings). Although there has been research investigating the impact of expert testimony on factors that influence eyewitness accuracy, the results are mixed with respect to its impact on jurors.

Jeffrey S. Neuschatz and Deah S. Lawson

See also Estimator and System Variables in Eyewitness Identification; Expert Psychological Testimony on Eyewitness Identification; Identification Tests, Best Practices in; Juries and Eyewitnesses

Further Readings

Brewer, N., Weber, N., & Semmler, C. (2005). Eyewitness identification. In N. Brewer & K. D. Williams (Eds.), *Psychology and law: An empirical perspective* (pp. 177–221). New York: Guilford Press.

Lindsay, R., Ross, D., Read, J., & Toglia, M. (Eds.). (2007). *The handbook of eyewitness psychology: Vol. 2. Memory for people.* New York: Lawrence Erlbaum.

Neuschatz, J. S., & Cutler, B. L (in press). Eyewitness identification. In H. L. Roediger (Ed.), *Learning and memory: A comprehensive reference.* New York: Lawrence Erlbaum.

Wells, G. L., & Olson, E. (2003). Eyewitness identification. *Annual Review of Psychology, 54*, 277–295.

EYEWITNESS MEMORY, LAY BELIEFS ABOUT

Lay beliefs about factors that influence the reliability of eyewitness testimony have been assessed with a variety of survey and experimental methods. When compared with expert opinion about the effects of these factors, the lay public frequently holds beliefs that would be considered incorrect in the light of psychological research on eyewitness memory.

A brief example provides the framework for understanding the relevance of lay beliefs about eyewitness memory to legal decision making and criminal justice procedures: A man presents a note to a bank teller and tells everyone to get on the floor. A security agent rushes the robber and is shot, but the thief escapes. Six weeks later, a man named Simon Chung is apprehended. His picture is included in a collection of photos that is shown to the teller, the wounded security officer, other employees, and the bank customers. The teller and four customers identify Chung as the robber, whereas the bank security guard and another three employees do not. Chung is charged with the crime and the case proceeds to trial. The prosecution believes that the five eyewitness identifications make up a strong case against Chung. At trial, Chung's defense team presents a cognitive psychologist who, if given the opportunity, will testify that a number of features of the robbery and of the defendant reduce the reliability of the identification evidence. Defense counsel argues that jurors need to be aware of these factors if Chung is to receive a fair trial. The judge considers the expert's testimony and, over the objections of the prosecution, decides that the expert should be allowed to give evidence.

The proffering of expert testimony at trial occurs frequently in common law countries. Judges decide whether an expert will be heard on the basis of several legal criteria, the most important of which for present purposes is the judge's assessment of the levels of lay or juror knowledge about eyewitness testimony. If the substance of an expert's presentation is deemed to be relevant to the case and to be outside the jurors' ken, experience, or their common knowledge, expert testimony intended to inform the jurors will likely be deemed admissible. Only an expert in the specific subject area may provide what is called *opinion evidence* on the matter. Based on his or her own knowledge and evaluation of the expert testimony, the judge decides whether members of the jury are, as a group, sufficiently informed and, if not, whether the quality and reliability of their deliberations will benefit from an expert's presentation. Given the adversarial nature of common law procedures, it is probable that opposing counsel may also proffer an expert who has a different interpretation of the importance of the relevant eyewitness factors.

Regardless of the decisions made by judges in these situations, there is little research that can tell us whether their assessments of jurors' lay beliefs about eyewitness factors are likely to be correct. Furthermore, although a topic of interest in its own right, few studies have assessed whether judges (or trial counsel) themselves hold correct beliefs concerning eyewitness issues. The question raised here, however, is the following: On what basis do judges decide whether jurors are sufficiently informed (or have "common knowledge")? Scientific investigations of lay beliefs about eyewitness memory have been conducted and, on occasion, the judges' assessments are informed by descriptions of this line of research.

To describe the history, methods, and results of that research, a few words are first needed about topics within the field of eyewitness psychology—topics about which the lay public may be examined as to their beliefs and knowledge. Briefly, the field of eyewitness memory research examines the myriad factors that *may* influence witnesses' recollections of an event, the people present, their behaviors, and the context in which the event occurred. The usual scheme for categorizing these factors is based on a distinction between (a) those that are under the control of the criminal justice system and, as a result, may be manipulated to improve the reliability of eyewitness evidence, such as the investigative interviews and the suspect identification procedures, and (b) those for which an impact on the reliability of testimony may only be estimated and that are not under the control of the justice system. This latter includes a very large group of factors, such as the age of the witness, lighting at the crime scene, witnesses' levels of stress, the confidence held by an eyewitness, and the presence of a weapon. Research has demonstrated that these factors can produce general memory impairments, but the effects are variable and unpredictable with regard to specific individuals.

Approaches to the Assessment of Lay Knowledge

Although the subject of scientific investigation of eyewitness memory is more than 100 years old, it is primarily the last 40 years of research that have provided a substantive and reliable foundation of data. To assess public beliefs concerning the eyewitness factors examined in this research, both *direct* and *indirect* methods have been employed. For examples, the introductory robbery scenario will serve. One factor that has long been considered relevant to the reliability of eyewitness identification is the correspondence between the race of the witness and that of the suspect. Identification reliability has often been found to be higher when both are members of the same racial group than when the two people belong to different racial groups—an outcome called the "other-race" effect. Using the *direct* or survey approach to the assessment of lay beliefs, respondents might be asked to agree or disagree with statements such as "People are better at recognizing members of their own racial group than those of a different race" or be asked to choose among a number of alternative formats to the following statement: "When people are asked to identify someone of a racial group different from their own, they are *just as likely* (or *more likely* or *less likely* or *don't know*) to be correct as when the person is of their own racial group." On the other hand, using an *indirect* approach, respondents may receive a brief written vignette in which the respective races of the witness and perpetrator are either not mentioned at all (a control condition), are described as being the same, or described as different. The vignette may in fact be a summary of an actual experiment in which identification rates were examined as a function of variations in the racial similarity variable. After reading the vignette, the respondents estimate the probability that the witness's identification decision is correct, an estimate that is often called a "postdiction" in relation to the actual experiment. Differences in the probability estimates from participants who received the different vignettes are taken to reflect public beliefs about the direction and magnitude of the relationship between witness-suspect race and eyewitness memory reliability. If, for example, Simon Chung is Asian, but the witnesses are Caucasian, juror beliefs about the

relevance of this distinction may be important to their assessments of the identification evidence. Of course, when compared with the effects of the variable on actual identification accuracy in research experiments, these response differences may reflect wholly erroneous beliefs.

These kinds of data from public samples will only be helpful to a judge if he or she has a basis for assessing the accuracy of the beliefs of survey respondents and research participants and, by extension, the public. Therefore, what is needed is a distillation of eyewitness research that provides the "correct" answer for each of the eyewitness factors present in a case. These correct answers have been made available to courts in two ways. In the first, survey researchers explicitly compare the public survey and research outcomes with their interpretations of what the scientific research literature has revealed. In the second, the survey researchers instead compare their findings with the results of surveys of "eyewitness experts" (themselves researchers) concerning the effects of variables on eyewitness reliability. The most recent of the expert surveys was completed in 2001 by Saul Kassin and colleagues, who tabulated the survey responses of 64 experts to each of 30 propositions about eyewitness factors including, for example, the effects of delay, weapon presence, other-race identification, stress, age, lineup construction techniques, and long term, to name but a few. To date, no factor has received complete unanimity from the experts as to its impact on eyewitness memory. Instead, to determine what is currently "correct," courts may look at general agreement among experts or a consensus of opinion. For example, of the 30 propositions presented to experts by Kassin, only 16 achieved a consensus of 80% agreement across experts. However, as a summarizing statement, when the responses collected from lay participants using both direct and indirect methods are compared with the consensual opinions of the experts about the factors, these comparisons frequently demonstrate significant differences between the beliefs of experts and those of members of the public.

Direct Methods

The earliest surveys were completed in the early 1980s and tested university students with multiple-choice questions. The majority of participants did *not* give the correct answer to most items, including the effect of violence on recall accuracy, the relationship between witness accuracy and confidence, memory for faces, effects of training or experience on identification performance, and the other-race effect. Subsequent surveys of other students, legal professionals, potential jurors, and community respondents in the United Kingdom, Australia, and Canada produced similar results: More than half the participants did not identify the known relationships between eyewitness accuracy and confidence, event violence, event duration estimates, trained observers, older witnesses, verbal descriptions, and child suggestibility. These surveys were followed by those in which Likert-type scale items (ratings on 7-point *agree-disagree* scales) were presented to samples of college students and community adults, with highly comparable results: Almost half the respondents disagreed with expert opinion on many items. Despite these differences, lay responses were, nonetheless, often similar to those of experts on a subset of the items: the effects of attitudes and expectations, wording of questions, weapon focus, event violence, and estimates of the duration of events. More recently, an assessment of the responses of potential jurors in Tennessee to items from Kassin's survey of experts produced a similar outcome: Jurors responded significantly differently than experts on 26 of 30 items, with magnitudes of disagreements ranging from 11% to 67%. A small sample of actual jurors from Washington, D.C., was also surveyed in 1990: Fewer than half the participants agreed with the correct responses. Furthermore, in a 2005 telephone survey, a large sample of potential jurors in Washington, D.C., were questioned about a smaller number of eyewitness factors. The authors argued that their results support the view that potential jurors often differ from experts in their opinions about and understanding of many issues. Finally, Canadian researchers recently constructed surveys in a manner intended to reduce jargon and professional terminology to improve understanding by survey respondents. Their results strongly suggest that assessments of lay beliefs are influenced by question format and that prior research may have underestimated current levels of lay knowledge concerning a number of factors, for example, the relationship between confidence and accuracy. Nonetheless, even with the friendlier survey format, disagreement with the experts was apparent for approximately 50% of the eyewitness topics.

Indirect Methods

The *indirect* approach to assessing lay knowledge is based on the distinction between *having* knowledge and *making use* of it. The direct-method survey research above has emphasized the former. With indirect methods, on the other hand, participant responses are used as the basis for determining whether existing beliefs appear to have influenced the respondents' judgments about the reliability of eyewitness testimony. In other examples of this approach, researchers attempt to increase the levels of knowledge of participants who serve as "mock jurors" and then ask whether such knowledge appears to be integrated in judgments about eyewitness reliability and defendant guilt.

In the first group of studies, research participants estimated the likelihood of accurate person identification by an eyewitness in situations that varied along several dimensions that had, in fact, been manipulated in actual experiments—for example, levels of witness confidence, crime seriousness, and lineup bias. To determine whether participants were sensitive to these factors as determinants of eyewitness reliability, their "postdictive" estimates were compared with the effects of these same variables in the laboratory research. In general, participants appeared to be quite insensitive to the manipulated factors: Estimates of identification accuracy were overly optimistic; considerable reliance was erroneously placed on witness confidence, and their estimates usually failed to reflect the real effects of variables. Another indirect approach examines data collected from "mock jurors" who reached verdicts (and other judgments of witness credibility) after reading case descriptions in which eyewitness variables that are known to influence identification accuracy had been manipulated. The results revealed that the factors recognized by experts as important determinants of eyewitness accuracy generally have not been shown to influence mock jurors' verdicts or credibility evaluations, and some of those known to be unrelated to witness accuracy (i.e., confidence) did affect such evaluations. Similarly, there is a disparity between mock jurors' judgments of factors that they say are important to eyewitness reliability and the impact of these factors on their decisions when case evidence is actually presented to them.

Furthermore, it is one thing to be able to identify correctly explicitly stated, general relationships between eyewitness factors and memory but quite another to have the depth of knowledge to appreciate conceptual distinctions made at trial by experts about these factors as they are presented in specific cases. To examine these questions, researchers have asked whether beliefs demonstrably held by mock jurors (without benefit of expert testimony) appear to be integrated into their decisions when they are presented with a case description that includes the relevant eyewitness factors (e.g., cross-race effect). In one of the few investigations of this question, Brian Cutler and colleagues found that even when jurors had specific knowledge of the limitations of eyewitness identification, the information was not well integrated into their decision making. Similarly, other researchers have recently found that mock jurors who have demonstrably more knowledge than others do not necessarily demonstrate sensitivity to the eyewitness factors relevant to a case. In summary, researchers have concluded that there is little evidence that the existing knowledge held by mock jurors is readily incorporated into their decisions regarding a written vignette.

Finally, Brian Cutler and colleagues have also attempted to improve levels of mock juror knowledge through the presentation of expert testimony prior to making judgments about cases in which eyewitness identification factors are manipulated. This research has been completed in laboratory settings with mock jurors, and as a result, its generalizability to courtrooms and jury deliberations is unknown. Nonetheless, these studies suggest that whereas the presentation of relevant expert testimony may increase low levels of juror knowledge or awareness of relevant eyewitness factors, the integration of this knowledge into juror decision making may or may not be successful, depending on the particular variables of interest. Thus, if expert testimony is recommended as a safeguard against weak juror understanding of eyewitness factors, it does not appear to be particularly effective.

Potential Difficulties With Evaluations of Lay Knowledge

A number of issues are relevant to the reliability and validity of the kinds of assessments of lay belief described above. First, in a temporal sense, public survey results have limited validity because public beliefs and knowledge will change over time. These changes likely result from improved scientific understanding and its dissemination to the general public through various media and by integration into formal education.

Second, considerably more research is required to determine the extent to which survey and mock trial responses accurately reflect the beliefs of jury-eligible participants. This issue concerns the sensitivity and reliability of the various assessment procedures described above and the extent to which lay responses

may be directly compared with those of experts. For example, even with ostensibly identical foci of the questions posed to experts and the public, the response options provided have not been identical. Similarly, if statements are written by experts and offered without change to survey participants, on what basis can we argue that the public understands the statements in a manner similar to that of the experts? Furthermore, the translation of the expert items into meaningful statements for lay respondents is difficult and suggests that real understanding of these issues by jurors (and by judges, trial counsel, and experts alike) will only be gained with more in-depth interviews, open-ended questions, and the use of techniques that can assess response consistency within individuals across both question formats and time.

A third question is whether the samples surveyed to date actually represent the members of a population of individuals who may be called for jury duty and who serve as jurors. Many studies have relied on undergraduate students, albeit jury-eligible in most cases, but who arguably are not representative of actual jurors: In fact, university students infrequently serve on actual juries. Additionally, even those studies in which community samples were included, nonetheless, suffer from weak representativeness because there may be important demographic and attitudinal differences between community members who, once called, appear versus those who fail to appear for jury duty. A more compelling approach would be to collect data from actual jurors who have participated in trials or to survey community members who have been called and appear for jury duty but have yet to be assigned to a particular case.

In summary, a fairly consistent description of juror knowledge emerges across a wide variety of assessment methods; specifically, jurors appear to have limited understanding of eyewitness issues and research findings.

J. Don Read and Sarah L. Desmarais

See also Cognitive Interview; Confidence in Identifications; Cross-Race Effect in Eyewitness Identification; Elderly Eyewitnesses; Estimator and System Variables in Eyewitness Identification; Expert Psychological Testimony; Expert Psychological Testimony on Eyewitness Identification; Exposure Time and Eyewitness Memory; Eyewitness Memory; Instructions to the Witness; Retention Interval and Eyewitness Memory; Simultaneous and Sequential Lineup Presentation; Weapon Focus

Further Readings

Benton, T. P., McDonnell, S., Ross, D., Thomas, W. N., & Bradshaw, E. (2007). Has eyewitness testimony research penetrated the American legal system? A synthesis of case history, juror knowledge, and expert testimony. In R. C. L. Lindsay, D. W. Ross, J. D. Read, & M. P. Toglia (Eds.), *Handbook of eyewitness psychology: Vol. 2. Memory for people.* Mahwah, NJ: Lawrence Erlbaum.

Benton, T. R., Ross, D. F., Bradshaw, E., Thomas, W. N., & Bradshaw, G. S. (2006). Eyewitness memory is still not common sense: Comparing jurors, judges, and law enforcement to eyewitness experts. *Applied Cognitive Psychology, 20,* 115–130.

Cutler, B. L., & Penrod, S. D. (1995). *Mistaken identification: The eyewitness, psychology, and the law.* New York: Cambridge University Press.

Devenport, J. L., Penrod, S. D., & Cutler, B. L. (1997). Eyewitness identification evidence: Evaluating commonsense evaluations. *Psychology, Public Policy, and Law, 3,* 338–361.

Kassin, S. M., Tubb, V. A., Hosch, H. M., & Memon, A. (2001). On the "general acceptance" of eyewitness testimony research. *American Psychologist, 56,* 405–416.

Schmechel, R. S., O'Toole, T. P., Easterly, C., & Loftus, E. F. (2006). Beyond the ken? Testing jurors' understanding of eyewitness reliability evidence. *Jurimetrics, 46,* 177–214.

FACIAL COMPOSITES

When a crime has been committed and the identity of the perpetrator is unknown, eyewitnesses are often asked to attempt to create a likeness of the face of the perpetrator. An eyewitness can do this by creating a facial composite, either through the assistance of a sketch artist or by using a mechanized composite system. However, facial composites tend to be poor representations of the intended face, even if it is a face that is very familiar to the composite creator. This is probably due to a mismatch between the way in which people encode faces and the way in which they attempt to recall faces when building a composite.

When facial composites were first introduced in the criminal justice system, eyewitnesses would work together with a sketch artist to create a likeness of the intended face. Today, law enforcement agencies typically use mechanized composite production systems, and computerized composite production systems are used more than twice as often as noncomputerized versions. The original mechanized composite production systems, such as the Identi-Kit and Photo-Fit, are composed of overlays of facial features (e.g., noses, eyes, chins, hair) that can be combined to create a face. Modern, computerized versions, such as E-fit, Mac-a-Mug, and FACES, consist of features that can be combined, and typically resized, in any order to create a face. Currently, however, composite production systems are being created that move away from producing a face at the feature level and, instead, focus on whole faces.

Many of the mechanized and computerized systems have attempted to increase the number of features available from which a composite creator may choose, the realism of the final product, and the user friendliness of the interface. FACES, for example, has more than 3,700 features, ranging from relatively prominent features such as hair, eyes, and lips to detailed features such as eye lines and mouth lines. The computerized systems result in a fairly realistic product and can be used after a minimal training session. However, even when people view a face that has been created with a composite system and attempt to re-create the face using the same system, thereby ensuring that all the features are available, they are still unable to create good likenesses of the intended face. Furthermore, composite producers themselves are poor judges of how well the composite that they have created matches the target face. Even if a person who creates a composite rates the composite's similarity to the face that it is intended to represent, this rating is not predictive of how others rate the similarity of the composite to the target face.

Researchers have typically assessed people's ability to create composites of faces through naming tasks, matching tasks, and similarity-rating tasks. Naming tasks show people a composite of someone who should be familiar to them (e.g., a famous person) and ask them to name the person the composite is designed to depict. Matching tasks have people choose which face the composite is designed to depict from a larger set of faces. Similarity-rating tasks have people rate the similarity between a composite and the face it is designed to depict. In general, facial composites tend to be poor likenesses of the faces that they are intended to represent, regardless of the composite production system and regardless of how the similarity of the composite to the intended face is assessed.

Although facial composites can be a helpful tool for law enforcement, they can potentially be problematic. This is because a composite that does not truly represent the perpetrator of a crime can lead the police to investigate innocent suspects who do resemble the composite. Additionally, creating a composite and viewing it can bias an eyewitness's memory away from the original face toward the composite face. Recent research has shown the advantages of morphing (averaging at the pixel level) composites of the same target face that have been created by different people. But, at best, morphing of composites can only be used in multiple-witness cases, and although a morphed composite does tend to resemble the target face more than do individual composites, there is only a modest increase in similarity.

The main reason why composites do not tend to resemble the faces that they are designed to depict appears to stem from the difference between the way in which people naturally encode faces and the way in which creating a composite forces them to retrieve information about the face. People tend to encode faces through a holistic process, which enables them to be better at facial recognition than facial recall. Composite-production forces people to recall faces at a feature level, as they attempt to piece together a face while looking at many different variations of the same feature.

Newer, whole-face production systems that are still in very early, experimental phases attempt to correct for this disconnect between the encoding and retrieving phases in composite production. These systems start by generating a random set of faces; the user selects the face that best matches the user's memory of the intended face. From that, a number of different algorithms are used that produce a set of faces that are variations of the initially selected face. The user again selects the face from this set that most closely resembles the intended face, and this process is repeated until the faces all resemble that target face equally well. Although the few comparisons to date of the whole-face systems with feature-level composite systems do not show the whole-face systems to be superior, they do present the composite creator with a retrieval task that is more similar to the encoding task than do the other systems. Consequently, these new systems may eventually prove to be a better tool for

eyewitnesses to create a likeness of the perpetrator for the police and the public.

Lisa E. Hasel

See also Confidence in Identifications; Eyewitness Descriptions, Accuracy of; Eyewitness Memory; Identification Tests, Best Practices in; Wrongful Conviction

Further Readings

Davies, G. M., & Valentine, T. (2007). Facial composites: Forensic utility and psychological research. In R. C. L. Lindsay, D. F. Ross, J. D. Read, & M. P. Toglia (Eds.), *Handbook of eyewitness psychology: Vol. 2. Memory for people* (pp. 59–86). Mahwah, NJ: Lawrence Erlbaum.

Frowd, C. D., Carson, D., Ness, H., Richardson, J., Morrison, L., & McLanaghan, S. (2005). A forensically valid comparison of facial composite systems. *Psychology, Crime, & Law, 11,* 33–52.

Hasel, L. H., & Wells, G. L. (2006). Catching the bad guy: Morphing composite faces helps. *Law and Human Behavior* [Electronic version]. Retrieved November 15, 2006, from http://www.springerlink.com

FALSE CONFESSIONS

A false confession is a narrative admission to a crime that is made, orally or in writing, by an innocent person. Research shows that innocent people may confess in different ways and for different reasons—resulting in three types of false confessions: voluntary, compliant, and internalized. From an empirical perspective, this entry addresses the evolution of our understanding of false confessions, the frequency of their occurrence, and the methods of interrogation that put innocent people at risk.

False confessions are an important problem in forensic psychology, especially when viewed in the context of their consequences within the criminal justice system. Historically, confession evidence is considered the most incriminating form of evidence that can be presented at trial, a belief that is supported by its effects on jury decision making. Even when disputed, uncorroborated, and contradicted by other evidence, confessions are a driving force for conviction.

Among the many notable examples of this phenomenon was the infamous 1989 Central Park Jogger case, in which five teenage boys confessed to brutally beating and raping a female jogger in New York's Central Park. Even though the boys were subjected to lengthy and harsh interrogations, gave confessions that were filled with factual errors, retracted their confessions shortly thereafter, and were excluded as donors of the semen by DNA tests, each was convicted at trial—solely on the basis that they had confessed. It was not until 13 years later that they were exonerated when a serial rapist stepped forward from prison to confess. His confession betrayed firsthand knowledge of the crime and was supported by a match to the original DNA sample.

Questions of Prevalence

The jogger case is notorious but not unique. Beginning with the Salem witch trials of 1692, numerous false confessions surfaced when it was later discovered that the confessed crime had not been committed (e.g., the alleged victim turned up alive) or that it was physically impossible (e.g., the confessor was demonstrably elsewhere) or when the real perpetrator was apprehended (e.g., by ballistics evidence). Indeed, as more and more wrongful convictions are discovered, often as a result of newly available DNA tests on old evidence, it is apparent that 15% to 25% of those wrongfully convicted had confessed. Moreover, many false confessions are discovered before there is a trial, are not reported by the police, are not publicized by the media, or result in plea bargains and are never contested—suggesting that the known cases represent the tip of an iceberg. In short, although it is not possible to know the prevalence rate of false confessions, it is clear that they occur with some regularity, making it important to understand how they come about and how they can be prevented.

Types of False Confessions

Both criminals and innocent suspects may confess, providing true and false confessions, respectively. Based on a taxonomy introduced by Saul Kassin and Lawrence Wrightsman, it is now common to further divide the latter into three types: voluntary, compliant, and internalized.

Voluntary False Confessions

In the absence of pressure from the police, voluntary false confessions occur when people freely admit to crimes for which they were not responsible. Sometimes innocent people have volunteered confessions in this way to protect the actual perpetrator, often a parent or a child. At other times, however, voluntary false confessions have resulted from a pathological desire for attention, especially in high-profile cases reported in the news media; a conscious or unconscious need for self-punishment to alleviate feelings of guilt over other transgressions; or an inability to distinguish fact from fantasy, a common feature of certain psychological disorders. As revealed in actual known cases, the motives underlying voluntary false confessions are as diverse as the people who make them.

A number of high-profile cases illustrate the point. In 1932, the aviator Charles Lindbergh's baby was kidnapped, prompting some 200 people to volunteer confessions. In 1947, Elizabeth Short, a young, aspiring actress, later called "Black Dahlia" for her black hair and attire, was brutally murdered in Los Angeles and her nude body cut in half, prompting more than 60 people, mostly men, to confess. In the 1980s, Henry Lee Lucas falsely confessed to hundreds of unsolved murders, mostly in Texas, making him the most prolific serial confessor in history. More recently, John Mark Karr was arrested in Thailand in the summer of 2006, after it appeared that he had voluntarily confessed to the unsolved 1996 murder of JonBenét Ramsey, a 6-year-old beauty pageant contestant in Boulder, Colorado. Karr was intimately familiar with the facts of the crime. Ultimately, he was not charged, however, after his ex-wife placed him in a different state and after DNA tests from the crime scene implicated another, still unidentified, man.

Compliant False Confessions

In contrast to cases in which innocent people confess without external pressure are the numerous false confessions that are elicited through pressure from family, friends, and most notably, the processes of police interrogation.

In many of these cases, the suspect surrenders to the demand for a confession to escape from the stress and discomfort of the situation, avoid a threat of harm or punishment, or gain a promised or implied reward. This type of confession is a mere act of public *compliance* by a suspect who comes to believe that the short-term benefits of confession relative to denial outweigh the long-term costs. American history contains numerous stories of this type of confession—as in the Salem witch trials of 1692, when some 50 women were tortured and threatened into confessing to witchcraft. This type of false confession is also illustrated in the Central Park jogger case, in which all the boys retracted their confessions immediately on arrest and said that they had confessed because they were scared and had expected to be allowed to go home. In the interrogation room, there are many specific incentives for this type of compliance—such as being allowed to sleep, eat, make a phone call, go home, or feed a drug habit. The desire to terminate the questioning may be particularly pressing for people who are young, desperate, socially dependent, or anxious about additional confinement. As discussed later in this entry, certain commonly used interrogation techniques increase the risk of police-induced compliant false confessions.

Internalized False Confessions

In some cases, innocent but vulnerable people, as a result of exposure to highly suggestive and misleading interrogation tactics, not only comply with the demand for a confession but come to internalize a belief in their guilt. In extreme cases, these beliefs are accompanied by detailed false memories of what they allegedly did, how, and why.

The case of 18-year-old Peter Reilly illustrates this phenomenon. Reilly called the police when he found his mother dead in their home. The police administered a lie-detector test and told Reilly that he had failed it, which was not true but which indicated that he was guilty despite his lack of a conscious recollection. After hours of interrogation, Reilly transformed from certain denial to confusion, self-doubt, a change in belief ("Well, it really looks like I did it"), and eventually a full confession ("I remember slashing once at my mother's throat with a straight razor I used for model airplanes"). Two years later, independent evidence revealed that Reilly was innocent. The case of 14-year-old Michael Crowe, charged with stabbing his sister, similarly illustrates the process. At first, Michael denied the charge. Soon, however, he conceded, "I'm not sure how I did it. All I know is I did it"—an admission that was followed by lies about the physical evidence. Eventually, the boy concluded that he had a split personality—that "bad Michael" killed his sister, while "good Michael" blocked out the incident. The charge was later dropped when a local

vagrant with a history of violence was found with the girl's blood on his clothing.

Why Innocents Confess

The reasons why people confess to crimes they did not commit are numerous and multifaceted. Sometimes, an individual may be dispositionally naive, compliant, suggestible, delusional, anxious, or otherwise impaired so that little interrogative pressure is required to produce a false confession. In these cases, clinical testing and assessment may be useful in determining whether an individual suspect is prone or vulnerable to confession. At other times, however, normal adults, not overly naive or impaired, confess to crimes they did not commit as a way of coping with the pressures of police interrogation. Indeed, social psychology research has amply shown that human beings are profoundly influenced by figures of authority and can be induced to behave in ways that are detrimental to themselves and others. In short, both personal and situational risk factors may increase the risk of a false confession.

Dispositional Risk Factors

Over the years, numerous studies by Gisli Gudjonsson and his colleagues have shown that not everyone is equally vulnerable to becoming a false confessor. For example, they note that suspects vary in their predispositions toward compliance (as measured by the Gudjonsson Compliance Scale) and suggestibility (as measured by the Gudjonsson Suggestibility Scale). People high in compliance desire to please others and avoid confrontation—which increases the tendency to capitulate in a highly adversarial interrogation. Those who are high in suggestibility are often less assertive, have lower self-esteem, and display poorer memories. In studies of crime suspects, those who confessed and later retracted their statements obtained higher suggestibility scores than the general population, whereas resistors, who maintained their innocence throughout the interrogation, obtained lower scores.

Also at risk are innocent juvenile suspects, who are overrepresented in the population of known false confessors. Juveniles are more likely to comply with authority figures and to believe false presentations of evidence. Research shows that they also exhibit less comprehension than adults of their *Miranda* rights, are less likely to invoke these rights, and are more likely to confess when under pressure to do so.

Mental retardation is also a substantial risk factor, as it is associated with increases in compliance and suggestibility. Research has shown that people with intellectual impairments do not comprehend their *Miranda* rights and are prone to answer "Yes" to a range of questions, particularly from those in positions of authority, indicating an acquiescence response bias. They are also highly influenced by misinformation, a suggestibility effect that increases the risk of internalized false confessions.

Mental illness can also increase the tendency for false confessions. Distorted perceptions and memories, a breakdown in reality monitoring, anxiety, mood disturbance, and lack of self-control are common symptoms of many categories of mental illness. These symptoms may lead people to offer misleading information, including false confessions, to the police during interviews and interrogations. Moreover, disorders that lead people to be more anxious can increase the likelihood of their making a false confession as a means of escape from interrogation.

Interrogation Risk Factors

Although there are subtle variations among approaches, the typical police interrogation is a multi-step event that involves an interplay of three processes: (1) isolation, (2) confrontation, and (3) minimization.

First, interrogators are trained to remove suspects from their familiar surroundings and question them in the police station, often in a specially constructed interrogation room. To some extent, interrogation time is a risk factor. Although most police interrogations last for less than 2 hours, a study of documented false confession cases in which time was recorded revealed that the mean of interrogation exceeded 16 hours.

Second, interrogators confront suspects with strong assertions of guilt that are designed to communicate that resistance is futile. As part of this process, interrogators are trained to block the suspect from issuing denials, to refute alibis, and even to present supposedly incontrovertible evidence of the suspect's guilt—even if such evidence does not exist. Historically, the polygraph has played a key role in this false evidence ploy. In numerous false confession cases, compliant and internalized false confessions have been extracted by police examiners who told suspects that they had failed a lie detector test—even when they had not

(as in the Peter Reilly and Michael Crowe cases described earlier).

The third step is to minimize the crime by providing suspects, who are feeling trapped by confrontation, with moral justification or face-saving excuses, making confession seem like a cost-effective means of escape. At this stage, interrogators are trained to suggest to suspects that their alleged actions were spontaneous, accidental, provoked, peer pressured, drug induced, or otherwise justifiable by external factors, as a way to encourage confession. Indeed, research shows that minimization tactics lead people to infer that leniency will follow from confession, even in the absence of an explicit promise.

Empirical Research on False Confessions

In recent years, researchers have sought to examine various aspects of false confessions using an array of methods—including aggregated case studies, naturalistic observations of live and videotaped interrogations, self-reports from the police and suspects, and laboratory and field experiments designed for hypothesis-testing purposes.

Saul Kassin and Katherine Kiechel developed the first laboratory paradigm to systematically examine the factors that elicit false confessions. In this experiment, participants working on a computer were accused of hitting the ALT key they had been instructed to avoid. In the original study, participants were rendered more or less vulnerable to manipulation by being paced to work at a fast or slow pace. In a manipulation of the false evidence ploy, some participants, but not others, were then exposed to a confederate who claimed to have seen them hit the forbidden key. Results showed that this false evidence ploy significantly increased the false confession rate, as well as the tendency of participants to internalize the belief in their own guilt—particularly among participants rendered vulnerable to manipulation. Follow-up studies using this computer-crash paradigm have replicated and extended this false evidence effect.

A second laboratory paradigm was developed by Melissa Russano and colleagues to investigate the effects of promises and minimization on both true and false confession rates. In their study, participants were paired with a confederate for a problem-solving study and instructed to work alone on some trials and jointly on others. In a guilty condition, the confederate asked the participant for help on an individual problem, inducing a violation of the experimental rule; in an innocent condition, the confederate did not make this request. Later, all participants were accused of cheating and were interrogated by an experimenter who promised leniency, made minimizing remarks, used both tactics, or used no tactics. The results showed that minimization was as persuasive as an explicit promise, increasing the rate not only of true confessions but of false confessions as well.

In light of the numerous wrongful convictions involving false confessions, as well as recent research, the time is ripe for law enforcement professionals, attorneys, judges, social scientists, and policymakers to evaluate current practices and seek the kinds of reforms that would not only secure confessions from criminals but also protect the innocent in the process.

Jennifer M. Torkildson and Saul M. Kassin

See also Confession Evidence; Interrogation of Suspects; Reid Technique for Interrogations; Videotaping Confessions

Further Readings

Drizin, S. A., & Leo, R. A. (2004). The problem of false confessions in the post-DNA world. *North Carolina Law Review, 82,* 891–1007.

Gudjonsson, G. H. (2003). *The psychology of interrogations and confessions: A handbook.* West Sussex, UK: Wiley.

Kassin, S. M. (1997). The psychology of confession evidence. *American Psychologist, 52,* 221–233.

Kassin, S. M. (2005). On the psychology of confessions: Does innocence put innocents at risk? *American Psychologist, 60,* 215–228.

Kassin, S. M., & Gudjonsson, G. (2004). The psychology of confessions: A review of the literature and issues. *Psychological Science in the Public Interest, 5,* 33–67.

FALSE MEMORIES

We do not necessarily remember our experiences the way they really happened—and what is more, remembering an experience does not necessarily mean it actually happened at all. In little more than a decade, scientists have discovered that people can have detailed, emotion-filled, and utterly false memories.

False memories are memories that are partly or wholly inaccurate. They are the product of second-hand information rather than genuine experience. Although the term *false memory* can be used to describe a wide range of memory phenomena, in this entry it is used to describe full-blown distortions of our own biographies: wholly false memories of unreal experiences. However, readers should be aware that two large and parallel scientific literatures show that people can misremember aspects of witnessed events, misidentify perpetrators, and falsely recall verbal information.

The Repression Phenomenon

According to the Harvard scientist and clinician Richard McNally, for many decades mental health professionals in the United States generally believed that once victims of childhood sexual abuse reached adulthood, they often did not like to talk about their abuse; yet by the end of the 1980s, he notes, the reluctance to disclose became an inability to remember. Many therapists, convinced that their clients were repressing experiences of long-ago trauma, began using techniques designed to dig up these buried memories—techniques such as imagination, guided imagery, hypnosis, and dream interpretation.

Many of these therapeutic techniques appeared in a mass-market book called *The Courage to Heal,* by Ellen Bass and Laura Davis. First published in 1988, it was the biggest gear in what Carol Tavris has called the "abuse-survivor machine." It still ranks among Amazon.com's bestsellers, and even a cursory browse through Amazon's customer reviews reveals that the book is surely among their most controversial. On the one hand, the book has given comfort to genuine victims; on the other, it encourages beliefs that can create a legion of pseudovictims.

For example, readers who wonder if they might be repressing memories of childhood abuse are told that the lack of such memories does not mean that they were *not* abused. In fact, memories are unnecessary: The *belief* that one was abused and the presence of certain symptoms in one's life are enough to confirm that the abuse happened. Other therapists concurred. A few years later, in 1992, Renee Fredrickson suggested that the very absence of memories was proof enough; that is, those who remember very little of their childhood or a period of their childhood (e.g., between the ages of 10 and 14) have repressed memories.

Scientific Research on False Memories

Lost in the Mall

As the notion of repression became more popular, some psychological scientists began asking themselves if these "recovered memory therapy" (RMT) techniques might be dangerous. Would it be possible, they wondered, for people to "recover" memories for false childhood events?

The answer was yes. In a landmark study in 1995, Elizabeth Loftus and Jacquie Pickrell showed that they could implant a false childhood memory using a seemingly innocuous RMT technique: asking people to try to remember a childhood experience. They asked people in their study to read descriptions of four childhood events. Three descriptions were genuine—having been provided by a family member—and one description was false. The false event described the reader being lost in a shopping mall and being rescued by an elderly lady. For example, one person in the study read this description:

> You, your mom, Tien, and Tuan all went to the Bremerton K-Mart. You must have been 5 years old at the time. Your mom gave each of you some money to get a blueberry Icee. You ran ahead to get into the line first, and somehow lost your way in the store. Tien found you crying to an elderly Chinese woman. You three then went together to get an Icee.

People were asked to write everything they could remember about all four events, and then they were interviewed twice over as much as 2 weeks. By the end of the study, approximately 25% of the people reported at least some information about the false shopping mall episode. Some of the memories were rich narratives, while others were less so—although perhaps even these may have developed if they had had more time to incubate.

The "Lost in the Mall" study was the first demonstration that everyday people could come to recall entirely false events, a finding that showcased the malleability of autobiographical memory and questioned the legitimacy of some of the recovered memories emerging in therapy. It also gave rise to a number of studies using the same basic paradigm. Since then, scientists have shown that people can recover memories of a wide range of false experiences, from being attacked by an animal to being saved by a lifeguard.

Photographs

Another RMT technique is photographic review, in which people look through photo albums as a way of triggering recall of their buried abuse memories. Scientists asked two questions about this technique: (1) Are photos powerful enough to elicit memories of false events? (2) Do photos add power to a false suggestion?

To answer the first question, Kimberley Wade and colleagues followed the "Lost in the Mall" procedure but swapped the written event descriptions for photographs. Again, one of the events was fake: taking a hot-air balloon ride. The people who took part in the study each saw a doctored photograph of themselves and at least one family member in the basket of a hot-air balloon. Each person was interviewed three times over approximately 2 weeks and asked to work at remembering the experience. Even in the absence of any narrative suggestion, by the end of the study, half the subjects came to remember something about the balloon ride. In short, photographs can lead people to remember experiences that never really happened.

Of course, as dubious an RMT technique as photographic review might be, it does not call for the use of doctored photos—instead, clients are encouraged to review family albums in concert with the suggestion that they might be repressing memories for childhood abuse. But suppose that suggestion is false. We have already seen that false suggestions can lead people to report false experiences. Would the combination of a false suggestion and a real childhood photo be especially dangerous? Stephen Lindsay and his colleagues addressed this question by asking one group of people to read descriptions about some grammar school experiences. One of the events was false and described getting in trouble for playing a prank on a schoolteacher. A second group also read descriptions—including the false story about the school prank—and received class photos corresponding to the age at which each event took place. As in previous studies, nearly half the "descriptions-only" people remembered something about the prank, but more than three quarters of the "descriptions-plus-photo" people remembered something. This study shows that the combination of familiar real photos and a false suggestion can be especially dangerous.

How Do False Memories Develop?

The scientific research now clearly shows that it is possible to change people's autobiographies by implanting false memories. How do these memories develop? One model of false memory development was proposed by Giuliana Mazzoni and colleagues. Their model contains components that are crucial to the formation of false memories. We focus on two of those here: the plausibility of the false event and the belief that the event really happened.

Plausibility

There are numerous real-life cases where people have reported implausible—some would say impossible—memories, ranging from being abducted by space aliens to being forced to breed for a satanic cult. How does the plausibility of a false event affect the likelihood that someone might come to believe it really happened? To answer this question, Giuliana Mazzoni and colleagues ran a four-part experiment over the course of several months. In the first phase, they asked people to rate the plausibility of various experiences, including a critical event: witnessing an incident of demonic possession. People also reported how likely they thought it was that they had actually witnessed such an incident when they were very young. At the end of this phase, the subjects reported demonic possession as both implausible and unlikely to have featured in their childhoods. In the second phase, some of those people read stories about cases of demonic possession and learned that it was a real phenomenon. In the third phase, these same people took a test that ostensibly measured their fears, and their results were always interpreted to mean that they might have witnessed a case of demonic possession. Finally, they completed the same measures as in the first phase. The key question was how responses at the final phase compared with responses at the first phase. People who had read about demonic possession and received the fear interpretations rated witnessing it as more plausible than they had initially. Giuliana Mazzoni and colleagues also found that even small changes in plausibility were enough to cause significant changes in people's belief that the experience had really happened. This study and, later, related research suggest that people can judge an event as implausible yet harbor the belief that it had really happened. The same is true of the relationship between plausibility and memory; for example, the world is riddled with adults who still remember hearing reindeer on the roof one Christmas Eve.

Increased Belief

The second component in the development of false memories is the belief that the experience really happened. On this front, scientists have discovered that a number of RMT techniques can increase belief.

One of the most common of these techniques is imagination. What is the consequence of imagining a false event? To answer this question, Maryanne Garry and colleagues first asked people to report their confidence that a series of childhood events had happened to them. Later, the same people were asked to imagine some of those events but not others and then report their confidence again using the same test. People were more likely to inflate their confidence for imagined events compared with nonimagined events, an effect known as "imagination inflation." Other scientists have produced imagination inflation for unusual or bizarre experiences. In fact, the same kind of inflated confidence can occur when imagination is replaced with some other kinds of activities, such as paraphrasing statements about fictitious events or writing a paragraph explaining how the event might have happened. Still other research shows that the act of imagination can also produce false memories, even in the absence of suggestive "Lost in the Mall" type of descriptions. In one study, when people imagined that they had participated in a bogus national skin-sampling test, they became more confident that the false procedure had occurred, and some people developed detailed memories of it.

Consequences of False Memories

Both false beliefs and false memories can affect behavior. In one study, people who received a false suggestion that they had become ill after eating strawberry ice cream during childhood said that they would be less likely to eat it at a party than before they received the false suggestion. In another study, people who imagined drinking fewer caffeinated soft drinks later believed (and reported) having done just that.

Richard McNally and colleagues discovered that false memories can also produce physiological signs of distress. They found that when people who believed that they had been abducted by aliens listened to their own accounts of some of their most terrifying encounters with the creatures, they showed an increased heart rate, skin electrical conductance, and muscle tension, all symptoms that people with posttraumatic stress disorder show when they remember their own traumas.

How Do We Figure Out If a Memory Is True or False?

In experimental settings, scientists know which events are true and which are false. Thus, they can tell people about their false memories at the end of the study. But what do people do in real life to determine for themselves whether a memory is true or false? In one study, people were asked if they had ever remembered an event that they later found out really did not happen. If so, they were asked to describe the episode, and the ways they tried to figure out if the event was true or false. The two most popular strategies were to consult another person about the event and to use cognitive techniques, such as thinking about or imagining it. These two approaches are not without risks. For example, the consulted person may remember the event partly or completely inaccurately. In addition, a quick review of earlier sections in this entry will make clear the perils of relying on imagination as a means to determining the veracity of an experience.

There are also real-life consequences to real-life false memories. In many countries, false memories have landed innocent people in prison, divided families, drained our health care resources, and clogged our courts. It is these consequences that compel psychological scientists to continue their work.

Eryn Newman and Maryanne Garry

See also Eyewitness Memory; Reconstructive Memory; Repressed and Recovered Memories

Further Readings

Garry, M., & Hayne, H. (Eds.). (2006). *Do justice and let the sky fall: Elizabeth F. Loftus and her contributions to science, law and academic freedom.* Mahwah, NJ: Lawrence Erlbaum.

Loftus, E. F., & Davis, D. (2006). Recovered memories. *Annual Review of Clinical Psychology, 2,* 469–498.

McNally, R. J. (2003). *Remembering trauma.* Cambridge, MA: Harvard University Press.

FINANCIAL CAPACITY

Financial capacity (FC) is a medical-legal construct that represents the ability to independently manage one's financial affairs in a manner consistent with personal self-interest. FC thus involves not only performance skills (e.g., accurately counting coins/currency, completing a check register, paying bills) but also the judgment skills that optimize financial self-interest.

From a legal standpoint, FC represents the financial skills sufficient for handling one's estate and financial affairs and is the basis for determination of conservatorship of the estate (or guardianship of the estate, depending on the state legal jurisdiction). Broadly construed, FC also encompasses more specific legal "financial capacities," such as contractual capacity, donative capacity, and testamentary capacity. Thus, FC is a very important area of assessment in the civil legal system.

From a clinical standpoint, FC is a highly cognitively mediated capacity that is very vulnerable to neurological, psychiatric, and medical conditions that affect cognition (such as dementia, stroke, traumatic brain injury, and schizophrenia). Financial experience and skills also vary widely among cognitively normal individuals and are associated with factors of education and socioeconomic status. Clinicians are increasingly being asked by families, physicians, attorneys, and judges to evaluate and offer clinical opinions regarding FC.

With the recent development of conceptual models of FC and associated assessment instruments, there is an emerging body of empirical research on this important civil capacity.

Importance of Financial Capacity

Impairment and loss of FC has important psychological, economic, and legal consequences for patients and family members. Similar to driving and mobility, the power to control one's finances is a fundamental aspect of individual autonomy in our society. Loss of financial control may result in psychological consequences such as increased feelings of dependency and depression. Declines in FC are also associated with immediate and long-term economic consequences. Failure to pay bills or difficulty in handling basic financial tasks may result in disconnection of services, property repossession, poor credit ratings, and even homelessness. Impaired financial judgment may also result in loss of assets intended for long-term care or inclusion in a will or trust. From a legal perspective, diminished FC is associated with increased risk of financial exploitation in the form of consumer fraud and other scams, as well as greater susceptibility to undue influence by family members and third parties. As noted above, some situations of financial incapacity may reach the courts and result in loss of decisional autonomy and the appointment of a conservator (or guardian) by the court to protect the person and his or her estate.

Conceptual Model of Financial Capacity

Early conceptual formulations of FC were anemic and limited to unelaborated descriptions such as "money management skills" or "financial management skills." In actual fact, FC is a complex, multidimensional construct representing a broad range of conceptual, pragmatic, and judgmental skills. This multidimensionality is reflected in the concept of limited financial competency recognized across state legal jurisdictions, where an individual may still be competent to perform some financial activities (e.g., handle basic cash transactions, write small checks) but no longer others (e.g., make investment decisions or asset transfers). In addition to multidimensionality, a conceptual model of FC should incorporate the dual performance and self-interest perspectives discussed above. For example, persons with schizophrenia may have adequate financial performance skills but lack FC because they consistently make poor judgments about how to spend their government entitlement monies.

Marson and colleagues have proposed a clinical model that conceptualizes FC at three increasingly complex levels: (1) specific financial abilities or tasks, each of which is relevant to a particular domain of financial activity; (2) general domains of financial activity, which are clinically relevant to the independent functioning of community-dwelling older adults; and (3) overall FC, or a global level. This conceptual model of FC currently comprises 9 domains, 20 tasks, and 2 global levels. The 9 domains include basic monetary skills, financial conceptual knowledge, cash transactions, checkbook management, bank statement management, financial judgment, bill payment, knowledge of personal assets and estate arrangements, and investment decision making. As discussed, each domain of financial activity is further broken down into constituent tasks or abilities that emphasize understanding and pragmatic application of concepts relevant to a specific domain. For instance, the domain of financial conceptual knowledge involves understanding

concepts such as loans and savings and also using this information to select advantageous interest rates. Similarly, bill payment involves not only understanding what a bill is and why it should be paid but also accurately reviewing a bill and preparing it for mailing. Finally, clinicians are usually asked by families and the courts to make clinical judgments concerning an individual's overall FC. Such global judgments involve integration of information concerning an individual's task- and domain-level performance, his or her judgment skills, and informant reports. Such global clinical judgments are particularly relevant for guardianship and conservatorship hearings.

Methods for Clinically Assessing Financial Capacity

At present, there are at least three major approaches to assessing FC: clinical interview, patient/informant ratings, and direct performance instruments. The clinical interview is the traditional, and currently the primary, method for evaluating FC. At the outset of an interview with a patient (and family members), it is important that a clinician first determine the patient's prior or premorbid financial experience and abilities. For example, it would be inappropriate to assume that a person who on testing demonstrates difficulty writing a check has suffered decline in this area if he or she has never performed this task and/or has traditionally delegated this task to a spouse. Once the premorbid experience level is established, clinicians need to identify the financial tasks and domains that make up the patient's current financial activities and differentially consider those required for independent living within the community. The level of impairment on a specific task or domain should be carefully considered. Individuals who require only verbal prompting to initiate or complete a financial task (e.g., paying bills) are qualitatively different from individuals who require actual hands-on assistance and supervision in paying bills; both, in turn, differ from individuals who are now completely dependent on others to pay their bills.

A second approach to assessing FC involves the use of completed patient and informant rating forms. Clinicians commonly use observational rating scales to supplement their clinical interview. Observational rating scales are typically completed by the patient and/or a knowledgeable informant, such as a spouse, parent, or adult child. They can provide valuable "real-life" information about an individual's current financial functioning and also about changes in functioning over time. At the present time, however, there are few rating forms available that are specific to FC. Most of the rating forms are designed to gauge performance across a spectrum of basic and advanced activities of daily living and therefore may yield only limited information specific to financial performance.

A weakness inherent in patient/informant rating forms (and also clinical interviews) is reporter bias. Both patients and informants can misestimate a patient's FC and other functional abilities, owing to a number of factors including lack of insight, denial, and psychiatric issues. Dementia patients and hospitalized elders have been found consistently to overestimate their functional abilities, including financial skills, relative to results of performance-based functional assessment measures. Similarly, even over a short period of time, spousal caregivers of persons with Alzheimer's disease (AD) can be unstable in their ratings of FC in their spouses. Despite these limitations, clinicians justifiably rely on interviews and informant reports of FC due to their ease of administration, minimal cost, and overall information yield.

Performance-based instruments represent a third approach to assessing FC. In contrast to clinical interview formats and observational rating scales, performance-based instruments are not subject to reporter bias. Instead, individuals are asked to perform a series of pragmatic tasks equivalent to those performed in the home and community environment. Performance-based measures are standardized, quantifiable, repeatable, and norm referenced, and thus results can be generalized across patients and settings. These measures, thus, can provide clinicians and the courts with objective information regarding the performance of specific financial tasks that can be highly relevant to the formulation of recommendations and treatment strategies.

Weaknesses of performance-based measures should also be noted. Performance-based measures conducted in a laboratory or clinical office setting cannot take into account either the contextual cues or the distractions within the home environment that may assist or interfere with a person's abilities to perform everyday financial tasks. These instruments are more difficult and time-consuming to administer. They usually require specialized equipment and training, which can make them costly relative to observational rating scales.

Research on Financial Capacity

The lack of conceptual models and assessment instruments specific to FC helps explain the relative lack of clinical research in this important area of civil competency assessment. Only recently have systematic empirical studies of FC been conducted in clinical populations. These studies have investigated patterns of FC impairment in patients with AD and mild cognitive impairment (MCI).

Studies by Daniel Marson and his group have demonstrated significant impairments of financial abilities in patients with both mild and moderate AD. At the domain level, patients with mild AD performed significantly below normal older adult controls on all domains of financial activity, with the exception of basic monetary skills. Patients with moderate AD performed significantly below controls and persons with mild AD on all financial domains.

At the task level, patients with mild AD performed equivalently with older controls on simple tasks such as naming and counting coins and currency, understanding the parts of a checkbook, and detecting the risk of mail fraud. However, such patients had difficulty performing more complex financial tasks such as applying financial concepts (i.e., choosing the best interest rate), obtaining exact change for vending machine use, understanding and using a bank statement, and making an investment decision. Patients with moderate AD were substantially impaired on all financial tasks, relative to both normal older adults and persons with mild AD.

At the global level, mild-AD patients showed substantial impairment in FC relative to older controls, and moderate-AD patients were impaired relative to both controls and mild-AD patients.

Based on these initial findings, Daniel Marson and his group have proposed preliminary clinical guidelines for assessment of FC in patients with mild and moderate AD:

1. Mild-AD patients are at significant risk of impairment in most financial activities, in particular complex activities such as checkbook and bank statement management. Areas of preserved autonomous financial activity should be carefully evaluated and monitored.

2. Moderate-AD patients are at great risk of loss of all financial abilities. Although each AD patient must be considered individually, it is likely that most moderate-AD patients will be unable to manage their financial affairs.

Declines in FC have also been observed in persons with MCI. Relative to normal older adults, individuals with MCI demonstrated mild impairment in the domains of financial conceptual knowledge, checkbook and bank statement, financial judgment, and bill payment. More specifically, persons with MCI had relative difficulty with tasks requiring practical application of financial concepts, understanding and using a bank statement, and prioritizing and preparing bills for mailing. However, persons with MCI performed significantly better than persons with mild AD on most domain-level financial activities and task-specific abilities. However, not all patients with MCI demonstrated these impairments, suggesting heterogeneity in financial performance in this prodromal dementia group. Nonetheless, these results suggest that a significant, albeit mild, decline in financial abilities is an aspect of functional change associated with MCI and may play a role in the eventual conversion of MCI patients to AD. Accordingly, clinicians should monitor over time the FC of individuals with MCI.

Daniel C. Marson and Katina R. Hebert

See also Competency, Foundational and Decisional; Financial Capacity Instrument (FCI); Forensic Assessment; Guardianship; Testamentary Capacity

Further Readings

Griffith, H. R., Belue, K., Sicola, A., Krzywanski, S., Zamrini, E., Harrell, L., et al. (2003). Impaired financial abilities in mild cognitive impairment: A direct assessment approach. *Neurology, 60,* 449–457.

Marson, D. C., Savage, R., & Phillips, J. (2006). Financial capacity in persons with schizophrenia and serious mental illness: Clinical and research ethics aspects. *Schizophrenia Bulletin, 32,* 81–91.

Marson, D. C., Sawrie, S. M., Snyder, S., McInturff, B., Stalvey, T., Boothe, A., et al. (2000). Assessing financial capacity in patients with Alzheimer's disease: A conceptual model and prototype instrument. *Archives of Neurology, 57,* 877–884.

Moye, J. (2003). Guardianship and conservatorship. In T. Grisso (Ed.), *Evaluating competencies: Forensic assessments and instruments* (pp. 309–389). New York: Plenum.

Wadley, V., Harrell, L., & Marson, D. (2003). Self and informant report of financial abilities in patients with Alzheimer's disease: Reliable and valid? *Journal of the American Geriatrics Society, 51,* 1621–1626.

FINANCIAL CAPACITY INSTRUMENT (FCI)

The Financial Capacity Instrument (FCI) is a conceptually based, standardized psychometric instrument designed to directly assess everyday financial activities and abilities relevant to community-dwelling adults. The FCI assesses financial skills at the task, domain, and global levels. The current version of the FCI (FCI-9) consists of 20 financial tasks, 9 domains of financial activity, and 2 global levels. The FCI is a reliable and valid measure of financial capacity that discriminates well between cognitively intact older adults and persons with mild and moderate Alzheimer's disease (AD). The FCI has also proven sensitive to identifying subtler changes in the financial abilities of individuals with mild cognitive impairment (MCI). In addition to older adults with dementia, the FCI has application to other patient groups with acquired cognitive and functional impairment, including patients with multiple scleroses, stroke, and traumatic brain injury. It is an instrument that has application in both clinical and forensic contexts.

Conceptualization and Development of the FCI

There continues to be a pressing need for conceptually based, standardized assessment instruments specific to the construct of financial capacity. The FCI was developed to help fill this need. The FCI is based on a three-level conceptual model that analyzes financial capacity at the task, domain, and global levels. Specifically, this model examines (a) financial abilities (or tasks), such as counting coins/currency, using a vending machine, or preparing bills for mailing; (b) broader domains of financial activity relevant to independent function in the community, such as conducting cash transactions, checkbook management, or financial judgment; and (c) global measures of overall financial capacity.

The original FCI (FCI-6) consisted of 14 specific tasks that assessed six domains of financial activity, including basic monetary skills (D1), financial conceptual knowledge (D2), cash transactions (D3), checkbook management (D4), bank statement management (D5), and financial judgment (D6). The FCI was revised in 2001 to include eight separate domains and 19 standardized, quantifiable behavioral tasks

(FCI-8). New domains assessed bill payment (D7) and knowledge of personal assets and estate arrangements (D8). An index of overall financial capacity was also introduced. The FCI was last modified in 2003 (FCI-9). Tasks pertaining to the detection and avoidance of telephone and mail fraud remained under the domain of financial judgment (D6). Investment decision making, which was included as part of D6 in earlier versions of the FCI, was accorded its own domain (D9).

Administration and Scoring of the FCI

Financial abilities and experience can vary substantially across individuals. It is important to identify an individual's prior level of financial skill and experience before administering the FCI or any other financial capacity instrument. For example, it would be misleading to test for checkbook management skills in a person who has never used a checkbook. An instrument for assessing prior financial experience is the Prior Financial Capacity Form. This rating form is completed by both patients and informants and assesses whether an individual could previously perform designated financial tasks and activities (a) independently, (b) only with assistance, or (c) not even with assistance.

FCI tasks are administered serially by domain. A system of prompts and recognition format questions is included to allow partial credit for persons with amnesia or aphasia.

Task-, domain-, and global-level performance scores are obtained using a detailed and standardized scoring system. Performance scores for each domain are obtained by summing task scores within that domain. Performance scores at the global level (overall financial capacity) are obtained by summing domain scores.

FCI performance scores can also be converted into capacity outcomes (capable, marginally capable, or incapable) using psychometric cut scores derived from normal control performance. These capacity outcomes are to be interpreted cautiously, as they are based on psychometric cut scores and are not equivalent to clinically or legally determined capacity judgments. However, the outcomes serve as a useful additional perspective for understanding performance on the FCI.

Reliability and Validity of the FCI

The original FCI-6 demonstrated adequate to excellent internal, test-retest, and inter-rater reliabilities at task and domain levels using small samples of older

adult controls and AD patients. Very good to excellent reliabilities were obtained for the FCI-8 at the domain level. At the task level, the FCI-8 demonstrated excellent inter-rater reliability but mixed internal and test-retest reliability. This probably reflected item reductions within tasks and reduced task range.

All versions of the FCI arguably have strong face and content validity. The FCI tasks and domains represent simple and complex financial abilities and activities that are commonly performed by older adults in the community. The FCI structure and contents were reviewed and approved by a panel of physicians, gerontologists, an attorney, and a judge with considerable knowledge of the financial capacity construct.

The FCI has also demonstrated construct validity. FCI domains and tasks have been found to discriminate well the performance of cognitively intact older adults from that of patients with mild to moderate AD and patients with amnestic MCI. In addition, impaired domain-level performance in MCI and AD has been correlated with deficits in cognitive functions of semantic memory, working memory, simple attention, and executive function. In the continuing absence of a clear criterion measure for assessing financial capacity, this research provides initial support for the construct validity of the FCI.

Future Research

Preliminary research on the reliability and validity of the FCI is promising. Its direct, standardized, and quantified approach to assessing financial abilities and activities represents a new and significant contribution to the area of functional capacity assessment. However, initial studies using the FCI have been limited to relatively small samples of cognitively intact older adults and persons with MCI and AD. No research has been conducted to date that examines financial performance among other populations, such as persons with serious mental illness. Therefore, studies with larger and more heterogeneous control and clinical samples are needed. Future validation studies should compare FCI results with the judgment of experienced clinicians based on clinical interviews.

Daniel C. Marson and Katina R. Hebert

See also Competency, Foundational and Decisional; Financial Capacity; Forensic Assessment; Guardianship

Further Readings

Earnst, K., Wadley, V., Aldridge, T., Steenwyk, A., Hammond, A., Harrell, L., et al. (2001). Loss of financial capacity in Alzheimer's disease: The role of working memory. *Aging, Neuropsychology, and Cognition, 8,* 109–119.

Griffith, H. R., Belue, K., Sicola, A., Krzywanski, S., Zamrini, E., Harrell, L. E., et al. (2003). Impaired financial abilities in mild cognitive impairment: A direct assessment approach. *Neurology, 60,* 449–457.

Marson, D. C., Sawrie, S. M., Snyder, S., McInturff, B., Stalvey, T., Boothe, A., et al. (2000). Assessing financial capacity in patients with Alzheimer's disease: A conceptual model and prototype instrument. *Archives of Neurology, 57,* 877–884.

Note: The FCI is owned by the UAB Research Foundation (UABRF) and is currently available as an instrument for clinical research. A commercial version of the FCI will be made available by the UABRF in late 2007 or 2008.

FINGERPRINT EVIDENCE, EVALUATION OF

Fingerprints and other friction ridges of the skin have a persistent structure that often leaves characteristic evidence at crime scenes. Latent print examiners compare this evidence with inked copies of friction ridge skin from a known suspect to determine whether these two patterns originate from the same source. This examination process uses computer databases for initial screening, but all evidence presented in court is based on human comparisons. Experts must establish their credentials in order to testify, and recent vision science work has suggested that experts possess visual mechanisms that novices do not. However, these experts have also shown evidence of biases, and critics have begun to question the evidentiary value of fingerprints.

Sources of Evidence

Impressions left by volar skin, or the ridged skin of the palmar surfaces of hands and fingers and plantar surfaces of feet and toes, play a major role in forensic science. Commonly known as fingerprints, palm prints, or footprints, recordings of this skin are often used as a form of physical evidence to link a person to a particular item or location, such as a crime scene. Perspiration, oil, blood, or other substances are often present on the skin and are deposited on surfaces such as plastic, wood, metal, or glass during touches, which might leave a recording of details of the ridge, crease, scar, and imperfection patterns from the skin. The evidence is recovered using a variety of development techniques to make the latent image, or undeveloped print, visible. These include powders, cyanoacrylate glue, chemicals, or stains that adhere to or react with the residues of the print. A variety of different lights and filters can also be used to visualize a latent print.

The basic challenge of fingerprint (more formally known as *friction ridge*) evidence derives from the fact that any latent print recovered from a crime scene will vary in appearance from every other latent print and from every standard print. A standard print can be obtained using a variety of techniques, from black-inked prints on a white card to electronic imaging of the volar surfaces. The intent of the standard recording is to obtain a clear set of prints from a known-source individual for comparison with the unknown-source latent prints. In some cases, these variations in appearances are trivial, and the match between an unknown latent and known inked print appears obvious. However, latent or standard prints with low quality or quantity of details are a challenge to examine, and thus the field of *forensic latent print examinations* uses established procedures, practices, guidelines, and methodology to support the examination of latent prints.

Friction ridge skin develops its structure in utero by means of biological, chemical, and physical processes of pattern formation known as reaction-diffusion. This process ensures that ridges form in a roughly parallel configuration and tend to orient orthogonally to lines of stress that occur during the fetal development of structures known as volar pads in fingers, palms, soles, and toes. The resulting ridges form patterns of loops, whorls, and arches in the pads of the developing finger tip (distal phalanges). Additional structure is provided by the development of ridges that form bifurcations and ridge endings, or minutiae. These minutiae are often coded when fingerprints are entered into computer databases such as the Integrated Automated Fingerprint Identification System, maintained by the U.S. Federal Bureau of Investigation.

The interactions of chemistry, physics, and biology in pattern formation in nature support the belief within science that no two natural patterns will ever be exactly alike. All the internal and external developmental noise, interactions, and timings that occur will cause the anomalies that become a part of the configurations within natural pattern structures. All natural patterns in volar skin will be unique. This includes the ridges, furrows, creases, and pores and their anomalies and textures that make up the skin. Scarring will provide new unique features to the skin. The homeostatic regeneration of skin maintains the form and function of the features of the volar surface in persistent configural and sequential arrangements.

Basis of Testimony

The uniqueness and persistence of friction ridge skin is the rule of support for the proposition that an individual can be determined as having touched a particular surface. With this rule or law, the next step is to examine the latent and standard prints and determine whether the latent print was made by the person who made the standard print. The two prints are comparatively measured with each other. The first-level detail of general direction of ridge flow is examined, followed by examination of the second-level detail of lengths of individual ridge paths with their endings and bifurcations and, if needed, the examination of the third-level detail of edges, textures, and pore positions of the ridges. The details are examined to determine whether they correspond in sequences, shapes, and configurations in both prints. The examination results either in a determination that the person made the latent print (individualization) or that the person did not make the latent print (exclusion), or no determination is made whether the person made the latent print (inconclusive). This individualization or exclusion determination has, in principle, a philosophical problem: Comparisons between the latent print and all prints in the world are impractical. However, in practice this has been overcome with a high degree of certainty (although there are criticisms of this conclusion, which we will discuss in a later section). The expert makes the determination that there is definite agreement between the configural and sequential arrangement of details in the two images, indicating that they were made by the same unique and persistent source. The individualization decision basically comes down to the expert judgment that the recovered latent print is so similar to the inked print that it could only have come from the same person. Stated in a different way, the claim is made that there is no more similar print from any other source among all the prints in the world, which is of course impractical to test. In practice,

the individualization often comes down to the expert rendering the opinion that the degree of match between the latent and the inked print is typical of known training, competency, and proficiency individualizations and casework peer-reviewed individualizations and is closer than any close correspondence from another source that the expert has ever seen or expects to see. Because this judgment is based on prior experience, presenting a conclusion in court depends on the expert establishing his or her credentials, which has become a major portion of latent print testimony and is discussed next.

The latent print expert examiner should have some basic knowledge before conducting case work, rendering conclusions, and testifying in court. This includes understanding the source of images, volar skin, and its unique and persistent features. The examiner also must understand the basics of fetal development, homeostasis, growth, aging, wound healing, scarring and imperfections of the volar skin, and the uniqueness of pattern formations in nature. Moreover, the examiner must understand distortions of the skin and variations in appearances of latent or standard prints or images. Latent and standard print development, capture, and imaging techniques must be understood to understand the variations in appearances. The examination method within the latent print community of analysis, comparison, and evaluation (ACE), possibly followed by verification (V), is the method used in conjunction with the sufficiency and judgment threshold of quality and quantity (QQ) of details in the images. Furthermore, the examiner must understand examination method and sufficiency and judgment thresholds. In addition, the examiner must understand the history of latent print examinations and latent print communities, the role of a community within science, and the role of the expert within a scientific community. Finally, the latent print examiner must be trained to be competent and demonstrate accuracy and proficiency within the community.

The goal of an examination is to judge whether developed unknown latent prints and known standard prints are sufficient for examination purposes and whether the considered source of the latent print can be determined or excluded. As noted earlier, three conclusions of the comparative examination can be reached: (1) the unknown print was determined to have been made by a specific source or person (individualization); (2) the unknown print was determined not to have been made by a specific source or person (exclusion); (3) no determination was made whether a specific source or person made the unknown print (inconclusive).

When testifying in court, the examiner must be able to present the reasons that qualify him or her to testify as an expert for rendering opinions of judgments of examinations. This qualification requires the judge's determination of sufficiency of expertise based on the training and experience of the witness. The witness must be prepared to answer questions on qualifications and on anything to do with the science and method of latent print examination.

Criticism of Fingerprint Evidence

Recently, fingerprint evidence has come under intense criticism, and below we discuss the different forms of attack on latent print evidence. Since the *United States v. Byron Mitchell* case of 2003, in which defense attorneys began challenging the admissibility of forensic latent print examinations, fingerprint evidence has come under attack as an admissible science in the courts. A major issue surrounding fingerprint evidence is in the information content that can be extracted and identified in a latent print. While rolled inked prints taken under controlled conditions are usually very clear and rich in detail and information, latent prints are often inherently less clear, are distorted, and contain considerably fewer details due to the commonly partial nature of the print itself. It is up to the examiner to use his or her expertise to determine whether the latent print contains sufficient information to determine usability. Then, the examiner determines whether the details in the inked print and the latent print agree and have a common source. An individualization is made when the examiner claims that the two prints contain a high enough level of similarity that surpasses the similarity between any two prints from different individuals. However, determining the level of similarity between two prints is left to the examiner to establish on the basis of his or her training, skill, and experience within the forensic comparative science community. This makes fingerprint evidence somewhat different from DNA analysis, which codes a limited range of chemical sequences to establish an identification. Unlike DNA analysis, which has a specific set of known features, fingerprints can be matched on the basis of many different types of features, including minutiae, ridge flow, and even shapes of pores. Because the useful features are more difficulty to quantify, it is more difficult to establish a

specific statistical model that would provide the probability of an erroneous identification. Thus, the procedures include a subjective element, albeit one that can be verified by third parties. The techniques of comparison and evaluation represent an objective application of documented procedures.

Despite this lack of statistical models, some examiners have made claims as to the "infallibility" of fingerprints, that identifications are "100% positive," and that the error rate of forensic fingerprint identification is zero. In fact, to date there have been approximately 20 known cases of misidentifications recorded, with some involving qualified examiners. Many of these misidentifications have been so widely publicized that the claim of "zero error rate" and infallibility has come under serious scrutiny. In addition, a series of tests conducted from 1995 to 2001 by a private independent testing service recorded misidentification rates ranging from 3% to 22%. As a result, authors have pushed for blind proficiency testing to reduce the amount of erroneous identifications. Many of these misidentifications are corrected with the use of additional fingerprint evidence, leading to the proposal that the criticism should fall on individual examiners rather than the science of latent print examinations as a whole.

Psychological Research Using Latent Print Examiners

An issue raised recently by Itiel Dror is the possibility that external sources of information about a case can affect the decision made by examiners. Known as confirmation bias or contextual biases, these sources of biases originate from knowledge such as whether other examiners called a particular individualization or whether other sources of evidence link the suspect to the crime. Once this information becomes known, it can be very difficult for an examiner to ignore this evidence. One fortunate aspect of fingerprints is that, unlike eyewitness testimony, they represent a form of physical evidence, and if confirmation is required or any bias is suspected, testimony from a new examiner can be sought.

Despite the attacks on fingerprint examiners and the push for fingerprint evidence to be omitted from the courts as scientific testimony, several authors have argued for demonstrable differences between expert examiners and novices. Recent behavioral and electrophysiological (electroencephalogram, EEG) research by Tom Busey and colleagues has shown that experts appear to perceive fingerprints using the configural process or a holistic process, in which the observer appreciates not only the presence of individual features but the spatial relations between them as well. This process is known to occur when humans process visual information for faces, which produces a characteristic pattern in the EEG trace. Fingerprint examiners demonstrate similar brain-wave activity regarding fingerprints as the general population shows with respect to faces, and this fact suggests that experts recruit similar brain processes to support expertise in the fingerprint domain. This suggests that trained latent print examiners have perceptual abilities not shared by the rest of the population.

John R. Vanderkolk, Bethany Schneider,
and Tom Busey

See also Expert Psychological Testimony, Admissibility Standards; Expert Psychological Testimony, Forms of; Expert Testimony, Qualifications of Experts

Further Readings

Ashbaugh, D. R. (1999). *Quantitative-qualitative friction ridge analysis: An introduction to basic and advanced ridgeology.* Boca Raton, FL: CRC Press.

Busey, T. A., & Vanderkolk, J. R. (2005). Behavioral and electrophysiological evidence for configural processing in fingerprint experts. *Vision Research, 45,* 431–448.

Cole, S. A. (2005). More than zero: Accounting for error in latent fingerprint identification. *Journal of Criminal Law and Criminology, 95*(3), 985–1078.

Cowger, J. F. (1983). *Friction ridge skin, comparison and identification of fingerprints.* New York: Elsevier Science.

Daubert v. Merrell Dow Pharmaceuticals, 509 U.S. 579, 113 S. Ct. 2786 (1993).

Dror, I. E., Peron, A., Hind, S., & Charlton, D. (2005). When emotions get the better of us: The effect of contextual top-down processing on matching fingerprints. *Applied Cognitive Psychology, 19,* 799–809.

United States v. Byron Mitchell, No. 02-2859 (3d Cir. September 9, 2003). Retrieved from http://vls.law .villanova.edu/locator/3d/April2004/022859p.pdf

Web Sites

Scientific Working Group on Friction Ridge Analysis, Study, and Technology: http://www.swgfast.org

FITNESS-FOR-DUTY EVALUATIONS

A fitness-for-duty evaluation (FFDE) is just what the term suggests, an evaluation of an individual's fitness to do his or her job. In high-risk occupations, such as the police and public safety, the need for psychological suitability and fitness is generally established by statute or case law. In fact, some courts have held that agencies are required to assess an officer's fitness when significant evidence suggests a lack of fitness.

The specifics of what constitutes fitness are defined, if they are defined, in very general terms, usually by state statute. The gist is that job holders should be free of psychological factors, traits, and problems that would prevent them from performing their duties safely and effectively. The specifics of how to assess the fitness of job incumbents and the decision-making standards have received limited research attention. Instead, the standards are based on the experience of police psychologists. The Psychological Services section of the International Association of Chiefs of Police (IACP) developed guidelines for FFDEs. Their revised guidelines were published in 2004.

The first issue in FFDEs is whether an evaluation should be ordered. This issue is important because although the FFDE can be an important tool in protecting public safety, it has the potential for misuse. The current consensus, including the recommendation of the IACP, is that there should be objective evidence that the employee may be unable to adequately perform the job and a legitimate basis for believing that the problems are due to psychological issues.

FFDEs are also being increasingly used in a variety of other occupations when concerns about potential violent behavior by an employee are said to raise concerns about the employee's psychological fitness for duty. This use of FFDEs is more controversial and less clearly protected by statute or case law. The practice can be particularly problematic in the absence of clear written policies outlining the circumstances and procedures for fitness evaluations. Relevant legal concerns include violations of the Americans with Disability Act and the individual employee's privacy rights. However, the practice can be important to defend an employer from "wrongful retention" or "negligent supervision" complaints when people are injured by violent employees.

For any occupation, experts agree that FFDEs should not be used as a substitute for the normal disciplinary process. However, employers may choose to use a psychological FFDE to mitigate discipline and develop rehabilitation or accommodation plans. It is best for this process to be outlined in the employer's written policies.

The FFDE begins with a referral. This referral normally involves a written summary statement of the employer's concerns and the evidence in support of those concerns. The referral also generally includes any specific issues the employer wishes to have addressed. It is best if the standards for triggering an FFDE and the process involved are in the employer's written policy. When accepting referrals for FFDEs, ethical concerns require evaluators to consider whether there are any dual-relationship or conflict-of-interest issues that interfere with the evaluator's ability to perform the evaluation competently and effectively.

The employer is normally considered the client in an FFDE, not the individual being evaluated. In most situations, employees referred for FFDEs are compelled to participate as a condition of employment. However, it is generally considered advisable to obtain the employee's written informed consent for the evaluation and the communication of the results of the evaluation to the employer. When informed consent is not sought, evaluators are still ethically obligated to inform the individual being evaluated of the nature of the evaluation and the expected use of the obtained information.

FFDEs include psychological testing, clinical interviews, and collateral information to enable the evaluator to determine if the incumbent employee is able to safely and effectively perform the essential job duties of the position or specialty assignment. The psychological testing frequently includes an objective psychological measure designed to assess psychopathology and an objective psychological measure designed to identify psychological strengths and weaknesses in nonpathological populations. Many evaluators also include some sort of measure of cognitive functioning. This test selection is similar to that used in pre-employment evaluations. However, in FFDEs, additional measures designed to assess relevant issues or problems may be included. The collateral information includes the job description (including any additional requirements of specialty assignments), employment and medical records, reports from supervisors and coworkers, and reports from family members and friends.

When the FFDE is complete, the evaluator must communicate the results, usually to the employer or the employer's legal representative. Many of the standards for what may be communicated to employers following an FFDE are regulated at the state level. Case law in some jurisdictions severely limits the information that evaluators may communicate to the employer without violating the employee's privacy rights. Without the written consent of the individual being evaluated, evaluators need to exercise caution in communicating any information about the individual other than fitness for duty to the employer. Even with consent, only essential and relevant information should be included. If a lack of fitness involves confidential issues or other people (e.g., a health problem in an employee's spouse), evaluators should ensure that the information communicated does not violate privacy standards in that jurisdiction.

Usually, the report will include an outline of the actions involved in the evaluation and the evaluator's conclusion concerning the individual's fitness for duty. The categories are fit for unrestricted duty, fit for restricted duty (which could include regular work activities with mandatory treatment), or unfit for any duty. Additionally, when the employee is unfit for unrestricted duty, it may be described as temporary or permanent. If the lack of fitness is temporary, recommendations for facilitating the return to fitness are appropriate. It is usually difficult to consider a psychological condition permanent without a treatment trial.

Nancy Lynn Baker

Further Readings

Borum, R., Super, J., & Rand, M. (2003). Forensic assessment in high risk occupations. In I. B. Weiner (Series Ed.) & A. D. Goldstein (Vol. Ed.), *Handbook of psychology: Vol. 11. Forensic psychology* (pp. 133–148). New York: Wiley.

IACP Police Psychological Services Section. (2004). *Psychological fitness-for-duty evaluation guidelines.* Alexandria, VA: Author.

FITNESS INTERVIEW TEST–REVISED (FIT–R)

The Fitness Interview Test–Revised (FIT–R) is an instrument designed for use by mental health professionals in evaluations of competence to stand trial.

Designed as a structured clinical judgment instrument that guides evaluators through an assessment of the specific psycholegal abilities required of a defendant to stand trial, the FIT–R demonstrates reliability and predictive validity and is useful for screening out individuals who are clearly competent to stand trial.

Competence (or fitness) to stand trial is a well-established legal principle designed to ensure that criminal defendants have the ability to participate in legal proceedings. Defendants must be able to understand the charges against them, understand the possible consequences of legal proceedings, and communicate with their attorney. Defendants whose ability to participate competently in their trial is in question are typically referred for a forensic assessment, since mental health issues are central to the evaluation. If the court later determines that a defendant is competent, legal proceedings are resumed; if the defendant if found incompetent, the legal proceedings are suspended until competence is restored.

There are a number of forensic assessment instruments designed to assist in this process, and the FIT–R, a semistructured interview and rating scale, is one of them. While initially designed for use with adult defendants, research has also shown that it can be used to evaluate competence in juvenile populations. The current version is a revised and updated version of an earlier edition. A thorough review of pertinent U.S. and Canadian legislation is included in the introductory section of the FIT–R manual, and a brief review of research on fitness to stand trial is provided. However, the authors have noted that the FIT–R can be used in most common-law jurisdictions due to the similarity in legal criteria for competence to stand trial.

Administration of the FIT–R takes approximately 30 to 45 minutes. The instrument is intended to serve as a tool for assessing legal issues in concert with other methods of assessing additional clinical issues, including mental status and diagnostic considerations. The format follows a semistructured interview, ensuring that all legally relevant aspects of fitness criteria are addressed while allowing clinicians the flexibility to probe and further question the specific knowledge and abilities of the accused. Following the interview, the evaluator completes a rating scale in which the relative degree of incapacity for each of the items is evaluated. This semistructured format allows evaluators to conduct more uniform competence evaluations while still providing for flexible assessments.

The FIT–R comprises 16 items divided into three sections that parallel the Canadian and U.S. legal criteria for competence to stand trial. The first section, Understanding the Nature or Object of the Proceedings: Factual Knowledge of Criminal Procedure, examines a defendant's understanding of the arrest process, current charges, role of key participants, legal process, pleas, and court procedures. The second section, Understanding the Possible Consequences of the Proceedings: Appreciation of Personal Involvement in and Importance of the Proceedings, examines a defendant's appreciation of the range and nature of possible penalties, available legal defenses, and likely outcomes. The third section, Communication With Counsel: Ability to Participate in Defense, examines a defendant's ability to communicate facts to a lawyer; interpersonal capacity to relate to lawyers; and ability to plan legal strategy, engage in the defense, challenge prosecution witnesses, testify relevantly, and manage courtroom behavior. Each section comprises a number of items reflecting the requisite psycholegal abilities required for competence in each area. An individual's degree of impairment on each item is rated using a three-point scale (no impairment, possible/mild impairment, and definite/serious impairment), which is clearly explained and defined for evaluators. The evaluator then rates the accused's degree of impairment in each of the sections. These ratings as well as an assessment of the defendant's mental status are used by the evaluator to make an overall determination of the individual's competence to stand trial. In scoring the FIT–R, the instrument does not rely on "cutoff" or "total" scores for making decisions about an individual's competence, largely because the weight assigned to any one item will likely vary across individuals.

It is important to recognize that the FIT–R was designed to reflect the relative competence status of an accused individual at the time of examination, and it can serve neither a predictive nor a retrospective assessment function. Research has shown that few of the accused individuals ordered to undergo fitness assessments are found incompetent to stand trial. The FIT–R can be used as a brief screening instrument for assessing fitness, where individuals who score at an "unfit" or "questionably unfit" level will be referred for a more thorough evaluation. Research has demonstrated that it yields good sensitivity (the probability that the predictor variable is positive given a recommendation of unfit) and negative predictive power (the probability of a recommendation of fit given that the predictor variable is negative) when used in this way and that it can reliably screen out individuals who are clearly competent to stand trial, thereby reducing the number of individuals referred for more lengthy and costly assessments. The FIT–R can also be used as part of a more comprehensive fitness evaluation.

Ronald Roesch and Kaitlyn McLachlan

See also Adjudicative Competence of Youth; Competency Screening Test (CST); Competency to Stand Trial; Evaluation of Competence to Stand Trial–Revised (ECST–R); Forensic Assessment; Interdisciplinary Fitness Interview (IFI); MacArthur Competence Assessment Tool for Criminal Adjudication (MacCAT–CA)

Further Readings

Grisso, T. (2003). *Evaluating competencies: Forensic assessment and instruments.* New York: Plenum Press.

Roesch, R., Zapf, P. A., & Eaves, D. (2006). *Fitness Interview Test–Revised: A structured interview for assessing competency to stand trial.* Sarasota, FL: Professional Resource Press.

Roesch, R., Zapf, P. A., Eaves, D., & Webster, D. (1998). *Fitness Interview Test–Revised Edition.* Burnaby, BC, Canada: Mental Health Law and Policy Institute.

Viljoen, J. L., Vincent, G. M., & Roesch, R. (2006). Assessing adolescent defendants' adjudicative competence: Interrater reliability and factor structure of the Fitness Interview Test–Revised. *Criminal Justice and Behavior, 33,* 467–487.

Zapf, P. A., & Roesch, R. (1997). Assessing fitness to stand trial: A comparison of institution-based evaluations and a brief screening interview. *Canadian Journal of Community Mental Health, 16,* 53–66.

FORCED CONFABULATION

Forced confabulation can occur if an individual erroneously incorporates into his or her memory of an event, self-generated information that was not actually part of that event. Forced confabulation most commonly occurs when an individual (a) experiences an event, (b) thinks about or talks about that event, and (c) later confuses what actually occurred with what he or she talked about or thought about afterward. Every time an individual makes an error of commission and remembers a detail of an event that did not actually

occur, it is not necessarily confabulation. In the research literature, forced confabulation is typically caused by (a) forcing an individual to answer an unanswerable question about an event (i.e., the relevant information to answer the questions was not actually part of the event) or (b) pressing an individual to answer a question even though the individual has indicated that he or she does not know or is unsure of the answer to the question. As a consequence, later, individuals will sometimes erroneously remember the information in their forced answer as part of the event itself. When this occurs, it is considered to be forced confabulation.

A number of studies have been conducted to assess how postevent information influences event memory. This research examines how memory of an event can be suggestively influenced by exposure to any related information about the event. In most of this research, the postevent information is other-generated (e.g., information in the interviewer's questions can be remembered as part of the actual event) rather than self-generated, but in fact, either would qualify as postevent information. Thus, forced confabulation is really a subtype of suggestibility that can occur from being forced to self-generate postevent information. A certain amount of self-generated confabulation will naturally occur as people think about and talk about events that they have observed. Although people rarely come to remember entire events that did not occur, it is common to confuse (a) what we correctly remember because we observed it with (b) what we erroneously remember from contemplating the event afterward.

A typical study of forced confabulation was conducted by Maria Zaragoza and her colleagues. They had adults and children view a brief video, followed immediately by a sequence of answerable and unanswerable questions. Unanswerable questions probed information that was not actually presented in the video. Half the participants were forced to answer every question and were told to guess if they did not know an answer. Control participants were told to respond only to questions for which they knew the answer; they were encouraged not to guess. One week later, all participants were asked whether they had seen various objects in the video. Individuals frequently misattributed to the video objects that they had self-generated.

One question of interest in the forced confabulation research is whether information is more likely to be incorporated into memory if it is (a) spontaneously self-generated or (b) forcibly self-generated—for example, by pressing eyewitnesses to answer questions about events that they are unsure of. Kathy Pezdek and her colleagues conducted several studies to examine this issue. In this study, individuals viewed a crime video and then answered open-ended questions that included answerable and unanswerable questions about the video. Half the participants were in the "spontaneous guess" condition; the "Don't know" response option was available to them, so they did not need to guess any answers. The other half of the participants were in the "forced guess" condition and did not have a "Don't know" response option. One week later, the same questions were answered with a "Don't know" option available for everyone.

The primary finding concerns the following question: If participants were forced to guess answers to *unanswerable* questions at Time 1, were the answers they generated likely to be recalled 1 week later at Time 2, when they all had the option of responding, "Don't know"? The responses to unanswerable questions are the most revealing in this study, because we know that the individuals did not actually observe the information relevant to answering those questions. The mean proportion of responses that received the same answer at Time 1 and Time 2 was significantly higher in the spontaneous guess condition ($M = .54$) than in the forced guess condition ($M = .40$). This result suggests that although false confabulation does occur, false information that resulted from forced confabulation is less likely to persist in memory than false information that individuals spontaneously provided because they thought they had observed it. Furthermore, when the same answer was given to an unanswerable question both times, the confidence expressed in the answer increased over time both for answers that were spontaneously guessed and those that were forced guesses. Thus, erroneous memories that occur from self-generated false confabulation are confidently held. This is of course problematic from the point of view of assessing the veracity of eyewitness memories because it suggests that it may be difficult to differentiate between true and falsely confabulated memories.

This topic is relevant to the specialty of psychology and law because virtually 100% of all eyewitnesses to crimes who eventually testify in court are interviewed by police officers at least once, and typically multiple times. Forced confabulation can occur in police interviews when officers press an eyewitness to answer a question even though the eyewitness has indicated that he or she does not know or is unsure of the answer

to the question. In addition, police interrogation typically involves techniques to pressure witnesses to answer questions they are reluctant or unable to answer. It is important to recognize that such techniques are likely to generate forced confabulations—even confidently held forced confabulations—as well as true information. Although no data exist documenting how frequently this practice occurs in real police interviews, Richard Leo has reported that this is not an unusual practice, that, in fact, forced confessions commonly occur under these circumstances.

Kathy Pezdek

See also Delusions; Eyewitness Memory; False Confessions; False Memories; Postevent Information and Eyewitness Memory

Further Readings

Ackil, J. K., & Zaragoza, M. S. (1998). Memorial consequences of forced confabulation: Age differences in susceptibility to false memories. *Developmental Psychology, 34,* 1358–1372.

Leo, R. A. (1996). Inside the interrogation room. *Journal of Criminal Law and Criminology, 86,* 266–303.

Pezdek, K., Sperry, K., & Owens, S. (in press). Interviewing witnesses: The effect of forced confabulation on event memory. *Law & Human Behavior.*

FORCIBLE MEDICATION

This entry discusses the involuntary administration of psychotropic medication, which continues to be one of the most controversial issues in mental health law. Whether mental patients in hospital, the community, jail, prison, or the judicial process may refuse psychotropic medication that the government would like to administer raises complex legal, clinical, moral, and social issues. Psychotropic medication is by far the leading treatment technique for patients diagnosed with mental illness. Although demonstrably helpful for many patients, it often imposes serious direct, often debilitating, and unwanted side effects that are beyond the patient's ability to resist and that may be long lasting. As a result, involuntary administration of these drugs raises serious constitutional questions.

Most states now have statutory and administrative restrictions on involuntary treatment. The limits imposed by the U.S. Constitution and its state counterparts are the most significant restrictions on state authority in this regard as they drive other legal restrictions. This entry discusses these constitutional limitations, the level of scrutiny the courts will apply in weighing right to refuse medication claims, and the standards that must be satisfied for involuntary medication to be authorized. To meet these standards, the government must show that treatment is both medically appropriate and the least-restrictive alternative means of accomplishing one or more compelling governmental interests. The patient is entitled to a hearing concerning the satisfaction of these criteria, typically occurring before treatment may be imposed. In an emergency, the hearing may take place thereafter.

Constitutional Bases for the Right to Refuse Medication

Constitutional limits on involuntary intrusive treatment of the kind represented by the psychotropic drugs derive from several sources. The U.S. Supreme Court has recognized that unwanted antipsychotic medication invades a significant liberty interest protected by the due process clauses of the Fifth and Fourteenth Amendments. Substantive due process protects a liberty interest in bodily integrity and personal security, as well as a liberty interest in personal autonomy in health care decision making that involuntary medication would invade. Moreover, such medication also may invade the First Amendment's protection of mental privacy and freedom of mental processes from significant governmental intrusion. When administered as punishment, involuntary medication may also raise questions of cruel and unusual punishment banned by the Eighth Amendment. Moreover, because medication is not administered on an involuntary basis to medically ill patients, for whom informed consent would be required, but is for those with mental illness, an equal protection question may be raised. In more limited circumstances, when refusal of medication is based on religious objection, forced medication may infringe the First Amendment's protection of the free exercise of religion.

The level of constitutional scrutiny of governmental attempts to impose involuntary treatment will vary with the intrusiveness of the treatment in question. Traditional antipsychotic drugs can induce a variety of Parkinson-like effects that are distressing and several serious and permanent effects such as tardive dyskinesia. Even the newer atypical antipsychotic

drugs impose serious risks, including diabetes and perhaps stroke. Although drugs used in the treatment of depression and bipolar disorder may raise fewer constitutional difficulties, their impact on mood and mental processes remains sufficiently significant to require some degree of heightened judicial scrutiny. Almost all these drugs intrude directly and powerfully into mental processes, bodily integrity, and individual autonomy and therefore would seem justified only on a showing of compelling necessity.

Constitutional Requirements for Forcible Medication

The Supreme Court's decisions in *Sell v. United States* (2003) and *Riggins v. Nevada* (1992), both involving criminal defendants seeking to refuse antipsychotic medication, seem to suggest a form of strict scrutiny. To justify the administration of antipsychotic medication, the Court required a finding that the involuntary medication was medically appropriate and the least intrusive means of accomplishing one or more compelling governmental interests. The government's interest in restoring criminal defendants to competence to stand trial and maintaining them in a competent state so that they may be tried will meet this test as long as the medication in question is clinically appropriate for the individual, no less intrusive treatments or medications will achieve this goal, and medication will not significantly impair the defendants' trial performance. When a criminal defendant seeks to refuse medication that the government contends is required to restore or maintain his or her competency, the criminal court will need to hold a hearing on whether these standards are satisfied and to make specific factual findings concerning them before medication may be imposed.

This strict scrutiny approach would seem generally applicable to the administration of unwanted, intrusive medication in hospital and community settings and even in jails that house pretrial detainees. A more relaxed standard will apply to sentenced prisoners, however. In *Washington v. Harper* (1990), the Supreme Court applied a reduced form of constitutional scrutiny to uphold the involuntary administration of antipsychotic medication in a prison hospital for an inmate who was found to be dangerous to other prisoners and staff. In prison contexts, as long as the medication is medically appropriate and reasonably related to the need to protect others from harm and to protect prison security, it may be imposed even if less restrictive alternatives, such as solitary confinement, might suffice to protect others from violence. Outside the prison context, however, involuntary medication will need to be justified as necessary to accomplish one or more compelling governmental interests.

Governmental Interests That May Justify Forcible Medication

What are the interests that count as compelling? As previously noted, the state's interest in restoring an incompetent criminal defendant to competency so that he or she may stand trial will count as a sufficiently compelling governmental interest. Other state interests that will be deemed sufficiently compelling to outweigh the individual's assertion of the right to refuse treatment will include the police power interest in the protection of others from harm. When mental illness renders an individual in an institution dangerous to self or others, including other patients or institutional staff, the government interest in preventing serious harm that is imminent will be deemed sufficiently important to outweigh the individual's interest in avoiding unwanted medication, at least when other standards of strict scrutiny are satisfied. The state's parens patriae interest in the well-being of individuals rendered incompetent by their mental illness to make treatment decisions for themselves also will meet the compelling interest test. When the individual has been determined to be incompetent to make such decisions, involuntary medication may be authorized if it is in the patient's best medical interests and no less restrictive alternative treatments are medically indicated.

State statutes or administrative rules frequently authorize treatment in these circumstances for those who have been civilly committed or who accept voluntary admission to a hospital. An increasing number of states now authorize court-ordered involuntary treatment on police power or parens patriae grounds under statutes allowing outpatient commitment or conditional release from hospitalization. Similarly, state statutes or administrative rules will authorize involuntary medication in such circumstances for those suffering from mental illness in jails and prisons.

Medical Appropriateness and Least-Restrictive Alternative Requirements for Involuntary Treatment

Even when these compelling interests are present, involuntary treatment must be medically appropriate and the least-restrictive means to achieve compelling state interests. The medical appropriateness requirement will necessitate a finding that the medication in question and the dosage sought to be imposed are clinically indicated for the individual. For purposes of applying the least-restrictive alternative test, the burden of establishing the futility of less restrictive treatments or their lack of success will be placed on the state. Treatments less restrictive than psychotropic medication, such as verbal, behavioral, or cognitive behavioral treatment, therefore should be attempted before medication is sought to be imposed, unless they are deemed to be unlikely to succeed in the circumstances. In addition, if the individual can show that an alternative medication that is less intrusive would suffice, or even a lower dosage of the medication sought to be imposed, then these less restrictive alternatives should be attempted. If alternatives other than treatment are available that would fully satisfy the governmental interest in involuntary treatment, such treatment may be impermissible. For example, in the case of the government's police power interest in protecting other patients or institutional staff from the violent acts of a mentally ill individual who is institutionalized, alternative means of containing the danger, such as seclusion and restraint, may be more preferable to the patient than medication and therefore should be used instead.

The Right to a Hearing

Even when involuntary medication is constitutionally permissible, procedural due process will require notice and a fair hearing before treatment may be imposed. Some states require a formal, adversarial judicial hearing, but most courts have accepted the constitutionality of permitting informal and nonadversarial administrative hearings. Procedural due process also will require periodic review of the need for continued medication. Even though it may be overwhelmingly likely that the outcome of such hearings will result in approving the need for medication or continued medication, the hearing can have important value in educating the patient concerning why medication is needed and providing him or her with a form of participation in the decision-making process that provides the patient with a voice and a sense of validation. When these participatory or dignitary values of procedure are accorded, the patient may be more accepting of the decision to impose medication and more compliant with it. The attitudes that procedural justice fosters may therefore increase the effectiveness of the medication that the individual is required to receive and the likelihood that he or she will continue to take it even when not forced to do so.

Waiver of Right to Refuse Treatment: The Informed Consent Doctrine

Of course, not all patients will refuse psychotropic medication. The right to refuse treatment may be waived as long as the requirements of the informed consent doctrine are satisfied. These include disclosure of treatment information, competency, and voluntary choice. In fact, when the requirements of informed consent are satisfied, patients may enter into advance directive instruments that express their wishes concerning the acceptance or rejection of treatment at a future time when they may become incompetent. Although not yet in widespread use for this purpose, advance directive instruments are likely to emerge as an important way for dealing with the right-to-refuse-treatment question in the future.

Professional Ethics and Therapeutic Jurisprudence

Apart from legal restrictions on involuntary medication, forced treatment raises ethical concerns for clinicians. The professional ethics of the various clinical disciplines strongly favor voluntary treatment. Moreover, psychological theory would suggest that voluntary treatment is more efficacious for many patients than coerced therapy. Coercion may spark patient resistance, whereas voluntary choice may engage the patient's intrinsic motivation and increase treatment compliance. As a result, the principles of beneficence and nonmaleficence, which are at the core of professional ethics, would strongly favor voluntary approaches and the use of less intrusive techniques before involuntary medication is attempted. Because psychological theory would predict that voluntary treatment will be more effective than coerced treatment and more likely to produce treatment compliance over time, considerations of therapeutic jurisprudence also would favor voluntary over involuntary treatment.

Of course, these therapeutic benefits of voluntary choice may not apply when the individual is incompetent to engage in rational decision making. However, even for patients rendered incompetent as a result of their mental illness, once medication has succeeded in restoring competency to make treatment decisions, these ethical and therapeutic jurisprudence concerns can present therapeutic opportunities.

Judges, attorneys, and clinicians called on to act in the forcible medication context, thus, should understand that they function as therapeutic agents in the way they treat the individual who seeks to resist unwanted medication. Judges and clinicians involved in involuntary treatment therefore should treat patients fairly, with dignity and respect, and accord them a sense of participation in the decision-making process. The hearing that often will be required before involuntary medication may be imposed, if structured to satisfy these conditions and properly conducted, can have a significant therapeutic value. Rather than resisting the patient's right to refuse treatment, clinicians should understand that recognition of such a right and the patient's participation in treatment decision making can present therapeutic opportunities.

Bruce J. Winick

See also Civil Commitment; Forensic Assessment; Mental Health Law; Therapeutic Jurisprudence

Further Readings

Riggins v. Nevada, 504 U.S. 127 (1992).
Sell v. United States, 539 U.S. 166 (2003).
Washington v. Harper, 494 U.S. 210 (1990).
Winick, B. J. (1997). *The right to refuse mental health treatment.* Washington, DC: American Psychological Association Books.
Winick, B. J. (2005). *Civil commitment: A therapeutic jurisprudence model.* Durham, NC: Carolina Academic Press.

FORENSIC ASSESSMENT

Forensic assessment is a part of the broader category of psychological assessment. The purpose of forensic assessment is distinct from that of traditional therapeutic assessment, and as such forensic evaluators have different training and practice guidelines. The settings in which forensic evaluations occur are vast, including law enforcement, correctional, and civil and criminal court settings. Forensic assessment may include traditional psychological assessments and specially designed forensic measures.

Psychological assessment refers to all the techniques used to evaluate an individual's past, present, and future psychological status. The primary goals of assessment involve providing explanations for past and present behavior and making predictions about the parameters of future behavior. Furthermore, psychological assessment may involve the use of psychological tests or measuring devices. Forensic assessment is a category of psychological assessment that is used to aid a legal fact finder and is one of the most common applications of psychology to the law, prevalent in a variety of legal settings. A relatively new specialty, forensic assessment is one of the fastest growing areas in clinical psychology. Increasing numbers of psychologists are conducting, analyzing, and presenting psychological data in various legal settings. It has been estimated that hundreds of thousands of forensic assessments are conducted annually by psychologists and other mental health professionals.

Differences Between Therapeutic and Forensic Assessment

Unlike therapeutic assessment, which occurs at the request of the patient, forensic assessment is commonly conducted at the bequest of the legal system. As such, forensic assessment is often not voluntarily sought by the person being evaluated and has more limited confidentiality than traditional therapeutic assessment. The person undergoing forensic assessment may resist the evaluation or may knowingly or unknowingly try to influence the assessment to further his or her legal situation. Attempts to feign mental illness or present oneself in a positive light are more common in forensic assessment than in traditional therapeutic assessment and should always be considered.

Traditional assessment is concerned primarily with the examinee's view of the problem or events. Although forensic assessment does pay attention to the examinee's perspective, it is more concerned with the accuracy of events than is traditional therapeutic assessment. Unlike therapeutic assessment, which casts the examiner in a supportive or helping role, the forensic evaluator's duty is to the legal fact finder, which may or may not assist the person being evaluated. In other words, the client in traditional therapeutic assessment is the person being evaluated, whereas in forensic assessment, the client is the legal fact finder.

Finally, the scope of the two types of assessment differs. Therapeutic assessment typically covers broad clinical issues such as diagnosis, personality, and treatment. Forensic assessment, in contrast, is solely determined by the legal question at hand and, as such, commonly concerns more narrowly defined issues or incidents than what is covered in traditional therapeutic assessment. Although an examinee's mental health and therapeutic needs may be discussed in forensic assessments, such discussions occur only in the context of the larger psycholegal referral question.

Training and Practice Guidelines

In most cases, forensic assessment is performed by mental health professionals who may or may not have had specialized forensic training. Recent years have seen a rapid increase in the teaching, training, and supervision of psychology graduate students, interns, and postdoctoral fellows. Numerous conferences and continuing education opportunities have proliferated as well. In the mid-1980s, the American Board of Professional Psychology (ABPP) began signifying psychologists who have advanced knowledge and competence in forensic psychology by the awarding of diplomate status, and in the early 1990s the American Psychological Association (APA) recognized forensic psychology as an APA specialty.

In addition to the ethical codes of conduct in psychological practice as well as standards for testing (e.g., Ethical Principles of Psychologists and Code of Conduct [EPPCC] and Standards for Educational and Psychological Testing), there are general and specific guidelines for forensic practice. The Specialty Guidelines for Forensic Psychologists (SGFP) were published in 1991, and a revision is under way. The SGFP are general in nature and apply to all areas of forensic psychological work. Unlike the EPPCC, which contain rules of conduct that are enforceable for APA members, the SGFP are aspirational and advisory. The SGFP inform psychologists about the nature and development of competent and responsible forensic practice with the goal of continuous improvement and enhancement. In addition to the SGFP, specialty guidelines and standards have been developed for certain areas of forensic work (e.g., Guidelines for Psychological Evaluations in Child Protection Matters and Standards for Psychology Services in Jails, Prisons, Correctional Facilities, and Agencies).

Several general instructions should be kept in mind when conducting forensic assessments. First, the conclusions and opinions need to be formed from a scientific basis. Quality forensic reports substantiate opinions with data and outline the reasons for the conclusions drawn. Forensic examiners must be prepared to defend the method of data collection and its scientific basis. Therefore, data should be collected carefully, and the limits of any data collected should be recognized and reported. Interpretations made during a forensic assessment should be based on multiple methods of data collection. The response style of the examinee should always be assessed for attempts to minimize or feign psychological impairment. The best method for conducting a forensic assessment and writing a subsequent forensic report is to imagine that all methods and conclusions are being critiqued by an opposing attorney. Finally, testing instruments, if used, should be related to the legal issue at hand and should be theoretically and psychometrically sound.

Forensic Assessment Settings

Typically, when people speak about forensic assessment they are referring to psychological assessments as part of civil or criminal court cases. The broad definition of forensic assessment used in this entry also encompasses forensic assessment in law enforcement and correctional settings. Overlap may exist between settings; also, a forensic assessment might be conducted for use in more than one setting or might be completed for one setting only to be used later in another setting.

Law enforcement is, of course, a broad term for the work of police officers in a variety of settings. Psychological assessment in law enforcement settings may involve criminal profiling and psychological autopsies as well as direct work with police officers. Psychological assessment of police officers can include screening of police candidates, fitness-for-duty evaluations, and promotional evaluations.

Psychological assessment in correctional settings may be involved at any phase of incarceration or correctional involvement. Forensic assessment might be conducted to provide insight into and predict criminal behavior with the goal of preventing future criminality. This area of risk or dangerousness assessment has been quite popular in both clinical and research arenas, with much attention given to isolating the variables associated with recidivism, especially violent recidivism. Assessment in correctional settings can also be used to assess amenability to treatment and/or rehabilitation and may be subsequently used in reaching sentencing

and parole decisions. Psychological assessment may also be used to evaluate the mental health needs of jail and prison inmates, as well as the psychological effects of imprisonment.

Both civil and criminal courts increasingly request and use psychological data. Civil courts handle disputes between citizens; criminal courts handle disputes between a citizen and the state. Examples of where forensic assessment might be involved in civil courts include divorce and child custody cases, competency to consent to treatment or provide care for oneself, examinations of testamentary competence, or civil suits where psychological or neurological injury might be involved (e.g., malpractice cases or automobile accidents).

Certain types of cases have been traditionally categorized as civil but, given the potential deprivation of liberty involved, have been labeled as "quasi-criminal" by scholars in the field. The two types of quasi-criminal cases are civil commitment hearings and juvenile delinquency cases. Forensic assessment is invaluable in civil commitment hearings, in which most states require a finding that the person is mentally ill and is a danger to self or others or in need of care or treatment. There are many stages in juvenile delinquency proceedings where forensic assessment can be of assistance. Issues that used to occur primarily in the adult criminal justice system, such as competency to stand trial, are increasingly being raised in juvenile cases. In addition, juveniles may be evaluated for their amenability to treatment in the juvenile justice system. If they are not considered amenable, their case may be waived to adult court. A child who is tried through the juvenile justice system may undergo a presentence evaluation to determine the best disposition of his or her case.

Forensic assessment can be involved at all levels of criminal proceedings, starting with evaluations of a defendant's capacity to waive *Miranda* rights at the time of arrest and concluding with evaluations of a defendant's competency to be sentenced or competency to be executed. Forensic assessment is most commonly requested in criminal cases to evaluate a defendant's competency to stand trial, with approximately 60,000 such evaluations performed annually. Evaluations of a defendant's criminal responsibility (insanity defense evaluations) are probably the second most common question posed in criminal forensic assessment, although the insanity defense is raised in less than 1% of all felony cases. Sometimes, *competency to stand trial* and *criminal responsibility* are confused, and the terms are used interchangeably. Competency-to-stand-trial evaluations focus on a defendant's current mental functioning, whereas criminal responsibility evaluations focus on the defendant's mental state at the time of the offense. Other types of criminal forensic assessment include evaluations of competence to waive counsel and competence to plead guilty.

Tests and Assessment Instruments

Forensic assessment, as mentioned earlier, may involve the use of psychological tests or assessment instruments. The decision about how and when to use a test as part of a forensic assessment involves consideration of the relevance of the test to the legal question or to the psychological construct that underlies the legal issue. Whether a given test is relevant should be determined by the specific issues involved in the psycholegal referral question. Only tests or instruments with a sound theoretical and psychometric base should be used. Forensic examiners should assess any research findings concerning correlations between testing results and legally relevant behaviors. Testing results and generated hypotheses should be corroborated with archival or third-party data. Corroboration is crucial in forensic contexts because examinees may knowingly or unknowingly present themselves in a manner that helps their legal situation. Third-party data are often more important than testing in cases that involve retrospective inquiries about a person's prior psychological functioning (i.e., criminal responsibility evaluations). Finally, examiners should be concerned about how the selected test will be received by the legal system and should take pains to ensure that the test and its applicability to the legal question at hand are fully explained. The volume of tests that may be used in forensic settings is so vast that it is impossible to mention all types or examples. However, three general classifications exist, reflecting the degree of direct relevance the test has to a specific legal issue.

The first category includes tests and assessment techniques that were developed for the assessment, diagnosis, and/or treatment planning of nonforensic populations in primarily therapeutic contexts. Research has shown that in addition to clinical interviewing, this test category is the one most commonly used in forensic assessment. However, despite their widespread use, caution is advised when selecting these tests to aid in forensic assessment. Conventional

psychological tests have limited use in forensic contexts because they were not devised to address psycholegal questions and typically do not use forensic populations in their development or validation. If such tests are used, it is essential that the link between the test and the legal issue at hand be adequately established. Examples of this category include tests to measure achievement, personality, or intellectual ability (e.g., Woodcock Johnson Tests of Achievement–Third Edition, Personality Assessment Inventory, Wechsler Adult Intelligence Scale–III).

The second category includes tests that were not specifically developed for addressing legal issues but are considered to be forensically relevant in that they address clinical constructs that are often pertinent to persons involved in legal situations. Perhaps the most popular of forensically relevant instruments are measures that assess an examinee's response style, specifically evaluating minimization or feigning of problems (e.g., Minnesota Multiphasic Personality Inventory–II or Structured Interview of Reported Symptoms). Other forensically relevant instruments include tests that may help in child custody assessments (e.g., Parenting Stress Index) or measures of psychopathy (e.g., Hare Psychopathy Checklist–Revised).

Forensic assessment instruments designed to address specific legal issues comprise the third category. These tests are directly relevant to the assessment of psycholegal capacities, abilities, or knowledge. Such instruments can enhance the quality of a forensic assessment by providing relatively standardized assessment procedures and methods for classifying or quantifying an examinee's responses. The use of forensic assessment instruments may serve to reduce examiner bias and/or error and may allow for meaningful comparisons over time or between different examiners. Forensic assessment instruments range from simple interview guides that help structure interviews around the appropriate legal issues to instruments that are constructed and validated with a solid research base. In conjunction with the rise in forensic assessment and the need for psychological input in legal cases, the development and validation of specialized forensic assessment instruments is becoming more critical.

Forensic assessment instruments exist in most areas of forensic assessment. For example, the Inwald Personality Inventory was developed to assess police officer candidates for behavior and maladjustments that might negatively affect their performance as police officers. The Jail Screening Assessment Tool was developed to identify inmates during intake who may require a more formal mental health assessment. In addition to their usefulness in law enforcement and correctional settings, forensic assessment instruments are especially prevalent in civil, quasi-criminal, and criminal settings. Instruments in civil settings include measures of parenting capacity, daily decision making, and competency to consent to research or manage health care decisions (e.g., MacArthur Competence Assessment Tool for Treatment). Quasi-criminal settings that use forensic assessment instruments are primarily juvenile justice proceedings. The majority of forensic assessment instruments used with juveniles were designed primarily for use with adults (e.g., Competence Assessment for Standing Trial for Defendants with Mental Retardation), although instruments created specifically for addressing forensic issues with juveniles are on the rise (e.g., Juvenile Adjudicative Competence Interview). Forensic assessment instruments are most well-known for their use in adult criminal court settings and are especially prevalent in the area of competency to stand trial (e.g., Fitness Interview Test–Revised, MacArthur Competence Assessment Tool–Criminal Adjudication, and Evaluation of Competence to Stand Trial–Revised), although measures exist for other areas of criminal forensic assessment (e.g., Grisso's Instruments for Assessing Understanding and Appreciation of *Miranda* Rights and Rogers Criminal Responsibility Assessment Scales).

A marked increase in commercially available forensically relevant and forensic assessment instruments has occurred in recent years, with this trend showing no signs of slowing down. Measures have been developed and published in two ways. The first is more methodical and scientific in that a test is made commercially available only after it has been researched, peer-reviewed, and refined with the normative data collected. The second, and more questionable, method involves publication of an instrument after only preliminary research has been conducted. Prevailing testing standards and the SGFP caution against the use of tests that have not undergone adequate research and development.

In addition to these cautions, each state has varying requirements for the admissibility of expert testimony. Until recently, the standard employed by all states was that established in *Frye v. United States* (1923), whereby the tests used in reaching expert opinions must have "general acceptance" in the field. In many

states, the *Frye* standard was supplemented by the standards established in three, more recent cases, *Daubert v. Merrell Dow Pharmaceuticals* (1993), *General Electric Co. v. Joiner* (1997), and *Kumho Tire Company v. Carmichael* (1999). These three cases increased the number of challenges made by attorneys regarding the instruments used by clinicians in reaching their expert opinions. Admissibility standards associated with these cases include increased scrutiny of the development, reliability, validity, peer review, and general acceptance of the tests or instruments used in forming expert opinions.

Virginia G. Cooper

See also Adjudicative Competence of Youth; Capacity to Waive Rights; Child Custody Evaluations; Civil Commitment; Competency, Foundational and Decisional; Criminal Responsibility, Assessment of; Ethical Guidelines and Principles; Fitness-for-Duty Evaluations; Juvenile Offenders; Malingering; Risk Assessment Approaches

Further Readings

American Association for Correctional Psychology. (2000). Standards for psychology services in jails, prisons, correctional facilities, and agencies. *Criminal Justice and Behavior, 27,* 433–493.

American Educational Research Association, American Psychological Association, & National Council on Measurement in Education. (1999). *Standards for educational and psychological testing* (3rd ed.). Washington, DC: American Educational Research Association.

American Psychological Association. (2002). Ethical principles of psychologists and code of conduct. *American Psychologist, 57,* 1060–1073.

Archer, R. P., Buffington-Vollum, J. K., Stredny, R. V., & Handel, R. W. (2006). A survey of psychological test use patterns among forensic psychologists. *Journal of Personality Assessment, 87,* 84–94.

Committee on Ethical Guidelines for Forensic Psychologists. (1991). Specialty guidelines for forensic psychologists. *Law and Human Behavior, 15,* 441–448.

Daubert v. Merrell Dow Pharmaceuticals, 509 U.S. 579 (1993).

Frye v. United States, 293 F. 1013 (D.C. Cir. 1923).

General Electric Co. v. Joiner, 522 U.S. 136, 118 S. Ct. 512 (1997).

Grisso, T. (1998). *Forensic evaluation of juveniles.* Sarasota, FL: Professional Resource Press.

Grisso, T. (Ed.). (2003). *Evaluating competencies: Forensic assessments and instruments* (2nd ed.). New York: Kluwer Academic.

Heilbrun, K., Marczyk, G., & DeMatteo, D. (2002). *Forensic mental health assessment: A casebook.* New York: Oxford University Press.

Kumho Tire Company v. Carmichael, 526 U.S. 137 (1999).

Melton, G. B., Petrila, J., Poythress, N. G., & Slobogin, C. (1997). *Psychological evaluations for the courts: A handbook for mental health professionals and lawyers* (2nd ed.). New York: Guilford Press.

Rogers, R. (Ed.). (1997). *Clinical assessment of malingering and deception* (2nd ed.). New York: Guilford Press.

Rogers, R., & Shuman, D. W. (2005). *Fundamentals of forensic practice: Mental health and criminal law.* New York: Springer.

Weiner, I. B., & Hess, A. K. (Eds.). (2006). *The handbook of forensic psychology* (3rd ed.). New York: Wiley.

Georgia Court Competence Test (GCCT)

The evaluation of competence to stand trial is by far the most common forensic evaluation conducted. It has been estimated that there are between 24,000 and 60,000 of these evaluations carried out across the United States each year. This entry describes the Georgia Court Competence Test (GCCT), an instrument used to assess competence to stand trial. The GCCT may best be used as a screening instrument at institutions that process numerous defendants each day. In this role, the GCCT can direct services to individuals who are showing clear signs that they may be incompetent to stand trial at that time. For the assessment of competence to stand trial during a criminal proceeding, however, a much more comprehensive evaluation is necessary.

In the landmark case of *Dusky v. United States,* the U.S. Supreme Court (USSC) established the legal standard for competence to stand trial. The USSC stated that "the test will be whether [the defendant] has sufficient present ability to consult with his lawyer with a reasonable degree of rational understanding, and whether he has a rational as well as a factual understanding of the proceedings against him." The court did not define the procedure for determining competence, and as a result, mental health professionals assess this construct in a variety of ways, including the use of forensic assessment instruments—for example, the GCCT. The current version of the GCCT is a 21-item interview that assesses a defendant's knowledge of very basic information related to competence to stand trial. Although the test has been available for 27 years, research on the measure is limited, and recently, it was recommended that it be used only as a checklist to identify potential areas of concern.

In all evaluations of competence to stand trial, the defendant is required to answer questions related to the trial process. Defendants' ability to communicate with counsel, to understand their legal proceeding and their role as a defendant, and to make relevant legal decisions are areas that are investigated. Research conducted over the past 20 years has demonstrated that these issues are best evaluated when one or more standardized measures of competence to stand trial are included in the evaluative process. One such measure is the GCCT, created in 1980 by Robert W. Wildman and colleagues.

The initial version of the GCCT consisted of 17 items and was developed as a screening instrument that would differentiate defendants who were clearly competent from those who required further evaluation. The instrument requires approximately 10 minutes to administer and score and is conducted in an interview format. The most recent version of the GCCT, known as the Mississippi State Hospital Revision (GCCT–MSH), consists of 21 questions that fall into three broad domains: (1) knowledge of the courtroom and legal proceedings, (2) knowledge of current charges and associated penalties, and (3) relationship with counsel. Like the original measures, the GCCT–MSH is accompanied by a pictorial representation of the courtroom, on which the defendant is asked to identify where courtroom personnel will sit during the trial. The measure is scored out of 100 (raw score multiplied by 2), and the recommended cut score is 69 or below; defendants who score in this range are recommended for further evaluation.

Research conducted on the GCCT–MSH has been limited, but that which is available suggests that the measure has good interrater reliability, has good internal consistency, and can be effective as a checklist to identify potential deficits in functional abilities. Three studies have looked at the factor structure of the GCCT–MSH, and the findings have indicated a lack of stability; consequently, the exact domains that are assessed by GCCT–MSH are not clear.

Much of the commentary regarding the utility of the GCCT–MSH relates to the narrow focus of the measure, specifically the almost exclusive focus on foundational competence (e.g., the ability to understand the purpose and process of the criminal proceedings) to the near exclusion of decisional competencies (e.g., knowledge of the legal options, capacity to engage in rational deliberations regarding legal strategy). Numerous scholars have discussed the relative importance of decisional competencies over foundational competencies, and they contend that foundational competence does not adequately capture what is required to demonstrate competence. Instead, they argue that it is the defendants' ability to function within the context of their own legal proceedings that is of paramount importance.

In addition to the narrow focus of the measure, concerns regarding the face validity of the GCCT–MSH have been raised and addressed in the literature. In 1995, Shayna Gothard and colleagues created the Atypical Presentation Scale to the GCCT–MSH. This scale is composed of 8 items that are scored on a 3-point scale (0 = *no*, 1 = *qualified yes*, 2 = *definite yes*). In the original study, scores of 6 or higher suggested atypical responding and the need for a more comprehensive evaluation of malingered incompetence. A more recent study indicated that the original cut score was too stringent, and it was suggested that the cut score be lowered to 3 or higher, or perhaps even 1 or higher.

The utility of the GCCT–MSH is limited to screening for possible concerns regarding the competence of the defendant. Although a cut score of 69 has been the recommendation for a further evaluation of competence to stand trial, this score should never be used as the sole criterion for such a determination. Like all forensic assessment instruments, the GCCT–MSH plays a small and unique role in the comprehensive evaluation of a defendant.

Karen L. Salekin

See also Competency to Stand Trial; Forensic Assessment; Presentence Evaluations

Further Readings

Bonnie, R. (1992). The competency of criminal defendants: A theoretical reformulation. *Behavioral Sciences and the Law, 10,* 291–316.

Dusky v. United States, 362 U.S. 402 (1960).

Gothard, S., Rogers, R., & Sewell, K. W. (1995). Feigning incompetency to stand trial: An investigation of the GCCT. *Law and Human Behavior, 19,* 363–373.

Rogers, R., Ustad, K. L., Sewell, K. W., & Reinhart, V. (1996). Dimensions of incompetency: A factor analytic study of the Georgia Court Competency Test. *Behavioral Sciences and the Law, 14,* 323–330.

GRISSO'S INSTRUMENTS FOR ASSESSING UNDERSTANDING AND APPRECIATION OF *MIRANDA* RIGHTS

The Instruments for Assessing Understanding and Appreciation of *Miranda* Rights were originally developed in the 1970s by Thomas Grisso as a research tool to inform public policy about juveniles' and adults' capacities to waive rights. The tool, composed of four distinct instruments, was subsequently adopted for use in juvenile and adult forensic evaluations, and the instruments were published for clinical use in 1998. A revised version of the instruments, the *Miranda* Rights Comprehension Instruments–II, has been developed and normed, and the manual is in preparation.

Development and Purpose

Grisso organized an expert panel of lawyers and psychologists to offer comments about, and reach a consensus on, the organization of the instruments, item structure, and scoring criteria. In 1980, Grisso published the results of a large-scale study employing these instruments and, in that article, included the instruments' norms and psychometric properties.

Although the instruments were designed for research purposes, their clinical utility quickly became apparent. The U.S. Supreme Court, in *Miranda v. Arizona* (1966), established that a valid waiver of rights must be provided *knowingly* (i.e., the suspect must demonstrate a factual understanding of the rights' meanings), *intelligently* (i.e., the suspect must demonstrate an appreciation of the consequences of waiving those rights), and *voluntarily* (i.e., the defendant must waive his or her rights without police coercion or intimidation).

Courts typically apply the *totality of circumstances* test to determine the validity of a suspect's waiver by considering multiple factors related to interrogation conditions (e.g., length of the interrogation) and suspect characteristics (e.g., age, intelligence, prior criminal history). The Instruments for Assessing Understanding and Appreciation of *Miranda* Rights may be used to provide a standardized assessment of a suspect's capacities related to the knowing and intelligent requirements of a valid waiver.

In addition to providing a reliable measure of an examinee's understanding and appreciation of *Miranda* rights through the use of standardized administration and scoring criteria, the Instruments for Assessing Understanding and Appreciation of *Miranda* Rights were created with sensitivity to developmental and contextual factors. For instance, visual stimuli are used for many items to maintain examinees' attention. In addition, because of the limited reading and verbal expressive skills of many adolescent and adult offenders, all items are read aloud, and examinees are offered multiple ways of demonstrating their knowledge.

Descriptions of Instruments

The measure is composed of the following four discrete instruments:

1. *Comprehension of* Miranda *Rights (CMR)* assesses an examinee's basic understanding of the four *Miranda* warnings. Each warning is read allowed to the examinee, and the examinee is asked to paraphrase each warning. Examinees' responses are scored 0 (*inadequate*), 1 (*questionable*), or 2 (*adequate*), and standardized questions are provided to probe questionable and inadequate responses. Total scores can range from 0 to 8, and administration requires approximately 15 minutes.

2. *Comprehension of* Miranda *Rights–Recognition (CMR–R)* also assesses an examinee's basic understanding of the four *Miranda* warnings but does so without relying on verbal expressive skills. Each warning is presented with three preconstructed sentences, and an examinee must determine whether the meaning of each preconstructed sentence is semantically identical to the

associated warning. Scoring is bimodal, 0 for incorrect responses and 1 for correct responses. Total scores can range from 0 to 12. Administration requires approximately 5 to 10 minutes.

3. *Function of Rights in Interrogation (FRI)* assesses more than basic understanding by targeting an examinee's appreciation of the significance of the *Miranda* warnings. Four separate illustrations of police, legal, and court proceedings are each accompanied by a short vignette. After reading each vignette, the examiner asks questions about the boy in the vignette (e.g., what he should tell his lawyer, what would happen if he does not talk to the police). There are 15 standardized questions that assess appreciation of three areas: the adversarial nature of police interrogation (NI subscale), the advocacy role of attorneys (RC subscale), and the entitlement to the right to silence (RS subscale). Scoring for the FRI employs the same 0-to-2 scale as the CMR; total scores can range from 0 to 30. Administration requires about 15 minutes.

4. *Comprehension of* Miranda *Vocabulary (CMV)* assesses understanding of six vocabulary words that are typically used in *Miranda* warnings: *consult, attorney, interrogation, appoint, entitled,* and *right.* Initially, nine words were included in the CMV. However, the vast majority of participants in a pilot study adequately understood three of the words, and consequently, those three words were discarded. To administer the CMV, the examiner shows a vocabulary word to the examinee while reading it aloud, using it in a sentence, and repeating it. The examinee is then asked to define the word. Scoring procedures are identical to those of the CMR and FRI, and the total score may range from 0 to 12 points. Administration time is approximately 10 minutes.

Application, Interpretation, and Acceptability

The instruments are appropriate for delinquent and nondelinquent youths aged 10 to 17 and for offending and nonoffending adults. There is no overall *Miranda* comprehension score, because the instruments were designed to assess different aspects of comprehension. Instead, scores on each instrument can be compared with the established absolute or relative standard. To meet the minimal absolute standard, an examinee must not have any *inadequate*, or 0-point, responses. To meet a higher absolute standard, an examinee must achieve all *adequate*, or 2-point, responses. To assess an examinee's scores using a relative standard, scores can be compared against norms.

The instruments have been strongly endorsed by forensic psychologists and are considered the gold standard by licensed clinical psychologists for use in forensic evaluations of capacities to waive *Miranda* rights. For instance, one survey of 64 diplomates of the American Board of Forensic Psychology revealed that these instruments, along with the Wechsler Adult Intelligence Scale–III (WAIS–III), were the only traditional or forensic assessment instruments that were recommended for use in *Miranda* rights evaluations by the majority of surveyed psychologists.

Although these instruments are well respected by experts in the field, several limitations should be considered. First, the instruments provide only an estimate of the examinee's understanding and appreciation of his or her rights at the time of the evaluation. Questions about the validity of a *Miranda* waiver typically are not raised at the time the waiver is offered, and a great deal of time may pass between the waiver and the evaluation. Thus, the examinee's understanding and appreciation of the *Miranda* rights may have changed in the interim as a result of discussions with the attorney, maturation, or experience.

Furthermore, although the instruments provide information about capacities related to the knowing and intelligent requirements of a valid *Miranda* waiver, they do not measure the validity of the waiver. Rather, the evaluator can use data from the instruments to inform the court about an examinee's capacities to understand and appreciate his or her rights. The court may then use this information, in conjunction with other factors considered in the *totality of circumstances* test, to determine the ultimate question of waiver validity.

Revised Instruments

Grisso's original instruments were developed nearly three decades ago using the language of the *Miranda* warnings in Saint Louis County, Missouri, the location of the instruments' development. Although there is no standardized wording of the *Miranda* warning, the language used in most jurisdictions today is far simpler than the warnings used in Grisso's instruments. In addition, many jurisdictions today include a fifth warning, informing suspects that they have the right to stop questioning at any time during a custodial interrogation to ask for an attorney.

To maintain the utility of the instruments, Naomi E. Sevin Goldstein, Lois Oberlander Condie, and Thomas Grisso have developed a revised version, the Miranda Rights Comprehension Instruments–II (MRCI–II). In addition to simplifying the wording of the rights and including the fifth warning, the updated instruments include additional vocabulary words in the CMVs and a supplemental instrument, Perceptions of Coercion During Holding and Interrogation Procedures (P–CHIP), designed to assess self-reported confession behavior in a variety of holding and interrogation situations. Research on the revised instruments has established updated norms for the 21st century, and the MRCI–II manual is in preparation.

Naomi E. Sevin Goldstein,
Rachel Kalbeitzer, and Heather Zelle

See also Capacity to Waive Rights; Forensic Assessment; Juvenile Offenders

Further Readings

Goldstein, N. E. S., Condie, L. O., & Kalbeitzer, R. (2005). Instruments for assessing juveniles' capacity to waive Miranda rights. In T. Grisso, G. Vincent, & D. Seagrave (Eds.), *Mental health screening and assessment in juvenile justice* (pp. 357–369). New York: Guilford Press.

Grisso, T. (1998). *Instruments for assessing understanding and appreciation of Miranda rights.* Sarasota, FL: Professional Resource Press.

Miranda v. Arizona, 384 U.S. 436 (1966).

GUARDIANSHIP

Guardianship is the process by which one individual (a legal guardian) is appointed by a court to care for the personal and property interests of another individual (a ward) in situations where the latter is unable to function independently. Guardians are appointed to represent children, developmentally disabled and mentally ill adults, and the elderly who have been deemed legally incompetent and to make decisions on their behalf. The appointment of a guardian represents a critical point in a ward's life as it essentially rescinds that person's right to make independent decisions.

Judges often rely on input from psychologists or other mental health professionals to help them determine whether guardianship is appropriate. Ideally, family members or close friends are appointed as guardians, keeping the ward's best interests in mind, though this is not always the case.

Guardianship statutes originate from the doctrine of parens patriae, which gives to the state the right and duty to protect people who cannot care for themselves due to infancy, disability, or incapacity. The request for guardianship often comes from a family member who petitions a court to be allowed to make decisions concerning a relative, though public guardians are sometimes appointed to represent the interests of wards who have no relatives or friends to assume that role. The appointment of a guardian essentially rescinds an individual's right to independence and self-determination and can result in the loss of freedom to make decisions about financial matters, health care, housing, education, employment, purchases and sales of property, travel, and marriage and divorce.

Guardianship practices are dictated by state statutes rather than by federal laws, resulting in subtle differences in the type and scope of guardianship arrangements, though nearly all statutes distinguish between protection of an individual and protection of an estate (in some jurisdictions, these responsibilities are termed *guardianship* and *conservatorship*, respectively) and between full (or "plenary") guardians, who make critical decisions in all realms of a ward's life, and partial (or "limited") guardians, who may act only in restricted domains as determined by a court. The intent of limited guardianship is to preserve a ward's autonomy as much as possible so that he or she may continue to function independently.

Guardianship of Children

In most jurisdictions, parents of a minor child are the legal guardians of that child, and they can designate the person or persons who would replace them in the event of their death. On occasion, parents are unable to care for and nurture their children, and the children are removed from their homes and placed in foster care. When neither reunification nor adoption appears to be feasible, alternative permanency options must be explored. Often, these arrangements involve a relative or a foster parent assuming the role of legal guardian of the minor child. In fact, kin care providers make up a large proportion of appointed guardians of children. Under

ideal circumstances, that arrangement provides a more stable environment for the child and also allows retention of connections to the birth family (legal guardianship does not require the termination of parental rights), which can enhance the general well-being of many children. If and when their circumstances change, birth parents can ask a court to vacate guardianship and to return the child to their custody.

The Adoption and Foster Care Analysis and Reporting System monitors trends in the guardianship of children and the characteristics of children transferred from foster care to guardianship arrangements. Compared with children who are adopted, those who become wards tend to be older and are more likely to be members of a minority group.

Guardianship of Adults

It is estimated that more than 1,250,000 adult citizens have had guardians appointed on their behalf. An important milestone occurs when a young person reaches the age of majority and parental rights are transferred from the parent to the child, unless the child has been deemed incompetent. Family members of disabled or incompetent individuals often petition for guardianship at this critical juncture. A prime concern is that the ward is unable to make wise financial decisions. The severity of the ward's disability determines the scope of guardianship: Those with only mild impairments are likely to have a limited guardian, and those with severe impairments are likely to have a full guardian.

As our population ages, the number of adults with chronic diseases, functional impairments, and dementia will increase as well. Thus, guardianship is an important mechanism for protecting older adults who cannot care for themselves. In assessing the need for guardianship of an elderly person, a court must decide whether that individual has the ability to manage daily activities and to make important decisions independently. Because the loss of decisional autonomy can have serious consequences for some elderly wards, affecting their mental health, sense of personal control, and physical well-being, some commentators have suggested that guardianship should always be considered as a last resort.

Psychological Issues

Guardianship raises a number of interesting and complex psychological issues. The first concerns the difficulty of assessing competence and determining the appropriateness of guardianship, especially in cases involving older adults whose functional and cognitive abilities and limitations fluctuate. Judges must balance an individual's right to self-determination against that person's and society's need to be protected. To assist them in these decisions, judges rely on evaluative data provided by medical or mental health professionals who have examined the proposed ward and may have conducted various psychological tests. Unfortunately, these evaluations often lack important information concerning diagnosis, prognosis, the strengths of the proposed ward, and his or her preferences.

A second concern is the ability of guardians to protect their wards without exceeding the bounds of their authority while also promoting the choices that the wards would make for themselves. Some data suggest that surrogate and proxy decision makers have difficulty predicting the choices and describing the status of the persons they represent.

A third issue concerns the impact of guardianship on the lives of the ward and the petitioner—namely, the extent to which guardianship enhances psychological and physical well-being. Undoubtedly, many people who become wards fare better with assistance than they would without, particularly in cases where abuse, neglect, or exploitation precipitated the petition. However, data also suggest that some older wards have felt angry, resentful, agitated, and upset by the guardianship proceedings and that the appointment of a guardian does not necessarily protect all of the interests of younger people with disabilities.

Edith Greene

See also Financial Capacity; Proxy Decision Making; Testamentary Capacity

Further Readings

Lisi, L., Burns, A., & Lussenden, K. (1994). *National study of guardianship systems: Findings and recommendations.* Ann Arbor, MI: Center for Social Gerontology.

Millar, D., & Rengazlia, A. (2002). Factors affecting guardianship practices for young adults with disabilities. *Exceptional Children, 68,* 465–484.

Moye, J. (2003). Guardianship and conservatorship. In T. Grisso (Ed.), *Evaluating competencies: Forensic assessments and instruments* (pp. 309–389). New York: Kluwer Academic/Plenum.

Testa, M. (2004). When children cannot return home: Adoption and guardianship. *The Future of Children, 14,* 114–129.

Wilber, K., Reiser, T., & Harter, K. (2001). New perspectives on conservatorship: The views of older adult conservatees and their conservators. *Aging Neuropsychology and Cognition, 8,* 225–240.

GUDJONSSON SUGGESTIBILITY SCALES

The Gudjonsson Suggestibility Scales (GSS 1 and GSS 2) are clinical instruments designed to assess levels of interrogative suggestibility. The scales provide a total score for suggestibility based on responses to leading questions and negative feedback. They also provide measures of memory recall and confabulation. The scales are used in forensic assessments and are also useful research tools, as they provide a quantifiable measure of levels of interrogative suggestibility and an extensive range of norms against which various hypotheses can be tested.

Description

Gisli Gudjonsson developed two scales of interrogative suggestibility designed to be used as forensic tools to help assess the reliability of confessions that have been retracted. The scales also help identify those individuals who may be particularly vulnerable to the pressures associated with police interviews and who, as a result, may require extra care during interviewing. As well as their clinical applications, the scales are also used for research purposes to investigate the social psychological processes that influence the levels of interrogative suggestibility. The GSS 1 and the GSS 2 are identical in structure; each comprises a spoken narrative and 20 questions about that narrative. The content of the GSS 2 narrative is less complex than that of the GSS 1 narrative, and for this reason, the GSS 2 is more commonly used with children or adults with learning disabilities. The scales are therefore parallel in form and produce closely comparable norms.

Administration

The narratives each contain 40 distinct pieces of information. Of the 20 questions for both scales, 15 are misleading, suggesting details that are not part of the narrative, and 5 are "true" questions, containing no misleading information. These 5 true questions are interspersed with the misleading or suggestive questions. Administration of the scales initially involves presentation of the narrative to the interviewee; the test administrator, or interviewer, reads out the narrative at a steady pace. Following this, the interviewee is asked to provide immediate free recall of the narrative. There is then a 50-minute delay, followed by the interviewee's providing delayed recall of the narrative. The 20 questions about the narrative are then asked. When all the questions have been answered, the interviewer gives the interviewee negative feedback. Regardless of level of accuracy, interviewees are told that they have made some mistakes and that it will be necessary to repeat the questions, and they are urged to try and be more accurate. This negative feedback is to be delivered both clearly and firmly so as to convey an appropriate level of interrogative pressure to the interviewee.

Scoring

Immediate recall and delayed recall are scored according to how many discrete pieces of information are recalled correctly. Information is scored as correct if the meaning is the same as the original item in the narrative. Each correct item earns 1 point, with the maximum score being 40. There is also a score given for Total Confabulation, which comprises a count of the number of distortions and fabrications included when recalling the narrative. A distortion represents a major change to an existing piece of information from the narrative, whereas a fabrication is the introduction of new material. There are four suggestibility scores obtained from the scales: Yield 1 is a measure of all leading questions that are answered affirmatively in the first round of questioning, with the range of possible scores being 0 to 15; Yield 2 is the number of leading questions accepted following the administration of the negative feedback, and again the range of scores is 0 to 15; Shift is a measure of any distinct changes in response to all 20 questions in the second round of questioning, with a range of 0 to 20; and Total Suggestibility is the sum of Yield 1 and Shift, giving a range of 0 to 35.

Reliability and Validity

Factor analysis of the GSS 1 and GSS 2 questions shows two clear factors, with items loading significantly on the appropriate Yield or Shift factors. The scoring of Yield and Shift are nondiscretionary in nature, and studies assessing interscorer reliability confirm that it is very high. Interscorer reliability for immediate and delayed recall is also very high. Scoring of confabulation is slightly less reliable, although correlations show that this is still relatively high. Owing to the nature of the scales, it is not possible to assess test-retest reliability within each scale, as any memory of the narrative and questions affects subsequent testing. However, comparison of the scores of individuals who have completed both the GSS 1 and the GSS 2 has shown high correlations. The scales can therefore be said to have temporal consistency.

Research

There has been extensive research using the scales to test the hypotheses derived from the theoretical model of interrogative suggestibility. The model postulates that interrogative suggestibility is largely dependent on individuals' cognitive appraisal of the interrogative situation. Research using the scales confirms that suggestible responding is related to cognitive abilities. For example, several studies have demonstrated that GSS scores are negatively related to intelligence and positively correlated with memory capacity. Studies have also shown that increases in the perception of psychological distance between the interviewer and the interviewee are related to increases in scores on the scales. Other research has demonstrated that there are intra-individual differences, such as self-esteem and self-monitoring, that also affect responses on the scales. The research using the scales demonstrates that interrogative suggestibility is a complex response mediated by a range of cognitive and social psychological processes.

Stella A. Bain

See also Competency to Confess; False Confessions; Forensic Assessment; Interrogation of Suspects; Postevent Information and Eyewitness Memory; Test of Memory Malingering (TOMM)

Further Readings

Bain, S. A., Baxter, J. S., & Ballantyne, K. (2007). Self-monitoring style and levels of interrogative suggestibility. *Personality & Individual Differences, 42,* 623–630.

Bain, S. A., Baxter, J. S., & Fellowes, V. (2004). Interacting influences on interrogative suggestibility. *Legal and Criminological Psychology, 9,* 239–252.

Gudjonsson, G. H. (2003). *The psychology of interrogations and confessions. A handbook.* Chichester, UK: Wiley.

Woolston, R., Bain, S. A., & Baxter, J. S. (2006). Patterns of malingering and compliance in measures of interrogative suggestibility. *Personality & Individual Differences, 40,* 453–461.

GUILTY BUT MENTALLY ILL VERDICT

The guilty but mentally ill (GBMI) verdict is a verdict option that enables juries and judges to find a defendant guilty of committing an offense while formally acknowledging that the defendant has a mental illness. The GBMI does not usually replace the insanity defense standard but presents an additional verdict option. The GBMI verdict has met with sound criticism and little empirical support; nonetheless, 20 states have adopted it.

Although the idea of holding mentally ill people "guilty" for their criminal acts has been brewing for some time, the single event that brought the guilty but mentally ill verdict to fruition may have been the Michigan Supreme Court's decision in *People v. McQuillan* (1974). In this case, the court held that it is unconstitutional to detain people who have been found not guilty by reason of insanity (NGRI) for indefinite periods, insofar as it violates their due process and equal protection rights. After some crimes were committed by those found NGRI and later released, the Michigan Legislature passed a law in 1982 introducing a new verdict—GBMI.

A defendant who receives a GBMI verdict is sentenced in the same way as if he or she were found guilty. The court then determines whether and to what extent the defendant requires treatment for mental illness. When, and if, the defendant's mental illness is deemed to have been stabilized, the offender is required to serve out the rest of his or her sentence. This is different from the case of individuals who have been found NGRI. In those cases, the insanity-defense acquittee is released from psychiatric commitment once he or she is deemed to be no longer dangerous.

Essentially, the GBMI verdict holds defendants criminally responsible for their acts but recognizes that the defendant is mentally ill. The GBMI verdict is typically employed as an option in addition to the NGRI and guilty verdicts, leaving it to the jury to decide, for example, if the defendant should be found guilty, not guilty, NGRI, or GBMI. The rationale for introducing the GBMI option was to reduce the number of insanity acquittals in Michigan and to prevent the early release of NGRI acquittees, which legislators feared would occur following the *McQuillan* case. The GBMI plea has been termed an "in-between classification," since defendants are neither acquitted nor found guilty in the traditional sense.

The introduction of the GBMI verdict has produced a rather tumultuous controversy. Proponents of the GBMI verdict assert that it provides for necessary treatment of mentally ill defendants while still ensuring that those defendants are punished for their crimes. Other supporters argue that the GBMI verdict protects the public because mentally ill defendants serve the remainder of their sentence in prison after they are well, which would not happen with defendants found not guilty by reason of insanity.

Some commentators argue that the verdict has been successful because it allows defendants to be held criminally responsible for their actions while also enabling them to seek treatment. In sharp contrast to these benefits, critics argue that the GBMI verdict is simply an overreaction to a problem that really does not exist—that is, that the insanity defense does not allow dangerous defendants to simply "get off." Moreover, research has not shown a reduction in the use of the insanity defense in states where the GBMI verdict has been introduced.

Similarly, critics argue that the GBMI verdict serves no necessary purpose and is a misleading verdict, introduced because of purely political reasons. It is argued that the verdict only confuses jurors and enables them to find a disproportionate number of defendants "guilty." Indeed, some mock jury research has found that mock jurors tend to use the GBMI verdict as a "compromise" verdict where members of the jury are torn between finding a defendant guilty or finding the defendant NGRI.

Perhaps the most significant criticism of the GBMI verdict is that the jury, when instructed about their verdict options, are not informed about the consequences of a finding of GBMI. Given the dearth of treatment services available for people in prisons with mental illnesses and the disproportionate number of prisoners who suffer from a mental illness, the reality is that many people with mental illnesses do not receive the treatment they require when they are in prison—regardless of whether they have been found GBMI or not.

Despite the criticisms of the GBMI verdict and the general lack of support for it, the verdict has proven quite popular with politicians. Since its inception 25 years ago, at least 20 states have enacted GBMI provisions.

James R. P. Ogloff

See also Insanity Defense Reform Act (IDRA); M'Naghten Standard

Further Readings

Blunt, L. W., & Stock, H. V. (1985). Guilty but mentally ill: An alternative verdict. *Behavioral Sciences and the Law, 8,* 49–67.

Melville, J. D., & Naimark, D. (2002). Punishing the insane: The verdict of guilty but mentally ill. *Journal of the American Academy of Psychiatry and Law, 30,* 553–555.

People v. McQuillan, 392 Mich. 511, 221 N.W.2d 569 (1974).

H

HALLUCINATIONS

Hallucinations are abnormal sensory perceptions of stimuli that occur in the absence of external stimuli. Hallucinations can be visual, auditory, tactile, olfactory, or gustatory. There are numerous disorders that are associated with hallucinations, including, but not limited to, schizophrenia, posttraumatic stress disorder (PTSD), substance use and withdrawal, and mood disorders. To determine appropriate treatment, the etiology of the hallucinations must be ascertained by conducting a thorough medical history, psychological assessment, and, if warranted, imaging studies.

Definition

Hallucinations can be defined as conscious abnormal sensory perceptions that do not have a source in the outside world. Hallucinations can involve one or more senses, including visual, auditory, gustatory, olfactory, or tactile. People who experience hallucinations report experiences such as seeing things that aren't there, hearing voices that no one else can hear, feeling that there is something crawling on their skin, smelling things that no one else can smell, or tasting things that other people cannot taste.

In one study, Johns and colleagues found that prevalence of hallucinations in a community sample ranged from 2% to 10%. There is currently no evidence that hallucinations occur more frequently in some racial or ethnic groups than in others, and gender does not appear to affect the presence or frequency of hallucinations.

Disorders Associated With Hallucinations

Hallucinations are associated with numerous disorders, illnesses, and states. Currently, there does not appear to be a single underlying cause that can explain all types of hallucinations. Several explanations and hypotheses have been put forth for various disorders, but to date, the causes of hallucinations are not completely understood.

Hallucinations are most commonly associated with schizophrenia, a mental illness characterized by disordered perceptions, thoughts, and behaviors. According to the National Institute of Mental Health, approximately 75% of individuals with a diagnosis of schizophrenia experience auditory hallucinations, visual hallucinations, or both. The auditory hallucinations may be command hallucinations, in which the person hears voices ordering him or her to do something.

Other disorders are that are less frequently associated with hallucinations include eye disorders such as macular degeneration or glaucoma; high fever, particularly in children and the elderly; late-stage Alzheimer's disease; migraine headaches; intoxication or withdrawal from alcohol or drugs; severe medical illness such as liver or kidney failure or brain cancer; severe mood disorders such as bipolar disorder and depression; post traumatic stress disorder; and temporal lobe epilepsy. In addition, hallucinations are also associated with normal sleep-wake cycles. Approximately one third of adults experience hypnagogic hallucinations, which occur as a person passes from wakefulness into sleep; another 10% to 12% of adults report hypnopompic hallucinations, which occur as the person is waking up.

Hallucinations and Violence

The relationship between hallucinations and violent behavior has been the subject of debate. Some research has found a modest positive relationship between hallucinations and violence, whereas other studies found no immediate relationship. Dale E. McNeil and colleagues studied the relationship between command hallucinations and violence in a sample of 130 inpatients who were diagnosed with schizophrenia. They found that 30% of the inpatients reported that they had experienced command hallucinations to hurt someone else in the past year, while 22% of the patients reported that they complied with those command hallucinations. These findings suggest that patients who experienced command hallucinations were almost twice as likely to engage in violent behavior as patients who did not experience command hallucinations. Other studies have reported compliance for command hallucinations of violence ranging from 39.2% to 88.5%. Compliance with command hallucinations has been found to be related to whether or not the person recognizes the hallucinated voice, with those recognizing the voice being more likely to obey the command.

Hallucinations and Schizophrenia

Hallucinations are most commonly associated with schizophrenia. Patients with schizophrenia may experience auditory and/or visual hallucinations. Some research suggests that auditory hallucinations can be caused by high levels of the neurotransmitter dopamine in the patient's brain. Researchers have found evidence, however, both to support and to refute the dopamine hypothesis. The evidence that most strongly supports the dopamine hypothesis comes from the effects of drugs such as amphetamines and cocaine. These drugs are known to increase the levels of dopamine in the brain and can result in psychotic symptoms, including hallucinations, when large doses are consumed over long periods. Several studies have found that when patients with schizophrenia were administered drugs that produce increased dopamine levels, up to 75% of them had significant increases in their hallucinations and psychotic symptoms, while control subjects without schizophrenia showed no effects on being administered the same drugs. Further evidence supporting the dopamine hypothesis was found following the discovery of a class of drugs known as phenothiazines, which include antipsychotic medications. These drugs bind to dopamine receptors and have been found to decrease the positive symptoms of schizophrenia, including hallucinations.

With the advent of more sophisticated brain imaging techniques such as positron emission tomography (PET) scanning, newer findings challenged the dopamine hypothesis. In PET studies with schizophrenic patients, researchers found that in some patients, more than 90% of the dopamine receptors were blocked by the antipsychotic drugs, yet there was no observed diminution in psychotic symptoms, including hallucinations. However, the patients in this study had been receiving treatment with antipsychotic medications for more than 30 years. In another study, researchers found that 90% to 95% of patients who were only recently diagnosed with schizophrenia responded to antipsychotic medications, and scans of their brains revealed that only 60% to 70% of the dopamine receptors were blocked. Finally, in recent years, atypical antipsychotic medications have been developed to treat schizophrenia. While equally as effective as the typical antipsychotic medications, these atypical antipsychotic medications block fewer of the dopamine receptors (about 60–70%). Thus, confronted by some evidence that supports and other evidence that refutes the dopamine hypothesis, research continues into the etiology of schizophrenia.

There has also been a great deal of research investigating the structural and functional abnormalities in the brains of patients with schizophrenia. Researchers have found that some people with schizophrenia have changes in the density of the brain's gray matter in the frontal and temporal lobes. If these differences in brain structure were present since birth, then they could result in dopamine hypersensitivity as described above, resulting in psychotic symptoms such as hallucinations.

Researchers have also noted abnormal patterns in brain activity among patients with schizophrenia. More specifically, abnormalities were found in the corollary discharge mechanism, which enables people to distinguish between internal and external stimuli. Studies with electroencephalograms (EEGs) of the brains of patients with schizophrenia that were taken while the patients were talking found that the corollary discharges from the frontal cortex of the brain (the area where thoughts are produced) did not provide information to the auditory cortex (the area in which sounds are interpreted) that the sounds that were detected were self-generated. Therefore, this dysfunction would lead patients with schizophrenia to perceive internal stimuli as being generated by external sources, thereby producing auditory hallucinations.

Finally, there is some evidence that auditory hallucinations may be related to tissue loss in the primary auditory cortex. The receptors in the auditory cortex process information and then send it to the thalamus, which filters the information before sending it to be decoded in the brain. These complex processes transform abstract sensory information such as sound and light waves into recognizable images and voices of the world around us. While dysfunctions in any of these structures alone would not explain the presence of hallucinations, it is possible that patients with schizophrenia may experience the malfunction of several of these neurotransmitter and receptors networks simultaneously. None of these defects alone would cause schizophrenia or trigger a psychotic episode; however, they do confer a predisposition for developing schizophrenia. Thus, individuals with these defects would be more likely to experience auditory or visual misperceptions, which would present themselves as auditory or visual hallucinations.

Hallucinations and Posttraumatic Stress Disorder

Trauma survivors who develop PTSD often report visual and auditory hallucinations. Hallucinations in trauma survivors are often referred to as *flashbacks*. During these flashbacks, the person relives the traumatic experience as if they were really there. Although these flashbacks can be described as hallucinations, they are nonpsychotic in nature. It is believed that flashbacks in patients with PTSD occur following abnormal memory formation patterns that occur during the traumatic experience. In cases of trauma, it is hypothesized that instead of being processed in the hippocampus, where memories are described using language, traumatic memories are stored in the amygdala, which stores the memory as an emotional experience. As a consequence, the traumatic memories are stored in the amygdala without words but only with intense emotions, and the memories are associated with vivid sensations and sensory perceptions that can manifest themselves as hallucinations during stressful situations.

Hallucinations and Substance Abuse

Hallucinations can be caused by overdoses of prescription drugs, illegal drugs, and alcohol or drug withdrawal. Substance-induced hallucinations seem to occur because of blocking of the action of serotonin, while phencyclidine induces hallucinations by blocking glutamate receptors. Interestingly, individuals who have used lysergic acid diethylamide (LSD) have reported flashbacks, or spontaneous hallucinations, which occur when the person is no longer taking the drug. This phenomenon is referred to as hallucinogen persisting perception disorder.

Withdrawal from alcohol can also result in hallucinations. These types of hallucinations usually occur if a chronic alcoholic suddenly stops drinking alcohol. Initially, on withdrawal, patients report auditory hallucinations, such as hearing threatening or accusatory voices. After several days of withdrawal, patients can experience delirium tremens, a condition in which they feel disoriented, depressed, and feverish and experience visual hallucinations.

Hallucinations and Mood Disorder

Hallucinations have also been associated with mood disorders. Approximately 20% of patients in the manic phase of bipolar disorder and almost 10% of patients with major depressive disorder experience auditory hallucinations. It is not clear what causes patients with mood disorders to experience hallucinations. There appears to be a genetic link, as psychotic mood states have been found to run in families. Additionally, elevated levels of the hormone cortisol have been found in patients who experience depression with psychosis.

Assessment of Hallucinations

To assess hallucinations, the general physician, psychiatrist, or psychologist should conduct a thorough medical and psychosocial examination to rule out possible organic, environmental, or psychological causes. Depending on the patient's symptoms and medical history, such an evaluation may also involve laboratory tests and imaging studies. If a psychological cause such as schizophrenia is suspected, a psychologist will typically conduct an interview with the patient and his or her family and administer one of several clinical inventories, or tests, to evaluate the mental status of the patient. This could include the Mini-Mental Status Exam (MMSE), the Psychotic Symptom Rating Scales, the Positive and Negative Syndrome Scale, or the Scale for Assessment of Positive Symptoms. A total score of 20 or lower on the MMSE is generally indicative of delirium, dementia, schizophrenia, or severe depression.

Treatment of Hallucinations

If hallucinations are related to schizophrenia or another psychotic disorder, then the patient should be under the care of a psychiatrist. For schizophrenia-related hallucinations, the patient should be prescribed antipsychotic medication such as thioridazine (Mellaril), haloperidol (Haldol), chlorpromazine (Thorazine), clozapine (Clozaril), or risperidone (Risperdal). Treatment for hallucinations that are not related to schizophrenia are dependent on the disorder associated with the onset of hallucinations and could include anticonvulsant or antidepressant medications, psychotherapy, brain or ear surgery, or therapy for drug dependence. Hallucinations related to normal sleeping and waking are considered normal and do not require intervention.

Elizabeth L. Jeglic

See also Delusions; Mental Health Courts; Police Interaction With Mentally Ill Individuals; Posttraumatic Stress Disorder (PTSD); Violence Risk Assessment

Further Readings

American Psychiatric Association. (2000). *Diagnostic and statistical manual of mental disorders* (4th ed., text revision). Washington, DC: Author.

Behrendt, R. P. (2006). Dysregulation of thalamic sensory "transmission" in schizophrenia neurochemical vulnerability to hallucinations. *Journal of Psychopharmacology, 20*(3), 356–372.

Johns, L. C., Nazroo, J. Y., Bebbington, P., & Kuipers, E. (2002). Occurrence of hallucinatory experiences in a community sample and ethnic variations. *British Journal of Psychiatry, 180,* 174–178.

McNeil, D. E., Eisner, J. P., & Binder, R. L. (2000). The relationship between command hallucinations and violence. *Psychiatric Services, 51,* 1288–1292.

Ohayon, M. M. (2002). Prevalence of hallucinations and their pathological associations in the general population. *Psychiatry Research, 97,* 153–164.

HARE PSYCHOPATHY CHECKLIST–REVISED (2ND EDITION) (PCL–R)

The Hare Psychopathy Checklist–Revised (2nd edition, PCL–R) is a 20-item rating scale for the measurement of the clinical construct of psychopathy. Although it was designed for use in research, its explanatory and predictive features have led to its widespread use within the criminal justice system. This entry describes the development of the PCL–R, its psychometric properties, and its use in the criminal justice system.

The PCL–R had its origins in the late 1970s at a time when a variety of clinical and self-report methods were being used to define what ostensibly was psychopathy. There was little evidence that these methods were conceptually or empirically related to one another, with the result that many research findings obtained with one method could not be replicated with other methods. The development of the PCL–R (and its predecessor, the PCL) was based on a rich clinical tradition that included the writings of, among others, Benjaman Karpman, Silvano Arieti, William and Joan McCord, and, especially, Hervey Cleckley. The selection of several items and the scoring protocols was influenced by the nature of the population with which the research was being conducted, namely incarcerated offenders. Prison populations continue to offer several advantages for the study and measurement of psychopathy: high prevalence and the availability of extensive amounts of "hard" information about the individual. The latter is particularly important, given that self-disclosed information (e.g., interviews, self-reports) typically is subject to impression management and often unreliable, not only in offenders but also in the general population.

The PCL–R scoring criteria first were distributed to researchers in 1985. With the subsequent accumulation of large amounts of empirical data, the criteria and accounts of the psychometric properties of the PCL–R were formally published in 1991. This was followed by a dramatic upsurge in the use of the instrument for both basic research and applied (clinical, forensic) purposes and the publication of a greatly expanded second edition in 2003, which contains data on more than 10,000 offenders and forensic psychiatric patients. Throughout, the scoring criteria have remained unchanged to ensure conceptual and measurement continuity.

Description and Psychometric Properties

The PCL–R uses a semistructured interview, case history information, and specific scoring criteria to rate each item on a 3-point scale (0, 1, 2) according to the extent to which the criteria are judged to apply to a given individual. Total scores can vary from 0 to 40 and reflect the degree to which the individual matches the prototypical psychopath.

There is good evidence that the PCL–R is a very reliable instrument when administered and scored by trained and experienced raters. Internal consistency is high (alpha coefficient is greater than .80). The intraclass correlation (ICC) typically exceeds .80 for a single rater (ICC_1) and .90 for the average of two raters (ICC_2). The standard error of measurement (SEM) of the PCL–R total score is approximately 3 for a single rating and 2 for the average of two ratings.

The PCL–R also has good generalizability across diverse forensic populations, although there may be sex, ethnic, and cultural differences in the way some features of psychopathy are manifested. Recent research suggests that the construct underlying the PCL–R is dimensional in nature, but a cut score of 30 has proven useful as a working definition of psychopathy. The utility of cut scores for clinical and forensic purposes will be influenced by the context in which the PCL–R is used (e.g., research, diagnosis, risk assessment, treatment options).

Although there is good evidence that the PCL–R measures a unitary construct, the items can be grouped, logically and statistically, into several correlated dimensions or factors. Recent confirmatory factor analyses of very large data sets clearly indicate that a four-factor model (18 items) fits the data well: *Interpersonal* (Glibness/superficial charm, Grandiose sense of self-worth, Pathological lying, Conning/manipulative); *Affective* (Lack of remorse or guilt, Shallow affect, Lack of empathy, Failure to accept responsibility for actions); *Lifestyle* (Need for stimulation/proneness to boredom, Parasitic lifestyle, Lack of realistic long-term goals, Impulsivity, Irresponsibility); and *Antisocial* (Poor behavioral controls, Early behavior problems, Juvenile delinquency, Revocation of conditional release, Criminal versatility). Two other items (Promiscuous sexual behavior, Many short-term marital relationships) do not load on any factor but contribute to the total PCL–R score. Some commentators have suggested that the Antisocial factor is a measure of criminality and that it is a manifestation of the more central features of psychopathy. In reality, it reflects a pattern of persistent and serious rule-breaking behavior. Clinical tradition, as well as recent findings from behavioral genetics and developmental research, clearly indicates that antisocial dispositions are an integral part of the construct and its measurement.

Association With Other Measures

Psychopathy, as measured by the PCL–R, is treated by some as being equivalent with the *DSM-IV* (*Diagnostic and Statistical Manual of Mental Disorders*, fourth edition) diagnosis of antisocial personality disorder (APD). However, the diagnostic criteria for APD place greater emphasis on antisocial behaviors than does the PCL–R and are more closely associated with the Lifestyle/Antisocial components of psychopathy than with its Interpersonal/Affective features. Most of those with APD do not have high PCL–R scores (i.e., in the 30+ range). Psychopathy and APD are related but not identical constructs.

The PCL–R is moderately correlated, in expected directions, with various self-report measures of psychopathy and with several omnibus personality scales. These instruments make it easy to collect large amounts of data and are beginning to play a role in delineating and elucidating the nomological network, behavioral genetics, and developmental pathways of psychopathy. They also provide support for the view that psychopathy is an extreme variant of normal personality dimensions.

Validity

The validity of the PCL–R in the criminal justice system is well established, a reflection of the central and pervasive role of psychopathy in criminal behavior. There is extensive evidence for the explanatory power and utility of the PCL–R in the prediction of recidivism, violence, and treatment outcome in criminals and in forensic and civil psychiatric populations. The PCL–R routinely is used in risk assessments, either on its own or, more appropriately, as part of a battery of variables and factors relevant to offending and violence. Besides forensic and applied areas, evidence for the validity of the PCL–R is provided by findings obtained from a wide variety of laboratory, cognitive/affective, and neuroscience paradigms, including functional magnetic resonance imaging.

Current Issues

The widespread acceptance of the PCL–R as the principal method for assessing psychopathy and its frequent description as the "gold standard" have led some commentators to express their concern that the measure has become the construct. The remedy is to introduce and validate supplementary or improved assessment methods. A more pressing concern is the potential for misuse of the PCL–R in the forensic context. Because assessments of psychopathy can have serious consequences for the individual and society, it is crucial that the PCL–R (and other instruments) be used in accordance with the highest professional and ethical standards and that such use be subjected to careful scrutiny by the stakeholders.

Robert D. Hare

See also Antisocial Personality Disorder; Hare Psychopathy Checklist: Screening Version (PCL:SV); Hare Psychopathy Checklist: Youth Version (PCL:YV); HCR–20 for Violence Risk Assessment; Psychopathic Personality Inventory (PPI); Violence Risk Appraisal Guide (VRAG); Violence Risk Assessment

Further Readings

Hare, R. D. (2003). *The Hare Psychopathy Checklist–Revised* (2nd ed.). Toronto, ON, Canada: Multi-Health Systems.

Hare, R. D. (2007). Psychological instruments in the assessment of psychopathy. In A. R. Felthous & H. Sass (Eds.), *International handbook on psychopathic disorders and the law* (pp. 41–67). New York: Wiley & Sons.

Neumann, C. S., Hare, R. D., & Newman, J. P. (2007). The superordinate nature of the Psychopathy Checklist–Revised. *Journal of Personality Disorders, 21,* 102–117.

Leistico, A. R., Salekin, R. T., DeCoster, J., & Rogers, R. (in press). A large-scale meta-analysis relating the Hare measures of psychopathy to antisocial conduct. *Law and Human Behavio*r.

Hervé, H., & Yuille, J. (Eds.). (2007). *The psychopath: Theory, research, and practice.* Mahwah, NJ: Lawrence Erlbaum.

HARE PSYCHOPATHY CHECKLIST: SCREENING VERSION (PCL:SV)

The Hare Psychopathy Checklist: Screening Version (PCL:SV) is a 12-item symptom-construct rating scale designed for use by expert observers to assess the lifetime presence and severity of symptoms of psychopathic personality disorder. It was derived from the Hare Psychopathy Checklist–Revised, or PCL–R. The PCL:SV is intended for use with adult males and females in a broad range of settings, including correctional, forensic psychiatric, civil psychiatric, and community settings. As its name implies, the PCL:SV also can be used in conjunction with the PCL–R as a screening test in correctional and forensic psychiatric settings, with elevated scores on the PCL:SV triggering administration of a more detailed and comprehensive assessment using the PCL–R. Because of its demonstrated association with future violence, the PCL:SV is most often used as part of a comprehensive violence risk assessment, using structured professional guidelines for assessing violence risk such as the HCR–20, the Sexual Violence Risk–20 (SVR–20), and the Spousal Assault Risk Assessment Guide (SARA).

Description and Development

Development of the PCL:SV took place between 1986 and 1994, funded in part by the John D. and Catherine T. MacArthur Foundation's Research Network on Mental Health and the Law, under the direction of John Monahan, School of Law, University of Virginia. Its development culminated in the publication of the test manual by Multi-Health Systems Inc. in 1995. Originally written in English, the test has been translated into Swedish and German.

The PCL:SV was developed to address several recognized limitations of the PCL–R. First, scale length was reduced from 20 items in the PCL–R to 12 items in the PCL:SV by combining PCL–R items with overlapping content. Second, PCL–R items defined in terms of specific socially deviant behavior were excluded from the PCL:SV. Third, PCL–R items reflecting antisocial behavior were redefined in the PCL:SV so that they could be scored without reference to an official criminal record (i.e., formal charges or convictions). Finally, item definitions were shortened from an average of about 200 words in the PCL–R to about 50 words in the PCL:SV.

Each PCL:SV item reflects a specific symptom (i.e., clinical feature) of psychopathy. Part 1 comprises 6 items that reflect an arrogant and deceitful interpersonal style and deficient affective experience. Part 2 comprises 6 items that reflect an impulsive and irresponsible behavioral style and a history of criminal conduct in adolescence and adulthood. Parts 1 and 2 are parallel to Factors 1 and 2 of the PCL–R. Items are scored on the basis of an interview and a review of case history information; in some circumstances, it may be possible to base ratings solely on case history information. Items are rated on a 3-point scale according to the lifetime presence and severity of symptoms (0 = *absent*, 1 = *possibly or partially present*, and 2 = *present*); items may also be omitted in the absence of relevant information.

Items are summed (and prorated when necessary) to yield Total scores that can range from 0 to 24, as well as scores on Parts 1 and 2 that range from 0 to 12.

PCL:SV Total and Part scores can be interpreted dimensionally, with respect to data collected from 586 people in correctional, forensic psychiatric, civil psychiatric, and community settings. Total scores also can be interpreted categorically, with scores of 18 and higher diagnostic of psychopathic; when the PCL:SV is used as a screening test, scores of 13 and higher reflect the presence of elevated psychopathic symptomatology, which may trigger a more detailed evaluation using the PCL–R.

Psychometric Evaluation

Evaluations based on classical test theory indicate that PCL:SV Total scores have good structural reliability. Mean corrected item-total correlations average about .55, mean interitem correlations average about .35, and Cronbach's alphas average about .80. Total scores also have good interrater reliability, with intraclass correlation (ICC) coefficients (based on two independent raters) averaging about .80.

Evaluations based on modern test theory also support the structural reliability of Total scores. Item-characteristic curves based on item response theory (IRT) analyses indicate that all the PCL:SV items are reasonably discriminating with respect to the latent trait and also that they discriminate across a broad range of the latent trait. Test-characteristic curves from IRT analyses indicate that test scores provide reasonable information across a broad range of the latent trait.

Exploratory factor analyses of the PCL:SV appeared to support a two-factor structure parallel to that of the PCL–R. Subsequent confirmatory factor analyses of both the PCL–R and the PCL:SV have found a hierarchical structure, in which three or four specific factors—reflecting interpersonal, affective, and behavior symptoms, plus a possible fourth factor reflecting criminality—underlie a superordinate factor of psychopathy.

Validity

The PCL:SV has good concurrent validity with respect to the PCL–R. First, IRT analyses indicate that scores on PCL:SV items are strongly related to the PCL–R items from which they were derived. Second, the correlation between Total scores on the two tests is about

.90, controlling for other facets of unreliability; similarly, in IRT analyses, the correlation between latent traits on the two tests is also about .90. Third, supporting its utility as a screening test, high scores on the PCL:SV have excellent sensitivity and good specificity with respect to PCL–R diagnoses of psychopathy.

The PCL:SV has been used in a wide range of research on psychopathy, including etiological and cross-cultural research. Numerous studies have examined its predictive validity, finding that PCL:SV Total scores typically have a moderate effect size with respect to institutional and community violence in various settings.

Stephen D. Hart and
Catherine M. Wilson

See also Hare Psychopathy Checklist–Revised (2nd edition) (PCL–R); HCR–20 for Violence Risk Assessment; MacArthur Violence Risk Assessment Study; Psychopathy; Sexual Violence Risk–20 (SVR–20); Spousal Assault Risk Assessment (SARA)

Further Readings

Cooke, D. J., Michie, C. E., Hart, S. D., & Hare, R. D. (1999). Evaluating the screening version of the Hare Psychopathy Checklist–Revised (PCL:SV): An item response theory analysis. *Psychological Assessment, 11,* 3–13.

Douglas, K. S., Strand, S., Belfrage, H., Fransson, G., & Levander, S. (2005). Reliability and validity evaluation of the Psychopathy Checklist: Screening Version (PCL:SV) in Swedish correctional and forensic psychiatric samples. *Assessment, 12,* 145–161.

Hart, S. D., Cox, D. N., & Hare, R. D. (1995). *Manual for the Hare Psychopathy Checklist: Screening Version (PCL:SV)*. Toronto, ON, Canada: Multi-Health Systems.

HARE PSYCHOPATHY CHECKLIST: YOUTH VERSION (PCL:YV)

The construct of psychopathy as applied to children and adolescents has received increasing attention in recent years. Many researchers and clinicians believe that psychopathic traits and behaviors are first manifested early in life, which has led to efforts to develop measures to identify psychopathic traits early in development. The Hare Psychopathy Checklist: Youth Version (PCL:YV) is a structured assessment instrument designed to assess psychopathic traits and behaviors in adolescents. It was adapted from the Hare Psychopathy Checklist–Revised, developed by Robert Hare, which is widely used in research, clinical, and forensic settings for the assessment of psychopathy in adults. The PCL:YV was published in 2003 to provide researchers and clinical users with a common metric to assess psychopathic traits in adolescents and to encourage systematic research. Future research and input from practitioners will play an integral role in clarifying and refining the construct, identifying the causal mechanisms, delineating the psychobiological correlates, and designing effective intervention programs.

The PCL:YV consists of 20 items that measure the interpersonal, affective, and behavioral dimensions considered to be fundamental to the construct of psychopathy. The PCL:YV manual provides a detailed item description and examples of sources of information to use when rating the item. Each item is scored on a 3-point scale: A rating of 2 indicates that the *item definitely applies*, 1 indicates that it *applies to some extent*, and 0 indicates that the symptom *definitely does not apply* to the individual. Several sources of information are needed to score the PCL:YV—namely, a semistructured interview with the youth and a review of available file and collateral information associated with the youth.

Because of the increasing importance of the PCL:YV in the juvenile justice systems, the manual recommends that it should be used and interpreted in combination with information from a number of sources and should never be the sole criterion for decision making about treatment and/or adjudication. In addition, because the consequences of misuse are especially serious, Forth and colleagues state that it is inappropriate to label a youth as a psychopath and that it is unethical to use scores for exclusion from available treatment programs. Finally, it is not appropriate to rely on PCL:YV scores alone to impose harsher sentences or to use the scores in determining whether a young offender should be tried as an adult.

Psychometric Properties

PCL:YV: Factor Structure, Reliability, and Generalizability

Confirmatory factor analyses suggest that a model with four correlated factors provided a very good explanation for the pattern of covariation among PCL:YV item scores. Four items loaded on an Interpersonal dimension (e.g., impression management, pathological lying) and 4 items on an Affective dimension (e.g., lack of remorse, callous/lack of empathy). Five items loaded on a Behavioral dimension (e.g., impulsivity, lack of goals) and 5 items on an Antisocial dimension (e.g., poor anger control, serious criminal behavior). However, a model with only three correlated factors also provided reasonable fit. The interrater reliability of PCL:YV total scores is high (single-rater ICC of .90 to .96). The internal consistency of PCL:YV total scores is high, with alpha coefficients ranging from .85 to .94. Research has been conducted with institutionalized young offenders, young offenders on probation, psychiatric inpatient youths, and youths in the community. PCL:YV total scores do not appear to be unduly influenced by youths' age, gender, or ethnicity.

PCL:YV Validity

High scores on the PCL:YV are associated with substance use, conduct disorder, oppositional defiant disorder, and attention-deficit/hyperactivity disorder in adolescents.

The PCL:YV has been related to a range of relevant correlates and outcome measures. High PCL:YV scores are associated with academic problems, early onset of antisocial problems, instrumental motives for violence, increased frequency and versatility of nonviolent and violent offenses, and increased institutional nonviolent and violent infractions. In addition, PCL:YV scores are correlated with measures of cognitive, emotional, and social cognitive anomalies largely similar to those identified with adult psychopathic offenders.

Several studies have been conducted to examine the predictive validity of the PCL:YV. PCL:YV scores were predictive of nonviolent and violent/sexual recidivism in juvenile sex offenders and nonviolent and violent recidivism in adjudicated male youths. Recent research has not found the PCL:YV to predict general or violent recidivism in adjudicated female youths.

No controlled evaluations of intervention programs for youths scoring high on the PCL:YV have been completed to date. Research with offenders referred to a substance abuse program found that PCL:YV scores correlated negatively with days in the program, quality of participation, number of consecutive clean urine screens, and researchers' ratings (from discharge summaries) of clinical improvement. There is some encouraging evidence that adolescent offenders with high PCL:YV scores who complete a treatment program have posttreatment violent recidivism rates that are lower than those who serve their dispositions in juvenile correctional facilities. Young offenders are more malleable than adult offenders, and early interventions are more likely to be effective than those directed at adults.

To date, much of the research has been conducted on older male adolescents who have been in contact with the juvenile justice system. Additional data are needed on female adolescents, younger adolescents, nonadjudicated community youths, and ethnically and culturally diverse groups.

Adelle E. Forth and David Kosson

See also Hare Psychopathy Checklist–Revised (2nd edition) (PCL–R); Juvenile Psychopathy; Psychopathy; Psychopathy, Treatment of

Further Readings

Forth, A. E., Kosson, D. S., & Hare, R. D. (2003). *The Hare Psychopathy Checklist: Youth Version.* North Tonawanda, NY: Multi-Health Systems.

Patrick, C. P. (2006). *Handbook of psychopathy.* New York: Guilford.

HATE CRIME

See BIAS CRIME

HCR–20 FOR VIOLENCE RISK ASSESSMENT

The HCR–20 Violence Risk Assessment Scheme is a 20-item violence risk assessment tool, accompanied by a 97-page user's manual. It is intended to structure clinical decisions about the risk for violence posed by adult forensic psychiatric patients, civil psychiatric patients, and criminal offenders (whether mentally disordered or not). The HCR–20 is relevant to the field of law and psychology because violence risk assessment is a psychological decision-making task that routinely transpires within legal and forensic settings. This entry describes the development, content, and conceptual basis of the HCR–20, its intended application, user qualifications, and a summary of evaluation research.

Description and Use

The 20 HCR–20 risk factors are dispersed across three scales: Historical (10 risk factors), Clinical (5 risk factors), and Risk Management (5 risk factors). The Historical scale focuses on past events, experiences, and psychiatric conditions (e.g., past violence, young age at first violence, major mental illness, psychopathy, personality disorder, childhood maladjustment), while the Clinical scale addresses recent functioning (e.g., negative attitudes, psychiatric symptoms, noncompliance, impulsivity). The Risk Management scale deals with factors such as feasibility of plans, stress, and support.

The HCR–20 can be used on a person's entry to a facility such as a forensic hospital, during the course of institutional tenure, on consideration for release to the community, and while a person is being supervised in the community. In all applications and settings, users are encouraged to consider risk management strategies that align with identified HCR–20 risk factors and to incorporate such strategies into their risk reduction efforts.

The HCR–20 was developed as one of the first instruments belonging to the Structured Professional Judgment (SPJ) model of violence risk assessment. Therefore, the HCR–20 structures clinical decisions through (a) specification of a minimum set of risk factors that should be considered in each case, (b) operational definitions of risk factors, (c) explicit coding instructions for risk factors, and (d) recommendations for making final risk judgments about the nature and likelihood of violence and its mitigation. Instruments developed using the SPJ approach share common elements, such as the method of development. Risk factors are selected using the *logical item selection approach* (sometimes called rational, or analytic, item selection) to instrument derivation. This method entails wide consultation of the scientific and professional literatures to select risk factors with broad support. Items are not selected on the basis of empirical associations within single samples because of the threat to generalizability and the risk of selecting sample-specific variables that a purely empirical item selection approach entails. Logical item selection is intended to promote both generalizable applicability and comprehensiveness in risk factor domain coverage.

In considering the individual manifestation of each risk factor for an evaluee, the user rates each item as *absent* (score of 0), *possibly/partially present* (score of 1), or *definitely present* (score of 2). The evaluator then makes a final summary risk rating of *low, moderate*, or *high risk for violence* depending on the number of risk factors present; their relevance to the individual case; and the degree of intervention, supervision, or risk management that is estimated to be necessary to mitigate risk. The HCR–20, like other SPJ instruments, provides a greater emphasis on risk management and risk reduction than do some actuarial approaches. It does this through the inclusion of *dynamic*, or changeable, risk factors (the C- and R-scale risk factors) and the recommendation that these be reevaluated at important decision-making junctures or according to some regular schedule.

Precise numeric algorithms or cut scores are not used for clinical decision making as they are in actuarial prediction methods because of the high likelihood of instability of such algorithms across settings and samples due to idiosyncracies (i.e., capitalization on chance associations) in their derivation.

User qualifications include expertise in violence and in mental health assessment. Common user groups include psychologists, psychiatrists, social workers, psychiatric nurses, and professionals in related fields. Some items (mental illness) may require users to possess advanced degrees (Ph.D. or M.D.), although other users can rate these under supervision or provisionally.

Evaluation Studies

Evaluation research primarily has focused on questions of interrater reliability and predictive validity of either the HCR–20 risk factors (numeric scores) or summary risk judgments. Studies of the risk factors and numeric scores are important to determine whether these can be rated reliably and whether, as they are defined by the HCR–20, they relate to violence. Studies of the summary risk judgments are important to test whether raters, on considering the HCR–20 risk factors and structured decision-making principles, are able to make reliable risk-relevant judgments that also are predictive of violence.

There have been several dozen peer-reviewed published evaluation studies on the HCR–20. These have been conducted across numerous countries (Canada, the United States, Sweden, the United Kingdom, Germany, the Netherlands) and settings (forensic psychiatric, civil psychiatric, prison). Although there is the expected variability in the findings, most research demonstrates acceptable interrater reliability of both the risk factors and the final summary risk judgment.

Similarly, on average, the HCR–20 demonstrates moderate to large effect sizes with violence. Studies have shown that the HCR–20 summary risk ratings of low, moderate, and high risk perform as well as, or better than, numerical (actuarial) use of the HCR–20.

The HCR–20 has been translated into 15 languages. It currently is on Version 2, and Version 3 will be published in 2008 or 2009.

Kevin S. Douglas

See also Risk Assessment Approaches; Violence Risk Assessment

Further Readings

Douglas, K. S., & Kropp, P. R. (2002). A prevention-based paradigm for violence risk assessment: Clinical and research applications. *Criminal Justice and Behavior, 29,* 617–658.

Douglas, K. S., Ogloff, J. R. P., Nicholls, T. L., & Grant, I. (1999). Assessing risk for violence among psychiatric patients: The HCR–20 violence risk assessment scheme and the Psychopathy Checklist: Screening Version. *Journal of Consulting and Clinical Psychology, 67,* 917–930.

Douglas, K. S., Webster, C. D., Hart, S. D., Eaves, D., & Ogloff, J. R. P. (Eds.). (2001). *HCR–20: Violence risk management companion guide.* Burnaby, BC, Canada: Mental Health, Law, and Policy Institute, Simon Fraser University and Department of Mental Health Law & Policy, University of South Florida.

Doyle, M., & Dolan, M. (2006). Predicting community violence from patients discharged from mental health services. *British Journal of Psychiatry, 189,* 520–526.

Webster, C. D., Douglas, K. S., Eaves, D., & Hart, S. D. (1997). *HCR–20: Assessing risk for violence* (Version 2). Burnaby, BC, Canada: Mental Health, Law, and Policy Institute, Simon Fraser University.

Hearsay Testimony

The rules of evidence regarding the admissibility of hearsay testimony are complex, but in general, the law treats hearsay as inadmissible evidence. A number of exceptions to this general rule exist, however, and psychologists have conducted research to examine how jurors evaluate and use hearsay testimony in their decision making. No simple conclusions can be drawn at this point from the research literature owing to the large number of variables that undoubtedly influence juror perceptions of hearsay witnesses.

Hearsay is an out-of-court statement made by an individual (the declarant) that is offered as evidence in court by another individual (the witness, but referred to here as the "hearsay witness" for clarity) to prove the truth of the matter asserted. Repeating a declarant's statement in court is hearsay if the witness is trying to convince the jury that what the declarant said is true, whereas it would not be hearsay if the witness is trying to show that the declarant speaks English, for example. Concerns about the trustworthiness of hearsay arise because the declarant was not under oath at the time of the statement, the demeanor of the declarant while uttering the statement cannot be observed by the jury, and cross-examination of the hearsay witness may not reveal shortcomings in the declarant's statement. The hearsay rule therefore establishes that hearsay is not admissible except in situations where there is some reason to believe that the declarant's statement is trustworthy. The Federal Rules of Evidence identify certain exceptions that are allowed only when the declarant is unavailable to testify (e.g., a statement made under the belief of impending death or a statement against self-interest), whereas other exceptions exist regardless of the declarant's availability (e.g., an excited utterance or statements made for purposes of medical diagnosis). The question of whether statements falling within these exceptions are truly more trustworthy (and thus more useful) to a jury than are statements currently excluded as hearsay is one potential avenue of research that has not yet been explored.

The vast majority of studies examining how jurors evaluate hearsay testimony have used either college students or adult community members as mock jurors, although at least one study presented written questionnaires to jurors who had just delivered a verdict in an actual case that involved hearsay. Evidence has been presented to mock jurors in a variety of ways; frequently, researchers provide participants with written trial summaries, but other studies have used either audiotapes or videotapes of trials or forensic interviews in which the critical variables are experimentally manipulated. Researchers have examined variables related to the declarant (e.g., the declarant's age), the hearsay witness (e.g., his or her relationship to the declarant), how the declarant made his or her statement (e.g., whether a suggestive or nonsuggestive form of questioning was used), and when the statement was made (e.g., the amount of time between the event and the declaration).

One basic question is whether jurors even distinguish between hearsay and nonhearsay evidence. Research into how jurors evaluate hearsay evidence began with studies comparing evidence presented by an eyewitness with the same information presented by a hearsay witness (therefore, the hearsay used in these studies would have been ruled inadmissible). Results suggest that jurors do not overvalue hearsay but instead seem to use the information in an appropriate way. The few studies examining the impact of judicial instructions to disregard inadmissible hearsay have led to mixed results regarding the instructions, but the results are generally consistent with the finding that hearsay is not overvalued as a form of evidence.

Many studies in recent years have focused on how jurors are influenced by hearsay testimony that is admissible either because it meets one of the standard exceptions to the hearsay rule or because of child hearsay statutes adopted by many states beginning in the 1980s. These statutes typically allow for hearsay in cases involving a child declarant who has been the victim of sexual abuse if a court determines that the hearsay information is reliable. The child hearsay statutes allow for hearsay only in cases involving sexual abuse, in part because the prospect of testifying in court in such cases may be especially terrifying to the child victim. Criminal defendants have the right to confront their accusers (provided by the Confrontation Clause of the Sixth Amendment to the U.S. Constitution), but facing the defendant may impair the child witness and reduce the accuracy of his or her testimony. Child hearsay statutes allow for an adult to present the evidence to the jury while sparing the child the trauma of testifying.

Research comparing the in-court testimony of the child victim with some form of adult hearsay witness testimony has yielded inconsistent findings; in some cases, conviction rates are higher when the child testifies, and in other cases the hearsay witness produces a higher conviction rate. No consistent patterns of how jurors evaluate hearsay have yet emerged, a fact that is likely due to the large number of potentially relevant variables and the relatively small number of studies conducted to date.

Consider the special difficulties facing a juror who is evaluating hearsay evidence. Like any other witness, the juror must consider how believable the hearsay witness is in terms of his or her perception, memory, and intention (e.g., is the witness trying to deceive the juror?). Unlike other witnesses, however, the juror must now make inferences as to the believability of the declarant (who may never be seen by the juror). In addition, the juror will need to consider the nature of the relationship between the declarant and the hearsay witness as well as the circumstances regarding how and when the information was shared. Clearly, the task of evaluating hearsay testimony is daunting for both jurors and researchers alike.

Peter Miene and Sarah L. Shurbert

See also Children's Testimony; Child Sexual Abuse; Inadmissible Evidence, Impact on Juries; Juries and Eyewitnesses

Further Readings

Hearsay Reform Conference [Special issue]. (1992). *Minnesota Law Review, 76*(3).

Ross, D. F., Warren, A. R., & McGough, L. S. (Eds.). (1999). Hearsay testimony in trials involving child witnesses [Special issue]. *Psychology, Public Policy, and Law, 5*(2).

HOMICIDE, PSYCHOLOGY OF

Computed across a lifespan of 75 years, there is a 1 in 200 chance that an individual in the United States will be murdered. The frequency of homicide and this startlingly high statistic warrant more concerted efforts to research the psychological underpinnings motivating homicide. The history of the study of the psychology of homicide is replete with theoretical shifts—some of which have led to empirical dead ends and others to tremendous advances. Explaining the motivations of a murderer historically has been a difficult task for psychologists because of the wide array of individual, situational, and cultural variables influencing the development of homicidal behavior. Recent psychological research includes both theoretical and methodological advances that have allowed for new, unprecedented insights into the psychology of homicide.

Theoretical Perspectives

Several theories have been developed over the brief history of psychology seeking explanations of the patterns of homicide. These theories have followed larger movements within psychology. Movements have proceeded from individualistic explanations of homicide in the late 19th and early 20th centuries to more environmental explanations throughout much of the past century. Modern theories seek to address the limitations of previous theories by accounting for a broader range of causes of human behavior. Rather than discussing all the theories, this entry expands on those that are particularly influential and provides an organizational framework to anchor and interpret the changes in these theories.

George Vold organized various theories of the mid 20th century into *spiritistic* and *naturalistic* explanations. To focus on scientific explanations of human behavior, we will not discuss spiritistic accounts of homicide. Naturalistic explanations include those that lend themselves to empirical scrutiny and include hereditary and defectiveness theories, mental deficiency theories, and mental illness theories. Hereditary and defectiveness theories view homicide as the product of biological and genetic causes. Mental deficiency theories argue that homicide is the product of low intelligence. Mental illness theories, espoused first by Sigmund Freud, have been better received than mental deficiency theories. Although Freud's psychoanalytic theory was a starting point for explaining the psychology behind homicide, psychoanalytic theory is now recognized as empirically barren. Freud's influence was lasting, however, with many later contributions revealing Freudian pedigree. Evidence of views of homicide as the product of psychopathology is revealed by the first study on homicide, published in 1898 in the psychology journal *American Journal of Insanity* by Charles Bancroft. Continuing to the present day is the perspective of understanding homicide as the result of pathological psychological manifestations. The theories mentioned so far focus primarily on characteristics internal to an individual that may influence homicidal behavior. There was a focus on more environmental explanations of homicide in the early to mid 20th century, largely in reaction to the previous focus on intra-individual explanations of homicidal behavior.

Environmental Theories

Environmental theories can be described generally as focusing on sources or causes of homicidal behavior outside the individual. Examples of such theories include socialization theories, symbolic interactionism, social structural theories, control theory, and social ecology theory. Socialization theories of homicide and aggression have historically been among the most popular and influential accounts of the motivations for homicide. The sex difference in the commission of violent crimes—including homicide—was one of the first and most obvious observations demanding explanation. Men are more often than women both the offenders and the victims of homicides. Socialization theories argue that men, more than women, have been socialized to view aggression as a permissible means to achieve certain ends. This differential socialization for aggressive behavior in men and women, it is argued, can explain the greater homicide rates among men. While this theory has been well received within psychology, there is growing evidence that an exclusive reliance on this theoretical position to explain homicide patterns leads to incomplete conclusions. Socialization theories push back one step many of the most intriguing questions psychologists working to understand homicide have tried to answer. Why are men and women differentially socialized to behave aggressively? Why are boys and girls differentially receptive to certain aspects of environmental input? Socialization theories cannot provide answers to such questions. Despite the limitations of environmental theories, insight has been gained from the research conducted by social scientists focusing on social and cultural influences. One notable finding reflecting the cultural and demographic variables within cultures has resulted from research on homicide rates across the United States.

Social scientists have identified key sociocultural beliefs and attitudes that vary by region and have analyzed homicide rates as a function of these different beliefs and attitudes. The Southern states in the United States adhere more strongly to a "culture of honor" than other regions. In the Southern states, men act more aggressively than men in the Northern states to protect their honor and their reputation. This difference is arguably generated by exposure to a culture in which honor and reputation are very important in protecting resources. Of the state executions that have occurred since 1977, 82% have occurred in the Southern region of the United States. In addition to these social explanations of homicide, recent breakthroughs have been made in understanding the biological roots of homicide.

Biological Theories

Advances in technology now provide researchers with an unprecedented window into the brain activity of murderers. These technological advancements include functional magnetic resonance imaging, electroencephalography, computed tomography, and positron emission tomography, all of which can be used to study neurological and neuroanatomical abnormalities in the brains of individuals who have perpetrated homicide. Research has shown distinct neurological activity in individuals who have homicidal thoughts or who exhibit violent behaviors.

One perspective explicit in the call for integration of biological (e.g., genetic predispositions), psychological (e.g., psychological disorders), and social (e.g., poverty) explanations of homicide has been aptly named the biopsychosocial perspective. There are limitations to this theory because many of the bidirectional relationships between these three metafactors have not yet been fully explored. Although this is a promising theoretical position, a wealth of new research is yet to be conducted exploring the links between these factors. Inherited predispositions for particular personality disorders may influence how an individual is perceived and treated by others. The way an individual is perceived and treated by others provides a feedback loop, altering cognitions about relationships with others that can influence personality. In sum, there are numerous potential pathways to homicide, and we will be better positioned to expand on these interrelationships with future research.

In many of the cases, links between abnormal cognition and brain activity have been documented. Murderers have been diagnosed with psychological disorders such as antisocial personality disorder or other personality disturbances, psychological stressors, various types of childhood trauma, and drug and alcohol abuse problems. Not all these psychological disorders, however, apply to all killers. Many known factors combine to result in individual differences in brain patterns and cognition and complicate our understanding of the psychology of homicide. We believe that insight gained from various areas of the psychological and other behavioral sciences will provide greater clarity into the motivations and development of homicidal thoughts and behavior. Various theories have recently shed light on homicidal psychology in ways that have previously escaped psychologists.

Evolutionary Perspectives

One particularly powerful theoretical perspective that has yielded insight has been the application of evolutionary perspectives to the study of homicide. An evolutionary psychological approach to homicide is relatively new and allows for stronger anchoring of the psychological sciences with the biological sciences. Evolutionary psychologists argue for distinctions between various types of homicide. Inroads into the psychology of homicide have been made by an attempt to understand the relationships between the victim and the offender. There is a debate among evolutionary psychologists on whether there exist evolved psychological adaptations for homicide or whether homicide occurs as a by-product of adaptations selected for in response to other sets of social adaptive problems (e.g., sexual jealousy, same-sex competition, aggression). An evolutionary psychological approach informs us of many areas in the psychology of homicide that have not been fully explored. If homicides were a recurrent feature of our ancestral environment, for example, selection would have favored antihomicide psychological adaptations (e.g., avoid being killed, minimize the threats posed by others). Research on the existence of these possible evolved psychological adaptations is currently under way.

In many homicides, the offender and the victim are individuals with a history of previously close romantic or familial relationships. There are many known factors linked with homicide among romantic partners, including sexual jealousy and prolonged abuse of women by their partners. These variables demand a deeper understanding of interpersonal relationships that can add to the body of research informing the psychology of homicide. A particularly dangerous time for many women comes when they terminate a romantic relationship. From an evolutionary perspective, this termination prompts psychological adaptations in men that may have functioned in ancestral environments to retain a mate. These adaptations may prompt behavior such as vigilance over the partner's whereabouts, reassessment of the relationship, or, more dangerously, stalking behavior and homicidal rage over the termination of the relationship and a newly established relationship with a rival male.

Among homicides occurring between parents and children, men are more likely than women to kill their children when the children are older, whereas women are more likely to kill their children when the children are younger. Many of the results of analyses of filicides follow from predictions made by evolutionary psychologists. Men, relative to women, may harbor psychological adaptations that monitor genetic relationships between themselves and their putative children (e.g., cues such as female infidelity and their own similarity to the child). The features of homicides by mothers perpetrated against children are very different from those of homicides perpetrated by fathers against children. Mothers more often than fathers kill their children because of factors related to current states (e.g., absence of investing father, resource demands from children) or future prospects (e.g., bias toward future children rather than current children). Prior to the work done by evolutionary psychologists, no research platform had identified the presence of stepparents as a risk factor for child homicide. Researchers have documented a risk factor of filicide that is 100 times greater when a stepparent resides in the household.

Siblicides account for only 1% of all homicides, but analysis of this type of homicide has given us glimpses into the psychology of sibships. Among siblicides, for example, older siblings are more often the perpetrators earlier in life. In contrast, younger siblings are more often the perpetrators later in life—perhaps as an attempt to secure larger portions of inheritance that might otherwise be channeled to older siblings. Additionally, features of the precipitating conflict within the relationship may be revealed by the method of murder. Among siblings, for example, full siblings use a less brutal method of homicide than stepsiblings or half-siblings.

Future Directions and Integration

In addition to the theoretical strides that need to be made in the area, there are many empirical obstacles to be overcome. Data found in national and city-level homicide databases often do not contain enough information relevant for more detailed analyses of homicides. These obstacles are correctable with greater collaboration between law enforcement and social scientists. Another problem with our collective understanding of homicide is media misrepresentations. Those murder cases that are relatively rare (e.g., homicide of women and children, serial murders) are often the cases covered the most by different media sources. Very little is known by the public of the actual risk factors and probabilities of homicide.

The prospect of future research on the psychology of homicide is bright, with the overarching goal of understanding the biological, psychological, and social triggers producing homicidal cognitions and behavior. More detailed pictures of the minds of murderers will be made through the collaborative efforts of criminologists, sociologists, anthropologists, forensic psychiatrists and psychologists, neuropsychologists, clinical/counseling psychologists, and evolutionary psychologists. With such collaborative efforts focusing on the interplay between the biological, psychological, and social correlates of homicide, further refinement of existing theories will lead to future discoveries in the psychology of homicide.

Jennifer Pryor and
Richard L. Michalski

See also Antisocial Personality Disorder; Child Maltreatment; Criminal Behavior, Theories of; Intimate Partner Violence; Media Violence and Behavior; Minnesota Multiphasic Personality Inventory–2 (MMPI–2); Mood Disorders; Psychotic Disorders

Further Readings

Bancroft, C. P. (1898). Subconscious homicide and suicide; their physiological psychology. *American Journal of Insanity, 55,* 263–273.

Buss, D. M., & Duntley, J. D. (2006). The evolution of aggression. In M. Schaller, J. A. Simpson, & D. T. Kenrick (Eds.), *Evolution and social psychology* (pp. 263–285). New York: Psychology Press.

Daly, M., & Wilson, M. (1988). *Homicide.* New York: Aldine de Gruyter.

Daly, M., & Wilson, M. (1997). Crime and conflict: Homicide in evolutionary psychology perspective. *Crime & Justice, 22,* 51–100.

Nisbett, R. E. (1993). Violence and U.S. regional culture. *American Psychologist, 48,* 441–449.

Smith, M. D., & Zahn, M. (2004). *Homicide: A sourcebook of social research.* Thousand Oaks, CA: Sage.

HOPKINS COMPETENCY ASSESSMENT TEST (HCAT)

The Hopkins Competency Assessment Test (HCAT) was developed as a brief screening measure for assessing a patient's capacity to provide informed consent and prepare advance directives regarding medical treatments. As mental health clinicians have increasingly recognized the importance of accurately assessing a patient's ability to provide informed consent, the need for measures to quantify this ability has grown. The HCAT represents one of the first such efforts at developing a standardized approach to evaluating the capacity to provide informed consent by providing a systematic measure of comprehension. Although primarily used in research settings, this measure has the potential to help inform clinical judgments about decision-making competence.

The HCAT, developed by Jeffrey Janofsky, consists of a short description of the informed consent process and the durable power of attorney, followed by six questions (e.g., What are four things a doctor must tell a patient before beginning a procedure?). These questions evaluate the patient's comprehension of the information disclosed and yield a score ranging from 0 to 10, with scores of 3 or lower signifying inadequate comprehension. In their validation study, Janofsky and colleagues provided interrater reliability for the HCAT by analyzing the ratings of two independent examiners on a series of 16 cases. Not surprisingly, given the simplicity of the scoring system, the authors found a correlation of .95, suggesting a high degree of consistency in HCAT scoring. Other forms of reliability, however, have not been analyzed and are potentially less salient. For example, because the clinical condition of many patients changes over time, test-retest reliability is not necessarily a meaningful index of scale reliability.

The content validity of the HCAT has been evaluated in several research studies. For example, Jeffrey S. Janofsky and colleagues compared the results of the HCAT with the opinion of an experienced psychiatrist who was not shown the HCAT results. All individuals whom the psychiatrist considered incompetent had received a score of 3 or less on the HCAT, whereas none of the individuals who "failed" the HCAT were considered competent by the psychologist (i.e., a 100% accuracy rate for determination of competence). Barton, on the other hand, found very little concordance between HCAT scores and clinician opinions regarding competence; however, the latter were based on hospital records indicating that a patient had been considered incompetent (which rarely occurred).

Subsequent studies have analyzed the association between HCAT scores and ratings of patient functional impairment, as well as performance on other measures of cognitive functioning. For example, Sorger et al. (2007) found markedly poorer decision-making ability, based on the HCAT, among elderly patients diagnosed with terminal cancer compared with a physically healthy elderly sample, even after controlling for other group differences (e.g., age, gender, etc). Nearly half (44%) of the terminally ill patients studied "failed" the HCAT compared with only 6% of an ambulatory nursing home comparison sample. Moreover, HCAT scores were significantly correlated with other measures of cognitive functioning including the Mini-Mental State Exam.

Despite strong preliminary data in support of the reliability and validity of the HCAT, this measure is rarely used in either empirical research or clinical practice. There are numerous reasons for the limited popularity of the HCAT. Foremost among them is the "generic" nature of the information presented and assessed, focusing on the concept of informed consent and durable power of attorney rather than a specific treatment decision. Clinical evaluations, and much of the emerging research on informed consent and decision-making competence, focus on a patient's ability to formulate decisions, not simply comprehension of the right to make such treatment decisions. In fact, understanding of informed consent may have little association with the ability to make a rational choice among a set of complicated options. Without tailoring the information disclosed to the patient's particular medical conditions and treatment options, HCAT scores have relatively little bearing on the patient's capacity to consent to a specific intervention. These disadvantages are likely the reason why the HCAT has been eclipsed by the MacArthur instruments, which are designed to assess capacity to consent to treatment and research: MacArthur Competence Assessment Tool for Treatment (MacCAT–T) and MacArthur Competence Assessment Tool for Clinical Research (MacCAT–CR), respectively.

On the other hand, the HCAT has several advantages for clinical research, including brevity, ease of administration, and the generic nature of information presented. Thus, this measure can be easily administered in the context of a battery of assessment instruments (in both research and clinical settings) and is applicable to all patients, regardless of health state or treatment needs. In clinical settings, the HCAT may, with further research, become a useful screening measure that can quickly identify patients who need a more thorough evaluation. Of course, further research is clearly needed before the HCAT gains acceptance as a useful clinical or research instrument. For example, a comparison of the HCAT with more focused measures of decision-making capacity, such as the MacArthur instruments, would help clarify the relationship between the general comprehension of informed consent and the specific decision-making abilities that typically form the basis of such evaluations.

Barry Rosenfeld and
Rebecca A. Weiss

See also Capacity to Consent to Treatment; MacArthur Competence Assessment Tool for Clinical Research (MacCAT–CR); MacArthur Competence Assessment Tool for Treatment (MacCAT–T)

Further Readings

Barton, C. D., Mallik, H. S., Orr, W. B., & Janofsky, J. S. (1996). Clinician's judgment of capacity of nursing home patients to give informed consent. *Psychiatric Services, 47,* 956–959.

Janofsky, J. S., McCarthy, R. J., & Folstein, M. F. (1992). The Hopkins Competency Assessment Test: A brief method for evaluating patients' capacity to give informed consent. *Hospital and Community Psychiatry, 43,* 132–136.

Jones, B. N., Jaygram, G., Samuels, J., & Robinson, H. (1998). Relating competency status to functional status at discharge in patients with chronic mental illness. *Journal of the American Academy of Psychiatry & Law, 26,* 49–55.

Sorger, B. M., Rosenfeld, B., Pessin, H., Timm, A. K., & Cimino, J. (in press). Decision-making capacity in elderly, terminally ill patients with cancer. *Behavioral Sciences and the Law.*

Hypnosis and Eyewitness Memory

The use of hypnosis to enhance the memory of a witness to a crime often results not only in some additional accurate recall of information about the event but also in the incorporation of additional misinformation into the witness's memory of the event and a general increase in his or her confidence in the veracity of recall. Research has shown that hypnosis increases the amount of information that is recalled about an event. This effect often occurs with other techniques also, such as the cognitive interview. When techniques such as hypnosis and the cognitive interview are used to enhance a witness's memory, the amount of new information recalled turns out to be a mixture of accurate and inaccurate information. Furthermore, once accurate and inaccurate information get mixed into a coherent narrative, the witness is typically not very good at distinguishing those aspects of the story that are true from those that are false. The additional information will make the narrative the witness is trying to construct more coherent, and his or her confidence in it will increase. The witness's memory has not been refreshed. A more coherent narrative has been constructed that the witness feels is a more accurate representation of the event he or she is being encouraged to remember.

Admissibility of Hypnotically Refreshed Testimony

The problems associated with hypnotically refreshed testimony have been recognized in hundreds of decisions by American courts. In 1987, the U.S. Supreme Court considered the admissibility of hypnotically refreshed testimony in *Rock v. Arkansas.* Following the per se exclusionary rule, the trial judge in this case determined that the hypnotically refreshed memories of the defendant were inadmissible. There was a growing trend in state courts at the time toward total exclusion of hypnotically refreshed testimony. In *Rock v. Arkansas,* the Supreme Court acknowledged that the possibility for contamination of the witness's memory increases significantly when attempts are made to hypnotically refresh the witness's memory; however, the court determined that the per se exclusionary rule cannot be applied if in doing so a defendant is denied his or her constitutional right to testify. State courts that have to deal with this kind of testimony generally recognize the problems associated with it and often apply the per se exclusionary rule to the hypnotically refreshed testimony of witnesses other than the defendant. Those courts that do not follow the per se exclusionary rule are usually willing to allow hypnotically refreshed testimony only if certain safeguards have been adhered to in the conduct of the hypnotic interview.

Theories of Hypnosis

A number of different theories have been proposed regarding the nature of the hypnotic experience and its relation to the behavior of the hypnotized subject. There are several characteristics of the hypnotic state that distinguish it from the normal waking state. Ernest Hilgard has proposed the following list: increased suggestibility, enhanced imagery and imagination, subsidence of the planning function, and reduction in reality testing. Hilgard contends that hypnotic phenomena often reflect a split in consciousness. It appears that the experience of the hypnotized subject is dissociated from the subsystems of control that are regulating the subject's perceptions and behavior. The major alternative to this point of view is sociocognitive theory. The emphasis in sociocognitive theory is on the social psychological relationship between the hypnotist and the subject. According to this theory, there is no need to propose that the subject has entered into some kind of trance state or that some kind of split in consciousness has occurred; the hypnotized subject is engaged in the performance of a role in a social situation that is largely under the control of the hypnotist. Hilgard acknowledges the fundamental importance of the social psychological aspect of hypnotic phenomena, but he contends that changes in consciousness occur when a subject is hypnotized that cannot be accounted for by efforts on the part of a compliant subject to please the hypnotist. In their theory of dissociated control, Erik Woody and Kenneth Bowers propose that hypnotized subjects are in a state temporarily like that of patients with frontal lobe damage. According to their theory, the perceptions and behavior of the hypnotized subject are under the regulation of lower-level subconscious systems that are not being monitored by the frontal lobe executive.

If hypnotized subjects process information primarily at a subconscious level, then the kinds of rules that are applied in the evaluation of information by hypnotized subjects are likely to be very different from those applied in the conscious rational analysis of information. Seymour Epstein has provided considerable support for the idea that much of the information processing that occurs in our everyday lives consists of rapid evaluations of environmental stimuli that depend largely on subconscious schemata associated with emotionally significant past events. What we might have with hypnosis is an exaggeration of this aspect of normal experience. If the subconscious experiential system dominates information processing during hypnosis, then what may occur is not that missing material gets dragged up from the unconscious to fill in the gaps in memory but that the gaps in memory are filled in with plausible information that is suggested either directly or indirectly during the hypnotic interview. It turns out that hypnosis tends to produce this kind of effect whenever the subject is required to produce a narrative reconstruction of a highly emotional event. In studies that employ stimuli of low emotional impact, hypnosis does not produce an increase in the amount of information recalled. Furthermore, it is with free recall that we see the effect of hypnosis on the amount of information recalled; when specific questions are asked or when the subject is asked to decide between various alternatives, responses are restricted so that the tendency to produce more is not revealed.

Research Findings

Some individuals are more susceptible to hypnosis than others, and there has been a good deal of research devoted to the investigation of the individual differences involved. Subjects who score high on tests of hypnotic susceptibility are generally more suggestible than those who are not very susceptible to hypnosis. Hypnotically susceptible individuals have also been found to have greater capacity for sustained attentional focus; they process information more rapidly and more easily, and they have a more active imagination and a more active fantasy life. It appears that the experiential system is particularly active in individuals who are highly susceptible to hypnosis. Subjects who are high in susceptibility to hypnosis appear to be particularly prone to accept misleading information, especially when the hypnotic interview is conducted by a trained hypnotist. Disturbingly, this is the situation where the greatest inflation of the subject's confidence in the accuracy of his or her memory is likely to occur also.

Subjects who are highly susceptible to hypnosis can be easily led to construct vivid and detailed false memories of childhood experiences in situations that are analogs to the clinical interview when various memory-enhancing techniques are used, including hypnosis, guided mnemonic restructuring, and visualization instructions. These kinds of results are particularly relevant to the courtroom battles based on repressed memories of childhood sexual abuse. Studies of hypnotic age regression show that hypnosis and other memory-enhancing techniques can produce fantastic memories of fictional events, such as vivid and detailed memories of the hospital environment the day after birth. Michael Nash and his colleagues were able to hypnotically age regress hypnotically susceptible subjects back to an event that allegedly occurred when they were 3 years old. The instructions that were used produced memories in the majority of subjects of a transitional object, such as a teddy bear, which when checked against the memory of the mother often turned out to be false. Subjects continued to believe in these false memories when they were questioned about them subsequently in a normal waking state. Thus, vivid and detailed memories of childhood events that never actually occurred can be produced with hypnotic age regression; however, Nash found that it does not appear that hypnotized subjects in these studies are transformed to a childlike state of mind.

The degree to which sexual trauma during childhood interferes with the victim's memory of the event or series of events is not a question that lends itself to experimental analysis. Even with the more general question of the effects of arousal on the memory of a witness, there are limits to the degree of stress that the subjects in our experiments may be exposed to. When staged events are used to examine the effect of high levels of arousal on a witness's memory of the perpetrator of a crime, it is generally found that arousal has a debilitating effect. During emotional events, the attention of the witness is often focused on those aspects of the environment that have the greatest significance for his or her well-being, such as a weapon used by the perpetrator in the commission of a crime. The evidence suggests that due to poorer encoding of target features during these kinds of events, the witness's ability to recognize the target in a subsequent lineup will be impaired.

When hypnosis is used to refresh a witness's memory of an emotional event, pressure is placed on the witness to remember aspects of the event that were not initially processed very well, if at all. Research has found that hypnotized witnesses do not perform any better on photographic lineups than witnesses who have not been hypnotized. Instead, the hypnotized witness may become particularly susceptible to cues that direct attentional focus to a particular individual in the lineup, leading in some cases to misidentification of an innocent suspect. Staged-event studies have also revealed that the level of anxiety experienced by a witness during a staged event is negatively correlated with the degree of confidence subsequently expressed by the witness in a decision he or she has made about the presence of the perpetrator in a lineup. This finding has important implications regarding the cohesiveness of memories of highly emotional incidents. Regardless of the actual accuracy of a witness's recollection of a stressful event, if he or she is less confident about it, then there is an increase in the probability that misinformation will be incorporated into the witness's recollection of the event when he or she is questioned about it. Several studies on the effects of hypnosis on memory have produced results consistent with this hypothesis. After exposure to emotionally arousing stimuli, subjects with high levels of hypnotic susceptibility showed an increased tendency to fill in the gaps in their memories while under hypnosis, taking information suggested by the hypnotist or confabulating on their own.

Robert K. Bothwell

See also Cognitive Interview; Eyewitness Memory; Postevent Information and Eyewitness Memory; Reconstructive Memory; Repressed and Recovered Memories

Further Readings

Deffenbacher, K. A., Bornstein, B. H., Penrod, S. D., & McGorty, E. K. (2004). A meta-analytic review of the effects of high stress on eyewitness memory. *Law and Human Behavior, 28,* 687–706.

Epstein, S. (1994). Integration of the cognitive and the psychodynamic unconscious. *American Psychologist, 49,* 709–724.

Hilgard, E. R. (1977). *Divided consciousness: Multiple controls in human thought and action.* New York: Wiley.

Kebbell, M. R., & Wagstaff, G. F. (1998). Hypnotic interviewing: The best way to interview eyewitnesses? *Behavioral Sciences and the Law, 16,* 115–129.

Kirsch, I., & Lynn, S. J. (1995). The altered state of hypnosis: Changes in the theoretical landscape. *American Psychologist, 50,* 846–858.

Nash, M. R. (1987). What, if anything, is age regressed about hypnotic age regression? A review of the empirical literature. *Psychological Bulletin, 102,* 42–52.

Ready, D. J., Bothwell, R. K., & Brigham, J. C. (1997). The effects of hypnosis, context reinstatement, and anxiety on eyewitness memory. *International Journal of Clinical and Experimental Hypnosis, 45,* 55–68.

Rock v. Arkansas, 483 U.S. 44 (1987).

Scheflin, A. W., & Shapiro, J. L. (1989). *Trance on trial.* New York: Guilford Press.

Spanos, N. P., & Chaves, J. F. (Eds.). (1989). *Hypnosis: The cognitive-behavioral perspective.* New York: Prometheus Books.

Spanos, N. P., Burgess, C. A., Burgess, M. F., Samuels, C., & Blois, W. O. (1999). Creating false memories of infancy with hypnotic and non-hypnotic procedures. *Applied Cognitive Psychology, 13,* 201–218.

Steblay, N. M., & Bothwell, R. K. (1994). Evidence for hypnotically refreshed testimony: The view from the laboratory. *Law and Human Behavior, 18,* 635–651.

Whitehouse, W. G., Orne, E. C., Dinges, D. F., Bates, B. L., Nadon, R., & Orne, M. T. (2005). The cognitive interview: Does it successfully avoid the dangers of forensic hypnosis? *American Journal of Psychology, 118,* 213–234.

Woody, E. Z., & Bowers, K. S. (1994). A frontal assault on dissociated control. In S. J. Lynn & J. W. Rhue (Eds.), *Dissociation: Clinical and theoretical perspectives* (pp. 52–79). New York: Guilford Press.

I

Identification Tests, Best Practices in

Perhaps the ultimate form of eyewitness evidence is the identification of a suspect from a live or photo lineup, as opposed to more general information provided by a witness, such as a verbal description of an event. Best-practice recommendations in this area are based on a combination of some good procedures used by law enforcement for decades, sound logic and probability theory, basic psychological principles, and dedicated psychology–law research. The primary goal of a good identification procedure is to let the witness's memory be the basis of his or her decision, rather than any implicit or explicit influences that derive from either the procedure used or the nature of the lineup itself. And, of course, the desired outcome of a good procedure is to secure either an accurate identification of a guilty suspect or a "Don't know" or "Not there" response if the actual offender is not in the lineup.

There are at least four techniques for obtaining an identification from an eyewitness, and most of the best-practice procedural recommendations apply in all of them (as opposed to filler-selection issues, for example, which don't apply for at least one of the techniques). The two techniques that have received the most attention by researchers and the legal community, and are the primary focus of this entry, are live lineups (also known as identification parades in the United Kingdom and some other countries) and photo lineups (also known as photo arrays or photo spreads and sometimes called a "6-pack" in the United States, in reference to the most common number of photos used). The other

two procedures are the field identification procedure (often called a "showup"), in which just one individual is shown to a witness, usually soon after an event has occurred and within close proximity to the scene, and the in situ procedure, in which a witness is asked to view a group of individuals in a relatively informal setting, such as the lobby area of a police station or a public location that a suspect is known to frequent, such as a bar or a place of employment.

The showup is thought by most eyewitness researchers, and some courts, to be "inherently suggestive," and few researchers would recommend it as a best-practice technique. The two most obvious potential advantages of a showup are that a potentially dangerous person could be detained on the basis of a positive identification, often with the aim of protecting a person who might be revictimized otherwise, and that an innocent suspect could be quickly exonerated. The showup procedure is included as a legitimate option in the U.S. National Institute of Justice (NIJ) document "Eyewitness Evidence: A Guide for Law Enforcement," published in 1999, and the Wisconsin Department of Justice's "Model Policy and Procedure for Eyewitness Identification," released in 2005. Despite the situations in which the potential advantages of a showup might outweigh the otherwise prudent decision to conduct either a live or a photo lineup with nonsuspect fillers, the best practice-recommendation is to think of a lineup as the default procedure. It is not unreasonable, for example, to expect that law enforcement can use current and near-future technology to construct an electronic photo lineup at a crime scene using a digital image of a suspect who was found in the vicinity and benefit from the immediacy associated with the showup and the safe-guards associated with a lineup.

The relatively informal in situ identification procedure tries to take advantage of a naturally occurring situation where a witness gets a chance to observe a suspect when the suspect does not know that he or she is being observed for that purpose. As mentioned, this often happens when a suspect is casually waiting in a police station regarding an incident, usually with a number of other people, and a witness to the incident is asked to look through a door or window to see if he or she recognizes anyone. Although this technique has received little attention in the eyewitness research literature, the legal community typically accepts the results, as long as the basic principles of the more common and formalized procedures discussed below are included. Also, it is common that a more formal identification procedure will follow if an identification is made.

Viewing mug shots could also be construed as an identification procedure, but the phrase *identification test* implies that the police have a suspect in mind and that they are "testing" their hypothesis that the suspect is the offender (as opposed to testing the witness's memory per se). A mug shot viewing is typically used when the police do not yet have a suspect, so they show potentially hundreds of photos of people who have been arrested in the past for a similar crime and/or who match a general description of the offender. The result of a mug shot viewing could be a relatively positive identification from an eyewitness, but typically, the procedure just helps to narrow down what the witness remembers about an offender (e.g., "He had beady eyes like Number 55, long blond hair like Number 132," etc.).

Finally, a witness could be asked to work with a sketch artist to create a likeness of the offender, or use a facial composite system, but these procedures are more in the realm of witness recall as opposed to an identification test.

Constructing the Lineup

This aspect of identification procedures has received the most attention from eyewitness researchers, and several of the issues are addressed in detail in separate entries. A prototypic lineup consists of one suspect and at least five known-innocent fillers (variously called distracters, foils, stand-ins, shills, and other terms). *Known innocent* means that the police have no reason to believe that the person could have committed the crime in question, as opposed to meaning that the

person has never committed a crime in general. The logical power of this single-suspect lineup is that the identification of anyone other than the suspect is a "known error," because that person could not have committed the crime. At that point, the police need to consider several possibilities—the suspect is not the offender, the witness's memory is not sufficient to recognize the offender if he or she is present, the offender's appearance is sufficiently different from the way he or she appeared at the time of the crime so that the witness cannot recognize the offender, or perhaps the witness is reluctant to identify the offender even if he or she is present.

The number of fillers is not as important as the degree to which the fillers serve to make the lineup unbiased against the suspect, yet they should not be so similar to one another and the suspect that it becomes very unlikely for even a witness with a good memory of the offender to recognize the offender if he or she is present. The best-practice recommendation here is that fillers be chosen based on their match to the witness's description of the offender, as opposed to their match with the suspect's actual appearance, with certain logical qualifiers. Suppose, for example, that a witness describes an offender as White, male, 30–35 years old, and with a distinctive feature, such as an "insect tattoo on his right cheek." Suppose further that the suspect in the case has a spider tattoo in the correct location. The other lineup members should also be White, male, 30 to 35 years old, but they need only have an "insect tattoo" on their right cheek (a bee, a scorpion, or even different kinds of spiders) in order to qualify as good fillers. Requiring the fillers to have the identical spider tattoo or covering up the suspect's tattoo and the corresponding spot on the fillers' faces serves only to remove a potentially useful memory cue for the witness to recognize the offender if he is in the lineup.

Instructions to the Witness

The most common instruction, recommended by eyewitness researchers since the early 1980s, is "The offender may or may not be present." The logic of this instruction, supported by empirical research, is that it provides witnesses with a "None of the above" alternative and counters to some extent any tendency of the witness to assume that the police wouldn't be bothering with an identification procedure if they didn't have the "right" person. This tendency might lead to witnesses guessing or choosing someone they don't feel very confident about, which is a primary concern because it is of course possible that the suspect is in fact not the offender. The NIJ Guide for Law Enforcement goes a step further on this specific point and includes the additional instruction, "It is just as important to clear innocent persons from suspicion as to identify guilty parties."

At this point, it is important to discuss the potentially confusing use of the terms *suspect* and *offender* in this context. Many law enforcement agencies have actually changed their wording of the caution that the offender may or may not be present to read that the *suspect* may or may not be present, most often with a well-intentioned motive not to bias witnesses, but that wording change is not a legitimate substitution. It is just that *suspect* has become a more acceptable term to use for many people in law enforcement and the media when referring to offenders. Television viewers are exposed to this tendency on a regular basis on shows where a person is on videotape driving at well over the speed limit on the wrong side of the road, crashing into other cars and sometimes attempting to run down or shoot at police officers, all the while being referred to as "the suspect" by the narrator (just saying "the driver" would solve the problem). Granted, in some cases, the term refers to the fact that the driver is *suspected* of being involved in the bank robbery that initiated the chase, but it can blur the line between describing a person who by all reasonable standards is currently committing a crime (an offender) versus someone who has been apprehended after a crime has occurred as a possible candidate for the offender (a suspect). It also comes up when the media report that the "police are looking for two suspects in the case; the first suspect is described as male, White, average build," when they really mean to say that the police are looking for two *offenders*, the first of whom matches that description. *Suspect* would only work in that example if there's some reason to believe that the crime did not really occur. Of course many law enforcement policies—and the NIJ Guide, for example—do use an appropriate alternative for offender, such as "the person who committed the crime."

There are other important points to include as instructions for witnesses prior to participating in an identification test, detailed in the NIJ Guide, the Wisconsin Model, and other sources. In some cases, the relevance of a particular instruction depends on the particular procedure used, but one that deserves special attention concerns witnesses' confidence in their decision. Eyewitness researchers are in general agreement that it is crucial to get some expression of witness confidence at the time of the identification decision, instead of relying on what is provided at trial, often many months later. The concern is that a witnesses' experiences after making an identification might influence their confidence, most likely in an upward direction. These experiences can range from the unavoidable implication that the witness has identified the suspect, when the witness is summoned to testify at the trial against that suspect (now the defendant), to something subtle, such as a smile or a nod, to something explicit, such as "Good, you've picked the right person!" Therefore, it is recommended that witnesses be told prior to viewing the lineup that they are expected to state, in their own words, and not necessarily on a scale of some kind, how certain they are of their decision and that this confidence rating be obtained prior to any kind of feedback from the person conducting the lineup, subtle or otherwise.

Conducting the Identification Procedure

Almost all the research on procedure concerns photo and live lineups. The instructions for the showup and in situ procedures are the most important part, assuming reasonable safeguards against influencing a witness to say "Yes" or "No" in the case of the showup and against choosing a particular person in the case of the in situ procedure. The most recommended safeguard for all identification tests, except the showup (where it is not possible), is the double-blind procedure, the rationale for which is to avoid unintentionally influencing the witness's decision and, thereby, the outcome of the lineup procedure. In general, a double-blind lineup can be accomplished in one of at least two ways: The person conducting the lineup does not know who the suspect is and/or cannot see which photo or person the witness is viewing or discussing at any particular time. In practice, it can be difficult if not impossible to conduct a live lineup in such a way that the administrator cannot see the lineup members, so the only reasonable option is usually to have another person administer the lineup. With a photo lineup, however, there are at least two ways for a person who knows the suspect to conduct the procedure in a double-blind fashion (assuming a sequential presentation, as detailed below). The first, low-tech, approach is to randomize the position of the photos (but ensuring that the first photo is a filler) and then use folders or envelopes to conceal the photos until the witness views them, at an angle (or with some sort of small obstruction) that blocks the administrator's view. This way, if the witness says something like "Number 4 looks a lot like the person I saw," the lineup administrator does not know whether the witness is referring to the suspect or a filler photo. The relatively high-tech approach is to use a computer to administer the lineup, with built-in randomization and with the screen positioned in such a way that the administrator can't see it. In fact, there are computer applications available to construct and present the lineup and record the procedure.

The other major recommendation is to present the members of a lineup one at a time (a sequential lineup), as opposed to all at once (a simultaneous lineup), and that the sequential presentation be done in a very particular manner (not *just* one at a time). The rationale for the sequential lineup is that it reduces the tendency of witnesses to choose the person from the lineup who looks *most* like the offender they saw (a relative judgment strategy), as opposed to choosing a lineup member only if he or she matches the witness's memory trace for the offender beyond some threshold level (an absolute judgment strategy). Of course, if the suspect is the offender, then the outcome from both strategies should be the same, but in the case where the suspect is not the offender, the relative judgment strategy can increase the chance of that person being chosen.

There is some criticism about the recommendation for a sequential procedure, based largely on the concern that the rate of witnesses accurately identifying guilty suspects might be lower. There are, in fact, some data showing that the rates for choosing suspects can be lower overall with the sequential procedure, but it is difficult if not impossible to determine if that means guilty people are being identified less often—the lower rate might mean that fewer innocent suspects are being chosen. Also, it has been argued that some of the "accurate" choices of guilty suspects from simultaneous lineups are essentially lucky guesses, which are less likely to occur with the sequential technique, and that lucky guesses are not a legitimate route to justice. So the best-practice recommendation is to use a double-blind, sequential procedure. Step-by-step details are available in the NIJ Guide and the Wisconsin Model.

Recording the Procedure

Ideally, the entire identification procedure would be video- and audiotaped. The camera(s) should be positioned such that the witness and the photos or persons in the lineup are viewable, and a microphone that can pick up any of the witness's spontaneous utterances should be used. This recommendation is not made with the intent of monitoring the conduct of the person administering the lineup but to capture the procedure and outcome in a way that provides as much information as possible, especially the confidence statement. In fact, most eyewitness researchers consider what happens during the identification procedure as the *only* relevant information, as opposed to what the witness says about it at trial. As mentioned previously, computers are ideal for administering the double-blind photo lineup procedure, with digital cameras that record directly to a disc or a hard drive, and for monitoring decision times and the order in which the photos were displayed.

John Turtle

See also Computer-Assisted Lineups; Confidence in Identifications, Malleability; Double-Blind Lineup Administration; Lineup Filler Selection; Lineup Size and Bias; Mug Shots; Showups; Simultaneous and Sequential Lineup Presentation

Further Readings

Kassin, S. M. (1998). Eyewitness identification procedures: The fifth rule. *Law and Human Behavior, 22,* 649–653.

Turtle, J., Lindsay, R. C. L., & Wells, G. L. (2003). Best practice recommendations for eyewitness evidence procedures: New ideas for the oldest way to solve a case. *Canadian Journal of Police and Security Services, 1,* 5–18.

U.S. National Institute of Justice. (1999). *Eyewitness evidence: A guide for law enforcement* (NIJ 178240). Washington, DC: Author.

Wells, G. L., & Luus, C. A. E. (1990). Police lineups as experiments: Social methodology as a framework for properly-conducted lineups. *Personality and Social Psychology Bulletin, 16,* 106–117.

Wells, G. L., Malpass, R. S., Lindsay, R. C. L., Turtle, J. W., & Fulero, S. M. (2000). From the lab to the police station: A successful application of eyewitness research. *American Psychologist, 55,* 581–598.

Wisconsin Department of Justice, Bureau of Training and Standards for Criminal Justice. (2005). *Model Policy and Procedure for Eyewitness Identification.* Retrieved from http://www.doj.state.wi.us/dles/tns/EyewitnessPublic.pdf

Inadmissible Evidence, Impact on Juries

What is the impact on juror verdicts of inadmissible evidence that surfaces in the courtroom and of judicial instruction to disregard such information? This question has been addressed in laboratory research by attention to its two component parts. First, the research establishes that the presence of inadmissible evidence has a significant impact on juror verdicts in line with the evidentiary slant of the information: The level of guilty verdicts rises with pro-prosecution evidence and decreases with pro-acquittal evidence. Second, the research demonstrates that once inadmissible evidence is present, a corrective judicial admonition does not fully eliminate the impact of the inadmissible information.

These conclusions come from a 2006 meta-analysis that summarized 175 experimental tests, from 48 studies and 8,474 research participants. Confidence in the findings is strengthened by the demonstrated convergence of data from multiple independent labs; 42 research teams contributed to the data set, no more than 6 tests coming from any one lab. Ninety-one percent of the tests involved criminal cases. Civil and criminal cases showed similar effects.

The greatest number of laboratory tests involve inadmissible evidence that favors the prosecution in criminal cases. When research participants heard problematic pro-prosecution evidence and were admonished to disregard it, the conviction rate was 10% higher than a no-exposure control group. Of additional interest is the finding that exposure to contested evidence that was subsequently ruled *admissible* accentuated that information, raising conviction rates 34% above the control group and significantly strengthening the impact of that evidence beyond its original influence.

Inadmissible evidence violates due process, and legal evidentiary standards dictate that a curative instruction is appropriate to minimize the risk that the jury is misled by the unacceptable information. Psychologists posit that jurors are likely to follow the prescribed corrective action only if motivated and able to do so. Research shows that jurors do attempt to use information in a fair manner and to align their decisions with the judge's instructions. However, juror motivation also may be affected by reactance—resistance to a judge's admonition when it is seen as constraining effective deliberation—unless the judge can offer a clear and compelling reason as to why the information is unreliable or irrelevant to the case. Jurors may resist giving up information that they find probative.

Even when they are motivated to do so, jurors' ability to effectively purge inadmissible evidence from their decision making is questionable. At times, the problem may be one of disentangling an inadmissible element from a broader coherent "story" that has developed in the juror's mind and of separating out any inferences that grow from that bit of evidence. Contamination of a juror's knowledge by inadmissible evidence may be exacerbated by simple source confusion: As the trial proceeds, jurors may misremember the origin of a piece of information—for example, nonevidentiary pretrial publicity versus testimony evidence—or fail to recall whether it is legally admissible. In addition, contested evidence is likely to become salient to jurors, and the judge's subsequent instruction to disregard the information may produce what researchers refer to as a "white bear effect"—an inability to *not* think of the "white bear" once the thought is forbidden.

Recent experimental research demonstrates that judges, like jurors, have difficulty ignoring inadmissible evidence. Specifically, the decisions of a sample of 265 judges in simulated cases were shown to be affected by nonevidentiary information from pretrial settlement proposals, conversations protected by attorney-client privilege, prior sexual history of a rape victim, prior convictions of a plaintiff, and defendant cooperation with the government. An impact on decisions was apparent even when the judges were reminded or they determined that the information was inadmissible. This sample of judges, however, was able to disregard information obtained in violation of a defendant's right to counsel and as the outcome of a search when deciding on probable cause issues.

Directed forgetting of inadmissible evidence prompts a very difficult cognitive task. Research firmly demonstrates the failure of judicial instruction to effectively eliminate jurors' use of inadmissible evidence, particularly in the absence of a good reason for rejecting the information. Far less research has addressed potential solutions to this problem. Jurors do respond to specific procedural information that they can understand and appreciate. Therefore, remedies may be found in the addition of up-front (pretrial) direction, clear explanations during trial admonitions, and reinforcing charges at the end of the trial. Lessons from broader memory research suggest that any means to intercept errant information before or at the time it is encoded into memory is likely to be more successful than an attempt to remove the inadmissible evidence after it is merged into memory. Jury deliberation also may be expected to limit the influence of inadmissible evidence; however, few studies have addressed this specific hypothesis. The research and legal communities will benefit from future research that attends to creative solutions for the problem of inadmissible evidence.

Nancy K. Steblay

See also Juries and Judges' Instructions; Pretrial Publicity, Impact on Juries; Story Model for Juror Decision Making

Further Readings

Steblay, N., Hosch, H., Culhane, S., & McWethy, A. (2006). The impact on juror verdicts of judicial instruction to disregard inadmissible evidence: A meta-analysis. *Law and Human Behavior, 30,* 469–492.

Wistrich, A,. Guthrie, C., & Rachlinski, J. (2005). Can judges ignore inadmissible information? The difficulty of deliberately disregarding. *University of Pennsylvania Law Review, 153,* 1251–1345.

Insanity Defense, Juries and

The insanity defense is one of the most controversial legal defenses in the U.S. legal system, as demonstrated through the constantly evolving insanity laws and the public response to insanity cases. There is extensive evidence to suggest that juror attitudes, preconceived notions, and case-relevant biases and beliefs affect their judgments in insanity defense cases. Research provides strong support for the finding that negative attitudes toward the insanity defense have a robust effect on mock jurors' verdict decisions. Additionally, there is evidence that jurors, rather than relying on instructions and legal definitions, tend to rely on their own commonsense notions of what is considered sane and insane and to use these in determining their verdicts. At the same time, a number of other factors, such as the severity of the crime, characteristics of the perpetrator, and knowledge levels, may moderate the relationship between attitude and

verdict, and these factors warrant further investigation. This entry briefly examines the evolution of insanity law, jurors' attitudes to and knowledge of the insanity defense, the influences on jurors' insanity verdicts, and the role of experts in insanity trials.

The insanity defense can be raised in criminal cases when a defendant has a mental illness that interferes with his or her capacity for criminal responsibility. The concept underlying the insanity defense is that it is fundamentally unfair to hold a person responsible for a crime when he or she lacks the capacity to form intent because of a mental illness. The idea that certain defendants should not be held responsible for their actions due to their mental state has been well established for centuries, starting with the "wild beast" test of the 1700s. Since then, the law has struggled to establish guidelines as to what constitutes insanity. This has led to a constantly evolving standard in these cases.

The changing standards for insanity reflect the difficult nature of the defense. The M'Naghten test, established in 1843, held that defendants were not responsible for their actions if they could not tell that their actions were wrong at the time they were committed. This test was subsequently criticized because it put heavy emphasis on the cognitive aspects of right and wrong but failed to take into consideration the issue of the defendant's volitional control. The M'Naghten test underwent many changes, each altering the balance of emphasis between the cognitive and volitional underpinnings of insanity and also changing the definitions of these concepts. Some of the standards currently in use include the M'Naghten test; the M'Naghten test with an allowance for the defendant having an "irresistible impulse"; the Durham or "product" rule, requiring only that the crime be the product of a mental illness; the American Legal Institute standard, which includes both cognitive and volitional reasons for insanity, and the Insanity Defense Reform Act of 1984, which includes only the cognitive element and requires the mental illness to be severe. Many of these changes in standards were in response to highly publicized insanity defense cases in which the verdicts were viewed unfavorably by the public. The most influential of these cases was the trial of John Hinkley for the attempted assassination of President Reagan.

Juror Decision Making in Insanity Cases

The changes in the law described above have resulted in multiple insanity standards, which raises the question of how jurors will respond to these variations and if they are able to distinguish among them. The standards that jurors are supposed to use in any specific insanity defense case are delivered to the jurors via jury instructions. Research has investigated jurors' responses to these various standards as presented in jury instructions. This research has shown that jury decision making is not substantially affected by the standard that is used or by variations in jury instructions. Additionally, jurors who are given instructions and those who are given no instructions do not seem to significantly differ in their decisions. Whether a standard is present and, if so, which type of standard is used appears to have little effect on jurors' ultimate decisions, even though the standards are based on very different legal notions. This should not be interpreted to mean that jurors do not take the instructions into consideration when they are deliberating, nor does it indicate that they do not take their duties seriously. Some scholars suggest that jurors interpret insanity cases based on their commonsense understanding of mental illness and of the defense itself. It is argued by Norman Finkel (1988) and others that jurors may not distinguish among the varying standards because they rely on their own interpretation of insanity when judging the appropriateness of the defense.

If jurors are basing their decisions in insanity cases in part on their commonsense understanding of the defense, it is important to determine what this commonsense understanding might be. Michael Perlin has written extensively about the common misunderstandings that might be relied on in decision making in insanity cases. He identified eight "myths" that drive public perceptions of the insanity defense. These myths include the belief that the insanity defense is overused, defendants who plead insanity are usually faking, the insanity defense is used almost exclusively in cases that involve violent crimes, pleading not guilty by reason of insanity (NGRI) is a strategy used by criminal defense attorneys to get their clients acquitted, there is no risk to the defendant who pleads insanity, trials involving an NGRI defense almost always feature "battles of the experts," NGRI acquittees spend much less time in custody than do defendants convicted of the same offense, and NGRI acquittees are quickly released from custody. Perlin's myths are examples of the flawed knowledge about insanity that exists in the public domain. Each of these myths has been refuted by empirical findings from multiple sources. However, this misinformation has the potential to negatively influence jurors' consideration of the insanity defense in specific cases.

In addition to the faulty knowledge that prospective jurors might have, jurors may also have preexisting attitudes about the insanity defense that could affect their decision making. Surveys as well as experimental studies have revealed that people hold strong negative attitudes toward this defense. Many prospective jurors report viewing the insanity defense as a loophole in the legal system through which dangerous mentally ill people could reenter society or by which truly guilty criminals who were not mentally ill could be acquitted. In addition, people perceive the insanity defense as one that is too frequently used as well as abused. Research also indicates that negative attitudes about mental illness are largely fueled by this misinformation about mental illness. For example, people have a tendency to overestimate the number of defendants who plead insanity and who are acquitted by reason of insanity, while they tend to underestimate the period of confinement for insanity acquittees. The relationship between insanity knowledge and attitudes is such that more accurate knowledge is related to more favorable attitudes.

Negative attitudes have been shown to decrease jurors' willingness to consider and to render NGRI verdicts. Research indicates that attitudes toward mental illness and the insanity defense exert significant influence on mock jurors' verdicts in insanity cases, even more so than the case facts. Jurors with negative attitudes are far less likely to render NGRI verdicts. Attitudes toward the death penalty are also related to decision making in insanity cases. Jurors with positive attitudes toward the death penalty are crime-control oriented, tend to hold negative attitudes toward the insanity defense, and are significantly less willing to render NGRI verdicts.

Another focus of research on the origins of potential jurors' beliefs about the insanity defense has been in the study of insanity prototypes, or the concept of the typical insanity defendant. In several prototype studies, researchers have found that jurors' notions of insanity included extreme impairments at the time of the offense as well as extreme psychosis. They tended to inflate symptoms of psychosis, as well as portray the offender as extremely violent. These prototypes could produce expectations about defendants in insanity trials that could in turn affect decision making, although there has been little research on this phenomenon.

Once a trial in which insanity is claimed begins, it is the responsibility of the jurors to assess the evidence presented to them and the viability of the insanity defense in that case. Research has investigated the impact of varying case facts on decision making in insanity cases. Mock jurors seem to construe case information differently depending on their prior beliefs and attitudes. As noted above, there is a tendency for jurors in insanity defense cases to rely more on their own notions of insanity than on the facts of the case. The type of mental illness can be influential, and much research has focused on schizophrenic defendants. Some case facts are also influential in insanity verdicts. For example, some research has found that defendants who had been more reckless, committed more gruesome crimes, and behaved with premeditation were found guilty more often.

Research has also investigated the impact of the personal characteristics of the jurors themselves. The importance of personal contact with mental illness (either through a personal experience or that of a relative or a friend) has been examined, with mixed results. For example, contact with people with mental illness has a somewhat positive effect on attitudes toward mental illness. Studies have shown that college students who had direct interactions with people suffering from depression or psychosis made more positive attributions about the causes of these illnesses. On the other hand, some research has found that those suffering from mental illnesses were less accepting of others who had mental illnesses. Juror gender has also been found to exert an influence on verdict in a limited number of studies; there is some indication that females may be more accepting than males of the insanity defense and of mental illness as a factor in determining criminal responsibility.

Expert Witnesses and the Insanity Defense

Expert testimony is typically proffered in trials where the defendant is raising an insanity defense. The typical successful insanity defense requires a showing of significant mental illness or impairment through expert testimony. The role of experts in insanity defense trials is somewhat unique. There has been substantial controversy about the role of expert psychological testimony in insanity defense trials, and some have advocated doing away with experts in these cases. The law places a number of constraints on experts in insanity trials. Psychologists in most instances testify about a diagnosis for the defendant and the symptoms associated with that diagnosis, and they give their opinions regarding the defendant's ability to understand the

difference between right and wrong. However, after the Hinkley case, the Federal Rules of Evidence were amended to disallow expert mental health testimony on the ultimate issue—whether or not the defendant was sane or insane at the time of the alleged offense. This decision was left to the trier of the fact. Limited research has examined the effect of expert testimony in general or of ultimate opinion testimony on juror decision making. A consistent finding is that the ultimate opinions proffered by experts do not have a significant effect on decision making, contrary to the concerns underlying their prohibition.

Jennifer Groscup and Tarika Daftary

See also Criminal Responsibility, Assessment of; Criminal Responsibility, Defenses and Standards; Expert Psychological Testimony; Extreme Emotional Disturbance; Guilty but Mentally Ill Verdict; Insanity Defense Reform Act (IDRA); Mental Illness and the Death Penalty; M'Naghten Standard

Further Readings

Finkel, N. J. (1988). *Insanity on trial.* New York: Plenum Press.

Hans, V. P., & Slater, D. (1984). "Plain crazy": Lay definitions of legal insanity. *International Journal of Law and Psychiatry, 7,* 105–114.

Perlin, M. L. (1996). The insanity defense: Deconstructing the myths and reconstructing jurisprudence. In B. D. Sales & D. Shuman (Eds.), *Law, mental health, and mental disorder* (pp. 341–359). Belmont, CA: Thomson Brooks/Cole.

Poulson, R. L., Braithwaite, R. L., & Brondino, M. J. (1997). Mock jurors' insanity defense verdict selections: The role of evidence, attitudes, and verdict options. *Journal of Social Behavior & Personality, 12,* 743–758.

Zapf, P. A., Golding, S. L., & Roesch, R. (2006). Criminal responsibility and the insanity defense. In I. B. Weiner & A. K. Hess (Eds.), *The handbook of forensic psychology* (3rd ed., pp. 332–363). Hoboken, NJ: Wiley.

Insanity Defense Reform Act (IDRA)

The Insanity Defense Reform Act (IDRA), passed by Congress in 1984, imposed a uniform standard for legal insanity that applies in all federal trials in which the defense is raised; it also established the burden of proof in such cases.

Although criminal law is primarily the province of the individual states, the federal government has independent jurisdiction to prosecute criminal activity that concerns the federal government. In 1984, all the states and the federal criminal law had some version of the insanity defense, but the federal criminal code did not contain an insanity defense. Instead, each of the courts of appeal in the 11 federal judicial circuits had judicially adopted an insanity defense that applied in that circuit.

Ten of the 11 circuit courts of appeal had adopted the American Law Institute's Model Penal Code (MPC) insanity defense, which permits acquittal by reason of insanity if

> at the time of [the crime] as a result of mental disease or defect [the defendant] lacks substantial capacity either to appreciate the criminality (wrongfulness) of his conduct or to conform his conduct to the requirements of law. (MPC, Sec. 4.01(1))

One circuit still used the traditional M'Naghten test, which permitted acquittal if the defendant, as a result of mental disorder, did not know the nature and quality of his or her act or did not know that it was wrong.

In 1982, John W. Hinckley Jr. tried to assassinate President Ronald Reagan. Reagan survived, and Hinckley was charged with the federal crime of attempted murder of the President. Hinckley raised the defense of legal insanity. The case was tried in the federal district court in the District of Columbia, which had adopted the MPC test quoted above, which placed the burden of proof on the prosecution to prove beyond a reasonable doubt that the defendant was *not* legally insane. A jury found Hinckley not guilty by reason of insanity.

The unpopular verdict unleashed widespread criticism of the insanity defense in Congress and in many state legislatures, especially of the "loss-of-control" prong of the MPC test. There were many proposals to abolish the insanity defense, including from the Reagan Justice Department. Five state legislatures did abolish the insanity defense, although in one, the state Supreme Court held that abolition unconstitutional. The American Medical Association favored abolition, but the American Bar Association and the American Psychiatric Association opposed abolition on the grounds that it would lead to unfair results and that it was unnecessary to protect the public.

Many of the criticisms of the insanity defense were unfounded. For example, the defense has not let large numbers of defendants "beat the rap." In fact, few defendants have succeeded with an insanity defense, and if those successful were not genuinely criminally responsible, then it would have been unjust to blame and punish them. Moreover, the arguments that all criminal defendants with severe mental disorder at the time of the crime were criminally responsible were morally and logically unpersuasive.

The Justice Department abandoned its call for abolition, and Congress decided to retain the insanity defense. The IDRA created a uniform insanity test applicable in all federal criminal trials in which the defense is raised. The test is as follows:

> It is an affirmative defense to a prosecution under any Federal statute that, at the time of the commission of the acts constituting the offense, the defendant, as a result of a severe mental disease or defect, was unable to appreciate the nature and quality or the wrongfulness of his acts. Mental disease or defect does not otherwise constitute a defense.

The IDRA also placed the burden of proof on the defendant to prove by clear and convincing evidence that he or she was legally insane.

The legal insanity test created is similar to the traditional M'Naghten test and thus is narrower than the MPC test, which had been "blamed" for Hinckley's acquittal. Criticisms of loss-of-control tests convinced lawmakers that they were unwise, and such a test was not included. Moreover, the federal test uses the phrase "unable to appreciate," which suggests that this is a bright-line, all-or-none, question, whereas the apparently more forgiving MPC test points to "lack of substantial capacity." Whether this wording difference makes a difference in practice is not clear.

Like M'Naghten, the federal test focuses on the defendant's understanding of the nature and quality of the act or its wrongfulness. The test is apparently broader than M'Naghten, however, because it uses the defendant's lack of "appreciation" rather than lack of "knowledge" as the operative criterion, and many think that appreciation includes an affective as well as a cognitive component. Whether this criterion is broader in practice is an open question. The test is also apparently narrower than M'Naghten because it explicitly requires that only a severe mental disease or defect will support a successful insanity defense.

Again, whether this restriction narrows the test in practice is an open question because few defendants suffering from less serious mental disorders were previously found not guilty by reason of insanity.

Perhaps the most important part of the IDRA was placing the burden of proof on the defendant, which makes it harder for the defendant to succeed. Placing the burden of proof on the defendant is constitutional because legal insanity is an affirmative defense rather than part of the definitional criteria for criminal offenses, and the Supreme Court has held that the prosecution must only prove the definitional criteria beyond a reasonable doubt. Jurisdictions are therefore free to impose the burden of proof for affirmative defenses on the defendant.

Later empirical research has confirmed that placing the burden of proof on the defendant is more successful in hindering insanity acquittals than narrowing the standard for legal insanity itself. This innovation is often criticized as unfair because it creates too much risk that a defendant who is genuinely legally insane will nonetheless by convicted, but it is constitutional, and Congress shows no inclination to change this rule.

The last sentence of the federal test quoted above has generally been interpreted by lower federal courts to mean that in federal criminal trials, evidence of mental disorder can also be used to negate the mental state required by the definition of most crimes, mens rea. Negation of mens rea using mental abnormality evidence is not considered an affirmative defense, so this interpretation is not inconsistent with the legislation. The Supreme Court held in *Clark v. Arizona* (2006) that jurisdictions are under no constitutional obligation to permit defendants to use evidence of mental disorder to negate mens rea, but most federal courts do permit this as a result of statutory interpretation of the IDRA.

Stephen J. Morse

See also Criminal Responsibility, Assessment of; Criminal Responsibility, Defenses and Standards; Mens Rea and Actus Reus

Further Readings

Clark v. Arizona, 548 U.S. ____ 126 S. Ct. 2709 (2006).

Morse, S. J. (1985). Excusing the crazy: The insanity defense reconsidered. *Southern California Law Review, 58,* 777–836.

Steadman, H. J., McGreevy, M. A., Morrissey, J., Callahan, L. A., Robbins, P. C., & Cirincione, C. (1993). *Before and after Hinckley: Evaluating insanity defense reform.* New York: Guilford Press.

Institutionalization and Deinstitutionalization

As recently as the mid-20th century, the U.S. public mental health system consisted largely of the state hospitals. These hospitals, originally constructed for the humane asylum and "moral treatment" of those deemed mentally ill, had evolved into overcrowded, understaffed, and inadequate responses to the general welfare burden of society. Since that time, there have been many attempts to change the world of psychiatric treatment, including the use of medication and deinstitutionalization. Unfortunately, most of the efforts to change the treatment of persons with mental illness have not been successful. Although policymakers have promised changes in the current mental health system, meaningful changes are not going to happen until it is realized that community-based care is necessary and there is no "quick fix." For deinstitutionalization to be successful, there must be adequately funded community alternatives—other than jail, prison, homelessness, or early death—for individuals diagnosed as mentally ill.

Historical Progression of Hospitalization of Persons With Mental Illness

Through the first half of the 20th century, state hospitals provided care, housing, employment (usually unpaid), and social control of people deemed unable to meet life's daily demands. Mental illness, alcoholism, mental retardation, advanced age, or chronic somatic illness, or a combination of these factors, were all reasons for admission. The census nationally peaked at 553,000 in 1955 and is today less than 10% of that number.

The evolution from small pastoral asylum to large, multiburdened institution—Pilgrim Psychiatric Center in New York had more than 14,000 patients in 1955—was less the result of a conscious, articulated social policy than a drift in policy by a relatively young nation struggling with immigration, urbanization, poverty, disability, and industrialization.

By the 1950s, several factors had combined to alter this approach to serious mental illness. First, institutional abuses became widely publicized, resulting in the creation of the Joint Commission on Mental Illness and Health in 1955. Six years later, this commission was to produce recommendations for a community mental health system in a book titled *Action for Mental Health* (1961).

Second, in 1952, the world of psychiatric treatment was to change profoundly with the development of the antipsychotic drug Thorazine (chlorpromazine) by Henri Laborit. The introduction of this drug meant that many people with serious mental illnesses could control their symptoms with medication.

Third, the Civil Rights Movement began to gather momentum. Initially focusing on persons of color, civil rights attorneys eventually turned their attention to other disenfranchised populations, including people with mental disabilities. Court decisions such as *O'Connor v. Donaldson* (1975) reinforced the liberty interests of psychiatric patients and limited the goal of involuntary hospitalization to prevention of harm, as opposed to the alleged best interests of the patient.

Eventually, these pressures resulted in the passage of the Mental Retardation Facilities and Community Mental Health Centers Construction Act in 1963. The bill was passed with optimism and fanfare and promised that high-quality mental health services in the community would be less expensive and more effective than hospital care. However, these promises were never kept.

Meanwhile, the cost of institutional care began to rise dramatically. In part, this too was due to the efforts of civil rights attorneys and federal courts. Eventually, large class actions such as *Wyatt v. Stickney* resulted in court-mandated improvements in institutional care, which dramatically increased staffing requirements and costs.

Deinstitutionalization

There was insufficient provision for the comprehensive needs of both discharged patients and future generations of people with serious mental illnesses. These needs—housing, social support, employment—were largely neglected in the early decades of deinstitutionalization. Treatment services were expanded but were often focused on those with less severe mental illnesses.

In many ways, the decades since the massive deinstitutionalization of the 1960s and 1970s have been devoted to repairing the flaws of that era. Community support systems and supportive housing were gradually increased—although demand vastly outstrips supply in every state. The growth of the family movement and consumer empowerment movement brought new advocacy to the needs of those attempting to manage and recover from severe mental illness.

The results of our nation's implementation of deinstitutionalization have been mixed. A recent study found that people with serious mental illness are dying 25 years earlier than the general population. Between one-fourth and one-third of America's 2.3 million homeless persons have a serious mental illness, such as schizophrenia, bipolar disorder, or major depression. Furthermore, 6% to 20% of the nation's more than 2 million incarcerated people are estimated to have a serious mental illness. The high prevalence of mental illness in local jails and state prisons eventually became known as the "criminalization" of mental illness.

Yet when deinstitutionalization is done thoughtfully, the results are impressive. In Vermont, Courtney Harding and her colleagues found that linking comprehensive rehabilitation programs, housing, and clinical support to hospital downsizing produced positive, measurable results: Over half the patients 30 years later were productive, living independently with little social impairment, and over two-thirds were functioning "pretty well."

Implications for the Future

There are many lessons to be drawn from the flaws and triumphs of deinstitutionalization. The first is that public policy implemented without consultation with those directly affected—patients and their families in this case—can lead to major folly.

A second lesson is the danger of overpromising. Policymakers overestimated the impact of medication alone, ignoring the need for housing, social support, and an empowered, productive role for patients, all of which are essential to the recovery process.

Finally, society needs to learn that today there is no quick-fix or inexpensive solution to devastating, severe mental illness. Hospitals cost more than community services, but coordinated, comprehensive systems that include treatment, housing, empowerment, social support, and employment are also costly. Convincing taxpayers to support such a system remains a major challenge.

Like it or not, community-based care is here to stay. The costs of hospital care remain prohibitive, and although some states have relaxed civil commitment statutes, in general, long-term hospital treatment remains targeted only at those with the most disabling conditions. Increasingly, the necessity for long-term hospital care is being questioned for anyone who has not committed a serious crime.

However, as our public policy remains committed to community living for persons with serious mental illness, the gap between needs and resources must continue to shrink. Alternatives to jail, prison, homelessness, and premature death must be funded and implemented if deinstitutionalization is to keep its lofty promises, and there is much work yet to be done.

Joel A. Dvoskin, James Bopp,
and Jennifer L. Dvoskin

See also Civil Commitment; Mental Health Law

Further Readings

Abram, K. M., & Teplin, L. A. (1991). Co-occurring disorders among mentally ill jail detainees: Implications for public policy. *American Psychologist, 46,* 1036–1045.

Kiesler, C. A., & Sibulkin, A. E. (1987). *Mental hospitalization: Myths and facts about a national crisis.* Newbury Park, CA: Sage.

O'Connor v. Donaldson, 422 U.S. 563 (1975).

Wyatt v. Stickney, 325 F. Supp. 781(M.D. Ala., 1971), 334 F. Supp. 1341 (M.D. Ala., 1971), 344 F. Supp. 373 (M.D. Ala., 1972), *sub nom Wyatt v. Aderholt,* 503 F.2d 1305 (5th Cir. 1974).

INSTRUCTIONS TO THE WITNESS

The instructions given to a witness prior to the presentation of a lineup have an important influence on how the witness views the identification task and how the witness makes a decision whether to make an identification or whom to identify.

Biased Versus Unbiased Instructions

Because the suspect in the lineup may be innocent, it is important that police officers instruct the witnesses that the actual perpetrator may or may not be in the lineup and that they are not obligated to make an identification. Because these instructions are unbiased with respect to the presence or absence of the perpetrator, they are typically called *unbiased* instructions. In contrast, instructions that explicitly state or imply that the perpetrator is in the lineup and that the witness should make an identification are called *biased* instructions.

It is not surprising that biased instructions result in more identifications. Witnesses who are led to believe that the perpetrator is in the lineup and that it is their "job" to identify him or her make more identifications. The question, of course, is whether they make more correct identifications or more false identifications. As simple as the question is, it does not have a simple answer. Some studies have shown that biased instructions lead to increases in both correct and false identifications, and some studies show only increases in false identifications with little or no change in correct identifications.

The consistent increase in false identifications arises because biased instructions lead to more identifications, and if the perpetrator is not in the lineup (i.e., the suspect is innocent), then any identification made by the witness will be an error. The most critical errors, of course, are the false identifications of the innocent suspect. The proportion of identifications of the innocent suspect (rather than one of the foils—i.e., an innocent person in a police lineup) depends on the composition of the lineup.

The question remains: Is there variation in the outcomes for correct identifications? Some of the variation is likely due to ceiling effects. Considering only those lineups in which the perpetrator is present, if the identification rate is fairly high under unbiased instruction conditions, then it cannot increase very much under biased instruction conditions. Consequently, the correct identification rate cannot increase very much either.

However, the variability in correct identification rates cannot be explained by ceiling effects alone. Results showing an increase in the overall identification rate (when the perpetrator is in the lineup), with no increase in the correct identification rate, suggest that the biasing effect of the instructions is not simply to lower the witness's decision criterion. Instead, in studies showing this pattern of results, the biasing instructions may induce witnesses to change their decision rule or change the way they compare the lineup members with their memory. Another explanation arises from the reasons why witnesses do not identify the perpetrator in the first place. If witnesses who are presented with a lineup that includes the perpetrator do not make any identification, it may be because their memories are quite distorted and inaccurate, such that if they are biased to make an identification, it is very likely that one of the lineup fillers will be a better match to their (distorted) memory of the perpetrator than the perpetrator himself (or herself).

Unbiased Instructions and Biased Lineup Administrators

Police officers may sometimes give witnesses a mixed message by reading an unbiased instruction but then follow that instruction with various encouragements and nudges, suggesting that they should make an identification and even who they should identify. Even seemingly innocuous comments to "take your time" or "look at each photograph carefully" can convey to witnesses that they should make, rather than not make, an identification. Other forms of prompting can direct witnesses as to whom to identify. The point here is that police officers can essentially "undo" their unbiased instructions with biased nudges and prompting.

The prompting may be explicit, or it may be quite inadvertent. Consider, for example, a police officer who knows that the suspect is in Position 4 and is quite certain that the suspect is the perpetrator. If the witness states, "Number 3 looks familiar," should that be considered an identification of Number 3 or a case of the witness thinking out loud? Because the police officer knows that Number 3 is a filler, he or she may interpret the witness's comment as thinking out loud and say something like "Take your time." Because of such interpretation problems, it is recommended that the police officer administering the lineup be blind to the identity and position of the suspect in the lineup.

Change-of-Appearance Instruction

It is also common to instruct witnesses, prior to the presentation of a lineup, that people can change their appearance. The perpetrator, as pictured in a photograph, may have lost or gained weight, grown or shaved a beard, and so on. (A booking photograph used in a photo lineup may have been taken years before or years after the witnessed crime.)

What effect does this instruction have? There is considerably less research on the effects of the appearance-change instruction than the "may or may not be present" instruction. However, one study by Steve Charman and Gary Wells showed that the appearance-change instruction had only one effect—to increase false identifications. They suggested that the appearance-change instruction may function to make witnesses more lenient and to decrease their decision criterion. What has not been shown is that the appearance-change instruction serves its presumably intended purpose of increasing the likelihood of correct identifications of perpetrators who have, in fact, changed their appearance.

Steven E. Clark and Anne K. Cybenko

See also Appearance-Change Instruction in Lineups; Eyewitness Memory; Identification Tests, Best Practices in

Further Readings

Charman, S. D., & Wells, G. L. (in press). Eyewitness lineups. Is the appearance-change instruction a good idea? *Law and Human Behavior.*

Clark, S. E. (2005). A re-examination of the effects of biased lineup instructions in eyewitness identification. *Law and Human Behavior, 29,* 395–424.

Steblay, N. M. (1997). Social influence in eyewitness recall: A meta-analytic review of lineup instruction effects. *Law and Human Behavior, 21,* 283–297.

INTERDISCIPLINARY FITNESS INTERVIEW (IFI)

The Interdisciplinary Fitness Interview (IFI) is a semi-structured assessment device designed to help examiners explore systematically the domain of psycholegal abilities associated with adjudicative competency. Originally developed by Stephen Golding and Ronald Roesch for a National Institute of Mental Health (NIMH)–sponsored comparative validity study of methods of assessing competency, the IFI was developed on the basis of three assumptions. First, the Competency Assessment Interview, which was the most promising and articulated assessment device available at the time, was outdated and did not include many of the psycholegal abilities associated with adjudicative competency that emerged from an extensive review of competency case law and research. Second, an approach was needed that stressed the possible, but not automatically assumed, linkage between psychopathology and incapacity. Third, an assessment approach needed to reflect the highly contextualized nature of adjudicative competence.

As originally designed and tested, the IFI manual stressed the linkage and contextual aspects of competency assessment and emphasized the importance of these aspects of competency evaluation by including both attorneys and forensic mental health professionals in the interview and evaluation process (hence the term *interdisciplinary*). It was a good, but impractical, idea. In the NIMH-funded pilot project, attorneys proved to be able to contribute in a meaningful and reliable fashion to the competency appraisal, but implementing their routine involvement proved difficult for financial and logistical reasons. In its modern form, the revised version (IFI–R) is designed so that the forensic examiner provides the linkage based on extensive training, knowledge of the legal issues, and consultation with both defense and prosecution about the particular context of a given case. The IFI–R is also designed to include a more extensive linkage analysis and includes additional psycholegal abilities associated with more modern competency cases. Thus, the IFI–R, in addition to the traditional competency domains, also focuses on competencies associated with the decision to proceed pro se or to plead guilty, the competency to comprehend and appreciate rights during a custodial interrogation, and the iatrogenic effects of medication.

The IFI–R organizes 35 specific psycholegal abilities associated with adjudicative competency into 11 broad domains. Thus, the IFI–R spans the entire domain of competency-related psycholegal abilities, ranging from fundamental issues such as understanding the prosecutor's adversarial role, through common competency concerns such as the ability to communicate relevant information to counsel, to higher-order decisional competencies such as the ability to make a reasoned choice of defense options. Special competency considerations that arise in the context of psychotropic medications, such as deficits in psycholegal abilities induced by such treatments and treatment refusal, are also addressed.

For each psycholegal ability, the IFI–R guides examiners through suggested inquiries meant to explore the linkage, if any, between psychopathological symptoms or cognitive deficits and impairment in each domain. While each psycholegal ability can be "scored"

as to degree of impairment, the inherent idiographic nature of the instrument means that the scores are specifically not designed to be summed into a "competency score" but rather are meant to guide a forensic examiner's structured judgment. Subsequent research across various competency assessment instruments has demonstrated the validity of this assumption.

The IFI–R has not been thoroughly examined from an empirical perspective. The original NIMH developmental and validational studies found that the IFI items were scored with good to excellent interrater reliability. Furthermore, competency judgments based on the IFI aligned very well with both independent assessments by a "blue-ribbon panel" and court judgments. However, it should be pointed out that these results were obtained with a group of interviewers who received intensive training in both the logic and the methodology of the IFI as well as a detailed review of relevant case law. When untrained examiners' evaluations (using unstandardized methods) are "coded" according to the IFI–R domain/ subdomain scheme or when untrained examiners are provided the IFI–R format *without training and supervision*, their assessments of individual domains or subdomains are quite unreliable. Thus, the IFI–R is meant to be used by highly trained and experienced forensic examiners. It has been favorably reviewed in terms of its conceptualization and its usefulness in guiding forensic competency assessments. Most research on the conceptualization of the IFI–R (i.e., using a contextualized semistructured interview to examine the linkage between psychopathology and articulated psycholegal ability domains) has been conducted with the Canadian cousin of the IFI–R, the Fitness Interview Test–Revised (FIT–R).

Unlike most other competency evaluation methods and procedures, the IFI–R and its Canadian cousin, the FIT–R, are the only procedures that have been examined with respect to their comparative validity in a real-world context. Most other competency instruments have been validated by showing that scores on the instrument are significantly different in groups adjudicated as incompetent versus those judged competent. Although such contrasted group designs do provide informative data, they are relatively weak tests of construct validity.

Stephen Golding

See also Competency, Foundational and Decisional; Competency Assessment Instrument (CAI); Competency Screening Test (CST); Competency to Stand Trial;

Evaluation of Competence to Stand Trial–Revised (ECST–R); Fitness Interview Test–Revised (FIT–R); MacArthur Competence Assessment Tool for Criminal Adjudication (MacCAT–CA)

Further Readings

Golding, S. L., Roesch, R., & Schreiber, J. (1984). Assessment and conceptualization of competency to stand trial: Preliminary data on the Interdisciplinary Fitness Interview. *Law and Human Behavior, 8*(3–4), 321–334.

Roesch, R., Zapf, P., & Eaves, D. (2006). *FIT–R: Fitness Interview Test–Revised: A structured interview for assessing competency to stand trial.* Sarasota, FL: Professional Resource Press/Professional Resource Exchange.

Viljoen, J., Vincent, G., & Roesch, R. (2006). Assessing adolescent defendants' adjudicative competence: Interrater reliability and factor structure of the Fitness Interview Test–Revised. *Criminal Justice and Behavior, 33,* 467–475.

Zapf, P. A., & Roesch, R. (2005). An investigation of the construct of competence: A comparison of the FIT, the MacCAT–CA, and the MacCAT–T. *Law and Human Behavior, 29*(2), 229–252.

INTERROGATION OF SUSPECTS

The interrogation of those suspected of wrongdoing, although of great importance to society, has not been researched extensively compared with other crucial topics in psychology and law. Effective interrogation (and therefore the prosecution and possible conviction) of guilty persons is of obvious and high relevance to this encyclopedia, as is the successful interviewing of those suspects who are, in fact, innocent. A number of different approaches to interrogation have been adopted in various countries around the world. Some involve a pressurizing, dominating, and possibly coercive approach; others involve a more humane approach. Research on what really happens in police interviews and on how interviewees view these experiences forms the background for consideration of the strengths and weaknesses of these respective approaches.

In many countries, the interrogation of suspects has had a strong focus on the obtaining of confessions. Although this may be, in general, a useful approach,

some psychology-law scholars have emphasized that false confessions do occur. Also, if the primary aim of interrogation is seen as the obtaining of a confession rather than an account from the suspect (which may include a confession), then it may be difficult to be sure that the confession is reliable. Psychological research has been helping the police forces in some countries to reassess how best to interview suspects.

The Reid Technique

In the United States (and many other countries), extensive guidance on how to interrogate suspects has largely come from a book (now in its fourth edition) written by John Reid and colleagues. This book advocates a two-phase approach. In the first phase, the interviewer seeks to obtain relevant information from the suspect. If during this phase the suspect does not either confess/admit to the crime or provide sufficient information to substantiate his or her innocence, or appears to be lying, then the second phase commences. During this phase, which is more of an interrogation than an interview, the interviewer is recommended to use a variety of tactics (involving a stepped approach) to get the (now presumed guilty) suspect to confess.

A major criticism made by some psychologists regarding this approach is that the symptoms/cues of deception/truthfulness that it recommends to be used to determine if suspects are lying have not been found to be valid by the many published studies on cues to lying. Indeed, recent research suggests that focusing on such cues could impair lie/truth-detection performance.

What Really Happens in Police Interviews?

Very few published studies exist regarding the actual effectiveness of the two-step approach. A seminal paper published in 1996 was based on 9 months of fieldwork with a large police department in the United States, during which the researcher sat in on more than 100 interviews with suspects (and observed another 60 that had been recorded on videotape). He found that the police used many of the interrogation tactics recommended in relevant publications. These he categorized into positive incentives (which suggest that the suspect will benefit/feel better if he or she confesses) and negative incentives (which suggest that the suspect confess because no alternative course of action is sensible). He concluded that the following techniques were very commonly used:

- Undermining suspects' confidence in their denial of guilt
- Offering justifications for their behavior
- Confronting suspects with fabricated evidence of their guilt

Some of the findings of this ground-breaking 1996 study were taken by others (along with their own reading of relevant guidance publications) to indicate that (a) police interviewing of suspects was a confrontational and accusatory process that purposely involved the application of considerable psychological pressure and (b) some of the recommended Phase 2 steps raised ethical questions (e.g., the discouraging/preventing of denials).

In the United Kingdom, a similar, if smaller, 1980 observational study found that among the tactics used were the following:

- Pointing out the futility of denial
- Minimizing the seriousness of the offense
- Manipulating the suspect's self-esteem
- Pretending that the police were in possession of more evidence than was, in fact, the case

In light of (a) this research finding, (b) some courts' decisions and judges' comments regarding inappropriate tactics and procedures being used, and (c) considerable media concern about the police interviewing of suspects, the government in England and Wales brought in legislation that from 1986 sought to discourage the use of unduly oppressive interviewing tactics (which could result in a confession not being deemed "voluntary") and required that all interviews with suspects be fully recorded (e.g., on audiotape).

Around this time, police forces in England and Wales were also becoming aware of research on detecting deception (some conducted by officers themselves, usually as part of their university studies) that was making it ever clearer that generally applicable, valid behavioral cues to deception are unlikely to exist.

The audiotaping of interviews with suspects (routine since 1986) set the scene for a series of studies conducted in the late 1980s to analyze these. Such studies found that while few interviews were now unduly oppressive, the extent and level of interviewing skill was not high. For example, a common tactic

was to inform suspects (truthfully) at the outset of the evidence against them. If such evidence was strong, many such suspects confessed. However, if the evidence was weak or moderate, many suspects did not readily confess when informed of the evidence against them. Analyses of the tape recordings revealed that when confessions did not occur in these situations, many police officers seemed not to know what to do next. (They would have been fully aware that the relevant legislation precluded undue pressure.) The primary tactic of revealing the evidence bears similarity to the first phase of the two-phase approach advocated in the United States (and many other countries). However, if this did not work, many British police officers seemed unaware of what could be done in Phase 2.

Reform of Techniques

As soon as the research analyzing the tapes revealed this problem, the Association of Chief Police Officers, with support from the government, set up a working party to design new training and philosophy regarding the interviewing of suspects. This working party based their recommendations (which were adopted) on the fundamental realization that there are many essential similarities between the effective interviewing of suspects and the effective interviewing of witnesses/victims. For example, both need to be designed to encourage the interviewee to talk on relevant topics using methods prescribed by the law and various conventions on human rights. Thus, from 1992 on, all police officers in England and Wales had to undergo new training programs (the extent of which was determined by their job role) in what was termed *investigative interviewing*. The emphasis now was on "skills," in particular skills relevant to (a) encouraging interviewees to provide accounts (including those that could corroborate a confession provided early in the interview) and (b) strategically (in a planned/prepared way) disclosing evidence (piece by piece) at appropriate points in the interview that would encourage the interviewee to provide more information and demonstrate to the interviewee that what he or she has said (or failed to confirm) contradicts the evidence.

Only a limited number of (relatively large) studies have been conducted/published that have analyzed interviews conducted by police officers who have received this new form of training. Among the major findings regarding interviews with suspects are the following:

- Although most make good efforts to encourage the suspects to give an account, few seemed good at building rapport.
- Use of leading questions and overtalking were relatively rare.
- Challenging what the suspects said did occur in most interviews, but this was often done poorly.
- Most interviewers did purposely provide, near the end of the interview, an opportunity for the suspect to correct or add to the officer's summary of what the suspect had said.
- Few interviews breached the law. (Of course, the officers who conducted these interviews did not know that later they would be analyzed in a research project.)
- The tactics of "intimidation," "situational futility," "minimization," and "maximization" (which would be of great concern to both psychologists and the courts) never or almost never occurred.

Even in interviews assessed as skilled (in terms of what the interviewer did and how this seemed to affect the suspects), however, some of the skills deemed important by police officers themselves were rarely present (e.g., empathy/compassion, flexibility, pauses/ silences). Nevertheless, almost all interviewers, even those who were less skilled, now successfully avoided releasing to the suspect all the evidence/information at the beginning.

Suspects' Views

Until fairly recently, the only information available from suspects about their interrogation/interviews were anecdotes. However, 2002 saw the publication of a pioneering Swedish study (conducted by a former police officer) of a large sample of (subsequently convicted) suspects' views about the police interviewing they had experienced. Many indicated via a postal questionnaire that their interviewers displayed impatience, condemning attitudes, and a lack of empathy— which the researcher classified as a "dominating" style. However, other suspects reported experiencing a more "humane" approach, and it was these whose confession rate was higher. This crucial finding could call into question the routine use of a dominating style. However, interviewee denial could cause a dominating style.

Importantly, subsequent research in Canada and Australia on suspects' views can be taken to confirm the Swedish finding. In Canada, a large number of men in a maximum security prison, 45% of whom had confessed to the police, filled in a number of questionnaires. When asked what motivates suspects *not* to confess, the inmates indicated that "the negative attitude of the police officer" and "lacking confidence in the police officer" were among the most important factors. The researchers also examined which of the inmates' questionnaire responses actually related to whether they had confessed or not and found that suspects' perception of the strength of the evidence against them was significant.

The research in Australia asked convicted sex offenders what interviewers should do to increase the likelihood of a genuine confession. Their responses included being compassionate, neutral, clear, and honest and not making false accusations. When asked what would make confessions less likely, the most common response was officer aggression.

In light of research at the psychology-law interface (e.g., on police interviewing), a number of European countries have decided that their police officers be trained in what they call the "British approach." While this approach may have a positive effect not only on minor criminals, who make up the vast bulk of police suspects, but also on major criminals (e.g., of the types studied in Sweden, Canada, and Australia), research on its effectiveness with the most dangerous perpetrators, such as terrorists, is not available. However, those who interview/interrogate suspects will want to be fully aware of what psychology and the law have to say.

Ray Bull

See also Behavior Analysis Interview; Detection of Deception in Adults; False Confessions; Reid Technique for Interrogations; Videotaping Confessions

Further Readings

Buckley, J. (2006). The Reid Technique of interviewing and interrogation. In T. Williamson (Ed.), *Investigative interviewing: Rights, research and regulation* (pp. 207–228). Cullompton, UK: Willan.

Bull, R., & Milne, R. (2004). Attempts to improve the police interviewing of suspects. In G. D. Lassiter (Ed.), *Interrogations, confessions and entrapment* (pp.181–196). New York: Kluwer.

Davis, D., & O'Donohue, W. (2003). The road to perdition: Extreme influence tactics in the interrogation room. In W. O'Donohue & E. Levensky (Eds.), *Handbook of forensic psychology* (pp. 877–996). New York: Elsevier.

Gudjonsson, G. (2003). *The psychology of interrogations and confessions.* Chichester, UK: Wiley.

INTIMATE PARTNER VIOLENCE

The phrase *intimate partner violence* encompasses a pattern of psychological and emotional abuse, physical abuse, sexual abuse, and stalking between past or present intimate romantic partners. Scientific and clinical evidence indicates that intimate partner violence can result in a plethora of mental health and physical maladies due to ongoing patterns of abuse within relationships, and those most at risk of victimization are women and their children. This entry reviews the incidence and definition of intimate partner violence, the risk factors, and the effects of violence on both victims and perpetrators. Interventions for such abuse now cut across multiple public and private sectors (criminal/ civil justice systems, the health care system, child services, battered women's shelters, etc.), and mental health professionals must know how to negotiate such systems in order to help victims and their children. Various prevention and intervention strategies are described below. Finally, current issues concerning intimate partner violence include the controversies surrounding batterer treatment, the unintended consequences of contemporary changes in the law (e.g., mandatory/preferred arrest), and the recent increase in effective yet damaging manipulation of criminal, civil, and family court processes by batterers.

Incidence of Intimate Partner Violence

According to the latest reports from the United Nations and the World Health Organization, intimate partner violence extends across class, culture, ethnicity, and nationality and results in devastating physical and financial costs to individuals, families, and communities across the globe. In the United States, it is estimated that nearly 5.3 million incidents occur each year among women 18 years or older, and 3.2 million occur among men. Fortunately, most intimate partner violence assaults within the United States are relatively minor and are limited to pushing, grabbing, or slapping.

Nevertheless, intimate partner violence results in nearly 2 million officially reported injuries and 1,300 deaths each year, with the overwhelming majority of perpetrators of such severe violence being men and the majority of victims being women. Even so, most intimate partner violence incidents are not officially reported to the authorities, and the Centers for Disease Control Injury Center estimates that only about 20% of intimate partner sexual assaults/rapes, 25% of physical assaults, and 50% of stalkings against women are reported. Thus, most authorities agree that available data nationwide are gross underestimates of the problem.

Defining Intimate Partner Violence

Research points to the importance of societal factors that influence individual and collective perceptions of the abuse. For some intimate partner violence victims, the abuse is perceived as a normal part of relationships and is not defined as criminal behavior. For many perpetrators, the abuse is perceived as the correct and most effective way to get their needs met within an intimate romantic relationship. This should not be surprising, because intimate partner violence has only recently been defined as criminal behavior. During the Civil Rights Movement in the United States during the 1960s and 1970s, intimate partner violence was named and brought out from behind closed doors. Prior to that time, violence between partners was viewed as private business and not a place for the state to intervene. Battered women's shelters and rape crisis centers sprang up across the country and are now located within every major metropolitan area in the United States. Due to the work of women's rights advocates, intimate partner violence is now defined as a crime worthy of police intervention and prosecution, similar to assaults that might occur on the street between strangers. Every state in the union now has some form of intimate partner violence law on the books (often referred to as "domestic violence" in the statutes), and many states now also include stalking within these laws. In addition, most states no longer require intimate partners to be married or living together for these laws to apply. Based on variation by state, a complex set of laws protecting intimate partner violence victims now exist (ranging from civil protective orders to mandatory/preferred arrest at the scene), and perpetrators can no longer abuse their partners with impunity.

Physical abuse is now defined as any act that is physically aggressive or violent against another, from slapping or shoving, up to and including homicide. Unfortunately, some of the best-known and widely used measurement tools (e.g., the Conflict Tactics Scale) do not differentiate between mild forms of such aggression and that which results in intimidation, coercion, and control, not to mention severe injury or death. Sexual abuse is defined as any sexual behavior that is imposed on another without that person's full consent, from sexual imposition or fondling up to and including rape. Psychological or emotional violence is defined as behavior meant to intimidate, control, and coerce. This would include things such as threats to harm, put-downs and insults, monitoring of actions, control of the environment, and inducing fear in others. Often, psychological violence will overlap with stalking behavior, such as following, tracking down, leaving unwanted phone calls at work or home, contacting coworkers or friends and family, and other unwanted contacts after being told to stop. As noted above, mild violence such as pushing, grabbing, or slapping is the most common form of intimate partner violence in the United States, leading some to label such actions as "common couple violence." These types of actions are reported about equally by both men and women. However, serious forms of intimate partner violence that result in patterns of abuse over time, coercion and control, sexual assault/rape, stalking behavior, injury, and homicide are overwhelmingly perpetrated by men (about 85–95% of all perpetrators). This latter type of intimate partner violence has been labeled by some as "intimate terrorism" or "battering" and constitutes a severe public health problem. As will be shown below, the primary perpetrators of such battering behavior are overwhelmingly male, while the victims are overwhelmingly female.

Risk Markers

While it is well-known that intimate partner violence is underreported, those incidents that are severe enough to come to the attention of public and private social service agencies (the police, hospitals, shelters, etc.) suggest that most victims are women, most perpetrators are men, and most are relatively young (15–39 years of age). In terms of ethnicity, some suggest that people of color are more likely to be involved in intimate partner violence than Caucasians. However, when socioeconomic status is controlled, these racial patterns tend to disappear. For instance, when one compares police and emergency room patterns with those found in more private services such as battered women's shelters or advocacy centers, public services seem to be used more often by those in poverty, while the more private services seem to be accessed by those who reflect the racial/ethnic proportions found in the general population. Thus, it is safe to say that intimate partner violence cuts across all races and ethnicities and is most likely to come to the attention of the criminal justice system within the context of poverty and the risks that are associated with being poor.

Substance use has also been shown to be a risk marker, and some researchers have suggested that intoxication lowers inhibitions and increases impulsivity, thus leading to a higher propensity for violence of all kinds (not just intimate partner violence); however, research has shown that substance use is correlational and not causal.

The single largest, repeatable risk marker for battering is being a man within our culture, leading many to suggest that the problem is largely one of patriarchal gender socialization concerning intimate relationships. Indeed, a recent national survey revealed that cohabiting with a man, whether in a heterosexual or a homosexual intimate relationship, was a much stronger risk marker for victimization than cohabiting with a woman. Others, however, reject this hypothesis because women can also be primary perpetrators. Nevertheless, severe intimate partner violence remains overwhelmingly a male problem.

Men who have been abused in childhood or witnessed violence in parents or caregivers are at higher risk of becoming a batterer in the teen years and adulthood than those who have not. Conversely, women who have been abused in childhood or witnessed violence in the home are at higher risk of being victimized. Thankfully, most individuals with such a history do not become abusive or victimized in the teen years or adulthood, and protective markers are similar to those for other types of violence (the presence of nonviolent peers and adults in the formative years, etc.). Nevertheless, it has been known for some time that children learn how to negotiate intimate relationships from adult caregivers of both genders, and if abusive relationships are the norm, there is a higher chance that such relationships will be repeated in their own lives into adulthood. This is known as the "intergenerational transmission" of violence. Disturbingly, estimates suggest that children are present in the home and know about, witness, or are directly involved in up to 75% of all intimate partner violence incidents between adults.

Lethality Assessment

Trying to predict severe injury or death as a result of battering is difficult. Many of the risk markers for severe violence never result in death because homicide has an extremely low base rate within the general population. In addition, some intimate partner homicides occur "out of the blue," meaning that others are unaware of problems within the relationship until after homicide has occurred. Nevertheless, there is amassed evidence for highly lethal risk markers from reviews of intimate partner homicides, whether or not prior knowledge of the problem was available. Such risk markers include severity of past violence (attempts/threats to harm or kill, sexual assault/rape, strangling/choking of partner, child and pet abuse, serious injury, etc.), other criminal behaviors (history of prior arrests, threats/harassment of others besides partner, etc.), failure of past interventions (others have intervened but violence continues, ignoring protective and court orders, numerous police calls, etc.), obsessive stalking behaviors (following, watching, monitoring, isolation, sense of ownership of partner, etc.), and psychological risk markers (previous suicide/homicide threats or attempts, military history or weapons training, depression or other mental health disorders, external life stressors such as job loss or death in the family, drug/alcohol use, etc.). *However, the single largest risk marker for severe injury and homicide is when the victim attempts separation from the perpetrator.* It appears that when batterers can no longer control their partners or the relationship, their violence escalates. Indeed, in the most extreme cases, batterers will kill their partners, their children, and then commit suicide rather than allow separation of any kind.

Negative Effects of Intimate Partner Violence

Similar to any other form of trauma, once the abuse stops, most victims will recover to the emotional and functional levels that were present before the abuse started. Indeed, most battered women will not enter into another abusive relationship in their lifetime. On the other hand, batterers often go from one violent relationship to the next and, without intervention, will often abuse a string of intimate partners. Not surprisingly, data have shown that among intimate couples reporting violence, women report significantly more fear of their partner and fear for their safety than do men.

Victimized women can present with cognitive disturbances due to repeated head banging or beatings, hyperarousal and anxiety disturbances, attentional deficits, seclusion, denial, minimization, somatization, depression, and classic posttraumatic stress disorder symptoms such as dissociation, nightmares, and flashbacks. These symptoms can unfortunately result in misdiagnosis if the effects of intimate partner violence are not taken into account. Such victimization can also cause changes in personality that usually remit on cessation of abuse and establishment of safety but that can also be easily misdiagnosed if the context of intimate partner violence is not taken into account. This is not to say that victimized women never have prior comorbid health issues, only that misdiagnosis is likely to occur if the abuse is not identified. Perpetrators, on the other hand, often cannot be distinguished from other men in terms of personality disorders, depression, anxiety, or any other mental health issue. They are more likely, however, to hold more traditional views concerning men's and women's roles than those who are not abusive.

The effects on children in a home where battering is present are quite negative. As mentioned above, children in such families are at higher risk of becoming future perpetrators or victims themselves. Children from such homes can also experience anxiety and depression, become withdrawn and secretive, struggle in school, have trouble with attention and memory, or begin to act out aggressively. If they attempt to intervene during an intimate partner violence incident, they can suffer mild to severe physical injuries. Perhaps most disturbingly, it has been estimated that in up to 60% of all homes where battering is present, child abuse in some form also occurs.

Types of Interventions

Similar to other types of public health problems, there are three classes of interventions that are currently being applied for the problem of intimate partner violence: (a) primary prevention strategies, (b) secondary prevention strategies, and (c) tertiary intervention strategies.

Primary Prevention

Primary prevention refers to public access educational efforts that attempt to reach most or all members of a population. Such efforts include educational material presented through the media (television, radio, newspapers, the Internet, etc.) that defines the problem of intimate partner violence and provides information about services available and how to access them and what to do if you or someone you know is a victim or a perpetrator.

Secondary Prevention

Secondary prevention refers to efforts that are tailored to those groups most at risk for perpetration (young males) and victimization (young females). Such interventions are usually presented within educational institutions, religious institutions, and other community organizations such as hospitals and include information similar to that found in primary prevention efforts.

Tertiary Intervention

Tertiary intervention refers to "after the fact" interventions directly targeting known victims and perpetrators. Such services include police intervention and prosecution of the batterer, probation and parole monitoring, civil and criminal protective orders issued by the courts, family divorce courts, legal advocacy centers, battered women's shelters and rape crisis hotlines, child protective services after abuse or threats of abuse, emergency room visits after injury, and access to private or public physicians and mental health workers after the abuse has occurred.

There is evidence that some medical and mental health professionals overlook intimate partner violence victimization in terms of information gathering and diagnosis, even though females nationwide access such health services in larger numbers than males. As noted earlier, misdiagnosis can result from a lack of professional knowledge about intimate partner violence, not to mention ineffective interventions and perhaps even an increase in risk to clients. Nevertheless, more and more health workers are dealing with the unique problems that intimate partner violence can pose in clients' lives, and there has been a call to increase the amount of training concerning such issues across health professions. In addition, the treatment of perpetrators has become a widespread concern, especially since many court jurisdictions now use batterer treatment as an adjunct to or instead of incarceration.

Victim Intervention

In terms of victim intervention, the single largest issue is safety. Mental health providers cannot assist victims and their children in overcoming the effects of

trauma if the abuse is continuing or they continue to live in fear of their batterers. Thus, providers must know how to design and monitor client safety plans, be aware of local resources for victims and how to access them, be well versed in lethality factors (especially recent separation), and be willing to call in outside resources such as the police if victims or their children report especially lethal behavior on the part of the batterer. While there are no mandated reporting requirements on the books because victims are enfranchised adults, standard lethality assessment requirements nevertheless apply. Of course, for child victims, mandated reporting is required. Once victim safety is established, mental health providers often serve in the triple roles of therapist, advocate, and case manager. This is because, as noted above, the tertiary interventions for intimate partner violence victimization now cut across multiple public and private systems. In addition to helping victims and their children cope with the psychological aftermath of abuse within an ongoing lethality analysis, therapists often find themselves assisting victims to access services such as shelters, crisis lines, and advocacy centers; helping victims navigate within the criminal, civil, and family courts and child protective services; and testifying in court.

Batterer Intervention

In terms of batterer intervention, many criminal jurisdictions require batterers to attend and successfully complete treatment in lieu of sentencing or jail time or as part of probation/parole requirements. Studies show that batterer treatment is relatively unsuccessful due to high drop-out rates nationwide. Unfortunately, courts are inconsistent and vary by jurisdiction concerning the penalties for such treatment failures on the part of batterers. Still, when court-ordered batterers do complete treatment, studies suggest that recidivism is reduced when measured as future arrests for intimate partner violence. However, batterer treatment remains controversial because of the high drop-out rates, the problems inherent in court-ordered treatment in general (similar to court-ordered drug/alcohol treatment), and the finding that following treatment, some batterers have learned to become more savvy in their abuse in order to avoid future detection by the authorities. Overall, studies suggest that if perpetrators are not personally ready to change their behavior at the time of treatment, at best treatment is ineffective and at worst it creates more savvy batterers. Nevertheless, for those ready to change, treatment is quite helpful as long as it is conducted within an ongoing lethality analysis. Once again, mental health providers who deal with batterers often find themselves in multiple roles. Therapists are not only expected to deliver antiviolence treatment to batterers, they are also usually required to interact with probation and parole officers, judges, child protective services, and victims to ensure that the violence has stopped. Not only are therapists required to play multiple roles, they must also be quite clear in identifying the "client" when providing batterer treatment. This means that, often, the client is the court and the goal is victim safety, not necessarily the "best interests" of the batterer.

Contemporary Issues

Sadly, with the advent of mandatory arrest policies, there has been an unintended increase in victim arrests at intimate partner violence scenes across the United States, and therefore an increase in victims being mandated for batterer treatment. Nationwide, the best estimates suggest that only about 2% to 3% of all intimate partner violence arrests are of actual primary female perpetrators, and the remainder of these women have been erroneously arrested. Therapists need to be cognizant that erroneous victim arrest can result in job loss, loss of aid and access to other services, charges of unfit parenthood, and future threats by batterers to have them arrested again. Furthermore, those therapists providing batterer treatment should provide thorough assessments of all referrals to ensure that primary perpetrators are identified and separated from their victims regardless of gender and that treatment is then tailored accordingly.

Yet another contemporary issue of which therapists should be aware is that harassing and manipulative behaviors on the part of batterers are becoming more and more commonplace within the criminal, civil, and family court systems. This can be seen not only in the recent increase in victim arrests as noted above but also in the increase in the number of batterers obtaining criminal and civil protection orders against their victims as well as the number of batterers using invalid "parental alienation" arguments in custody battles in the family courts. Even though many states and local communities forbid the issuing of dual protective orders, batterers are nevertheless obtaining them because of the lack of communication across most jurisdictions resulting in inadequate tracking of such

cases. Similarly, batterers are using the family courts during highly conflictual custody proceedings to make unjustified claims against their victims concerning unfit parenthood, with the children caught squarely in the middle. Mental health professionals need to be cognizant of such manipulative batterer behavior in the treatment of victims, perpetrators, and their children.

Kathy McCloskey

See also Child Custody Evaluations; Child Sexual Abuse; Conflict Tactics Scale (CTS); Criminal Behavior, Theories of; Posttraumatic Stress Disorder (PTSD); Reporting Crimes and Victimization; Stalking; Victimization

Further Readings

Centers for Disease Control and Prevention. (n.d.). *Intimate partner violence: Overview*. Atlanta, GA: Author. Retrieved May 2, 2007, from http://www.cdc.gov/ncipc/factsheets/ipvfacts.htm

Geffner, R. A., & Rosenbaum, A. (Eds.). (2001). *Domestic violence offenders: Current interventions, research, and implications for policies and standards*. New York: Haworth Press.

Hamburger, K. L., & Phelan, M. B. (2004). *Domestic violence screening and intervention in medical and mental healthcare settings*. New York: Springer.

McCloskey, K., & Grigsby, N. (2005). The ubiquitous clinical problem of adult partner violence: The need for routine assessment. *Professional Psychology: Research and Practice, 36*(3), 264–275.

Mills, L. G. (2003). *Insult to injury: Rethinking our responses to intimate abuse*. Princeton, NJ: Princeton University Press.

United Nations General Assembly. (2006). *In-depth study on all forms of violence against women: Report of the Secretary-General*. New York: United Nations Organization. Retrieved May 1, 2007, from http://www.springtideresources.net/resources/show.cfm?id=161

World Health Organization. (2005). *WHO multi-country study on women's health and domestic violence against women: Initial results on prevalence, health outcomes, and women's responses*. Geneva, Switzerland: Author.

INVOLUNTARY COMMITMENT

See CIVIL COMMITMENT; OUTPATIENT COMMITMENT, INVOLUNTARY

JAIL SCREENING ASSESSMENT TOOL (JSAT)

The Jail Screening Assessment Tool (JSAT) is a screening tool developed for the purpose of identifying mentally disordered offenders in jails and prisons. The JSAT is administered by a mental health professional during a brief interview. Initial studies support the JSAT's validity and use as an effective screening device to identify inmates' mental health needs.

Incontrovertible evidence now exists to show that the prevalence of mental disorder among those in the criminal justice system (prisoners, offenders on community orders, and accused on remand) is significantly greater than is found in the general population. Despite the prevalence of mentally disordered people in the criminal justice system, and the potential consequences of failing to adequately address the related issues, relatively few services exist either in prisons or in the community to help identify these people and prevent them from entering or remaining in the criminal justice system.

A number of contributing factors have been identified that help explain the high numbers of people with mental illnesses in the criminal justice system. Considerable concern has been raised about the capacity of community-based mental health services to address the needs of mentally ill offenders. Community-based mental health services work best for those who have reasonable connections and support within the community. While the presence of mentally ill people in the criminal justice system presents challenges and raises concerns, the fact is that the justice system provides an opportunity to identify and deliver

treatment to people who are otherwise likely to remain outside the reach of services. As such, it has been suggested that mental health services in the judicial system present an opportunity for identifying those with mental illnesses and making services available to them that would otherwise be nonexistent.

Estimating the prevalence of mental disorder in the criminal justice system is a somewhat inexact practice as the population is inconsistently defined and markedly heterogeneous. Differences may exist on the basis of age, gender, diagnosis, or culture. The prevalence of mental disorder in the criminal justice system indicates that identifying such disorders is of paramount importance. Nonetheless, given the volume of prisoners admitted to jails and prisons on a daily basis, it is not possible to conduct a comprehensive mental health assessment with every person who enters the institution. Thus, screening is vital to identify those who do require a comprehensive evaluation. The aims of screening are to identify mentally disordered offenders and provide the necessary treatment, prevent violent and disruptive incidents in institutions, allocate resources for those with the greatest or most immediate need, and reduce the cycle of admissions to the criminal justice system. To ensure that those requiring mental health treatment are seen by mental health professionals in jails and prisons, screening processes should aim to minimize the number of "false negatives" (failing to identify an actually mentally disordered person), even at the expense of making "false positives" (those identified as possibly being mentally disordered who are not).

The JSAT was developed and refined over a 10-year period that included screening assessments on almost 50,000 prisoners. According to the authors of the JSAT, there are several aims involved in screening for mental disorders in the criminal justice system: identifying mentally disordered inmates for the purpose of treatment, preventing violent behavior, allocating limited resources for the inmates most in need of services, and reducing the demands on the criminal justice, health, and social welfare systems.

Mental health screening should normally be completed within the first day of admission to jail. The purpose of this screening is to detect serious mental disorder requiring rapid management, treatment, or further evaluation. It is desirable to minimize false-negative errors at this screening stage (inmates who have a mental disorder that is not detected). It will allow those inmates who do have a mental illness to be evaluated further.

Administration of the JSAT involves a brief interview with the prisoner (i.e., approximately 20 minutes) and consideration of relevant history. Although the interview is brief, the JSAT is designed to elicit sufficient information to make initial decisions about the mental health needs of incoming inmates. The JSAT is designed to be administered by a mental health professional, most typically a psychiatric nurse, a clinical psychologist, or an intern.

The screening procedure includes completion of a brief semistructured mental status interview and a revised version of the Brief Psychiatric Rating Scale. The interview covers 10 content areas: personal/demographic information and social background, legal status, mental health assessment and treatment, suicide and self-harm risk, violence issues, criminal history, recent social adjustment, recent mental status, substance use and abuse history, and mental health history. Following the administration of the JSAT, the clinician makes recommendations for any prisoner needs if mental health concerns are identified. Typically, a more comprehensive assessment is then recommended and undertaken.

The JSAT is not a standardized psychological test and does not use cut scores for identifying people requiring further assessment. Rather, the JSAT is an example of structured professional judgment, a decision-making approach in which professional judgment is guided by a formal, standardized structure. The JSAT is also unique in that it involves screening inmates for violence and victimization as well as self-harm, suicide, and mental disorder.

Validation data reported by Nicholls and colleagues indicated that the JSAT has a very high degree of validity. The JSAT has been validated for both male and female prisoners. Indeed, 100% of those identified as having psychotic illnesses, obsessive compulsive illnesses, or suicide risk were subsequently referred to a mental health program.

James R. P. Ogloff and Michael R. Davis

See also Risk Assessment Approaches; Structured Assessment of Violence Risk in Youth (SAVRY); Violence Risk Appraisal Guide (VRAG)

Further Readings

Nicholls, T. L., Lee, Z., Corrado, R., & Ogloff, J. R. P. (2004). Women inmates' mental health needs: Evidence of the validity of the Jail Screening Assessment Tool (JSAT). *International Journal of Forensic Mental Health, 3,* 167–184.

Nicholls, T. L., Roesch, R., Olley, M. C., Ogloff, J. R. P., & Hemphill, J. F. (2005). *Jail Screening Assessment Tool (JSAT): Guidelines for mental health screening in jails.* Burnaby, BC: Simon Fraser University, Mental Health, Law, and Policy Institute.

JUDGES' NONVERBAL BEHAVIOR

Early studies by Martin Orne on demand effects and Robert Rosenthal on experimenter expectancy effects established the impact of a sender's nonverbal communication and the way in which it might alter the behavior of others. In the courtroom, judges' nonverbal behavior (e.g., tone of voice, demeanor) often communicates their expectations (sometimes termed *leakage*) about the case at hand. Jurors, for instance, may interpret a judge's nonverbal cues as evaluations of evidence, attorneys, and parties. In some circumstances, these inferences may become information that affects jurors' decisions, in ways not recorded in the trial record. One meta-analysis of studies examining the impact of trial judges' nonverbal behavior on juror verdicts found a significant and nontrivial relationship ($r = .14$). Therefore, depending on the nature and extent of the nonverbal cues, the due process rights of defendants (that is trial fairness) may be impacted.

Research examining judges' nonverbal behavior has found four distinct "global" styles (general behavior that governs interactions that may be verbal or nonverbal): judicial, directive, confident, and warm. These global styles were found in content-present and content-absent channels. Judges high in the "judicial" style are viewed as concerned with fairness and propriety; conversely, the "directive" style is seen as managerial and task oriented. Judges high in the "confidence" style are seen as comfortable and patient, and judges themselves have noted that patience is an important quality that helps avoid tyranny in the courtroom. Finally, judges high in "warmth" are seen as supportive and accepting of other trial participants.

The impact of these global styles reaches beyond the abstract perceptions that jurors may have of trial judges. They also predict the "micro"-level, nonverbal behaviors (e.g., eye contact and body posture) that jurors perceive and use as information regarding judges' perceptions of the trial, trial participants, and evidence. These perceptions, in turn, may affect jurors' own perceptions of the trial, trial participants, and evidence and thereby influence their decision making.

Studies using field-based, quasi-experimental, and experimental methodologies have demonstrated that trial judges form expectations about likely jury verdicts that are related to characteristics of the case, the parties, and the jury. Judges are more likely to expect jury verdicts of guilt when the defendant has a more serious criminal history or is of lower socioeconomic status. Jury characteristics also influence judicial expectations. Judges are more likely to expect that the jury will return a guilty verdict on the first count of indictment (a higher charge) when jurors are more educated and a guilty verdict on the second count of indictment when jurors are younger. Moreover, the nonverbal behavior of judges (as rated by study participants viewing tapes of judges during actual trials) is related to these expectations; more specifically, judges expecting a guilty verdict are rated as less warm, less competent, less wise, and more anxious when they deliver jury instructions. When these studies investigated the impact of judges' nonverbal behaviors, they found them to be related to jury verdicts but not consistently so.

Concerns that judges' nonverbal behavior influences juror decisions, thereby compromising trial fairness, have led to research investigating ways to mitigate such an impact. One study examined the complexity of jury instructions and judges' expectations for trial outcomes. Mock jurors were more likely to vote in accordance with judicial expectations when standard instructions were given. However, when simplified jury instructions were presented, participants were more likely to decide in opposition to the judges' expectations.

As is evident, then, existing literature suggests that the effect of judges' nonverbal behavior on jury verdicts is a complex issue. Part of the impact relates to the context in which jurors make their judgments; while interpretations of behavior may be predictive in everyday social situations, they often are less predictable in novel contexts, such as in trial settings. Generally, people are adept at interpreting explicit and implicit nonverbal messages in a variety of social contexts. For the nonlegal professional though, a courtroom is a novel context. The formality of the situation in which jurors find themselves and the novel instructions governing behavior make usual judgments of behavior often inapplicable. Maintaining stoic behavior when one is faced with accusation is not usually seen in social contexts; in a courtroom, such behavior on the part of a defendant may be governed by circumstances or even explicit directions from one's attorney or the judge. Importantly, jurors may infer such behavior to reflect "cold" or "calculating" characteristics, and these inferences may influence their interpretations of other behavior and testimony—and ultimately their decisions.

Other studies show that the courtroom context matters. In one study, participants were exposed to mock trials that simulated British or American trial procedures. British procedures are generally less adversarial, with attorneys more constrained in their participation. British judges (rather than attorneys) issue objections and summarize the evidence at the end of a trial. Though it was hypothesized that the less adversarial environment would provide fewer distractions and thus diminish the influence of judges' nonverbal behavior, the opposite was found to be the case. Perhaps in British trials, the trial judges are more involved in the trial proceeding, which places them even more under the watchful eye of the jury.

In sum, assessing the determinants of juror decision making and judges' nonverbal behavior is complex. Trial judges' interpretations of evidence, parties, and expectations of the verdict appear to relate to their behavior during the trial. In turn, judges' behavior is apparent to observers (e.g., jurors). Jurors' decisions are not strongly predicted from judges' nonverbal behavior alone (as should be the case), and it is possible that this mitigated effect is because jurors are not always accurate at interpreting nonverbal behaviors in the courtroom. This view is consistent with demonstrations showing that changing trial contexts relates to jurors' reliance on judges' nonverbal behaviors and increased reliance occurring when judges have more active roles.

Meera Adya and Peter Blanck

See also Detection of Deception: Nonverbal Cues; Scientific Jury Selection

Further Readings

Blanck, P. D. (1991). What empirical research tells us: Studying judges' and juries' behavior. *American University Law Review, 40*(2), 775–804.

Collett, M. E., & Kovera, M. B. (2003). The effects of British and American trial procedures on the quality of juror decision making. *Law and Human Behavior, 27*(4), 403–422.

Halverson, A. M., Hallahan, M., Hart, A. J., & Rosenthal, R. (1997). Reducing the biasing effects of judges' nonverbal behavior with simplified jury instructions. *Journal of Applied Psychology, 82*(4), 590–598.

Searcy, M., Duck, S., & Blanck, P. (2005). Nonverbal behavior in the courtroom and the "Appearance of Justice." In R. Riggio & R. Feldman (Eds.), *Applications of nonverbal communication* (pp. 41–61). New York: Lawrence Erlbaum.

JURIES AND EYEWITNESSES

The role of an eyewitness can be extremely important in the legal system, as eyewitness testimony and eyewitness identifications play a major role in the prosecution of a criminal defendant. Often the courts are left to rely solely on an eyewitness because there is no other physical evidence. This leaves the jury to rely on a witness's testimony. Jurors are asked to determine the credibility of an eyewitness at trial when rendering a verdict, and jurors have been found to place more emphasis on eyewitness testimony than on any other kind of evidence. However, there are numerous documented cases of mistaken identifications, and erroneous identifications have been regarded as a leading cause of wrongful convictions. One of the reasons for juries' wrongful convictions based on eyewitness misidentifications is that jurors are not sensitive to the factors that affect identification accuracy. Because jurors rely heavily on eyewitness testimony, it is important to determine what lay people understand about eyewitness performance.

Laypeople's Intuitions About Eyewitness Memory

Psychological research has used various methods to evaluate potential jurors' intuitions concerning eyewitness memory. For example, some studies have used multiple-choice questions that ask potential jurors about the factors that have been found to influence the accuracy of an eyewitness's performance. Another method that has previously been used by researchers is to ask mock jurors whether they agree or disagree with statements concerning eyewitness performance—for example, "Do you agree or disagree that confidence is a poor predictor of an eyewitness's identification accuracy?" The final method researchers use to assess juror knowledge of the factors that influence eyewitness identification testimony is trial simulations. In these simulations, researchers have participants play the role of jurors in a trial, and the researchers manipulate various factors. The goal of these studies is to test either how sensitive the mock jurors are to the factors or how the factors influence perceptions of eyewitness identification accuracy. Certain factors have a significant impact on eyewitness accuracy, while others, such as an eyewitness's confidence rating, are weak predictors of accuracy.

Researchers who began studying mock juries in the late 1970s quickly discovered that participants were unable to distinguish between accurate and inaccurate witnesses. No matter which method was used, the studies indicate that potential jurors' intuitions are correct about some factors that affect eyewitness accuracy but are often incorrect concerning other factors. This unpredictability of jurors' knowledge means that prospective jurors vary widely in their responses when assessing an eyewitness's credibility and rendering a verdict in cases involving eyewitness testimony.

Accuracy and Confidence

Studies have determined that potential jurors' intuitions are not correct concerning certain factors that affect eyewitness accuracy. One factor that jurors overestimate is the power of hypnosis. Mock jurors overestimate the capability of hypnosis in helping memory retrieval. Another factor they overestimate is the relationship between confidence and accuracy. Confidence has been found to have, overall, a somewhat weak relationship to eyewitness identification accuracy. However, mock jurors consistently believe that highly confident witnesses are more likely to make an accurate identification than less confident witnesses. Consequently, potential jurors' verdicts are predicted by the confidence of the witness. Thus, mock jurors are more likely to believe confident eyewitnesses, but confident eyewitnesses are not more likely to be accurate than less confident witnesses. A common finding is that confidence of the eyewitness is the overriding determinant of the weight mock jurors give an eyewitness when rendering the verdict, regardless of whether or not the identification is accurate.

Lineup Procedures and Situational Characteristics

In relying heavily on confidence, which is a weak predictor of accuracy, jurors simultaneously ignore other variables that have a stronger relationship to eyewitness reliability. Such factors include both lineup procedures and characteristics of the witnessing situation. Mock jurors predict far fewer false identifications in a target-absent lineup (i.e., one in which the perpetrator is missing) than in a target-present lineup (containing the perpetrator), which contradicts empirical evidence. Another lineup factor that laypeople do not consider important when predicting accuracy, but which does in fact influence the accuracy of a witness, is lineup instructions. Mock jurors are able to identify when lineup instructions, as well as foils (innocent persons in a lineup), are suggestive; however, they do not consider these factors important when rendering their verdicts.

Jurors also tend not to consider sufficiently aspects of the witnessing situation that can have a significant impact on eyewitness performance. For example, they underestimate the effect of the amount of time an eyewitness has to view the culprit. Research has determined that the longer the exposure to the culprit, the better the accuracy of the eyewitness. Thus, jurors underestimate the importance of lineup selection procedures and exposure time when evaluating the accuracy of an eyewitness.

Cross-Race Identifications

Jurors also may fail to consider individual characteristics that affect eyewitness behavior. One common area of misidentifications is the "cross-race effect," which refers to a person's tendency to be better at identifying a member of his or her own race than members of a different race. Although the cross-race effect influences an eyewitness's accuracy, many potential jurors are unaware of the effect. In one survey, only half the participants agreed that a White eyewitness would be worse than a Black eyewitness at identifying a Black culprit.

Although jurors are not knowledgeable about some factors, there are other factors that laypeople are intuitively knowledgeable about. For instance, they correctly believe that an eyewitness tends to overestimate the duration of an event, that the presence of a weapon negatively affects memory, and that the wording of a question influences an eyewitness's report. Potential jurors also understand that the attention paid to the criminal during the crime, the opportunity to view the criminal, and the amount of time between the crime and the identification of the suspect are important factors concerning the reliability of eyewitness identifications.

In summary, laypeople's intuitions when determining the credibility of an eyewitness vary depending on the factors present in a specific case, but they are often inaccurate. This failure to appreciate many of the factors that affect identification accuracy has significant implications for jurors' verdicts in eyewitness cases. If jurors do not appreciate that a factor, such as cross-racial identification, can influence eyewitness accuracy, then they will not use the information correctly when deciding a defendant's guilt.

Jurors' Intuitions and Their Verdicts

Another question to consider is whether laypeople use their intuitions correctly when rendering a verdict. For example, laypeople have knowledge—some correct, some incorrect—about the various factors that influence the accuracy of an eyewitness. Do they use these intuitions when weighing an eyewitness's credibility and rendering a verdict? To what extent do jurors follow their intuition in reaching a verdict?

Several trial simulations have assessed whether jurors are sensitive to the impact of various witnessing and identification conditions that do and do not influence eyewitness identification accuracy. Specifically, these studies examined the influence on mock jurors' judgments of the perpetrator's wearing a disguise, the presence of a weapon, the use of violence during the crime, the length of the retention interval, the presence or absence of instruction bias, foil bias, and the level of witness confidence. Results indicated that none of these factors influenced the verdict except the level of witness confidence. Therefore, even though mock jurors indicate that they have knowledge concerning the impact of these factors (e.g., weapon focus), they do not use the information correctly when rendering the verdict.

In many cases, mock jurors report knowledge of some relevant factor, such as the cross-race effect, and that factor influences their evaluation of the eyewitness's credibility but does not affect their verdict. It is also the case that mock jurors who are relatively knowledgeable about eyewitness memory—both in general and with respect to specific factors—are not more likely to use this information when rendering their verdict than those who are less knowledgeable. This raises the possibility that expert testimony on eyewitness memory would improve jurors' fact-finding ability.

Expert Testimony

Would providing expert testimony aid the jury in using the factors found to increase or decrease identification accuracy? Several surveys have collected opinions from eyewitness experts. When the experts were asked what the role of an eyewitness expert was, 77% of them said that their primary purpose was to educate the jury. There was also a high rate of agreement among the experts concerning many (though not all) eyewitness phenomena as being reliable enough for presentation in court. The majority of the experts polled believed that eyewitness experts generally have a positive impact on juries.

Apart from the opinions of the experts, a line of research has looked at the impact expert testimony has in a trial scenario involving eyewitness testimony. For example, participants might watch a videotape of a trial in which the primary evidence was an identification of the defendant (a robber) by an eyewitness. Half the participants would be exposed to a *poor* witnessing condition, in which the perpetrator was disguised, the robber was carrying a weapon, the identification took place 14 days after the robbery, and the lineup instructions were suggestive. The remaining participants would be exposed to a *good* witnessing condition, where the robber was not disguised, the weapon was hidden, the identification took place 2 days after the robbery, and the lineup instructions were not suggestive. In half the trials, an expert provided testimony concerning the effect of the factors on eyewitness accuracy. The results showed that the expert testimony increased the sensitivity of the participants to the eyewitness evidence. However, the jurors who

were not presented with expert testimony did not rely on the witnessing conditions when evaluating the accuracy of the eyewitness. These results provide justification for the use of expert testimony in trials that rely heavily on eyewitness testimony.

In summary, despite the fact that mock jurors are aware of many of the limitations of eyewitness identification, they seem to be unable to apply this knowledge in a trial situation, or they use it in assessing witness credibility without applying it further to their verdicts. Jurors consider eyewitness testimony to be highly credible, but their understanding of the topic is fragmentary and often erroneous. Previous findings suggest that expert testimony could be beneficial in improving jurors' understanding of eyewitness memory and aid them in using the evidence properly to arrive at a more informed decision.

Cindy Laub and Brian H. Bornstein

See also Confidence in Identifications; Cross-Race Effect in Eyewitness Identification; Expert Psychological Testimony on Eyewitness Identification; Hypnosis and Eyewitness Memory; Lineup Filler Selection

Further Readings

Abshire, J., & Bornstein, B. H. (2003). Juror sensitivity to the cross-race effect. *Law and Human Behavior, 27,* 471–480.

Boyce, M., Beaudry, J. L., & Lindsay, R. C. L. (2007). Belief of eyewitness identification accuracy. In R. C. L. Lindsay, D. F. Ross, J. D. Read, & M. P. Toglia (Eds.), *Handbook of eyewitness psychology* (Vol. 2, pp. 501–525). Mahwah, NJ: Lawrence Erlbaum.

Devenport, J., Penrod, S. D., & Cutler, B. L. (1997). Eyewitness identification evidence: Evaluating commonsense evaluations. *Psychology, Public Policy, and Law, 3,* 338–361.

Kassin, S. M., & Barndollar, K. A. (1992). The psychology of eyewitness testimony: A comparison of experts and prospective jurors. *Journal of Applied Social Psychology, 22,* 1241–1249.

JURIES AND JOINED TRIALS

Joinder is a legal term that refers to the combination of several counts, parties, or indictments in a single trial. Although there has been limited empirical research examining joinder trials, the research that has been conducted has focused almost entirely on the influence of the inclusion of additional indictments on juror decision making. In this context, a joinder trial refers to a trial in which one defendant is tried for multiple offenses that have similar characteristics or arise from the same incident. The court has the discretion to try a defendant for each offense individually in separate trials or combine the offenses into a single trial if the offenses are related. However, there has been a general consensus among researchers that trials with joined offenses lead to a proconviction bias; jurors are more likely to vote for conviction when offenses are joined than when the defendant is tried separately for each offense. Although the courts have addressed the potential prejudice inherent in joining offenses or defendants by specifying safeguards to protect defendants, the adequacy of these safeguards is still subject to debate.

The Law Concerning Joined Trials

Rule 8(a) of the Federal Rules of Criminal Procedure allows for defendants to be tried for two or more offenses in a single trial if the offenses are similar in character or are part of a single scheme or plan of action. Furthermore, Rule 8(b) allows for two or more defendants to be tried in a single trial if they are accused of jointly engaging in the same criminal transaction. Although these rules are for federal courts, many states have patterned their own rules of criminal procedure after these federal rules. The primary purpose of the combination of offenses is judicial expediency. Separate trials for each offense or defendant would result in many more trials, increasing court costs. In essence, the issue becomes balancing the need to conserve resources with providing defendants fair trials.

The law does recognize that joining offenses and/or defendants may result in a pro-prosecution bias. Rule 14 of the Federal Rules of Criminal Procedure states that the court must protect defendants from the prejudice that may arise from joined trials by separating the charges into separate trials, severing the trials of two or more defendants, or employing any other remedy necessary. If defendants wish to be tried for each of the charges separately or be tried separately from other defendants, they can make a motion for severance of the offenses or from the defendant. However, judges frequently will rule in favor of joining offenses and defendants, unless a case can be made that a joined trial will prejudice the jury. Prejudice may be inferred if the defendant would be likely to rely on contradictory defense strategies if the

charges were severed, if the jury would be likely to infer from one of the charges that the defendant has a criminal disposition, or if the jury would be likely to accumulate evidence across charges when determining the defendant's guilt.

Judges may be disposed to join offenses or defendants because case law argues that any prejudice that does arise from joinder can be easily remedied. Specifically, the U.S. Supreme Court has ruled that prejudice from joining offenses or defendants in a single trial can be prevented by instructing jurors to consider the evidence for each charge individually and decide independently the verdicts for each of the charges or defendants.

Empirical Evidence

Researchers have sought to determine whether the courts' assumptions about the ways that jurors decide verdicts in joined trials are supported by empirical evidence. Although there has been limited research in the area, the studies that have been conducted produced relatively consistent findings. Some researchers have posited that joining offenses may lead to a deprivation of the defendant's right to an unbiased trial. The empirical evidence suggests that when offenses are combined in a single trial, defendants are more likely to be convicted than if the offenses were tried separately. Several jury simulation studies show that trials with joined offenses result in higher conviction rates than if each offense was tried in separate trials. Moreover, although the courts have opined that the prejudice that results from joining offenses can be prevented by proper judicial instruction, most studies suggest that judicial instruction is insufficient to prevent this bias toward conviction. In addition, other factors can affect the nature and degree of the prejudicial nature of joined trials.

In one of the first studies to examine the effects of joining offenses in a single trial, researchers examined the differences in conviction rates when mock jurors made judgments in severed trials, where the defendant was charged with a single count of rape in each of two trials, or in a joined trial, in which the defendant was tried for two charges of rape in the same trial. When the offenses were joined, the judge also instructed the mock jurors that they were to consider each charge with its respective evidence separately. Despite the judicial instruction, the jurors were more likely to find the defendant guilty of the first offense when the offenses were joined than when the offenses were severed. Joinder did not influence rates of conviction on the second offense, but of course, in real cases, the same jury would never hear evidence for both of the severed offenses. This bias toward conviction has been demonstrated across a number of studies that vary on a number of dimensions, including participant type, the presence of deliberations, and the medium used to present the trial (written, audiotaped, or video-taped stimulus).

Studies have also examined the mediators of this pro-prosecution bias in joined trials. As noted previously, courts have acknowledged three possible sources of prejudice in a joined trial: (1) confusion in relating the evidence to the charges, (2) the accumulation of evidence across the charges, and (3) jurors inferring that the defendant has a "criminal disposition" because he or she is being tried for multiple crimes. As early studies merely demonstrated that joining offenses increased convictions and did not address how joining offenses altered juror evaluations that lead to verdicts, researchers such as Sarah Tanford and Steven Penrod began to examine empirically whether various attributes of the joined trial, such as charge similarity, evidence similarity, and judicial instruction, increase jurors' confusion about which evidence relates to which charges, their accumulation of evidence across charges, and their tendency to draw inferences about the defendant's criminal disposition. After watching a videotaped mock trial in which the similarity of the charges, the similarity of the evidence, and the presence of judicial instructions were manipulated, jurors were more likely to render a guilty verdict when the offenses were joined than when they were tried separately, which is consistent with earlier research. In contrast, evidence similarity had no effect on verdicts, and charge similarity was related to verdicts in some studies and not others. Across studies, joining offenses did result in confusion of the evidence, an accumulation of prosecution evidence, and negative inferences about the defendant's criminality. Although the jurors' perceptions of the defendant's criminality mediated the effects of joinder on verdicts, confusion of the evidence did not. Early research by this research team using representative jurors suggested that elaborated judicial instruction designed to reduce the prejudicial effects of joinder had no effect on verdicts; however, follow-up research conducted with undergraduate students found the same instructions to have an ameliorative effect.

Edie Greene and her colleagues have explored other potential mediators of the prejudicial effect of joinder on verdicts. In two experiments, these researchers replicated previous findings that conviction rates are higher in joined trials. They also tested several previously examined mediators of these effects, including negative inferences about the defendant and evidence confusion. Their findings comported with previous research findings that jurors' inferences that a defendant had a criminal disposition seem to drive the increased conviction rate in joined trials. They also examined previously untested mediators of the joinder effect. They hypothesized that jurors who possess the knowledge that the defendant is charged with multiple offenses may be more distressed than jurors who are aware of only a single offense. This increase in distress may lead jurors to lower their criterion required for a conviction; that is, jurors in joined trials may have a lower threshold for finding a defendant guilty than jurors who hear the severed charges. It is also possible that joining offenses creates a greater memory load for jurors in joined trials and this greater load leads to less accurate or detailed memories of the trial evidence. A third hypothesis is that the greater amount of information presented at joined trials may cause jurors to remember only the more salient information that confirms their verdict choice. There was no evidence to support the viability of any of these additional potential mediators of the prejudicial joinder effect.

Although there are some areas in which the empirical evidence is equivocal, there are certain findings about the effects of joinder on jurors that have been repeatedly demonstrated. There is consensus that the joinder of offenses in a single trial results in a pro-prosecution bias. There is also consensus that the effects of joining offenses on the verdict are mediated by jurors' perceptions of the defendant's criminality rather than by confusion over the evidence. Similarly, although the courts have stated that judicial instruction is an adequate safeguard against prejudicial joinder, there is consensus that the judicial instructions generally provided when offenses are joined in one trial are ineffective in protecting jurors' decisions from the prejudicial effects of joinder. There is some evidence that alternative judicial instructions that are designed to reduce the prejudicial effects of joinder may work under certain circumstances; however, further research is needed to replicate these findings and to determine the limitations of these elaborated instructions in reducing the prejudicial effects of joinder on juror decisions.

D. David Barnard and Margaret Bull Kovera

See also Juries and Judges' Instructions

Further Readings

Greene, E., & Loftus, E. I. (1985). When crimes are joined at trial. *Law and Human Behavior, 9,* 193–207.

Horowitz, I. A., & Bordens, K. S. (1985). Joinder of criminal offenses: A review of the legal and psychological literature. *Law and Human Behavior, 9,* 339–353.

Tanford, S., & Penrod, S. (1984). Social inference processing in juror judgments of multiple-offence trials. *Journal of Personality and Social Psychology, 47,* 749–765.

Tanford, S., Penrod, S., & Collins, R. (1985). Decision making in joined criminal trials: The influence of change similarity, evidence similarity, and limiting instructions. *Law and Human Behavior, 9,* 319–337.

Juries and Judges' Instructions

When a jury trial is conducted, community members who typically have no special legal training or knowledge are called on to serve as jurors. During the trial, the judge instructs jurors as to the relevant law and the procedures to be used to determine an appropriate verdict in the case. Unfortunately, jurors do not always render a verdict congruent with the law. Frequently, jurors misunderstand a large portion of the instructions that are presented to them. In some cases, jurors may also decide to disregard the instructions they have been given. A variety of factors contribute to instruction ineffectiveness, including the language used to convey the instructions, jurors' education level, and jurors' preexisting "commonsense" beliefs about the law. A number of proposed improvements to the instruction process, such as rewriting the instructions, changing the timing of delivery of instructions, providing written instructions, and providing a special verdict form or flow chart/decision tree, have been empirically evaluated. The effectiveness of each of these potential solutions is discussed.

Purpose of Instructions

During a trial, the judge delivers relevant substantive and procedural instructions to jurors. Substantive instructions refer to laws that apply to the specific case at hand (e.g., the definition of first- and second-degree murder, manslaughter, sexual assault, and arson; relevant civil laws, etc.). Procedural instructions refer to the general duties of jurors and are relevant across cases (e.g., legal thresholds such as "reasonable doubt" in criminal cases or "clear and convincing evidence" in most civil cases in the United States, the decision rule to be used—either a unanimous or a majority decision, concepts such as burden of proof, etc.).

Development of Pattern Instructions

Historically in the United States, judges would create jury instructions on a case-by-case basis with input from the attorneys involved in the case. However, this process was time-consuming and led to frequent objections on the ground that the relevant law had been incorrectly explained to jurors. In addition, there was not always consistency in the instructions used in cases of a similar nature. Finally, there was concern that jurors did not understand the instructions they were presented with due to the complexity of the law and because judges were forced to focus their attention on delivering instructions that were legally accurate rather than on explaining the law in a manner that jurors could easily understand, to avoid having cases appealed.

To resolve these problems, prewritten "pattern jury instructions" were developed. Pattern instructions are instructions that have been preapproved by relevant sources (legislatures, state bars, commissions) and can be used repeatedly. In 1938, California was the first state to adopt a set of pattern instructions. This practice quickly spread to jurisdictions across the United States at both the state and the federal level.

Pattern instructions were efficient for judges to use, reduced the number of appeals due to the use of erroneous instructions, and successfully ensured that jurors in similar cases heard consistent instructions. However, a well-established body of social science research has demonstrated that jurors still have considerable difficulty in understanding the law when pattern instructions are used.

Jury Instruction Comprehension Rates

Instruction comprehension problems have been found in jurisdictions throughout the United States and in other countries that use laypersons as jurors (e.g., Canada, New Zealand, Australia, Scotland, and England). Many studies have found that jurors typically understand a little more than half the instructions they are presented with and that in some cases there is no difference in comprehension rates between participants who receive pattern instructions and those not instructed at all. Some studies have found comprehension rates below 40%, and some have found comprehension rates in the 70% to 80% range. This variability may be due in part to the measure used to assess comprehension, with higher rates obtained when True/False or other multiple-choice recognition questions are used and lower rates when participants are asked to paraphrase instructions.

Comprehension problems exist for both substantive and procedural instructions. In terms of substantive law, a variety of criminal instructions have been shown to be problematic, including those on murder, assault, robbery, theft, and insanity. For example, research has shown that about one third of jurors are unable to articulate that intent is an essential part of first-degree murder. In addition, other research has shown that jurors are not sensitive to the subtle, but important, differences between different insanity standards (i.e., the M'Naghten Standard, the American Law Institute standard, and the Guilty but Mentally Ill standard). Instead, jurors tend to use their own beliefs about insanity in their decision making.

Death penalty instructions appear to be particularly problematic to jurors. In death penalty cases, jurors are typically asked to weigh aggravating factors (specific aspects of the crime that must be present to sentence a defendant to death) against any mitigating factors (aspects of the crime or the defendant's life that make life imprisonment an appropriate verdict). Although the concept of aggravation appears to be reasonably well understood by jurors, mitigation (a critical safeguard that prevents the defendant from being unjustly executed) is not. Jurors sometimes confuse the factors as well (i.e., erroneously believe a mitigating factor to be an aggravating factor).

Research has indicated that jurors have considerable difficulty in comprehending a variety of concepts from civil trials, such as negligence and liability, and have difficulty in determining appropriate damage awards as a result. Some problems associated with civil instructions are likely a result of the complexity of civil law. Difficulties with civil instructions may also occur because jurors are less familiar with civil legal standards than criminal law concepts (as civil issues are portrayed less frequently in news reports and fictional legal stories presented on television, in films, and in books). In addition, in the United States, civil jurors are typically given minimal guidance as to how abstract concepts such as pain and suffering should be transformed into specific monetary amounts for damages.

Procedural instructions are also problematic for jurors. Some research has shown that jurors do not fully comprehend the meaning of presumption of innocence and burden of proof in criminal cases. There is confusion in the minds of jurors as to whether the burden of proof rests entirely on the prosecution and the defendant does not have to present any evidence.

In addition, jurors do not appear to have a complete understanding of the different "standards of proof." The standard of proof is the level of certainty necessary for a fact finder (i.e., the jury) to find that charges against a defendant in a criminal case or the claims against a defendant/respondent in a civil case are true. In the United States, "beyond a reasonable doubt" is the standard used in criminal trials. Individuals in the legal community have estimated this standard to mean requiring approximately a 90% certainty of guilt. It is the highest standard of proof required, reflecting the belief that it is far worse to convict an innocent person than to acquit a guilty one, yet absolute certainty need not be achieved for a conviction. "Preponderance of evidence" is the standard of proof used in most civil cases and requires that the plaintiff establish a certainty above 50% that the allegations against a defendant are true. In addition, in cases of deprivation of liberty, such as civil commitment, denaturalization, deportation, and termination of parental rights, the standard of "clear and convincing evidence" is also used. This third standard is intended to be an intermediate threshold that falls between the other two and has been interpreted as requiring a certainty level between 67% and 75%. Although some research has shown that jurors provide estimates of the meaning of reasonable doubt that are close to those given by members of the legal community, there is still considerable variability in the estimates provided. In addition, jurors express considerably more variability (reflecting greater uncertainty) when asked to estimate the meaning of the preponderance of evidence and clear and convincing evidence standards. Courts do not typically elaborate on the meaning of standards of proof when jurors are instructed. In cases where definitions of the concepts are given, the explanations typically do not shed much light on the concepts (e.g., for reasonable doubt: a doubt "that is not trivial or imaginary" or a doubt "that would cause a reasonable man to hesitate in making an important decision").

Instructions that caution jurors as to how to use evidence are also problematic. For example, some research has shown that jurors exposed to eyewitness testimony cautionary instructions (commonly known as "Telfaire" instructions) are no more sensitive to the problems associated with eyewitness testimony than jurors not given instructions. Periodically, the judge must instruct jurors to ignore inadmissible information that they have heard in court or in the form of pretrial publicity. These types of instructions have been typically shown to be ineffective. In some cases, jurors may actually pay more attention to evidence that has been ruled as inadmissible than if the judge had said nothing at all about it. This tendency has been termed the "backfire effect" and may be the result of either a sense of resistance (i.e., reactance) building up in jurors because they feel that their freedom to consider the evidence is being threatened or cognitive factors causing a person to pay more attention to information that he or she is actively trying to ignore.

Factors Affecting Instruction Effectiveness

A number of factors have been identified that affect the overall effectiveness of instructions. Comprehension issues are a primary problem and result from the language used to convey the instructions. As previously noted, historically, the focus of instructions has been on stating the law in a legally accurate manner rather than on creating instructions that are designed to maximize comprehensibility. In addition, this problem may be compounded in complex trials in which difficult legal concepts must be explained and a greater amount of instructions must be given. Education level has also been consistently shown to relate to instruction comprehension, with higher instruction comprehension rates found among well-educated jurors, although a number of researchers have found that even law students have difficulty in comprehending the instructions they are presented with.

As previously mentioned, in certain cases, jurors may decide to ignore the instructions they are given. This may happen in cases where a judge rules certain information as inadmissible. In addition, jurors may ignore the law and decide that even though a defendant has broken the law (as they understand the law to be), it would be morally wrong to render a conviction, because the defendant did not violate the spirit of the law or because the law is viewed to be unjust. This phenomenon is known as "jury nullification."

Finally, jurors' beliefs about the law may also interfere with the effectiveness of instructions. There is evidence that jurors tend to rely on their own beliefs regarding the meaning of legal concepts rather than on the specific instructions they are given. This process is known as using "commonsense justice." Jurors may use commonsense justice in their decision making because their beliefs regarding certain legal concepts such as insanity may be particularly strong or because jurors are forced to rely on whatever relevant concepts they possess when given instructions that are unclear.

Improving the Jury Instruction Process

Social science researchers have examined a variety of techniques for improving jurors' comprehension levels for instructions. The most effective technique appears to be rewriting the instructions using general psycholinguistic principles. A variety of research teams across the United States have successfully improved comprehension rates using this approach, with improvement gains between 20% and 30% often detected. It is unclear whether additional revisions to instructions would lead to even higher gains.

In the process of revising instructions, researchers have focused on revisions such as breaking down complex sentences and reorganizing the material using a more logical structure, in addition to replacing legal jargon and uncommon words with more familiar language and replacing abstract words (e.g., "plaintiff") with more concrete terms or specific names (e.g., the plaintiff's actual name). Other changes include eliminating negatively modified sentences, using the active rather than the passive voice, removing prepositional phrases, and replacing nominalizations (nouns that have been constructed from a verb) with verbs (e.g., change "the thinking of" to "think about"). In the process of applying these psycholinguistic principles and improving comprehension, the legal accuracy of instructions has not been sacrificed.

Jurors typically are given instructions just prior to deliberations. However, several studies have found that delivering instructions twice, once at the beginning of the trial and again after the evidence has been presented, improves comprehension somewhat. In addition, delivering pretrial-instructions gives participants a framework for interpreting the evidence, making them more attentive to due-process issues designed to protect the defendant such as burden of proof. However, comprehension has not been improved on a reliable basis when jurors are only given pretrial instructions (that are not repeated following attorneys' closing statements).

Traditionally, the judge delivers instructions to jurors orally. However, an alternative delivery approach is to provide written instructions to the jurors that can be brought into the deliberation room. Several studies have shown that comprehension levels are increased when written instructions are provided, and that jurors are better able to apply the law. However, other studies have produced contradictory findings and have not found improvements for comprehension or verdict differences when written instructions are used.

Special verdict forms may be used to ensure that jurors attend to key elements that are conveyed in jury instructions. A special verdict form consists of a series of questions regarding separate issues of fact to which jurors must respond. These forms are used in both civil and criminal trials in the United States and in other countries. Similarly, flow charts (also known as decision trees) indicate the order in which decisions regarding different legal questions should be answered and the appropriate verdict that should be rendered as a result of those decisions. It is possible that instruction comprehension can be improved through the administration of these forms and charts because jurors are required to attend to key legal questions that must be resolved. To date, only a few studies have examined the effectiveness of special verdict forms and flow chart/decision-tree models, and those studies have produced mixed results. Some research has shown that instruction comprehension is improved by these techniques and that jurors believe that special verdict forms are helpful in improving their understanding of instructions and rendering a verdict that they are confident in and satisfied with. However, other research has shown that comprehension is not increased by these techniques and that jurors do not use flow charts when they are provided during deliberations.

When jurors are unsure as to the meaning of instructions, they may attempt to resolve their confusion during deliberations by discussing the matter with each other. If one or more jurors have a very good understanding of the instructions, it may be possible for them to clarify the instructions for others,

thus improving the overall comprehension level of the jury. Research has indicated that jurors have some discussion regarding the meaning of instructions in most trials. Unfortunately, jurors are unable to clarify misunderstood points on a regular basis and, as a result, deliberation does not appear to be a successful remedy for comprehension problems. Rather, it has been demonstrated that jurors are as likely to replace an initially correct understanding of instructions with an incorrect one as to correct a misunderstood point of the instructions.

Jurors may also turn to the judge to clarify instructions. Although judicial clarification may be the best possible solution to instruction comprehension problems, judges typically either re-read the problematic instructions or do nothing at all and simply allow jurors to proceed relying on their best memory and understanding of the instructions originally delivered. The lack of judicial responsiveness to jurors' requests for clarification is based on concerns regarding appeals. It is unlikely that a decision will be reversed on the basis of the instructions provided when the judge restricts his or her comments to the pattern instructions. However, if he or she deviates from the specific wording in the pattern instructions, it can be argued that the language used to clarify the instructions was inappropriate.

The "Plain English" Movement and the Future of Jury Instructions

The primary problem associated with judicial instructions is that they have traditionally been conveyed in a manner that emphasizes legal accuracy, with minimal attention paid to comprehensibility among a nonlegal professional audience. The development of pattern instructions was seen as an improvement to the instruction process, and it did reduce the time judges spent developing instructions for jurors as well as the number of appeals based on instructions while increasing instruction consistency across cases. However, pattern instructions did not serve to remedy comprehension problems.

Recently, states have begun to respond to the recommendations of social scientists by redrafting pattern instructions using a "plain English" approach and applying psycholinguistic principles. For example, in 2003, California approved approximately 800 new civil jury instructions and special verdict forms and revised its criminal jury instructions in 2006. Other states are either considering or in the process of making similar revisions (including Delaware, Iowa, Michigan, Minnesota, Missouri, North Dakota Arizona, Florida, Vermont, and Washington). It is hoped that in the future, continued assessment and revision of instructions accompanied by the application of theoretical perspectives from cognitive and social psychology will continue to improve the jury instruction process, leading to verdicts that are based on a true understanding of the law by jurors.

Joel D. Lieberman

See also Damage Awards; "Dynamite Charge"; Inadmissible Evidence, Impact on Juries; Jury Nullification; Jury Understanding of Judges' Instructions in Capital Cases

Further Readings

Ellsworth, P. C., & Reifman, A. (2000). Juror comprehension and public policy: Perceived problems and proposed solutions. *Psychology, Public Policy, & Law, 6,* 788–821.

Elwork, A., Sales, B. D., & Alfini, J. J. (1982). *Making jury instructions understandable.* Charlottesville, VA: Michie.

Finkel, N. J. (2000). Commonsense justice and jury instructions: Instructive and reciprocating connections. *Psychology, Public Policy, and Law, 6,* 591–628.

Greene, E., & Bornstein, B. (2000). Precious little guidance: Jury instruction on damage awards. *Psychology, Public Policy and Law, 6,* 743–768.

Lieberman, J. D., & Sales, B. D. (1997). What social sciences teaches us about the jury instruction process. *Psychology, Public Policy, and Law, 3,* 1–56.

Ogloff, J. R. P., & Rose, V. G. (2005). The comprehension of judicial instructions. In N. Brewer & K. D. Williams (Eds.), *Psychology and law: An empirical perspective* (pp. 407–444). New York: Guilford Press.

JURY ADMINISTRATION REFORMS

Over the past half-century, courts have implemented a host of reforms to the administrative processes involved in qualifying and summoning prospective jurors for jury service. These reforms have largely focused on improving the demographic representation of the jury pool and alleviating the burden of jury service on citizens. This entry describes the legal and theoretical basis for administrative reforms and the specific efforts that courts have made to ensure that the jury pool is broadly inclusive of the entire population and reflects a fair cross-section of the community.

Legal and Theoretical Basis for Administrative Reforms

The U.S. Supreme Court first ruled that African Americans could not be systematically excluded from the jury pool on the basis of race in 1880, but widespread efforts to ensure a demographically representative jury pool began in earnest only with the civil rights and women's rights movements during the mid-20th century. The legal principle requiring a racially and ethnically diverse jury pool derives mainly from the Sixth Amendment requirement that criminal defendants be tried by "a fair and impartial jury," which the U.S. Supreme Court has interpreted as a jury selected from "a fair cross-section of the community."

The principle is premised on the belief that a jury that reflects a broad spectrum of life experiences and viewpoints is less likely to succumb to unchallenged assumptions or biases during deliberations. This understanding is supported by a substantial body of empirical research concerning the implications of the story model of juror decision making, which posits that jurors filter trial evidence as it is presented through a preexisting framework of life experiences, opinions, and attitudes (e.g., how the world works, how people interact, etc.), which in turn affects the inferences that each juror takes away from that evidence. During deliberations, jurors have the opportunity to present competing interpretations of evidence and discuss their credibility in the context of the entire case and come to a consensus about the facts and the appropriate application of law to those facts in their verdicts. Due to the widespread public acceptance of this premise, courts have also justified administrative reforms to the jury system to bolster public perceptions of the fairness and legitimacy of jury verdicts produced by diverse and representative juries.

A secondary principle—tangentially related to the first—is that jury service is a civic obligation that all citizens must be prepared to undertake if the American justice system is to continue to uphold its democratic ideals. This principle derives less from specific constitutional requirements and more from the belief that a well-functioning democracy engages citizens across every dimension of cultural identity, socioeconomic status, and political orientation in a process of shared decision making. Thus, no segment of society should be considered too marginal or too elite to be spared from the basic task of jury service.

A number of institutional and social factors affect citizens' ability and willingness to serve, and they often have a disproportionate effect on minority populations. For example, voter registration lists, the most popular source list for compiling the master jury list, have long been criticized for overrepresenting populations that are older, more affluent, and highly educated and being less representative of minorities. The high mobility rates of youth and lower-income individuals result in substantial numbers of jury summonses—on average, 15% nationally—being returned as undeliverable by the U.S. Postal Service. Some qualification criteria, such as citizenship and English language fluency, disproportionately exclude Hispanic, Asian, and other immigrant populations. Occupational exemptions for various types of professionals place a disproportionate burden of jury service on those who do not qualify for an exemption. The length of time that citizens are required to serve can last up to 6 months or more in some jurisdictions, and juror fees rarely cover more than daily travel and out-of-pocket expenses. Consequently, an average of 9% of prospective jurors are excused for hardship. Another 9% of individuals— again disproportionately lower income and less educated—fail to respond to their jury summonses.

Specific Reforms

To address these myriad issues, state and federal courts have gradually implemented various improvements in jury administration that are designed to expand the jury pool to encompass all jury-eligible citizens, equalize the burden of jury service across the entire population, and make it possible for all jury-eligible individuals to serve if summonsed. For example, half of all state courts now use both registered voters and licensed drivers lists to compile the master jury list, and 20% of courts use three or more source lists. Each new source list adds unique names that were not found on the previous source lists, thus expanding the pool of prospective jurors. Many courts also employ sophisticated mailing list management tools, such as those developed by mail order retailers, to verify and update addresses and reduce the proportion of undeliverable summonses. Several jurisdictions have eliminated occupational exemptions; 12 states and the District of Columbia provide exemptions only for previous jury service.

To reduce the burden of jury service on individuals, nearly one in four courts (23%), whose collective jurisdiction encompasses more than half the U.S. population, now employs a "one day/one trial" term of service. That is, if a person reports for jury service and is impaneled as a trial juror, he or she serves until the completion of that trial and then is released for some statutorily defined period of time. If the juror is not impaneled as a trial juror by the end of the day, he or she again is released from jury service for the statutorily defined period of time. Many courts have also enacted deferral policies that permit citizens to select a new reporting date if the original summons date conflicts with a prior obligation. From a purely logistical standpoint, a shorter term of service in which jurors are used and released, rather than reused in subsequent jury trials, requires courts to summon more citizens for jury service to ensure a sufficient number of prospective jurors to try cases. Thus, this arrangement simultaneously relieves the burden of jury service on individual jurors and distributes the burden more equitably among the jury-eligible population of the community.

Other jurisdictions have increased juror fees to more adequately reimburse jurors' out-of-pocket expenses. Because the fiscal implications of these changes on state and local governments can be quite substantial, many jurisdictions are moving away from a flat daily payment for jury service and toward a graduated payment system in which jurors receive a reduced fee, or no fee, on the first day of jury service and then an increased fee on subsequent days. This type of payment arrangement works well in jurisdictions with one day/one trial terms. It minimizes the cost of jury service incurred by courts on the first day of service, when large numbers of jurors report for jury selection, but provides somewhat better compensation to those citizens who serve for longer periods of time as sworn trial jurors. Some states have also coupled improved juror compensation systems with legislation mandating that employers compensate employees while on jury service for a given period of time (usually 3–10 days), thus minimizing the financial hardship jurors might experience due to lost income. Finally, Arizona, Louisiana, Mississippi, and Oklahoma have enacted legislation authorizing a "Lengthy Trial Fund" to reimburse jurors who are impaneled on longer trials (e.g., 10 days or more) for lost income up to a statutorily defined maximum ($100 to $300 per day).

Along with efforts to reduce the burden of jury service, many courts have stepped up enforcement proceedings on citizens who fail to respond to the jury summons. Nearly two thirds of courts report some form of follow-up on nonresponders, most often in the form of a follow-up letter or second summons that informs jurors that they have failed to report for jury service and assigns them a new reporting date. Courts that have formally evaluated this approach find that the response rate to a second summons ranges from 35% to 50% and that individuals responding to a second summons qualify for jury service in roughly the same proportion as those responding to the first summons. If a juror fails to appear a second time, sanctions can increase in severity from civil contempt proceedings and fines to arrest and incarceration. Practically, serious juror scofflaws constitute a relatively small proportion of the population in most communities. Thus, these more aggressive enforcement measures often are conducted sporadically, but with a great deal of publicity, as a deterrent to future jurors who might ignore the summons.

The result of these efforts has been a remarkable improvement in the diversity of jury pools over the past three decades. Although some disparity in racial and ethnic representation still occurs in most communities, typically the difference between the proportion of a given minority in the community and the proportion of that minority in the jury pool ranges from 2 to 4 percentage points. These changes, especially expanding the inclusiveness of the master jury list and reducing the term of service, have also dramatically increased the proportion of the American population that has experienced jury service—from 6% in 1977 to 29% in 2004. It may be this direct and personal experience with jury service that has continued to bolster popular support for the institution even in light of the precipitous decline in the proportion of cases tried by jury over the past 30 years.

Paula Hannaford-Agor

See also Jury Deliberation; Jury Reforms; Jury Selection; Story Model for Jury Decision Making; Voir Dire

Further Readings

American Bar Association. (2005). *Principles for juries and jury trials.* Chicago: American Bar Association.

Hannaford-Agor, P. L., Waters, N. L., Mize, G. E., & Wait, M. (2007). *The state-of-the-states survey of jury improvement efforts: A compendium report.* Williamsburg, VA: National Center for State Courts.

Hastie, R., Penrod, S. D., & Pennington, N. (1983). *Inside the jury.* Cambridge, MA: Harvard University Press.

Munsterman, G. T., Hannaford-Agor, P. L., & Whitehead, G. M. (Eds.). (2006). *Jury trial innovations.* Williamsburg, VA: National Center for State Courts.

Jury Competence

Many observers praise the abilities of juries in making decisions in both criminal and civil cases. Others, however, criticize the competence of juries, arguing that juries are not effective legal decision makers. Psychologists have conducted a variety of studies to evaluate how juries make decisions, using simulation and field experiments, archival data, and interviews of jurors and judges. Overall, juries show a relatively high degree of competence—jurors take their decision-making tasks seriously, understand the nature of the adversary process, attempt to make decisions that achieve many (sometimes conflicting) goals simultaneously, and perform at a level that is similar to that of judges. However, there are clear areas in which jury performance could be improved, and a variety of procedural mechanisms have been developed to assist juries in their decision-making tasks.

Models of Juror Decision Making

Research has shown that jurors attend to the trial evidence presented and show relatively high levels of comprehension and recall of the facts at issue. Mathematical models of juror decision making—i.e., Bayesian models, algebraic models, and stochastic process models—posit that jurors begin with a preliminary judgment and update that judgment as evidence is introduced throughout the trial. In contrast, the "story model" of juror decision making is an explanation-based model of juror decision making that contends that jurors construct a narrative story that best accounts for the (often conflicting) trial evidence and then select the verdict option that best fits that narrative.

Jurors' Use of Evidence

In reaching their verdicts, jurors endeavor to make decisions that account for the evidence and that follow the law. Research has shown that in doing so, jurors do tend to make use of the evidence that the law defines to be relevant to their decisions. For example, jurors use evidence about offenders' conduct in determining criminal guilt and civil liability and evidence about the severity of plaintiffs' injuries in setting compensation. Indeed, the substantive trial evidence turns out to be the best predictor of verdicts.

Extralegal Evidence

In some instances, however, jurors may use information that has been held to be legally irrelevant. First, research has demonstrated that jurors sometimes use information that is related to the case but that is not part of the legally admissible evidence. For instance, jurors have difficulty ignoring evidence to which they are exposed but that is ruled to be inadmissible by a judge—even when they are explicitly told to disregard such evidence. In addition, jurors are influenced by information about a case that that they obtain through the media—pretrial publicity—but that is not part of the evidence admitted in the court.

Second, jurors sometimes use evidence that is appropriately offered for one purpose to inform another decision for which that evidence is legally irrelevant. For example, evidence about a criminal defendant's prior record is not admissible to establish guilt, but it may be admitted to discredit the defendant's testimony. However, jurors have difficulty in limiting their use of such information. In the same way, jurors have been shown to conflate their liability and damages decisions, using evidence that is relevant to one in making decisions about the other. Similarly, there is evidence that jurors take into account their assessment of a plaintiff's own fault in determining the level of damage that plaintiff has suffered. Because these decisions are supposed to be made separately and then combined by the judge, this can result in a "double discounting" of the plaintiff's damages.

Third, jurors have also been found to rely on preexisting cognitive schemas about the law in ways that may be inconsistent with legal rules. For example, jurors may bring with them ideas about offenses or verdict categories that may conflict with the relevant law. Similarly, in the absence of guidance from the court about whether or how their decisions should take into account the possibility that a party is insured or will incur attorney fees, jurors must rely on their own notions about the likelihood and nature of any insurance or fees and about how their decisions should be informed by these possibilities.

Some, but not all, of the difficulties that jurors have in appropriately dealing with these evidentiary issues may be related to difficulties that they have in understanding jury instructions (see below). In addition, some studies have shown that jurors are better able to avoid misusing evidence in some of these ways when given instructions that explain the rationale underlying the legal rules. For example, jurors are better able to keep evidence about plaintiff or defendant culpability from influencing their damage awards when the reasons for doing so are explained.

Hearsay Evidence

There has also been research examining how jurors use particular types of evidence. For example, some studies have examined how jurors assess hearsay evidence—testimony by a witness relaying what was said by another person (the "declarant") that is used to prove the truth of the matter asserted. Jurors appear to be able to competently assess hearsay evidence, distinguishing more reliable hearsay testimony as more accurate, more helpful to their decisions, and of higher quality than less reliable hearsay testimony.

Confession and Eyewitness Evidence

How jurors assess incriminating evidence, such as confession evidence or eyewitness testimony, has also been studied. With regard to confession evidence, there is some evidence that jurors are not influenced by factors—such as evidence of coercion—that are associated with the reliability of confessions. There is similar evidence with respect to eyewitness testimony. Psychological research has documented a number of factors that can influence the accuracy of an eyewitness, including the presence of a weapon, the use of a disguise, or other conditions under which the eyewitness observed the suspect. However, unaided, juror decisions—such as verdicts, culpability judgments, or assessments of the accuracy of the eyewitness—may not be influenced by these factors. In addition, juror decisions can be insensitive to differences in lineup procedures. In contrast, there is evidence that jurors are influenced by the confidence of the testifying eyewitness, even though confidence is only weakly correlated with witness accuracy. Expert testimony about the influences on eyewitness accuracy (e.g., witnessing conditions), however, has been shown to increase juror sensitivity to such factors and to decrease the effect of witness confidence. When experts testify for both sides, however, jurors appear to become skeptical of all eyewitness testimony, including identifications made under relatively good conditions.

Scientific and Statistical Evidence

Finally, it has been found that jurors can have particular difficulty with certain types of complex evidence, such as statistical, scientific, or other forms of expert testimony. On the one hand, expert evidence often proves helpful to juries—for example, helping them better evaluate other evidence, such as eyewitness testimony or confessions (see above). In addition, there is evidence that jurors carefully evaluate such expert testimony, approaching expert witnesses with some skepticism and working to evaluate both the experts (e.g., their credentials and motives) and the substantive testimony. On the other hand, it has been found that jurors sometimes have difficulty in understanding and using such evidence properly. For example, there is evidence that jurors are not skilled at identifying flaws in the design of scientific research studies and may not discount the value of such research appropriately. Studies with confounding variables, missing control groups, problems with the validity of measures, and the opportunity of experimenter demand are as influential as better-designed studies, and witnesses presenting such flawed research are not seen as any less credible than witnesses presenting studies without such flaws. Similarly, interviews with jurors as well as experimental studies have shown that jurors experience difficulty in reasoning about and making inferences from statistical evidence, such as probability estimates and information about population base rates. Recent research, however, suggests that improved judicial instructions may help jurors better understand scientific testimony.

Civil Decision Making

Civil juries in particular have been criticized as unpredictable, arbitrary, biased against plaintiffs, and prone to making large damage awards. Data from actual cases, however, provide little evidence of juries that are out of control; most jury awards are modest. However, while jury damage awards are appropriately influenced by legally relevant factors, they can also be highly variable, such that different amounts are awarded in cases involving what seem to be similar injuries. In addition, studies have found that juries tend to overcompensate small injuries but undercompensate large injuries. Moreover, there is evidence that for noneconomic damages, such as damages for pain and suffering, and for punitive damages, jurors have some difficulty in translating their judgments into dollar figures and can be influenced by cognitive biases such as anchoring.

Concern is often expressed that juries are biased in favor of plaintiffs and against defendants, particularly those defendants with "deep pockets." However, there is evidence that jurors are relatively skeptical of plaintiffs and their claims. In addition, there is little evidence that the wealth of the defendant influences jurors' liability determinations or their compensatory damage awards. In contrast, however, corporate defendants do seem to be held to a higher ("reasonable corporation") standard of conduct than are defendants who are individuals.

Jury Instructions

The primary way in which juries are schooled in the requirements of the law is through the legal instructions that trial judges give them to guide their decisions. These instructions explain the jury's role, inform the jury about the legal rules that govern the case that it is to decide, define the standard and burden of proof, and define the possible alternative verdicts available to the jury. Typical instructions focus on stating the law precisely rather than on comprehensibility; contain many legal terms of art; and consist of lengthy, complex sentences. Perhaps not surprisingly, therefore, a large body of research has demonstrated that while jurors perform relatively well at understanding and remembering the factual evidence presented at trial, they often have difficulty in understanding, remembering, and applying these legal instructions. For example, jurors have particular difficulty in understanding the "beyond a reasonable doubt" standard in criminal cases, the "negligence" standard in civil cases, and legal terms such as "aggravation" and "mitigation" in capital punishment instructions. Similarly, typical instructions limiting the use of particular evidence or indicating that particular evidence is to be ignored are poorly understood.

Significantly, there is evidence that the comprehension of and ability to follow instructions is improved when instructions are rewritten following the basic principles of psycholinguistics. Removing legal jargon, negatives, and words with multiple meanings; using more common words; replacing abstract concepts with concrete terms; using party names; simplifying sentence structure; and providing an analytical structure to guide decision making can all help make instructions more comprehensible. In addition, there is some evidence that providing jurors with written copies of instructions can lead to improved memory for and comprehension of the legal instructions. As noted above, research has also shown that jurors are better able to follow legal instructions when they include explanations and reasons for the underlying legal rules.

Deliberation

Much research examining jury competence has been conducted by examining the decisions and judgments of individual jurors. Indeed, the predeliberation preferences and judgments of individual jurors are predictive of ultimate jury verdicts. Juries, however, operate as group decision-making bodies. Thus, it is important to consider the ways in which the deliberative process might influence jury competence. Importantly, juries may be advantaged over an individual decision maker (such as a judge) in that they can draw on the memories and understandings of the collective. Research has demonstrated that jurors who deliberate are more likely to engage in complex reasoning about the law and the evidence and make more counterarguments, have better memory for the trial evidence, are less susceptible to some judgmental biases, and reach more consistent decisions. On the other hand, group deliberation has been found to worsen judgmental biases in some circumstances, and group decisions can become more extreme.

Comparing Jurors With Judges

Any discussion of jury competence must consider the standard by which competence is to be evaluated. One common standard by which to evaluate jury competence is to compare jurors with the most likely alternative—trial court judges. In general, research has shown that judges and jurors show substantial agreement in their decisions. High rates of agreement are found both in cases classified by judges as relatively easy to understand and in cases involving a high degree of legal and factual complexity. Moreover, in those cases in which there is disagreement between jury and judge, the judges do not attribute the disagreement to jury misunderstandings of the case. Rather, judges are more

likely to disagree with jury decisions in cases that are "closer calls"—that is, in cases in which there are credible arguments to support either decision. Several studies have also shown relatively high rates of agreement between juries and other expert decision makers; for example, jury verdicts in medical malpractice cases tend to correlate with the judgments of physicians.

In addition, research has shown that judges and jurors engage in similar decision *processes*. For example, judges and jurors consider the same factors in assessing plaintiffs' pain and suffering in personal injury cases, rank the severity of cases in similar ways, take into account similar factors in setting punitive damage awards, and are influenced by the same variables when assigning blame in criminal cases. Judges also suffer from many of the same difficulties that jurors do. For example, judges, like jurors, are typically not trained in math or science and have difficulty in evaluating statistical and scientific evidence. In addition, judges, like jurors, have been shown to be unable to ignore inadmissible evidence. Similarly, judges are subject to the same sorts of cognitive illusions as are jurors; their decisions are influenced by anchoring, outcome and hindsight bias, and other heuristics.

Judges—as the trial participants who are in a position to most closely observe the jury—are also well suited to comment on jury competence. When asked their opinions about juries, judges report high levels of satisfaction with juries and believe that juries understand the issues and attempt to follow the legal instructions.

Aids to Jury Decision Making

A variety of aids have been proposed to assist juries with their decision tasks. Many of these aids have been controversial, but over time more courts have become willing to incorporate some of these procedures into their processes. This increased openness has also facilitated empirical assessments of the effects of these reforms in field settings. These reforms attempt to improve jury decision making through a range of mechanisms. First, a number of reforms are aimed at assisting jurors in making sense of and remembering the evidence. For example, instructing juries about the law prior to the introduction of evidence provides jurors with a framework that helps them structure the trial evidence as they hear it. Similarly, allowing jurors to take notes and ask questions of witnesses helps jurors understand the testimony presented and remember it better. Providing access to trial transcripts, witness lists, or trial summaries helps jurors refresh their memories, allows them to clarify the evidence when memories differ, and makes it more likely that they will systematically process the evidence. Allowing jurors to discuss the case throughout the trial may help jurors comprehend the evidence and formulate useful questions.

Other reforms are targeted at helping jurors follow the legal rules. For example, bifurcating the trial—that is, separating trials into multiple parts at which different questions are considered may help jurors focus on the evidence that is most relevant to the separate decisions at hand. For example, decisions on punitive damages could be postponed until after the jury has determined liability and compensatory damages. Then, evidence relevant to punitive damages could be heard at a separate proceeding. Similarly, asking jurors to respond to a series of questions ("interrogatories" or a "special verdict") can be used to focus jurors on the relevant legal questions. Reforms directed at judicial instructions are also likely to improve jurors' ability to understand and follow the law. Rewriting judicial instructions to make them more understandable and easier to follow, drafting instructions to assist jurors with scientific and statistical evidence, and formulating reason-based instructions may all help jurors comprehend and apply the law better.

Jennifer K. Robbennolt

See also Chicago Jury Project; Confession Evidence; Damage Awards; Expert Psychological Testimony; Expert Psychological Testimony on Eyewitness Identification; Hearsay Testimony; Inadmissible Evidence, Impact on Juries; Juries and Eyewitnesses; Juries and Judges' Instructions; Jury Decisions Versus Judges' Decisions; Jury Deliberation; Jury Reforms; Statistical Information, Impact on Juries; Story Model for Juror Decision Making

Further Readings

Greene, E., Chopra, S., Kovera, M. B., Penrod, S., Rose, V. G., Schuller, R., et al. (2002). Jurors and juries: A review of the field. In J. R. P. Ogloff (Ed.), *Taking psychology and law into the twenty-first century* (pp. 225–284). New York: Kluwer Academic/Plenum.

Hans, V. P. (Ed.). (2006). *The jury system: Contemporary scholarship.* Aldershot, UK: Ashgate.

Kalven, H., & Zeisel, H. (1966). *The American jury.* Boston: Little, Brown.

Lieberman, J. D., & Sales, B. D. (Eds.). (2000). The jury instruction process [Special issue]. *Psychology, Public Policy, & Law, 6*(3).

Robbennolt, J. K. (2005). Evaluating juries by comparison to judges: A benchmark for judging? *Florida State University Law Review, 32,* 469–509.

Robbennolt, J. K., Groscup, J., & Penrod, S. D. (2005). Evaluating and assisting civil jury competence. In I. Weiner & A. Hess (Eds.), *The handbook of forensic psychology* (pp. 392–425). New York: Wiley.

Vidmar, N. (1998). The performance of the American civil jury: An empirical perspective. *Arizona Law Review, 40,* 849–899.

Vidmar, N., & Hans, V. P. (2007). *American juries: The verdict.* New York: Prometheus Books.

JURY DECISIONS VERSUS JUDGES' DECISIONS

In American trials, the verdict is reached by either a judge or a jury, raising questions as to how these two fact finders reach their decisions and whether their decisions systematically differ. Most research has focused on the jury, though some key studies have compared the decisions of judges and juries. The available archival studies, case-specific judicial surveys, and experimental research reveal substantial similarities and a few differences.

Before a civil or criminal trial begins, the parties decide whether it will be a trial by jury or a trial by judge ("bench trial"). A bench trial occurs if both sides waive the right to a jury. Although rates vary across jurisdictions, approximately one third of felony trials and one in four civil trials in the United States are bench trials. Outside the United States, a mixed tribunal consisting of both lay and professional members may determine the outcome of a trial. Some critics of the American jury suggest that the justice system would be improved by transferring more decision-making responsibility to professional judges. Thus, in evaluating the performance of the jury, the policy-relevant comparison is not some hypothetical ideal decision maker, whatever characteristics that model might have, but rather the professional, legally qualified judge. Yet most research on trial court decision makers has focused on the jury rather than on the judge, perhaps because the jury is both a cultural icon and a favorite whipping boy, because relying on conscripted amateurs rather than professionals to decide outcomes of important conflicts raises questions, and because laypersons are more accessible than judges as subjects for research on decision making.

Judges and juries differ in several potentially important ways. Modern judges are legally trained professionals, while jurors are not. Although the modern jury may include members with legal training, most jurors are legal novices. Although some members of a jury may be more educated than the judge or have more expertise in a particular trial-related topic, the judge is typically more educated than the average juror. While the trial judge sits and deliberates alone, jury members have an opportunity to pool their experiences and opinions and to correct misunderstandings. Jurors, unlike judges, must reach a group decision. Finally, the judge is a repeat player, employed by the state to preside regularly over legal matters. In contrast, for the citizen selected to serve as a juror, jury service is an unusual event. The differences between the decisions of judges and juries may be due to one or a combination of these factors.

Direct comparisons of judge and jury decision making are challenging to make, and whether the data are obtained in the field or the laboratory, the implications of the results are sometimes ambiguous. Nonetheless, they are necessary to draw policy conclusions about the decision-making behavior of these two parties. Although still rare, their number is increasing, providing some systematic evidence on two central questions. First, do judge and juries differ in the likelihood of their deciding on conviction or liability or in the level of sentence severity or damage amounts they choose? Second, do juries and judges consider different factors or weigh them differently in reaching their decisions?

Researchers compare the decisions of judges and juries using three methods: archival analyses examining outcomes in jury versus bench trials, judicial surveys in which the judge indicates how he or she would have decided the case that a jury decided, and experiments in which judges and jurors respond to the same (or similar) simulated evidence. All three methods have strengths and weaknesses. A picture of current knowledge about judge–jury similarities and differences emerges from a composite of these findings.

Archival Research

Archival studies capture the real decisions of judges and juries, but they must attempt to control statistically for differences between the cases tried by judges and those tried by juries. Because the tribunal that hears the case is determined by the choice of the litigant not to plead guilty or to settle as well as whether or not to waive the jury, the selection of cases is far from random and must be modeled for successful control. Most of the archival research comparing judge and jury verdicts has been conducted on civil trials. Researchers have not found consistent differences in overall liability rates between juries and judges. They have shown, however, that differential win rates on liability in federal civil trials vary across categories of cases, with plaintiffs winning more often in bench trials than in jury trials in some major types of tort cases and less often in bench trials than in jury trials in others. Before concluding that these patterns indicate that the win rates on the decisions of the judge and the jury do not differ on average or differ systematically by case type, it is necessary to determine how much of the apparent similarity or difference is attributable to selection effects. A key difficulty is that in attempting to control for selection differences, researchers do not have even an approximate measure of the strength of the evidence for liability and must rely on the limited case characteristics that have been recorded in the archives.

The same modeling problem arises for comparisons of judge and jury verdicts on damages. Several archival studies report that damage awards from jurors tend to be higher than those from judges, although a substantial portion of the apparent difference disappears when controls for differences in the cases they decide are introduced. Other studies have found no overall differences. Similarly, some researchers using archival data to study punitive damages and the size of punitive damage awards have found more frequent and higher awards given by juries, while others have found no differences.

Case-Based Judicial Surveys

Nearly 50 years ago, to address the selection problems that plague archival comparisons of judge and jury verdicts, Harry Kalven and Hans Zeisel developed the innovative approach of a case-based judicial survey for their classic national study of the American jury. In each of the 7,500 cases they studied, the trial judge completed a questionnaire describing the characteristics of the case, the jury's verdict, and how the judge would have decided the same case in a bench trial. Studies using this approach depend on the independence of the judges' personal verdict reports—that is, whether the judge reports a personal verdict preference before learning the jury's verdict or, if the report comes after, whether the judge has been affected by that knowledge. Nonetheless, the case-based judicial survey ensures that the judge and jury verdicts being compared come from equivalent cases because the judge in each case is providing a judicial verdict in precisely the same real trial that a jury decides. The judge and jury in the Kalven-Zeisel survey of 3,500 criminal cases agreed in 78% of the cases on whether or not to convict. When they disagreed, the judge would have convicted when the jury acquitted in 19% of the cases, and the jury convicted when the judge would have acquitted in 3% of the cases—a net leniency rate of 16%. Disagreement rates were no higher when the judge characterized the evidence as difficult than when the judge characterized it as easy, suggesting that the disagreements were not produced by the jury's inability to understand the evidence. Disagreement rates did rise when the judge characterized the evidence as close rather than clear, indicating that disagreement cases were, at least in the judge's view, more likely to be those cases that were susceptible to more than one defensible verdict. Primary explanations offered for the overall differences were differences in judgments about the credibility of witnesses and a different threshold of reasonable doubt. Two smaller, more recent studies using the Kalven-Zeisel method have shown remarkably similar patterns in criminal cases, obtaining 74% to 75% agreement, with a greater leniency of 13% to 20% from the jury. Studies outside the United States have shown similarly high levels of agreement between professionals and juries or lay judges in criminal cases.

For the 4,000 civil trials in their judicial survey, Kalven and Zeisel obtained the same agreement rate of 78% on liability, but disagreement was almost equally divided, so that in 12% of the cases, the jury found for the plaintiff, while the judge favored the defense and in 10% of the cases, the jury found for the defense, while the judge would have made an award. Awards by juries were 20% higher on average than awards by judges. Several smaller, recent studies of civil jury cases in several locations have indicated agreement rates on liability between 63% and 77%, but it is unclear whether any overall change has occurred over time because no national study comparable with the Kalven and Zeisel study has been conducted. Because punitive damages are awarded so rarely (in roughly 3% of contract and tort cases), researchers conducting case-specific judicial surveys

have not been able to compare judge and jury decisions on punitive damages.

Simulations and Experiments

A third approach comparing judge and jury decision making asks judges and laypersons to reach decisions based on simulated trial materials in the form of written materials or videotaped presentations. Comparability is ensured by having the judges and laypersons read or view precisely the same stimulus. In addition, by experimentally varying the stimulus within each group, researchers have tested how specific variations in the evidence (e.g., exposure to inadmissible evidence) affect judges and laypersons differently. The extent to which these simulated decisions reflect what the decision makers would do in a real trial is contingent on the extent to which the simulation captures the relevant factors that would affect trial judgments. The materials in these studies generally must be brief to obtain judicial participation. Trial elements such as jury instructions are often truncated or missing. Mock jurors frequently are not asked to deliberate, so that the judicial responses are compared with those of individuals rather than the group decisions of multiple jurors. Nonetheless, the few experiments comparing judges and laypersons reveal a striking overall similarity between their decisions.

Experiments showed that exposure to inadmissible evidence influenced judges and laypersons similarly, and both groups were reluctant to impose liability based on mere statistical evidence. In several experiments involving personal injury cases, both professionals and laypersons responding to the same cases used the severity of injury in determining pain and suffering awards, but in one study, laypersons were more variable in their awards. It is unclear how much, or whether, variability in decisions by lay decision makers would drop if their awards were determined by group verdicts rather than individual judgments. In determining criminal sentences in a series of cases, laypersons favored lower penalties than judges did, indicating that the same greater leniency was shown by juries in criminal conviction cases in case-based judicial surveys.

In a few of the experiments directly comparing the judgments of judges and laypersons, the samples tested raise questions about the representativeness of the findings because the laypersons were students or the judges sampled came from a unique subgroup (e.g., those who had signed up to attend a law and economics seminar). Much more research is needed to map experimentally the differences and similarities between the judgments of judges and juries before concluding that judges are better than juries at specific tasks (e.g., assessing risk) or that deliberations enable juries to outperform judges on other tasks (e.g., assessing conflicting testimony).

Finally, in addition to the few studies that have exposed judges and laypersons to the same stimulus, in several experiments with judges, researchers conducted conceptual replications of the impact of heuristics (e.g., anchoring, hindsight, framing) or of extralegal factors, which had previously been tested on laypersons. With a few exceptions, these experiments have revealed that judges show a similar susceptibility to these cognitive illusions.

Shari Seidman Diamond and Pam Mueller

See also Juries and Judges' Instructions; Jury Competence; Jury Deliberation; Jury Selection; Leniency Bias

Further Readings

Diamond, S. S., & Rose, M. R. (2005). Real juries. In J. Hagan (Ed.), *Annual Review of Law & Social Science* (Vol. 1, pp. 255–284). Palo Alto, CA: Annual Reviews.

Eisenberg, T., Hannaford-Agor, P. L., Hans, V. P., Waters, N. L., Munsterman, G. T., Wells, M. T., et al. (2005). Judge-jury agreement in criminal cases: A partial replication of Kalven and Zeisel's *The American Jury*. *Journal of Empirical Legal Studies, 2*, 171–207.

Guthrie, C., Rachlinski, J. J., & Wistrich, A. J. (2001). Inside the judicial mind. *Cornell Law Review, 86*, 777–830.

Kalven, H., Jr., & Zeisel, H. (1966). *The American jury.* Boston: Little, Brown.

Robbennolt, J. K. (2005). Jury decision making: Evaluating juries by comparison to judges: A benchmark for judging? *Florida State University Law Review, 32*, 469–509.

JURY DELIBERATION

Jury deliberation begins when a trial ends and the jury moves to a secluded location to discuss the evidence and arrive at a decision. Understanding how juries reach their decisions is a prerequisite for answering the question of how well they serve their function in a democratic society. Jury deliberation has been studied empirically by social science researchers for more than 50 years now, but direct access to the jury room has been always greatly limited due to a concern that any

"external" presence in the deliberation room could influence the jury's decision. As a result, researchers have relied on two other methodologies to study jury deliberation: experimental studies with mock juries and posttrial reconstructions of actual deliberation via surveys of and/or interviews with former jurors.

This entry summarizes what has been learned about jury deliberation using these two methodologies. The picture that emerges is one in which juries take their task seriously and generally do a good job of reviewing the evidence, although they often struggle with their instructions. Influence in juries is a function of information exchange and the pressure to conform. An excellent predictor of the jury's final verdict turns out to be the distribution of verdict preferences on the jury's first vote; the verdict favored by the initial majority ends up being the jury's final verdict about 90% of the time. However, the initial majority does not always prevail, and these "reversals" represent some of the most interesting products of jury decision making.

A General Model of Deliberation

A simple stage model provides a reasonable framework for thinking about jury behavior in many, if not most, deliberations. In the first stage, jurors get oriented toward each other and their task. They settle in, introduce themselves, select a foreperson, and discuss how they will do things. In the second stage, which takes up the bulk of the time spent in deliberation, jurors discuss the evidence, take opinion polls (or "votes"), and confront disagreement among members. During this stage, conflict often surfaces, efforts are made to persuade other jurors to change their minds, and the jury moves toward a consensus. In the final stage, the jury achieves sufficient agreement (usually unanimity) to reach a verdict, followed by attempts to smooth ruffled feathers, reconcile individuals to the group's decision, and help everyone feel good about the collective verdict. Jury deliberations vary considerably in length, but most last somewhere between 2 and 4 hours.

The Foreperson

Juries typically receive little instruction regarding how they ought to deliberate, but one thing they are all told to do is choose a foreperson. Forepersons are usually selected early, often immediately after members assemble in the jury room but occasionally not until the end of deliberation. Most of the time, the selection process is brief and even perfunctory, particularly in criminal juries. Forepersons tend to be White, male, better educated, seated at the end of the table, and the first to speak or the first to identify the need to select a foreperson. This profile suggests that juries tend to eschew confrontation and rely on stereotypes and subtle interpersonal cues (such as seating and order of speaking) to identify a "natural leader." Only two task-relevant characteristics have been found to be associated with forepersons: They tend to have previous experience as jurors, and they sometimes have a relevant occupational background in civil settings (e.g., an accountant being chosen in a trial featuring complex financial transactions). Much of the research on forepersons was conducted before 1970, however, and it is unclear if the findings related to a foreperson's demographic characteristics still hold in the wake of systematic efforts to increase the demographic diversity of juries as well as significant changes in societal attitudes over the last 40 years.

Speaking and Discussion Content

In general, research has shown that speaking during deliberation is not spread evenly across jurors—several individuals tend to do the lion's share of the talking, while a few members typically say little or nothing (especially in larger juries). As might be expected, forepersons generally speak more than the typical juror. Although there has been a pervasive fear that juries will get sidetracked easily and end up spending much of their time talking about irrelevant topics, this apprehension appears to be unfounded. A robust finding has been that juries (both real and mock) take their jobs very seriously and try to stay focused on the task at hand. Indeed, most of the deliberation time is taken up with discussion of legally relevant topics, such as the evidence (around 75%) and the jury's instructions (around 20%). Juries also generally do a good job of correcting inaccurate statements made by their members, exhibiting good collective recall. Furthermore, when individual jurors introduce legally irrelevant considerations (e.g., the similarities between the current trial and a recent movie), this is often noted and sanctioned (corrected) by other members.

Initial Distribution of Verdict Preferences

One of the strongest and most reliable findings about juries is that the distribution of verdict preferences at the beginning of deliberation is a very good predictor of the jury's ultimate verdict. Specifically, the verdict option favored by the initial majority tends to be the jury's final verdict about 90% of the time. This finding is based on extensive research with mock juries where individuals were asked to provide an explicit verdict preference prior to deliberation, as well as several field studies where the first vote was reconstructed later and used as a proxy for the initial preference distribution in real trials. This robust phenomenon has often been referred to as the "majority effect."

A good deal of research on "social decision schemes" in the 1970s and 1980s aimed to identify the specific probabilities associated with the various verdicts that occurred given every possible initial distribution of juror verdict preferences. Early studies suggested that factions within the jury would usually "succeed" in getting their preferred verdict in the end if they began with a strong majority or a higher share of the vote (defined as two-thirds or more). If no two-thirds majority existed initially, juries were theorized to acquit or hang with high probability. Subsequent work provided support for the majority effect but also identified an asymmetry in the probabilities working in favor of the defendant in criminal trials—a so-called leniency effect. The leniency effect essentially corresponds to an increase in the likelihood of a prodefense verdict for any given preference distribution relative to what would be expected if the nature of the verdict had no impact on the majority's chance of succeeding. For example, a weak majority of 7 people in a 12-person jury is considerably more likely to succeed if it favors acquittal as opposed to conviction. This prodefense shift is consistent with the explicit value placed on giving the defendant the benefit of the doubt in criminal trials and the strict standard of proof needed to convict (i.e., "beyond a reasonable doubt").

Consistent with both the majority and the leniency effects noted above, a recent meta-analysis of studies measuring early-verdict preference distributions (i.e., predeliberation or first vote) and final verdicts in criminal trials identified two critical thresholds of member support related to potential verdicts. When there existed a strong early majority favoring conviction (i.e., 75% or more of the jury), a "guilty" verdict was the usual result. Conversely, if 50% or less of the jury initially supported conviction, a "not guilty" verdict was extremely likely. The only time the jury's final verdict could not be forecasted correctly was when a weak initial majority favored conviction, in which case "guilty," "not guilty," and "hung" verdicts were all relatively common.

The Dynamics of Consensus

In most deliberations, it becomes obvious at some point that all members do not favor the same verdict and some jurors will have to change their minds if the jury is to accomplish its task. A number of studies have examined how juries go from an initial nonunanimous distribution of preferences to a consensus verdict, and two general sources of influence have been identified: informational and normative. *Informational influence* is associated with the content of the jury's discussion; it stems from the articulation of case "facts," interpretations, and arguments supporting a particular verdict. *Normative influence* comes about from a desire by individuals to fit in with others and not be seen as deviant, incorrect, or even disagreeable. In essence, normative influence represents a pressure to conform that is rooted in the desire to avoid the social costs associated with standing apart from the collective.

Research on the dynamics of deliberation has shown that majority factions exert both informational and normative influence on minority (i.e., dissenting) jurors. In particular, several different theoretical models of majority influence converge on the conclusion that the degree of influence exerted is proportional to the size of the majority faction. In addition to exerting normative influence in direct proportion to their size, majority factions exert informational influence as well. In this regard, majority factions have a "sampling advantage" over minority factions during deliberation in that they have more members to draw on for evidence-related recollections, observations, and views consistent with their preferred verdict. Conversely, in keeping with their smaller size, minority factions are forced to rely primarily on informational influence. Research has also shown that juries tend to move away from their initial distribution slowly at first but with increasing speed as the majority faction grows and its influence increases in a snowball-like fashion. In essence, as the majority is given time to deploy its normative and informational advantages, it becomes harder and harder for the minority to prevail. Interestingly, though, a few studies have observed a momentum effect as well: Once the jury begins moving in either direction toward a verdict (whichever it happens to be), it rarely stops and changes direction. This suggests that

a key event underlying a "reversal" of the early majority is when the *first* juror to change votes joins the minority faction.

Opinion polling is one procedural variable that may influence the dynamics of deliberation. Polling during deliberation can vary on several dimensions, including timing (e.g., early vs. late) and secrecy with regard to individual votes. In particular, early opinion polls conducted in a "public" fashion (where members can observe how other jurors vote) may bring considerable normative pressure to bear on members of the minority faction to change their vote. In one clever series of studies using mock juries with known verdict preference distributions (i.e., an even 3:3 split or a 4:2 weak majority), polling was structured so that all members of one faction voted first in sequence. Consistent with the research on conformity, the first member of the second faction was much more likely than chance to switch his or her vote and join the faction that voted first. This was particularly so when the vote was taken early and when the first faction voted "not guilty." Of note, some research suggests that minority factions may have more influence if subgroups emerge (or are specifically formed) before a general collective discussion and the minority faction finds itself having a "local majority" in one or more of the subgroups. Taken together, these findings support the notion that the *order* in which things are done may distort the influence of faction size by affecting how obvious the factions are.

Another stream of research on the dynamics of deliberation has identified two general deliberation "styles" that juries may adopt as they go about their task: evidence driven and verdict driven. *Evidence-driven* juries work toward the goal of establishing the "facts" of the case as they see them before any discussion of the appropriate verdict. They spend a great deal of time in reviewing the evidence and take their first (and sometimes final) vote relatively late in the process. On the other hand, *verdict-driven* juries take an early first vote to get a sense of their members' standing and then organize their discussion around the verdict options and which one seems more appropriate given what seems to be generally accepted by the group. Research suggests that a substantial number of juries (perhaps 33–50%) adopt a verdict-driven style, and studies in which deliberation style was manipulated suggest that its influence on the final verdict may depend on other variables, such as the required legal elements for the available verdicts.

Sometimes the influence process fails to produce a critical mass of opinion, however, and the jury cannot reach a verdict (i.e., it "hangs"), resulting in a mistrial. In a classic early study in the 1950s, the frequency of hung juries was found to be about 5%. More recent work with samples of juries drawn from several large metropolitan areas suggests that the frequency rate varies considerably across jurisdictions and may be as high as 15% to 20% in some places, although the observed frequency rate depends on whether hanging is defined at the level of the defendant as a whole or the specific charge. A primary determinant of hanging is the ambiguity of the evidence, with trials involving moderately strong evidence producing initial preference distributions without strong majorities. Small minority factions—especially those composed of only one individual—are rarely able to hold out.

The Dynamics of Monetary Award Decisions

Research on civil juries has increased dramatically since the 1980s, but the study of how juries arrive at damage awards is still in its infancy. Nonetheless, experimental research using mock juries has established a number of influences on both the likelihood and the amount of compensatory damage awards, including whether or not the trial is bifurcated (divided into liability and award phases), the characteristics of the two parties (e.g., the number of plaintiffs and the variability of their injuries), trial complexity, the explicit mention of "appropriate" damage awards by the attorneys, and the actual severity of the plaintiff's injury. However, relatively little attention has been devoted thus far to the issue of how juries arrive at a specific figure, and at least three models are possible: (1) juries begin with a salient benchmark figure explicitly identified by one party or the other during the trial and modify it based on the content of the deliberation; (2) juries break down the award into components, assign dollar values to the various elements of the claim through discussion, and then sum the component values to achieve a total value; and (3) juries simply choose an amount that seems appropriate in a holistic fashion. Distinct from the issue of when these models might apply is the question of whether they would be executed by individual jurors, the jury as a whole, or both in a mixed fashion. Research examining the relationship between the amounts preferred by individual jurors and the collective jury award has shown that jury awards tend to be (a) larger than the central tendency of their constituent individual members and (b) less variable than individual award preferences (particularly in 12-person juries as opposed to 6-person juries). Related to the first point, some research suggests that the median of the individual award preferences (as opposed to the mean or mode) is the best predictor of the actual collective award.

Deliberation Quality

Much of the research on juries can be viewed as a search for variables that influence the nature of the verdicts observed (i.e., guilty vs. not guilty). Relatively little attention has been directed at the question of how *well* juries deliberate and the extent to which this influences the nature of their decision, but several notable empirical findings bear on the issue. First, considerable research on the impact of jury size and assigned decision rule (e.g., unanimous, critical majority, simple majority) has generally shown these procedural variables to have little influence on verdict distributions. However, larger juries and those required to reach unanimity tend to take more time, generate a greater exchange of information, produce more satisfied members, and show less variability in their damage awards—all characteristics that might be taken to indicate a higher quality of deliberation. Second, evidence-driven deliberation styles tend to be associated with longer deliberations, a more thorough examination of the evidence, and less normative influence. In other words, juries that are larger, evidence driven, and/or required to be unanimous may be more likely to have higher-quality deliberations than smaller, nonunanimous, and verdict-driven juries.

Another question related to the notion of deliberation quality is whether the deliberation process amplifies or suppresses the biases of individual jurors. An early, well-known hypothesis was that the biases of individual jurors would tend to manifest themselves when the evidence was ambiguous and not clearly supporting any verdict, but the empirical research has been mixed. In some situations, deliberation seems to reduce the biases of its members, but in other situations it appears to magnify them. Most likely, there is no simple, straightforward answer to this question—whether deliberation accentuates or attenuates individual bias probably depends on the strength of the evidence as well as how that bias is distributed across jurors (and particularly whether it is concentrated in an early majority).

Finally, it is worth noting that a variety of initiatives intended to improve the functioning of juries have been identified, implemented, and occasionally examined in the past 25 years or so. These initiatives include rewriting and simplifying legal instructions, providing copies of the instructions to jurors, allowing jurors to take notes and/or ask questions through the attorneys, and allowing jurors access to exhibits and/or transcripts during deliberation. Most recently, jurors in some jurisdictions have been allowed to discuss the evidence prior to deliberation so long as all members are present. Most of these initiatives have been aimed at making jurors' jobs easier by reducing their cognitive burden and removing any constraints on the process. While these changes have generally not been found to systematically influence the nature of observed verdicts and jurors almost always react positively to them, there have been few efforts to evaluate how the deliberation process itself is affected.

A Final Thought

An unfortunate consequence of an early (and well-known) likening of jury deliberation to the development of a predetermined photographic image appears to have been a squelching of scholarly interest in the dynamics of the deliberation process. After all, what value is there in studying what juries do if the final outcome is so reliably predicted by the preference of the initial majority? However, even though reversals of the initial majority preference are relatively rare, their absolute occurrence is still considerable given the thousands of jury trials held each year. In a free and democratic society, and with so much at stake for the individual participants as well as the community, it is clearly important that we understand how juries go about making their decisions. Furthermore, in a large number of those trials, deliberation itself is a critical determinant of what those decisions are.

Dennis J. Devine

See also Chicago Jury Project; Jury Size and Decision Rule; Leniency Bias

Further Readings

Davis, J. H., Kameda, T., Parks, C., Stasson, M., & Zimmerman, S. (1989). Some social mechanics of group decision making: The distribution of opinion, polling sequence, and implications for consensus. *Journal of Personality and Social Psychology, 57,* 1000–1012.

Devine, D. J., Clayton, L. D., Dunford, B. B., Seying, R., & Pryce, J. (2001). Jury decision making: 45 years of empirical research on deliberating groups. *Psychology, Public Policy, and Law, 7,* 622–727.

Ellsworth, P. C. (1989). Are twelve heads better than one? *Law and Contemporary Problems, 52,* 207–224.

Hastie, R., Penrod, S. D., Pennington, N. (1983). *Inside the jury.* Cambridge, MA: Harvard University Press.

Kalven, H., & Zeisel, H. (1966). *The American jury.* Chicago: University of Chicago Press.

Tanford, S., & Penrod, S. (1986). Jury deliberations: Discussion content and influence processes in jury decision making. *Journal of Applied Social Psychology, 16,* 322–347.

JURY NULLIFICATION

Juries have the implicit power to acquit defendants despite evidence and judicial instructions to the contrary. This power, called *jury nullification,* is embedded in the jury's right to return a verdict by its own moral compass and has historically permitted sympathetic juries to acquit those whom the jurors perceive as legally guilty but morally upright. The criminal jury's power to deliver a verdict counter to both the law and evidence resides in the fact that a general verdict requires no explanation by the jury. Some citizens' groups and some legal scholars believe that the jury not only should have the ability to nullify but also the right to be explicitly informed of this right. However, the majority of the legal community, with near unanimity among sitting judges, prefers the status quo—juries are not informed of this nullification power but are free to exercise it without prompting when the jury believes that a guilty verdict clearly violates community sentiment. Research has shown that juries informed of their nullification power are more likely to consider extralegal factors and may be more prone to be persuaded by emotional biases.

A Short History of Jury Nullification

Judges uniformly instruct the jury that they must apply the law as provided by the court. However, jurors traditionally have been able to act as the "conscience of the community," a long-standing role that implicitly enabled juries to return verdicts that fly in the face of the proffered law. Depending on one's point of view, this much-disputed power of the jury has served the interest of justice or has led to injustice and chaos in the legal system.

Juries in England historically had been constrained by the King. The jury's power to deliver an unfettered verdict was essentially nonexistent, although there is evidence that the English jury, in its various guises, refused to convict defendants who were unfairly charged or for whom the sentence was wildly disproportionate to the crime. However, juries did this at great peril. The Crown had the means and the will to punish the jury for verdicts of which it disapproved. Juries could be incarcerated, without food or drink, until they returned a suitable verdict. Indeed, their very fortunes and families were put at risk.

In 1670, this state of affairs began to change. A seminal case, known as *Bushell* (the name of the jury foreman), prohibited the Crown from punishing the jury for verdicts deemed unlawful or rebellious. *Bushell* involved a trial in which the famous Quakers, William Penn and William Mead, were charged with fomenting revolution by preaching in the streets. Against all expectations, the jury returned a not-guilty verdict and maintained their stance against the King's fearsome intimidation. The result was revolutionary: an independent jury.

Juries in the American colonies often served as a buffer between colonists and unpopular British laws. Famously, an 18th-century jury acquitted the printer John Peter Zenger of sedition when he had certainly violated the local law prohibiting criticism aimed at representatives (New York's Mayor) of the Crown. Colonial juries routinely acquitted smugglers (most notably, John Hancock) and others who defied unpopular laws. Jury power was rather untrammeled from the Revolution until the middle of the 19th century. And in the absence of a highly professional legal community, juries often decided on the basis of their own notions of what was just, the law notwithstanding. The proponents of the jury's right to nullify the law suggest that juries have historically had that power and right.

It is clear that the nullification power was extant during the early days of the Republic. It was perhaps not as ubiquitous as presumed. In very few colonies was the nullification power explicit, and according to one scholar, there are indicators that there was no such right for much of the colonial era in Georgia, Maryland, and Massachusetts.

Some historical indications suggest that the jury's right to nullify moved only in one direction—toward mercy, but some scholars disagree. This power did not include the power to legislate new law. American juries that stood against the oppressive power of the British King were held in high esteem, as were the fiercely independent agrarian juries in the early part of the 19th century. It is no coincidence that concerns about the power of the jury began to surface primarily in the middle of the century, when immigration from Europe increased at a remarkable rate. By the 1850s, powerful legal figures, such as Justice Joseph Story, were arguing vigorously against an unfettered jury.

Despite the attempts of a number of state legislatures to sustain jury power, an increasingly professional legal community, through a cascading series of appellate cases, began to rein in the power of jurors to decide cases with little or no concern for the relevant law. In 1895, the U.S. Supreme Court offered its only opinion on the jury's nullification power. In *Sparf and Hansen v. United States*, the Court proscribed the jury's explicit power and authority by indicating that the jury's obligation was to follow the law as received from the Court and to apply that law to the facts. Nevertheless, the issue of nullification resurfaced at various times, almost always during periods of social and political unrest. Some Northern juries refused to convict violators of the Fugitive Slave Act in the 1850s. Juries refused to convict labor organizers of conspiracies during the 1890s. The Eighteenth Amendment, known as the Volstead Act, which prohibited both the manufacture and the consumption of intoxicating liquor, was widely violated by both the public and the criminals who illegally imported or manufactured the banned substances. Citizens who violated this act during the period known as Prohibition often walked out of the courtroom free men because juries were opposed to what they perceived as unwelcome government interference in their daily life and pleasures. In the tumultuous 1970s, juries sometimes set free those who had illegally avoided the draft during the later, more unpopular stages of the Vietnam War, and other juries refused to convict physicians for euthanizing the terminally ill. Jury behavior in these circumstances either made the laws moot or convinced prosecutors not to bring cases that they would surely lose.

Without question, the jury's nullification power also has a dark side, most notably when (mostly) Southern juries from the Reconstruction onward acquitted transparently guilty Whites for depredations committed on Black citizens. This disturbing side of nullification ("jury vilification") was seen when juries returned verdicts that reflected prejudiced or bigoted community standards and violated the benign standard of nullification proponents that such verdicts should be merciful rather than vindictive. In fact, one nullification scholar notes that the difference between vengeance and mercy is an unprincipled one and that, while nullification may have had some legal basis in colonial days, it is now a legal anachronism. Modern proponents of jury power argue that the jury has both the right and the power to judge both the defendant and the law. It is an obvious understatement to say that the right of the jury to nullify has more support among legal academics than among judges.

Some legal scholars and jury activists argue that judges and courts are actively attempting to constrain the jury's unfettered right to return a verdict according to its own views. One scholar points to the antinullification section appended to the California Jury Instructions. Proponents want judges to inform jurors directly that they can exercise their right to nullify. Indeed, much of the empirical research on nullification has focused on the effects of providing just such an instruction to the jury. One practicing attorney eloquently argues that defense attorneys should aggressively seek nullification in cases where their technically guilty clients are morally blameless. Proponents believe that nullifying juries inform the legal process and militate against unjust laws. Furthermore, the pronullification argument contends that research shows that laypeople are more sophisticated than the courts assume and that anarchy emanates not from jury disobedience but when laws are in conflict with community sentiment.

Jury Research and Nullification Instructions

The modern debate as to the limits of the jury's power was most clearly limned in *United States v. Dougherty* (1973), in which a 2:1 majority rejected a defense request that the nullification instruction be permitted in this trial of antiwar activists. Judge Harold Leventhal, writing for the majority of the D.C. Court of Appeals, while noting that the pages of history abound with shining examples of juries that refused to convict virtuous defendants, nevertheless suggested that if juries were given explicit nullification instructions, their behavior would be anarchic. Such an instruction would result in "chaos" because the verdict would not be predicated on the law. Furthermore, an explicit declaration of the jury's power to nullify would, in Judge Leventhal's view, require the jury to "fashion" the law. Judge Leventhal argued that without explicit knowledge of nullification, juries would use their implicit power more carefully and judiciously, not chaotically.

A number of researchers have explored the impact on verdicts of jury instructions that include a nullification clause. These are laboratory-based studies of varying levels of similarity to legal processes. Results suggest that juries that received nullification instructions spent less time deliberating the evidence and focused more on defendant characteristics, attributions, and personal experiences. Jurors in receipt of nullification instructions were more likely to take account of the extralegal factors of race, gender, and social class. One researcher reported that mock jurors were significantly less likely to return a guilty verdict for an individual accused of murder in a context where the act might be characterized as euthanasia. When in receipt of nullification instructions and when the act was committed out of compassion (such as disconnecting a respirator or increasing a morphine drip), the jury verdicts were the same as those returned by juries given standard instructions. Note that much may depend on the nature of the nullification instructions, which are usually appended to the standard instructions. Thus, what we see in many studies is a fairly circumscribed use of jury power, as Judge Leventhal had suggested.

However, researchers have reexamined this "chaos" hypothesis by examining situations that evoke jurors' emotional biases. These biases are evoked by information that strongly affects jurors' emotions (e.g., gruesome crime-scene photos) but that implies nothing directly about the guilt or innocence of the defendant. In several experiments, researchers have found that nullification instructions can indeed change and intensify jurors' responses to such emotionally biasing information. For example, in one study, information about the victim of a crime affected jurors' emotions so that they were much more upset at the alleged murder of an upright, admirable person than that of a less-worthy citizen. When mock jurors were given standard jury instructions (which tell them that they must follow the law as it is explained by the trial judge), these emotional reactions did not affect their verdicts.

In another research example, mock jurors heard one of two versions of a trial in which a physician was charged with murder. In the first version, the physician had euthanized a patient he knew (to relieve suffering); in the second version, the physician was charged with murdering the patient for financial gain. In other words, while the euthanatizing procedure was the same—increasing a drug dose beyond the recommended dosage, the motive for that act was different in the two circumstances. When jurors were given standard instructions, the apparent motive of the surgeon had no effect. Jurors found the defendant guilty irrespective of the motive. However, when the jury was in receipt of nullification instructions, a surgeon who increased the drug dose to relieve suffering was less likely to receive a guilty verdict. Nullification instructions induced jurors to attend to emotionally biasing information (e.g., how sympathetically the victim was portrayed). Proponents of jury nullification would likely argue that these results sustain their view that juries will use their right to nullify judiciously. Those opposed to jury nullification would suggest that the law should determine trial outcomes, not the whims, however well meant, of the jurors.

Irwin A. Horowitz

See also Juries and Judges' Instructions; Jury Competence; Jury Deliberation

Further Readings

Brown, D. K. (1997). Jury nullification within the rule of law. *Minnesota Law Review, 81,* 1149–1200.

Conrad, C. S. (1998). *Jury nullification: The evolution of a doctrine.* Durham, NC: Carolina Academic Press.

Finkel, N. J. (1995). *Commonsense justice.* Cambridge, MA: Harvard University Press.

Horowitz, I., Kerr, N. Park, E. S., & Gockel, C. (2006). Chaos in the courtroom reconsidered: Emotional bias and juror nullification. *Law and Human Behavior, 30,* 163–181.

Horowitz, I. A., & Willging, T. E. (1991). Changing views of jury power: The nullification debate, 1787–1988. *Law and Human Behavior, 15*(2), 165–182.

Howe, M. (1939). Juries as judge of criminal law. *Harvard Law Review, 52,* 582–616.

Sparf and Hansen v. United States, 156 U.S. 51 (1895).

St. John, R. R. (1997). License to nullify: The democratic and constitutional deficiencies of authorized jury lawmaking. *Yale Law Review, 106,* 2563–2597.

United States v. Dougherty, 473 F.2d 1113 (1973).

JURY QUESTIONNAIRES

Jury questionnaires are often used during the voir dire process to help judges and attorneys identify prospective jurors who are not suitable for jury service. Jury questionnaires typically include items dealing with hardship or medical issues that may make it difficult for some individuals to serve as jurors. Often, at the discretion of the court, jury questionnaires may delve into experiences or opinions related to the case, sometimes in considerable detail. Of course, jury questionnaires are self-report measures that are vulnerable to forgetting, distortions, or deception. Lengthy jury questionnaires completed by a large group of prospective jurors can make it difficult to extract useful information in a short amount of time. Moreover, there are situations where trial attorneys would be ill-advised to request a detailed jury questionnaire.

The Sixth Amendment of the U.S. Constitution provides defendants with the right to an impartial jury. Often a part of the voir dire process, jury questionnaires may help identify sources of bias in prospective jurors that may interfere with their impartiality or ability to follow the law. The fundamental assumption underlying the use of jury questionnaires is that people are more likely to disclose information on a survey than in open court, particularly information about sensitive issues. There is a general tendency for people to appear open-minded and to provide socially desirable responses to questions posed during attorney- or judge-conducted voir dire. In theory, jury questionnaires serve to measure more accurately the relevant attitudes, expectations, and experiences related to the case.

Generally used at the discretion of the court, generic jury questionnaires have become much more common throughout the United States. The format, content domain, and scope of the items vary considerably, but there is some common content. Most jury questionnaires tap into factors that may lead to a challenge for cause, reflecting a legitimate difficulty or problem with jury service. These items include hardship issues, such as having to care of an infant or elderly parent, serious financial difficulties, or other related factors. Other items common to jury questionnaires include those dealing with medical problems, disabilities, and the use of medication that might interfere with a prospective juror's ability to serve as a trier of fact. Most include a question relating to difficulties in reading or understanding the English language and difficulties with following the law as provided by the court. Finally, most jury questionnaires include some measures dealing with familiarity with the case (particularly if there was some pretrial publicity) and knowledge of the witnesses, lawyers, parties, or others associated with the case.

Beyond these typical items, jury questionnaires may delve into a number of other topics. Demographic items are common and often include those dealing with race or ethnic affiliation, gender, place of birth, and so forth. General experiences are also often measured: These usually include service in the U.S. military; jury experience; and prior involvement in the criminal or civil justice system as witness, plaintiff, defendant, or other party. Sometimes jury questionnaires delve into case-related experiences, such as having experience with complex business transactions, having been a victim of a workplace accident, or having personal experience with a drug dependency problem. Jury questionnaires may also include attitudinal items that could tap into constructs such as legal authoritarianism, juror bias, or beliefs about a just world, although entire scales are rarely included. More often, there is a focus on more narrow, case-related attitudes (e.g., Do you believe that politicians should be held to a higher standard of moral or ethical conduct than other people?). Finally, some jury questionnaires are quite detailed and delve into leisure activities, bumper stickers (presumably, these reflect jurors' values or concerns), newspaper readership, television-viewing habits, and other items in the same vein. Indeed, jury questionnaires can be relatively short (10 items) or remarkably lengthy (exceeding 200 items).

Of course, attorneys are typically looking for red flags or any information that might raise concerns so that they can decide whether to explore these issues during attorney-conducted voir dire (if permitted), whether to use a challenge for cause in an attempt to excuse the juror from jury service, or whether to exercise a peremptory challenge (typically in the event that an initial attempt at using a challenge for cause is unsuccessful). Trial attorneys may also use jury questionnaires to look for indicators of leadership and receptivity to a case, relying on the assumption that a juror who exhibits leadership potential may guide the jury toward a particular view of the case.

When trial teams provide input into jury questionnaires, they often consider a number of strategic issues. First, to the extent that the survey is lengthy or acquires a lot of information, trial teams will face challenges in gathering the relevant information and evaluating each juror in time for jury selection. The lengthier the survey, the more difficult it is to make sense of the information and formulate a strategy and the greater the need for ample time to examine the surveys. In some cases, trial teams might receive 40 to 50 completed jury questionnaires and have only a short time to examine them before jury selection begins. Well-developed coding sheets are often helpful in these situations.

Jury questionnaires are particularly helpful when prior jury research reveals that certain characteristics can predict verdicts and these predictors can be incorporated into the juror questionnaires. It is possible then to estimate the probability that a particular juror will favor one side or the other. Of course, there are myriad factors that make these sorts of predictions tenuous at best.

Strategically, detailed jury questionnaires may not always be advantageous to a party. Some courts permit juror questionnaires at the expense of attorney-conducted voir dire, leaving lawyers with little opportunity to explore the responses further. If a party believes that jurors are likely to support its view of the case, a juror questionnaire may reveal supportive jurors, giving the opposing side an advantage.

Jury questionnaires suffer from the self-report problem; people are not very accurate at reporting their thoughts or behaviors because of memory or social desirability problems. Few people would disclose their use of illegal drugs, production of child pornography, or history of spousal abuse, for example. Occasionally, individuals respond dishonestly in an attempt to survive the jury selection process and serve as jurors on a case. Responses should be considered in light of these limitations.

There are a number of different ways in which jury questionnaires are administered. In some areas, individuals who are summoned for jury service complete the surveys online and submit them in advance of the trial date. In other areas, the jury questionnaire is mailed to prospective jurors, who complete it and return it to the court. Typically, the trial teams prefer to have sufficient time to examine these completed surveys before the voir dire process begins.

Veronica Stinson

See also Jury Selection; Legal Authoritarianism; Pretrial Publicity, Impact on Juries; Scientific Jury Selection; Voir Dire

Further Readings

Posey, A. J., & Wrightsman, J. S. (2005). *Trial consulting.* New York: Oxford University Press.

JURY REFORMS

Over the past 15 years, courts have begun implementing a host of reforms to the jury system in response to growing criticism about jurors' competence to decide cases. Of particular concern was the ability of jurors to set aside preexisting biases and to understand increasingly complex evidence and legal principles. This entry describes the efforts undertaken by the courts to address these concerns. In particular, the section on voir dire focuses on efforts to elicit complete and candid information from prospective jurors during jury selection while balancing competing interests in courtroom efficiency and juror privacy. The second section focuses on the techniques employed by judges and lawyers during trial to enhance juror comprehension and performance.

Voir Dire

The process of selecting trial jurors from a panel of prospective jurors is called *voir dire*, a term derived from 14th-century legal French, which, loosely translated, means "to speak the truth." Typically, voir dire consists of a limited question-and-answer period in which the trial judge and attorneys examine prospective jurors to determine if they can serve fairly and impartially on that trial. If the judge concludes from this examination that a particular juror has life experiences, opinions, or attitudes that would prevent him or her from serving impartially, that juror will be removed "for cause." After all the "for-cause" jurors have been excused, the attorneys have the opportunity to remove those jurors who they suspect may be predisposed against their clients by using a statutorily defined number of "peremptory challenges." After all the for-cause and peremptory challenges have been executed, the jurors who remain are sworn as the trial jurors. The amount of time needed to select a jury varies according to the type of case to be tried (e.g., felony, misdemeanor, civil), the legal requirements and mechanics of voir dire, and the local legal culture, but it generally ranges from 1 to 3 hours.

A number of concerns about the voir dire process have risen in recent years. Some of these focus on the legitimacy of the criteria that judges and attorneys employ when deciding to remove or retain jurors. Most often, these debates take place in the context of proposals to reduce the number of peremptory challenges in order to minimize the opportunity for attorneys to discriminate on the basis of race, ethnicity, or gender—a practice ruled unconstitutional by the U.S. Supreme Court in *Batson v. Kentucky* (1986) and its subsequent progeny. The counterargument by the practicing bar is that peremptory challenges are needed as a remedy for the failure of trial judges to grant challenges for cause, even when a juror's responses to voir dire questions indicate bias or prejudice. Thus far, Maryland is the only state to successfully reduce the number of peremptory challenges, and that legislation was driven as much by cost considerations as by concerns about the discriminatory use of peremptory challenges. However, several other jurisdictions—notably California, New Jersey, and the District of Columbia—are seriously considering legislation that would substantially reduce the number of peremptory challenges.

Other proposals for improving voir dire focus on the efficacy of the voir dire process in eliciting candid and useful information from jurors. Empirical studies have repeatedly found that up to one in four prospective jurors fail to disclose case-relevant information during voir dire. In some instances, jurors are reluctant to reveal personal or sensitive information to a courtroom full of strangers. In other instances, jurors are unwilling to disclose information that they believe is not relevant to the case. Often the mechanics of the voir dire process—for example, whether the judge or lawyers question the jurors, whether jurors are told to raise their hands or respond orally to questions—send subtle messages about the judge's desire, or lack thereof, for complete disclosure by jurors.

Attorney-conducted voir dire, which is the predominant practice in most state courts, but not in federal courts, is considered the better practice insofar as jurors are more likely to respond with candid, rather than socially desirable, answers to questions posed by lawyers rather than judges. Moreover, attorneys typically are more familiar with the nuances of the case and thus are in a position to question jurors about issues that a judge might not immediately view as relevant. Another technique that is gaining in popularity is the use of written questionnaires asking either general background information or case-specific information, which gives jurors the opportunity to disclose sensitive information to the judge and attorneys without having to do so orally in open court. This technique is also useful for trials involving substantial pretrial publicity because it permits jurors to disclose their knowledge of the case without tainting other jurors who may not have read or heard as much about it.

Many judges now invite jurors to indicate if they would prefer to respond to questions about potentially embarrassing or sensitive information (e.g., criminal background, substance abuse, or criminal victimization) privately in a sidebar conference or in chambers with the attorneys; approximately 30% of jurors take advantage of this opportunity. A small, but increasing, number of judges now advocate giving all prospective jurors an opportunity for individual voir dire, regardless of the nature of the case or the questions to be posed, as it alleviates some of the intimidation of the courtroom environment and invites jurors to disclose any information that they believe relevant to their impartiality even if no question has directly solicited that information.

In spite of increased awareness about how traditional voir dire techniques can discourage fully candid and complete self-disclosure by jurors, trial judges in many areas of the country have been reluctant to embrace voir dire reforms, largely out of concern over the additional time and effort that they might cause in the jury selection process. Many judges also voice skepticism about the need for a more expansive voir dire, claiming that lawyers' desire for more information about jurors' backgrounds too often intrudes on jurors' privacy without actually eliciting useful information about jurors' ability to serve impartially. Because of the traditional deference given to judges' management of the voir dire process by reviewing courts and legislatures, reforms to voir dire have taken place more slowly and incrementally than reforms to other stages of the trial process.

Jury Comprehension and Performance

The most dramatic reforms to jury trials in recent years are those designed to enhance juror comprehension and decision making during the trial and deliberations. The growing popularity of these reforms among judges, lawyers, and policymakers reflects a change in the traditional understanding of how jurors perceive and process evidence and what, given this new understanding, the appropriate role of jurors should be in the trial.

Traditional jury trial procedures were developed with the intent of reinforcing juror passivity, which was believed essential to maintaining their neutrality throughout the evidentiary portion of the trial. Consequently, jurors were traditionally discouraged from taking notes because it might distract them from observing the witnesses' demeanor or they might confuse their own notes with the evidence actually presented. Jurors were prohibited from asking questions of witnesses because they might become inappropriately adversarial. They were prohibited from discussing the evidence among themselves or with others because they might begin to draw conclusions before hearing the entire case. And they were not informed about the legal principles that they would be required to apply until just before deliberations because it might cause jurors to disregard evidence that seemed unrelated to those principles. All these restrictions were intended to ensure that nothing interfered with jurors' ability to accurately remember, understand, and consider all the evidence presented to them at trial.

A substantial body of research from the field of social and cognitive psychology emphatically contradicts this traditional understanding of juror decision making. Empirical studies have conclusively established that jurors are not simply "blank slates" or "empty vessels" waiting to be filled but instead actively process and interpret information as it is received during the trial, in spite of the restrictions imposed on them. Indeed, many of those restrictions have been found to actually hinder jurors' ability to efficiently and effectively process information. Thus, the reforms that have been introduced in recent years are intended to capitalize on jurors' natural ability to understand and process information while emphasizing to jurors the continued importance of their neutrality during trial.

The least controversial reform, and the one that appears to have caught the attention and support of the legal community most strongly, is permitting jurors to take notes during trial, which helps jurors remember evidence. In a recent study of jury trial practices nationwide, jurors were permitted to take notes in 70% of trials in state and federal courts. Moreover, jurors in 64% of the trials were actually given notepaper and writing instruments with which to do so. Only two states—Pennsylvania and South Carolina—prohibit juror note taking in criminal trials, and only South Carolina prohibits it in civil trials; all other states either mandate that jurors be permitted to take notes (Arizona and Indiana) or make the practice discretionary.

Other techniques have encountered somewhat greater resistance in actual practice, in spite of empirical studies documenting their effectiveness, favorable reports from jurisdictions that have implemented those techniques, and endorsement by prominent judicial and bar organizations (e.g., the American Bar Association, the Conference of Chief Justices). Two of the techniques involve permitting jurors to submit questions in writing to witnesses and permitting jurors to discuss the evidence among themselves during trial provided that they refrain from making conclusions about ultimate issues (guilt/innocence, liability/no liability). Both of these techniques are intended to provide jurors with an opportunity to clarify confusing or ambiguous evidence while it is still reasonably fresh in their minds. The vast majority of states (37 in civil trials, 36 in criminal trials) grant trial judges the discretion to permit juror questions to witnesses; however, only 15% of judges routinely exercise this discretion. Only 11 states permit civil jurors to discuss the evidence before the final deliberations, and only 10 states permit criminal jurors to do so. Nationally, juror discussions were permitted in less than 2% of all trials.

Juror comprehension of instructions also continues to be a challenging area for many courts. Unlike disagreements over factual issues, in which jurors routinely combine their collective memories and judgments to make accurate conclusions, jurors' unfamiliarity with the form and substance of the law often prevents them from correctly interpreting and applying the law. In addition to poorly drafted jury instructions, the form and timing of their delivery—typically orally and immediately before deliberations—also contributes to juror confusion. To address these issues, the majority of judges and lawyers (69%) now provide jurors with a written copy of the instructions—if not during the oral delivery of the jury charge, at least for their use during deliberations. Increasingly, judges are delivering jury instructions earlier in the trial. More than 40% of judges instructed juries before the closing arguments in their most recent trial, and 18% gave preliminary instructions on substantive issues before the evidentiary portion of the trial. In addition to providing jurors with the legal context in which to consider the evidence and closing arguments, the repetition of instructions at different points in the trial also helps jurors understand and retain that information. Finally, judicial and bar leaders have become increasingly aware of the importance of pattern jury instructions, especially their credibility to trial judges, lawyers, and reviewing courts in terms of both legal accuracy and clarity to jurors. This has led to efforts by pattern jury instruction committees across the country to improve the comprehensibility of instructions for laypersons and to increased education for trial judges on the appropriate use of pattern jury instructions.

Empirical studies of these various techniques present a mixed picture of their effectiveness. Juror note taking has conclusively been found to enhance juror recall of evidence, but it has a less apparent effect on juror comprehension. Studies of juror questions and juror discussions have arrived at differing conclusions about their impact on juror comprehension—most finding a small effect in longer, more complex cases but little or no impact in routine trials. Improvements in the clarity and organization of jury instructions have been found to improve juror comprehension of the law, but recent revisions to pattern jury instructions have not been rigorously evaluated. Virtually all investigations of these techniques have reported greater juror satisfaction in jury service and confidence in their verdicts, and concerns initially raised about these techniques—for example, that they would disrupt the trial process or undermine juror impartiality—have been unfounded.

Paula L. Hannaford-Agor

See also Juries and Judges' Instructions; Jury Competence; Jury Deliberation; Jury Questionnaires; Jury Selection; Pretrial Publicity, Impact on Juries; Story Model for Juror Decision Making; Voir Dire

Further Readings

American Bar Association. (2005). *Principles for juries and jury trials*. Chicago: Author.

Batson v. Kentucky, 476 U.S. 79 (1986).

Dann, B. M. (1993). "Learning lessons" and "speaking rights": Creating educated and democratic juries. *Indiana Law Review, 68,* 1229–1279.

Hannaford-Agor, P. L., Waters, N. L., Mize, G. E., & Wait, M. (2007). *The state-of-the-states survey of jury improvement efforts: A compendium report.* Williamsburg, VA: National Center for State Courts.

Hastie, R., Penrod, S. D., & Pennington, N. (1983). *Inside the jury.* Cambridge, MA: Harvard University Press.

Munsterman, G. T., Hannaford-Agor, P. L., & Whitehead, G. M. (Eds.). (2006). *Jury trial innovations.* Williamsburg, VA: National Center for State Courts.

Jury Selection

Before a jury trial begins, attorneys must select a jury from a panel of community members who have reported for jury duty. Rather than choosing jurors to sit on the jury, attorneys choose people to exclude from the jury. The attorneys may excuse anyone who exhibits demonstrable bias that would interfere with his or her ability to serve as a juror. Attorneys are also given a limited number of challenges that they may exercise for any reason except an attempt to exclude members of certain identifiable groups. When attorneys make their decisions to exclude potential jurors based on intuition or experience, the process is known as traditional jury selection. Scientific jury selection refers to the process where attorneys rely on social science surveys of community members to determine which types of jurors will be most favorable to their case.

Definition of Jury Selection

Jury selection is the process of choosing a petit jury of independent fact finders from a pool of venire members for a criminal or civil trial. Potential jurors are subjected to a system of examination known as voir dire, which allows judges and attorneys to obtain information about individual venire members. During voir dire, the judge and attorneys pose questions to individual jurors and the panel as a whole. Although the term *jury selection* gives the impression that the people are selected to remain seated on the jury, the process actually involves removing prospective jurors for a number of reasons. The Sixth Amendment of the U.S. Constitution gives defendants the right to be tried by an impartial jury. To fulfill the requirement of impartiality, jurors who harbor biases or cannot be fair to both sides are excluded from the jury through challenges. Individual venire members certainly have various expectations, beliefs, and experiences, but the legal system requires that members of the jury agree to set aside any preexisting biases and decide the case solely on the evidence. Although the Sixth Amendment states that jurors must be chosen from a representative cross-section of the community, this does not mean that the petit jury is representative of the

community once the jury selection is finished. However, there are rules in place to protect against discrimination in the jury selection process, such as the Jury Selection and Services Act of 1968, which was created to ensure nondiscrimination in federal jury selection and services.

During jury selection, there are two types of challenges that attorneys can use to remove venire persons from the jury: challenges for cause and peremptory challenges. A challenge for cause is a request to remove a potential juror when there is reason to believe that he or she cannot serve as an impartial juror. When challenges for cause were first introduced, very few circumstances warranted their use. Only jurors who were related to the defendant by blood or marriage or those who possessed an economic interest in the case were excused for cause. Apart from those reasons, a juror could not to be removed from the jury for cause. In 1911, the Sixth Amendment was codified, and it provided both parties the right to challenge jurors for cause. Currently, the challenge for cause may be used to exclude prospective jurors who possess biases and are unable to follow the law in a given case. In addition, most states now acknowledge that potential jurors may be challenged for cause if they have a relationship with anyone involved in the trial, if the juror has prior experience with a similar case, or if an obvious bias or disability exists that would warrant removal. Judges are usually in charge of exercising the challenges for cause and striking out those people who appear to have a conflict with the case that cannot be corrected through juror rehabilitation.

The peremptory challenge is the second type of challenge offered to attorneys during voir dire. Peremptory challenges allow attorneys to remove a prospective juror without having to offer a reason for doing so. Attorneys from each side of the case are afforded a predetermined number of peremptory challenges with which to eliminate jurors and the number of peremptory challenges allowed varies depending on the state, the case, and even the judge. Initially, the peremptory challenge was permitted only in capital cases, and only the prosecution was allowed to use this device. Now, however, defendants are also afforded the use of peremptory challenges, and depending on the nature of the case, they may be allowed a greater number of peremptory challenges than the prosecution. Although the adoption of the Federal Rules of Criminal Procedure in 1946 attempted to reduce this prodefense advantage for capital, noncapital, and felony cases, the prosecution is still typically awarded fewer challenges than the defense. Once judges have struck ineligible jurors for cause, attorneys may still have concerns about prospective jurors that are insufficient to justify a challenge for cause. The peremptory challenge is intended to serve as a curative device for removing potentially biased jurors who cannot be removed for cause. For example, this type of challenge is appropriate to remove a juror who has avoided answering questions to remain on the jury, when the attorney suspects that the juror holds a bias that could not be demonstrated.

Peremptory challenges are legitimate provided that attorneys are not targeting people who are members of cognizable groups. According to the ruling in *Batson v. Kentucky* (1968), attorneys may not use peremptory challenges to exclude prospective jurors on the basis of race. The Supreme Court recognizes that excluding certain populations from jury service is a form of discrimination and jeopardizes the integrity of the justice system and has extended the *Batson* rule to include other cognizable groups such as gender, sexual orientation, and religion. Accordingly, if a peremptory challenge is contested by the opposing side, a reason for the removal must be stated, and the rationale for the challenge must be neutral to the cognizable groups. More commonly known as the *Batson* test, there are three steps taken to remedy the misuse of peremptory challenges. First, complainants have to demonstrate a prima facie case of discrimination, then the court needs to uncover the prejudice motives, and finally the attorney has to provide a valid reason for removing the prospective juror. Recently, the Supreme Court's decisions have supported a more stringent enforcement of *Batson*'s requirements after a challenge was found to be racially motivated, in which a prosecutor excluded 10 of 11 qualified Black venire members from the panel. Some insist that the courts are unable to control the mandated use of peremptory challenges appropriately and suggest that they should be eliminated altogether to constrain attorney discretion. However, others argue that peremptory challenges provide parties with essential protection from the risk of partiality.

Many attorneys believe that the ability to sculpt a jury can have considerable bearing on the outcome of the trial. Currently, attorneys employ both traditional jury selection and scientific jury selection techniques to shape the jury. However, research is inconclusive as to which approach is more likely to achieve a desired outcome or result in a less "biased" jury. Traditional jury selection entails reliance on attorney experience and intuition to identify undesirable jurors, whereas scientific jury selection identifies unfavorable jurors by collecting case-relevant attitudes and demographic information from the community and analyzing it using statistical techniques. Each party then attempts to use peremptory challenges to exclude the prospective jurors who have been identified as possessing a bias, an opinion, a trait, or a characteristic that may be injurious to that party. Attorneys can use challenges to remove a potentially harmful juror; however, there are legal limitations to these challenges. That is, attorneys are not legally permitted to remove whomever they like for whatever reason. While the legal purpose of peremptory challenges is to eliminate jurors who may be biased, in practice, peremptory challenges are used for a variety of goals. Attorneys' objectives may not necessarily be to obtain a fair jury but instead to obtain the jury that is most advantageous for their side of the case. In contrast, the court aims to seat a jury that best replicates the collective sentiment of the community and that is able to be fair to both sides of the case.

Traditional Jury Selection

Traditional jury selection refers to the strategies and techniques that derive from attorney experience and legal folklore. Traditional jury selection encompasses strategies such as previous experience with juries, common sense, expectations, intuition, and implicit stereotypes. Simply put, attorneys attempt to collect as much meaningful information as they can during voir dire and rely on stereotypes, instinct, hunches, and common sense to interpret that information. However, critics of this approach opine that in some cases, commonsense stereotypes can lead to opposite conclusions about the favorability of a particular of a juror. On the one hand, a prosecutor might assume that females are ideal jurors for a rape case because women are more inclined to identify and sympathize with the victim and are more likely to render a guilty verdict. On the other hand, a defense attorney might prefer female jurors on a rape case because women may need to believe that the victim put herself in a vulnerable position so that they can continue to believe that the world is just. Some civil attorneys assume that poor jurors should be avoided because they are more likely to make large awards of money due to their resentment of their own situation, whereas other civil attorneys assume that poor people would be less likely to award such large sums because they are not accustomed to that amount of money. These examples highlight the difficulties inherent in using stereotypes to formulate reliable assumptions about juror favorability.

Another factor that attorneys often consider during jury selection is juror nonverbal communication. It has been suggested that factors such as posture, pitch of voice, and willingness to express opinions go into the decision of who should stay on the jury and who should be removed. Other attorneys use information such as facial expression and perceived level of friendliness or extroversion to make decisions about prospective jurors. Although research has not proved traditional jury selection to be superior to other methods, it does not necessarily follow that the traditional approach should be abandoned. It is quite possible that in individual cases, attorneys may use their implicit theories about jurors based on years of experience to exercise peremptory challenges in their favor.

Scientific Jury Selection

Scientific jury selection refers to the use of community surveys and data analysis to yield probabilities that different types of prospective jurors will be favorable to a particular side. Scientific jury selection is a systematic method for identifying information that would be useful to elicit during the voir dire process and to rely on when deciding which jurors to challenge. The core of this approach assumes that different people who view the same evidence may render different verdicts and that verdict preference can be predicted by individual juror characteristics. This approach also assumes that attitudes and individual differences can be measured accurately; the attitudes themselves or proxies for the attitudes, such as demographic characteristics, must be discernable during voir dire. In addition, this approach requires that these attitudes and characteristics can ultimately be used to predict verdicts.

When conducting a community survey, trial consultants recruit a random sample of participants from the same pool from which an actual jury is being selected. These surveys are often conducted over the telephone by using a random digit dialing sampling technique. Respondents are asked questions that measure demographic characteristics, attitudes toward the legal system, knowledge of case facts, and case-relevant attitudes. Participants may also be provided with evidentiary information about the case. Participants are then asked to render a verdict. By using statistics to test for significant relationships between demographic

characteristics, general attitudes, and case-relevant attitudes, trial consultants can educate attorneys about the likelihood that prospective jurors with certain attitudes or demographic characteristics will be favorable or unfavorable to their side. The techniques used during scientific jury selection must take into account the nature and scope of voir dire. For example, the information gleaned from a community survey that indicates that political affiliation is likely to be a strong predictor of verdict preference is helpful only if the judge allows the venire panel to be questioned about political affiliation. Because the judge determines which questions attorneys are allowed to pose to the venire panel, the scope of voir dire can vary widely. When only minimal voir dire is permitted, attorneys may not have any opportunity to pose any questions to the potential jurors, let alone questions that have been identified through the community survey to be predictive of verdicts. In more expanded voir dire situations, attorneys may be allowed to administer a questionnaire to the panel that could contain questions known to predict verdicts.

Individual Characteristics as Predictors of Verdicts

An abundance of research has been conducted on the relationship between individual juror characteristics and jurors' verdict preferences. Research generally suggests that there is no single set of personality or demographic predictors that can be used for all types of cases. Unfortunately, those characteristics that are the most visible, such as gender and race, tend to be weakly correlated with verdict across cases. Although these characteristics are not good predictors in general, race and gender may be good predictors in specific types of cases in which these racial and gender issues are salient. For example, although juror gender is important when gender is an issue in the trial, such as in rape or sexual harassment cases, gender is not a stable predictor of verdicts in other types of cases. There is also evidence that personality characteristics such as authoritarianism, liberalism, and the need for social approval affect juror decisions. For example, jurors who score high on measures of authoritarianism are more conviction prone. It is arguable that group membership and political beliefs may have a greater influence on verdict judgments than race or gender because, unlike gender and race, people choose their affiliations. Jurors are affected by their cultural backgrounds, prior experiences, and personal affiliations. These factors influence the manner in which they understand and judge the details of the case. Social psychological research on in-group/out-group bias suggests that jurors may have an inclination to judge a witness who is similar to them as more credible and reliable than a witness who is dissimilar to them. However, research on the black sheep effect indicates that jurors may perceive in-group members more negatively than out-group members when the in-group member has committed a transgression. Therefore, the nature of the interaction between jurors' group memberships and the defendant and witnesses' group memberships will depend on the context of the particular case.

Although demographic and personality variables are not stable predictors of verdict judgments across cases, research suggests that case-relevant attitudes, such as death penalty attitudes or attitudes about business, predict verdicts. Studies on death penalty attitudes indicate that those who are pro–death penalty are more likely to render a guilty verdict than those who are against the death penalty. Finally, some research indicates that attitudes toward business and tort reform predict verdicts and awards in civil cases.

Efficacy of Jury Selection

A number of mock jury studies and field studies have been conducted to investigate the influence of jury selection strategies on jury verdict. In general, the research in this area indicates that the evidence accounts for the greatest amount of variance in juror verdicts, and that juror's individual characteristics account only for approximately 5–15% of the variance. However, in cases such as capital cases where defendants have a possibility of receiving the death penalty, it can be argued that factors influencing this small percentage of variance become very important to study. Research has also demonstrated that case-relevant attitudes, such as attitudes toward the death penalty or attitudes toward the insanity defense, are better predictors of verdicts than general attitudes or demographic characteristics.

Investigating the utility of scientific jury selection is often done using mock jury simulations. Critics of this method argue that mock jury studies provide little practical utility for real jury selection because it is virtually impossible to replicate every aspect of a trial. Because participants know that their decisions in a study have no impact on a defendant in a real case,

they may find it easier to render a guilty verdict because there are no real consequences for doing so.

Jury selection research has not conclusively established the superiority of one technique over another, in part because research in this area is difficult. To demonstrate that scientific jury selection is efficacious, it is necessary to establish its superiority over traditional jury selection and the random selection of jurors. However, some research suggests that traditional jury selection may result in a jury with attitudes similar to a jury composed of the first 12 jurors to be considered for the jury or a jury that is randomly selected from the jury pool. Nevertheless, instead of trying to identify which approach is more useful, it may be possible that a combination of an attorney's experience and a trial consultant's advanced research methodology would prove to be the most effective approach. Because the role of the jury is an integral part of the legal system, the process of selecting the jury is important and needs further empirical evaluation.

F. Caitlin Sothmann, Caroline B. Crocker, and Margaret Bull Kovera

See also Scientific Jury Selection; Voir Dire

Further Readings

Batson v. Kentucky, 106 S. Ct. 1712 (1986).

Diamond, S. S., & Zeisel, H. (1974). A courtroom experiment on juror selection and decision-making. *Personality and Social Psychology Bulletin, 1,* 276–277.

Hepburn, J. R. (1980). The objective reality of evidence and the utility of systematic jury selection. *Law and Human Behaviour, 4,* 89–101.

Horowitz, I. A. (1980). Juror selection: A comparison of two methods in several criminal cases. *Journal of Applied Social Psychology, 10,* 86–99.

Kovera, M. B., Dickinson, J. J., & Cutler, B. L. (2003). Voir dire and jury selection. In A. M. Goldstein (Ed.), *Handbook of psychology: Vol. 11. Forensic psychology* (pp. 161–175). New York: Wiley.

JURY SIZE AND DECISION RULE

Both the size of the jury and the number of jurors who must be in agreement for a verdict to be concluded (the group's "social decision rule") have been the subject of litigation at the U.S. Supreme Court as well as a subject of research by psychologists and other social and behavioral scientists. The number of jurors and the minimum proportion of them who must be in agreement are set by formal legal rules (e.g., state statutes, federal rules of civil procedure), and those rules are in turn subject to constitutional requirements. The Supreme Court has framed its analysis of jury size and decision rule questions in terms of the effects of those variables on jury behavior. Thus, the findings of research on group decision making as a function of group size and social decision rule are of central relevance to the Court's constitutional analysis. Yet a considerable tension exists between the Court's conclusions and the empirical findings.

Jury Size

For 600 years of common-law history and 200 years of American constitutional history, the jury was considered to have 12 members. But several states and federal districts in the United States began to use smaller juries, and in the 1970s, challenges to the use of juries with fewer than 12 members reached the U.S. Supreme Court. The Court analyzed the constitutionality of smaller juries by rejecting the guidance of history, tradition, and its own precedents. Instead, the Court reasoned that because the size of the jury was not specified in the Constitution and the framers' intentions regarding jury size could not be divined, the answer would have to be found through a "functional" analysis of the jury's purpose: If smaller juries did not behave differently from juries of 12, then they were their functional equivalent and therefore were constitutional.

In a series of cases—*Williams v. Florida* (1970) (state criminal juries of 6), *Colgrove v. Battin* (1973) (federal civil juries of less than 12), and *Ballew v. Georgia* (1978) (state criminal juries numbering 5)— the Supreme Court held smaller juries to be constitutionally permissible because it found no important differences between 6- and 12-member juries in the reliability of their fact finding, the quality or quantity of their deliberation, their cross-sectional representation of the community, the ability of jurors in the minority to resist the social pressure to conform, or their verdicts. These findings were reached through a combination of judicial intuition, misconstruing nonstudies as empirical studies, misreading the findings of actual empirical studies, and failing to see elementary flaws in actual empirical studies.

What the empirical research findings actually indicate is that smaller groups foster behavior that is beneficial in some respects, but in view of the purposes for which juries are employed, most of the advantages appear to favor keeping juries at 12. On the positive side, in smaller juries, members share more equally in the discussion, find the deliberations more satisfying, and are more cohesive.

A meta-analysis of studies specifically of juries (both simulated and actual) found that larger juries are more likely than smaller juries to contain members of minority groups, deliberate longer, hang more often, and recall trial testimony more accurately. Turning to studies of small-group behavior generally, one finds that larger groups tend to discuss and debate more vigorously, collectively recall more information, and make more consistent and predictable decisions. The latter finding means that as juries grow smaller, they will tend in criminal cases to make more errors of acquitting the guilty or convicting the innocent; and in civil cases, not only will the rate of erroneous verdicts rise, but juries will tend to render damage awards that are more variable and unpredictable. (Because such differences will be small, very large sample sizes would be necessary to detect them.) In accord with classic research on the psychology of conformity, because in larger groups there is greater likelihood that a dissenter will have at least one ally, a dissenter in larger juries will usually find an ally and therefore be better able to resist the pressure to submit to the majority.

In short, the *Williams* Court had scant support for its conclusion that "there is no discernible difference between the results reached by the two different-sized juries"; the little research evidence that existed then and most of the evidence that developed later supported the opposite conclusion: that 6-person juries did behave differently from 12-person juries and most of those differences represented less-desirable decision-making processes.

In the *Ballew* case, the Supreme Court drew the line, holding juries of 6 to be the constitutional minimum. Justice Harry Blackmun's opinion announcing the judgment of the Court extensively reviewed the empirical research on the subject, much of it having been prompted by the *Williams* decision. Curiously, although the research summarized in the opinion mostly compared 6- and 12-person juries and indicated that the former did not perform as well as the latter, the Court did not reverse its earlier holdings. Instead, it reaffirmed the earlier decisions finding equivalence between large and small juries, but it now held that juries smaller than 6 were unconstitutional because, in Justice Blackmun's opinion, the studies raised serious concerns about the performance of juries of fewer than 6 members.

The research findings have been recognized in other legal settings. The Standing Committee on Federal Civil Rules recommended 12-person juries for federal civil trials (a recommendation not adopted by the Judicial Conference). During the administration of President Reagan, the Department of Health and Human Services promulgated a model medical malpractice statute for the states that specified 12-person juries (specifically for their greater predictability). And the New Hampshire Supreme Court—citing the factual findings of *Ballew* but rejecting its legal holding—ruled that a reduction in jury size below 12 would violate the New Hampshire State Constitution (which similarly did not specify a jury size).

Social Decision Rule

From the 14th century in England until the latter part of the 20th century, juries had been required to reach unanimous verdicts. Several American states began to permit quorum verdicts, and in the 1970s, challenges to the constitutionality of quorum verdicts came before the U.S. Supreme Court.

The principal motivation for eliminating the unanimity rule seems to have been a desire to reduce the incidence of hung juries. Without quorum verdicts, hung juries occur at a national rate of about 5% or 6%, and allowing quorum verdicts reduces that rate by a few percentage points.

In *Apodaca v. Oregon* (1972) and *Johnson v. Louisiana* (1972), the Supreme Court held verdicts split as widely as 9:3 to be constitutional, and in *Burch v. Louisiana* (1979), the Court held that the verdicts of 6-person juries had to be unanimous. The Court's reasoning was much the same as in the jury-size cases: As to the social decision rule for a jury verdict, the Constitution does not say and the intentions of the framers are unknown, so the "inquiry must focus upon the function served by the jury in contemporary society."

The main issues about group behavior that were debated in the Court's functional analysis were whether juries required to reach only quorum decisions would pay less attention to the arguments of the unneeded minority, whether the jury's verdicts would be less accurate, and whether the weight of evidence sufficient to produce a conviction would be reduced. The last of those questions is an especially interesting one. The standard or proof (preponderance, beyond a reasonable doubt) is directed at individual jurors, seemingly separate from the issue of the rules for combining individual views into a group decision. But the two together will surely have a bearing on the group's collective confidence in their verdict and on the quantum of proof needed to lift the jury over those several individual-to-group decision thresholds to a verdict.

The Supreme Court's opinions assert that jurors will not behave differently when a nonunanimous decision rule is in place—at least not when the jury numbers 12—or not differently enough to matter. Less research has been done on social decision rules than on group sizes, but what research has been conducted does not generally support the Court's majority.

Compared with unanimous rule juries, juries operating under a nonunanimous decision rule deliberate for a shorter time, do not let dissenters have sufficient say so as to change the minimum consensus once it is achieved (while in unanimous rule juries, jurors in the minority participate disproportionately in the deliberation), are more vote oriented and less evidence oriented, are less certain of the defendant's guilt when convicting, and are less likely to end in a deadlock. In research on group decision making generally, groups required to reach unanimous decisions are found to be more likely to reach correct solutions (on problems with clear right/wrong answers) than groups working with less-demanding social decision rules.

Notwithstanding the Supreme Court's rulings permitting nonunanimous verdicts under the federal Constitution, the great majority of states continue to require unanimous verdicts in felony trials, and all do in capital murder trials.

Michael J. Saks

See also Jury Deliberation; Jury Reforms; U.S. Supreme Court

Further Readings

Apodaca v. Oregon, 406 U.S. 404 (1972).

Arnold, R. S. (1993). Trial by jury: The constitutional right to a jury of twelve in civil trials. *Hofstra Law Review, 22*, 1–35.

Ballew v. Georgia, 435 U.S. 223 (1978).

Burch v. Louisiana, 441 U.S. 130 (1979).

Colgrove v. Battin, 413 U.S. 149 (1973).

Hastie, R., Penrod, S., & Pennington, N. (1983). *Inside the jury.* Cambridge, MA: Harvard University Press.

Johnson v. Louisiana, 406 U.S. 356 (1972).

Saks, M. J. (1977). *Jury verdicts: The role of group size and social decision rule.* Lexington, MA: Lexington Books.

Saks, M. J., & Marti, M. W. (1997). A meta-analysis of the effects of jury size. *Law and Human Behavior, 21,* 451–467.

Williams v. Florida, 399 U.S. 78 (1970).

Zeisel, H. (1971). . . . And then there were none: The diminution of the federal jury. *University of Chicago Law Review, 38,* 710–724.

Jury Understanding of Judges' Instructions in Capital Cases

Research has shown that jurors in many types of cases frequently fail to understand the jury instructions they receive. However, this failure to understand has special implications in capital, or death penalty, cases. As in other cases, juror comprehension of instructions in death penalty cases is very low, and the difficulty of some of the terms and concepts used in the death penalty context exacerbates their confusion. But this misunderstanding carries with it an additional set of consequences in capital cases. Not only will jurors who misunderstand a judge's instructions in a death penalty case have difficulty in applying the law accurately, but these jurors may also be more easily influenced by bias or prejudice in their decision-making process and may be more likely to vote for a sentence of death.

Guided Discretion

In 1972, in *Furman v. Georgia*, when the Supreme Court held that the death penalty was unconstitutional, it based its decision in part on the fact that the jury's decision-making processes in capital cases at the time seemed "arbitrary" and "capricious." When the Supreme Court approved new death penalty laws 4 years later, in *Gregg v. Georgia* and several other cases, it was because the Court felt that the new laws provided jurors with a framework intended to guide their decision-making process, guaranteeing that the jury's discretion was controlled or channeled. Because this sort of guided discretion (communicated to the jury through jury instructions) was central to the

Court's decision to bring back the death penalty in the United States, it is important that jurors in capital cases actually understand the jury instructions intended to provide that guidance.

Several components of death penalty cases make the jurors, the trials, and the jury instructions in those trials unique. During the jury selection process, for example, the death qualification process eliminates from service those potential jurors who have such strong views about the death penalty that those views might affect their ability to make an unbiased decision in an individual case. In addition, a capital trial is frequently divided into two phases: a "guilt phase," in which jurors are asked to decide if the defendant is guilty or not guilty, followed by a "penalty phase" if the defendant was found guilty during the first phase. In the penalty phase, the same jurors are asked to decide whether a defendant should be sentenced to life in prison without the possibility of parole or to death.

Penalty Phase Instructions

A significant amount of research has focused on the jury instructions used in the penalty phase of capital trials. This research has focused on several concepts that are central to the penalty phase and the structure approved by the Supreme Court. First, the term *aggravating circumstances* is used in death penalty cases to describe the evidence that suggests that the defendant should receive a death sentence. This evidence is usually presented by the prosecution. Aggravating evidence includes those aspects about the crime or the defendant that, if true, should encourage jurors to vote for the death penalty. Aggravating factors are frequently limited to those listed in state statutes and can include things such as prior felony convictions or the circumstances of the crime in question. The term *mitigating circumstances*, on the other hand, describes the evidence to be considered by jurors that weighs in favor of a life sentence. Mitigating evidence is information about the crime, the defendant, or his or her life circumstances that, if true, should encourage a life sentence. Sometimes, specific examples of mitigation are included in jury instructions (e.g., the age or mental capacity of the defendant or social history), but mitigating evidence is not limited by law. The Supreme Court has said that jurors in death penalty cases should be able to consider any and all mitigating circumstances. As a result, death penalty statues frequently include a "catch all" category to let jurors know that mitigating evidence can include anything they believe should weigh in favor of a life sentence.

Both aggravating evidence and mitigating evidence are presented during the penalty phase of a capital trial, to inform the jury's life and death decision. Although most jury instructions refer to these terms, many instructions do not provide definitions of the terms for jurors. Similarly, some states provide a list of "factors" that can be considered in the penalty phase but do not indicate whether the individual factors should be considered as aggravating or mitigating. In most jurisdictions, jurors are instructed to "weigh" aggravating and mitigating evidence in order to decide on the appropriate punishment. However, no specific formula for this weighing process or information about how it should take place is provided to jurors.

Juror Confusion

Evidence from mock jury studies, case studies, and interviews with actual jurors in death penalty cases shows that jurors have a great amount of trouble understanding these terms and applying the concepts. In some studies, jurors understood less than half the instructions they heard. This confusion extends beyond a failure to understand the words used; it also affects the ability of jurors to identify whether particular types of evidence should be used in favor of a life sentence or a death sentence and their ability to weigh the evidence presented in a legally appropriate manner. For example, studies have shown that many jurors believe that they are required to impose a sentence of death in certain situations, when in fact a death sentence is never required by law.

Many possible explanations for this confusion have been advanced. For example, some explanations focus on the use of confusing, passive language and the excessive use of jargon in the instructions. Others have suggested that jurors may become confused because they hold incorrect assumptions about crime and punishment at the time of the trial and these assumptions prevent them from understanding the accurate legal meanings of terms and instructions.

It is significant to note that in addition to the general lack of comprehension of instructions in the penalty phase of capital cases, the confusion does not seem to be evenly distributed, or to have a neutral impact. Although jurors have trouble with all these concepts, they seem to have more trouble understanding the concept of mitigating (the evidence that should

be used in support of a life sentence) than aggravating circumstances. There are several possible explanations for this confusion. For example, in cases where the terms are not defined, jurors may rely on their personal knowledge of the terms. Because *aggravating* is a term we use more often than *mitigating* in our daily lives, it may be more familiar to jurors. No matter what the reason, this confusion means that sometimes jurors may not recognize mitigating evidence as being relevant to their decision. At other times, jurors may mistake mitigating evidence as being aggravating instead and use it against the defendant (to vote for death) rather than in his or her favor (by sparing the defendant's life). This sort of error, a direct result of juror confusion, can have significant consequences for the accuracy of the decision-making process and for the defendant's future.

Jury Decision Making

This lack of comprehension affects the jury decision-making process in capital cases in both direct and indirect ways. For example, as described above, research suggests that the skewed nature of the confusion may bias jurors toward death, rather than life, sentences, although the specific impact of juror comprehension on verdict choice is currently unclear. There is also some concern that this bias toward the death penalty embedded within the jury instructions works in combination with several other aspects of the capital-sentencing structure (including the use of two phases with the same jury for both and the death qualification process) to make death verdicts even more likely.

In addition to the direct impacts of juror confusion on verdict choice, research shows that jurors who are confused by the instructions will rely instead on the things they know and understand—if jurors do not understand the judge's instructions, they are more likely to make their decisions based on their personal schemas and stereotypes. While a juror with a good understanding of the instructions is likely to base his or her decision on the relevant evidence and adhere to the weighing process in a legally appropriate way, the confused juror's reliance on stereotypes allows for bias and prejudice to enter the decision-making process. Research has shown, for example, that mock jurors with lower comprehension levels are more likely to sentence a Black defendant to death than those with higher comprehension levels. In addition, mock jurors with lower comprehension levels find mitigating evidence to be more persuasive in the case of a White defendant than in the case of a Black defendant. Mock jurors with high comprehension levels do not exhibit the same discriminatory behaviors.

Finally, above and beyond the impact of low comprehension on juror verdict choices, it is clear that jurors—citizens who are being called away from their everyday lives and asked to make a very difficult decision—experience frustration with the instructions themselves, and many feel confused and upset during the decision-making process.

Improving Comprehension

Despite the limitations of the capital-sentencing instructions being used today, several studies have demonstrated that it is possible to improve comprehension levels using a variety of techniques. For example, several studies using psycholinguistic improvements designed to simplify and clarify the language in the penalty phase instructions have shown improved comprehension levels in jurors. Similarly, researchers have experimented with penalty phase instructions that incorporate case-specific details, instructions that include definitions of the terms *aggravating* and *mitigating*, enhancements designed to improve both the declarative and the procedural knowledge of jurors, and other innovations, all of which have been successful in improving jurors' comprehension of penalty phase instructions to some degree.

Although there is a significant body of social scientific evidence documenting the limitations of juror comprehension in capital cases, and providing techniques and suggestions for improvement, juror comprehension of capital penalty phase instructions continues to represent an area of tension between psychology and the law. The Supreme Court has consistently upheld the death sentences of defendants challenging the instructions used in their trials, reasoning that there is a presumption that the jury both uses and understands the instructions provided in any case.

Amy E. Smith

See also Aggravating and Mitigating Circumstances, Evaluation of in Capital Cases; Aggravating and Mitigating Circumstances in Capital Trials, Effects on Jurors; Death Penalty; Death Qualification of Juries; Juries and Judges' Instructions

Further Readings

Diamond, S. (1993). Instructing on death: Psychologists, juries, and judges. *American Psychologist, 48*(4), 423–434.

Furman v. Georgia, 408 U.S. 238 (1972).

Gregg v. Georgia, 428 U.S. 153 (1976).

Haney, C., Sontag, L., & Costanzo, S. (1994). Deciding to take a life: Capital juries, sentencing instructions, and the jurisprudence of death. *Journal of Social Issues, 50*(2), 149–176.

Luginbuhl, J. (1992). Comprehension of judges' instructions in the penalty phase of a capital trial: Focus on mitigating circumstances. *Law and Human Behavior, 16*(2), 203–218.

Lynch, M., & Haney, C. (2000). Discrimination and instructional comprehension: Guided discretion, racial bias, and the death penalty. *Law and Human Behavior, 24*(3), 337–358.

Ogloff, J., & Chopra, S. (2004). Stuck in the dark ages: Supreme Court decision making and legal developments. *Psychology, Public Policy and Law, 10,* 379–416.

Wiener, R. L., Rogers, M., Winter, R., Hurt, L., Hackney, A., Kadela, K., et al. (2004). Guided jury discretion in capital murder cases: The role of declarative and procedural knowledge. *Psychology, Public Policy, and Law, 10,* 516–576.

JUVENILE BOOT CAMPS

Correctional programs designed to be similar to military basic training are called "boot camps." Although there are some programs for youths at risk of delinquency, these vary widely, and most juvenile boot camps are designed for children adjudicated as delinquent. This entry describes the program and operations of typical boot camps for adjudicated youths, reviews the development of correctional boot camps, and examines how they have changed over time. It then discusses controversies concerning the risks and benefits of boot camps, including the issue of net widening, and reviews research on their effectiveness.

Most boot camps for adjudicated juveniles require that they serve 3 to 6 months in a boot-camp-type facility. The programs resemble those of military boot camps; for example, staff are usually called drill instructors, and staff and juveniles wear military-type uniforms. Youths must say "Yes, sir" or "Yes, ma'am" in response to staff, and they cannot speak unless spoken to or given permission to speak. There is a rigorous daily schedule of activities. Strict rules govern all facets of the juveniles' activities and comportment. They are required to respond immediately to staff commands. Rule violations are punished immediately, referred to as summary punishments, often with some physical activity (e.g., pushups, running laps). If they do not comply with the rules of the program, the juveniles may be required to serve a longer period of time in another type of juvenile detention facility.

A Day in a Boot Camp

On a typical day in a boot camp, participants arise before dawn, dress quickly, and march in cadence to an exercise area, where they do calisthenics and other physical exercise. They return to their dormitory for quick showers and then march to the dining hall for breakfast. After breakfast, they may practice drill and ceremony until they march to their classrooms for the required educational activities. Later in the day, they may have other classroom activities such as cognitive skills training or drug treatment. Before dinner, they may again be required to practice drill and ceremony or participate in additional physical exercise. Evenings may include additional therapeutic programming or required homework. They are not permitted to watch television unless it is an educational program, nor do they have access to radios, other musical devices, or computer games.

Strict rules exist at mealtimes. Participants are required to stand at parade rest when the serving line is not moving and execute crisp military movements and turns when the line does move. They are often required to approach the table and stand at attention until ordered to sit and eat. Frequently, they must eat without conversation.

The Development of Correctional Boot Camps

Boot camps began in the adult correctional systems of Georgia and Oklahoma in the early 1980s. By the early 1990s, there were more than 21 programs for adults in 14 state correctional systems. Juvenile boot camps developed in the late 1980s. By the mid-1990s, approximately 35 juvenile boot camps were operating. The number of camps keeps varying because some of the old camps have closed down while other new camps have opened.

Several factors account for the rapid growth of correctional boot camps. One important influence was the conservative political climate of the 1980s. Politicians felt the need to be tough on crime. Many sanctions appeared to be "soft" on the criminal. Boot camps were a different story. Boot camps appealed to the "gut instincts" of a public that wanted criminals punished swiftly and harshly in a place where they were required to respect authority and obey rules.

Another important factor influencing the rapid development of the camps was the media. Boot camps provided powerful visual images of juveniles snapping to attention in response to staff members. The tough drill sergeant yelling at the young street thug made great television for a public that wanted to get tough responses to crime. It was ideal for the 60-second feature in the evening news.

Differences in Boot Camps

Juvenile boot camps have changed dramatically over time. The biggest change was in the move away from an emphasis on the basic training model. The first boot camps emphasized the basic military training with strict rules and discipline, physical training, and hard labor. Later, the camps began to emphasize other aspects such as education, leadership training, drug treatment, or cognitive skills. In fact, many of the camps no longer referred to themselves as "boot camps." They used a variety of other names for the programs, such as leadership academy, leadership development, highly structured program for juveniles, or challenge program. While these programs still had strict rules and discipline, physical training, and drill and ceremony, they placed a greater focus on leadership, education, and other therapeutic activities.

Camps differ greatly in the amount of time devoted to different activities. Some still emphasize basic training, and the juveniles spend a great deal of time in physical training and drill and ceremony. Other camps focus on therapeutic activities such as drug treatment, cognitive skills training, vocational training, or education, and the daily schedule reflects this emphasis. Furthermore, the follow-up supervision and aftercare vary among camps. Some have a long-term aftercare program with therapeutic activities, other camps may have intensive supervision, and others may have little follow-up supervision or care. These differences depend, in part, on the philosophy of those who manage the programs or the correctional administrators who oversee the programs. Money available for programming is also an important factor in determining the type of activities included in the boot camp; therapeutic programming and aftercare may greatly increase the cost of the program.

Controversies Over Juvenile Boot Camps

Boot camps have been controversial since they first opened. Advocates believe that the strict discipline and control in these camps is what these youths need. Many adults who have spent time in the military argue that this was a life-altering and positive experience for them, and camps can have the same impact on juvenile delinquents. Others point to the fact that the orderly environment and control help the youths focus on their problems and make positive changes in their lives. They believe that these undisciplined youths will prosper in an environment that requires them to obey and respect adults.

Critics of boot camps have other concerns. Correctional psychologists argue that the confrontational nature of the interactions do not reflect the type of supportive interpersonal interactions that are conducive to positive change. They maintain that 90 days of verbal abuse, push-ups, and marching cannot be expected to address the problems related to addiction, low educational attainment, or gang membership and other problems faced by these juveniles. In their opinion, boot camps do not include components that are associated with effective correctional treatment, such as therapeutically trained staff and individualized treatment. Furthermore, military training in the armed forces is followed up by 2 years or more of service that emphasizes the skills learned in basic training. Juvenile boot camps do not continue to give participants such long-term follow-up services and treatment.

The Problem of Net Widening

Boot camps appear to be a deceptively seductive alternative for youths with behavior problems. Thus, there is a good chance that low-risk juveniles may be sent to boot camps when they would otherwise have been given a community alternative such as probation. This essentially widens the net of control over juveniles. Net widening is viewed as a disadvantage because increased numbers of juveniles are incarcerated in facilities when there is little advantage in incarcerating

them. There may be little risk that they will commit future delinquencies. Also, these low-risk youths may be negatively affected by the programs. From the perspectives of both costs and the impact on youths' lives, there may be little advantage in widening the net of control.

Dangers of the Boot Camp Environment

The rigorous physical activity, confrontational interactions, and summary punishments in boot camps carry with them the chance of abuse or injury. The environment is apt to be mentally and physically stressful for the participants. There have been several deaths in the juvenile camps, and law cases are pending regarding responsibility for the deaths. Many people question whether the dangers of the boot camp atmosphere outweigh any benefits of the programs. While physical activity can be healthy, some of the camps have been criticized for requiring activities that are beyond the health status of the participants (e.g., the required long-distance running for overweight juveniles). This is a particular concern if the staff has not had adequate training to be able to determine when juveniles are experiencing extreme mental or physical stress.

Do Juvenile Boot Camps Work?

The effectiveness of correctional programs can be measured in many ways. For example, boot camps may have an impact on the conditions of confinement. From this perspective, research may investigate whether boot camps are safer than other facilities or whether they increase positive changes such as increased educational attainment or decreased antisocial attitudes. Often the major interest of policymakers and the public is whether correctional programs reduce the recidivism or future criminal activities of participants.

There is some research examining the effectiveness of correctional boot camps in reducing recidivism. MacKenzie and her colleagues conducted a meta-analysis comparing the recidivism of boot camp participants with the recidivism of comparison groups. A meta-analysis is a statistical analysis that uses studies as the unit of analysis. The meta-analysis of boot camps included 44 different studies of adult and juvenile boot camps. The studies used different measures of recidivism, including rearrests, reconvictions, and reincarcerations. For each study, an effect size was calculated. The effect size indicates whether recidivism was lower for the boot camp participants or the comparison group and how large this difference was. The researchers found that the recidivism rates of the participants and of the control group that did attend a boot camp were almost exactly the same. This was true for both the adult and the juvenile programs. Thus, from this research, it does not appear that juvenile boot camps are effective in reducing the later criminal activities of juvenile delinquents.

Some research has indicated that boot camps have a positive impact on participants' attitudes. In this research, the participants were found to have become less antisocial and develop better attitudes toward staff and programs. However, these results are not consistent. It may be that the results differ depending on the emphasis of the camp. Boot camps that emphasize therapeutic treatment may have a more positive impact on attitudes than camps that emphasize basic military training, consisting of physical training, drill and ceremony, and hard labor. We don't have enough research to clearly assess whether the camps have a positive impact on attitudes.

Another way the effectiveness of boot camps can be studied is to examine the cost of the programs. It is costly to build and operate facilities. If the boot camps widen the net by putting juveniles in facilities when they would otherwise have been in the community, there may be a substantial cost to the programs. On the other hand, if the camps reduce the amount of time juveniles spend in facilities, they could reduce costs. Most juvenile programs are relatively small, so the costs of the programs may not have a large impact on the jurisdictions operating them. This may be the reason why there is no research investigating the issue of the cost of juvenile boot camps.

The Future of Juvenile Boot Camps

Boot camps were a popular correctional approach that fit the philosophy of the conservative 1980s and 1990s. The programs appeared tough on crime and therefore answered politicians' needs to show that they supported tough programs. They answered the public's desire to punish juveniles instead of coddling them. The media liked them because they made good short news pieces for national television. But will they last? This is a question that many people are asking. There have been deaths of both staff and juveniles in the boot camps; as a result, people are beginning to question whether this is good correctional practice. Critics continue to advocate the elimination of the camps because they do not follow the principles of effective correctional practice. It is impossible to tell at this point whether boot camps will continue to operate. Given the disappointing results of the recidivism analyses, it appears that there is little reason to continue to operate the camps. Unless some additional justification for the camps is discovered, most likely there will be fewer and fewer juvenile boot camps in the future.

Doris Layton MacKenzie

See also Antisocial Personality Disorder; Juvenile Offenders

Further Readings

Gover, A. R., MaccKenzie, D. L., & Styve, G. J. (1999). The environment and working conditions in juvenile boot camps and traditional facilities. *Journal of Criminal Justice, 28*(1), 53–68.

Lutz, F., & Murphy, D. (1999). Ultra-masculine prison environments and inmate adjustment: It's time to move beyond the "boys will be boys" paradigm. *Justice Quarterly, 16*(4), 709–733.

MacKenzie, D. L. (2006). *What works in corrections? Examining the criminal activities of offenders and delinquents.* Cambridge, UK: Cambridge University Press.

MacKenzie, D. L., & Armstrong, G. S. (Eds.). (2004). *Correctional boot camps: Military basic training or a model for corrections?* Thousand Oaks, CA: Sage.

JUVENILE OFFENDERS

Interest in juvenile offenders has increased in the past few decades due to the large number of youths coming into contact with the law and the rising violent crime. Research by Howard Snyder and Melissa Sickmund provides extensive juvenile population and crime statistic data, and some of their pertinent information is summarized here to provide a rough picture of the characteristics of juvenile offenders in the United States. From 1989 to the mid-1990s, juvenile violent crime was on the rise, and it peaked in 1994. From 1994 to 2003, the juvenile crime rate decreased, with a particularly steep decline of 48% in the juvenile violent crime arrest rate. Juvenile offending remains a significant social problem, and subgroups of juveniles engage in different levels of criminal behavior. Specifically, the arrest rate for female juveniles has increased over this 10-year period, while the juvenile male arrest rate has declined. Furthermore, while the violent crime arrest rate for Black youth has declined, it still is greater than the rate for any other racial group. Several environmental factors, social factors, and personal traits contribute to the persistence or desistance of juvenile delinquency. While different developmental trajectories for the progression of delinquency and different risk factors for male and female juveniles exist, juvenile offenders generally are at greater risk for mental health problems, less education, substance abuse problems, and low socioeconomic status.

Juvenile Population and Crime Statistics

In 2002, the juvenile population in the United States was nearing 73 million. Just over 2 million juveniles (i.e., under age 18) were arrested in 2003, but fortunately, over the 10-year period from 1994 to 2003, juvenile arrests declined by 18%. Property crimes (e.g., burglary and larceny), which accounted for 463,300 juvenile arrests in 2003, constituted the largest crime category, and violent crimes, such as murder, accounted for 92,300 juvenile arrests. The overall trend for very young offenders, but not for juvenile female offenders, mirrored that for juvenile offenders in general. In fact, the rate of offending for girls increased. Additionally, arrest rates differed by racial group but were similar to the overall pattern for juveniles.

Very Young Juvenile Offenders

Marked differences in the rate of offending across age exist, and there are also general trends in the extent to which very young people engage in antisocial conduct. Very young offenders are of particular concern because it is not expected that young children would be breaking laws. This phenomenon might also signal substantive problems with our parenting practices and broader problems with communities in that both may be less than effective in developing prosocial behavior in youth. Recent trends show that among very young juvenile offenders (10–12 years of age), the arrest rates for violent (+27%) and drug-related (+105%) crimes increased, while their overall arrest rate declined, from 1980 to 2003. Furthermore, for most offense types,

more females were arrested than males in the 10- to 12-year age range. For example, the violent crime index for young juvenile female offenders increased by 135% between 1980 and 2003, while it increased only by 14% in the same time period for young juvenile male offenders. Very young juvenile offenders form a unique subgroup in that they are particularly at risk for substance use and gang affiliation.

Gender Trends

Taking into account the total number of arrests in 2003, the arrest rate for juvenile females was higher than that for juvenile males (20% vs. 15%). Additionally, from 1994 to 2003, the arrest rate for juvenile males declined by 22%, which is greater than the decrease in the juvenile female arrest rate (–3%) over this period. Additionally, the juvenile female arrest rate either increased more or decreased less than the juvenile male arrest rate for most offense types. For example, simple assault arrests increased by 1% for juvenile males and by 36% for juvenile females from 1994 to 2003. Juvenile females accounted for 29% of all juvenile arrests and were disproportionately arrested for prostitution (69%) and running away from home (59%). These findings indicate the importance of examining gender differences in juvenile offenders and that trends found with boys do not necessarily reflect what will occur with girls who are offending in the community and vice versa.

Race Trends

White juveniles accounted for 71% of all juvenile arrests in 2003, while Black youths were responsible for 27% of juvenile arrests. Sixteen percent of Black and of White arrests in 2003 were attributed to juveniles. However, Black juveniles, who represented only 16% of the juvenile population (ages 10–17), accounted for 63% of the arrests for robbery, 48% of murder arrests, and 40% of the arrests for motor vehicle theft. The proportion of juvenile arrests varied across offense type. For example, 9% of all arrests for murder involved juveniles, while 51% of all arrests for arson involved juveniles. The proportion of White and Black juvenile arrests also differed across offense types. Juveniles were responsible for a larger proportion of Black arrests than of White arrests for robbery (27%) and motor vehicle theft (33%), while the proportion of White arrests attributed to juveniles was greater for arson (53%) and vandalism (41%). However, Black and White juveniles were both responsible for the same proportions (9%) of Black and White arrests for murder in 2003. Although there has been some discussion about the inequity in charges across race, it is difficult to determine the specific causes of these disparities.

Violent Crime Trend

As mentioned, the violent crime rate varied across years, with the late 1980s to early 1990s evidencing high rates of juvenile violent crime. The Violent Crime Index for juveniles was generally stable from 1980 to 1988, but by 1994, it had increased to 61%. By 2003, the Violent Crime Index for juvenile arrests had dropped below its level in the early 1980s. The juvenile male arrest rate, which was 8.3 times the rate for juvenile females in 1980, dropped to 4.2 times the female arrest rate in 2003. From 1988 to 1994, the increase in the arrest rate for juvenile females (98%) was larger than it was for juvenile males (56%). Additionally, the greater decline in the male than the female rate (51% vs. 32%) from 1994 to 2003 was largely responsible for the decline in the overall rate of juvenile violent crime. While some of these statistics are encouraging, there continue to be a large number of juvenile offenders.

Surprisingly, the murder arrest rate increased 110% from 1987 to 1993. For juvenile males, the arrest rate for murders increased 117% in this time period, which accounted for the overall rise in the juvenile murder arrest rate. The juvenile female arrest rate did not contribute to the overall increase because this rate increased only by 36% during this time period. In 2003, the murder arrest rate for both juvenile males (78%) and juvenile females (62%) declined the most since 1980 or earlier. The violent crime trend for several minority groups, including Black, Asian, and Native American, mirrored the trend for White juveniles, with each group's arrest rate peaking in 1994. The rate for Black juveniles declined the most, but their violent crime arrest rate was still higher than the rate for any other racial group in 2003. In 2003, the violent crime arrest rate for Black juveniles, which had decreased by 35%, was approximately four times the rate for White juveniles, which was the next highest rate (800 arrests vs. 200 arrests per 100,000 juveniles, respectively). The large number of youths who come into contact with the law, which affects their own personal mental health, ability to excel in school,

and other aspects of life that could lead to well-being, has led researchers to attempt to better understand youths with conduct problems. This research has led to further efforts to understand juvenile offenders and, thus, further subtyping of juvenile offenders and of youths with conduct problems.

Developmental Pathways of Delinquent Behavior and Juvenile Offending

Childhood- Versus Adolescent-Onset Antisocial Behavior

According to Terrie Moffitt, childhood-onset or life-course-persistent antisocial behavior has a different developmental pathway from adolescent-onset antisocial behavior. Early-onset antisocial behavior is the result of a child's characteristics and a poor family and social environment. Traits increasing a child's risk of antisocial behavior include a difficult temperament, cognitive deficits, developmental motor delays, and hyperactivity. Environmental influences include weak or broken familial bonds, poverty, poor parenting, and strained relationships with teachers and peers. Childhood-onset antisocial behavior commonly persists into adulthood, and these children have much poorer prognoses than children with adolescent-onset behavior. Additionally, the life-course-persistent group of antisocial youth, which is much smaller than the adolescent-limited group, is responsible for a disproportionately large amount of crime. In contrast, adolescent-onset antisocial behavior is considered developmentally normal and occurs in otherwise healthy children. Adolescent-onset antisocial behavior is deemed normal because it is a means by which youths establish independence from their parents, and these children generally outgrow this behavior as they progress into young adulthood. However, desistance in adolescent-onset youths may be delayed if they encounter problems, such as addiction.

Triple-Pathway Model

Rolf Loeber and David Farrington identified three categories of troublesome behavior in children aged 7 to 12 years. These authors developed a triple-pathway model to explain the links between various pathways in the context of increasingly severe delinquency. First, children exhibiting disruptive behaviors, such as aggression, should be considered at risk of becoming juvenile offenders because they frequently exhibited similar behaviors early in life. Approximately, one quarter to half of these children are at risk of progressing to delinquency. Next, low-level juvenile offenders commit less serious and generally nonviolent crimes (e.g., shoplifting), but these delinquent behaviors frequently serve as precursors to more serious crimes. Serious juvenile offenders, who have committed homicide, rape, or arson, are of greatest concern because they are responsible for 10% of all juvenile arrests. Additionally, this subset of offenders committed 2%, or 600, of the murders attributed to juveniles, and weapons were used in more than 50% of these murders. Furthermore, juveniles who had access to weapons began committing crimes at a younger age than those juveniles without access to weapons.

The development of delinquent behavior in boys has been shown to occur through three pathways—overt, covert, and authority conflict. Juveniles on the overt pathway initially engage in low levels of aggression but graduate to physical fighting and then violence. In contrast, the covert pathway is associated with the commission of minor acts of delinquency (e.g., shoplifting) before 15 years of age and progresses to property damage (e.g., fire setting) and then to moderately severe forms of delinquency (e.g., fraud). Finally, in juveniles under 12 years of age, the authority conflict pathway is characterized by defiant behavior at low levels and by avoidant behavior (e.g., running away) at the highest level. For these boys, higher levels of avoidant behaviors are associated with a greater risk of covert and overt delinquent behaviors. In all three pathways, as the severity of behaviors increases, the number of juveniles engaging in these behaviors decreases. Additionally, juvenile males with an earlier onset of delinquency are more likely to progress to the more severe behaviors within each pathway. Another trend in the development of delinquent behavior is the expansion of such behavior from the home to the community. However, normal levels of disruptive behavior are commonly seen in 2- and 3-year-old children and, therefore, must be distinguished from problematic levels. Two major indicators of future delinquency are developmentally inappropriate (i.e., elevated) levels of disruptive behaviors in terms of frequency and severity and the persistence of these behaviors beyond 3 years of age.

Gender Differences in Risk Factors for Developing Antisocial Behavior

Female and male juvenile offenders share many risk factors, including poor academic histories, living in high-crime neighborhoods, family dysfunction, and poverty. However, female juvenile offenders are more likely than male juvenile offenders to have experienced physical or sexual abuse. For girls, having at least one parent with a criminal record greatly increases the likelihood that they will be arrested by age 15.

While the overall juvenile female arrest rate exceeds the rate for juvenile males, young females are less likely than boys to possess the risk factors associated with the life-course-persistent trajectory of antisocial behavior. For example, female children exhibit fewer developmental motor delays, temperamental difficulties, and neuropsychological and cognitive problems, including learning and reading difficulties. As predicted, fewer females than males were classified as life-course-persistent, but their backgrounds were similar in that they shared several of the life-course-persistent risk factors. However, adolescence-onset antisocial girls are expected to be more numerous than their life-course-persistent counterparts because they are exposed to the same antisocial peers as are adolescent boys. Yet the opportunities to engage in antisocial behavior may be more limited for adolescent girls than for adolescent boys because girls are more likely to experience physical harm (e.g., sexual assault), which may reduce their involvement in delinquent behaviors.

Predictors of Desistance and Persistence

The initial commission of a criminal act by age 13 is associated with a 2 to 3 times greater risk of chronic, violent offending. Depending on environmental factors and personality or behavioral traits, criminal behavior in juveniles can be prolonged. The presence or absence of snares (e.g., delinquent peers) could respectively limit or promote desistance of criminal behavior in juveniles. For example, economically depressed neighborhoods have high rates of juvenile crime and violence, and they have more risk and fewer protective factors. Within neighborhoods, additional sources of influence include a youth's family and peers, and the interaction of these microsystems must be collectively considered to gain a more complete understanding of juvenile delinquency. Additional environmental factors associated with juvenile offending include poverty, tenuous community bonds, minimal social control from other residents in the neighborhood, and low parental supervision. A consistent finding in juvenile delinquency research is that associating with a delinquent peer group is a strong predictor of serious, chronic offending. In contrast, protective factors include consistent discipline and positive, warm parental interactions.

Personality traits of juveniles also influence the frequency and severity of their committing delinquent or criminal acts. Callousness and impulsivity have both been linked to future juvenile delinquency. Low restraint (e.g., impulsivity) and high distress (e.g., anxiety) are associated with rearrest. However, high-restraint youth committed fewer but more severe crimes.

Callous and unemotional traits (e.g., lack of empathy) have consistently been linked to a subgroup of antisocial youth with particularly severe aggressive behavior. Furthermore, callous children also express a preference for arousing, dangerous stimuli and have lower levels of reactivity to threatening or emotionally upsetting stimuli.

Consequences of Juvenile Offending

Several consequences of juvenile offending exist, and they are particularly salient for juveniles with early-onset of delinquency. Early-onset juvenile offenders are more likely to continue engaging in delinquent behavior, and the repeated commission of such acts throughout childhood is also a factor in persistent delinquency. In other words, involvement in delinquency precludes juveniles from engaging in prosocial behaviors and is associated with low educational attainment, inadequate social skills, limited employment opportunities, low socioeconomic status, and, for males, early parenthood. These juveniles also have higher rates of externalizing behaviors (e.g., aggression), internalizing behaviors (e.g., depression), substance abuse, and suicide. The increased number and severity of mental health problems in juvenile offenders lead to their greater involvement with child welfare service, mental health providers, and the criminal justice system. Juvenile offenders and their victims have more psychological and occupational problems and, overall, a lower quality of life. Moreover, juvenile delinquents who develop into chronic offenders cost society $1.3 to 1.5 million. Because of the

great impact juvenile offending has on the children involved in criminal activity and on society, further research into prevention and intervention needs to be conducted.

Haley L. Ford and Randall T. Salekin

See also Juvenile Offenders, Risk Factors; Juvenile Psychopathy

Further Readings

Grisso, T., Vincent, G. M., & Seagrave, D. (2005). *Mental health screening and assessment in juvenile justice.* New York: Guilford Press.

Loeber, R., & Farrington, D. P. (2000). Young children who commit crime: Epidemiology, developmental origins, risk factors, early interventions, and policy implications. *Development and Psychopathology, 12,* 737–762.

Moffitt, T. E. (1993). "Life-course-persistent" and "adolescence-limited" antisocial behavior: A developmental taxonomy. *Psychological Review, 100,* 674–701.

Snyder, H. N., & Sickmund, M. (2006). *Juvenile offenders and victims: 2006 national report.* Washington, DC: U.S. Department of Justice, Office of Justice Programs, Office of Juvenile Justice and Delinquency Prevention.

JUVENILE OFFENDERS, RISK FACTORS

Broadly defined, a risk factor for juvenile offending is any experience, circumstance, or personal characteristic that increases the probability that a given youth will commit a legal transgression. No single risk factor *causes* offending; many youths who have been exposed to various risk factors never commit a crime. Rather, juvenile offending typically emerges as a result of complex interactions among a wide variety of risk and protective factors that vary from child to child. Combined risk factors tend to exhibit additive effects, with the likelihood of offending increasing as the number of risk factors increases. Also, the impact of a given risk factor varies across the life course; some may have an effect only at a particular developmental stage. Attempts to mitigate possible risk factors must, therefore, take into account a youth's developmental status. The risk factors for different types of offending vary as well. Studies have found that juvenile offenders tend to follow one of two possible patterns of offending. The majority exhibit *adolescence-limited* offending, which begins during adolescence and subsides during the transition to young adulthood. *Life-course-persistent* offenders, in contrast, tend to exhibit conduct problems early (prior to adolescence) and continue to offend into adulthood.

Risk factors for juvenile offending are numerous and wide-ranging. Some (such as gender) are unalterable. Others (such as neighborhood conditions or family dynamics), though changeable in theory, are systemic and difficult to control. Nevertheless, by understanding the wide range of risk factors for juvenile offending, prevention programs and treatments can be tailored to meet the unique needs of the various populations of youths they aim to help. The predominant factors can be grouped into three broad categories: individual characteristics, social influences, and community conditions. This entry describes well-established risk factors in these domains.

Individual Characteristics

Antisocial Behavior

One of the best predictors of future delinquency is a history of antisocial behavior in childhood. Adolescents who engage in antisocial behavior (e.g., theft, fighting, vandalism, fire setting, etc.) before puberty (prior to age 13) are more likely to be delinquent than those who have not engaged in these acts prior to puberty. Research also suggests that violent careers often begin with relatively minor forms of antisocial behavior that escalate over time. Those with an early arrest (before age 13) are more likely to become chronic offenders by age 18. Such chronic offenders make up a small percentage of the offending population but are responsible for the majority of serious violent crimes. In addition, youths whose delinquent careers begin early tend to engage in a broad range of antisocial behavior rather than specialize in a particular type of offending. Early childhood may thus be an important developmental period to target for the prevention of juvenile delinquency.

Substance Abuse

Chronic abuse of drugs and alcohol is a precursor to other dangerous behaviors, including criminal activity. Although some degree of experimentation with drugs and alcohol is not unusual during adolescence, excessive use is a risk factor for delinquency.

Cognitive Deficits

Cognitive deficits have also been implicated as a risk factor for delinquent behavior. Low intelligence quotient (IQ) scores, weak verbal abilities, learning disabilities, and difficulty with concentration or attention have all been associated with subsequent delinquent behavior. Social-cognitive development is especially important because it affects one's ability to learn social norms and expectations. For example, studies have shown that delinquent youths are more likely than their peers to think that other children's behavior is deliberately hostile, even when it is not. Though not conclusive, studies suggest that such cognitive deficits usually precede the development of delinquency and not vice versa.

Psychological Factors

Youths who are impulsive, hyperactive, and engage in risk-taking behaviors are more prone to delinquent acts than those who are not. In fact, self-control (or the lack thereof) has been suggested by some to be the root individual-level determinant of crime throughout the life course. Persons with low self-control lack diligence, find it difficult to delay gratification, have little tolerance for frustration, lack interest in long-term pursuits, and have little ability to resolve problems through verbal rather than physical means. While youths who react to new stimuli with anxiety or timidity tend to be less likely to commit antisocial acts, youths who approach new stimuli impulsively or aggressively tend to be more likely to offend. Interestingly, motor restlessness (fidgeting, or the inability to sit still) in kindergarten is a stronger predictor of delinquency between 10 and 13 years of age than low anxiety or a lack of prosocial behavior. In fact, children who become persistent offenders are more likely than their peers to suffer from attention-deficit/hyperactivity disorder (ADHD).

Brain Development

Neuropsychological deficits (often initially manifested as subtle cognitive deficits or a difficult temperament) have been linked to delinquency and chronic offending. Anatomical, chemical, and neurological abnormalities are more prevalent among chronic criminal offenders and those exhibiting recurrent antisocial behavior than among the general population. These abnormalities may be caused by damage to a specific brain region (i.e., through injury) or by a variety of behavioral or environmental factors (e.g., poor nutrition, exposure to violence, substance abuse). For example, research has found that prenatal and perinatal complications have been associated with later antisocial behavior. Adolescence is a time of marked brain development in many regions, including areas implicated in various aspects of self-control. As such, neurological development during adolescence has a significant effect on emotion regulation. Researchers are actively investigating the complex interrelations among biological and psychological factors as correlates of conduct problems.

Social Influences

Family

Family structure, family characteristics, and family dynamics have all been connected to juvenile offending. The effect of family characteristics is most pronounced in early childhood. While some research has reported that children from single-parent households are at increased risk of delinquent behavior, these differences are often found to be negligible when differences in socioeconomic status are taken into account. Interestingly, family size has been connected to juvenile offending, with youths having more siblings being more likely to engage in delinquent behaviors. The most powerful family-level predictors of juvenile delinquency include lack of parental supervision, inconsistent discipline, and hostile or rejecting parenting styles. Also, children who witness or are victims of abuse in the home are at even greater risk of engaging in antisocial behavior. Aggressive behavior has been found to run in families: Having an antisocial sibling, especially one who is close in age, increases a child's likelihood of engaging in delinquent behavior, and youths whose parents engage in antisocial behavior are more likely to do so themselves.

Peers

The importance of peers in youths' social networks grows substantially during adolescence. It is thus not surprising that most youths commit crimes in groups and that certain characteristics of a youth's peer group increase his or her likelihood of offending. Foremost, individuals with delinquent friends are more likely to offend than individuals without delinquent friends. While peers are known to influence an individual's behavior (known as *socialization*), research also demonstrates that adolescents who are delinquent are more likely to seek out and befriend other delinquents (known as *selection*). Antisocial peer influence can thus be self-reinforcing. The age and gender of an adolescent's peers are also important factors; having older friends is associated with a greater likelihood of offending, and male peers are generally more likely to encourage antisocial behavior than female peers. Gang membership reflects the most extreme example of deviant peer influence on offending. Interestingly, aggressive children who are universally rejected by their peers are at greater risk of becoming chronic juvenile offenders than are aggressive children who are not rejected.

The negative influence of peers tends to arise as a key risk factor later in development, whereas family influences typically are most important during earlier stages. Nevertheless, the influence of peers is magnified when the family environment is not healthy.

Community Conditions

Neighborhood

Children raised in disadvantaged neighborhoods are at greater risk of becoming juvenile offenders than children from more affluent neighborhoods. This neighborhood effect remains significant even when differences in school quality and family socioeconomic status are taken into account. Since disadvantaged neighborhoods have weak social controls due to isolation and high residential turnover, delinquent behavior is more likely to go unnoticed or be ignored by others in the community. The lack of social control in poorly monitored neighborhoods not only provides more opportunities for antisocial behavior but also increases youths' exposure to criminal behavior by others in the community. Such exposure is yet another risk factor for subsequent offending.

School

Youths who experience problems at school are at increased risk of becoming delinquent. Problems at school can include a wide range of experiences, such as poor scholastic performance, weak connections to school, and low educational aspirations. Such factors are associated with delinquent behavior even when cognitive factors (such as intelligence or attention deficits) are taken into account. Youths who drop out of high school are more likely than those who graduate to engage in delinquent activities. School policies such as suspension and expulsion have been found to exacerbate delinquent behavior among at-risk youths.

Prediction

Risk factors combine in complex ways to influence individual behavior. Although these factors can be used to predict the relative probabilities of offending in large groups with similar characteristics, they cannot be reliably used to predict the behavior of specific individuals. Even among groups with numerous risk factors, the majority of youths generally do not offend, making it extremely difficult to use such factors to identify individual future offenders with meaningful accuracy. The number of "false positives" from such predictions would exceed the number of "true positives," and the potential stigma of being labeled as a "future offender" would itself be detrimental.

Elizabeth Cauffman

See also Child Maltreatment; Child Sexual Abuse; Classification of Violence Risk (COVR); Conduct Disorder; Criminal Behavior, Theories of; Divorce and Child Custody; Extreme Emotional Disturbance; Juvenile Offenders; Juvenile Psychopathy; Mental Health Needs of Juvenile Offenders; Risk Assessment Approaches; Substance Use Disorders; Victimization

Further Readings

Farrington, D. P. (1995). The development of offending and antisocial behavior from childhood: Key findings from the Cambridge Study in Delinquent Development. *Journal of Child Psychology and Psychiatry, 36,* 929–964.

McCord, J., Widom, C. S., & Crowell, N. A. (2001). *Juvenile crime, juvenile justice. Panel on juvenile crime: Prevention, treatment, and control.* Washington, DC: National Academy Press.

Moffitt, T. (1993). Adolescence-limited and life-course-persistent antisocial behavior: A developmental taxonomy. *Psychological Review, 100,* 674–701.

Office of the Surgeon General. (2001). *Youth violence: A report of the Surgeon General.* Washington, DC: U.S. Department of Health and Human Services, Office of the Secretary, Office of Public Health and Science, Office of the Surgeon General. Retrieved from http://www .surgeongeneral.gov/library/youthviolence/toc.html

Tremblay, R. E., & LeMarquand, D. (2001). Individual risk and protective factors. In R. Loeber & D. P. Farrington (Eds.), *Child delinquents: Development, intervention, and service needs* (pp. 137–164). Thousand Oaks, CA: Sage.

JUVENILE PSYCHOPATHY

Despite disagreement about its exact contours, most conceptualizations of psychopathic personality disorder emphasize traits of emotional detachment, including callousness, failure to form close emotional bonds, low anxiety proneness, remorselessness, and deceitfulness. Nevertheless, most measures of psychopathy go beyond these interpersonal and affective features to assess repeated involvement in antisocial behavior, which many scholars view as peripheral to the construct. Chiefly, this is because most measures are based on the Psychopathy Checklist–Revised (PCL–R), which weighs past violent and antisocial behavior as strongly as traits of emotional detachment. Over the past decade, researchers have extended this adult measure of psychopathy downward to adolescents and children, with the goal of assessing "juvenile psychopathy." This research has gained considerable momentum, despite ongoing controversy about the appropriateness of diagnosing psychopathy before youths' personalities have reached a period of relative developmental stability. Most contemporary research and virtually all practical interest revolve around the reliability and utility of measures of juvenile psychopathy in forecasting youthful offenders' violent and antisocial behavior. In this entry, this movement is noted, but research on the validity of extending this construct to youths is emphasized. Theoretically driven research on the potential mechanisms that underpin psychopathy reveals the importance of emotional detachment as a likely manifestation of psychopathy in youths. However, there is no compelling evidence that the purported traits of psychopathy (a) remain stable during the transition to adulthood or (b) do not respond to treatment. This limits the utility of measures of psychopathy for informing legal decisions with long-term consequences concerning youth. Although relevant measures have been developed for children as young as 3 years, the focus of this entry is on preteens and adolescents.

Extending Psychopathy From Adults to Youths

Several factors have encouraged the extension of psychopathy from adults to youth. Foremost among them are (a) the recognition that the chief tools for diagnosing psychopathy predict violence and criminal recidivism and (b) the juvenile justice system's increasingly punitive policies, which have created a demand for identifying inalterably dangerous youths. Although researchers hoped that psychopathy assessments would be used to identify a subgroup of at-risk youths to target for intervention, recent legal reviews suggest that the youths identified are likely to be excluded from treatment and set up for harsh sanctions.

Most measures of juvenile psychopathy modify the PCL–R items and scoring criteria to reference youths' peer, family, and school experiences. They are built on the assumption that the features of psychopathy manifested by adult psychopaths will, when exhibited in youths, identify a small subgroup of offenders who are maturing into psychopaths. That is, psychopathy is manifested similarly, whether one is 13 or 33 years old. This assumption is challenged by a study of clinical psychologists' conceptions of juvenile psychopathy. Clinicians viewed some of the features of adult PCL–R psychopathy (e.g., impulsivity, the failure to accept responsibility, a parasitic lifestyle, criminal versatility) as nonprototypic of juvenile psychopathy. Although this raises the possibility that the manifestations of psychopathy differ as a function of developmental stage, no "bottom-up" measures of juvenile psychopathy have been developed.

Reliability and Predictive Utility of Juvenile Psychopathy Measures

The most widely validated measures of juvenile psychopathy were derived from the PCL–R, including the Psychopathy Checklist: Youth Version (PCL:YV), the Antisocial Process Screening Device (APSD), and the Child Psychopathy Scale (CPS). Like its parent measure, the PCL:YV is based on a clinical interview and file review; the other measures are based on self- or collateral report. Perhaps, given these method differences, the PCL:YV correlates only moderately with the remaining measures.

These measures share two general strengths. First, each has been shown to be reliable (interrater, internal consistency, and/or short-term test-retest). Second, each has demonstrated some utility in predicting youths' violent or antisocial behavior. The typical degree of association with these behavioral outcomes is similar to that observed in adults (i.e., $r \neq .25$). Although most prospective studies follow youths for only 1 to 2 years, one retrospective study indicates that youths' (mean age = 16) file-based PCL:YV scores moderately predict violent recidivism over an average 10-year follow-up period. Most of the PCL:YV's predictive utility in this study, however, was attributable to its assessment of an impulsive, antisocial lifestyle rather than traits of emotional detachment. This finding is consistent with much of the adult literature and challenges the assumption that the measure's association with violence is an indication that emotionally detached psychopaths use violence to prey on others. Instead, the measures may tap traits of aggression or externalizing features that predict violence but are not specific to psychopathy.

Construct Validity of Juvenile Psychopathy: Potential Mechanisms and Etiology

For such reasons, predictive utility (which seeks clinical utility) cannot be mistaken for construct validity (which seeks construct identification). To determine whether psychopathy is a valid construct when applied to youths, juvenile psychopathy must be (a) evaluated against a validation hierarchy dictated by a theory of the disorder and (b) shown to be a stable personality disorder that does not dissipate as youths become adults.

Despite the differences among them, most theories describe psychopathy as a largely inherited affective or cognitive processing deficit. These theories dictate a validation hierarchy that places pathophysiologic and etiologic mechanisms at the top, as they offer the greatest potential for explaining the disorder and potentially altering its course. The question is whether diagnostic criteria for juvenile psychopathy identify a homogeneous group of youths with clearly delineated deficits and largely genetic pathophysiology.

Paul Frick and his students have begun to address this question. Their work highlights the importance of features of emotional detachment, or "callous/ unemotional" (C/U) traits, in defining juvenile psychopathy. Theoretically, traits of emotional detachment are underpinned by a fearless temperament and deficient processing of emotionally distressing stimuli, which causes insensitivity to socializing agents and interferes with the typical development of conscience. At the symptomatic level, Frick and his colleagues have found that youths with traits of emotional detachment tend to be fearless, thrill and adventure seeking, and low in anxiety. At the pathophysiological level, they have found that emotionally detached traits identify— among a *pool* of youths with early and persistent antisocial behavior—those who possess information-processing and emotional deficits similar to those found among psychopathic adults. These include reduced sensitivity to cues of punishment when a reward-oriented response set is primed and diminished reactivity to threatening and emotionally distressing stimuli. Although such results might be interpreted as evidence that psychopathy is genetically influenced, caution should be exercised in drawing premature inferences because the heritability of these laboratory variables is unclear.

Only one behavioral-genetic study of psychopathy has been conducted with youths to date. In this study, psychopathy was operationalized using teachers' ratings of C/U traits on an unvalidated but internally consistent scale. Based on a selection of 661 7-year-old probands with extreme C/U traits (>1.3 *SD*), the authors found concordance rates of 39% and 73% for dizygotic and monozygotic twins, respectively, yielding an estimate of moderate heritability for C/U traits ($h = .67$). Although observational studies suggest that childhood maltreatment relates more strongly to antisocial behavior than features of emotional detachment per se, more research is needed to determine whether features of emotional detachment are more highly heritable.

In summary, existing research provides some support for the validity of emotional detachment or C/U traits in defining juvenile psychopathy. The importance of these traits is bolstered by psychometric studies. Studies that apply item response theory indicate that interpersonal and affective items convey more information about the underlying juvenile psychopathy construct than items that tap aggressive and antisocial conduct. Some of the recently developed measures of juvenile psychopathy (e.g., the Youth Psychopathic Traits Inventory; the Inventory of Callous Unemotional Traits) focus on emotional detachment, de-emphasizing antisocial behavior. It remains for future research to determine whether these measures more "cleanly" assess the construct than their predecessors.

Malleability of Juvenile Psychopathy

The fact that we can reliably assess features of emotional detachment in youths that relate in a theoretically coherent manner to cognitive and affective deficits provides some support for extending psychopathy measures downward from adults to youth. Presently, however, we lack the necessary collateral evidence that what we are assessing in youths is psychopathy, a personality disorder that will remain stable into adulthood.

Scholars have expressed two main concerns about the stability of juvenile psychopathy. First, downward translations of the PCL–R include normative and temporary features of adolescence such as impulsivity, stimulation seeking/proneness to boredom, poor behavior controls, and irresponsibility. At least one study indicates that measures of juvenile psychopathy correlate moderately with measures of psychosocial maturity. To the extent that measures of juvenile psychopathy tap construct-irrelevant variance related to psychosocial maturity, a youth's score will gradually decrease as he or she matures. It is possible that recent measures of juvenile psychopathy that focus specifically on emotional detachment may capture less construct-irrelevant variance related to psychosocial maturity. Indeed, a cross-sectional item-response theory study indicates that PCL:YV items that assess emotional detachment are more defining of psychopathy across age groups than items that tap impulsive, antisocial behavior.

The second concern is that there is no compelling evidence that youths assessed as psychopathic will mature into psychopathic adults. Because personality and identity may not be well formed until adulthood, our nosological systems generally forbid applying diagnoses of personality disorders to children and adolescents. Although psychopathic adults probably manifested similar traits when they were younger, relatively few youths with psychopathic features may mature into psychopathic adults. Reasoning by analogy, the majority of children with conduct disorder desist acting out and do not mature into adults with antisocial personality disorder.

Three relevant studies have been conducted. In the first, the APSD was repeatedly administered to 100 nonreferred fourth graders. Across a 4-year period, the stability of APSD scores and rank order was excellent (interclass correlation [ICC] = .80), suggesting that parent ratings change little from late childhood to early adolescence. The two remaining studies focused on the transition from adolescence to adulthood. In the second study, more than 200 youths were administered the CPS at age 13 and a screening version of the PCL at age 24. Over this 10-year period, there was relatively poor stability (ICC = .27), and most of the shared variance was between the CPS and PCL's antisocial scale. Of the adolescents who obtained extremely high CPS scores (i.e., the top 5%) at age 13, less than one-third (29%) were classified as psychopathic at age 24. In the third study, PCL measures were repeatedly administered to approximately 200 adolescents and 100 adults. Over a 2-year period, the stability of adolescents' PCL:YV scores was limited (ICC = .34). Adolescents' PCL:YV scores decreased significantly more than adults' PCL–R scores, indicating that psychopathy assessed during adolescence is less stable than that assessed during adulthood.

The apparent features of psychopathy can change not only as a function of maturity but also as a function of intervention. The results of recent research challenge the long-standing therapeutic pessimism about psychopathy. Although three studies of youth have been conducted, only one is prospective and includes a control group. In this study, of approximately 150 youths with pronounced PCL:YV scores and long histories of acting out, those who participated in an intensive treatment program were 2.4 times *less* likely to recidivate violently the year after release than those who participated in treatment as usual.

Legal Implications

Although juvenile psychopathy is a promising construct, the available evidence cannot support its application to legal decisions about youth that have long-term consequences. First, given the lack of evidence that these measures identify inalterably dangerous youths who will mature into adult psychopaths, it is inappropriate to apply these measures to determine whether a youth should be tried in the adult court system. Second, these measures should not be used as an exclusion criterion for treatment programs. Indeed, juveniles with high psychopathy scores should be reframed as high-risk cases in need of intensive treatment rather than hopeless cases to incapacitate.

What legal uses of these measures might be appropriate? Given their predictive utility, one might use a measure of juvenile psychopathy as a risk assessment tool to inform short-term decisions about placement (particularly levels of security). However, risk assessment tools that have been designed and validated for youth are available. Before selecting a diagnostic measure of psychopathy over a validated risk assessment tool, one must consider the potential for stigmatizing a child or an adolescent with the unsavory label "psychopath." Studies of juvenile justice professionals and mock juries alike indicate that this label invites assumptions that the youth is inalterably dangerous. Although this assumption does not enjoy empirical support, it pushes decision makers away from rehabilitative efforts toward harsh sanctions and incapacitation. Because adolescence is a time of significant developmental change, it is imperative to learn more about the stability, nature, and manifestations of psychopathy before embracing this construct as a component in the evaluation of juvenile offenders.

Jennifer Skeem, Eva Kimonis, and Sarah Vidal

See also Conduct Disorder; Hare Psychopathy Checklist–Revised (2nd edition) (PCL–R); Hare Psychopathy Checklist: Youth Version (PCL:YV); Psychopathy

Further Readings

Edens, J. F., Skeem, J. L., Cruise, K. R., & Cauffman, E. (2001). Assessment of "juvenile psychopathy" and its association with violence: A critical review. *Behavioral Sciences and the Law, 19,* 53–80.

Frick, P. J., & Dickens, C. (2006). Current perspectives on conduct disorder. *Current Psychiatry Reports, 8,* 59–72.

Salekin, R. T. (2006). Psychopathy in children and adolescents. In C. J. Patrick (Eds.), *Handbook of psychopathic traits* (pp. 389–414). New York: Guilford Press.

JUVENILES AND THE DEATH PENALTY

The controversy surrounding the juvenile death penalty is not new; the courts have struggled with the issue for decades. Meanwhile, psychologists have presented research results on both the capabilities of juveniles and the public's support for the juvenile death penalty. Although the Supreme Court has not consistently relied on psychological findings, those findings are relevant to the legal debate.

Supreme Court Rulings

In 1988, the U.S. Supreme Court in *Thompson v. Oklahoma* overturned a death sentence for a 15-year-old offender because it violated the Eighth Amendment prohibition against cruel and unusual punishment. The Court found that the community's "evolving standards of decency" were incommensurate with the execution of a juvenile. The Court considered four factors: the number of state statutes prohibiting the juvenile death penalty for 15-year-olds, jury sentencing statistics, the opinions of national and international organizations, and the Court's analysis of whether the juvenile death penalty accomplished the goals and purposes of the punishment.

A year later, the Court reexamined whether the death penalty should be available for 16- or 17-year-olds in *Stanford v. Kentucky* (1989). This time, the Court failed to find consensus in state statutes and held that the death penalty for these youths was not in violation of the Eighth Amendment. Surprisingly, the Court ignored all other measures of evolving community standards that were considered in *Thompson.*

Making matters even more confusing, the Court did an about-face in 2005, finding the juvenile death penalty unconstitutional in *Roper v. Simmons* and determining that the community's standards of decency had evolved to oppose executing juveniles of any age. Furthermore, relying on psychological research, the Court found that the juvenile death penalty did not satisfy the punishment goals of deterrence and retribution, due in part to juveniles' immaturity and their inability to make rational judgments that consider the outcomes of committing violent crimes.

Psychologists have contributed to these legal developments in two ways. First, they have conducted polls to measure community support for the juvenile death penalty. Second, they have conducted research testing the development of juveniles.

Public Opinion Research

The Supreme Court has sometimes referred to the results of public opinion polls measuring the "evolving standards" of the community. Polls have shown changing support over time. Although 28% of respondents supported the juvenile death penalty in 1936,

only 19% supported the punishment in 1953, and only 11% were supportive in 1957. Surprisingly, a 1965 poll reported 21% support for juvenile executions, despite declining public support for the death penalty in general. Demonstrating even more variability, a 1988 poll showed 44% support and a 1989 poll showed 57% support for juveniles over 16. At the same time, another 1989 poll found 25% to 30% support for executing offenders as young as 14 years. More recently, a 2002 Gallup poll found 31% support for juvenile executions. Exhibiting regional differences, a 1991 poll in the southeastern United States found that 64% supported executing juveniles aged 16 or over and 35% supported executing those under 16. Still, the level of support (83%) for executing adults was much higher.

Support is not uniform, however, as Whites and conservatives are typically more supportive of the death penalty in general than their counterparts. Similarly, participants who are older, male, White, and conservative are more supportive of the juvenile death penalty.

Despite this variability among polls, the trend indicates a general disfavor among respondents especially when it comes to executing juveniles as compared with executing adults. The *Roper* ruling did not rely on polling results; nevertheless, findings from this research do agree with the Court's judgment that the juvenile death penalty now does offend the community's evolving standards of decency.

Research on Juvenile Development

A second line of psychological research argues against executing juveniles because their limited developmental judgment capacities mitigate their culpability. The American Psychological Association filed an amicus brief in the *Roper* case that referred to research demonstrating that juveniles are biologically, psychosocially, and cognitively less developed than adults. These differences suggest that the death penalty does not fulfill its purposes when the state invokes it against juveniles who commit homicide. It is not possible to deter juveniles from committing homicide if they do not engage in a rational cost-benefit analysis before engaging in violence.

As adolescents progress to adulthood, they develop capabilities, attention, information-processing skills, and memory, which makes them more reasoned decision makers. Some research suggests that older juveniles are similar to adults in their reasoning skills, at least when tested in laboratory settings (e.g., participants imagine how they would react to hypothetical situations). However, critics argue that differences between adult and juvenile judgments are much more likely to emerge in real-world settings than in laboratories.

Some researchers concluded that juveniles' psychosocial development remains immature even in later adolescence. As a result, juveniles are more susceptible to peer influence, are ineffective in weighing the risks and rewards of their behavior, have difficulties in reasoning about the long-term consequences of behavior, and have a lower capacity for self-management (e.g., impulse control). These deficiencies affect their cost-benefit analysis, leading them to make immature decisions.

A growing body of neuropsychological research has confirmed that juveniles differ from adults in important ways. For instance, recent research has indicated that the areas of the brain that control reasoning (e.g., the prefrontal cortex) are the last to develop. As such, juveniles are less competent than adults, with less-developed capabilities for concentration, control of impulsivity, self-monitoring, and decision making. Because these areas of the brain are underdeveloped, juveniles rely more heavily on the amygdala, the area of the brain that processes emotions. Thus, juveniles are biologically different in ways that may decrease criminal culpability.

In sum, the age at which an offender is legally eligible for the death penalty is 18. At least for now, the legal debate surrounding the juvenile death penalty is settled, due in part to the work of psychologists studying public opinion and the development of cognitive, emotional, and neurological capacities.

Monica K. Miller and Richard L. Weiner

See also Death Penalty; Mental Illness and the Death Penalty; Mental Retardation and the Death Penalty; Racial Bias and the Death Penalty; Religion and the Death Penalty

Further Readings

Boots, D. P., Heide, K. M., & Cochran, J. K. (2004). Death penalty support for special offender populations of legally convicted murderers: Juveniles, the mentally retarded and the mentally incompetent. *Behavioral Sciences and the Law, 22,* 223–238.

Kalbeitzer, R., & Goldstein, N. E. S. (2006). Assessing the "evolving standards of decency": Perceptions of capital punishment for juveniles. *Behavioral Sciences and the Law, 24,* 157–178.

Roper v. Simmons, 543 U.S. 551 (2005).

Stanford v. Kentucky, 492 U.S. 361 (1989).

Steinberg, L, & Scott, E. S. (2003). Less guilty by reason of adolescence: Developmental immaturity, diminished responsibility, and the juvenile death penalty. *American Psychologist, 58,* 1–10.

Thompson v. Oklahoma, 487 U.S. 815 (1988).

Index

Entry titles are in **bold.**

AAI (Adult Attachment Interview). *See* **Adult Attachment Interview (AAI)**

Abandonment, of elderly, **1**:249

Abidin, Richard, **2**:540

Abuse. *See* Child abuse; **Elder abuse**; Sexual abuse

"Abuse excuse," **2**:740, **2**:742

"Abuse-survivor machine," **1**:310

Acamprosate, **2**:776

Accommodation, under Americans with Disabilities Act, **1**:24, **1**:25

Ackerman-Schoendorf Parent Evaluation of Custody Test (ASPECT), 1:1–2
 limitations of, **1**:2

Ackerson, Imberley, **1**:114

ACLU, Ashcroft v., **2**:530

Acquittal, jury nullification, **1**:412–415

Actuarial decision making, **2**:850–851

Actuarial prediction, risk assessment, **2**:699–700, **2**:725

Actus reus, **1**:35, **2**:487. *See also* **Mens rea and actus reus**

ACUTE–2007, **2**:726, **2**:751–753. *See also* **STABLE–2007 and ACUTE–2007 Instruments**

AD (Alzheimer's disease). *See* Alzheimer's disease (AD)

ADA (Americans with Disabilities Act). *See* **Americans with Disabilities Act (ADA)**

Adam Walsh Act, **2**:724

Ad damnum, **1**:183

ADHD (attention deficit hyperactivity disorder). *See* Attention deficit hyperactivity disorder (ADHD)

Adjudicative competence
 criteria for, **1**:105–106
 Interdisciplinary Fitness Interview, **1**:4, **1**:121, **1**:377–378
 societal values and, **1**:106
 of youth, **1**:2–5
 See also Competence

Adjudicative competence of youth, 1:2–5
 assessment of, **1**:3–4
 interventions for remediating incompetence, **1**:4–5
 legal standards for competence, **1**:2–3
 MacCAT–CA, **1**:12, **1**:121, **2**:464–466
 sources of incompetence, **1**:3

Adjustment, **2**:448

Admissibility of evidence, **1**:332
 Daubert standards, **1**:224, **1**:267, **1**:271, **1**:272, **1**:273–274
 Frye standards, **1**:224, **1**:271–272, **1**:274, **1**:332

General Electric Co. v. Joiner, **1**:271, **1**:273, **1**:332

hypnotically refreshed testimony, **1**:361

Kumho Tire Company v. Carmichael, **1**:271, **1**:273–274, **1**:332, **2**:828

Adolescents. *See* **Juvenile offenders**

Adoption and Foster Care Analysis and Reporting System, **1**:339

ADR (alternative dispute resolution). *See* **Alternative dispute resolution** (ADR)

Adult Attachment Interview (AAI), 1.5–6
 areas for future study of, **1**:6

Advance directives, **1**:255, **1**:256, **1**:359, **2**:633. *See also* **Psychiatric advance directives** (PADs)

Affective disorders. *See* **Mood disorders**

Aggravating and mitigating circumstances, evaluation of in capital cases, 1:6–9
 mitigation specialist, **1**:7–8
 sentence and, **1**:6–7

Aggravating and mitigating circumstances in capital trials, effects on jurors, 1:7, 1:9–11
 aggravating factors, **1**:9–10
 mitigating factors, **1**:10–11

Aggravating circumstances, **1**:426

Aggravating factors
 antisocial personality disorder, **1**:28–33
 defined, **1**:7
 evaluation of in capital cases, **1**:6–9
 jurors, effect of on, **1**:7, **1**:9–11

Aggressive behavior, media violence and, **2**:482–486

Alabama, prison overcrowding in, **2**:618

Alabama ex rel T.B., J.E.B. v., **2**:856

Alaska
 electronic recording of interrogation, **2**:845
 registration of sex offenders, **2**:722

Alcohol, myopia theory of effects of, **1**:12

Alcohol abuse, by police, **2**:591

Alcohol addiction
 ADA and, **1**:24
 death penalty and, **1**:10

Alcohol consumption
 criminal behavior and, **1**:155–156
 effects of, **1**:12
 by police, **2**:591
 See also Alcohol intoxication

Straus, M. A., **1:**145
Stress
    critical incidents, **1:**171–172
    eyewitness memory and, **2:**769–770
    litigation stress, **2:**460–461
    malpractice lawsuits, **2:**461
    Parenting Stress Index, **2:**540–541
    police stress, **2:**583, **2:**587–590, **2:**591, **2:**594
Stress and eyewitness memory, 2:769–770
Stress response syndrome. *See* **Posttraumatic stress disorder (PTSD)**
Structured Assessment of Violence Risk in Youth (SAVRY), 2:770–771
Structured Clinical Interview for *DSM-IV* Axis II Personality Disorders (SCID–II), **1:**30
Structured Interview for *DSM-IV* Personality Disorders, **1:**30
Structured Interview of Reported Symptoms (SIRS), 1:267, **2:**772–773
Structured professional judgment, **2:**851
Structured risk assessment, **2:**699–701
Substance abuse
    in adult sexual assault victims, **1:**151
    criminal behavior and, **1:**155–156
    hallucinations and, **1:**347
    juvenile offending and, **1:**436
    treatment of, **2:**775–777, **2:**779, **2:**802–804
    See also **Substance use disorders**
Substance abuse treatment, 2:775–777, 2:779, **2:**802–804
Substance-induced psychotic disorder, **2:**653
Substance use disorders, 2:778–780
    biopsychosocial model, **2:**778–779
    cues or triggers, **2:**779
    death penalty and, **1:**10
    diagnosis of, **2:**780
    impact of, **2:**778
    rehabilitated drug abusers and ADA protection, **1:**24
    therapeutic communities for treatment of, **2:**802–804
    treatment for, **2:**775–777
    See also Substance abuse
Substantive competence, **1:**260
Substantive legal psychology, **1:**236
Substantive psychology, **1:**235
Substituted judgment. *See* **Proxy decision making**
SUE technique, **1:**205–206
Suicidal intent, **2:**783
Suicide, **2:**513–514, **2:**785
    prevention of, **2:**784
    in prisons, **2:**781–784
    risk factors, **2:**781–784
    suicide by cop, **2:**786–787
Suicide assessment and prevention in prisons, 2:781–784
Suicide Assessment Manual for Inmates (SAMI), 2:785–786
Suicide by cop, 2:786–787
Suicide ideation, **2:**783
Suicide notes, **2:**514
Suicide plan, **2:**783–784
Suicide prevention, **2:**784

Sullivan, Thomas, **2:**845
Sundowner Offshore Services, Inc., Oncale v., **2:**736
Superego, **1:**155
Superior Court, Hovey v., **1:**191
Supermax prisons, 2:787–790
    conditions of supermax confinement, **2:**788
    effects of supermax confinement, **2:**789
    legal regulation of, **2:**789–790
    population of, **2:**788–789
Support groups, for substance abuse, **2:**776
Supreme Court. *See* **U.S. Supreme Court**
Supreme Court Forecasting Project, **2:**828
Surveillance model of supervision, **1:**102
Susceptibility to suggestion, **2:**759
Suspects
    defined, **1:**367
    interrogation of, **1:**379–381
SVA (Statement Validity Assessment). *See* **Statement Validity Assessment (SVA)**
SVR–20 (Sexual Violence Risk-20). *See* **Sexual Violence Risk–20 (SVR–20)**
Swanson, J.W., **2:**636
SWAT team (special weapons and tactics team), **1:**168, **2:**579, **2:**581

Tanford, Sarah, **1:**394
Tapp, June, **2:**451, **2:**452
Tarasoff v. Regents of the University of California, **2:**850
Tavris, Carol, **1:**310
Taylor, William v., **1:**62
TBI (traumatic brain injury). *See* Traumatic brain injury (TBI)
TC (testamentary capacity). *See* **Testamentary capacity (TC)**
TCC (treatment consent capacity). *See* Treatment consent capacity (TCC)
Technical competence, **1:**260
Television, media violence and behavior, **2:**482–486
Temporary insanity, **1:**162. *See also* Insanity defense
Tender years doctrine, 2:791–792
Tennessee, Payne v., **2:**832
Terminal illness. *See* **End-of-life issues**
Termination of parental rights, 2:792–795
    child maltreatment and, **2:**794
    ethical standards and, **2:**794
    forensic assessment, **2:**793–794, **2:**795
    legal and regulatory standards, **2:**793
Terrorism, 2:795–798
    crisis and hostage negotiation, **1:**167–170, **2:**579, **2:**581
    psychology of, **2:**796–797
Terrorist mindset model, **2:**796
Testamentary capacity (TC), 2:798–801
    attorney observations of, **2:**799–800
    clinical evaluation of, **2:**800
    insane delusions and, **2:**799
    legal elements of, **2:**799
    research on, **2:**800–801
    retrospective evaluation of, **2:**800
    undue influence, **2:**799